CHRISTIAN CELEBRATION

PUBLISHER'S NOTE

THIS one-volume edition of the three books in the CHRISTIAN CELEBRATION series by J. D. Crichton is published to keep in print an important work for liturgists and students alike. The pagination of each of the three constituent volumes has been retained both so that this work can be made available more quickly and at less cost to the student, and so that the many references in other works of scholarship to these texts remain valid.

CHRISTIAN CELEBRATION:
THE MASS

First published 1971
This edition 1975
Reprinted 1976

Nihil obstat: John M. T. Barton, STD, LSS, *Censor*
Imprimatur: Victor Guazzelli, *V.G.*, Westminster, 20 July 1971

The *Nihil obstat* and *Imprimatur* are a declaration that a book or pamphlet is considered to be free from doctrinal or moral error. It is not implied that those who have granted the *Nihil obstat* and *Imprimatur* agree with the contents, opinions or statements expressed.

CONTENTS

	Preface	xi
	Abbreviations	xii
ONE	Liturgy and Contemporary Man	1
TWO	The World of Symbols	16
THREE	The Worshipping Community	31
FOUR	The New Order of the Mass	45
FIVE	The General Instruction	50
SIX	The Structure of the Mass	68
SEVEN	The Calendar	107
EIGHT	The Roman Missal of 1970: A Description of its Contents	115
NINE	Celebration	135
TEN	Celebration and the New Order of the Mass	146
ELEVEN	Liturgy and the World	159
	Index	177

PREFACE

BOOKS, like the liturgy, should be self-explanatory, and I hope this one is. It is a study of the new Order of Mass and of the various documents that attended its promulgation. There is one omission. Within the compass of this book, it did not seem possible to give extended treatment to the Lectionary. In any case, much of the introductory work on it has been done by Father P. Coughlan and Father P. Purdue (*Commentary on the Sunday Lectionary*, Vols. I, II, III, 1969, 1970) and to it I happily refer readers who are in search of further enlightenment.

I hope the book will be useful to the clergy, clerical students and those who have to teach the liturgy to others. It is these I have had much in mind while writing it.

The book really started its life in the diocese of Northampton in 1969 when the Bishop, the Right Reverend Charles Grant, invited me to speak to his clergy on the new Order. I have the happiest recollections of their kindness and hospitality.

In the course of planning and writing the book I have been constantly helped and encouraged by Mrs Sue Chapman of Geoffrey Chapman, Publishers. I am grateful to the Very Reverend F. G. Thomas, Rector of Oscott College, for reading the first chapter, and to the Reverend J. R. Ainslie for helpful suggestions on chapter 10. I wish to thank also Mrs Olive Yeo for valuable help with the typing of the book.

J. D. CRICHTON,
Pershore

May, 1971

ABBREVIATIONS

CL = Constitution on the Liturgy.

GI = General Instruction of 1969/70 attached to the *Missale Romanum* of 1970.

OM = *Ordo Missae* (as above).

Other conciliar and post-conciliar documents are given their full title. A number in brackets ( ) after a statement refers, in the case of the conciliar documents, to the section in which it occurs; in the case of GI to the relevant article. The Instruction is divided into chapters but its articles are numbered throughout from beginning to end (1–341).

For CL I have used the translation of Father Clifford Howell, S.J. (Whitegate Publications, Cirencester, 1963) with occasional reference to the Latin as given (with French translation) in *La Maison-Dieu*, no. 76, 1963.

For other Council documents I have used the translations of *The Documents of Vatican II*, ed. Walter M. Abbott, S.J. (Geoffrey Chapman, 1966).

Translations of GI are generally my own. I have occasionally referred to that given in *The Order of Mass*, the copyright of the International Committee on English in the Liturgy (ICEL), 1969. The Latin text there translated is that of OM, 1969, and differs from that to be found in the *Missale Romanum* where the revised version is given.

Editions of the Verona (Leonine) and Gelasian Sacramentaries are those of Mohlberg, Rome, 1956 and 1960 respectively.

N.R.K.
velociter scribenti

CHAPTER ONE

LITURGY AND CONTEMPORARY MAN

A FACT of our time is the mass abandonment of regular Sunday worship. Once, not so long ago, it was remarked upon and deplored. Now it is taken for granted. Yet it is a very extraordinary phenomenon. Throughout recorded history man, in community and publicly, has worshipped in one way or another. Until the nineteenth century the majority of people felt the need to do so and, if not always very regularly, they did in fact join with their fellow human beings in public worship. In this century this practice has ceased. Only a minority in almost every country of the world worship publicly.

To attempt to establish the causes of this phenomenon would require enormous research, the results of which would occupy many volumes. Whether anyone has done so I do not know, but some explanation is required. In the first place, the abandonment of public worship is a function of the abandonment of organized religion. If the 'churches' no longer say anything to you or if you cannot accept their claims, clearly you are not going to join in their worship, except occasionally and for reasons that are not always religious. At a deeper level, it is said that there has been a massive loss of faith in Christianity and this, too, needs careful examination. The faith that some people lost deserved to be lost, for sometimes it was a barrier between them and God, just as the 'image' some people had and have of God is something that ought to be destroyed. On another plane, and without wishing to suggest a reductionist or LCM view of Christian truths, the churches have often been too slow in abandoning impossible positions. One thinks of the Galileo affair in the seventeenth century and the tangled debate over evolution in the nineteenth century and indeed later. The cosmology churchmen have simply assumed and the notions of divine providence they have put about have proved to be incompatible with the scientific world-picture of contemporary man. This is not to say that all he holds is necessarily true or that the church has to adapt her faith (as opposed to her theology). As the Second Vatican Council made plain, the church wishes to enter into dialogue with the modern world, and it is to be supposed that there will be some modification of ideas on both sides. In brief, the credibility gap between the modern man and the church has become too great for him to give his allegiance to it.

1

Where liturgy is concerned, the difficulties are different and in some ways greater. The Christian liturgy exists in a realm that is hardly open to the intellectualist and sometimes highly rationalistic mind of modern man. If he works in the physical sciences he is concerned with measurement and the exact application of tested principles to a problem, and if he is engaged in technological processes he knows that the *correct* application of scientific principles is vital to the success of his project. His reasoning mind is at work all the time, he is dealing with what he believes to be solid reality (though the picture physicists give of its solidity, in normal terms, hardly justifies such notions), and even if he does not do so, he knows that everything he is concerned with can be tested and proved. The world of liturgy is, on the other hand, a world of poetry, of symbol, a world where one thing often means another. In the eucharist the church says that the bread is not bread but the Body of Christ and then goes on to act in a certain way towards it, bowing to it or kneeling to it or holding it aloft. Water, oil and other elements are used in a quite non-utilitarian fashion, men are invested with mysterious powers and wear strange clothes as a sign that they have such powers. It all looks very much like magic or, more respectably, primitive religious practices that he has read about at one time or another.

Is this world closed to modern man? Or need it be? If the writing of verse has declined in our time, it is perhaps the only art that has. Music the plastic arts, drama, to mention no others, are in a flourishing condition and there are many with a wholly scientific training who take a keen interest in them. They are aware, too, that the considerable powers of science and technology are at the service of highly sophisticated forms of entertainment on television and radio. Like all of us, they are daily confronted with various art-forms which communicate to them over the whole range of mind, will and the senses. What is in question at the moment is not the quality of the communication but the style of it. If it does not engage the *whole* of the personality it is useless. With a little reflection we realize that we are not just reasoning beings, that there are values that cannot be scientifically analyzed or accounted for and that there is a world beyond the pedestrian necessities of everyday life. We become aware that we have *needs* that cannot be satisfied by a multiplicity of material goods or economic prosperity or political power and it is at least a fair guess that much of the emotional and psychological disorders of our age is to be attributed to the fact that man *is* trying to live on bread alone. There seems to be a wide measure of agreement that the protests and demonstrations of our time and the feverish searchings for something other *in kind* than the materialistic system in which we live are the symptoms of a spiritual malaise. It is distressing to older people to hear that the young who are demonstrating all over the world are doing so because they are rejecting the materialistic way of life that so many have assumed was a good thing in itself. Even the scourge of drug-taking witnesses to a desire for the Good Life, although the means to achieve it are and must be totally unacceptable. Drugs may be mere escapism of the crudest and most destructive kind, there are indeed many, too many, unscrupulous characters who are concerned simply to make money by 'pushing' the stuff, there are many of the young who are moved by fashion or the social pressure of their contemporaries, but the whole phenomenon cannot be explained by simply saying that the young are more vicious than their forefathers.

All this does not add up to saying that religion in general and worship in particular, if adopted, will settle all these troubles. On these terms religion would become simply another drug, the opium of the people indeed. What is necessary is an attempt on the part of Christian thinkers of various competences to show that there are values in religion which are authentic, which accord with the deepest needs of man. If people today can be brought to see this, they will be delivered from the narrow world of materialism and begin to realize what is their situation *vis-à-vis* that world and from this self-realization will come a confrontation with Reality. Such a confrontation may not lead to God or to worship, but it will inevitably pose ultimate questions.

Part of this work has already been done, and while it would be absurd to suggest that existentialist philosophies are going to be the bedside reading of the ordinary man, they do offer a way into reality which theologians, whether orthodox or unorthodox, have been exploring for some years. The great virtue of the existentialists is that they do not start with large and abstract notions but with man in the concrete predicament of his historical situation. Modern people are aware more or less clearly that they are involved in a world of 'things' over which they seek to gain the mastery, but when they have done so they become conscious of the absurdity of everything: what is it all for? This situation may be experienced with greater or less anxiety, with greater or less concern and a man may feel hemmed in, limited, frustrated. There seems to be a good deal of evidence that this is so among modern people. This is to experience what Heidegger calls the 'throwness' of man: he is thrown into a world to exist there in his situation, but his whence or his whither are concealed from him and, to lose his anxiety, he can take flight *into* things, into the 'instrumental' world which he constructs for himself, only finally to lose his identity in them. Or, having experienced the void of *things*, he can open himself out to being, and this 'unconcealedness' is for Heidegger simply truth. But before this happens he will have to experience 'nothingness', the absurd, or the great void that the world of things seems to be when he has turned from it. There is one further stage: he now becomes open to being and then the way lies open to him to feel the need for the Being Christians call God. This is not exactly Heidegger's conclusion, but it is where certain theologians have seen his argument to lead, and since he seems to be describing what is the predicament of so many people today we may suppose that this is the way they will find to God.[1]

But there are one or two more things to be added. If a man underwent this experience and found God, it is true, I think, that he would find him in encounter and not through a process of reasoning or abstraction. This might well come later. It is this element of encounter that we find in another, more specifically religious philosopher, Martin Buber. As is well known, he holds that man can have a twofold attitude, the first an 'I—Thou' one and the second and 'I—It' one. Only the first can be a truly personal relationship, involving the whole being. The second is concerned with the world of experience, the world of objects about which man reasons or thinks, or which he imagines or investigates. It is Heidegger's 'instrumental' world. With this man cannot have a relationship which involves his whole being. On the other hand, the 'I—Thou' attitude is precisely a relationship that is total and complete, a relationship that is expressed and maintained by the exchange that is called dialogue.

This relationship Buber describes as 'meeting' or 'encounter' and is expressed and maintained by the exchange that is called dialogue and represents a true reciprocity. 'Such a relation is direct, and it is also mutual, as involving a response which is absent in the detached objective attitude which may be taken up in experience. It is, furthermore, a relation of the whole person.'[2] This is the relationship we must look for and strive after, a relationship that for Gabriel Marcel involves commitment, and as with Heidegger, so with Buber, every 'I—Thou' relationship can degenerate into an 'I—It' relationship. Buber's thought then is intensely personal and it is not surprising that for him 'every particular "Thou" is but a glimpse through to the eternal "Thou"' who enters into a direct relation with us men in creative, revealing and redeeming acts, and thus makes it possible for us to enter into direct relation with him.[3] Martin Buber writes as a Jew and his sense of the co-inherence of human and divine relationships, the glimpse *through* the particular 'thou' to the eternal 'Thou' strongly reminds one of the gospel: 'In so far as you did it to them, you did it to me.' Buber's thought was no doubt born of a prolonged meditation on the Bible and it is the same source that has produced the 'encounter' theology of Catholic theologians since. As we shall see, this is a necessary basis for thinking about liturgy.

So far, we note that these thinkers (and, in fact, many others) provide an approach to God that is at once intensely personal and concrete. It is an approach that involves the *whole* personality in all his sheer human-

---

[1] The above summary is based on John Macquarrie's account in *Twentieth Century Religious Thought* (London, 1963), pp. 353–5.

[2] John Macquarrie, *op. cit.*, p. 196.

[3] *Op. cit.*, p. 197.

ness and over the whole range of his possibilities. It is the concrete 'I' in his here and now situation who, out of the meaninglessness of his world, looks for meaning and who, whether he is fully conscious of the fact or no, is seeking God with whom he would enter into a living personal encounter. This, it seems to me, is exactly what Christ was saying in all that teaching about the presence of the kingdom or in the Johannine vocabulary about the 'judgement' that is *now*, the *crisis*, the challenge that involves a decision and possibly a division. But in thinking about Christian worship it is on the wholeness of the personality, body, mind and spirit, in its approach to God that I would wish to insist. Man goes to God or seeks to go to God with all that he has. It is not just an intellectual or rational process. You can produce all the arguments from reason in the world, but if a man is not aware of his concrete situation both in what he himself is and where he finds himself, unless he realizes the ultimate absurdity of that situation *in itself*, he will not be moved by reasons. It is not that way that *in fact* he goes to God.

We are the heirs of a long tradition that owes more to Descartes than to St Thomas Aquinas. For Descartes, man was 'an angel in a machine', made up of two constituents of which the mind or soul was all-but a foreign body in the composite. Aquinas's simple teaching that the human soul is not a disembodied angel, was never intended to be such and will never be such, seems to have gone mostly unregarded if one examines the reams of pious literature that have been written in the last four centuries. The notion that a human being is a body-soul composite in which it is impossible to discern the 'seams', whose soul is precisely *human* and whose mode of operation is totally conditioned by the body, seems to be largely unknown to this day. Aquinas's thought may have been 'essentialist' or, rather incautiously, has usually been represented as if it were, but he was in fact fully 'humanist' and saw the importance of the body in every department of human living. It is because this teaching, too simply sketched here, has been disregarded that the body in recent centuries has been virtually excluded from worship. The thought that we can worship God with our bodies has hardly occurred to anyone. Worship in particular and religion in general has been regarded as something mental, interior and private and the more interior, the more genuine. The Mass-liturgy of the last eight or nine centuries has, of course, driven the laity to this attitude, for it was a liturgy that they could only see (though not always) and hear (though again not always) and in which their own activity was reduced to walking to the altar rails for communion. The devout occupied themselves with books of devotion and later, under the influence of the first phase of the liturgical movement, with their missals, and the undevout spent the time as best they could. This situation, I believe, more than anything else, is responsible for the resistance to the 'new' liturgy which is in fact very old.

From what we have said so far, it might seem that this existentialist approach to God is purely personal. In a way it must be. Everyone has to discover God for himself and if he discovers him out of his own experience God will be real for him in a way that no argument can make him real. But does the 'I—Thou' relationship involve *nothing* but God? As we have seen, Martin Buber already suggests that this is not so and Gabriel Marcel carries the matter a stage further. He distinguishes between *Having* and *Being*. *Having* is 'an external egocentric relationship' which gives us power over objects, including our own ideas. This is the 'instrumental' world of Heidegger. We cannot, of course, obliterate it or, in the last analysis, do without it. So *Having* has to be transformed into *Being* 'which brings us into different kinds of relationships, in which the sharp distinction of the self and its objects gives way to reciprocity and existence transcends any narrow egocentricity'.[4] For Marcel *being* involves not only commitment but community: 'In Marcel's view what is typical of a person is that he is continually engaging himself—for instance, he says "I'll see you tomorrow at three o'clock". But in doing this, he is already existing in community. Like Buber, Marcel finds the *locus* of human existence not in the isolated "I" but in the "we".[5] Perhaps it could be put in this way: it is only in encounter, between two persons with all the reciprocity that goes with it, with dialogue and mutual giving, that they realize the being or existence that is theirs, that they *are*. Man is not naturally an isolated being, and a sane view of things must reject Sartre's despairing 'Hell is others'. We need to recall the conventional teaching that individualism is not personalism, that, as Gerald Vann said somewhere many years ago, individualism is a kind of materialization of the person, emphasizing what is particular and turning the person into a being who exists only for himself. Two persons find themselves in each other, become persons, and what is true of interpersonal relationships is true in its measure of the relationships that are set up by community. A community is not a miscellaneous collection of individuals but an assembly of those who have relationships between them and who through community come to achieve not merely in measurable output what individually they could not achieve, but an enhancement of personality. They become fuller, richer beings with a firmer grasp on existence and a deeper realization of what they are. This, too, is part of the human situation and through reflection on it in communion with others they will come to a realization of God. It may be that one of the reasons why Godlessness, whether willed or not, has become endemic in modern industrialized civilization is that society has been atomized, people do feel desperately alone, cannot solve their problems because they are isolated from any real and really personal relationships with their fellows.

---

[4] *Op. cit.*, p. 360.
[5] *Op. cit.*, p. 360.

One of the inferences that may be drawn from the above view of reality is that man discovers God from out of the depths of his personality as it exists in the concrete situation of his life and if, by reflection on this situation, he does in fact go to God, he does so with his whole being and with all its potentialities. You can distinguish in him, if you like, body and soul, but in *fact* he exists in the wholeness of his being and it is with this that he approaches God and it is with his whole being that eventually he will embrace God. But this is as far as he can get. His whole being can cry out for God, but is there a possibility of real encounter with him of the person-to-person kind? Can he enter into communion with God? Will he in fact be able to commit himself to God without at the same time fearing that he is ultimately committing himself to himself and no more? If man needs to approach God with the whole of his being, there must be an answer that transcends the limits of human-ness.

The Christian answer is that since man needs to go to God in this way, God has approached him in a way that meets the deepest needs of his nature. The transcendent God became a man, involved in the whole human predicament, and far from this being a 'condescension' to the lowliness of humankind, it is, in the mind of Aquinas, the *highest manner* that God could communicate himself, give himself to man.[6] The purest religion therefore is not the solitary contemplation of The Other, it does not consist of lonely musings on the Divine nor yet of an effort to slough off the materiality of the person. The self-communication of God resulted in an 'enfleshment', the Word became flesh, and it is those who receive him who become sons of God: 'no one can come to the Father except by me'. And the 'religion' that Jesus inaugurated in the world was an 'enfleshed' religion; it is, by the very exigencies of the case, a *sacramental* religion through which man can go to God because he is that sort of being.

Even our knowing of God is 'sacramental'. Christ is the 'sacrament' of God, what St Paul calls 'the mystery' of God: 'the mystery *is* Christ among you' (Colossians 1:27) and, as he shows, the purpose of the mystery is to *reveal*, to manifest the richness of God's love that has been at work among the old people of God from the beginning, though that love is so great and so rich that in the last analysis it must remain a mystery. We come to know God in and through Jesus Christ: 'Philip, he that has seen me has seen the Father' and, as we have seen, there is no other way. We may read and study and theologize—and all these things are necessary at

---

[6] S.T., III, q.I., a.i. His argument is that since God is the *summum bonum* it is congruous with his nature that he should communicate himself to man in the best way possible: this happened in the incarnation because he united a human creature to himself and 'personalized' that nature: 'one person was made out of three things, the Word, the soul and the flesh'.

one time or another—but if we are to know God existentially we can only know him in and through Christ.

But we do not merely *know* God through Christ, we are able to make an encounter with God through Christ. He is not only the revelation of the Father, he in himself is the communication of the Father's love. Christ makes God present to men with all his redeeming power and love and this he did in his life, passion, death and resurrection. His passion and death were a self-giving, both to his Father and to us, a *total* giving of himself to his Father and to us, and through that self-giving he makes available to us and to men of all time the love of his Father. To this self-giving we are called, invited, urged to respond with a self-giving of faith and love, and in that exchange we meet God, we come to 'know' him in St John's sense, to enter into a communion with him that makes dialogue possible, the dialogue of prayer in which, for St Paul, the Spirit of God is present. The whole life of the Godhead indeed can be seen as a dialogue, but a dialogue at the infinite depth of divine life in which there is a perpetual giving and receiving of love, without loss or diminution, and it is through the encounter we make in Christ with God that we are drawn into the vital dialogue of Father, Son and Holy Spirit that is the life of the Trinity itself. This is the end-purpose of all worship and we see that it occurs 'in community' and through the total response of the human person, body, soul and all.

From a slightly different viewpoint, we also see that the *manner* of salvation was through community. God called a people and made them a holy and priestly people (Exodus 19:5–6; and cf I Peter 2:4–9 and Revelation 1:6) to whom he could communicate his love. Jesus came as the head of a people, the whole human race; he summed up in himself the experience of the old people of God and identified himself with the human predicament, feeling in himself the impact of sin (Mark 14:32–42; 15:34 and parallels, cf II Corinthians 5:21) and from within the human race lifting it up to a new life (John 3:13–15), so that man could enter into union with his Father. In this way he brought into existence a new people of God whose purpose would be to show to the world the redeeming love of God and whose function would be to make Christ present to every succeeding generation of man. The people now became the 'sacrament', totally dependent on Christ, but *sent* with his word and his redeeming love to all mankind (Matthew 28: 18–20). In language that has long been traditional and adopted by the Constitution on the Liturgy (6), 'it was from the side of Christ as he slept the sleep of death on the cross that there came forth "the wondrous sacrament of the church"'.

Clearly, it is this sheer visibility that is the sacrament of Christ, revealing that he, with the Holy Spirit, is active in the world; and visibility means institution, structures, among other things liturgy. And here we encounter all the scandal of particularity. Man's large aspirations, the most spiritual of his desires, his longing to be in contact with Being, these, he now realizes, are to be satisfied in and through the materiality of institution and rite. Not only that, but the institution and the rite can become opaque. The one can become complicated, weighed down with legalism, appearing to be an end in itself and, since the institution is a people, it can be defaced by all the sins and follies of humankind. The rite can become encrusted with non-functional elements, it can degenerate into the meaningless performance that is called ritualism, it too can appear to be an end in itself. All this is not only possible but has happened and then Christ is not proclaimed, Christ is not made visible to the world and the institution and the rite become barriers to the encounter with Christ. The church becomes a 'scandal', a stumbling block.

But what is the alternative? Even the purest religion of the word can degenerate into formalism, the freest form of prayer can petrify and large aspirations can vanish in clouds of unrealism. Either way, the seeds of human imperfection can mar the vaunting idealism of man. He, too, is part of the scandal of particularity. It is part of the human condition and he has got to come to terms with it. If he does, he should find that the material, the particular, the humble element can become for him a theophany. Without, for the moment, going into the nature of the liturgical mystery, there is a St Francis to bear witness that the sun and the moon, fire and water and even the humble body can in Christian eyes be the images, the far-off echoes, of divine Beauty. This, it seems to me, is as genuine an intuition of Being as is that born of the anguish that seems to be have been the *point de départ* of the existentialists.

Of course the church must always be purifying herself—*semper reformanda*—of course there must be a constant moral effort within the church to seek Christ and to make him visible to the world. But not even the church can abolish the concrete, the symbolic, the sacramental. These are of the stuff of the Christian way of life and, one may think, are, whatever the danger of corruption, the singular means by which man can make religion real to himself, by which he can grasp it so that in effect he can live by it. It is possible, I suppose, for a man and woman to agree wordlessly that they are married, but throughout history, if they have not declared this publicly and if the community has not borne witness to it, not only do they hardly realize that they are man and wife but the community is not willing to accept them as such. We can go to God directly in repentance and we must, but unless that repentance is 'sacramentalized', until we are faced with God and ourselves in the process of confession, we have a weakened realization of sin that can eventually disappear. We can, as the Lord commanded us, seek God in private prayer, but if we never join with a community in praying, if even in private prayer we regularly shut out the community to which we belong, then our prayer will become a self-regarding activity, a species of what a former Bishop of Oxford called 'a self-regarding soul culture'. It, too, will deteriorate and may disappear altogether.

Can man then come to an *experience* of God in community? To suggest that he can and does seems to run counter to so much that has been held, both by non-Christians and even some Christians, in recent centuries. Religion has appeared to be mental, interior and solitary and worship to be private if it is to be true and genuine. In the Catholic church even the Mass was turned into a kind of meditation, the occasion when people thought holy thoughts and silently made their prayer to God. But if man is the concrete personal being we have seen he is, if *by his very nature* he needs 'I—Thou' relationships if he is to come to self-realization and if, as is suggested, these inter-personal relationships inevitably involve community, it would seem that it will be normal for him to find God in community worship.

How this may happen is indeed a little difficult to describe and where Christian worship is concerned it can be regarded as no more than an indication that it is possible. For in Christian worship man is presented with realities, with the reality of the human condition which is a fallen condition, but also with the reality that he has been lifted out of it or can be if he accepts in living dynamic faith the divine reality that is present in worship. All these realities, however, are matters of faith, of the self-communication of God to his creatures, a self-communication that invites and makes possible a response and a commitment. If, then, man realizes his personal existence, comes to know what and who he is, in inter-personal relationships with other human beings, it would seem to follow that he is going to come to a knowledge of God that is deeper and more embracing than purely intellectual knowledge through his dialogue with God in worship.

But there is another sense that goes much deeper in which we can say that man comes to God in worship and here we have to do with the deepest things of Christian reality. We move out of the world of psychological experience into the world of being, of reality, the reality of the intimate life of God. It is only through the relationships we have with the *persons* of the Holy Trinity, says Dom Alban Stolz, that we enter into the life of God: 'It is in fact of the essence of these relations that we are incorporated into the Son by the Holy Spirit and led to the Father by the Son.' But all this occurs within the church that is the body of Christ, union with whom is the very basis of mysticism. Because we are made members of Christ, because we have to be conformed to him, because there has to

---

[7] K. E. Kirk, somewhere in his vast study called *The Vision of God*. This, of course, does not mean that mystical prayer is invalidated but, as Dom Alban Stolz insisted, Christian mysticism is always ecclesial (*Théologie de la Mystique*, Fr. trans, 2nd ed. 1947), and he was not afraid to say that it was basically liturgical, sacramental and eucharistic, pp. 249–52.

be an *imitatio Christi* in the depths of our being, we have to undergo a transformation. We have to make the passover of the Lord from death to life our own:

'In the eucharist our insertion into Christ, that is, the passage of our whole sinful being into the transfigured being of Christ, becomes a *sacramental* reality. Our union with Christ delivers us from our sinful condition. Christ disentangles those who have become like him from the restrictions of this world and leads them before the face of God, as he himself preceded them at the ascension. By sharing in the eucharist the Christian is snatched out of himself and out of the world and is led by the Son to the Father. . . . The assimilation to Christ and the union with him that are effected sacramentally in the eucharist set the Christian (in Christ) in the presence of God.'[8]

At this level of Christian faith, then, the eucharist is a transforming process. As St Leo says somewhere, we are transformed into what we receive. This is what happens, though it is only faith that can perceive it. Whether and in what circumstances Christians can experience this process are questions that would take us very far but *that* it is possible can hardly be doubted. There are the experiences of the saints recorded sufficiently often, and particularly those of the Benedictine St Gertrude whose whole spiritual and mystical life was centred on and sustained by the liturgy. Mystical experience and liturgical celebration were for her almost one thing and, apart from a single occasion, there were no outward manifestations. Yet *what* she experienced she was able to express in the (dictated) writings of hers that survive.[9] There can hardly be any doubt that she achieved the highest mystical union.

There were, of course, several co-efficients at play here. Gertrude was a Benedictine nun, the whole framework of her life was the liturgy and she lived at the time of a 'mystical invasion' which in itself is so difficult to understand. But she brought to her worship an unusual spirit of self-giving and openness and it was this, humanly speaking, that made it possible for her to know God in and through the liturgy experientially. But the fact that, apart from that one occasion, there were no outward manifestations puts us on the right track. A recent writer usefully distinguishes the 'empirical' and the 'experiential' and he says that to look for the former in worship (or in the spiritual life in general) is to put the secondary for the primary. Empirical experience, something that is tangible and almost palpable and much sought after today, is 'a kind of overflow and a bonus

---

[8] A. Stolz, *op. cit.*, pp. 249–50.

[9] J. Leclercq, F. Vandenbroucke, *Histoire de la Spiritualité*, 2 (Paris, 1961), p. 539, and C. Vagaggini, *Il Senso Theologico della Liturgia* (2nd ed. 1958), pp. 578–627. The single occasion was at Mass, at the introit, when she was so moved that she found she was not following the movements of the choir and she besought the Lord to let her do so!

if it is genuine'. Since he summarizes much of what we have been trying
to say, the whole passage is worth quoting:

'The stress on the experiential provides a new insight into the
primacy of the inner, contemplative, transcendent dimension of life
and thus supplies the impetus to move out of a pedestrian, lifeless,
"ho-hum" style of religion that bores people to death. The christian life
is a thrilling adventure, a call out of the living death many people endure
into the exuberant life of freedom and love that is thoroughly personal.
The christian life is God's answer to man's search for transcendence; it
responds to man's desire and hope to live for something bigger than
himself, to move out of and beyond the limitations and imprisonment of
his own body and psyche. Every man is embarked on that search; most
take the road of experiences. This is the road of the empirical rather
than the experiential. The two are by no means the same. The empirical
is the observable, the tangible and measurable aspect of human life. It is
prayers as opposed to prayer, feeling sorry rather than being sorry, kind
acts compared to charity, experiences rather than experience. The first
member of these doublets ideally contains and is a manifestation of the
second. But it is not always so. And to confuse the two can be disastrous
in religious thinking. For those who fail to make the distinction, a
"meaningful liturgy" has to be a "happening" every time, deeply
moving, imaginatively enriching and emotionally rewarding. This is too
much to ask from a daily liturgy. It is to want something approaching a
mystical experience wherein there is an immediate touching and sensing
of transcendent realities. Empirical experience of this kind is an overflow
and a bonus if it is genuine. When it occurs, it is an integral and rewarding part of a religious experience, *which is a depth reality and consists
in insight and personal commitment*. The experience may be present in
the worshipper without any observable sign other than the peace and
desire of the person to be there in the presence of the Lord.'[10]

This is a very balanced statement and the writer does not scorn, as some
Catholic writers have, the incidence of 'empirical experience' but, like
St Thomas in fact, sees it as the overflow, the *redundantia*, or something
much deeper. However the process may be described (and it may be indescribable), the worshipper receives an insight into the faith, into the will
of God for himself or into the ways of God with man and through this
understanding (*intus-legere*) he realizes that he is making an encounter with
the living God. He is drawn into closer union with him and this may produce *ex redundantia* an experience of which he is conscious. *But even if it
does not*, it remains true that worship can and does have effects in the order
of experience: it deepens faith and kindles love, and though these effects
are often not immediately perceived by the worshipper, they are observable

---

[10] Ernest E. Larkin, 'The Search for Experience', in *The Way* (Vol. 11, no. 2,
April, 1971), p. 102.

in their lives. It is a matter of pastoral experience (and a subject for grateful wonder) that Christians who have no intellectual pretensions frequently acquire a depth of insight into the faith and what St Thomas called a 'connaturality' with the things of God through their faithful worship Sunday by Sunday. Oddly enough, this we should expect, and it is even odder that we should be surprised when we see it happening. Even under the old order of things this was observable, but now that the word of God is so much more adequately laid before the people, it is reasonable to expect that that deepening of faith will become an ever more important result of worship. For it is, I believe, the deepening of faith that provides the basis for the sort of 'experience' which we have been considering. More will be said about the relationship of word to sacrament later in this book, but immediately it is clear that the movement of the worshipper in faith and through faith in the first part of the Mass leads to an encounter in love in the second.

There is another aspect of the matter. Modern people have been saying for some time that they cannot, or cannot easily, find God in silent prayer or even perhaps in vocal prayer. The whole business of 'meditation' is repugnant to them. There have even been those who have said that prayer was a waste of time, that instead of praying for people we should get out and help them. It is of course always possible to make prayer a surrogate for the active service, in love, of others, but to abandon prayer in the interests of action is to fall into the heresy of activism, which means 'good works' without 'faith'. As I have written elsewhere, 'unless we are "in communication" with God by prayer, we shall have no true love to offer'.[11] Love needs constant purification if it is not to become either possessive or dominating, a *self* seeking (however disguised) instead of 'other' seeking. And that Other is both God and man. Modern people are quick to say that they can find God in others, and philosophers and some theologians have been suggesting that God's transcendence is meaningless. They, too, have perhaps been the victims of spatial images, for transcendence as Christians have understood it means the complete otherness of God and not that he is *somewhere else*, absent from the universe he has made and occasionally visiting it, as it were, to see how it is getting on. There is a co-inherence of God in creation and of created things in God which respects his complete otherness yet at the same time affirms that he is present. If we do in fact find God in other people, we find *God*, because he is here, and not just people. But it is not at all as easy as people think.

Worship, it seems to me, is the privileged moment (*kairos*) where we can meet both God and man. *In community* we become aware of the divine realities that are present first in the word and then in the sacrament but also in the hearts of our fellow-worshippers. They with us have heard God's

---

[11] *Liturgy*, April, 1968, p. 35.

call, they with us have received God's word into their hearts, they with us receive the one Bread that makes us, though many, one body in Christ and all establish the horizontal relationship that ties man to man. In the service that various members of the worshipping community do for each other, whether it be reading or serving or singing or even the humble task of welcoming brethren at the door, they are acknowledging the presence of God in each other. This is brought to its clearest expression in the sign of peace that is exchanged before communion and in the act of communion itself when by gesture and song the community recognizes that all share one faith in the one Spirit through Jesus Christ. No doubt we need to be more keenly aware of our relationship one with another, no doubt individual-istic attitudes can atomize the community and no doubt there are still people who regard their Christian brethren almost with hostility as they kneel alongside them. But the realities are there and it remains true that we can find God in others at a deeper level in our worship than anywhere else.

Of course the faith and love we find in worship has to be carried into the world we live in where in hard fact our service of others begins, but it may be thought that if modern man is looking for what I might call a credible God, if he is looking for a personal encounter with God, if he wants to come to a God who is not the conclusion of a metaphysical argument, he should not discount worship as the place where he will find him. It goes without saying that the style of worship he encounters will have much to do with whether he does meet God or not, but every human institution is weighed down with imperfection, with the sheer materiality of human existence, and while Christians must seek constantly to purify themselves and their institutions, the God-seeker (hypothetically a non-Christian) must learn to be patient and tolerant not merely of the shortcomings of Christians but of the limitations of his own human nature when he is approaching God. If it is true, as we have suggested, that man goes to God humanwise, through people and symbols, there will be times when both people and symbols become opaque, but that does not invalidate the way. It merely means that it is fraught with all the limitations of human existence as we know it.

For those who have experienced in faith the divine realities that are expressed in the liturgy, a further step is possible. However improbable it may seem, this earthly, indeed earthy, liturgy is but the sacrament of the heavenly liturgy, a reflection of the heavenly liturgy of the 'city of the living God', the new Jerusalem where Jesus is the supreme *leitourgos*, celebrating in festival with the angels and with 'the whole church in which everyone is a "first-born son" '. There is a continual come-and-go between heaven and earth but it is through the concrete community and the symbols of its worship that we are able to penetrate into the new and better temple not made with hands, where Jesus is ever living to make intercession for us.[12] The vision of the writer of the Letter to the Hebrews is very remarkable, for in it the earthly church and the heavenly are hardly distinguishable: through the one he sees the reality that is present in the other. This is what the earthly assembly meant for him, this is what he *saw* in it. We may suppose, too, that the John of Revelation who had his visions on the Day of the Lord (1:10), the day of Christian worship, had a similar insight into the co-inherence of the earthly and the heavenly liturgy (4 and 5). It is an aspect of worship that is very strongly marked in the Orthodox and Eastern traditions generally[13] and although it is less marked in the Roman tradition, there are the typical Roman prefaces to remind us that always we celebrate with the *whole* church in heaven and on earth. Nor are these, at least for men of faith, idle dreams or merely poetical expressions. That the earthly church inheres in Christ who not only suffered and died but also rose and is now enthroned in glory with his Father is an elementary truth that Western theology has never wholly forgotten, though the *theologia crucis* of both Catholic and Lutheran traditions has not always given sufficient emphasis to the theology of the Risen Christ. As sober a theologian as St Thomas Aquinas could see the church as the sacrament of our communion with God. One of the finest commentators on his ecclesiology can sum up the matter like this:

'(For St Thomas) the church is concerned with communion in the mystery of God. The deepest reality of the church, by which she achieves her greatest extension, the element that will remain eternally when all else is gone, is divinizing communion with *God*. But in our earthly, physical and historical situation, this can only be achieved through Christ, the incarnate Word, and through what he has given to us: faith, sacraments, institutions. . . . The church is fundamentally and supremely union with God in his godhead. In heaven, glory and vision; here below, grace and faith. But grace is the seed of glory and faith of vision so that in principle there is on the one hand a unity of existence between the angels and the *comprehensores*,[14] that is the heavenly church, and on the other, the faithful or the earthly church.'[15]

Whether and how far we experience these realities in worship is another matter, but there they are and perhaps the mere fact that we are aware of them may help us gradually to pierce the envelope of symbol and sacrament to God whom they convey to us but whom (because they are inevitably opaque) they also obscure.

---

[12] Hebrews 12:22–5; 8:2; 9:11; and cf CL 8.
[13] Cf Erik Peterson, *The Angels and the Liturgy* (Eng. trans. London, 1964).
[14] In Aquinas's language, these are all those who now *see* God.
[15] Yves Congar, *L'Eglise de Saint Augustin à l'époque moderne* (Paris, 1970), pp. 232–3.

THE WORLD OF SYMBOLS

IN THE previous chapter I have attempted to show that liturgy is fundamentally in accord with the nature of man. The matter can be stated in Christian terms: God has approached man in Christ who is the embodiment of the divine love and this God did because if man is to have something more than a merely mental apprehension of God, he must be approached in this way. On the other hand, man needs to approach God in the wholeness of his personality and if he is able to do this the relationship that he desires and needs to establish with God can in its turn become embodied, made concrete. It is in this area of reality that liturgy exists and it would not be too much to say that it is an embodied relationship if always we see that relationship as based on faith and love. That is, there is nothing automatic about it. It follows from this that liturgy exists in a world that is neither that of pure speculation or meditation, nor yet on the other hand of mere feeling. The realities it contains and conveys are embodied in certain gestures and in certain things that are used in a special way. We have, in other words, to understand the world of symbol if we are to understand liturgy.

As we have seen, modern man by the conditions of his culture is not adjusted to this world—or at least he may think he is not. In fact, he is living in a world of images which, it is true, are not always symbols—though unwittingly they may refer to hidden values, such as the making of money—and a great part of his life is controlled by signs. He has only to take out his car to be confronted with a forest of signs that condition and control his driving. Something, then, must be said about symbol and sign, though it is important that symbol should come first. There is a danger of intellectualizing signs that has not always been avoided by Catholic sacramental theology. The sign-value, the sheer power of significance, of the

---

[1] The bibliography on the subject is enormous. See Mircea Eliade, *Myths, Dreams and Mysteries* (Fontana, London, 1968). Yves Congar, ed., *La Liturgie après Vatican II*: M. D. Chenu, 'L'Homme de la Liturgie'; P. Colin, 'Phénoménologie et herméneutique du symbolisme liturgique'. L. Bouyer, *Rite and Man* (Eng. trans., London, 1963), which summarizes much that has been written on the subject. I. H. Dalmais, *Introduction to the Liturgy* (Eng. trans., London, 1961), which is, in fact, a very good introduction to the matter.

sacraments has been diminished by casuistry (how *little* water must flow for a 'valid' baptism) and by a faulty liturgical practice. The very liturgy in the books, the wealth of signs to be found there, was often disregarded and the minimum done to secure a basic validity. Even under the old order, it was impossible to understand what the church was saying about baptism unless one took into account both the whole ritual to be found in the book and the basic context that was (and, of course, still is) to be found in the Easter Vigil.[2]

In opposition to the Reformers' views of sacraments, Catholics emphasized the *efficiency* of the sign, they were causes of grace and sometimes the metaphors used to enforce this teaching gave the impression that they were utensils, tools. St Thomas's simple teaching that *sacramenta significando causant*, their very efficiency is by way of signification, was too little known. Attention then concentrated on 'matter' and 'form', both no more than analogical notions where the Christian sacraments are concerned, and *all* that was required was the proper 'application' of the latter to the former. The wider and deeper significance of the gestures done and things used just did not enter into the picture. That was possibly piety or, worse still, poetry, and you can't let poetry into the liturgy! Bread no longer looked like bread, oil was dabbed on only to be wiped off, the supplicatory attitude of the *orante* who held his hands palms upturned to beseech God's mercy was reduced to a hugging of the ribs, an attitude that was fiercely insisted on by 'Roman' rubricists. As a modern Thomist has said,[3] analyses of the sacraments along the lines of cause and validity led to a sort of rationalism. The sacrament looked very much like a machine; you could take it to pieces and (almost) evacuate the mystery.

The case with symbols is even worse. If you say 'symbol' it is immediately assumed that you mean 'empty symbol', that it has no content. It is reduced to rather less than a metaphor. If you say that the bread and wine are symbols of the eucharist, people immediately think you are saying that they are *no more* than symbols and that you are endorsing a receptionist and subjective theology of the eucharist. The usual view is that the bread and wine with the words are *efficient causes* of the Real Presence and so you get a eucharistic theology that concentrates on the words of institution

---

[2] In speaking in various places in the last year or so about the new baptismal Order, I was at first puzzled by the constant questioning about original sin: doesn't the new Order then say that baptism takes away original sin? One had to reply that it has very little to say about it (e.g. the prayer of exorcism). Then I realized that for a great number of people baptism simply meant 'the taking away of original sin', just like that. It apparently had no further or other consequences and any question of delaying the baptism was regarded as improper. The giving of the Holy Spirit, the incorporation into Christ and all the rest about which the Order has so much to say seem to have been widely unknown in any real sense of knowing.

[3] Père A. M. Roguet, OP, *Somme Théologique, Les Sacrements* (Paris, 1945), pp. 255–379.

to the exclusion of almost all else. Yet there are those disturbing expressions of the Fathers of the Church, of Origen and Ambrose, to mention no others, who speak of the bread as being the *homoioma* (likeness), the *figura*, of the body of Christ.[4] But the Fathers were right. The bread *is* a symbol of the body of Christ who is 'the bread of life' and who said 'Take and *eat*'. There is nothing abstruse here and the answer to the question why Christ took bread and wine at the Last Supper is simply that they are symbols, which everyone can understand, of nourishment. As Masure wrote long enough ago now:

'Thus it is through the enactment of a sacramental sacrifice of *bread and wine* that the Mass becomes the symbolic and moreover the *veridical* affirmation of the sacrifice of the cross. The bread and wine were admirably chosen by Christ to *show forth* to us not only that he died but that in dying he has given us life, and that by his resurrection he imparts it to us for ever. For the eucharist is both his flesh delivered up to the cross for the salvation of the world and *the bread of life come down from heaven.* . . .'[5]

These matters are now becoming clearer. The terminology has been changing for some time, the eucharist is referred to as a 'meal', a term to be found in the General Introduction to the Order of the Mass (e.g. 48, 56), and 'meal' indicates eating and drinking, whatever else may need to be added for a full statement of Catholic doctrine. The restoration of communion from the cup for the laity and, in many countries, of communion in the hand, all emphasize in liturgical, that is, symbolic language that the eucharist is a meal of which the chief symbols are the bread and wine. For an Origen, for an Ambrose and a host of other Fathers, the bread *was* the symbol of the body of Christ. *Of its very nature* it led the communicant to think of eating and drinking. Thus it was, and is, something much more than a sign of the Real Presence; it indicates, as far as it can, the real meaning of the eucharist, namely that it is an eating of the Lord's body and the drinking of his blood. But even that is not the whole truth. The symbols of bread and wine are, in a certain context, that of the *paschale convivium*, to use the term of the General Introduction, and this again has a special framework: as at the Last Supper the eucharist was instituted in the context of the paschal *berakah*, the prayer of blessing and thanksgiving, so the bread and wine are in the same context. They are elements of a whole action which is comprised of gestures (the taking and breaking of the bread) and of words which give their ultimate significance to the bread

---

[4] The English translator of Jungmann's *Missarum Solemnia* was indeed so disturbed by the introduction of *homoioma* into a paragraph quoting Origen on the eucharist that he purposely mistranslated it. Or perhaps it was the Censor librorum who insisted on a 'modification'.

[5] E. Masure, *The Sacrifice of the Mystical Body* (London, 1954), p. 63. My italics.

and wine as symbols: they no longer signify natural life, they are transformed so that they may become the means by which Christians enter into
the death and life of Christ. They become what the Roman Canon says
they are, the Bread of Life and the Cup of Everlasting Salvation. But
they need to undergo this 'transignification' if they are to achieve their
purpose as *sacramental* symbols.[6]

Symbolism, then, is an integral part of the liturgy, but if we are to
understand it more fully it is necessary to put the matter in a wider context. Symbolism is not a quality of the Christian liturgy merely. As scholars
have revealed for some long time now, it is part of all religious worship as
they have investigated it in its origins or in its more primitive state.

It will be best to begin at the beginning. Here we meet the ambiguous
word 'myth' which, as used by the phenomenologists, does not prejudge the
question whether its content is true or not. Myth is concerned with primordial events, in particular creation, when primitive man believed that the
gods or hero figures were reducing chaos to cosmos (the organized universe)
which was the *real* world, the world in fact of the sacred. But the activity
of the gods represented for him an abundance of life and energy. It was his
desire to make contact with the primordial event so that he could lay hold
of its life and energy not simply for himself as an individual, for a sense of
individuality was weak, but for the whole community of which he was a
member or, rather, with which he was con-corporate. It was vital to the
survival of the community that it should be in contact with that power and
so he was led to *mimesis*, the imitation in ritual of the primordial events.
Mimesis involved the re-enactment of the primordial events in gesture,
dance, song and the use of objects that were necessary for the 'drama'. It
is at this point that symbolism, gestures and objects became part of worship. Both gestures and objects referred away from themselves to the events
they were recalling but *at the same time* arrested the attention of the participants in such a way that they knew they were being put in touch with
those events. This is the first function of symbol. As opposed to sign (which
is 'thin') the symbol is solid, even opaque, something on which the senses
can rest and which, because as yet undetermined by word, can suggest a
whole range of meaning that the sign cannot. As I have written elsewhere,
symbol is more apt to convey the breadth of the liturgical mystery. Its
very opacity makes it possible for it to suggest mystery; it contains within itself echoes of the infinite. It arouses our interest, gives the mind

---

[6] To this extent and irrespectively of what conclusions theologians draw or do
not draw, the 'new' theology seems to me to have emphasized an element in the
eucharist that is important. As far as I can see, too, they are to this extent traditional. Unless I am mistaken, they are saying that whereas in the first instance
bread and wine signify simply ordinary food and drink, if they are to signify what
the eucharist intends, the body and blood of Christ, they must be 'transignified' so
that they become signs of the everlasting life that comes from Christ.

something to work on, but it also stimulates the whole affective side of the personality.[7]

Yet the use of symbols has its dangers. Just as the sign can become so 'thin', concerned with merely intellectual processes, giving no more than information, the symbol, because it is concrete and opaque, can draw all the attention to itself, making impossible the passage from itself to the thing symbolized. This is what happens, has happened, when ritual is seen as an end in itself, when it is not reflected on, when its meaning and purpose are not discerned, when it becomes divorced from the reality it is meant to convey. For it is of the essence of the symbol to be different from that which is symbolized as well as having a certain likeness to it. This 'difference from' has been called 'the symbolic hiatus'; you have to make a leap from the symbol to the reality symbolized. Anointing in the New Testament signifies the giving of the Holy Spirit and yet how vast is the distance between the symbol and the reality! Yet it is in this hiatus precisely that the power of symbols lies, as can be seen when we look at the Mass:

'We no longer know it simply in the nakedness of its essence (as if we knew the doctrine of the Mass as defined by the Council of Trent), but we know it as something radiating relationships with other elements of the world, clothed in analogies and likenesses with other things. It is thus that the "symbolic hiatus" constitutes the power and richness of the symbol: to knowledge pure and simple (given by the sign) it adds an impression of life and mystery, a value of delight and sentiment. These the thing alone or merely signified could not give. The symbol which is concrete, more immediate to us—we might say coarser—evokes them and transfers them to the thing that is symbolized.'[8]

Symbols, then, belong to this concrete world and enable man to concretize his relationship with his origins, to get in touch with the events that lie at the origin of his world and to bring their power into the present so that he can lay hold of it. Symbols are concerned with reality (not with *un*reality), but in worship they transcend themselves and lead men to a world that would otherwise be beyond his grasp. They are related to the world of poetry and indeed metaphor which is unreal only to those for whom all things can be measured, analyzed and weighed. The poet, the lover, says 'My love is a consuming fire'. That does not mean that his love is unreal but that it is so real that he can only express it by what might seem an extravagant metaphor. Likewise, we say not that God's word is *like* a seed but that it *is* a seed: 'Is there here simply a literary artifice? In a sense, yes, but it expresses by a metaphor the leap of the mind and

---

[7] 'Signs, Symbols and Mysteries' in *Worship* (USA), vol. 39, no. 8, Oct.–Nov., 1965, which summarizes much of what A. M. Roguet has to say in Appendix II of his trans. and commentary, *Somme Théologique, Les Sacrements* (Paris, 1945).

[8] A. M. Roguet, *loc.* and *art. cit.*

heart. Hence the realism of the symbol, particularly of the symbolic gesture for which no explanation is adequate even if (later) it becomes necessary. . . . It is indeed true that according to the condition of man mystery finds in the symbol its homogeneous expression', that is an expression that is in accord with the nature of man.[9]

It is in this world of symbol that the liturgy exists, a world that is other than the world of science and reason, and yet that is real. Wholly in accord with man's nature, it enables him to communicate, first with his fellows (the kiss, the handshake) and then with another world where he has glimpsed the *mysterium tremendum et fascinans* that for him is God.[10] When we come to the Christian liturgy, the symbolism achieves a density of reality that is based on God's action and on the symbols chosen by Christ that become efficacious by his power. If the Christian is able to make contact with the events by which the Christian community was brought into being, it is because God has made this possible. He has approached man in Christ who is 'the mystery of God among us' (Colossians 1:27).

We find, then, that there are three terms now in play, sign, symbol and mystery, and each needs to be understood if we are to understand what liturgy is. The Constitution says that 'in the liturgy man's sanctification is signified by signs perceptible to the senses' but 'signs' here need to be taken in all their density and not in the somewhat etiolated sense of recent sacramental theology. These signs are not just 'indicators' like a road sign, nor simply efficient causes; they are pregnant with reality, they are 'solid', addressing man in the wholeness of his personality, inviting him to make the leap from their humble materiality to the transcendent realities they show forth and convey. In other words, they are symbols that express a whole range of meaning and through that very expression effectively lead men to an encounter with God. They are efficacious, yes, but efficacious because they are full of reality which of their nature they can convey. This traditionally is called their 'causality', but even the causality is reduced if it is thought of as the efficiency of a tool. Human beings are not raw matter on which God carves his purpose, but free, willing, believing people who concretize their faith in the sacraments and who through this concrete, *human* approach to God come to meet him.

What, then, is the importance of 'sign' as such? It is here that 'word' becomes of crucial importance. Symbols remain vague in the sense that they can signify several things. Water symbolizes both life and death, for it is necessary if man is to live and it can suffocate him to death. How, then, does it symbolize life in baptism if not through the sign that makes of it the sacrament of life? But, further, how can it become the symbol-sacrament

---

[9] M. D. Chenu, 'Anthropologie de la Liturgie' in *La Liturgie après Vatican II*, ed. Y. Congar (Paris, 1967), p. 173.

[10] R. Otto, *The Idea of the Holy* (Eng. trans., O.U.P., 1923, and Penguin Books, 1959).

of death and life *in Christ* unless it is used in the Christian context? The meaning of water in baptism is part of the proclamation of the Gospel. Its meaning is only known to the believer, as St John Chrysostom said so long ago:

'Here the believer judges differently from the unbeliever (who) learns about baptism and thinks it is nothing but water. *But I do not think merely of what I see* (it is a symbol). I think of the purification of the soul which has been effected by the Holy Spirit. The unbeliever thinks that baptism is no more than a simple washing of the body, but I believe that it makes the soul pure, and holy, and I think of the tomb, of the resurrection, of sanctification and redemption and the adoption of sons, of our heavenly inheritance, of the kingdom of heaven and the gift of the Holy Spirit' (it is a Christian symbol).[11]

So the believer must have the gospel preached to him, the word must be communicated, but that word has the task of making clear to him also what exactly is the meaning of this symbol here and now:

'Precisely because the supernatural saving reality, veiled in historical events, and surrounded by the darkness of mystery, is present to us only in earthly form (*sacramentum*), it demands the revealing word (*verbum*) as the interior aspect of its earthly appearance. Only in and through the prophetic word is the divine dimension of saving history brought to light. "Word" and "sacrament" are therefore constituents for revelation in the Old Testament as well as in the New, and, after this revelation has been brought to an end, for the life of the Church which grows out of it.'[12]

But we need to go a step further. What is the exact significance of this action that is being performed? Oil is used in the ordination of bishops and priests, in baptism and confirmation, for the consecration of objects as remote from these as churches and chalices. Sign is not opposed to symbol, it is 'the illuminating point of the symbol'[13] but is still one with it. The symbol does not lose its density and yet it achieves that significance that is necessary if it is to play its part in liturgy. It is only when symbol is dismissed and sign is left in all its thinness that it begins to be less than adequate in suggesting the range of the mystery that it is its function to express and convey. Object-symbols are indeed used in the Christian liturgy and the burning paschal candle during the Masses of Easter-time or during baptism carries its own message as a symbol of the Risen Christ, the light of the world. But this is only because it has formed part of a rite that proclaims the message of salvation of which the passion and resurrec-

---

[11] Quotation in J. D. Crichton, 'Signs, Symbols and Mysteries', *art. cit.* I regret that I have misplaced the reference.

[12] E. Schillebeeckx, 'The Sacraments: An Encounter with God', in *Christianity Divided* (London and New York, 1961), p. 246.

[13] J. D. Crichton, 'Signs, Symbols and Mysteries', *art. cit.*

tion of Christ is the climax. It is true, too, that simple gestures and actions like a genuflexion can and do convey worship, but this again only in the context of Christian faith in the eucharist. However, normally and especially for the heart of the liturgy which is made up of the eucharist and the other sacraments, it is the *word* that is the illuminating point of the symbol. If the meaning of the different uses of oil is to be apparent it is only through the word that this can be so. Anointing with chrism at baptism signifies, as the prayer accompanying it makes clear, incorporation into Christ who is priest, prophet and king. But neither does the word remain separate from the symbol; it is indeed in a fashion incarnated in it and nowhere does human word operate at so high a potential as when it is combined with the objects and gestures of the eucharist where the Word who is proclaimed in the scriptures becomes bodily present in the bread and wine. These in turn become luminous through the word so that their *sacramental* significance can be grasped.

From another point of view, word is of the greatest importance in the liturgy. It saves it, as nothing else can, from the automatism that is always ready to overtake it. In the traditional phrase, now brought back to Catholic consciousness, we are saved by faith and the sacraments of faith (CL 59) and the word first expresses the faith of the church of which the whole sacramental action is the embodiment and, secondly, enables the Christian to express his faith in response to that declared by the liturgical action. It is the word that makes the celebration of the liturgy an encounter with God through which we enter into the redeeming work of Christ. Perhaps it is not necessary to repeat that through the sign-symbol this encounter is an embodied one and, as we have seen at the beginning of this chapter, the relationship that man desires with God is an embodied one so that we can say that liturgy is the 'incarnation' of the union of man with God.

The word is pre-eminently revelatory of the meaning of the symbol and so points to the reality it symbolizes. In more conventional language, the liturgy (the sacraments) declare the faith of the church but this faith is not declared in propositions or in an intellectualized manner. It is a faith that points to Christ and to his saving acts, the whole Christ whom the Christian embraces in the liturgical action. St Paul saw baptism as the 'revelation' in action of the death and resurrection of Christ and the New Testament accounts see the eucharist as the showing forth (and making present) of the Christ who first under the signs of bread and wine gave himself to his apostles, a giving that was the sacrament of his complete and total self-giving on the cross. That is why St Paul could say that when we celebrate the eucharist we are proclaiming the Lord's death until he comes again.

It should not be surprising (or offensive) that primitive man found something very similar in his worship. Dom Odo Casel, who pondered the meaning of the Christian mystery for years, writing on 'The Notion of

Festival',[14] singles out the element of epiphany, manifestation, in celebration:

'What is characteristic is that the divine life comes down, in some fashion effectively, among those who are taking part in the solemnity. This is not a simple recalling; it implies a presence. The divinity is present in the festival procession,[15] visible or recognizable by his efficacious action. For all this, the rich terminology of Hellenism has the word "Epiphany". God has appeared among those who serve in the liturgical worship. He has been summoned: listen, come, show yourself—and he has come, he is present: *advenit, epephanē, adest*. His presence is in no way passive: he has come to act, to rescue, to conquer through suffering, as at his first epiphany he suffered, fought and overcame. But his followers act with him in the liturgy because he is with them and their action becomes a sacred imitation (*mimesis, imitatio*) of the divine events which ensure the life of the community. It is a sacred action, a religious drama. Through it his followers appropriate to themselves divine life and so are renewed. . . . Here, then, there is play but play of a life incomparably richer and deeper than anything we have found hitherto. The play becomes mystery because in symbol it makes God present. Celebration of the religious feast ends in a liturgy in which is to be found its climax.'

It may be thought that Dom Casel has unconsciously christianized hellenistic worship, but in fact his description is in accord with the findings of much later experts, such as G. van der Leeuw and Mircea Eliade who relate myth, mystery, symbol and 'epiphany' to worship. Thus 'the myth relates a *sacred history*, that is, a primordial event that took place at the beginning of time, *ab initio*. But to relate a sacred history is equivalent to *revealing a mystery*. . . . The myth, then, is the history of what took place *in illo tempore*, the recital of what the gods . . . did at the beginning.'[16] The myth contains the 'mystery' that is revealed in the recounting of it and this narrative 'is the attempt of primitive man to express *in a symbolic way*, namely, in a symbolic story [and we could add through gesture, dance and song], a fundamental experience of his existence, that is, an aspect of his connection with the world or his relationship to the mystery of being'.[17]

We may note in passing that this view is closely related to the existentialist approach of man to God that we have sketched out in the previous chapter and also to the 'encounter' theology that has come in recent years from a deeper consideration of the Bible. This, too, is found to be the basis

---

[14] *La Maison-Dieu*, No. 1, 1945, pp. 25–6.

[15] *Paneguris*, the same word that is used in Hebrews 12:22, quoted in the previous chapter.

[16] Mircea Eliade, *The Sacred and the Profane* (New York, 1959), cited in *Phenomenology of Religion*, ed. Joseph D. Bettis (London, 1969), p. 209.

[17] Albert Dondeyne, *Faith and the World* (Eng. trans., Dublin, 1963), p. 103.

of a theology of the liturgy. What is of more immediate interest is that this analysis of worship shows that mystery is at once something hidden and yet also revelatory of the divine action that it is re-enacting. The 'epiphanic' aspect of the liturgy has been too little regarded in recent centuries but it is a matter of immense importance. How do we know that God is present among us, active among us? The liturgy is the concrete sign of the divine presence enabling us to grasp existentially the reality of that presence and, in the case of the Christian liturgy, actually conveying to us the richness of redemption. If man's mind can be opened by faith to all this, he has an evidence of the reality of God and of his presence in the world. In the Christian liturgy, too, the 'epiphany' of God is spelt out in the recounting of the saving events in the word of the scriptures which in its own mode is a revelation of God, for there is never any liturgy without the proclamation of the word, even if it is very brief. We may say, then, that liturgy is a symbolic action that re-enacts the sacred events of saving history and makes God present with his redeeming power. Liturgy lives in the world of symbol and it is in this sense that we should interpret the words of the Constitution that 'the sanctification of man is signified by signs perceptible to the senses and *is effected* in a way which corresponds with each of these signs' (7). We may add, as the Constitution does in many places, that at the same time man gives glory to God, *in the same way* he goes to God through signs and symbols and he goes to him in the wholeness of his being. As Irenaeus said, *Gloria Dei, vivens homo*: it is the whole, living man who has encountered God in the concreteness of the liturgy and in the concrete situation of his being who can give him the glory. The Christian is a sign of God's presence.

We are now in a position to consider 'mystery', which lies at the heart and origin of liturgical celebration. As we have seen, for Eliade myth is practically to be identified with mystery, the sacred events, real or imaginary, that were recounted in a sacred history which was acted out in various ways. There are differences of opinion as to whether myth or ritual came first and also as to what content primitive man found in the rituals that he performed. This is of no importance for our purposes here, for with Judaism and, above all, with Christianity we move into a different world which is characterized by historical time. Events really did happen and we can tie them to specific times, persons and places. Eliade, who more than anyone else has emphasized the importance of the elements of primitive worship we have considered, is equally emphatic about the difference between the Judaic-Christian *Weltanschauung* and all others. He speaks first of Judaism where he finds historical time as the mark of the religious outlook and actions that are the actions of a Personal God: 'His gestures are *personal* interventions in history and reveal their deep meaning *only for his people*, the people that Yahweh had chosen. Hence the historical event acquires a new dimension: it becomes a theophany.' God reveals himself in these particular, never-to-be-repeated events and it is here that the Hebrews found him. But

'Christianity goes even further in valorizing *historical time*. Since God was *incarnated*, that is, since he took on a *historically conditioned human existence*, historical time acquires the possibility of being sanctified. The *illud tempus* evoked by the Gospels is a clearly defined historical time—the time in which Pontius Pilate was Governor of Judaea—but it was *sanctified by the presence of Christ*. When a Christian of our day participates in liturgical time, he recovers the *illud tempus* in which Christ lived, suffered, and rose again—but it is no longer a mythical time. . . .'[18]

This shows the great difference there is between primitive, non-Christian (and non-Jewish) worship and our own, but the manner in which we 'recover the *illud tempus*' remains the same. When we make the memorial of what the Lord did at the Last Supper, when we recount the sacred history and perform the same gestures, when in short we do once again in symbol what he did long ago, we come into his presence or he makes himself present to us with all his power and love. There is 'epiphany', *adest*, he is present.

It is into this thought-world that the theology of the Christian mystery can without difficulty be fitted. The Constitution may be thought to be somewhat sparing in its use of the phrase and no doubt the Council Fathers had no intention of committing themselves to any particular theory of 'mystery-presence'. But it does see the mystery of Christ as mediated through the liturgy to the lives of men (CL 2) and says that the mysteries of Christ's redemption are 'in some way' made present to the people who are put in contact with them and are filled with the grace of salvation (CL 102).[19] If the differences between the pagan mystery-celebration and the Christian mystery-presence must be emphasized, the likenesses between the two cannot be overlooked. But mystery, fundamentally, is what the Constitution says the liturgy is and it goes on to make the necessary concrete applications. The climax of the history of salvation (sacred history) was the paschal mystery (Christ's passion, death and resurrection) and it is this that is the centre of the church's liturgy (CL 5).

So we have the historical mystery, rooted in time, and we have its liturgical celebration in which the original events by which the Christian community is established (CL 5), are recalled and made present. But since we are dealing with the Christian mystery the whole matter needs to be set in a wider context.

The history of salvation does not begin with the New Testament. Throughout the ages God by event and word had been revealing himself and offering his love to mankind represented by the people of Israel. This

---

[18] J. D. Bettis, *op. cit.*, p. 217. Italics Eliade's.

[19] I follow here the French translation which seems to do full justice to the Latin, which is not without its difficulties. Cf *La Maison-Dieu*, no. 76, 1964, pp. 118–9.

self-revealing was brought to its culmination in the sending of the Son, the Word, the very utterance of God, made flesh, who made God's love present to men in this world by his passion, death and resurrection. It is this same redeeming love that the liturgy conveys to us by its celebration in sign, symbol and sacrament. So we have three levels on which the mystery of Christ exists:

1. The Mystery is God, 'dwelling in light inaccessible' (I Timothy 6:16) and in the plenitude of a love that is always giving itself, always being communicated from Father to Son and Holy Spirit and back again. This love God freely communicated outside himself first in creation and then in redemption so that all could share that love.

2. The mystery exists in the historical order. As we read in I Timothy 3:16, Christ is the mystery of God, showing him forth:

'Great indeed, we confess, is the mystery of our religion:

He was *manifested* in the flesh,
vindicated in the Spirit,
seen by angels
preached among the nations
believed on in the world,
taken up in glory' (RSV translation).

The mystery of God was made visible in Christ, the only-begotten of the Father whose glory John and the other disciples had seen (in his risen state and in his ascension). He came in 'the fulness of time' and not only summed up in himself the whole history of salvation but gave that history meaning. It was God's plan to unite all men and all things in himself through Christ who 'in his body of flesh, by his death, reconciled' mankind to his Father so that we could be holy and blameless and irreproachable before him. In him is revealed the mystery of God's saving love and through his passion, death and resurrection he made that love present among men and available for their salvation.[20]

Here mystery is essentially *event*, in the terms of Eliade, the primordial event, Christ's redeeming work by which the Church came into existence. But it, too, looked back to the past which it interpreted and on to the future, the emergence of the Church through which the saving power would be mediated to the world, which would be indeed the sign to the world that God is present to it and at work in it. It looked on further into an undetermined future when God's plan would have been fully worked out and all things would be renewed and restored in Christ.

3. But the event has to be experienced in the present. Christ, as Dom Odo Casel liked to say (and apparently Kierkegaard before him), has to become man's contemporary. This is achieved by the liturgy which so many of the older prayers of the Roman sacramentaries called the *mysterium*.

---

[20] Ephesians 1:9; Colossians 1:22; 2:2 and cf ibid. 1:27.

Christ's passion, death and resurrection are present to us *in mysterio* and are active among us through the mystery:

'The religious experience of the Christian is based upon an imitation of Christ as *exemplary pattern*, upon the liturgical repetition of the life, death and resurrection of the Lord and upon the *contemporaneity* of the Christian with *illud tempus* which begins with the Nativity at Bethlehem and ends, provisionally, with the Ascension . . . the liturgical time in which the Christian *lives* during the divine service is no longer profane duration but is essentially sacred time, the time in which the Word is made flesh, the *illud tempus* of the Gospels. A Christian is not taking part in a commemoration of the Passion of Christ, as he might be joining in the annual celebration of the Fourth of July. . . . He is not commemorating an event but *re-actualizing a mystery*. For the Christian, Jesus dies and resurrects before him *hic et nunc*.'[21]

Apart from the last sentence which offers a number of theological difficulties[22], this passage by the most famous scholar of religion in our time is a very clear description of what is meant by the liturgical mystery. It looks to the past to recover the power of the primordial event, it makes this power present in the here and now and enables the worshipper to come into contact with the Person and the power that were active and present in the beginning. Through the sign-symbols it uses it manifests the presence of Christ's action and because these are sacraments to which Christ committed himself, they convey the saving power of his passion and resurrection.

In more conventional language, the liturgy is the sacrament of Christ showing him forth as present and conveying the power of his redeeming work to Christians who are living here and now and who through the liturgical action (which involves faith) are taken up in his saving activity. Although the terminology of mystery may seem strange and perhaps 'pagan' to some, it is not new. St Leo the Great was constantly using *sacramentum* in this pregnant and comprehensive sense and a phrase of his has had considerable currency in recent years: *Quod nostri redemptoris conspicuum fuit, in sacramenta transivit* (what our Redeemer did visibly, has passed over into the sacraments).[23] The sacraments (meaning here in particular the eucharist, I think, though not exclusively) contains what Christ did and the fact that in Leo's mind it was (saving) actions that were in question is clear from the context. The above phrase is the conclusion of a passage in which he says that Christ, after the forty days of his resurrection-life, in the presence of his apostles was lifted up to remain at the right hand of his Father until the number of the sons of the church should be fulfilled. *Now*

---

[21] Mircea Eliade, *Myths, Dreams and Mysteries* (Eng. trans., Collins, Fontana ed., 1968), pp. 30–1.

[22] Christ cannot die again, and his self-offering was once-for-all.

[23] *Serm.* LXXIV, *De Ascens.* II, PL 54, c. 398.

all that he did in his earthly life is to be found in the *sacraments*, the liturgy that he and his hearers were celebrating.[24]

The purpose of the mystery-theology of the liturgy is to preserve the realism of the liturgical action and to deliver it from the narrowness of mere efficient causality (which is never denied) and to show that it has a richer and broader range and significance that meets the human condition. Man, in the whole richness of his own being, wishes to meet God, desires that God should be real and present to him. He achieves this in the first instance by faith but it is in the symbolic-liturgical action that faith is concretized. The church in the use and celebration of the liturgy is declaring that Christ the Redeemer is present and active and man through involvement in the celebration can make encounter in the whole of his being with the living God who comes to him in signs and symbols and mysteries. Perhaps the whole matter of the liturgical mystery can best be expressed by saying that it is the concrete (symbolic) and manifold expression of God's presence and action among his people now.

It has a further advantage. Not being restricted by the theory of efficient causality, the liturgy is thereby given a range of reference that would otherwise be impossible. The Catholic liturgy does not consist just of the eucharist and the sacraments. Nor does the eucharist itself consist simply of the words of consecration and the reception of the elements. Christ is present in the proclamation of the word, he is present in the prayer of Christians when they gather for it and all the rites and gestures of the liturgy show him forth and in one way or another make him present. The numerous aspects of his life, teaching, death and resurrection can be shown, brought to the attention of worshippers, through the very various actions of the liturgy. The paschal candle moving into the darkened church is visibly Christ, the Light who has overcome the darkness of death, the ashes placed on the head on Ash Wednesday are a symbol of repentance, the oil of chrism signifies the entrance either into the Christian community or consecration for its service. The instances could be multiplied; what is important is that all these are efficacious of Christ's redeeming love and power at different levels and in different ways. They are addressed to the different needs of the human person and have the power totally to penetrate his life. Thus spelt out, it may be thought somewhat laboriously, this is what the Constitution is saying when it teaches that man is sanctified by a (variety) of signs in ways that correspond to each of them (7).

If the Constitution speaks only sparingly of mystery as such, it has no hesitation about taking for the foundation of almost the whole of its first,

---

[24] It is well known, of course, that Leo constantly used the word *mysterium* also, whether in the singular or the plural, and it is a nice question exactly what he meant on each occasion. But that he used it in the active-symbolic sense cannot be doubted. For a study of the whole matter see Dom Maria B. de Soos, *Le Mystère Liturgique d'après Saint Léon le Grand* (LQF, Heft 34, Münster, 1958).

and most important, chapter the paschal mystery. It is the climax of Jesus' life as it is the culmination of the history of salvation. It is the 'primordial event' that brought the sacrament-church into existence and it was the heart of the apostolic preaching. By baptism men 'are plunged into the paschal mystery of Christ, they die with him, are buried with him and rise with him'. When they eat the supper of the Lord they proclaim his death until he comes again and in celebrating the eucharist in which *the victory and triumph of his death are again made present* they are able to 'give thanks to God through him to the praise of his glory' (CL 6 (II Corinthians 9:15; Ephesians 1:12)). Through the liturgical, symbolic re-enactment of the primordial events by which it was brought into being, the Christian community throughout the ages can transcend time and space and make encounter with the living, Risen Christ who is the same yesterday, today and for ever. It is by this that the community exists and it is because of this that the liturgy is the summit of the church's activity and the source of all her power (CL 10).

Ineluctably the church is concerned with the paschal mystery. It is not only the centre of her life but the pattern of her existence. Because she is the body of Christ extended in space and time she will be 'in agony until the end of time' and her resurrection will only be seen in those who through the enactment of the paschal mystery are themselves able to undergo resurrection. It will not be until the Christian community is able to celebrate the heavenly liturgy, of which the earthly is but a foretaste, that the power of the Christ's resurrection will be finally and completely effective and all will be able to share the glory that is his now. Meanwhile, we journey as pilgrims towards the heavenly Jerusalem where Christ is in glory, the *leitourgos* of the temple not made with hands, and we through the earthly liturgy are able to join in his in which eternally he intercedes for us (CL 8; cf Hebrews 8:2, 7:25).

THE WORSHIPPING COMMUNITY

FEW areas of theology have seen such considerable and rapid development in recent years as ecclesiology. When Pius XII's encyclical on the liturgy (1947) spoke of the 'church' it meant almost exclusively the hierarchical church. The Constitution on the Liturgy (1963) emphasized the community aspect of the church and during the Council itself there was a development of thought. The Constitution on the Church (1964) saw the church as above all the ministerial, the servant church. This in turn affected the redaction of the documents on the bishops' pastoral charge and that on the ministry of priests. All this and the course of events since the Council have considerably affected the way in which Catholics are now thinking and speaking of the Christian community whether inside or outside worship. In writing of the liturgy this may not seem to be a matter of primary concern, but the Constitution on the Liturgy has the germinal and, as one is inclined to think, prophetic statement right at the beginning: 'the liturgy is the outstanding means whereby the faithful may express in their lives, and manifest to others, the mystery of Christ and the real nature of the true Church' (2). The liturgy is the *sign* and, according to the same document (41), 'the pre-eminent manifestation of the Church'. If this is so, then all that is going on in the church, the movement towards the change or modification of structures or different ways of doing things that remain fundamentally the same, is of interest for both the celebration and formation of the liturgy. No doubt the liturgy cannot and should not reflect every detail of the church's changing life but the Council delivered the church from a form of worship that had become immobilized and that for four centuries had been incapable of manifesting its life.

Already the teaching of the Council on the status of lay-people is changing practice. In various parts of the church they and religious women

---

[1] Summary bibliography: Yves Congar, ' "L'Ecclesia" ou Communauté Chrétienne, sujet intégral de l'action liturgique', in *La Liturgie après Vatican II* (Paris, 1967), pp. 241–82. Yves Congar, *Lay People in the Church* (Eng. trans., 2nd ed., London, 1965). J. D. Crichton, 'The Worshipping Community', in *The People of God*, ed. L. Bright (London, 1965), pp. 75–97. A. G. Martimort, 'The Assembly', in *The Church at Prayer* (Eng. trans. Shannon, Ireland, 1968), pp. 77–97. J. Gelineau, ed., *Nelle Vostre Assemblee* (Brescia, 1970), pp. 45–192.

are now performing liturgical functions—giving communion whether inside church or outside it, presiding over services of the word—that a few years ago would have been regarded as inalienably the right and duty of the ordained minister. Somewhat reluctantly, women have been allowed first to read at euchatistic celebrations and then in the same place as lay*men* or the clergy![2] The Constitution itself recognized that a wide variety of lay-people exercise a liturgical function in celebration and, if that document is to be consistent with itself, that means a priestly function. The style of liturgy has changed beyond recognition and it is not surprising that Père Congar can say that the 'subject' of celebration was changed by the Council. The celebrants of the liturgy are the people even if we must add, with the Constitution, that it is an ordered people who celebrate with bishop or priest. It is, in fact, this change that makes it possible for the liturgy assembly to be the sign and manifestation of the church.

The journey to this point—and it has been a return journey—has been a long one, and practice still limps behind theory. Priests still need to realize that in celebration they are the servants of a community (GI 60) and the people still need to make efforts to establish the bonds that will make it a living community. Both need to realize that the liturgical assembly is as much 'a reality of the order of salvation'[3] as the rite they are celebrating. It is part of the mystery, for it is, as we have said, the sign of Christ who is the head of the body with whose members he celebrates the liturgy.

But, as we have tried to show in previous chapters, liturgy is human, though transcending human categories, and the same is true of community. Much has been written about community from a sociological as well as a theological point of view and the matter is very complex. We cannot go into it here. We must confine our attention to those aspects of it that are relevant to worship.

Everyone is aware that people gather together for various purposes from the simplest domestic celebration to elaborate assemblies through which it is hoped to achieve some common purpose. This is a sign that people need each other both for the fulfilment of their personalities and to promote a cause they all believe in. Community is a fundamental human phenomenon, so well known that it hardly seems necessary to mention it. Yet in worship there is still strong resistance to the notion and people still come to church thinking that they are isolated individuals who cannot possibly have any relationship with their fellow-worshippers, except those who have been carefully inspected and approved of. Yet normally people do reach out to each other, do feel the need of contact and intercourse with their fellow-human beings and express that need through gestures. This is (very summarily) the basis of community as it exists in worship. But it has this to tell

---

[2] Third Instruction, 7 (*Notitiae* 60, January, 1971), p. 19.
[3] J. Gelineau, *op. cit.*, p. 54.

us, that community is basically what has been called a face-to-face relationship. People need to *know* each other and as modern life becomes more and more impersonal, and as church life in so many places suffers from the same disease, it is ever more difficult to establish and maintain community in worship. This means that we have to make efforts to do so. Such efforts bring an air of artificiality to the whole business and it may be that it is this sense of strain and unnaturalness that some find offensive. Yet this again is but another sign that modern life *has* become unnatural—inhuman—and it must be the church's task to re-establish a human value that is of enormous importance.

In any case, the way of salvation has been communal and was and is to be found in community.

'If we turn to the history of salvation we find that God enshrined his promises of redemption in a people. It was to a people that he gave the law, a people who responded to his love with obedience to that law and with sacrifice by which they sealed the covenant with him . . . when the fulness of time came, it was with the establishment of the new Israel of God that salvation became possible for the individual. If the New Testament is radically personalist it is as radically communal. . . .'[4]

In the Old Testament, God made the Israelites the *qahal*, the assembly, by covenant, law and sacrifice. This became *ecclesia* in the New Testament but only through Christ

'for all that had happened in the past was recapitulated in him and, to adapt a statement from St Paul (Romans 9:4–5), the Israelites, adopted as God's sons, are now Christ. He is the presence of God made visible to men; he is the covenant; he is the law; he is the promise fulfilled; he the temple; he first the new holy people who came into existence on the cross. If we have inherited the promises it is through Christ we have done so. If we are a covenanted people, it is because we are united to him. If we are a holy people, it was he first who was holy, the Holy One of God. If we are a priestly people, it was because he first was the high priest. If we are body, if we are bride, it is because he is head and because he, the bridegroom, has united us to himself as bride. What lies behind Ephesians 5:25–27 is that the Christian people are Christ's body, his bride, a consecrated people, holy, the temple of God'.[5]

The Christian people are a community and Christ's salvation is mediated through it, though each has to appropriate it to himself. But, as the New Testament makes clear, it is a community that is constantly in the making. As it was called, convoked, by God in the beginning, so it has to be called again and again in the present. Every time the Christian community gathers for worship, it is called by God—that is the purpose of the entrance rite and the word that accompanies it. It is at this point that it begins to be the

---

[4] T. D. Crichton, 'The Worshipping Community', *art. cit.*, p. 84.
[5] *Ibid.*, p. 85.

sign of Christ and of the church (*ecclesia*) scattered throughout the world. By the proclamation of the word (and the reception of the word in faith) and by the celebration of the eucharist, which according to St Augustine is the 'sacrament of the sacrifice' of Christ, the community becomes existentially the body of Christ offering itself to God.[6] Indeed, we can say that in celebration the church becomes a *Christian* community or, better, communion (*koinonia*): the church makes the eucharist and the eucharist makes the church.

But if the church is, through its worship, an organic union, it has to become a union of *persons*. There can be nothing mechanical about it. The faith and love that are generated in worship have to be appropriated, the worshipper must respond to the word of faith that is proclaimed and take to himself the love that is made present. Since it is the Holy Spirit who distributes the gifts in the body, it is through him that the worshipper will be able to appropriate the faith and love that is offered to him and it is in the Spirit that he is able to respond. This is why worship is dialogue and this is the sort of dialogue it is. It is not a mere saying of prescribed words or the singing of hymns, it is a dialogue at the level of life, the life of the Spirit, in him it is a dialogue with God.

Emphasis on the work of the Holy Spirit in the church and in worship has not been common in the West and even in the Constitution on the Liturgy it is not marked. The balance was partly corrected by the Constitution on the Church (12) where it is said that the laity, too, possess the gifts (*charismata*) of the Holy Spirit. Although the expression has not been familiar, it is none the less true that the church is to be described as a charismatic church and the people exercise their *charismata* in the general life of the church but also in worship. The *charismata* are extraordinary (I Corinthians 14) and ordinary (Romans 12:4–8). The former gave St Paul a good deal of trouble, though he did not deny their validity, but it is the latter that are exercised in worship. All the services, 'ministries' that various people do are exercises of the gifts of the Holy Spirit for the building up of the community and its worship.[7] Such gifts will often be conspicuous in music, singing, organ-playing and so on, and it should be realized that they *are charismata* and are to be encouraged. Further, the contributions the people can make to the celebration will also be the fruits of their *charismata* and means must be provided for them to exercise them.[8]

But this community is also by its nature a liturgical, that is, a priestly community. It came into existence by the sacrifice of its head who as priest of the whole human race offered himself in a total self-giving to his Father. It inherited the priesthood of the Old Testament, though only through

---

[6] *De Civ. Dei*, X, 20.

[7] Cf Gelineau, *op. cit.*, p. 98.

[8] See below.

Christ, who transcended and transformed that priesthood.[9] In a passage that is filled with liturgical overtones, the community-church is described as being a house of the Spirit of which the 'living stones' are a holy priesthood who have to offer 'spiritual sacrifices' (*pneumatikas thusias*), to God through Jesus Christ (I Peter 2:1–6). The house, the priesthood and the sacrifices all correspond to each other. They are 'pneumatic', not merely 'spiritual' in the weak modern sense, but 'of (the Holy) Spirit'. All the materialistic worship of the old Israel has gone, all the old sacrifices of bulls and goats, the old sacral priesthood and with them all the exclusiveness and the taboos that made Israel a *separate* people.[10] Nor is the Christian priesthood in any way comparable with the pagan priesthoods that filled the ancient world. It lies not so much between them as beyond them. It is a 'spiritual' priesthood that is at the service of a worship 'in spirit and in truth', not tied to Jerusalem or to any earthly location. The priesthood is indeed visible (in the first instance the church itself) but it has no sacrifice of its own. Its sacrifice is that of Jesus Christ who is the Priest that now offers it, the 'minister in the sanctuary . . . which is not set up by man but by the Lord' (Hebrews 8:2). The church's sacrifice is the 'memorial' of that sacrifice and makes it present. It does so by the operation of the Holy Spirit 'who is the principle in virtue of which the faithful become the church (*ecclesia*) and (thus) in their organic unity as body of Christ, the subject of liturgical actions'.[11]

The church is the Spirit-filled (pneumatic) body of Christ and in this sense its worship is and must be 'spiritual', of the Spirit. One is inclined to say that the nearest we can get to the 'spiritual' of the New Testament is 'sacramental', for it is through the symbolic-sacramental liturgy that the Spirit is communicated to the church and through which the church is able to establish contact with the Spirit. This may not be the only way the Spirit is communicated. There is faith and love, there are the *charismata*, the special gifts, but faith is 'sacramentalized' in baptism, love in the eucharist (*signum amoris*) and ordinary *charismata* are exercised in the celebration of the liturgy. The repentance of the sinner is actualized in the sacrament of penance and filled with the love of God that forgives sins. This last is the most striking example of how the free movement of the Spirit, who is, of course, not confined either to the liturgy or the church, can be concretized in the liturgy. And this is why the liturgy is the mystery-sacrament of Christ and the Holy Spirit who are present among

---

[9] See, in *The Christian Priesthood*, ed. Nicholas Lash and Joseph Rhymer (London, 1970), John A. T. Robinson, 'Christianity's "No" to Priesthood', and Robert Murray, SJ, 'Christianity's "Yes" to Priesthood'.

[10] See Gelineau, *op. cit.*, p. 58. Christianity 'pure and undefiled' is without taboos though some apparently have turned Christian practices into taboos or tribal customs and would like to retain them. Hence a certain falling away from religion. Cf Mary Douglas, *Natural Symbols* (London, 1970).

[11] Y. Congar, ' "L'Ecclesia" ou Communauté Chrétienne', *art. cit.*, p. 259.

men invisibly but whose presence becomes in a sense visible in the celebration of the liturgy.

The people of God, then, are a priestly people, or simply, as the New Testament says, a priesthood,[12] and on the other hand there is the ordained priesthood. The two are not opposed but complementary. The ordained priesthood is a *ministry*, a *diakonia*, a service of the people, that is, of the whole body of Christ. There is but one priesthood, that of Christ in which both people and ordained priests share in different ways. Massively the church is at the service of Christ's priesthood which consisted of word and saving work and it is this word and this work that the priestly church exists to prolong in space and time until the consummation. But because the ordained minister has a special relationship to the whole people, he is appointed and constituted by a special sacramental act for the service of the people. His relationship is, if you like, sacramentalized. But he is also specially related to Christ and shares in his teaching, priestly and ruling office. As the Council documents proclaim tirelessly, the ministry of God's word is a primary obligation of the ordained ministry. This has a priority not so much of time but of importance for the ordained minister, by his participation in Christ's priesthood, has to continue the work of proclaiming the Good News of salvation to those who have not yet heard it and to those who have, in the name of God summoning them at the beginning of worship to assemble as the Christian community and evoking their faith and love during its course. It is his function, too, to form the people so that they may be fitted for their task of carrying the gospel to the world in which they live and work. Finally, he presides at liturgical services and especially at the eucharist where his role is irreplaceable.

As we have seen, the whole people have as their vocation the offering of 'spiritual sacrifices', their lives and work (and so has he), and this offering, which is basically self-offering, is realized and expressed in the liturgical offering of the eucharist where they offer not merely through the priest-celebrant but with him (GI 62). They have a real, active part in that offering, for both 'priesthoods' are necessary for the building up of the church and both *together* make the sign, the eucharist, that in a pre-eminent way manifests the church. But the ordained minister has a special, a representative function, not of the people, but of Christ, the head, and it is through this that he is able to perfect the spiritual-sacramental offering of the people:

'While the priesthood presupposes the sacraments of initiation [which he, as well as the people, has received, making him one of them], the sacerdotal office of priests is conferred by that special sacrament through which priests, by the anointing of the Holy Spirit, are marked with a .

---

[12] *Hieratuma* (I Peter 2:5); *hiereis kai basileian* ('priests and a kingdom') (Rev. 1:6; 5:10).

special character and are so configured to Christ that they can act in the person of Christ the Head.'

But his participation in the priesthood of Christ must not be interpreted in any narrow, exclusive sense, as if he were only a eucharistic offerer. It is through his preaching of the gospel as well as through his purely eucharistic role that he is able to perfect the people's offering:

'They (priests) shoulder the sacred task of the gospel, *so that* the offering of the people can be made acceptable through the sanctifying power of the Holy Spirit.[13] For, through the proclamation of the gospel, the People of God is called together and assembled so that when all who belong to this People have been sanctified by the Holy Spirit, *they can offer themselves* as "a sacrifice, living, holy, pleasing to God" (Romans 12:1). Through the ministry of priests, the spiritual sacrifice of the faithful is made perfect in union with the sacrifice of Christ, the sole Mediator.'[14]

We need not go into the theological complexities that are connected with the relationship of the two 'priesthoods'. The documents of the church state that they exist and that they differ in kind and not in degree.[15] But it will be useful to pursue the question of 'active participation' which is often misunderstood. At one level participation is simply the means by which it is achieved, the recitation of prayers, responses, the singing of chants of various kinds and the making of gestures. But at a deeper level these are all symbols of the active *offering* of the people through which, and with the priest-celebrant, they may enter into the sacrifice of Christ. The means can vary, they can be richer in symbolic expression or weaker. There *is*, at the level of means, a difference between a eucharist celebrated in a house and one celebrated in a large church with choir and servers. But the end remains the same.

Some of the difficulty has, I think, come from regarding 'sacrifice' as a *thing* (the-thing-that-has-become-sacred-by-immolation). As St Augustine said long ago, it is first an attitude and then an action that externalizes the attitude.[16] In the eucharist the attitude is that of self-offering. This is not a 'pious' extra nor of course is it only the people who have to offer themselves. The priest must do likewise. It is of the very stuff of the eucharist, for it is the very condition of the insertion of Christ's sacrifice into the

---

[13] Romans 15:16. This reference to St Paul here is very remarkable. He sees the preaching of the gospel and its consequences in the life of the people as a *liturgy*. The Council took this up and applied it to the priest's ministry of the word which it relates to the people's eucharistic offering.

[14] Decree on the Ministry and Life of Priests 2 (*Documents of Vatican II*, ed. Abbott (London, 1966), p. 535).

[15] See Grillmeier in *Commentary on the Documents of Vatican II* (London, 1967), p. 158; David Power, *Ministers of Christ and his Church* (London, 1969), chapters VIII and IX.

[16] 'Sacrifice is the visible sign of the invisible offering (*sacrificii*)', *De. Civ. Dei* X, c. 5; and cf St Thomas, ST, II–II, 85, 2.

church's offering. When this is achieved, as it is through the sacramental-liturgical re-enactment of the eucharist, Christ's sacrifice can become hers and *then* she is in a position to offer herself, to be united with Christ's sacrifice and so come to union with the Father. It is only on account of the identity of the church's offering with Christ's sacrifice that she can 'offer' and in this offering become herself.[17] The whole body of the people is lifted up into the sacrifice of Christ and in this the priest has *his* sacramental role to play because of his special relationship with Christ. This relationship is a sacramental one (by Holy Orders) and through it he enables the people to bring to sacramental expression their self-offering and so to enter into the sacrifice of Christ.

All this expresses the vertical relationship of the people of God in the community. But a horizontal relationship is of the very essence of community. People are related to one another and give service to one another. This is pre-eminently true of the liturgical assembly, and one of the less noticed features of the reformed rite of the Mass, not to mention other sacraments, is that this horizontal relationship is built into its very structure. In the Constitution (CL 26–31) it is the first principle of the reform of the liturgy and is expressed in three principle ways:

1.   *All* liturgical services are celebrations of the community and, among other things, this must include the sacrament of Penance which offers peculiar problems for its reformation.

2.   Within the community there are different services which are necessary for the proper celebration of a liturgical service and which are liturgical, i.e. priestly functions.[18] Each must be allowed to perform his or her function which may not be absorbed by anyone else, least of all the priest-celebrant.

3.   These and the whole community exercise their priestly role by taking an active part.

This last is again not an optional extra but is necessary if the local community is to construct the liturgical sign that is a manifestation of the church itself. The sign that the liturgical service requires is a great deal wider (and richer) than the 'matter' and 'form' that used to be regarded as the sign of the sacraments. The sign is people, the worshipping community, and it is only they that can construct the sign that is going to manifest the real nature of the church. You may *say*, if you will, that the eucharist is the sign of the unity of the mystical body, but it remains mere theology if the people do not speak, act and sing and if the various ministers of the rite do not perform their services. This is why 'active participation' is in an entirely different

---

[17] Cf St Augustine: 'Of his self-offering (*oblatio*) Christ willed that the church's sacrifice should be the daily *sacramentum* and since she is his body, she learns to offer through him (*De Civ. Dei*, X, 20). Or again: 'In that which she offers, she herself is offered' (*ibid.*, X, 6).

[18] This means that women can (and do) in this sense perform priestly functions.

order from secular participation. *That* goes no deeper than the psychological needs that a gathering has or is conceived to have and it may be that because some think active participation is of that order they resist it. They do not wish to be associated with a football crowd.

Yet there is an interior aspect of active participation that is not always given its due. Although it has always been denied, Catholic liturgical worship has often in the past *looked* mechanical. It was a thing to be done, it was done and that was the beginning and end of it. The Constitution demands that the participation shall not only be active, exteriorized, but conscious and devout (CL 14, 41); the people are to come to worship 'with proper dispositions' and 'their minds should be attuned to their voices'. A whole programme of spiritual formation is in the background here, and at the lowest level people should be brought to realize that worship is not just the performance of pieces of ritual. But what we are concerned with is something deeper than psychological dispositions of a merely human kind. Now it is realized once more[19] that we are saved by faith and by the sacraments of faith and that *this faith is in play in the celebration of the liturgy.* Everyone knows that we need faith if we are to receive the sacraments fruitfully, but what is perhaps not always realized is that the liturgy declares in concrete fashion the faith of the whole church and conversely the people express their faith in the liturgy. It is a declaration *in sacramento,* in the celebration itself, of their faith in Christ. Here the proclamation of the word, as we shall see, has a peculiarly important role to play, for it evokes faith and strengthens it. It is out of faith that we are able to respond to the message of faith that is proclaimed and it is through faith thus enriched that we are able to meet Christ at a deeper level, more wholeheartedly and with a greater sincerity.

The liturgical assembly is a community of faith, shared by all and professed by all. The recitation of the creed is the most obvious expression of this. But the assembly is also a community of love because the eucharist itself is the 'sacrament of love, a sign of unity and a bond of charity'.[20] This love, and the union that comes from it, is expressed in the common reception of the body of Christ in holy communion and in the signs that accompany it, the sign of peace, the communion procession and the singing of the communion chant. But the service the various ministers of the assembly perform is also a sign of love, the manifestation of the *charismata* that are distributed in the community by the Holy Spirit for its 'edification'. Of this the most striking liturgical expression is the Washing of the Feet on Maundy Thursday when the priest as the president of the community does a service which is the symbol of his whole relationship to the people who

---

[19] Once more, for even St Thomas was merely summing up the tradition when he said that we are saved by faith and the sacraments of faith (cf III, 62, 6; 64, 2, ad 3 and CL 59).

[20] CL 47, quoting St Augustine.

are represented by certain members of the congregation. As the texts indicate, this is all done in the spirit of the service of love of the Last Supper (John 13 : 4–16, 34, 35).

As far as eucharistic celebrations are concerned, all this is summed up in the General Introduction to the new Order of the Mass (62–64). The people are the royal priesthood who give thanks to the Father, who offer themselves and the victim not only through the priest but with him. Their union is expressed in the hearing of God's word, in common prayer and song, in the common offering of the sacrifice and in the sharing of the Lord's table. Even the bodily attitudes they adopt and the gestures they make are signs of their unity. But the unity is not a uniformity and the different groups (the choir who are at the service of the congregation and individuals, cantors, readers, servers and the rest) all in different ways express different aspects of the community and together build up the 'sacrament of the church'.

How all this is to be done in practice is a matter of local judgement and organization (GI 5, 6), but one of the more striking features of the conciliar and indeed post-conciliar documents is their emphasis on the local church and, within the broad limits laid down, the principle of adaptation (CL 39–40). This has, of course, a practical value: not everything can be done everywhere in the same fashion. The General Instruction, which is remarkably flexible in its directives, has made it possible to organize a truly community Mass even where the resources are of the most limited. To have a celebration that is full of life it is not necessary (or desirable) to do a sort of mock-up of cathedral worship. Indeed, it is being found that in the circumstances of the smaller group, whether at home or elsewhere, it is possible to achieve a sense of community and intimacy that is often wanting in the celebration of the eucharist in a large parish church.

The emphasis on the local church, then, is not only leading to different styles of celebration but is revealing the need so many Christians feel for a genuine experience of community. As has been remarked, the sociologists think of community as that assembly of people where there is a face-to-face relationship. People *know* each other. As everyone is aware, it is very difficult if not impossible to establish such a relationship in a large city parish. Hence the felt need for decentralization even within the parish, with the consequence that eucharistic and other celebrations in people's houses are desired. Such celebrations, it is felt, are necessary to express at a deeper level than mere good fellowship the sense of unity in the community thus gathered.

There are those who fear the separatist tendencies that such assemblies might set up. But all will depend on the spirit in which they meet and the guidance (and instruction) they receive from their clergy. Separatist tendencies can be avoided if the house-groups realize that the celebration of the Mass among them is the sign of their missionary work for the neighbourhood. No mission, no Mass. That is to say, they must be groups that in various ways are reaching out to the people among whom they live. They are trying to serve them in whatever way is open to them and they are willing to gather people into their houses where questions of religious faith can be discussed. On these terms, they will be the most dynamic places within the parish community which, in fact, though often invisible, they will be building up. Finally, if they bring to parish worship on Sundays the experience they have had in their smaller communities, they will do much to turn the parish worship into a genuine expression of the whole parish community.

We naturally think of the parish as 'the local church' but it is not autonomous. It belongs to a wider grouping, the diocese, and is dependent for the sources of its Christian life on the bishop. In the documents 'the local church' seems to mean primarily the diocese and some have described, perhaps not too happily, the parish as 'the particular church'. Certainly, the Constitution on the Liturgy (41) sees the diocese as the key grouping. It is the liturgy of the bishop when celebrated with his priests, ministers and people that is 'the pre-eminent sign' of the whole church. But on the one hand, the picture suggested by this statement is that of a diocese that is a credible community and not merely a jurisdictional area 'ruled' by an ecclesiastical official called a bishop. For a liturgy that is going to be the sign of the church as community, smaller dioceses would seem to be a necessity. On the other hand, the picture leaves out of account the ever-increasing part the parish plays and has played for a very long time in the lives of the people. Some may not be very closely attached to it, but it is here normally that people come to know what the Catholic church is and it is here that they 'experience' church. Regrettably, the bishop is an occasional, if welcome, visitor.

There is, too, something of a theological problem about the relationship between the bishop and the priest.[21] One Council document speaks of him as making the bishop present but it is agreed that he is no mere delegate. He depends on the bishop in various ways, but what is more important is that the basis of his union with him is a sacramental one. *Both* share in the one priesthood of Christ and both have the common task of proclaiming the gospel and bringing people to God through the celebration of the liturgy. None the less, the parish liturgy makes the sign of the church: 'Parishes, set up locally under a pastor *who takes the place of the bishop* . . . in some manner . . . represent the visible church constituted throughout the world' (CL 42). This is sufficient to point up the importance of parish liturgy. It may well be that it cannot construct as full a sign of the church as the episcopal liturgy, but it *is* such a sign and everything should be done to show that it is.

---

[21] See David Power, *Ministers of Christ and his Church* (London, 1969), chapters VII, VIII, IX.

There are various ways in which the sacramental union that exists between bishop, clergy and people can be demonstrated. In some dioceses the Holy Oils, consecrated in a typical episcopal liturgy on Maundy Thursday, are carried to the parish church and placed before the altar at the evening Mass. This shows the link between the parish clergy and the bishop because the oils the former use in baptism (exceptionally in confirmation) and in the anointing of the sick are consecrated by the bishop. This is an ancient tradition and even where, as in the Eastern churches, priests regularly confirm, the chrism must always be consecrated by the bishop. In the new regulations concerning confirmation and baptism—they may be conferred during the Mass—it is possible for the bishop to preside at the parish eucharist and to show by the celebration of these sacraments that he is indeed the president of the whole diocesan liturgy. Where the adult catechumenate is established, he is able to celebrate the sacraments of initiation in the order in which they are intended to be given. Again, it has become an established custom to confer the sacrament of Holy Orders in parish churches and here the sign of the church is very plainly made. Not only are there the necessary ministers of various ranks but it is a truly community occasion when the parish gathers together to celebrate what is realized to be an important event. The bishop is the source in some sense of the Christian life of the whole diocese (CL 41) and it is in ways like this that he can bring home to the people that this is so.

The eucharistic liturgy is the sign of a church that is a community and this is to be achieved by allotting to the laity those roles or ministries that belong to them. These ministries are listed in the General Instruction 66–71 (and for the choir 63). We are familiar with some but the list includes others that do not seem to be common in most churches in this country. Choirs exist, though it is becoming ever more difficult to maintain them. For the General Instruction they exercise a truly liturgical function—as we have suggested above, a *charisma*—and it is for them to undertake those parts of the liturgy that are proper to them and to serve the people by assisting their active participation in song. There are altar-servers, too, of course, but there are also other officers who serve the community in different ways and help to construct the sign of community. Even at parish level the liturgy is 'hierarchical'. Among these we may note the cantor or what the Instruction (GI 67) calls the *psalmista* whose special task is to intone the psalms or other biblical canticles of the liturgy but who, as experience shows, can animate and carry with him a whole congregation if he has the necessary *charisma* (a combination of nature, art and grace!). There is a strong case for training such people since the difficulties in the way of training and maintaining choirs are becoming so great.

There are also humbler officers, those who take up the collection and those who welcome people to the church. These last are to be found all too rarely and yet their role, given the impersonality of modern life, is all the more important. Such officers can welcome people, indicate or show them to their places, and hand them whatever literature they may need for the celebration of the Mass. It is in these humble ways that a crowd begins to be a community, a community of people sharing a common faith and engaged on the common task of making Christ present in the here and now. It remains for the president to realize that he, too, is the servant of the community and to do his all-important part in bringing this local gathering of people to a realization that they are the people of God.

As we have seen, there is no doubt about the church's teaching that liturgical services are celebrations of the Christian community, ordered under its bishop and clergy. There is no doubt about the church's desire that all should take their proper part in the celebrations and the different roles have been generously allotted. But have the laity any other contribution to make to the liturgy? The complaint has been heard often enough in recent years that the new liturgy has been imposed on the people without their advice or consent. If formal consultation is meant, there is a degree of truth in the complaint. But it also implies that the priests, bishops and a considerable number of lay people who have been involved in the shaping of the new liturgy are in no way representative of the church. In fact, opinion had been forming for a great number of years on what our worship required and if some bishops, priests and laity chose to ignore what was being said and done in the church until the Vatican Council, they are not in a very strong position now to complain of what has happened. However, the decentralization of the church in recent years has made it possible for the local church, and that includes everyone, to make its contribution to the formation of the liturgy. This is not only possible, but is in certain circumstances required. Thus the General Introduction to the new Order of the Mass (GI 73) says that in the preparation of the liturgy, the rector of the parish should consult with his choir, his servers, his other helpers and also the people, at least for those matters that directly concern them. And this consultation is to concern itself not merely with liturgical matters in the stricter sense but also with pastoral matters. This means that the whole circumstances of the parish and its people must be taken into account when shaping the liturgy for the needs of the local church. This will cover a very wide range of matters indeed and will have a decisive effect on the worship of a particular parish.

In detail, the people are to be invited to contribute to the General Intercession of the Mass by proposing petitions and by reciting them before the congregation. According to the Order of Holy Week, there may be several such persons among whom are to be included those recently baptized (49). When smaller groups come together for the Mass they may choose (from the Lectionary) texts that are appropriate to the occasion (e.g. anniversaries of weddings). *Before* baptism the parish clergy are required to consult with the families concerned who will choose from the ritual the texts they prefer. The same is true of the marriage rite.

But there will be those who think that is insufficient. In the present situation little more is possible, but in the future that is opening out to us there remains the possibility of creative liturgy. Not in the sense of liturgical free-lancing (people deserve to be protected from that awful fate) but in the sense of consultation with bishop and clergy who will in discussion discover what are the needs of the people, will be willing to accept from them various suggestions (the people, too, have their charism) and finally will be able to shape the forms of the liturgy so that they will be truly expressive of the people's needs and desires. All somewhat utopian, some may think, but it would seem to be the condition of a living liturgy that continues to speak to the people and through which they will be able to give themselves in worship to God.[22]

---

[22] See J. D. Crichton, 'Liturgical Forms', in *The Way*, Supplement 11 (London, 1970), pp. 35–7. For a condemnation of unauthorized experimentation see the Third Instruction from the Congregation for Worship in *Notitiae* 60, January, 1971, pp. 12–25. However, the same document says that it is for bishops 'to control, direct, and *stimulate* the liturgical life of the diocese, as well as rebuking if necessary'.

CHAPTER FOUR

THE NEW ORDER OF THE MASS

THE Order of the Mass that was promulgated in 1969 was the fruit of several years' work of the *Consilium* set up shortly after the promulgation on 4 December 1963, by the Second Vatican Council, of the Constitution on the Liturgy. The terms of reference of the *Consilium* were the principles of reform laid down in the Constitution, 21–40, and in particular for the eucharist, 49–55. The *Consilium* as such had no independent authority. It was answerable to the Congregation of Rites and to other congregations, to the bishops of the world who had voted the Constitution into existence and, of course, finally to the Pope. At all stages there was widespread consultation and among the members and consultors of the *Consilium*, there were not only liturgical and other scholars but a considerable number of diocesan bishops and priests engaged in pastoral work. In addition, through the process of experimentation promoted by the *Consilium* itself, various rites were tested in actual pastoral situations and the results were collated for the final redaction of the texts. In this way the laity, too, have been able to make their needs known.

In view of certain misunderstandings of the procedures of liturgical reform it is necessary to give this summary account of them. The new rites that have been issued in recent years are not the work of a few liturgical bureaucrats who by unscrupulous intrigue have managed to impose dubious liturgies on an unsuspecting and unwilling church. At every stage the *Consilium*'s work has been scrutinized, sometimes over prolonged periods of time, and, among other things, documents have to be sent to the Congregation for Doctrine as well as, of course, to the Pope for his final approval. This is by no means a formality. The church has committed herself to these liturgies and they thus become authentic expressions of her faith. To complete the recent story, the *Consilium* became the Congregation for Worship in April 1970, and as a recent writer has said: 'The new Congregation for Worship is a more permanent version of the postconciliar *Consilium*.' But the work is not yet finished and will not be finished for some years to come. Not only are there further liturgical texts to be issued but the liturgy is now in a state of change. There is the adaptation now going ahead in Africa, India and elsewhere, and although the main lines of the rites have been fixed, it is very likely that even in

Europe and North America there will be considerable adaptation over the years. As the same writer observes: 'The liturgy can never be regarded as static, fixed and complete. An awareness is visible [in the Congregation for Worship] that liturgy is alive, evolving, adapting like any living organism to its environment. Like all living things, it adapts to a continually evolving world or it dies.'[1] The role of the Congregation will be to control the procedures of adaptation but also, no doubt, to stimulate them as and when necessary.

Another feature of the current liturgical reform is that more and more discretionary power is being given to local conferences of bishops. They, too, must work within the limits of the Council and post-conciliar documents, but they have a certain power of initiation even if their projects and *desideranda* must be submitted to the Congregation. As the nature of the case demands, translation is almost entirely in their hands. Each of the great language zones of the world have their episcopal committees and a working committee under them whose texts they either accept or reject. Each local conference of bishops must give their approval for their own areas and this by a two-thirds majority vote. In judging new rites it is necessary to make a distinction between the Latin texts that come from the Congregation and the vernacular versions that come from the episcopal conferences. Liturgical translation is a very hazardous business and, incidentally, inevitably involves some adaptation, but all this is controlled both at the local level and at the Roman level and it is unlikely that anything unorthodox will get through.

It may be questioned, and has been questioned, whether the policy of having uniform versions for given language zones is a wise one. The differences in idiom and mental association in the English-speaking world are certainly very great and impose difficulties, but with the flexibility that Rome itself recognizes these can be largely overcome. Only those texts that are common to the *people* must be uniform. The rest, scripture versions and the like, can differ. In any case, all texts are subject to revision after a period of time laid down by the respective episcopal conferences.[2]

It may be said that liturgical reform has been done by way of authority while on the other hand liturgy is said to be a living, growing thing. In the circumstances of the modern church it is difficult to see how the reform could have been done in any other way. Either it would not have been done at all or we should have been the victims of individual caprice. There are

---

[1] P. Coughlan, 'Consilium to Congregation' in *Life and Worship*, April, 1971, p. 25.

[2] ICEL, the International Committee for English in the Liturgy, has come in for a good deal of criticism in the course of years. Some of their work earlier on perhaps deserved it, but it remains to be proved that there is any other body in the English-speaking world that can do as good a job of work as, on the whole, they have done.

those, of course, who say there was no need of reform, but they must recognize that the general sense of the church is against them.

For nearly fifty years before the Council the Liturgical Movement, eventually involving a vast number of bishops, priests, scholars and lay people, had been working to bring the liturgy to the people and to encourage the people to take an active part in it. At first there was no question of liturgical reform, but experience showed that if the people were to take that active part in the liturgy that its nature demands, some change was necessary. The very shape of the liturgy and perhaps as much as anything the current style of celebration made it impossible for ordinary people to *use* it. More often than not they were just present at it. The language, Latin, was a barrier to true prayer and in the liturgy itself there were obscurities, obsolete rites and duplications that made it impossible for the ordinary Christian to appreciate its true significance. As is well known, the draft on the liturgy was the first presented to the fathers and was the only one they accepted as a basis for discussion without radical re-shaping.[3] After a strenuous and lengthy debate that took up nearly the whole of the first session and part of the second, the Council finally decreed that, as far as the eucharist was concerned, its liturgy should be reformed, certain rites simplified and the whole to be of such sort that all could easily understand it. Above all, 'the aim to be considered before all else' in the reform of the liturgy was 'the full and active participation' of *all* the people in its celebration. Active participation, even if not the happiest of expressions, is no mere psychological or 'popular' gimmick but in the words of Pius X in 1903 (so long ago!) 'the primary and indispensable source from which the faithful are to derive the true Christian spirit'.[4] If the new Order of the Mass has done nothing else, it has provided the means to make this possible.

In the *Missale Romanum* of 1970 there are three introductory documents: the Apostolic Constitution of Paul VI, the Proemium and the General Instruction, first issued with the *Ordo Missae* of 1969 and now appearing in a revised version.[5] It may seem strange that a new rite should need such a barrage of introductory material. Obviously, a papal document was needed to promulgate the new Order and the missal to the church and the General Instruction, which, as we shall see, is a document of the greatest interest and importance, was necessary to convey to both priests and people the deeper significance of the new rite. But it is to be regretted

---

[3] See P. Coughlan, *art. cit.*, p. 26.

[4] CL 14. Psychological and popular needs are not to be despised and one wonders how much longer ordinary people would have gone on tolerating the sort of liturgy they had. There were signs of restiveness *before* the Council. But, as we have tried to show, active participation goes a great deal deeper than the satisfaction of psychological needs.

[5] The Calendar is considered in Chapter eight below, the General Instruction in Chapter five.

that the Proemium, a controversial statement, intended to rebut the criticisms of the new Order and in the nature of the case a very ephemeral document, should have a place between the other two. We may regret, too, that for the same reason the Order itself had to undergo revision. After due consideration I have decided that since the Proemium does not add to a liturgical understanding of the new Order, there was no need for me to treat of it in this book. I have, of course, had to take into account the revision of the General Instruction which it occasioned and the principal modifications that have been introduced are considered in the next chapter.

The Apostolic Constitution

Apostolic Constitutions are legal instruments, well known in Roman practice, by which important decisions of the Holy See are promulgated. At times, they may seem to be no more than a formality, but the one that is to be found in the *Missale Romanum* of 1970 is no formal piece of writing. It breathes an air of personal conviction and concern, and if those who had objected to the new Order had read it, they would have found many of their objections answered. The suggestion heard, for instance, in certain quarters that Paul VI had no right to undo what Pius V had done or, more bizarrely, that he had sold the church out to the Protestants, would never have been made.

After mentioning the fruitful results that had come from the missal of Pius V, the Pope recalls the words of Pius XII that the liturgical movement was a sign of God's providence and of the work of the Holy Spirit in the church, and points out that his predecessor had in fact initiated the revision of the Roman Missal by his reforms of the liturgy of Holy Week. Further, the revision of the missal was not the result of a sudden decision. Liturgical study, a better knowledge of the ancient liturgical texts (many of which have only been edited in modern times), and, above all, the decisions of the Second Vatican Council, had made possible and necessary the revision of the eucharistic liturgy. He patiently lists the main principles of the reform (the texts and rites must express more clearly the realities they convey, the proper relation of part to part must be set out, the active participation of the people must be facilitated, a more generous provision of holy scripture must be made and facilities for concelebration provided), points out that the addition of three new eucharistic prayers is an innovation which is justified as an enrichment of our appreciation of the mystery of the eucharist, that the simplification of the offertory was necessary to eliminate useless 'repetitions' and that the importance of the homily and the restoration of the prayer of the faithful are examples of a return to an older tradition. A long passage is devoted to the importance of the new lectionary and urges in moving tones upon clergy and laity alike a serious study of God's word which is a source of the spiritual life, the main theme of doctrine and the heart (*medulla*) of all theology. As far as the eucharist is concerned such a study will ensure that the people will come to it properly prepared.

After drawing attention to certain other features of the missal (e.g. new Masses for modern needs) he recommends it to the church:

'When our predecessor St Pius V promulgated the *editio princeps* of the Roman Missal he presented it to the Christian people as an instrument of liturgical unity and as a monument of sincere worship in the church. We do the same and although we have admitted into the new missal legitimate variations and adaptations, according to the prescriptions of the Second Vatican Council,[6] it is our confident hope that it will be received by the Christian people as a means by which they will be able to bear witness to and strengthen the unity existing among them. In this way, and though uttered in a great variety of languages, one and the same prayer will ascend from all to the heavenly Father through our high priest, Jesus Christ in the Holy Spirit. . . .'

The document concludes as usual in the *stylus curiae*, but it is important to realize that it enshrines a legal decision formally abrogating the missal of Pius V. What Pius could do, Paul can undo. If the primacy of the Pope does not mean that, it means nothing.[7]

---

[6] CL 38–40 where the above phrase is to be found.

[7] It may, however, be questioned whether this legal language and the rubric that heads both Pius V's Constitution and that of Paul VI *Ad perpetuam rei memoriam* does not overdo it a bit. Paul XXVI could abrogate what Paul VI has done. When does 'perpetual' mean 'perpetual'?

CHAPTER FIVE

THE GENERAL INSTRUCTION

PUBLISHED together with the new Order of Mass is a document called *Institutio Generalis*, or General Instruction, which takes the place of the old *Ritus Servandus* of the 1570 missal and of the other rubrical injunctions that were added to it from time to time. The difference in spirit and character between the two is startling. Whereas the old rubrics were concerned with the minutiae of ritual and, with two exceptions,[1] with what the priest did at the altar, the new Instruction must be described as a liturgical document of the first importance. It goes far beyond rubrical direction and is concerned with the nature of eucharistic celebration. Each major section of it is prefaced by a theological statement about the Mass or about that part of it for which it is giving directives. True, these statements are for the most part summaries of Council documents, but they are very skilful and sometimes clarify the statements of the documents. Their great value is that they make the Mass appear as a totally meaningful action and those who are being trained for the ministry and laity who have to teach, or, indeed, would know what the Mass is, will find here a theology they can assimilate without difficulty. As far as seminarists are concerned, it is one that will form them for celebration. It will be impossible in the future to train people for the celebration of the Mass without at the same time teaching them what the Mass in general and particular is. With one blow this document kills rubricism stone dead.

Since the *Ordo Missae* is a long document consisting of 341 articles, divided into eight chapters covering a vast amount of detail, it will be as well to give a summary of it. Experience shows that since it is not as yet indexed, it is often necessary to spend a considerable amount of time tracking down a single item.

Chapter I, 'On the Importance and Dignity of the Eucharistic Celebration', is the principal though not the exclusive liturgico-theological statement of the Order.

Chapter II, 'On the Structure of the Mass, its Elements and Parts', is a *rationale* of the new rite (though so very different from that of a Durandus!), giving the meaning of each part. It is the most important chapter in the whole Instruction and to it we shall return.

---

[1] The elevation and the communion.

Chapter III, 'On the Functions and Ministries', deals with all those engaged in the celebration of the Eucharist from the priest through deacon and subdeacon, to readers, cantors, commentators, people and choir (the people being placed immediately after the deacon in order and before the subdeacon and lesser ministers).

Chapter IV, 'On the Different Forms of Celebrating the Mass', covers Mass with the people in its typical form together with the directives on the functions of deacon and subdeacon, concelebrated Masses, Mass in the absence of a congregation and 'Certain more general rules' about ceremonial (veneration of the altar and gospel book, genuflexions and bows, incensations, the cleansing of the hands and vessels and the various ways of administering communion in both kinds).

Chapter V deals with the arrangement and furnishing of the church for eucharistic celebration, largely repeating the directives of the Instruction of 1964.

Chapter VI gives directives about the bread and wine, the vessels to be used in celebration and the vestments.

Chapter VII sets out the principles on which liturgical texts are to be chosen for different Masses, and

Chapter VIII those concerning Ritual Masses, Votive Masses and Masses for the dead.

The eucharistic theology of the Ordo Missae

The form of the Mass that is given in the Order itself expresses the theology of the eucharist that is set out more formally in the Instruction, but for practical purposes it will be best to examine first what the Instruction has to say and then go on to see how its theology is reflected in the Order.

The three main features of this theology are that it is firmly anchored in what the Lord said and did at the Last Supper, that it speaks a language that goes back beyond the Council of Trent and belongs to the Fathers and liturgies of the early Christian centuries, and that it is set in a community context.

This teaching is found principally in articles 7 and 48 of the Instruction, both of which have undergone some re-writing, occasioned by the objections of its critics (see above, p. 47). It will be instructive to set out both versions:

1. 'The Lord's Supper or the Mass is the sacred synaxis or gathering[2] of the people of God who come together to celebrate the memorial of the Lord under the presidency of the priest. The saying of Christ that "where two or three are gathered together in my name, I am in the midst of you"

---

[2] *Synaxis* and *congregatio* are synonyms.

(Matthew 18:20) is thus eminently verified in the local gathering of holy church' (1969).

2. '*In* the Mass, that is the Lord's Supper, the people of God *are called together* to celebrate the memorial of the Lord, *that is the eucharistic sacrifice*, under the presidency of the priest *who acts in the person of Christ*. The saying of Christ that "where two or three are gathered together in my name, I am in the midst of you" is thus eminently verified in the local gathering together (*coadunatione*) of holy church. *For in the celebration of the Mass, in which the sacrifice of the cross is perpetuated, Christ is made really present in the congregation gathered in his name, in the person of the minister, in his word and indeed substantially and continually in the sacramental species*' (1970).[3]

The procedure is obvious: every time there is an incriminated expression, what may be called for short a 'Tridentine' phrase is put beside it. Thus 'memorial' is 'corrected' by 'eucharistic sacrifice', the presidency of the priest by 'acting in the person of Christ' and it is not safe/acceptable to say that 'the Mass or the Lord's Supper *is* the sacred synaxis of the people of God'. This, it may have been thought, looks like some sort of Congregationalism, though I do not know that any Congregationalists have ever held anything of the sort.

Although the commentators on the new version of the Instruction say that nothing new has been added,[4] the picture is subtly changed. They indeed say elsewhere that the *teaching* is the same.[5] If this is so, we can take the changes as simply so many warning signs that should be borne in mind but which do not affect the teaching of the Instruction.

But before we do, it will be as well to look at some of the other emendations in the above paragraph.

1.   We may speculate on the reasons why the description of the Mass as

---

[3] Since there are witch-hunters about, perhaps I had better give the Latin for the last phrase: '*substantialiter et continenter sub speciebus eucharisticis*', which literally is '*under* the eucharistic species'. For want of this proviso, I may be accused of holding the Lutheran theory of impanation! The phrases in italics represent the additions of 1970.

[4] G. Pasqualetti and S. Bianchi in *Notitiae*, 54, May, 1970, p. 177: 'Nihil autem ex novo confectum est'.

[5] E.g. The 'Memorial of the Lord' says the same as 'eucharistic sacrifice', indicating perhaps that it is all a matter of semantics, though they go on to say that this phrase eliminates any notion that the Mass is merely a symbolic representation. It may indeed be wondered why the Constitution on the Liturgy avoided the word 'represented' which is found in the *Capitulum* on the Mass of the Council of Trent (Sess. XXII. Denz. 938, ed. 17a) which on the other hand did not use '*perpetuaret*' of Vatican II. As I remarked in *The Church's Worship* (p. 133, n. 2) it seems to be a neutral word, deliberately chosen, perhaps to avoid words like '*renovare*' which is to be found in the Proemium. 'Represented' is perfectly respectable. It was thought sufficient by the Council of Trent, it was used by St Thomas (*Summa*, III, 83, 1) and by at least one of his Jesuit commentators, Vasquez, in the sixteenth century.

'the sacred synaxis of the people of God under the presidency of the priest' was objected to and the commentators indeed say that the revised version is more accurate, though, they also say, it was never the intention of the Order to give a doctrinal definition of the Mass (*loc. cit.* 178). They point out that it gives a description of the general liturgico-ritual structure of the Mass and state that the structure of the eucharistic celebration is drawn from the community Mass (*Missa communitaria*), that is, one celebrated with the people in which is fully verified the principle (to be found also in CL 7) that the eucharist is the 'action of Christ and the Church', namely of 'the hierarchically ordered people of God'. Here is but one example of what the commentators mean when they say that nothing new was added to the Instruction. Patiently, and one does not know with what irony, they are spelling out its meaning and, in fact, giving nothing away. What in fact is in conflict is two totally opposed theological worlds, what E. Schillebeeckx called the essentialist theology as opposed to the existentialist theology at Vatican II. The objectors want to cling to a static essentialist theology of the Mass which cheerfully abstracts from its liturgical forms and celebration. On the contrary, the Instruction sees it as something in action, a celebration, and it is perfectly legitimate to describe it as the 'sacred synaxis of the people of God who come together to celebrate the memorial of the Lord under the presidency of the priest'.[6] This is what it in fact is, this is what you can discern and, as the liturgical documents affirm, it is from the Mass-in-action that you can see what it is and indeed what it is saying about the church.[7] The people gathered by God and acting with and under the presidency of the priest are the sign of the church, explicitating its meaning. They are part of the total sacramental sign of the eucharist itself and that is why it can be said that 'the structure of celebration is drawn from the community nature of the Mass'. It is this 'hierarchically ordered people' who celebrate the eucharist, bring it into existence in the here and now and who consequently should not be excluded from any comprehensive definition of the Mass. The eucharist, like the other sacraments, is the legitimate object of theological reflection but it, like them, is an existent thing and its nature will only be known in celebration.

---

[6] Dom Henry Ashworth in *Notitiae* (53, April, 1970) points out that this description (to use a neutral term) of the Mass simply reflects I Corinthians 11:20–26: St Paul indicates that the eucharist was the *Cena Dominica* (GI 7), the people were gathered together (GI 7, the *synaxis* or *congregatio*) 'to make the memorial of the Lord' (Do this in memory of me) (GI *memoriale Domini celebrare*). The term 'The Supper of the Lord' (*Cena Domini*) was, of course, long current (cf the *Missale Romanum*, Maundy Thursday) but Father Ashworth notes a peculiarly pregnant expression in the Leonine Sacramentary which is older than the Gregorian: '*ut et in caenae mysticae sacrosancto convivio*': 'in the holy meal of the mystical supper'.

[7] Cf CL 2.

Along with their concern over the sacrificial nature of the Mass, the objectors show a certain fussiness about the role of the priest in the eucharist. Perhaps they have been used to defining the priesthood in the terms of cult and 'powers'; the unique 'power' of the priest is to celebrate the sacrifice of the Mass, to be a 'sacrificer' in fact, although the whole analogous nature of the terms fails to impress them. No doubt they are not much concerned with modern theological reflection on the ministry, but there are the documents of the Vatican Council (on the church, on bishops and on the life and ministry of priests, to mention no others) that give a rather different emphasis.

The objectors are concerned to emphasize that in 'sacrificing', the priest acts in the person of Christ but they nowhere state that he is acting in the same way when he is preaching God's word, when he is visiting the sick or consoling the bereaved. And yet in one way or another the Council documents do say this. Thus the decree on the Ministry and Life of Priests (4) can say 'that the *primary* duty (of priests) is the proclamation of the gospel of God to all'. This they have to do both by word and by their life, but their preaching in the liturgy is of special importance:

'Such is especially true of the Liturgy of the Word during the celebration of Mass. In this celebration, the proclamation of the death and resurrection of the Lord is inseparably joined to the response of the people who hear, and *to the very offering* whereby Christ ratified the New Testament in his Blood. The faithful share in this offering both by their prayers and by their recognition of the sacrament for what it is.'

In prayer, especially that of the Divine Office, they pray *in the name of the Church* (5), they have the task of forming Christian communities leading them *through Christ* and in the Spirit to God the Father (6) and, not to prolong the list, they have to care for the poor and lowly, an apostolate that is 'a sign of Messianic activity' in which they are following Christ (6). A comprehensive paragraph sums up the whole life of the priest, and if it does not say that in all his priestly tasks he is acting in the person of Christ, it says much the same thing when it says that they 'result from Christ's Passover':

'The purpose, therefore, which priests pursue by their ministry and life is the glory of God the Father as it is to be achieved in Christ. That glory consists in this: that men knowingly, freely, and gratefully accept what God has achieved perfectly through Christ, and manifest it in their whole lives. Hence, whether engaged in prayer and adoration, preaching the Word, offering the eucharistic sacrifice, ministering the other sacraments, or performing any of the works of the ministry for men, priests are contributing to the extension of God's glory as well as to the development of divine life in men. Since all these activities result from Christ's Passover, they will be crowned in the glorious return of the same Lord when he himself hands over the kingdom to his God and Father' (2).

We need not delay over the last part of this article. The concern for the Real Presence in or 'under the eucharistic species' is hardly necessary within the confines of the Roman Catholic Church and, in fact, the Proemium simply points to the *practices* of the liturgy, the elevation and the feast of Corpus Christi, as sufficient proof of the church's unwavering faith. We merely remark that the revisers have strengthened the statement of the Constitution on the Liturgy about the presence of Christ in different parts of the liturgy (CL 7): 'Christ is *really* present in the assembly, in the celebrant, in the word. . . .' As we know, the Council's teaching here startled some people, so used had we become to thinking of only one kind of presence of Christ. The reason for its inclusion here is obvious but again it is unnecessary.

The second place where there is some change is in article 48 which introduces 'The liturgy of the Eucharist'. It is slight, though showing the same concern: 'Christ, at the Last Supper, *instituted the sacrifice and paschal banquet by which the sacrifice of the cross* is continually made present in the church. . . .' The words italicized are the ones added to the original article that read: 'The Last Supper, at which Christ instituted the memorial of his death and resurrection is made continually present in the church when the priest, representing Christ, does what the Lord himself did and gave to his disciples to do in memory of him thus instituting the paschal sacrifice and banquet.' The addition, which is not much more than a re-arrangement of the words, was hardly worth making and the need for the change is found in the inability or unwillingness of the objectors to accept the ancient and wholly traditional language of 'memorial'. The memorial of the death and resurrection of Christ is the memorial of the paschal mystery by which he redeemed the world and when the church makes the memorial, it is making present in the here and now the effects of the redeeming work of Christ.

What picture of the eucharist, then, emerges from a study of the Introduction and of the rite itself? It will be convenient to take the Introduction first and then the rite.

The Mass in the Instruction

The first thing emphasized is that the Mass is a community celebration. Especially since the Constitution on the Liturgy, this is a theological platitude.[8] It is, however, worth pointing out that it is a complete change from the picture given by the rubrics of the Pius V missal. These were concerned almost wholly with the actions of the priest who is envisaged as concentrated on what he must do and say almost regardless of the people. Although the term is harsh, he appeared as the minister of a mysterious cult of which he alone had the secret. Even the gestures he was required to

---

[8] See *ibid.* 14, 26–31, 34, 41, 42, 48, 50, etc.

make were regarded as a clerical secret, and when in the seventeenth century the first translations of the missal and breviary were made, they were condemned as profanations.[9] Even educated people would read a book of devotions, one of the many *Manières d'entendre la Sainte Messe* or the Hours of Our Lady, during Mass and all were thought to be devoutly kneeling looking in wonder at the mystic rite (if they could see it) as it unrolled before them. The rubrics instructed the celebrant to 'show' the Host to the people after the consecration (by raising it over his head) and likewise the chalice, but frequently this was so badly done that they could not be seen. The people are spoken of in the *Ritus Servandus* once again, at the time of communion, and in spite of the strong recommendations of the Council of Trent to frequent communion, the rubric assumes that it is going to be rare: '*If* there are any to be communicated' (*si qui sunt communicandi* . . .). If to this we add that the custom grew up that people were communicated either before or after Mass (a custom that remained until about fifty years ago), it will be seen that the part of the people in the Mass was visibly non-existent.

How different the picture of the Mass as given by the *Ordo Missae* of 1969: the celebration of the Mass is the action of Christ and of the hierarchically ordered people of God, or in the words of the Constitution, the action of Christ in his church (CL 7). The celebration must be so ordered that all, ministers and people, in their various roles, may be able to take their part so that they may receive as copiously as possible the fruits of the Mass. It was to this end that Christ the Lord instituted the sacrifice of his body and blood and entrusted it as the memorial of his passion and resurrection to his beloved Bride, the church. Nor is this left in the realm of exhortation: since the eucharist requires and uses visible signs for its celebration, the greatest care must be taken to select those forms and elements that in local circumstances are best adapted to secure the full and active participation of the people (GI 3, 5). Celebration must be the visible sign of the worshipping eucharistic community and this community is the sign or sacrament of the Church. It reveals its nature, it shows and teaches that the church is the union of those who love one another in Christ and who through him are lifted up to the Father in praise and thanksgiving. As article I of the Order says, the eucharist is the centre of the whole Christian life both for the church as a whole, for the local church and for the individual, and is the culminating point of its existence. By it God in

---

[9] The terms of the brief of Alexander VII condemning Voisin's translation of the missal are very severe: the people might not apparently know the sacred words of the Canon, even in translation. It is no comfort to learn that the document was canonically 'surreptitious', i.e. obtained on the false charge that the translator intended to say Mass in French! The condemnation exerted a baleful influence until it was withdrawn by Leo XIII at the end of the nineteenth century. (See L. Bouyer, *Liturgical Piety*, University of Notre Dame, USA, 1955, p. 51.)

Christ sanctifies the world and men give their worship to the Father through him.

The teaching that the local church in its eucharistic celebrations is the sign of the great church is repeated at the opening of the long chapter on the structure of the Mass and the revised version does nothing to minimize it (GI 7). The people are *called together* to celebrate the memorial of the Lord and the whole body, under the presidency of the priest who represents Christ, is a conspicuous manifestation of the truth that 'where two or three are gathered together in my name, there I am in the midst of them' (Matthew 18:20). As we shall see, this, that has always been true, is made plain in the rite itself.

This teaching about the local church, whether the diocese or, less perfectly, the parish, is of both theological and practical importance. Theologically it suggests that the church, the *Una sancta*, is made up of innumerable communities throughout the world, each related to the other because they are parts of the Body of Christ in which the Spirit dwells and is active. Each has a different function and each casts a different light on the church as a whole. More important still, it is here in these local communities that the church really exists.[10] Until the modern renewal of the church and of its theology, we tended to look on it as a vast institution or organization, spread indeed throughout the world, propagating, in ways that were not very particularly examined, Catholic truth and getting (some) people into heaven. There was some temptation to see the church as a vast propaganda machine and many of those outside it in fact saw it as that. Rome and the Pope dominated the scene. What it came to, in fact, was an ecclesiastical institution that made itself present in different parts of the world largely juridically. The renewed theology of the church, the Second Vatican Council and now the *Ordo Missae*, make it clear that the great church exists and acts in and through the local church and principally through the celebration of the liturgy. It is here that God's word comes alive and is proclaimed, it is here that through Christ glory is given to God, it is here that men are sanctified and ultimately saved.

Practically, the teaching is important for it means that those in charge of the liturgy in a local community have to consider their own situation, have to decide what, within the limits of the Order, is right and possible. They have to construct a local liturgy that is adapted to the capacities and needs of the local church. This might seem too obvious to mention and everyone is more or less aware that it has always been necessary to adapt the liturgy to circumstances. No one can be unaware of the difference between a cathedral and a small parish church, though this awareness has

---

[10] There has been much writing about this in recent years. Apart from the council documents and those of the popes insisting on the importance of the subsidiary function, there is, for example, the essay of Karl Rahner, 'Theology of the Parish', in *The Parish*, Eng. trans. 1958 (Maryland, USA).

not always been sufficiently vivid to prevent priests and choirmasters from emulating those they have thought were their betters. Nor was adaptation (lawfully) easy under the old régime. It was a case of all or nothing. You either had a low Mass or a 'pompous' high Mass. The principle of adaptation has been built into the new Order. Incense may or may not be used at any kind of Mass and its use within the Mass may be varied from one kind to another (GI 235). The suggestions (they are nearer to this than to rules) about singing are even more flexible (GI 19). This or that rite may be done 'if convenient'. For instance, there should normally be an offertory procession but there are circumstances in which this is impossible. So you need not have one—but it would be against the spirit of the Order to decide that *nothing* can be done. What is required is that *some* gesture of offering on the part of the people (collectors or others can bring the elements to the altar) should be made. The mind of the Order is that the Mass should be a community action. Like the Constitution on the Liturgy, it says again and again that the *purpose* of the new rite is that the full, conscious and devout participation of the people should be made possible, a participation to which they have a right by baptism (GI 3, 5). Through this kind of celebration 'in which those elements of the rite are chosen to secure the active participation of the people' (GI 5) the 'real nature of the true church' will be manifested (CL 2) and the work of Christ's redemption will be effected (*ibid.*). The image of the church, the community of Christ, will be reflected in such a celebration and will be truly discernible. It will not be distorted.

What, then, does this community come together to do? The answer falls under three heads: 1) to celebrate the memorial of the Lord; 2) to meet Christ in his word; 3) to receive him in holy communion.

The phrase 'to celebrate the memorial of the Lord' is at once the simplest and most profound way of describing what the Christian community does at Mass. It is to say no more, but *no less*, than what Christ said at the Last Supper: 'Do this in memory of me' (*touto poieite eis tēn emēn anamnēsin*).[11] When the Christian community *makes* the eucharist, it is making the memorial of the Lord and of all he did from the Supper to the resurrection to redeem mankind. It should not be necessary to re-affirm, but apparently it is, that 'making the memorial', *anamnesis*, in fact, is not to be understood in the weak modern sense of just recalling to the mind a past event. All scripture scholars[12] and liturgists[13] are agreed that it is to

---

[11] Luke 22:19. As against those who for long have held that the shorter reading, omitting these words, is the better one, I find the case put up for the longer reading by Jeremias (*The Eucharistic Words of Jesus*, p. 138) and Benoît (*Exégèse et Théologie*, I, p. 163) completely convincing.

[12] See, for example, Max Thurian, *The Eucharistic Memorial*, Part I, The Old Testament (London, 1960). After a close analysis of the O.T. material the author states that 'memorial' means recalling before God a past event of his saving mercy

be understood in the active sense: by 'making the memorial' we are 'in some way', as both the Constitution and the Order say (CL 102 and GI 1), making present the redeeming work of Christ. When celebrating the eucharist, the church is put in possession of the power of Christ's redeeming actions from the Supper to the resurrection (what the documents call 'the paschal mystery'). Or, you can put it another way round, Christ, faithful to his promise, comes to his church once again, makes himself present to it and communicates to it his saving life. It is then, and only then, that we are able to give that worship to the Father through Christ of which the Order speaks (GI 1) and which alone is acceptable to God.

Needless to say, if the people have or are given a sense of the active, redeeming Christ in the Mass, their appreciation of it as 'sacrifice' will in no way be weakened. They will realize that sacrifice is not an inert object immolated and offered to God but that it is in its very essence Christ's act of self-giving[14] that continues in heaven where he is ever-living to make intercession for us (Hebrews 7:25). This same teaching, too, will evoke from them that other important New Testament teaching that our response to Christ's self-giving is a giving of ourselves to him and through him to the Father 'offer your living bodies as a holy sacrifice truly pleasing to God' (Romans 12:1).[15]

Emphasis on 'memorial' also makes the pattern of the whole eucharist action more comprehensible. There is the age-old problem of the relation of the 'once-for-all' sacrifice of the cross and the sacrifice of the Mass. Various words have been used, 'renewal', 're-enactment' and so on, all of which give the impression (at least) that the Mass is in some way a *separate* sacrifice. This will not do, as it at least seems to derogate from the uniqueness of the cross. Then again, the Mass has often and perhaps usually been called 'the renewal or re-presentation of the *cross*', but this over-simplifies

---

and through this 'memorial' making it present here and now. In Part II of the same work he applies this to the eucharist, 'The eucharistic memorial is a recalling of the Son to us, a recalling by us to the Father and a recalling to the Father for us'. We may add that because we are making the memorial according to the command of Christ, he makes himself present because like his Father in the Old Testament he is *faithful* to his covenant, to the new covenant of which the eucharist is the memorial. Thurian puts it this way: 'This memorial is not a simple subjective act of recollection, it is a liturgical *action*. But it is not just a liturgical action that makes the Lord present, it is a liturgical action that recalls as a memorial before the Father the unique sacrifice of the Son, and this makes Him present in His memorial, in the presentation of His sacrifice before the Father and in his intercession as heavenly High Priest' (pp. 35–6).

[13] See Louis Ligier, 'From the Last Supper to the Eucharist', in *The New Liturgy*, ed. Lancelot Sheppard (London, 1970), pp. 136–40. In a brief phrase he sums up the meaning of *memoria-anamnesis*, 'It is the whole narrative-anamnesis which constitutes both celebration and action'.

[14] See Letter to the Hebrews 10:7: 'I come to do your will'.

[15] See Chapter three.

things. This direct relationship of the Mass to the cross was not without its influence on the unhappy practice of looking for events of the passion and death of Christ in the Mass. Christ did not say on the cross 'Do *this* in memory of me'. It was after the Supper, in which he declared the meaning of what he was to do next day, that he said 'Do this in memory of me' and as the Council of Trent carefully said, by so doing he left a *memorial* of his sacrifice to the church. What we are doing in the Mass is to make the memorial of what Christ did at the Last Supper and through the making of that memorial we are able to make encounter with the sacrifice of Christ, which, as St Thomas said, is perpetual.[16] The church was put in possession of the means by which the men and women of all time could enter into the redeeming work of Christ. These means remain within the initiative of the church which, in obedience to Christ's command, inaugurates in the here and now the rite of the Mass. These successive 'inaugurations' can obviously be numbered, these can be called 'Masses' and the Proemium (2) can call the Mass a '*sacramental* renewal' where full weight must be given to the word 'sacramental'. It is the sacramental, ritual, liturgical action that remains within the competence of the church and through which, to repeat, it makes the memorial of the Supper, which in turn makes the sacrifice of the cross present to people here and now.

Even to narrow the memorial of the Mass to the cross is to say less than the truth of the matter. As the documents of the church affirm again and again, the Mass is the memorial of the Lord's death and resurrection, what the Constitution calls the paschal mystery (CL 5), by which he brought his 'worshipping' church into existence, redeemed mankind and gave glory to the Father. Because it is this kind of memorial, the church *now* can enter into the redeeming work, can make its own the effects of the redemption. In the Mass we encounter the Risen Christ, who has suffered and died. It is he who enfolds our self-offering in his, unites it to his own and offers us to his Father. Once this is achieved the whole community through the operation of the Holy Spirit (as the epicleses of the new eucharistic prayers make clear) is able to offer that sacrifice of praise, thanksgiving and propitiation of which both the Council of Trent and the Proemium speak. When the church speaks of 'active participation' it is all this it has in mind, not merely a voicing of certain formulas. These and actions and gestures and a dozen other things are merely the means by which the community may enter into union with God.

This is a rather different picture of the Mass from that that sees it as an offering of some object 'out there' to which people can attach themselves by pious thoughts or devout desires. This view of the Mass, which is not new but very old, means that the community must be involved in its action 'as the very nature of the celebration demands', to quote the Instruction (GI 3).

---

[16] 4 Sent. 12: *Hostia illa perpetua est.*

It is an action not an object to be contemplated, it is by definition a community action and normally the effects of Christ's redeeming work upon the participants will be in proportion to their active involvement. The church documents say this over and over again, but not all as yet realize that this is what they mean.

The role of the priest

The worshipping community is a 'hierarchically ordered' people made up of many 'ministries' united under the presidency of the priest. Thus the Council and other documents.[17] This means that in the celebration he is *visibly* head of the assembly, occupying the chief place and pronouncing certain texts, above all the eucharistic prayer, that belong to him alone.[18] But that is to describe no more than his material function. During celebration it is for him to *animate* the community, to set the tone for the act of worship and throughout to maintain the action of the people and of all the other 'ministries' that collaborate in the celebration of the eucharist. His mentality, attitude and general bearing are of crucial importance. He must be concerned not for himself but for the community he is leading. In his presidency he is above all the *servant* of the people, helping them not merely to say prayers and sing chants, but to move towards God and be united with him, which is the purpose of the whole action. The various ways by which he may do this will be considered later.

But if he is to achieve this presidency *in worship* he will also have to exercise it before worship in preparing all those people and things that are necessary for celebration, combining and harmonizing the work of choir, servers and readers especially. Of diocesan bishops the Decree on the Bishops' Pastoral Office in the Church (15) says that they are the principal dispensers of the mysteries of God and the '*governors, promoters* and *guardians* of the entire liturgical life in the church committed to them'. What is true of the bishop is true also of the pastoral priest within the limits of his own sphere and in dependence on his bishop and the regulations of the church. He is not just the performer of certain rites that can be found in the official books. Nor does he exercise this leadership-service without the collaboration of his people. They have their various functions to perform which may not be taken away from them (CL 28, 29) and they must be 'trained to perform their functions in a correct and *orderly* manner' (*ibid.*).

But the presidency of the priest goes much further. He is very much more than the organizer of ceremonial or the reciter of words. He is the *minister* of Christ 'who in the liturgy exercises his priestly office on our behalf by the action of the Holy Spirit' (Decree on Priests 5). He is first the minister of God's word both outside the liturgical sphere but especially

---

[17] Cf CL 41, Decree on Priests 5, GI 7.
[18] See the Instruction of 1970 where the point is re-emphasized.

inside it: 'In the Christian community itself, especially among those who seem to understand or believe little of what they practise, the preaching of the Word is needed for the very administration of the sacraments. *For these sacraments are sacraments of faith, and faith is born of the Word and nourished by it*' (*ibid.*, 4). Thus through his ministry of the word he is the minister of faith which leads men and women to Christ, who exercises his priestly office in their regard in the celebration of the sacraments.

In the eucharist there is the closest possible connection between the word and the sacrament. The priest leads the people into the sacrament by his ministry of the word: 'In this celebration, the proclamation of the death and resurrection of Christ is inseparably joined to the response of the people who hear, and to the very offering whereby Christ ratified the New Testament in his blood. The faithful share in this offering both by their prayers and by the recognition of the sacrament for what it is.' As we have seen (in Chapter three) by his total ministry the priest leads the people in the offering of the eucharist and makes it possible for them to unite themselves and their whole lives to the sacrifice of Christ.

All of this is comprised in 'the presidency of the priest' at the eucharist and it will be seen that the other phrase used in the Council documents and in the Order of the Mass 'the priest acts in the person of Christ' is merely a more concrete, and shorter, way of putting the matter. The priest is indeed 'configured to Christ' so that he can act 'in the person of Christ' (Decree on Priests 3), but he is so acting both when he is proclaiming the word and when he is leading the people into the offering that includes the offering of themselves. His action is indispensable but it does not obliterate that of the people. The whole community celebrates, the whole community offers, the whole community receives into itself the self-offering of Christ and the whole community is made one by communion in the Body and Blood of Christ. The 'presidency of the priest' is a leadership of service, making it possible for the whole community, of which he is a member, to be enfolded in the eternal sacrifice of Jesus Christ. Such collaboration may indeed be regarded as the model of that relationship between priest and people which the Council has called for and it irresistibly reminds one of St Paul's teaching of the need that one member of the body has of the others (I Corinthians 12:12–26).

The eucharistic action

The third feature of the theology of the Order we mentioned above, namely that it remains firmly rooted in what Christ did and said at the Last Supper, can best be seen in GI 48 which summarizes much that has gone before and expresses it with great succinctness:

'Christ instituted the memorial of his death and resurrection at the Last Supper. This is continually made present in the church when the priest, representing Christ, carries out what the Lord did. When he instituted the paschal sacrifice and meal (*convivium*), he handed it over (*tradidit*) to his disciples for them to do it in his memory.'

Simply, the memorial, paschal meal that Jesus instituted at the Last Supper is the recalling (in the full sense) or the 'making the memory' of the Lord's death and resurrection. Through it his sacrifice is made present to us. This is the ancient and traditional way of speaking of the Mass, and the Order goes on to draw out the consequences as they are shown in the liturgy itself:

'Christ took bread and the cup and, giving thanks, broke and gave to his disciples, saying: "Take and eat, this is my body. Take and drink, this is the cup of my blood. Do this in memory of me". The church has arranged the celebration of the eucharistic liturgy *to correspond to these words and actions of Christ*:

1. In the preparation of the gifts, bread, wine and water are brought to the altar, the same elements which Christ used.

2. The eucharistic prayer is the hymn of thanksgiving to the Father for the whole work of salvation, and in it the offerings become the body and blood of Christ.

3. The breaking of the one bread is a sign of the unity of the faithful, and in communion they receive the body and blood of Christ as the Apostles did from his hands.'[19]

This apparently simple description of the eucharistic action in fact isolates its main features: the presentation of the gifts, the recitation of the eucharistic prayer, the breaking of the bread and the communion. These are the basic structural elements on which any liturgy of the eucharist must be built and while faithful to the New Testament data, they do not slavishly repeat them. The description in the Order closely follows the pattern discerned by the late Dom Gregory Dix, now some long time ago. He observed that with absolute unanimity the liturgical tradition reduced the 'seven-action scheme' of the New Testament to the four-action scheme with which we are familiar:

1) 'The offertory; the bread and wine are "taken" and placed on the table together. 2) The prayer; the president gives thanks to God over the bread and wine together. 3) The fraction; the bread is broken. 4) The communion; the bread and wine are distributed together.'[20]

The first example of this 'absolute unanimity' is to be found in the earliest description of the eucharist we possess, written by St Justin the Martyr about the middle of the second century:

---

[19] We have used the ICEL translation here, which gives the version of the *Ordo Missae* of 1969, without, then, the revision. But on reflexion I have felt that the revision neither adds nor subtracts anything from this perspicuous text and that therefore it was best left in its simplicity. (Translation copyright © 1969, International Committee on English in the Liturgy, Inc. All rights reserved.)

[20] *The Shape of the Liturgy* (London, 1945), p. 48. The 'seven-action scheme' comes, of course, from the separate consecrations and communions.

a) bread, wine and water are brought to the table at which the president (*proestōs*) is standing;
b) he 'sends up' the prayer of thanksgiving to which the people give their assent with Amen;
c) communion is given and taken to 'those who are absent'.[21]
What is missing is the fraction which, however, must have taken place. On the other hand we note that the celebrant is called 'president' and that it is he who performs the eucharistic action.

In certain Reformed liturgies of the sixteenth century the fraction was made at the words of institution and it may be asked why the early church never adopted that position for it. The answer is, I think, to be found in the fact that the church was precisely making the memorial of the Last Supper and in the eucharistic prayer wished to dwell on the fact and draw out its consequences. Now, after Calvary and the resurrection, the eucharist was the 'memorial' (*anamnesis*) that made the power of the whole redeeming work of Christ present to the community. Hence the prolongation of the eucharistic prayer after the consecration, and we may suppose that before the *epiclesis* of the Holy Spirit was introduced (not generally until the fourth century), the fraction will have taken place at that point.[22]

Holy communion

This section of the Instruction does not in fact begin with one of its more lengthy statements, but its doctrine can be gathered from its interpretation of the rites that go to make up the communion act (GI 56, b, c, i).

It is a curious fact of religious history that for centuries Christians have not generally realized the full implications of the word 'communion'. Yes, it means communion with the Lord, but this has been thought of for the most part as a private conversation with him, often to the exclusion of other members of the Christian community. The Instruction is concerned to bring back the fundamental and ancient connotation of the word. It emphasizes that it means *koinonia* (inadequately translated 'fellowship'), which signifies communion with Christ *but also* with the members of Christ, with the *community* that is assembled in church.

1.   Thus, the sign of peace expresses the peace and unity of the church,

---

[21] Justin, *Apology* I, 65 and 67. The words of institution are suggested in 66 where he gives an account of Christian belief in the eucharist. He also mentions that a collection was taken at the end of the service—so collections are not a modern invention either!

[22] There is a fraction in the *Ap. Trad.* (xxi) of Hippolytus but the bishop broke the bread immediately before giving communion. But this was an exceptional service: it was the first Mass of those who had been baptized and after the eucharistic prayer there was a series of blessings. In the place where he gives a specimen eucharistic prayer, there is an *epiclesis* of the Holy Spirit, the doxology and at this point the text comes to an end (iv). [Numbering as in Dix (London, 1937).]

the mutual love that members of the church must have for one another before receiving the one bread, and it is also a prayer for the peace and unity of the human family. The implications of this last observation are far-reaching. It is meant to bring before the minds of Christians, precisely at communion, that they are part of the human family, that they have obligations to it and that at least they must pray for it. The Mass, in fact, is the vital centre of peace, love and unity in the world. The love that Christ had for mankind on the cross is mediated through the Mass to the world, even if it is not the only way it is so mediated.

2.   The next statement deepens the notion of unity-in-fellowship: the fraction is not just a practical action to break the bread so that it may be distributed; it is the sign that we, though many in number, are by the one Bread, which is Christ, made one body, and the text refers to I Corinthians 10:7. This is one reason why the Order requires that the bread, or at least some of it, should be sufficiently large to be broken and that it should be broken before the eyes of the people. Here is one of the many instances in the reformed liturgy where we find a real revalidation of symbols. The practical will say, 'It does not matter whether the bread is broken or whether you can see it broken. You receive Christ all the same.' But they (and we) need to reflect that Christ himself thought this action to be of immense significance[23] and the early church saw it was so. The earliest name for the eucharist is 'the breaking of bread'.[24] Critics of the new liturgy often say that there has been a reduction of symbolism, that all is dull and pedestrian, but it would seem that their notions of symbolism are those of the allegorists of the ninth and subsequent centuries who overlaid the Mass with all sorts of arbitrary meanings. The symbolism of the Mass as Christ instituted it is what is all-important.

3.   All this is spelt out in the communion act. The Instruction assumes that there is going to be a procession and it sees this and the chants that accompany it as means of promoting the 'spiritual union of the communicants' and of the brotherly love that exists (should exist) between them. As, then, the Christian people move towards the altar, singing chants taken either from holy scripture or from other sources, they are expressing in action the meaning of the whole rite: though many, they are being made one through the one Bread that is Christ.

Thus is brought back into currency by an official document of the church the most ancient and profoundest teaching on the meaning of holy communion. It will no doubt take time before this becomes the normal thinking of most Catholics and there will be (is) resistance to a change in one of the most intimate of people's devotional habits, but one can but feel that the change is long overdue. The practice of holy communion has too often been divorced from Christian living and the teaching given by the Instruction

[23] See e.g. Luke 24:30–31: 'They knew him in the breaking of bread.'
[24] Cf Acts 2:42 and many other places.

provides at least a point of entry into a fuller and richer use of holy communion.

Another aspect of communion is also high-lighted by the Instruction (GI 56, h). The people are to be communicated from the hosts consecrated at Mass 'to make it clearer that they are participating in the sacrifice that is actually being celebrated'. The Mass is a unity and communion is an integral part of it, and yet for many centuries there have been factors making for a separation of the sacrifice from communion. The fear of profanation in pre- and post-Carolingian times and the complications of the penitential system led to infrequent communion. All through the Middle Ages people did not receive it very often. One result was that the holy eucharist was divided into three things: Mass, communion and the adoration of the host (at the elevation) and towards the end of the Middle Ages, outside the Mass altogether. The strong recommendation of the Council of Trent to frequent communion did little to correct the situation and the custom of receiving it apart from the Mass grew. One of the greatest difficulties the early promoters of the liturgical movement had to overcome was to persuade both clergy and laity that communion is part of the Mass and normally should be received during it. Then, with the growing frequency of communion in this century, it was thought that there should always be a considerable reserve of hosts in the tabernacle and people even at Mass were communicated from that reserve. For a very long time now, from the time of Benedict XIV in the middle of the eighteenth century, recommendations have been made that the people should be communicated from hosts consecrated at the Mass. This recommendation has been renewed several times in recent years, by Pius XII in 1947 (*Mediator Dei* 128), by the Second Vatican Council (CL 55) and by the Instruction on the Eucharistic Mystery of 1967. The first battle has been won: people normally receive communion at Mass and in great numbers. Communicating attendance has largely replaced non-communicating attendance that was such a strange feature of Catholic life years ago. The second battle has still to be won, although the practice of communicating the people from hosts consecrated at the Mass is now very widespread. It is another case of fundamental symbolism that comes from the Last Supper itself. Jesus said 'Take and eat, take and drink' and what is needed is that the people should be able to see the Mass-liturgy as a coherent whole coming from what Christ said and did at the Last Supper. Any practices that obscure the basic lines of the eucharist must be condemned by this principle.[25]

One of the more remarkable features of modern liturgical reform is that it has restored to the liturgy (not merely to the eucharist) the eschatological dimension. As the General Instruction says (240) communion from the cup expresses more clearly 'the relation of the eucharistic banquet to the heavenly banquet' and it refers to the Instruction on the Eucharistic

---

[25] For communion in both kinds for the laity, see below, Chapter five.

Mystery of 1967 where we find a reference to Matthew 26:27-9, 'From now on, I tell you, I shall not drink wine until the day I drink new wine with you in the kingdom of my Father.' No doubt the first reference is to the eschatological banquet that is so frequent a figure for the consummation of God's work at the end (cf Matthew 22:1 ff. etc.) and it is to this that three out of the four acclamations after the consecration and the phrase immediately before communion refer. But the church also comes into the perspective. The 'kingdom' begins to come into existence after the resurrection when we find Jesus present among his followers (Luke 24:13-35 and cf Acts 1:4 and 10:41) with whom he had eaten and drunk. And we know that in the earliest days of the church there was a vivid sense of Christ as present among the gathered community. These words, then, refer to the church as the beginning of the kingdom, for it is through the celebration of the eucharist in the community of Christ that we shall come to celebrate the eternal banquet in heaven. A modern writer combines both perspectives very skilfully:

'This eschatological perspective is an integral part of the eucharist. At the eucharist Christ appoints a kingdom unto the Church, which participates in it in advance, and in that communion with God which it involves; *the Church already sits at table with Christ to eat and drink with him* and enter into communion with him as in the Kingdom. As through the eucharist they participate in this communion of the Kingdom and are admitted to the table of Christ, *the faithful are assured of their entrance into the Kingdom of God at the Last Day* that they may enjoy eternal communion with the Lord. They receive the sign of their belonging to the coming Kingdom at the eucharist; they are given the pledge that they will be able to enter in and have the right to sit at Christ's table "to eat and drink" with him in eternity.'[26]

Expectation of the Last Day and the Triumph of Christ is the fruit of Christian hope and while we are used to saying that the eucharist is supremely the sacrament of love, both God's towards us and ours towards him and our neighbour, we can see now that it is also the sacrament of hope. This means not simply that we long for the consummation (and how many of us do!) but that through our celebration of the eucharist and our communion in the Lord we are working towards his final victory. The power of Christ's final victory is already, through the eucharist, exercising a sort of 'pull' so that we and the whole church are able to have part in the working out in time and for the world of the divine plan of total salvation.

---

[26] Max Thurian, *The Eucharistic Memorial*, Part II, pp. 66-7 (London, 1961) (italics added). Theories on eschatology differ a good deal among the scripture experts and the note in Jerusalem Bible (*in loc.*) simply refers our Lord's statement to the end of all things. Thurian's view, which I have held for a long time, seems to be perfectly tenable and is, I think, the true meaning of this and similar statements in the gospel.

CHAPTER SIX

THE STRUCTURE OF THE MASS[1]

THE structure of the Mass as given in the *Ordo Missae* is the liturgical expression of the doctrine that is to be found in the General Instruction and this we have briefly considered. However, it is necessary from time to time to turn to the Instruction to discern the mind of the revisers, and this we shall do in what follows.[2]

The Mass, said the Constitution (CL 56), is made up of two parts: the ministry of the word and the ministry of the eucharist.[3] Each of these parts is broken down into its constituent elements: the first consists of the three readings, the responsorial psalm, the alleluia (or acclamation), the homily, the creed and the general intercession (GI 33). It is preceded by an entrance rite. The second consists of everything that runs from the presentation of the gifts to the completion of the communion rite, though the Order gives due prominence to its main elements: the eucharistic prayer and the rite of communion. It and the whole Mass is concluded with a brief rite of dismissal.

From this summary description the main lines of the Mass stand out clearly: fundamentally it consists of the proclamation of the word and 'the thanksgiving' with its necessary completion in holy communion. Nothing could be simpler, nothing nearer to the eucharist of the primitive church, and in the discussion about liturgical reform which some say must come from further experiment it is to be hoped that it will be realized that these are all indispensable elements and that the very order in which they occur is something that cannot be changed.[4] Other elements, entrance rites and rites of dismissal, are variable and could be changed without any essential damage to the structure of the Mass. But, if we see things this way, it does mean that the revisers have been faithful to their brief which was given to them in the Constitution on the Liturgy (50): 'The rite of the Mass is to be revised in such a way that the intrinsic nature and purpose of its several parts, as also the connection between them, may be more clearly manifested,

---

[1] GI 7–57.

[2] It is likely that the Order was worked out first and that the Instruction was then written as a liturgical commentary on what had been done.

[3] I use the word 'ministry' instead of 'liturgy' as the former has a long tradition in the English language. For me it has no theological overtones at all.

[4] See J. D. Crichton, 'Liturgical Forms', in *The Way*, special number, Autumn, 1970.

and that the devout and active participation by the people may be more easily achieved.' Keeping, then, the main structure of the Mass in mind, we can go on to consider its various parts.

The entrance rite

Of the various elements that go to make up the entrance rite some are old and some are new, the oldest being the entrance chant and the collect.[5] The new elements, the greeting and the brief address, unfold the meaning and the purpose of the oldest elements. It is a traditional Christian belief that when the people come together for worship they are called by God— they are *ecclesia*, the assembly of God, the people of God, and his word is first heard in the entrance chant, especially when it is taken from holy scripture. The collect is the first prayer said by the president when they are assembled so that they may respond to God's call. But in the course of centuries not only have these truths been obscured by a faulty liturgical rite, but it has been felt that they were not sufficiently explicit. At the psychological level, too, there is a case for saying that if a crowd of people are to become a community they need to be made aware of their relationship to each other, they have to move from being a crowd to being a community. It is the first function of the president to help them to do this. Moreover, if worship is a Christian action (divine worship, as it used to be called) it has first to be a human action, and it is the most human thing in the world that celebrant and people should feel that they are related to one another. A first contact at this point, then, is of considerable importance.

By our standards now, the old Mass began almost brutally. The Mass began from cold. The priest appeared (sometimes out of a side-door on the sanctuary) with server or servers, went to the altar, turned his back on the people and then began the prayers. Sometimes the people could hear what these were and sometimes they could not. A few moments later he turned to them briefly to address a more or less hurried *Dominus vobiscum* and they did not see his face again until, on Sundays, he turned round to read the epistle and gospel in English and to preach to them. It was assumed that the people did not need any preparation for Mass, that they were fully aware of what the feast or Sunday was, of what texts would be read and so on. It was assumed that they were an instructed and devout congregation that was ready in all respects to celebrate the greatest act of worship that there is. Possibly this was true in some places and at certain times. It is no longer generally true and, in any case, we have discovered new needs in worship, and one of them is that there should be a relationship between celebrant and people.

---

[5] If we take the old (pre-1955) Good Friday liturgy as being the liturgy of the church of Rome in the fourth century, we see that it began without either. The entrance chant and the collect would both seem to have been added to the Mass in the fifth century. (See Jungmann, *Missarum Sollemnia*, French trans., t. II, pp. 72ff.)

If community then means a relationship between a group of people and a relationship between them and their leader, the Order has been faithful to its teaching as given in the Instruction. Here, right at the beginning, the Order of the Mass endeavours to create community, a community in which Christ is present and is going to renew his presence in a variety of ways. The Instruction sums up the whole matter very briefly: the entrance rites have the qualities of preparation and introduction, but, more purposefully and more concretely, they enable the people to realize they are a community and to prepare to receive the word of God and to celebrate the eucharist itself (GI 25). The purpose of the entrance chant in particular is to 'foster the sense of union of the gathered people' (GI 26). It helps to do this because, among other things, it introduces the whole community to the liturgy of the day and provides the accompaniment of the celebrant's procession to the altar (ibid.). It does indeed 'open their minds' and where minds are meeting in the same thoughts, expressed in song, there community is beginning to be formed.

The truth that the assembly is gathered by the word of God is made explicit in the greeting. This is especially clear in the first and longest: 'The grace of our Lord Jesus Christ and the love of God and the fellowship of the Holy Spirit be with you all', but it is also clear in the shortest and best known: 'The Lord be with you . . .' as the modern interpretation of this obscure phrase shows: 'He (the celebrant) expresses the wish that the Lord, or peace, or grace, should be with them (the people) in their worship, and they return his greeting specifying that the Lord (peace or grace) may be with him in the exercise of his ministry—should be with the special charism he has received so that he may worthily perform his duty.'[6] These phrases are precious reminders that the liturgical community is not just any kind of assembly and that the dialogue that takes place within it during celebration is a dialogue with God through the presence of his Spirit.

The General Instruction has no doubt about the nature of the worshipping community and sees in this first greeting a sign of God's presence with his people, who through it become a sign, a 'sacrament' of the mystery of the church. It thus echoes the Constitution's teaching that the celebration of the eucharist 'is the outstanding means whereby the faithful may . . . manifest to others the mystery of Christ and the real nature of the true church' (CL 2 and cf CL 41, 42).

The brief address that follows, apart from its psychological appropriateness, can also be seen as a communication of the Spirit to the community. The celebrant will select a phrase from the liturgy of the day to concentrate people's thoughts and to help them to realize that the Spirit is present with them. He may and should announce as briefly as possible the liturgical theme of the day or feast and will give such information as may be neces-

---

[6] Paulinus Milner, OP, 'Et cum spiritu tuo', in *Studies in Pastoral Liturgy*, ed. Placid Murray, OSB (Dublin, 1967), pp. 202–10.

sary about the penitential act and the eucharistic prayer that are to be used. It is regrettable that some celebrants are neglecting this opportunity to make contact with the people and some never seem to have used it at all. No doubt it is equally regrettable to overlay the liturgical action with floods of verbosity. Preparation of the texts and an effort towards economy of words will prevent that unhappy situation.

For centuries the Roman Mass had no penitential formula at all and then when it first acquired one (the *Agnus Dei* introduced by Pope Sergius I c. 700) it was rather the accompaniment to an action, the breaking of the bread which in the papal rite was a prolonged affair. It was even later that a penitential act was introduced into the Mass (Ps. 42 with the *confiteor*—missal of 1570), and even this was overlaid at High Mass by the singing of the introit. So far as the people were concerned there was no penitential act on such occasions.[7] It is not surprising, then, that in the discussions of liturgical experts that went on for nearly twenty years before the Council[8] various solutions were debated. It was agreed that the existing rite was unsatisfactory: the psalm made it more like a duplicated entrance rite and the length and doubling of the *confiteor* made it unduly cumbersome. Its position in the rite, especially at High Mass, was also agreed to be unsatisfactory. But it was not so easy to see what should be done. One suggestion was that it should be put later in the Mass, either before the offertory, where in liturgies other than the Roman the kiss of peace takes place, or before the communion. Another, that has won the day, is that its form should be simplified and that it should be made part of the entrance rite of the Mass. It is a comprehensible solution: we need to be open to God both to hear his word and to receive his body and blood in holy communion. We have offended God in many ways and as we approach him once more we ask his forgiveness. The relationship is primarily between God and the community. If we interpret the sign of peace now made before communion in the light of Matthew 5:23, 24, here reconciliation between the members of the community is the lesson that is given.

It does mean, however, that the entrance rite is somewhat overloaded, and the whole situation is complicated by the retention of the *Kyries* in this place. This does ensure that the musical settings current for many centuries can still be sung where choirs are capable of doing so and on fitting occasions, though it does prolong the entrance rite unduly. It is indeed difficult to justify the presence of the *Kyries* in this place when they are taken as a separate piece. They are, of course, the remains of a whole litany which, as is well known, was shortened by Gregory the Great, at

---

[7] In practice, of course, they read the *Confiteor* out of their books and those who were 'liturgical' tried to lend an ear to the text of the introit. Psalm 42 with a confession was used in the later Middle Ages but the former was usually said either in the sacristy or on the way to the altar.

[8] E.g. at Lugano (1953), Assisi (1956).

least for some occasions. However, they have been integrated into the third penitential act and have thus become part of a litany of repentance. This new arrangement offers interesting possibilities of musical development and pulls together this part of the Mass. The General Instruction indeed envisages a further development here and speaks of 'tropes' being inserted between the *Kyries* (GI 30), but it is a procedure which will have to be used with great discretion.

There is little need to say anything about the *Gloria in excelsis* here. It is not primitive to the Mass, it is true, but it is the means by which on great feast days the community, now 'gathered by the Holy Spirit', can express its joy, praise and adoration 'to God the Father and to the Lamb' as well as making supplication to him, as indeed the General Instruction says (GI 31).

The final element of the entrance rite and one that brings it to a climax is the collect, which is pre-eminently the prayer of the gathered community now 'aware that it stands in the presence of God' (GI 32). It is the prayer of the community but led by its president, who summons them to 'rehearse silently' their petitions which are then summed up by the president in the prayer that gathers or 'collects' the desires, aspirations and needs of the community and presents them to the Father through the Son in the Holy Spirit. The silence between 'Let us pray' and the collect itself is thus given its meaning and in practice it is important to give the people time to ponder on their petitions.

Through all the various and sometimes apparently disparate elements of the entrance rite, its purpose is clear. The people come and then by God's word they are gathered into a community in which the Holy Spirit is present. This is the truth about the Christian assembly and the various texts are there to enable its members to realize that they are in fact gathered by the Holy Spirit and made one.

The ministry of the word

The restoration of an adequate ministry of the word to the Mass-liturgy is one of the most satisfactory parts of the liturgical reform. Apart from a few of the older and greater feasts and seasons, the lectionary of the old missal was so jejune that it is a wonder that we were able to put up with it for so long. What is more, the way the Mass had come to be celebrated over the centuries and the use of the Latin, which ever-decreasing numbers of people understood, resulted in a devaluation of the importance of the word in the eucharist that led to a considerable distortion of the whole rite. From the beginning the eucharist has been celebrated in the context of the proclamation of the word and was always in antiquity regarded as an integral part of it.[9]

---

[9] See Oscar Cullman, *Early Christian Worship* (London, 1953), pp. 26–31. The view, still widely held, that the ministry of the word was added to the eucharist in

We shall see why this was so, but immediately it can be said that because it was neglected, the people came to think of the Mass as a holy action which they watched, as an object of adoration and as a means for 'getting' holy communion. Their piety did something to substitute for the approach that it is necessary to make when we worship God, but apart from that, the word, unintelligible and often inaudible, failed to touch their hearts. This is one of the reasons why the present pattern of the ministry of the word gives some people a good deal of trouble, and it may be admitted that the church has restored it just at a time when people are apparently becoming less capable of listening than at any time in the history of mankind. If defence of the new ministry of the word is necessary, it can be said that even the old Mass, when turned into the vernacular, provided a fair slice of reading material: epistle, gradual (sequence—and that interminable one on *Corpus Christi*), Alleluia and verse. What is more, these texts were often enough not related to each other in any coherent pattern. If imbalance between word and eucharist is the charge, the old Latin High Mass was a bad offender when it was sung *in full*—and how rare that was! A gradual and Alleluia with verse could take seven minutes, *Glorias* and creeds fifteen or more minutes when sung to elaborate settings. But, it is suggested, no one complained.[10]

The root of the objection to the new ministry of the word is to be found in the prevalent practice of people before the liturgical reform. Ordinarily they went to a low Mass, the murmuring of the Latin at the altar did not disturb them and they 'got on' with their own prayers or, as often as not, they just gazed around. Now that they are required to listen, they feel disconcerted.[11] In fact, there has been no change in the balance of the Mass. Simply, the ministry of the word has been made more coherent and more intelligible.

---

some dark period between, say, 80 AD and 150 AD (Justin's *Apology*) seems to rest on a confusion between a word-service, probably very free and informal, and the synagogue service, something analogous, that may well have influenced the Christian service of the word as we see it when it emerges into history. After all, Christ instituted the eucharist in a context of dialogue and conversation, the 'prayer of blessing or thanksgiving' was almost certainly long and was a proclamation of the saving deeds of God, and if even only some of the discourses of St John (13–17) were uttered at the Last Supper, as is generally supposed, this would indicate that the eucharist was celebrated in a context of the word. In any case, there is Acts 20:7–12 recording that St Paul did celebrate it in the context of a service of the word.

[10] In fact, ordinary people just contracted out and in certain continental places where you could witness these performances, the local people just drifted in for twenty minutes or so and then drifted out.

[11] There is another objection that goes deeper. The modern Mass strongly suggests that the congregation should be involved, they are constantly being invited to commitment and those who have regarded the Mass as the ritual of a private club are naturally very upset.

The first thing to be said about the new ministry of the word is that it provides a pattern for the absorption of God's word so that its message can become part of ourselves. The reading is proclaimed, facing the people, and they are enabled to respond to it by a psalm that continues the theme of the reading, turning it into prayer. A second reading, often giving moral instruction relevant to the Christian life, follows, and then comes the climax in the salutation to the coming of Christ in the word of the gospel, and the proclamation of the gospel. The purpose of the homily that follows is to expound the meaning of the texts and relate them to the life-situation of the gathered community. To the whole of the ministry of the word they make their assent of faith in the creed, and in the General Intercessions turn their reflections on the word into prayer for the church and the world. Reading, psalm, acclamation and response are the oldest elements of Christian (and, indeed, pre-Christian) prayer. If to these is added, as the revised Order for Holy Week suggests, silent meditation after the readings or one or two of them, you have the combination of public and private prayer and the charge that the new Mass is a stream of verbiage is removed.

What then is the deeper purpose of the ministry of the word?[12] A full discussion would take us very far and it will be best to give the answer in the terms of the Constitution (CL 7, 33) and of the General Instruction (GI 33): 'in the liturgy God speaks to his people' and 'when the holy scriptures are read in church' Christ 'is present in his word'. First, then, through the readings (and, indeed, the other texts of the liturgy but pre-eminently in the scripture readings), God speaks to the assembled people. He is conveying his word just as really and, if we are willing to have it so, just as effectively as he did when he spoke through the prophets or when his own Son spoke to men. The words are the means, the envelope, the sign-sacrament of the saving truth that is to be found in God's word in itself. It comes in many forms, narratives, poetry, prophecy and the aphorisms of wisdom literature, and these different forms need to be understood if the essential meaning is to be discerned, for it is this that is of final importance.

The reading of the scriptures, then, at Mass is not just a form of giving information *about* God and his dealings with man, nor is it a kind of class-room instruction about 'the truths of faith'—for that purpose it would be supremely inefficient. What we need to realize before all else is that the reading of the scripture in the Mass is an *event*, it is a happening, it is the intervention of God in the here and now, in the affairs and minds of this gathered community. In Hebrew *dabar* means *both* word and event and it

---

[12] Cf Hubert J. Richards, 'God's Word in the Liturgy', in *The Mass and the People of God*, ed. J. D. Crichton (London, 1966). Paulinus Milner, OP, 'The Purpose and Structure of the Liturgy of the Word', in *The Ministry of the Word*, ed. P. Milner (London, 1967).

is sometimes a little difficult to know which is meant. The bible is *both* a record of events and words, words that were indeed indispensable to the interpretation of the events, but all told it was the events that mattered. For salvation history as a whole is action, the breaking through of God into this worldly order so that he can redeem it. But salvation history continues. It is not finished and will not be finished until the end of time. We are living in the last age over which Christ is Lord and in which the Holy Spirit is present. God still intervenes in the world, the history of salvation is continued in the church and by the church and it is primarily in the liturgy, and nowhere more effectively than in the Mass, that it is continued.

The matter can be put in what perhaps are more conventional terms. Through the readings and other texts (especially the responsorial psalm) God communicates his grace. He offers himself to us once again. By the readings and the homily the people's minds are opened so that they may accept the word in faith. Through the whole ministry of the word their hearts should be stirred by love and it is perhaps the function of the homily principally to do this and, further, to draw people on to commitment. Within the context of the Mass this is made in the creed in which the people renew their faith in God, Father, Son and Holy Spirit. The event, the 'happening' then can be seen as the communication of grace which enlivens the faith and love of the hearers and stimulates them to action.

This is not a theology invented to fit the liturgy. It has always been presupposed, as we can see from the ceremonial that has surrounded the proclamation of the word in all liturgies. The book of the Word has been (and is) carried in procession, surrounded by lights, saluted by incensations, reverenced in various fashions and all this would be sheer idolatry if it were not to be understood as a complexus of signs by which the Christian community bear witness to their belief in the presence of God in his word. For their part, the people hail Christ present in the gospel by Alleluia and acclamation, by the response they make as its title is proclaimed: 'Glory to you, Lord', and as it comes to its conclusion: 'Praise to you, Lord Jesus Christ'.

But as well as making God present to the people, the proclamation of the scriptures also unfolds to them 'the mystery of redemption and salvation' (GI 33). God has redeemed us through Christ, foreshadowing that redemption throughout the Old Testament and, as we can see now, bringing it ever nearer until it was finally achieved in Jesus Christ. The long and tortuous history of Israel is a record of the many ways in which God approached his people with love, offering them salvation. That history, however brutal and sordid at times, is also a gradual unfolding of God's nature, a *revelation* of what he was like, and if that revelation was always partial, it was in Jesus Christ that its meaning was made clear. It is in the light of Christ's revelation in the New Testament that we are able to understand the Old. The two march together and this is the fundamental reason why an Old Testament reading has been restored to the liturgy of the Mass.[13] It is through this use of the Old Testament, in conjunction with the gospel reading (and the two are usually related in the Lectionary) that the mystery of salvation will be unfolded to the people.

A third purpose given by the General Instruction (33) for the ministry of the word is the 'spiritual instruction' of the people. The Apostolic Constitution at the beginning of *Missale Romanum* refers to this (see p. 48 above) and we may ask how it will do it. The pope speaks of a better knowledge of holy scripture as a means of deepening the spiritual life, and if people are aware that in the scriptures they are in contact with God's word, that it is still communicating to them his grace and love, it will surely stimulate them to spiritual effort. The spiritual life is not *just* meditation; at its deepest it is action, the action of God in the depths of our being and a response to him from those same depths. It is on this that all else is built. God's word is then the *essential* nourishment; the early church lived by it, and as the years go by, and as people become ever more familiar with the scriptures, they will come to an ever deeper understanding of God and his saving actions and gradually enter into a closer union with him.[14]

The homily

For a very long time the homily was regarded as an intruder in the Mass. Priests used to remove the maniple before preaching and some even the chasuble as if to say 'This has got nothing to do with what has gone before or is coming afterwards'. Nor, for the most part, had it. It was customary to preach at the High Mass on Sundays but low Masses were celebrated without a sermon, and the odd thing was that there were those who thought that the 'Solemn High Mass' (as some called it) with deacon and subdeacon positively excluded it. Nor was the discourse necessarily related to the texts of the day. It was an oratorical exercise that happened to take place during the Mass. Even when it was agreed that the sermon should at least be concerned with the Mass of the day, there was a curious notion that the Council of Trent had said that only the gospel was to be expounded. Hence the tired homilies that were so often repeated year after year. In fact, the Council of Trent said that all the texts of the Mass (meaning principally the 'Proper') were to be the subject of the homily.

---

[13] The only exception is the Easter season, for then the church is celebrating its birth from the crucified and risen Christ. Hence the readings are from Acts and Revelation (Apocalypse) which have been used at this time since the fourth century (cf certain sermons of St Augustine).

[14] It cannot be said with absolute certainty that the nourishment of the spiritual life is the purpose of the *second* reading, usually from St Paul, but more often than not it serves this purpose. For the purpose of preaching it often has to be neglected, but no doubt as years go by and as the main themes of salvation-history become more familiar we shall be able to pay greater attention to it.

The Second Vatican Council put an end to this unhappy state of affairs and the Constitution on the Liturgy has firmly integrated the homily into the liturgical action and insisted on its necessity (CL 35 (2) and CL 52). At the same time it has indicated in a general way its nature and function.

a) It is part of the liturgical service, that is, in itself it is a liturgical action. Normally the Mass is incomplete without it.

b) Its content should be drawn mainly from scriptural and liturgical sources. It is not a literary essay about Christian doctrine or morals, nor is it a discourse about general questions of the day.

c) Its literary form is that of a *proclamation* of the deeds of God recorded in the history of salvation or of the mystery of Christ made present and active within the Christian, especially in the celebration of the liturgy.

Two things principally go to make up the liturgical homily: [15] its content and its form, namely proclamation.

1. The Constitution, not to mention other documents, leaves us in no doubt about the *content* of the homily: it is primarily the scripture readings of the day, though seen in the context of the whole history of salvation. It is here that we learn of God's saving deeds and it is this that is 'actualized' in liturgical celebration: 'The liturgy is in fact nothing other than a way by which Christ, in the intermediate time that runs from pentecost to the parousia, that is, in this eschatological time already in act, communicates the fullness of his divine life to individuals, reproduces his mystery in them and draws them into it.'[16]

This implies that the history of salvation is understood—it is the record of God's saving acts in Christ that are continued in the church—and that the scripture readings for the day are studied in this context.[17] The readings, again, are part of a liturgical context, feast, season or special occasion, and have a particular reference to it. These two factors, then, the history of salvation and the liturgical context condition the nature of the liturgical homily and so the use the preacher must make of the texts. A scripture expert's exegesis of them, apart from being unduly lengthy, is inappropriate, for it will almost certainly ignore the liturgical context. There must be a real penetration of the reasons why these particular readings are set for this day or occasion and the clue to this can be found through an attentive reading of the Bible and, where Old Testament passages are con-

---

[15] The word 'homily' apparently means 'familiar discourse' and is suggestive of a certain approach to preaching at the liturgy, but it does not seem to offer grounds for a distinction between 'sermon' and 'homily'. St Leo's discourses on the feasts of the year are called *sermones*, at least in the printed editions, and it is difficult to distinguish in St Augustine between *sermones* and *homiliae*.

[16] See C. Vagaggini, *Il Senso Theologico della Liturgia* (Rome, 1958), pp. 27, 33, 85–6, 369, etc.

[17] For the history of salvation see the CL 5, 6, 7, 8 and a commentary in J. D. Crichton, *The Church's Worship* (London, 1964), pp. 27–41.

cerned, some understanding of scriptural typology.[18] A further clue will be found in an examination of the non-scriptural texts of the liturgy, of which the readings form a part, even if the most important part. It goes without saying that mere moralizings occasioned by the readings are totally inadequate to the situation.[19]

2.   It is, however, *proclamation* that is decisive of the literary form of the homily, and the Constitution, as we have seen, says quite firmly that it is such. What, then, is it?[20]

The homily is proclamation first because it continues the proclamation of the scripture readings which themselves continue the *kerygma* of the New Testament. The gospels were *kerygma* or proclamation before they were written books, and it is widely agreed by theologians of the Catholic and Reformed traditions that it is in proclamation that the scriptures become the living word of God.[21] The models of *kerygma* are, as is well known, to be found in the New Testament, especially in Acts. Thus, in the first Christian sermon, Peter proclaims Christ, announces who he was, what he did and what he meant. He links this proclamation with the event that has just happened, and with a skilful use of the Old Testament[22] seeks to interpret the whole complexus of events in terms that his audience could be expected to understand. In a word, he proclaims the mystery of Christ who was sent by God and lived, died and rose again so that the sons of Israel might receive the Spirit whom Peter and his companions had already received. There was, too, the result: repentance, baptism and the coming of the Spirit (Acts 2:22–41).

The Constitution comes very close to this in its statement that the homily is 'the proclamation of God's wonderful works in the history of salvation, that is, the Mystery of Christ' (CL 35 (2)).[23] The primary function, then, of the homily is to isolate the core of the Christian mystery set forth in the readings and clearly and succinctly to announce it to the people. But this will usually require elucidation and so we get exposition, what is called in

---

[18] See, for instance, J. Danielou, *The Bible and the Liturgy* (London, 1956) and modern introductions to the Bible.

[19] At least one book of commentaries on the readings has appeared that falls into this category. On the other hand, the *Commentary on the Sunday Lectionary* (so far four volumes) by Peter Coughlan and Peter Purdue, one a liturgical expert and the other a scripture expert, has entirely the right approach and, though short, provides the right orientation for the preacher. The combination of the *two* expertises should be noted.

[20] See J. D. Crichton, 'The Nature of the Liturgical Homily', in *The Ministry of the Word*, ed. Paulinus Milner (London, 1967), pp. 27–44; the same: 'The Function of the Homily at Mass', in *Liturgy*, April, 1967, pp. 25–33.

[21] Oscar Cullman, 'Scripture and Tradition', in *Divided Christianity* (London, 1961), pp. 7–33.

[22] At least six quotations—which, of course, may have been the work of St Luke.

[23] 'History of salvation' and 'mystery of Christ' are separated by *seu* in the Latin, the weakest of distinguishing words, and is best translated 'that is'.

the New Testament *catechesis* or *didache*. This will take as its point of departure the scriptural readings and its style will be conditioned by the language of the Bible rather than that of theological manuals. But both the proclamation and the exposition will have as their aim the deepening of the Christian life of the people and will thus have a practical issue. In the first instance, it will seek to lead them into the celebration of the eucharist —and this is called by the rather formidable word 'mystagogy', an initiation into the mystery—and beyond the liturgical celebration into the living of the Christian life in the world.

These four elements, it is agreed, go to make up the liturgical homily,[24] though it by no means follows that they must follow one after another in the order suggested above. It may indeed be that in a given homily one or two of these elements will play a much smaller part than others. Often on the greater feasts any extended exposition is unnecessary. It may be that any explicit leading of the people into the eucharistic celebration is unnecessary. Proclamation can often be combined with exposition and to the hearers will be indistinguishable from each other. These are all matters of literary ability and pastoral sense that the preacher has to learn, not least from contact with people and knowing how their minds work. But this is what the church means by the liturgical homily and it is this style of preaching and this alone that is in tune with liturgical celebration.[25]

The creed and the General Intercessions

The creed, as we have said, is the principal assent of the people to the word of God proclaimed in the scriptures and in the homily. It brings to an end a process that has gone on since the beginning of the ministry of the word: God has been speaking, the people have been responding in various ways and now they sum up their response by a commitment of faith to God, Father, Son and Holy Spirit. As faith is more than an assent to a number of doctrines, so the creed is more than an audible recitation of those things that a Christian must believe. The General Instruction rightly calls it 'the profession of faith' (GI 43) and a profession of faith is an adherence to Christ as a living person as well as to all he taught and requires of us. Understandably, the Instruction insists that normally (*de more*) it is to be recited by all, either together or responsorially. Musical settings that take

---

[24] See J. Gelineau, 'L'homélie, forme plenière de la prédication', in *La Maison-Dieu*, 82, 1965, and J. D. Crichton, 'The Nature of the Liturgical Homily', *art. cit.*, pp. 33–42.

[25] The above is not to be regarded as a recipe for constructing homilies. The four elements should normally condition their shaping but, of course, the preacher is left complete liberty to shape his discourse as he thinks best for the circumstances in which he is working. It should not be thought that the liturgical homily is a piece of disincarnated biblico-liturgical theology without connection with the life-situation of the people. It must speak to them as they are and where they are.

it away from the people are not suitable to its purpose and, anyway, are far
too long for the likes of people nowadays.

Of the General Intercessions[26] three things are to be said:

1.   It is part of the ministry of the word (GI 33). The people, opened
up to the word of God and nourished by it, are now in a position to think
of the needs of the church and the world and to pray for them. It is an
interesting point of view, valid for prayer at any time. We do not rush into
the presence of God to demand this and that. We listen to his word and try
to discern his will. Then, humbly, we may address him. Practically, the
Instruction thus indicates that the theme of the readings and the homily
should be reflected in the intercessions. This, too, is a fundamental pattern
of Christian prayer. We speak and we turn our speaking into prayer. The
reflexion of the word of the day in the prayer of the day is the condition of
these intercessions remaining fresh, unstereotyped and in touch with the
life of the people.

2.   In these prayers the people exercise 'their priestly function' by praying for all mankind (GI 45). We are reminded of I Timothy 2:1, 2, 8,
where the writer says that prayers, petitions, intercessions and thanksgiving
should be offered for everyone and especially for kings, and others in
authority, and of his conclusion 'I want all men to lift up their hands [the
ancient gesture of supplication] reverently in prayer. . . .' These are the
prayers *of the people*, under the presidency of the priest who introduces
and concludes them, providing, incidentally, a classical pattern of liturgical
celebration. But since they are the prayers of the people they should have
some part in them.[27] This may be done in various ways, but the people
should at least be encouraged to send in their petitions. Normally, too, they
will be announced by a lay-person with, of course, the people responding.
This is a second condition of these intercessions remaining alive.

3.·   The form. A broad pattern of subjects is laid down (GI 45):
prayers are to be made for the church, for earthly rulers, for those in any
kind of need and for the local community. Normally the petitions will
reflect these intentions but there is no need to be over-rigid about them.
Circumstances alter cases and the emphasis can be now here and now there.
What the church requires is that the intercessions should be concerned with
the wider community and not concentrated on the particular concerns of
the local community. These, too, play their part, and in practice the intelligent discernment of such local needs again ensures that the prayer is going

---

[26] This is the translation ICEL have opted for and it is a good one. A possible
alternative is 'Prayer for the whole world' (*oratio universalis*) which may be thought
to be a little cumbersome. In England the title is 'Bidding Prayers', which seems
to be deliberately archaic.

[27] The revised Holy Week Order in the *Missale Romanum*, 1970, uses these
words of the newly-baptized who, it is envisaged, are taking full part in the
eucharist for the first time.

to be alive. By experience one finds that the people are more alive to current needs, whether of the world or of the local community, than the clergy, and this is another reason why they should have a notable part in the intercessions. In detail, the prayer is made up of four parts, an introduction and a conclusion (both by the celebrant), the *invitation* to prayer (by a lay-person) and the response of the people. Of these a word needs to be said about the third.

In the booklet issued by the then *Consilium*[28] for guidance on these intercessions, the basic forms of these invitations to prayer are laid down and these make it very clear that they are invitations and not prayers. If they are prayers the lay-person is in fact usurping the function of the celebrant whose business it is to pray in the name of the community.[29] The *Consilium* was in no doubt about this matter. What we have called 'invitations' are called in the booklet *propositiones intentionum*: intentions to be prayed for are proposed by the reader. They are not prayers themselves. The booklet lays down three possible forms: (Let us pray) *for* such and such *that* . . .; or simply (Let us pray) *that* such and such a favour may be granted; more simply still (Let us pray) *for* so and so. Different kinds of petition suggest the different uses of one of these three forms. They offer no difficulty and are beyond question the right ones to use. Fortunately a considerable degree of liberty is left open to the local clergy who within the limits laid down by the *Consilium* may compose their own prayers.[30]

It should be noted, too, that while the responses of the people on any given occasion should be the same (naturally to avoid confusion), they may be varied from one service to another and there is much to be said for doing so. The repetition of even short prayers, such as these, without variation soon becomes boring.[31]

The liturgy of the eucharist

The eucharistic liturgy should not be regarded as in some way cut off from the ministry of the word. As we have seen, word and eucharist have

---

[28] *De Oratione Communi seu Fidelium* (Vatican, 1965).

[29] It is unfortunate that this is the form adopted in such printed collections of intercessions as have been issued in this country. They have given people a quite wrong notion of the nature of this form of praying and, in fact, have led to an almost intolerable verbosity.

[30] The *Missale Romanum* (1970), pp. 893, provides some specimens of these general intercessions and have naturally used the forms given above though they have opted for the use of the second and third forms rather than for the first. Since the *Missale Romanum* is an official book, the obligation to follow it seems clear.

[31] Again, the English bishops have hitherto been very rigid about this matter. Officially the response is still 'Lord hear us (reader), Lord graciously hear us' (people). The second is so nasty a noise that one wonders how anyone can go on tolerating it. It may be noted here that on special occasions (marriages, funerals) the pattern suggested above (church, world, etc.) need not be rigidly adhered to (GI 46).

gone together since the beginning and one of the purposes of the proclamation of the word is to lead people into the fitting celebration of the eucharist.
Even the General Intercessions may legitimately be regarded as an anticipation of, and, indeed, a sharing in, the Great Intercession that from one
point of view the Mass is.[32]

Yet, of course, the eucharistic liturgy has an identity all its own and the
General Instruction (48) lays out its principal phases: the preparation of
the gifts, the eucharistic prayer and the fraction and communion.

1.   The preparation of the gifts

As is well known, the offertory rite of the Roman Mass of the 1570
missal was elaborate and yet at the same time inadequate for its purpose.
Fundamentally, it was a *priestly* rite. The celebrant said and did almost
everything and the prayers he was required to say, if adverted to by the
people, were somewhat misleading. They spoke of the bread and wine as
a 'sacrifice' which was 'offered', giving the impression that there was an
offering here somehow independent of the act of offering that occurs in the
eucharistic prayer. In many places the offertory was known as the 'Little
Canon'. In the new rite the emphasis is wholly different.

First, the rite has been renamed. It is a presentation and a preparation.
The offerings (bread, wine, money and possibly other things) are merely
brought to the altar (*afferuntur*) and the Order recommends that this should
be done by the people. It goes on to say that although the link between the
bread and wine presented by the people in former times and the elements
that are now placed on the altar has been broken, the gesture none the less
retains a spiritual significance (GI 49). So the emphasis is on preparation
rather than on offering. The gifts are considered to be set apart so that they
may be used in the *eucharistic* offering. They have no intrinsic value and
only acquire value when they become part of the eucharistic offering. They
are signs of the people's desire to give themselves in eucharistic worship,
and since self and life and work are really one, they are signs, too, of the
surrendering to God of what man has. This is the sense of the prayers of
offering now said over the bread and wine. These prayers, which are
modelled on Jewish forms of blessing prayers, state the all-important truth
that all we have comes from God's bounty. Of ourselves we have nothing.

---

[32] This would seem to be the sense of the somewhat tortuous statement that
Pope Innocent I (died 417) made in his famous letter to the Bishop of Gubbio
which is so difficult to interpret. He wanted the intercessions to take place in *ipsis
mysteriis*, during the eucharistic prayer, and said this was the Roman (indeed
apostolic) custom. On the other hand, the question whether the General Intercessions belong to the ministry of the word or to the ministry of the eucharist is a
little difficult to determine historically. In the fourth century (*Apostolic Constitutions*, viii, 8), there were prayers (and a blessing) for the catechumens who were
then dismissed. The rest were apparently regarded as the 'prayers of the faithful',
as they are still so called in modern Roman documents.

Yet the desire of self-giving is so strong and psychologically so necessary to us that we feel we must make the gesture. Bread and wine are offered in view of the eucharist ('that it may become the bread of life . . .') so that the offering is at once a plea for the coming of Christ to the community in the eucharistic action and a thanksgiving for all that we have and are, but a thanksgiving that will only acquire any value when it is enfolded in the self-offering of Christ.[33]

If the rite is called 'the preparation of the gifts', its description might be extended, 'that are brought to the altar by the people', for though the Order makes no obligation of it, it urges that they should be brought to the altar by the people. How this is to be done and, in some churches, whether it can be done at all, are practical matters to be decided by the local clergy. The important thing is to see the rite as yet another sign of community. The action is to be a *procession* accompanied by a chant. It is here that the people, usually through a representative group, are able to express the gesture of offering we have spoken of and, as the Instruction observes, to unite with the bread and wine their money or even other gifts in kind that are to be given to those in need (GI 49). This is an important aspect of the whole Mass and of the presentation of the gifts in particular. The Christian community exists to worship God but also to serve the world, and a community that is shut in on itself is not making the sign of the church that the Constitution says it should. The whole validity of a money offertory at this point has been questioned,[34] but if at least part of the offerings, of whatever kind, are given away, the practice is not only fully justifiable but continues the practice of the church in its first days.

What in any case needs to be avoided is any suggestion that we have anything to give to God, and the consequence must be that the liturgical arrangement of the offertory must be sober and never allowed to get out of hand. In the recent past there has been a tendency to over-rate it, perhaps because the offering, the real offering, that takes place during the eucharistic prayer was obscured by a silent canon which left the people no room for expression.

The eucharistic prayer

The most interesting point the Order makes about the eucharistic prayer is that 'it is the centre and climax of the whole celebration' (GI 54). It is to be noted that it does not say this of the consecration which, *theologically*

---

[33] J. C. Buckley puts this point very well: 'All is gift, free and unmerited, on the part of God. All we can do is to thank him and our offering can only be thanksgiving.' See 'Money and the Offertory', in *The Mass and the People of God*, ed. J. D. Crichton (London, 1966), p. 97. This thanksgiving element is clearly expressed in the people's response, 'Blessed be God for ever' for understood, and in Jewish blessings expressed, is the phrase 'for all his wonderful works'.

[34] See J. Duncan Cloud, 'The Theology of the Offertory Collection', in *op. cit.* ed. J. D. Crichton, pp. 108–21.

speaking, may be regarded as the climax of the eucharist (though one has doubts: the theology of the eucharist that has been based on what can be called the 'consecration mentality' has been far from happy). In so doing the Order returns to the oldest tradition of eucharistic celebration. For centuries, roughly up to the eleventh, Christians were not concerned about 'the moment of consecration', and until the addition of the elevation of the host at the end of the twelfth century, they were largely unaware when it occurred. Until this time, then, the church thought of the whole eucharistic prayer as the *action* which was to achieve the purpose for which it was instituted. We are reminded of this by the phrase in the missal of certain insertions into the Roman canon, *infra actionem*, which is found in the Gelasian Sacramentary, in all medieval missals, in that of 1570 and retained in the latest edition.[35] The whole eucharistic prayer was regarded as effecting the eucharist and this meant that the early church had a much wider and, as one may think, a deeper understanding of it. They saw the prayer as not just bringing about the presence of Christ but as making the great thanksgiving-memorial that made the great redeeming actions of Christ present and enabling the community to enter into them. They did not at all sharply distinguish 'real presence', 'sacrifice' and 'communion' (as was common in the later Middle Ages); they saw the eucharistic prayer as effecting the whole *opus redemptionis*.[36] The prayer, and the action, ran from thanksgiving through consecration to memorial, offering, intercession and communion. All this and much more is the content of the action that is set in motion by the eucharistic prayer.

We have, then, to do with action and the eucharistic prayer unfolds the various phases of that action which constitutes the essence of the eucharistic celebration. The Order (GI 55) gives a liturgical analysis of the eucharistic prayer which is really a description of the principal phases of the action. They are as follows: Thanksgiving, acclamation, *epiclesis* (or invocation), the words of institution, *anamnesis* (or memorial), offering, intercessions and doxology. To these could be added proclamation. Merely to list the various parts of the eucharistic prayer is to reveal how much richer it is than has been commonly supposed for many centuries.

Proclamation

The proclamation of God's word does not cease with the reading of the scriptures and the homily. The church has taken into herself God's message

---

[35] For the Gelasian Sacramentary see *Liber Sacramentorum Romanae Aeclesiae Ordinis Anni Circuli*, ed. L. Mohlberg (Rome, 1960).

[36] Prayer over the Offerings for Maundy Thursday, Evening Mass, and formerly 9th Sunday after Pentecost. It is found in the Gelasian Sacramentary (nos. 170, 1196) belonging to the seventh century and therefore expressing the ancient theology of Rome. The Constitution on the Liturgy (2) thought good to use it as a summary definition of the liturgy and in particular of the eucharist.

and now, almost exclusively in her own words, proclaims the meaning of the message. In the Roman tradition this is done in the first place by the 'preface' and the most plausible interpretation of that word (Lat. *prae-fatio*, a speaking out before God and his people) is that it means 'proclamation'.[37] In the Eastern tradition much of the first part of the anaphora is given over to a proclamation of the saving works of God, resuming the main phases of the history of salvation. This proclamation, with which is combined the invocation of the divine names, continues the action of the ministry of the word and shows that the eucharistic celebration itself is part of the history of salvation carrying it forward until the *parousia* which is announced in the acclamation after the consecration.

But it is also the proclamation of the church's *faith*.

'The eucharistic prayer is the principal proclamation made by the church of what the eucharist is. It has an absolutely crucial teaching function, for it is here in the first place that we must look for the faith of the Church in the eucharist. It is to this prayer we must go if we would know what the church wishes to affirm about the eucharist. . . . We discover too what the church is saying about herself, for as we know from the Constitution on the Liturgy, the eucharist is the principal expression of the church's life and activity and the manifestation of its true nature. The church is not primarily an institution or a society that has parallels with earthly societies. It is above all a communion, a *koinonia*, which is lifted up to God through the eucharist, the dynamic centre of the church's unity, in praise and thanksgiving to the Father. It is in the eucharist that the community, the *Qehal Jahve*, is actualised and is able to lay hold of the saving work of Jesus Christ and so make itself, if only slowly and with pain, what he would have it be. The church, it has been said often enough, makes (celebrates) the eucharist; it is even truer that it is the eucharist that makes the church.'[38]

All this and indeed much more the church is saying about the eucharist and herself, though not everything can be said in one eucharistic prayer. Hence the need for several.

Thanksgiving

Thanksgiving, eucharist, is the dominant note of the prayer and takes us right back to its institution when Christ brought the sacrament into being in the course of the 'thanksgiving' that he pronounced at the Last Supper: Mark 14:22, 23 (*eulogēsas* over the bread and *eucharistēsas* over the cup);

---

[37] Cf Jungmann, *Missarum Sollemnia*, French trans., t. III, p. 12 (Paris, 1954).

[38] See J. D. Crichton, 'The New Eucharistic Prayers', in *Liturgy*, October, 1968, p. 90.

Luke 22:19, 20 (*eucharistēsas* over the bread); Matthew 26:26, 27 (*eulogēsas* and *eucharistēsas* as in Mark).[39]

The origins of 'thanksgiving' are to be found in the prayers of blessing that Christ pronounced at the Last Supper. These were two: a very brief blessing of the bread at the beginning of the meal and the longer one for the blessing of the cup. Even before the end of New Testament times, it would seem, the former had been swallowed up by the latter and the consecration of both bread and wine took place during the one prayer called *eucharistia*. But the second table-blessing was no ordinary one. The Last Supper was a Passover celebration (whether exactly a passover meal is another question) and the eucharistic prayer over the cup contained special elements appropriate to the occasion: God's passing-by, the *midrash*, that is the account of the Exodus given to the guests by the head of the family, the eschatological passage, the expectation of Elijah and the verses speaking of the pouring out of wrath over the nations who know not God.[40] If we take this view, says Ligier,

'it is easy to reach a conclusion by situating the principal stages of the Last Supper within the framework of the Passover meal or *seder*. The verses of Luke 22 (15–18), the words of the Master and the first cup corresponded to the "blessing of redemption" which was already followed by a cup. In accordance with the Passover tradition, in it Jesus expressed his joy in taking part in this Passover; but instead of then, according to custom, showing his desire to take part in the approaching festivities he stated that for him this was the last Passover before the coming of the Kingdom. Then came the rite of the bread, coinciding with the blessing of the unleavened bread,[41] since it occurs directly afterwards and marks the beginning of the festal meal. Lastly, the consecration of the chalice, postponed to the end of the meal according to the traditions of Paul and Luke, occurred at the time when the father of the family offered the long prayer of thanksgiving. It was only after saying it that Jesus offered the cup and said the sacramental words in the presence of his apostles, at the moment when they were getting ready to recall the

---

[39] There seems to be little difference in meaning between the two words. *Eulogein* is closer to 'blessing' (Lat. *benedicere*), the 'saying of good things' about God which was very much the Jewish way of 'giving thanks'. However, the use of the two words in Mt and Mk would seem to indicate the existence of the separate and differing 'blessing' prayers said over the bread and the cup at the Last Supper. Luke, and more particularly Paul (I Corinthians 11:24), have put both under the one term 'thanksgiving' (so Ligier, 'From the Last Supper to the Eucharist', in *The New Liturgy*, ed. L. Sheppard (London, 1970), p. 118.

[40] Ligier, *op. cit.*, p. 123.

[41] With the formula 'Blessed be you, Lord, our God, king of the world, you have made us holy by your commandments and have commanded us to eat unleavened bread'. As Ligier points out (*op. cit.*, p. 125, n. 46), this formula opened the way for Christ to insert 'a new commemoration' into it (Do this in memory of me), a point which Paul and Luke emphasized in their accounts of the institution.

verses of wrath. Christ the Redeemer had transformed the cup of wrath into the chalice of mercy for the multitude of nations.'[42]

What emerges from all this is that the eucharistic prayer derives from the Jewish table-prayer of 'blessing', though all the elements of the latter are completely transformed. But it is this prayer that gives the Christian prayer its dominant character: it is a proclamation of thanksgiving (blessing) for the wonderful works of salvation that are recalled in greater or less detail in the course of it. In the Christian prayer the saving deeds of God wrought through Christ continue the recalling of the saving events of the Old Testament and lead naturally into the narrative of the institution. Even this, then, exists in the perspective of thanksgiving, as does the *anamnesis*, the making of the memorial with offering that follows the words of institution (see Eucharistic Prayers II and III). The prayer ends in *doxa*, giving glory to God through the Son in the Holy Spirit. *Doxa* is always associated with 'blessing'. 'thanksgiving' and 'praise' which, with petition, are found in Jewish prayers of blessing (*berakoth*). They are also found in the Christian eucharistic prayers in different ways.

Acclamation

Although the eucharistic prayer is uniquely the prayer of the president of the community and although he, in the name of the people, voices the thanksgiving, there is also within it a certain dialogue. The greatness, the glory and the love of God are proclaimed in the first part of the prayer and the people make their response with the *Sanctus*, which is a singing of the glory (*doxa, kabod*) of God who is seen as resplendent among the heavenly beings. But the dialogue goes on at an even deeper level. The church recalls and makes present the saving deeds of God so that she may receive into herself the 'eucharist', the thanksgiving of Christ, her head. For it is only then that she can return, bearing her gift of thanksgiving, to the Father through the Son and in the Holy Spirit. This response is made in the acclamation after the consecration, in the doxology at the end of the prayer and finally in the communion.

Epiclesis or invocation I

The Jewish prayers contained supplication and the eucharistic prayer has one of a rather different kind. Since the fourth century the Roman canon has had a prayer beseeching the Father to accept the offering of the community so that it may become the body and blood of Jesus Christ.[43] In the three new prayers there are invocations of the Holy Spirit asking

---

[42] *Op. cit.*, pp. 124–5. Ligier goes on to show that supplication (intercessions) and epiclesis are both suggested by the Jewish texts. It is not our purpose, however, to give a complete literary analysis of the eucharistic prayer but merely to indicate its nature.

[43] St Ambrose, *De Sacramentis*, IV.

that the people's offerings may become the body and blood of Christ.[44]

The importance of this supplication lies not so much in the fact that it invokes the Holy Spirit as in the fact that it integrates the 'offertory' into the action of the eucharistic prayers. The gifts the people have presented as the sign of their self-giving are now to be integrated into the offering of Christ which the eucharistic action makes present. In the New Testament view (cf Romans 12: 1, 2, etc.), self-offering, the offering of one's whole life and activity, is always associated with sacrifice and here in the eucharist it receives expression.

The institution narrative

The words of institution are the heart of every known eucharistic liturgy with the possible exception of the eccentric liturgy of Addai and Mari.[45] They constitute of course the real *anamnesis* of the Mass, for the church is here doing visibly what Christ commanded her to do at the Last Supper 'in memory of' him. This is the reason why they are effective. This has not always been understood by some of the critics of the new Order, and no doubt the passage (GI 55) has been 'edited' in the version of the General Instruction to be found in the *Missale Romanum* (1970)[46] to satisfy these critics.

---

[44] This invocation before the consecration seems to be an Alexandrian or Egyptian peculiarity. See *Sarapion's Sacramentary* (English trans., *Bishop Sarapion's Prayer-Book*, 1910).

[45] At least in the state in which it survives at present. For text, in translation, see Lucien Deiss, *Early Sources of the Liturgy* (London, 1967). It may be of the third century (Botte) or of the fifth century (Raes). Dom Botte thinks it once had the words of the institution.

[46] The revised version runs: 'The narrative of the institution and *the consecration*. The sacrifice is effected by the words and actions of Christ. This sacrifice he instituted at the Last Supper when he offered his body and blood under the appearances of bread and wine and gave them to his apostles to eat and drink and left to them his command to perpetuate the same mystery.' The translation given in the ICEL (1969) text runs as follows: '*The narrative of the institution*: the Last Supper is made present in the words and actions of Christ when he instituted the sacrament of his passion and resurrection, when under the appearances of bread and wine he gave his Apostles his body to eat and his blood to drink and commanded them to carry on this mystery (translation copyright © 1969 International Committee on English in the Liturgy, Inc. All rights reserved).'
The differences between the two are obvious. In the revised text 'consecration' and 'sacrifice' are inserted—corresponding with the obsession some have that if these words are not included every time the eucharist is spoken of, the statement will not be orthodox—the 'sacrament of the passion and resurrection' is removed, thus weakening the theology of the passage and it is at least suggested that the *narrative* of the institution does not effect the eucharist, as the Order of 1969 (Latin) says. In this thinking a narrative cannot be the 'form' of a sacrament. On the other hand, the ICEL translation hardly does justice to the Latin. Since the version of 1969 is thoroughly traditional in the best sense, we propose to follow it here.

The order of 1969 (GI 55) then says this:

a)   In the words (narrative) of institution the Last Supper is made present (*repraesentatur*) by the words and actions of Christ;

b)   in the Supper, Christ instituted the 'sacrament of his passion and resurrection';

c)   this he gave to his apostles, namely his body and blood under the appearances of bread and wine;

d)   at the same time he left to them the command to perpetuate the same mystery.

We note the identification between the 'narrative of institution' and 'the words and actions of Christ'. It is these that make present what Jesus did at the Last Supper. But what Jesus made present at the Last Supper was much more than bringing about a Real Presence under the appearances of bread and wine, more, in fact, than constructing a sign that was simply a memorial of his death. As the gospel narratives make clear, our Lord's mind was moving on towards the future, to the passion and the death, but also to the resurrection and the glorification. Indeed, he was looking on to the kingdom that would come into existence as a result of his death and resurrection, and all this was his redeeming work. When, then, he said 'Do this in memory of me' he was not restricting his vision to the passion and the death. The eucharist was to be in memory of *him* suffering and dead, yes, but also risen, ascended and glorified with his Father. The eucharist is the sign, the sacrament, the mystery of all this. St Paul, whose whole experience was of the risen, glorified Christ, had no doubt about it. For him the celebration of the eucharist was a proclamation of the redeeming death of Christ until he should come again. This, in fact, is what Jesus commanded his apostles to do so that the 'sacrament of his passion and resurrection' might be perpetuated in the church.

This, it seems to me, is a perfectly satisfactory way of speaking of the 'words of institution' or consecration, and I believe it to be thoroughly traditional. The church perpetuates the sacrament of the passion and resurrection precisely by saying and doing what Christ did at the Last Supper. She has nothing else to do. As Maurice de la Taille said a very long time ago, the 'newness' of the sacrifice of the Mass is totally on the part of the church: the power (of the Mass) is totally on the part of Christ.[47] The church has nothing to handle but the *sacramentum*, but Christ committed himself to it—it is the sign of the covenant, the new covenant—he is faithful to his promises and when the church, in obedience to his command, constructs the sign, makes or celebrates the sacrament, then Christ with all his redeeming power is present to her.

---

[47] *Mysterium Fidei*, Elucid. XXIII (p. 296), Paris, ed. 1921. And again: *Novitas sacrificii Missae respectu crucis desumenda est tantum ex parte Ecclesiae*: the newness of the Mass-sacrifice is to be found only on the part of the Church. Further on he says that 'the church makes her own' the sacrifice of Christ (p. 299).

What, however, has changed the perspective for Catholics of the Roman rite is the introduction of three new eucharistic prayers which may be used severally as alternatives to the Roman Canon. We shall consider each of them briefly lower down. What needs to be said here is that though in the narrower sense, the words of institution (what scholastic theologians have called the 'form') are the same in all four prayers, the narratives in which they are set are different in each case. That of the Roman Canon retains its elaborate description, Jesus took bread into his hands, he looked up to heaven (Matthew 14:19) and the Supper took place on the *day* before he suffered (a peculiarity of the Roman rite). The second takes from Hippolytus the phrase (that comes from John 10:18) saying that Jesus freely accepted his death, while the third adds no more than that it was on the *night* before he died that Jesus took the bread and cup. The fourth is markedly Johannine (John 13:1 ff): Jesus loved those who were his own and the eucharist is the proof of his love. To the words over the cup it adds 'filled with the fruit of the vine'. These variations will not only enrich people's notions of the eucharist but will be a constant reminder that the New Testament accounts themselves vary, each one throwing a different light on the mystery of eucharist.

As for the words of institution in the narrower sense, authority decided that they should be uniform in all four prayers. It was said that this was for pastoral reasons, presumably not to confuse the people. But the four longer narratives are already there to confuse them (if anyone is going to be confused) and one must suppose that all Catholics are aware that the New Testament accounts differ from one another. However that may be, two things have happened to this set of words: 'which will be given up for you' have been added to 'This is my body' and the famous (or notorious) 'Mystery of faith' has been removed from them in the Roman Canon and appears in the acclamation after the consecration. The first is borrowed from Luke 22:19 (and cf I Corinthians 11:24, margin, *klōmenon* = 'broken') and underlines the sacrificial aspect of Jesus's action ('This is my body which is to be delivered over to suffering and death for you'). This must be said to be a distinct enrichment of the rite and from a literary viewpoint it provides a better balance with the words over the cup. The removal of the words *mysterium fidei* from the words over the cup occasioned, it will be remembered, a considerable outcry, though needlessly. It was certainly not a confession of faith in the Real Presence. If it had been, it ought to have appeared in the words over the bread too, and in any case it was not until the twelfth or thirteenth centuries that the word 'mystery' was used of the Real Presence. Before that it meant the whole mystery of salvation or of the eucharist. That the words are an interpolation is certain, they seem to have come in somewhere during the sixth century, though how they got there is a matter of scholarly speculation.[48] The insertion of these words

---

[48] B. Capelle, *Travaux Liturgiques*, II, pp. 283–4 (Louvain, 1962).

into the acclamation is a very happy stroke and the responses of the people very evidently interpret their meaning: they acclaim the mystery of salvation, death, resurrection and second coming (the last in all but one).[49]

The anamnesis *or memorial prayer*

The words of institution are the real *anamnesis* of the eucharist. By these words that come to us from Christ we at once recall and make present his redeeming action. But the church from the time of the earliest eucharistic prayer we possess (that of Hippolytus, c. 215)[50] has always and everywhere drawn out the implications of the *anamnesis* in a prayer that bears that name. Verbally it varies a good deal but the sense is always this: by making the memorial (*anamnesis*) the church is brought into the presence of the redeeming Christ who suffered, died, rose again, ascended to the glory of his Father whence he will come again at the end of time. The power of the redeeming events is available to the church, she is able to 'make his sacrifice her own' and he unites her self-offering to his own. So the church is able to say: 'We make this sacrifice in the memory of Christ, we recall his passion, death, resurrection and ascension'[51] and so we are able to offer 'from your own gifts to us'[52] the bread that is now the Bread of Life and the Cup that is now the Cup of Salvation, namely the 'holy and perfect sacrifice',[53] Jesus Christ our Lord.

But the theme of thanksgiving is to be understood to be there, too, and this is often made explicit. This is very marked in the Liturgy of St John Chrysostom. After the phrase 'we offer you your own of what is your own', the choir (or the people) cry out: 'We praise you, we bless you, *we give you thanks*, Lord. . . .' But it is also found in the third eucharistic prayer: 'we offer you in thanksgiving this holy and living sacrifice'.[54] Objectively, the sacrifice of Christ by which he took away the sin of the world is the cause of all Christian rejoicing and 'eucharist'; subjectively, here in the Mass he makes his self-offering available to the offerers and they, thus being united with him, give thanks for the 'work of redemption' that is taking place within them. *Anamnesis*, offering and thanksgiving all go together.

---

[49] ICEL's translation of the first is very successful. It has turned a mere statement into an enthusiastic acclamation. ICEL has often been the target of bitter criticism. It is right to give credit where it is due. On the other hand it is odd that in English we have *four* acclamations and that there are only three in the *Missale*.

[50] And perhaps St Paul's 'announcing the death of the Lord' indicates a primitive *anamnesis*.

[51] In most prayers the second coming is mentioned.

[52] Roman canon '*de tuis donis ac datis*' which echoes the *ta sa ek tōn sōn*, lit. 'your own from your own', of the liturgy of St John Chrysostom, a phrase used also in Alexandria, it would seem, and that expresses the truth that the church has nothing of her own to offer.

[53] Roman canon.

[54] In E.P. II it is less emphasized: 'We thank you for counting us worthy to stand in your presence and serve you.'

In the presence of Christ's offering, however, we have 'to learn to offer' ourselves so that through him our Mediator we may be drawn day by day into an ever more perfect union with God and with each other.[55]

Epiclesis *or invocation of the Holy Spirit* II

As far as we know, the Roman canon has never had an invocation of the Holy Spirit. The third prayer (*Supplices*) after the consecration is certainly a prayer for the acceptance of the sacrifice and for the fruitful reception of holy communion on the part of the worshippers. But all efforts to show, by reconstruction, that it contained an invocation of the Holy Spirit have proved vain. Nor is it possible to show that the earliest eucharistic prayers had one. It is true that it is to be found in the present text(s) of the Apostolic Tradition of Hippolytus, though its authenticity has been contested.[56] The *epiclesis* of the Holy Spirit in this place is generally considered to have come into the prayer during the fourth century in the Syrian area.[57] In the light of all this it cannot be said, then, that an *epiclesis* of the Holy Spirit is a *necessary* element of the eucharistic prayer. But if we see the eucharist as the sacrament-sign of the church, there is a high appropriateness in having such an invocation. The church is the Spirit-filled body of Christ, in that body the Holy Spirit is regarded as the animating principle and it is to him that the fruitfulness of Christ's saving work in the hearts of Christians is attributed. Now that people can *hear* the invocation they become aware of the work of the Spirit in their midst and the eucharist becomes a more adequate sign of the church. From a practical point of view, the insertion of *epicleses* of the Holy Spirit into the Roman rite will do much to remind Western Catholics of the work and importance of the Holy Spirit in the church. To this extent it should have an ecumenical value, for the East has always had a stronger grasp of this truth than the West.

But what is the exact purpose of this *epiclesis*? There is no need here to go into the very vexed question of the consecrating power of the invocation of the Holy Spirit if only because the *epicleses* inserted into the last three eucharistic prayers for use in the Roman rite have carefully avoided all

---

[55] CL 48; GI 55, f, and see above, Chapter three.

[56] Botte (ed. Münster, 1963) strenuously maintains its authenticity and Dix (*Shape*, p. 158, and his ed. of *Ap. Trad.* (1937), pp. 75 ff.) is strongly inclined to reject it. If one is allowed a view in so learned a controversy, I would say that the passage is authentic. In any case, Dix's willingness to cut about liturgical texts to suit his own notions does not seem to be a very happy method of dealing with them, even if his analyses are sometimes illuminating.

[57] See the Mystagogical Discourses of St Cyril of Jerusalem, *Catéchèses Mystagogiques*, ed. A. Piédagnel (Paris, 1966), III, 3, 5. Does the existence of an *epiclesis* of the *Logos* (the Word) in the Sacramentary of Sarapion (c. 350) witness to an uncertainty about the whole business?

suggestion of consecration.[58] In the eucharistic prayers added to the Roman rite we find three elements: 1. the church asks that through the reception of holy communion 2. all may be filled with the Holy Spirit so that 3. all may be made one in Christ. The *epiclesis* of Eucharistic Prayer III sets this out the most clearly: 'Grant that we, who are nourished by his body and blood, may be filled with the Holy Spirit, and become one body, one spirit in Christ' (cf I Corinthians 12: 12, 13). Eucharistic Prayer IV adds 'into the one body, *a living sacrifice of praise*', thus relating the offering of the people to the sacrifice of Christ. This seems to echo the General Instruction (55, f) which remarks that in the memorial the church offers the victim to the Father in the Holy Spirit. So there is the upward and downward movement of the Holy Spirit, upward so that the very work of the church, the offering, is effected in the Holy Spirit and downward, for it is through his operation that the communion can become fruitful in the hearts of men.[59]

The intercessions

As we have seen, the Jewish form of blessing-prayer admitted supplication—it usually came towards the end of it—though it is impossible to say whether this influenced the insertion of intercessions into the Christian eucharistic prayers. They may not have been there from the beginning and the sample prayer given by Hippolytus does not contain them. On the other hand Justin[60] has them, though *before* the eucharistic prayer begins, and there are references to prayers for various categories of people in the works of Tertullian. But if they were not included from the beginning the church soon saw the appropriateness of interceding for the needs of mankind during the eucharistic prayer. Perhaps the best statement of the matter is to be found in the *Mystagogical Catecheses* of Cyril of Jerusalem.[61] This moment is most appropriate to make intercessions since the 'spiritual sacrifice' (*pneumatikēn thusian*) has just been accomplished and 'over the victim we call upon God and pray and offer it for all who are in need, for

---

[58] The solution of the problem whether the *epiclesis* is consecratory probably depends on an assessment of what the Easterns held in the fourth century and later about the 'moment of consecration'. It is generally held that in the fourth century and until a good deal later the 'moment of consecration' was not isolated. The whole prayer, enshrining an action, the action of the church, was regarded as consecratory. This was certainly so in the West, as the reference in the Roman Canon to the elements as *sacrificia* before the consecration suggests. Indeed, the whole notion was extrapolated into the 'offertory' as the ancient prayers over the offerings also suggested.

[59] This is suggested by GI 55, c, where it says that the *epiclesis* is an invocation that the victim may become the source of salvation to those who receive holy communion.

[60] *Apol.* I, 65, and cf I Timothy 2:1, 2.

[61] V, 8, 1-8; 9, 6-7; 10, 10-12. I assume, with the latest editor, Piédagnel, the high probability that these *Catecheses* were Cyril's, though possibly worked over by his successor, John.

the peace of the church, for the well-being of the world, for rulers, for armies, for the sick and the afflicted'. 'While the holy and dread sacrifice[62] is present' those who are prayed for 'greatly profit' from its offering.

The General Instruction (55, 9) yields a similar though less impressive teaching: the church at this moment celebrates the eucharist in union with the whole church both earthly and heavenly (Cyril includes this, too) and makes the offering for all its members, both living and dead, who are called to share in the redemption and salvation of Christ acquired by his body and blood. Unlike Cyril it does not emphasize the presence of Christ's sacrifice, yet the sense that intercessions should be made within the eucharistic prayer is ancient in the Western church. It was the sense of Pope Innocent I's letter (415) to Decentius of Gubbio, and it is clear from the same letter that some time before Innocent (perhaps not very long before) the intercessions had been brought within the Roman canon. There they still are, distributed before and after the consecration, though the *Memento* of the dead did not become a fixed element of the prayer until after the Carolingian adaptation of the ninth century. The Roman canon thus made the point, at a very early date and in a manner wholly liturgical, that intercession during its course is of special efficacy.[63]

The compilers of the new eucharistic prayers have preferred to place the intercessions after the consecration, no doubt to make clear the fundamental character of such a prayer: it is a single prayer, made up of proclamation, thanksgiving and praise, taking up in its course the enactment of the 'thanksgiving' which is the memorial of the Lord's passion, death and resurrection. Intercession, however appropriate within the prayer, is a sort of consequence of the pleading of the Lord's sacrifice and is therefore better placed at the end.[64]

As for the content of these intercessions, the Roman canon is notably rich. It has a strong sense of the communion of saints and its lists of saints are nicely graduated (thought by some to be the work of St Gregory the Great), though one could wish that they had not been so rigidly fixed. The ability to insert either the saint of the day or the saint of the place of celebration would help to make the prayer live for the time and the place. The

---

[62] 'Dread' = 'hair-raising', literally, a word much used in liturgies coming from the Syrian region and found also in St John Chrysostom.

[63] If one may refer to the 'moment of consecration' business again, it seems clear that for Pope Innocent the main point was that the intercessions should be within the prayer, though it did not matter to him whether they were before or after the consecration. This fits in with the whole tenor of the Roman canon.

[64] The Roman position, intercessions *before* the consecration, is not unique. They are found in the same position in an ancient Alexandrian prayer—one more instance of the strange similarities between Rome and Alexandria which liturgical scholars have noticed for years. (For a discussion of the Alexandrian prayer, see L. Bouyer, *Eucharistie, Théologie et Spiritualité de la Prière Eucharistique* (Tournai, 1966), pp. 191–6.)

emphasis, too, on the power of the intercession of the saints is more clearly marked in the Roman prayer than in the others ('May their merits and prayers gain us your constant help and protection'). That of E.P. II is briefer, less explicit, though in intention all-inclusive. It is difficult to understand why the laity were not included with the clergy, for the phrase 'have mercy on us all' is hardly sufficient. Mary and the saints are merely mentioned, though the earthly church is seen as joining with them in the praise of God. The intercessions of E.P. III have evidently been carefully thought out. They run out of the offering of sacrifice, they are explicitly inclusive of the universal church and of the local church gathered for worship and they end with an eschatological emphasis ('We hope to enjoy for ever the vision of your glory') that is so strongly marked in all the new liturgy. This part of the intercession is preceded by another in which the prayer of Mary, the saints and that of the saints of the place and the feast is sought. The commemoration of the dead is particularly rich and expresses a truly Christian theology of death. The intercessions of E.P. IV, if shorter than those of E.P. III, are none the less rich. Pope, bishop, clergy and laity are all prayed for explicitly and an ecumenical dimension is given with the prayer for 'all who seek you with a sincere heart'. The prayer for the dead is also generous in its scope: 'all the dead whose faith is known to you alone'—and how many there must be of that kind! The last petition is for the perfecting of the communion of saints when all, 'freed from the corruption of sin and death', will sing God's glory with every creature through Christ our Lord.

These intercessions must be said to be one of the most valuable additions to the liturgy of our day. It is one thing to be told from the theological manual or catechism that the Mass is a 'sacrifice of impetration' (language that tempts one to go heretical without further ado) and it is another to hear the eucharist being pleaded for the well-being of the whole church and the world.

The doxology

The eucharistic prayer began with giving praise and thanksgiving to God through Jesus Christ. Now it ends with giving God the glory through the Son and in the Holy Spirit for the showing forth of his continuing love made present in the eucharist. The church has received Christ's 'thanksgiving' into herself with the co-operation of the Holy Spirit. The covenant has been renewed, the bridal relationship between Christ and his church has been strengthened and the Spirit, with a new infusion of life, has come to her again. So she can now through Christ her head and Bridegroom and in the Holy Spirit give all glory and honour to the Father. This is made particularly clear in the doxology of the Roman canon which seems to bear a family relationship to that of Hippolytus: 'Glory and honour to you (the Father) through him (Christ), with the Holy Spirit in the holy church, now

and for ever'.[65] The fragmentary prayer of Der-Balyzeh combines the
doxology with a prayer for communion and in language lies somewhere
between that of Hippolytus and that of the Roman canon: 'Give (thy
servants) the power of the Holy Spirit, the confirmation and increase of
faith, the hope of eternal life to come, through our Lord Jesus Christ.
Through him, glory to thee, Father, with the Holy Spirit for ever.'[66] With
this seems to be related the doxology in the Sacramentary of Sarapion:
'Through him (Christ), glory to thee and power, in the Holy Spirit, now
and for ever and ever'.[67] There are others, and I have quoted one or two
here to show that if the Roman doxology is good, it is not unique, and it
is perhaps a pity that for pastoral reasons the Roman version is the only
one used in all four eucharistic prayers. Variation, of course, offers musical
difficulties and this is one of the texts the celebrant is urged to sing,[68] but
the single text rather limits the possibilities of musical settings that at least
some celebrants could sing and that could be of considerable interest.

From the time of Justin the Martyr the people's response 'Amen' has
been given at this point and usually in a loud voice or in song. It is the
affirmation of the people to what has been done in the eucharistic action;
by this response they express their participation in the thanksgiving and in
the offering of Christ. The revisers have set their face against repetitions
in the liturgy, but perhaps there was a case here for at least a triple Amen,
which musically can be very effective and is easier for the people to sing.[69]

The communion rite

One of the undeniable advantages of the new Order is that it has made
it perfectly possible to see, without explanation, what are the great structural lines of the Mass: the ministry of the word, the celebration of the
eucharistic memorial and the communion. It has thus replaced the old
'three parts of the Mass': the Offertory (which you had to be present for
to avoid mortal sin), the Consecration and the (Priest's—*sic*) Communion.
And even the liturgists' division of the Mass into the Mass of the Catechumens and the Mass of the Faithful is now shown to be inadequate.
Revision of the communion rite was very necessary, for no part of the Mass
was as confused as this. Missals continued the heading *Canon Missae* over
the whole section giving the communion rite, the breaking of the bread

---

[65] Trans. Brian Newns in *Liturgy*, January, 1968, p. 14.
[66] Lucien Deiss, *Early Sources of the Liturgy* (Eng. trans., London, 1967),
pp. 193–4. It is described as a 'communion prayer' in this edition, with what
justification I do not know.
[67] *Early Sources of the Liturgy*, p. 129.
[68] Instruction on Sacred Music (1967), nos. 7, 16; and cf GI 19.
[69] If, of course, the celebrant says the doxology perfunctorily or drops his voice,
there will hardly be any reply at all. The commentary of GI 55, h, seems hardly
adequate. The people confirm and conclude the giving of glory to God. Rather,
they give their assent to the whole eucharistic prayer and action.

that came during the embolism of the Lord's prayer, the elaborate signing of the chalice with a portion of the host, the *Agnus Dei* that had become completely divorced from its original purpose (an accompaniment to the breaking of the Bread which in the papal rite was very elaborate—and lengthy) and the kiss of peace (restricted in fact to the clergy) embedded in the celebrant's private prayers before communion.

The new Order now makes it quite clear that the Communion rite begins with the Lord's prayer, and even the printers have been instructed to put here the heading *Ritus Communionis*. All is now orientated towards the act of communion: the whole community prays the Lord's prayer, asking for the Bread of Life and that their sins may be forgiven so that, as the Instruction says, holy things may be given to those who are truly holy.[70] The embolism has with advantage been shortened and the action goes straight to the sign of peace which is prefaced by a prayer giving (part of) its meaning and the sign of peace is extended to the whole community. The Bread is now broken during the *Agnus Dei*, as it was when Pope Sergius I introduced it into the Mass at this place and for this purpose c. 700. A single prayer of preparation follows and after the invitation the community move in procession to the altar for communion. It is a comprehensible pattern.

In the copious commentary provided by the Instruction (56, a–k) certain features stand out. The church is concerned to emphasize brotherly love, the spirit of reconciliation that goes with it and the unity of Christians who are made one by the one Bread that is the body of Christ.

In the Lord's prayer we ask for our daily bread which for Christians is principally the body of Christ. Perhaps Western Christians ought to ask also that through the generosity and ingenuity of modern man the people of the Third World should be fed. The reconciliation theme is not prominent in the commentary here, though it is implicit in all it has to say about the communion act itself. We should do well to recall that, as the Lord said, when we are bringing our gift to the altar and if we remember that a brother has something against us, we should first be reconciled with him and only then may we offer our gift (Matthew 5:23–24).[71] If through the strength given us in holy communion we could go out and be reconcilers in the secular community we should be doing no more than is implied by the whole eucharistic action.

The sign of peace and the fraction are closely associated. The first is seen

---

[70] This phrase comes from the Liturgy of St John Chrysostom where it is said immediately before communion. It is one of the oldest expressions used in connection with the reception of the eucharist, and one could wish that it had been introduced into the revised liturgy either as an alternative to or in conjunction with the *Ecce, Agnus Dei*.

[71] In Orthodox practice it is the custom to do this before confession. See J. D. Crichton, in *Penance: Virtue and Sacrament*, ed. J. Fitzsimons (London, 1969), pp. 28–9.

as a prayer for the peace and unity of the church and of the whole of mankind (here the reconciliation theme appears) and as an expression of mutual love among the worshippers before they receive the one Bread that makes them one body in Christ. At this point the Instruction quotes I Corinthians 10:17, and remarks that the gesture is not merely for practical purposes to divide the hosts for the communicants but that it has this significance: we, though many, by communion in the one bread of life are made the one body which is Christ.

This is very satisfactory teaching and coming in a document that is primarily practical is very gratifying. But practice still limps behind preaching. Until the bread that is used for the people is much more substantial and the portions larger it is difficult to make the rite of the fraction as significant as the church now says it should be. For concelebration larger altar-breads have become common (though their papery quality is not satisfactory) and we now need something of the kind for the communion of the people. Such bread could be broken and the breaking would be visible to the people. If the ceremony were somewhat prolonged, so much the better. For far too long the people's communion in the Roman tradition has been too clinical. Small white 'hosts' which bear little resemblance to bread are hastily inserted into the mouths of the communicants. The whole rite is done as quickly as possible. There are, no doubt, practical difficulties to be overcome—there always are—but, as the Instruction observes elsewhere (56, h), there are certain things that are highly desirable in themselves and that even if difficult should be done. At least some of the bread the people receive should be broken from the large host or hosts. This is now required by the *Ordo Missae*. What is necessary is larger and more substantial altar-breads.

The mingling of the consecrated bread and wine, about which the Instruction is completely uninformative, has been retained, though its significance is not at all apparent. Its history is extremely complicated and cannot be gone into here.[72] The Order has retained the rite but has simplified the text, removing the awkward word *consecratio* (which probably witnessed to primitive notions of consecration by contact) and turning it into a prayer for the communicants.

In the new Order the administration of communion to the people is quite elaborate and the commentary in the Instruction rich in content. The

---

[72] It derives from *two* minglings in the papal rite of the *Ordines* (I and II), the earliest of which represents the mingling of the *Sancta* consecrated at a previous Mass (to signify the continuity of the sacrifice). The formula accompanying the mingling in the 1570 missal seems to have been inserted by a Syrian pope (unknown) and the mingling of the consecrated bread and wine was seen as the re-uniting of the body and blood of Christ, as it were a 'resurrection' taking place on the altar (the Syrians were much given to an exaggerated realism). But, more satisfactorily, it remains as a prayer for communion in the whole Christ. (See *L'Eglise en Prière*, ed. A. G. Martimort, Tournai, 1961, pp. 416–20.)

communion act is a *procession*, one of the three of the Roman rite (entrance, 'offertory' and communion), it is accompanied by song and *together* these express the unity of the communicants, their spiritual joy and brotherly love. Holy communion is no longer, therefore, *at this point* an act of private devotion; it is the action of the community whose members are praying that they may be drawn into a closer unity with Christ and through him with their fellow-worshippers and with all their fellow Christians throughout the world. In recent centuries we have reflected too little on the meaning of the word '*com*-union' which expresses one of the deepest truths about the church, namely that it is *koinonia*, a sharing of the common life of the body of Christ, the church. The church is communion long before it is institution and at a much deeper level than can be created by juridical bonds. Of this *koinonia* holy communion is the most conspicuous and pregnant sign. It is at this moment that the church is made one and as St Thomas Aquinas said seven hundred years ago, the ultimate, the *real* effect of the eucharist is the unity of the mystical body.[73]

This teaching remains true *however* communion is administered, though it is an interesting reflection on the power of liturgical gestures that where the communion procession has been absent, the notion that holy communion is an act of private devotion has prevailed. The communion procession is then not merely a matter of good order in the assembly (though that has its importance), it is a symbolic gesture signifying that communion is the action of the community, that by it its members are drawn more closely to each other and in practice it should give them an awareness of their solidarity with those outside their community. The communion procession should therefore be regarded as a normal part of the Mass and not as a ceremonial extra.

The rite of administration of communion is rich in meaning: the celebrant shows the host to the people and *invites* them to receive communion: 'This is the Lamb of God . . .' (John 1:36) to which has been added, from Revelation 19:9, 'Happy are those who are called to the (wedding) supper of the Lamb' and the people respond with further words from the gospel: 'Lord, I am not worthy . . .' (Matthew 8:9). It is interesting to observe that the whole invitation and final preparation for communion are in the words of scripture. The formulas of administration ('The body of Christ . . . the blood of Christ') with their response 'Amen' are very ancient, being found already in the writings of St Cyril of Jerusalem in the East and of St Ambrose in the West.[74] The latter's comment is the

---

[73] The expression occurs throughout his treatise on the eucharist, ST, III, qq. 73–83.

[74] *Catech. Myst.* V, 21, 5; *De Sacramentis* IV, iii, 25. In a note to his edition of *De Sacr.* (*Des Sacrements, des Mystères*, Paris, 1961), Dom B. Botte notes that it occurs in the third century, in a letter (3) of Pope Cornelius (died 252). Cf Eusebius, *Hist. eccles.* 6, 43.

best interpretation of the phrase: 'Not idly therefore do you say "Amen" for you are confessing that you receive the body of Christ. When, then, you present yourself, the priest says "The Body of Christ" and you answer "Amen", that is, it is true. *What you confess with your lips, keep in your heart.*'

As is well known the *manner* of receiving the eucharist has varied in the course of ages. The earliest records show that the people stood and received the Bread in their hands and drank from the cup.[75] From the ninth century in the West, to avoid profanation and out of respect for the Sacrament, people were communicated directly into the mouth. Even later, from the thirteenth century onwards, the custom of kneeling for communion came in. Habits and ways of thinking are changing again and now there is a great desire among the laity to receive in their hands and standing. The latter has become very common and the bishops of a region may give permission for the former.[76] Standing may be regarded as no more than a convenience and the natural thing to do when people are walking in a procession and singing. Communion in the hand is also the more natural way to take food and is a gesture helping people to remember that the eucharist is a meal.

The desire for communion in both kinds is even greater and the documents on this matter since (and including) the Second Vatican Council are numerous.[77] In certain communities, mostly of religious, full use has been made of the permissions so far granted. Bishops have, however, been sending in repeatedly petitions that the facilities should be extended. This has now been made possible by the last Instruction (1970) issued by the Congregation for Worship. This gives permission to local conferences of bishops to determine, within the limits set out in the document, when communion in both kinds may be given. The tendency seems to be setting that communion in both kinds should be normal practice and communion in one kind abnormal, that is, practically impossible on account of the great number of communicants. We have not yet arrived at that situation and meanwhile it seems worth saying that in smaller parishes communion in both kinds should present no very great difficulty and certainly at week-day Masses, where the number of communicants is small, one would have

---

[75] It would seem that at Alexandria in the time of Clement (c. 200) some walked up to the altar and communicated *themselves* there. But this may have been an abuse as Clement mentions the custom only to disapprove of it. See R. Berger, *Kleines Liturgisches Wörterbuch* (1969), s.v. 'Kommunion', p. 225.

[76] See below p. 102 for the Instruction.

[77] CL 55, *Ritus Communionis* . . . (1965) *Eucharisticum Mysterium* (1967, Eng. trans., CTS, *Instruction on the Eucharistic Mystery*), repeated in *Ordo Missae* and *Missale Romanum* (1970). The latest document is of 1970 from the Congregation for Worship: *Instructio de Ampliore Facultate s. Communionis sub utraque specie administrandae.*

thought that it ought to become normal practice. As people learn to appreciate the significance of the practice, it is likely to be extended. But the documents insist on instruction beforehand and certain lines of it are suggested in a semi-official commentary attached to the Instruction 1970.

While this, as might be expected, draws attention to the traditional doctrine, summed up at the Council of Trent, that communion under either kind is sufficient and that the whole Christ is present under the appearances of either the bread or the wine, it is interesting to observe that instead of the metaphysico-theological principles that have been to the forefront for centuries to justify communion in one kind, it now appeals to *significance* and *symbolism*. Communion in both kinds expresses more fully what Christ did at the Last Supper when he said 'Take and eat' and 'Take and drink'. The communicants, that is, at least in principle, the whole community, are making a more *exact* memorial of what Christ did at the Last Supper. Likewise, the practice shows up more clearly that the eucharist is a *meal*—at a meal one both eats and drinks—and in this way, too, the memorial aspect of the eucharist is made clearer. There is an even deeper reason for it. In celebrating the eucharist the church gives thanks so that she may receive within herself the self-giving of Christ by which he not only redeemed mankind but gave praise and glory to his Father (John 17). The bread that was broken and 'given up' for us is certainly a sign of that self-offering, but it is more vividly expressed by the significance of the blood 'which is to be poured out for you and for all mankind for the taking away of their sins'. As the Old Testament had it, 'the life is in the blood' and Jesus was visibly indicating the pouring out of his life when he took the cup and said 'This is the cup of my blood of the new covenant which is to be poured out for you'. If this is our understanding of the sacrificial nature of the Last Supper and of the Mass, which is its memorial, then it follows that the communicants, by receiving the cup, will be associated all the more closely with Christ's sacrifice, with his self-giving, which enables the Christian to give himself and his life to the Father.[78]

In fact, communion in both kinds has, as far as one can tell, caused no difficulties among the people. They see the point of it very quickly and in a country such as ours, where communion in both kinds has been customary in other Christian churches since the reformation, they are more familiar with it than Christians of some continental countries who have had no knowledge of it at all. At the same time, an extension of the practice would

---

[78] See *Notitiae* (57), Sept.-Oct., 1970, pp. 326–8. The last consideration is my own. The commentary goes on to say that part of the catechesis should show that the practice of not communicating people from the cup is to be explained on historical and practical lines. Dogmatic considerations did not come into play—at least not until the fourteenth century. In a note at the end it remarks that if communion by intinction is chosen as the *safer* way of communion, this is not to be regarded as the *better* way.

give much better opportunities for instruction and so would deepen the people's appreciation of the Mass.

Communion in the hand is now widespread in the church[79] but among traditionalist Catholics it seems to raise more objections than communion from the cup. No doubt it is a change from a practice that is some thousand years old and devotional habits, especially those connected with the reception of holy communion, change very slowly. This is very understandable but it is also clear from experience that there has been a faulty instruction about the manner of Christ's presence in the eucharist. Some people show themselves to be unable or unwilling to distinguish between an altar bread and a 'host'. What lies at the bottom of this attitude is a failure to distinguish between the *sign* and the reality it signifies (the body of Christ). Sight, taste and touch are in the eucharist deceived, said the author of the *Adoro te*, it is *faith* that perceives the reality. On the other hand, bread and wine are there precisely to support the senses; they are *signs*, symbols, telling us that here is the Bread of Life and the Cup of Salvation. It is not necessary to go to the long and elaborate treatise of St Thomas on the eucharist to learn that when we touch the sign we do not touch the Body. The teaching is for all to read in the Corpus Christi hymn, generally attributed to St Thomas, the *Lauda Sion*: when you break the host you do not break the Reality; only the sign (the bread) is broken and such a fraction in no way affects him whom the bread signifies.[80]

However, as the document sent to bishops on the subject and made public in 1969 observes, what touches the people so closely must be dealt with very carefully.[81] In this Instruction we note that the bishops are given permission to allow communion in the hand with proper safeguards. All danger of irreverence is to be avoided and conditions for a proper respect for the Real Presence are laid down. Previous instruction is one of them and such instruction would, one thinks, enlighten those who do not wish to receive in their hands. As the instruction makes clear, no one is to be pressed to do so. Still, there are considerable numbers of people who do wish to receive in their hands—it seems a more natural and adult way of taking food, even when it is the body of Christ—and it would seem that

---

[79] For *some* permissions, see *Notitiae*, 6, June, 1970.

[80] It is almost impossible to emulate in English the succinctness of the hymn's statement: 'Nulla *rei* fit *scissura; signi* tantum fit fractura; qua nec status nec statura *Signati* minuitur.' It has been to me a perpetual surprise that the teaching of Aquinas on the Presence of Christ in the eucharist has not, apparently, entered ordinary Catholic consciousness. And whenever modern theologians or priests (some of them) are accused of irreverence or diminishing the doctrine of the Real Presence, one suspects that the objectors have not absorbed Aquinas's doctrine

[81] *Notitiae*, 5, 1969: *Instructio de Modo Communionem Administrandi*, pp. 347–351. It was based on a questionnaire sent to all the bishops of the world, and in *Notitiae* is followed by a letter in the vernacular from the then President of the Congregation for Worship, Cardinal Gut.

permissions should be granted more readily than they are at present. Anglicans receive in the hand and *their* reverence is very striking. It is difficult to suppose that ours would be less.

The rest of the communion rite nicely balances the needs of public worship and private devotion. During the procession there may be song and then, when it is over, there is silence. If there has been no singing during the procession, the silence may be concluded with a chant sung by all.[82] Two observations may be made here.

1.   While it is highly desirable—and should be normal practice—that the people should take part in the communion chant, it is also perfectly proper that the choir should sing more elaborate chants that are calculated to assist the private prayer of the people. If the texts are familiar there is no reason why they should not be in Latin and this would ensure a place for Latin and certain kinds of music in our present liturgy. It goes without saying that the music should be of good quality and that the choir is capable of singing it *well*. It is difficult to see the virtue of badly-sung music. Mass is not the time, nor is it the function of the choir, to mortify other people's flesh.

2.   People probably need to be taught that *silence* as such is a good and prayerful thing and we all know that there is too little of it in the modern world. Sometimes they do not profit sufficiently from the silence after communion because they are saying words, even if only in their minds. Silence if willed leads to prayer, prayer that is quite wordless, a mere dwelling on the reality of God.

Anyway, this silence and other periods of silence that are permissible in the new rite, e.g. after the readings, should be treasured and if they do play the part in the celebration that they should, the complaint of some (quite unjustified) that the modern Mass is 'all talk' would fall to the ground.

The Dismissal

Since the Last Gospel and the Leonine Prayers were dropped, some have complained that the Mass comes to an end rather abruptly. There is some truth in this and no doubt they will not be consoled to be told that before 1570 it was even more abrupt. There were no Leonine Prayers, there was no Last Gospel and no blessing (both these being uttered by the priest, if at all, on his way back to the sacristy). The Roman Mass has always ended abruptly and the reason is that Rome (and the other great centres) saw the Mass as *the* eucharistia. The Mass is the 'thanksgiving' of the church which she is able to make to God through Christ and once she had asked in the prayer after communion for the effects of communion in the assembly she thought that the action was over: *Ite, missa est!*

---

[82] Other combinations are permissible according to GI 56, i.

But devotional habits change[83] and the church, in the new missal (pp. 495–506) has provided blessings *in addition* to the postcommunion prayer. These are combined with prayers (*orationes super populum*) which were a normal feature of the Mass in the Gelasian Sacramentary but which survived only for Lent in the Gregorian Sacramentary. Those in the new missal are of good quality and a translation of one or two of them may be of interest to the reader.

1.   (For Paschaltide): The celebrant addresses the people: 'Bow your heads for the blessing.' He continues (and the prayer is addressed *to the people*):

By the resurrection of his only Son, God has graciously redeemed you, making you his adopted children;
may you always rejoice in his blessing.
By Christ's redeeming work you have received the gift of perpetual freedom.
By his grace may you be co-heirs with him in eternal life.
By faith and baptism you have been raised to a new life;
may you, by your good life here below, be united with him in the heavenly city.
And may the blessing of almighty God, Father, Son and Holy Spirit. . . .[84]

2.   (For any Sunday in the year):

May the God of all consolation guide you through life so that you may enjoy his peace and blessing.
May your hearts be untroubled, established in his love.
Rich in faith, hope and love, may you pass through this present life, doing good and rejoice at the end in the happiness of eternal life.
And may the blessing. . . .

For ordinary use also there is the Aaronic blessing (Numbers 6:24–26) and the passage from Philippians 4:7: 'May the peace of God which surpasses all understanding keep your minds and hearts in the knowledge and love of God and of his Son, our Lord Jesus Christ.'

One feels that a judicious use of these blessings will do much to take away the reproach that the Roman Mass ends too abruptly.[85]

---

[83] Not, however, as much as some people think—and say. I can remember the clergy more than fifty years ago deploring the neglect of the people who did not stay to 'make their thanksgiving' after Mass—and this is just the time when some would have us think that people were so very devout and did. I suspect it was those who had servants to get their breakfast who stayed!

[84] One notes with gratification that this longer form has been chosen. It is so much easier to translate into acceptable English.

[85] The translation of these texts presents something of a problem. How literal can they, should they, be? Should they strike a 'modern' note? Perhaps one is influenced by the blessings pronounced by Anglican bishops and dignitaries *avec empressement* and in rhythmical prose, but one feels that here a little archaism is justified. I cannot imagine that the Aaronic blessing will sound very well in *any* modern version.

Critical observations on the new Order of the Mass

It will, I trust, be clear that I have given a positive evaluation to the new Order of the Mass. But liturgy-making is a human activity and consequently fraught with imperfection. No liturgy that ever was is perfect, if only because it can never adequately express the mystery of the eucharist and of the church of which it is the sign. In the last chapter of this book I have considered liturgy in the context of the modern world and I have suggested certain requirements of a liturgy that will, I believe, be suitable to that world. There is a number of smaller matters that deserve comment and that is done here.

The introductory rites

The main criticism of the Order here must be that it is unduly cumbersome. Normally, it is made up of eight different elements, some of which seem to duplicate each other: the sign of the cross, the greeting, the brief address, the confession with absolution, the *Kyries*, the *Gloria* and the collect. The sign of the cross and the greeting *could* have been alternatives and, as I have suggested above, the confession (combined with the *Kyries*) could have been placed at the end of the General Intercession.

The preparation of the gifts

The insertion of 'offertory' prayers, as of obligation, has unduly complicated what is, according to the General Instruction and the Roman tradition, an essentially simple rite. Apart from the prayers over the bread and the cup, the rest are for the private devotion of the celebrant. Perhaps they could have been prescribed for celebration when there is no procession, on weekdays, for instance, but as it is, it is difficult to combine them with the procession.

The eucharistic prayers

The chief criticism that is to be made of these is that they do not reflect the daily concerns and life of people today who in various documents are exhorted to offer themselves and their work through Christ to God. There are one or two references to the created universe, but they are insufficient and make little impression. Nor, as we shall see, is the balance corrected by the new prefaces.

The rite of communion

This is much improved but there is one feature, whose significance is heavily underlined by the General Instruction (GI 56), that still appears as a secondary rite. The Bread is broken so that all, receiving from the one loaf, may become one body in Christ. The original place of the fraction was immediately at the end of the eucharistic prayer, a place it retains in one Western rite, the Ambrosian. Its place in the Roman rite is due to the exigencies of papal ritual. After the doxology the Pope left the altar, went to the throne and there sang the Lord's prayer. Gregory the Great wished to sing it over the consecrated elements and moved the fraction to where it is now. It is to be supposed that such a return to tradition was too much for the responsible authorities who felt, that apart from a certain straightening out of the rite, it had better be left alone.

The significance of the mingling with its accompanying (though revised) text remains obscure. It is a rite that could have been omitted without any impoverishment of the communion act.

CHAPTER SEVEN

THE CALENDAR

IT WAS evident once the liturgical reform, initiated by the Second Vatican Council, got under way that sooner or later a new missal would be needed. What has perhaps been forgotten is that the radical revision of the calendar promulgated by Pope John XXIII in 1960 rendered a good deal of the existing Roman Missal obsolete so that even without a council a good deal of revision would have had to be made. A calendar is an integral part of liturgical celebration. It largely dictates how and when a liturgical book is to be used and hence the new Roman Missal has its calendar (pp. 100–12).

By nature a calendar is a dull enough document, nothing more than a long list of feasts to be observed at certain times and, what is even more boring, a body of usually complicated rules dictating the precedence or otherwise of certain festivals. The *Calendarium Romanum* issued by the Congregation for Worship in 1969, and now attached to the *Missale Romanum,* is a document of a very different kind. If you looked at (and still more, used) the calendar of about sixty years ago, you would have got the impression that the church was mainly concerned to celebrate the feasts of saints.[1] An ordinary saint's feast (a double, in technical language) could obliterate the celebration of Sunday and usually did. There were a considerable number of votive Masses that could be celebrated on Sunday and the ferial days of Lent were usually overlaid with votive Masses of the 'Holy Winding Sheet' and such like. It was Pius X who restored the celebration of Sunday, and during the next fifty years there was gradual pressure to ensure a better observance of Lent. By the *Simplification of the Rubrics* (1955) it became possible to choose the daily Lenten Mass in preference to a saint's feast[2] and the *Corpus Rubricarum* of 1960, by upgrading the Lenten ferias, made it possible to celebrate the Mass of the day almost throughout Lent.[3]

---

[1] When in the nineteenth century some bold spirit suggested that saints' feasts should be reduced in number, he brought down on his head the fulminations of Abbot Guéranger who said the holy Catholic faith was being attacked.

[2] See J. B. O'Connell, *Simplifying the Rubrics,* a commentary on the Decrēe *Cum Nostra* (London, 1955).

[3] The exceptions were great feasts like that of St Joseph, the Annunciation and a few others.

The old, unhappy order of things was decisively abolished by the Constitution on the Liturgy (102–108) and by the Calendar of 1969 which has
faithfully interpreted the injunctions of the Council.[4] The former (CL 108)
said that 'the minds of the faithful must be directed primarily towards the
feasts of the Lord whereby the mysteries of salvation are celebrated in the
course of the year. Therefore *the proper of time must be given the preference which is its due* over the feasts of the saints, so that the entire cycle
of the mysteries of salvation may be suitably recalled.' This the Calendar
has carried out. A simple inspection of it is sufficient to show that now the
celebration of the mysteries of salvation dominates the whole year. A few
figures will indicate the change of emphasis. Up to 1960 there were over
three hundred saints' feasts in the calendar, not counting those of the Lord,
Our Lady, the Apostles and certain New Testament saints. In the new
Calendar there are only sixty-three obligatory celebrations of saints and
ninety-five *ad libitum*.[5] What is even more significant is that Sundays have
now an almost unique position in the Calendar. They may only be superseded by 'solemnities' and feasts of the Lord, and in Advent, Lent and
Paschaltide they have absolute priority. With the celebration of the Lord's
paschal mystery on Sunday is closely linked that of the liturgy of Holy
Week, and it is to this that we now turn.

In the Introduction to the Calendar we find exactly the same emphasis
as is to be found in the Constitution on the Liturgy.[6] Like all the other new
liturgical documents it sets what formerly would have been a piece of dry
legislation in a liturgico-theological context. During the year the church
celebrates the 'saving work' of Christ on certain days and of these celebrations that of Holy Week/Easter is the most important, though it is this same
paschal mystery that is celebrated every Sunday of the year. At these times
the church 'makes the memorial' (*agit memoriam*) of the passion and death
of Christ for, as the Constitution said (CL 102), by so doing, the mysteries
of redemption are in a certain way made present to the people who are thus
enabled to lay hold of them.

There was some debate years ago about when the Liturgical Year began,
whether on the First Sunday of Advent or some other time. The Calendar
does not even glance at this debate. The paschal celebration of the Lord's
passion and resurrection (at Eastertime) is the culminating point (*culmen*)

---

[4] All sorts of wicked things have been said of the *Consilium* and of the Congregation for Worship that has superseded it. A prolonged examination of the work
and documents of both convinces me of their astonishing fidelity in interpreting
the decrees of the Council. If charges are to be brought against them, they must be
fairly laid at the doors of the bishops who by an almost unanimous vote brought
the Constitution into being.

[5] For these statistics see *La Maison-Dieu* (100, 1969) and J. D. Crichton, 'The
New Calendar', *The Tablet*, 10 January, 1970, pp. 46–7.

[6] *Calendarium Romanum: Normae Universales de Anno Liturgico et de Calen-
dario*, numbered in articles from 1–61 (Vatican Press, 1969), pp. 11–22.

of the whole Liturgical Year, it has absolute precedence over all other feasts or celebrations, it is put first in the list of precedence (59 (1)) and, to re-establish that it is a unitary celebration of the one Passover, it has been renamed. It is not merely the *Sacrum Triduum* (lit. 'sacred three days') but the *Paschal Triduum* and 'begins with the Evening Mass of the Lord's Supper (on Maundy Thursday), is centred upon the Paschal Vigil and ends with vespers on Easter Day' (18). Thus is restored to us in its full significance the most ancient celebration of the Christian church.[7] The impression has been finally removed that we were merely celebrating three holy days that 'commemorated' the last events of Christ's life. The three days form a whole in which the church celebrates the whole paschal mystery which is reflected (and participated in) in different ways throughout the period.

Next in order of importance comes the celebration of the Christian Sunday (4). This is the first and original (*primordialis*) feast of the church, celebrated by the apostles, and from which even the annual paschal celebration derives.[8] It is a festal day and should be kept as such. Because it is the weekly celebration of the paschal and saving mystery it has precedence over all feasts of saints (except a very few of the highest rank) and in Advent, Lent and Paschaltide it has absolute precedence over every kind of feast however great.[9] There are a few apparent exceptions during the year (Holy Family, Baptism of the Lord, Holy Trinity and Christ the King), but these are all 'feasts of the Lord', at least in the broad sense, and for the most part fit in well with the Sunday celebration of the paschal mystery. Other exceptions found in some countries, Epiphany, the Ascension and Corpus Christi, which are celebrated on the Sundays following the feast, are due to the exigencies of local situations: these feasts cannot be kept as real holidays, so the bishops of those countries have transferred these feasts to the following Sunday. There is much to be said for this policy.

Second only in importance to the annual and weekly celebration of the paschal mystery is the time after Easter (22–26). This is the oldest known season of the church's year. It is the sacred Fifty Days, already in existence in the second century, long before anything like Lent had evolved. It was regarded as a continual celebration of the paschal mystery and as St Athanasius called it 'The Great Sunday'.[10] Its observance, too, is kept intact

---

[7] For an account of how the paschal liturgy was broken down into *two* 'three days' (Thursday, Friday and Saturday/Sunday, Monday and Tuesday, the old 'Days of Devotion'), see Balthasar Fischer, in *Paschatis Sollemnia* (Freiburg i. Br. 1959), pp. 146–56; for a more summary account see J. D. Crichton, in *A Catholic Dictionary of Theology* (London, 1967), s.v. 'Easter, the Feast of', pp. 202–4.

[8] CL 108. For some commentary on the Christian Sunday, see J. D. Crichton, *The Church's Worship*, pp. 203–5.

[9] These are to be celebrated on the previous Saturday (5).

[10] Quoted *in loc., Epist. fest.* 1 (PG 26, 1366).

by the rules of the calendar and, as will be seen in a later chapter, the revisers have gone to great lengths to enrich this season of the year with new texts, both for the Sundays and the days of the week.

The season consists of seven Sundays that are evidently to be counted as 'Sundays of Eastertide'. 'Low Sunday' (as it has been called for long in the English tradition) is Easter II, since the Easter Octave ends with the Saturday. The following Sundays are numbered III, IV, V, VI, VII and Whitsunday is the last day of the *Pentecostē* or Fifty Days. Its octave, ancient as it is, is suppressed[11] and there can henceforth be no doubt that Pentecost, the Easter season, ends with Whitsunday.

Lent, as we have observed, had already been restored to its original observance—at least as far as the calendar is concerned—but the teaching of the Introduction unfolds its meaning: it is a preparation for the celebration of the paschal mystery. The main features of this preparation are the (organized) catechumenate and works of penitence. In addition, its limits are sharply defined: it runs from Ash Wednesday to the Evening Mass of Maundy Thursday exclusively. The sense of such a limitation is that on Thursday evening the church begins the celebration of the paschal mystery. Passion Sunday has been abolished[12] and the Sundays re-numbered accordingly from I to V, the sixth being what has been called for centuries Palm Sunday. This day is the prelude to Holy Week and the last act of Lent is the consecration of the Holy Oils at the morning Mass of Maundy Thursday (27–31).

It is necessary perhaps to say that the catechumenate element of Lent is not just an archaeological revival. In several countries now the catechumenate has been restored to meet a new pastoral need, and a new document on the subject is awaited from Rome at the time of writing. Nor is what the Introduction calls 'the keeping of the memorial of baptism' an archaeological attitude. As we have learnt in more recent years, baptism is a beginning and not an end and we have to live out its implications throughout our lives.

Lent, too, is a privileged time and its observance is now virtually uninterrupted.

Thus are established the main lines of the church's year, and it is plain for all to see that it is essentially a celebration of the redeeming work of Christ.

'The church recalls the whole mystery of Christ throughout the year' (17), but the one mystery is broken down into its various aspects. Of these the most important is Christmas, which runs from the celebration of the Lord's birth beginning on the eve of 24 December and running to the Sunday after Epiphany or after 6 January if the latter feast is kept on a

---

[11] It was in fact a pseudo-octave and the week was originally concerned with fasting, prayer and the offering of the first-fruits of the harvest (cf *L'Eglise en Prière*, ed. Martimort, p. 743).
[12] The title is combined with that of Palm Sunday.

Sunday (32–38). Christmas retains its octave (apart from Easter, the only one in the year). The 'mysteries' of the infancy are kept (Sunday after Christmas is the feast of the Holy Family and the scripture readings of the season concentrate on what might be called the pre-history of Jesus) and it comes to an end with the beginnings of the public ministry at the Baptism of the Lord. The season is marked (1 January) by the celebration of the oldest feast of Mary as the Mother of God.

Advent (39–42) has until now been somewhat ambiguous in significance, no doubt thanks to the very various sources from which it was derived.[13] The new calendar dispels the ambiguity and states firmly that Advent is made up of two elements: a preparation for the first coming of Christ, celebrated at Christmas, and secondly the season when *by means of that event* we are led to look for his second coming at the end of time. The season is to be kept in a spirit of devotion and joyful expectancy. The penitential element is thus suppressed.

The season has two clearly defined parts, the first running from its beginning to 17 December and the second from that date until 24 December. This second part is totally taken up with the preparation of the coming of Christ in his nativity, and Mary, Joseph and John the Baptist have a prominent place in it.

To all this there remains only to be added the time of the Sundays of the Year which, says the Introduction (43–44), are celebrations of the 'mystery of Christ in its fulness'. There are thirty-four such Sundays, the exact number in any year being dictated by the date of the First Sunday in Advent. Some may regret the disappearance of their ancient titles 'Sundays after Epiphany' and 'Sundays after Pentecost'. The new system is, however, simpler and may be easier to fit into a liturgical year for which there will one day be a fixed Easter.

The new arrangement for Rogation and Ember Days (45–47) reveals that the church now realizes that a liturgy based on a Mediterranean culture is not adapted to a church that is universal, many parts of which have a quite different cycle of natural life. The Introduction also realizes, but perhaps not sufficiently, that vast areas of the world are no longer agricultural. These occasions are described as times when the church prays for harvests, the work of man's hands and for the different needs of mankind. They are also times of thanksgiving (45). Now they are to be adapted to the different conditions of time and space and local conferences of bishops are to determine them and to work out forms of service. Mass-formulas

---

[13] The penitential element seems to have come from Spain and the famous *Rotulus* of Ravenna seems to indicate a season of expectation of the first coming of Christ. Rome was late in adopting the season. See P. Suitbert Benz, *Der Rotulus von Ravenna* (LQF, 45, Münster, 1967). For the provision of prayers for seventh century Rome in the Gregorian Sacramentary, *Das Sacramentarium Gregorianum*, ed. D. Hans Lietzmann (LQF, 3, Münster, reprint of 1967), nos. 185–193.

are provided for these occasions in the new missal (Masses and Prayers for Various Occasions, III: 25–31).

This change, which was adumbrated in the *Corpus Rubricarum* of 1960 (346–7), presents an opportunity to work out suitable services for these occasions. A Bible Service is the obvious solution, but now that we have a form of Divine Office much more suitable for use by the people, it would be very appropriate to compose intercessions to be used in conjunction with the morning and evening offices of the new breviary. This should be perfectly feasible as the new breviary makes it possible to combine an office with the Mass. Praise, intercession and eucharist combined into one service would be a most suitable liturgical expression of these occasions and should ensure that a sufficient number of people attends them.

There remains the question of the *Sanctorale*, the calendar of saints, an infinitely contentious subject. A writer in *La Maison-Dieu* (no. 100, December 1969) gives a useful hint to help keep a sense of proportion: he says that it is naïve to suppose all the saints of paradise are or ever were in the calendar, that no human action is entirely free from arbitrariness and choices are always disputable.[14] Within the limits the revisers set themselves, one notices a genuine effort to make the calendar universal, both geographically and chronologically. Geographically, all five continents are now represented if, in the nature of the case, somewhat thinly: Japan, North America, Oceania and Africa (Uganda) all being represented by martyrs and South America by St Martin Porres ('very popular with Negroes and coloured people' says the commentary, p. 75), St Turibius, Archbishop of Lima, as well as St Rose of the same place. England in particular appears with the feast of St John Fisher and St Thomas More, which may be celebrated everywhere in the church on 22 June. The commentary on them suggests that their example of fidelity should be offered to Christians of our time. St Bede, however, has been reduced to only a permitted celebration, though St Boniface of Devon retains his status, no doubt on account of his importance as the apostle of the Germanies.

Chronologically, the selection of commemorations covers the whole period of the church's history from the beginning until recent times, St Maria Goretti (5 July) being the latest to be included as a permitted *memoria*. There is noticeable a certain emphasis on the early martyrs whose acts are authentic and those with dubious legends for the most part disappear. St Cecily, 'on account of her popularity', is a notable survivor, even though her legend is one of the most questionable. The Fathers of the Church are well represented and so are the 'Doctors'. Among the chief casualties are a number of early popes who appeared in former calendars as martyrs and who are now known not to have been so. Perhaps the chief weakness is the representative value of the more modern saints, or rather,

---

[14] This and the following paragraphs on the saints first appeared in *The Tablet* (10.i.1970) and are reproduced with permission.

of the failure of the church to produce really great characters in the last hundred years or so. No bishop later than St Charles Borromeo (sixteenth century) seems to rate an obligatory celebration, and although he was a great man in his time, he was very much of his time.

The total picture is a little odd and one is led to ask whether the canonization processes are all that they should be. Great numbers of holy foundresses have been canonized (or beatified) in the last one hundred and fifty years and only two bishops. St John Vianney stands out in solitary glory as the one parish priest, and there are no modern married women. What is supremely anomalous is that Cardinal Newman, a man who has had more influence in and outside the church for a hundred years, should be kept, apparently interminably, waiting in the wings.

However, the austerity of the saints' calendar is mitigated by the suggestion that here, too, diversity in unity is part of the vision of the church, and it rests with regions, dioceses, and religious families to construct their own local calendars. This has always been so, but this document gives the matter a notable impetus. Here in England, where we have an exceptionally rich hagiography (thanks to men like St Bede), where we have a roll of saintly men and women reaching from the earliest centuries until the seventeenth, it would seem to be our bounden duty to construct a calendar that will reflect the long tradition of English (and British) sanctity. If such a calendar were carefully constructed, I believe that the sixteenth-century martyrs could be incorporated without offence to anyone. Perhaps, too, some way could be found of honouring men of traditions other than our own: for example, Keble for the Church of England and Wesley for the Methodists.

To conclude, the new Calendar is broadly satisfactory, its teaching is important and of considerable pastoral value, and the balance held between the celebration of the Year of the Lord and that of saints is about right. What the future will hold is anyone's guess and no doubt attempts will be made once more to infiltrate saints' feasts into the Proper of Time. It is to be hoped that they will be resisted.

Much of the Introduction is naturally taken up with technical matters (e.g. 8–16, 49–55 (local calendars), table of precedence, 59), which are hardly of general interest. It is well enough known by now that the highly complicated system of the former calendars has been very much modified since 1955. Clashes of feasts and interweaving octaves are now a thing of the past. The new calendar has sought to exclude such confusion in the future by working out a quite simple system of precedence. There are three classes, described as 'solemnities', feasts and 'commemorations',[15]

---

[15] The Latin is *'memoriae'* and presents difficulties of translation though it is a term long used in the monastic calendar. 'Commemoration' as above gives to older people the sense of a second feast, kept on the same day, and commemorated in the

these last being either obligatory or *ad libitum*. Particular (i.e. local or 'religious') calendars have, broadly, to harmonize with the general calendar (49–55). The rules seem to be sufficient to prevent any undue invasion of the Proper of Time while at the same time making provision for local celebrations. One of the features is that locality, as in so many other documents, is firmly written into the system. For example, the general rule is that only saints with a genuine local attachment are to be celebrated in any diocese or region.

However, the whole matter of keeping saints' feasts of minor grades (obligatory commemorations and the permitted ones) needs re-examining. The rules (referred to in Chapter ten) do preserve one principle that is very important: normally the daily course of scripture can be read on such days. But in effect the observance of these minor days does mean that it is only priests and religious who keep them. Even with the now-established custom of evening Masses the people are for the most part not able to do so. On the other hand the calendar would certainly be bleak without saints' feasts. I do not see any solution to the problem unless it be that local saints are celebrated locally, whether in the parish or the diocese (on the assumption that we have smaller dioceses) and that these celebrations are truly festivals, marked by some 'secular' rejoicing. This would indeed keep before people that 'feasts' are festivals, and we can be well content that most of the saints in the general calendar are 'commemorations'.

Mass and the office. Since this practice is virtually obsolete, 'commemoration' can do service and since the term is applied only to saints' feasts, whose *historical* entry into heaven is being 'commemorated', it is not inappropriate.

CHAPTER EIGHT

THE ROMAN MISSAL OF 1970;
A DESCRIPTION OF ITS CONTENTS

CLERICS have probably forgotten that there was once a time in their lives when the old missal appeared to be a very complicated book and that when as laymen they were 'following the Mass with a missal' they had considerable difficulty in finding their way about it. Even after they were ordained many, regrettably, never explored its content sufficiently and neglected large parts of it. However, they got used to it and on coming to a new missal will no doubt renew some of their youthful dismay. For though the new missal does in some ways follow the pattern of the Roman missal that was based on the *missalia plenaria*[1] of the eleventh century, its arrangement is somewhat different from that of the 1570 missal. Further there are certain *new* features that make some description, however summary, a necessity.[2]

Physically the *Missale Romanum*[3] is a very beautiful and noble book. The paper is of excellent quality, the typeface agreeable and easy to read, the rubrics are in a true terra-cotta red and what is more important than all, the lay-out of the pages is generous—plenty of space around the individual items. Normally, the texts of a Mass lie before one: no turning over is necessary. The binding is solid and opens very well in almost all parts. With the various documents, already mentioned, that come at the beginning, the whole book makes a volume of 966 pages.[4]

The first feature that will strike the reader is that it is fundamentally a sacramentary in the tradition of the Gelasian and Gregorian. It is without

---

[1] That is, missals containing not only the prayers but also the choral parts and eventually the lectionary.

[2] In what follows I am much dependent on an article of Mgr Jounel's in *La Maison-Dieu* (103, 1970), 'Le Missel de Paul VI', pp. 16–45. Among other things I take my statistics from him.

[3] Vatican Press, 1970.

[4] My only reservation is about the illustrations which presumably purport to be 'modern' but are often at once dull and mannered. It is unpardonable that the prefaces should be divided from the eucharistic prayers by a full-page illustration of the crucifixion. For two generations liturgists have been trying to inculcate into the people that the eucharistic prayer runs from the beginning of the preface to the doxology, and here this teaching is virtually denied.

lectionary and contains the prayers to be used at the eucharist. It differs only in pattern from the sacramentaries in that it has included the entrance and communion texts.[5] Its spine is, of course, the liturgical year (as set out in the calendar)[6] and the 'Proper of Time' is organized around the great feasts and seasons of Advent, Christmas, Lent and Paschaltide, ending with Whitsunday.

The Proper of Time

Advent. As before, there are four Sundays which retain their old introits and communion texts but are endowed with four new collects. For week-days there are six new Mass-formulas for the days from the beginning until 16 December with collects (and other prayers) for every day in the week. From the 17–23 December there is a Mass formula for each day.

Christmas begins with 24 December, Christmas Eve (the Mass intended only for use in the evening). Christmas Day has the midnight, dawn and day Masses as usual (alternative introit for the midnight Mass). The rest of the period is provided with the formulas for the feast of Holy Family, the solemnity of Mary the Mother of God, and three ferial Masses for 29, 30 and 31 December. (The feasts for 26, 27, 28, for England 29, and the *memoria* of 31 December are to be found in the 'Proper of Saints'.)

There is a Mass-formula for II Sunday after Christmas, which is fol-lowed by those for Epiphany and the Baptism of the Lord. Six ferial Masses with alternative collects to be used before and after Epiphany are provided for the days from 2 January to the Saturday before the Baptism of the Lord.

Lent follows with a Mass-formula for every day as before, but there is a proper preface for each Sunday of Lent, included in the Sunday texts.

Holy Week. The liturgy of Holy Week from Palm Sunday to Easter follows.

Eastertide. Mass formulas are provided for the ferias in Easter week and for the seven Sundays of the season. The Ascension appears after VI Sun-day and Pentecost (with a Saturday evening Mass and the Mass of the day) concludes the Easter season and the Proper of Time. The formulas for ferias during the weeks of Easter time appear after the feast of Pentecost.

The Sundays of the Year. Thirty-four Mass-formulas for these Sundays are placed next. It is to be noted that alternatives are given for the com-munion verse, the second for the most part being taken from the gospels and is to be used when the gospel text appears in the Mass for the day.

---

[5] The offertory verses have disappeared.
[6] See above.

The Solemnities of the Lord (occurring during the year).   These consist of the feasts of the Holy Trinity, of the Body and Blood of Christ (formerly Corpus Christi), the Sacred Heart and the Kingship of Christ.

The Order of the Mass.   This appears at this point, rather less than half-way through the book. It consists of the Order of the Mass with the people and that when there are no people present. It includes 51 of the prefaces out of the 82 all told, the rest appearing in their proper places in the course of the missal. The four eucharistic prayers appear after the prefaces and before the Rite of Communion. An appendix follows, giving the alternative greetings of the Mass, the alternative acts of penitence, alternative beginnings and conclusions of prefaces that may be used in the making of vernacular versions, the alternative acclamations after the consecration, the Solemn Blessings (to which we have referred) and Prayers over the People which may be said before the blessing at any Mass during the year.

The Proper of Saints.   This runs from 1 January to 31 December (not from November–December as in the old missal). Each solemnity and feast has a proper Mass-formula and almost every *memoria* has at least a proper collect.

The 'Commons'.   This has been completely reorganized. It is made up as follows: Dedication of a Church (regarded as a feast of the Lord), the Blessed Virgin Mary, Martyrs, Pastors, Doctors, Virgins, men and women saints (six formulas), religious (two formulas), those conspicuous for works of mercy, educators or simply holy women. If it be thought that these last groups are superfluous, the intention is that they should be used as models for the construction of Mass-formulas for local calendars (cf Instruction *De Calendariis*, 1970).

Ritual Masses.   This is a new title and to all intents and purposes a new section. All the sacraments and some other ecclesial acts may now be celebrated within the Mass and this section provides for this new situation. It has Mass-formulas for the various stages of Christian initiation, the catechumenate, baptism, and confirmation. There are others for ordination, for the administration of Viaticum, for weddings (three formulas), wedding anniversaries (also three), for the consecration of virgins and for the renewal of religious vows.

Masses and Prayers for Various Occasions.   Although the old missal had a section something like this, this is really new both in its texts and in the variety of occasions it provides for. The Pope in his Constitution refers to it specially as showing the concern of the church for all the needs of modern man. There are three sections that cover what are substantially public needs and may be used in public Masses. A fourth section gives formulas for more private needs (e.g. for a family) and may not normally be used in public Masses. There are 46 titles in all and many of them show the influence of the Second Vatican Council, some of their texts apparently being taken from council documents.

Votive Masses. These, says the General Instruction (329), are to serve the devotion of the people (and so not primarily the devotion of the priest). The texts given are for Holy Trinity, the Eucharist, the Name of Jesus, the Precious Blood, the Sacred Heart, Our Lady (a reference is given to the Common), Angels, St Joseph, Apostles, Sts Peter and Paul, one Apostle and All Saints. It will be seen that this section is much reduced and the slightly bizarre Masses for things like the Holy Winding Sheet or the Holy Lance and Nails have gone.

Masses for the Dead. This has been not only completely revised but completely re-thought. It is now an immensely rich anthology of scripture texts and prayers about Christian death, clearly reflecting its paschal character in accordance with the Constitution on the Liturgy (81). Not only this, but every possible category of person has been thought of. There are Masses for pope, bishops, priests (and deacons), of course, but also for a young person ('May he enjoy perpetual youth in heaven'), for one who has been suddenly taken away, for one, on the other hand, who has died after a long illness and, not to mention others, for a child and for parents who have lost an unbaptized child.

Appendix. The appendix gives the formulas for blessing water (it may be done in place of the penitential act in the Mass on Sundays), specimens for the General Intercessions (for every season of the year and for funerals), the preparation before Mass and thanksgiving after it (the prayers are the traditional ones, so traditional that the one beginning *Ad mensam* still bears the title *Oratio Sancti Ambrosii*!, only the list is a little shorter), the plainsong for various texts of the liturgy, and finally three indexes: one, alphabetical, of all the 'celebrations' (i.e. solemnities, feasts, etc.), two, of the prefaces (necessary because some of them may be used on a variety of occasions) and three, a general index of the whole book.

It will be seen that the job has been done competently and efficiently and represents a quite herculean labour.

Collects

A missal, however, which is the euchology or prayer-book of the church is going to stand or fall by the quality of the prayer-texts that are to be found within it. The revisers were fully aware of this and in the General Instruction is indicated their sense of its importance:

'Among the prayers that belong to the priest the eucharistic prayer has first place because it is the climax of the whole celebration. After that come the prayers, that is the collect, the prayer over the offerings and that after communion. These prayers, said by the priest who presides over the people, acting in the person of Christ and in their name and in that of the whole people, are directed to God. They are therefore rightly called presidential prayers' (GI 10).

We must then give these prayers some consideration, though it is manifestly impossible to consider them all, especially when we remember that there are 187 collects from the beginning to Advent to the last Sunday of the year, not counting Holy Week.[7] There are of course, in addition, prayers over the offerings and those after communion. We shall confine ourselves to some remarks on the collects and one or two brief comments on the prayers over the offerings.

An examination of the Proper of Time reveals that from Advent to Pentecost all the Sunday collects are 'new' (even those from the Gregorian Sacramentary for Advent have been replaced) and one is immediately prompted to ask: where do they come from? A brief investigation showed that some have come from the Gelasian Sacramentary, though it is very difficult to discover how many since the lists of *incipits*, now regularly printed in modern editions of sacramentaries, do not always or often give the clue. Mgr Jounel, who was on the sub-commission for the redaction of the new missal, tells us that they made a complete investigation of all the sources of the Latin liturgy, the Gregorian, the Gelasian (in both its editions), the Verona (or Leonine) as well as the Ambrosian books and those that are compendiously called 'Gallican'.[8] Wherever they found prayers of good quality they laid them under contribution for the formation of the new euchology.

This does not mean, however, that they have merely 'lifted' prayers from the ancient sources. Anyone who has browsed in, say, the Gelasian or the Leonine Sacramentaries, knows that the texts are often visibly corrupt, that the 'authors' were often content with an approximation to what they wanted to say and, indeed, were sometimes the victims of the *cursus* which dictated what they in fact said. The revisers, then, have corrected them in the light of all that is known of this kind of prayer and especially by comparing the versions as they appear in different sources. But they have also done something bolder. Discreetly but quite firmly they have adapted the prayers wherever they judged that they could enrich their content and improve their message. If the purist is inclined to shudder, let it be said that an examination of the revisers' work fully justifies their procedures.

Thirdly, the revisers have used the sources as a quarry from which to build new prayers. They soaked themselves in the prayer-language of the

---

[7] So Jounel, *art. cit.*, p. 18.

[8] And including those called 'neo-Gallican', drawn up mostly in the eighteenth century. At least one collect is based on a prayer of the Nîmes Missal.

sacramentaries so that they were able to recall almost at will phrases that have been incorporated into new prayers which, in fact, are entirely in the best Roman tradition.[9]

A good example of the first kind of correction and adaptation is to be seen in the collect for Easter Day, long known to have been 'edited', perhaps by St Gregory. The only way to show the methods of the revisers is to set out in Latin the three variations of the prayer.

Missal of Pius V (and Greg).	Missale Gallicanum Vetus (and Gel).	Missal of Paul VI
Deus, qui hodierna die, per Unigenitum tuum, aeternitatis nobis aditum devicta morte reserasti,		
vota nostra quae	da nobis, quaesumus,	da nobis . . . .
praeveniendo aspiras,	ut qui resurrectionis	. . . .
etiam adiuvando	dominicae sollemnia	. . . .
prosequere.	colimus, per innova-	. . . .
	tionem Spiritus *a mortis*	*in lumine vitae*
	animae resurgamus.	resurgamus.

For some reason, unknown to us, the last part of the prayer was diverted from asking for a paschal grace into something that looks like an anti-Pelagian prayer. The phrase 'that we who celebrate the mysteries of the Lord's resurrection' is obviously more appropriate to the day and the petition that follows from it is the right sort of thing to ask for at this time: 'By the renewal of the Spirit may we rise. . . .' But the revisers were rightly not very happy with '*a mortis animae*', from the death of the soul. This is too restricting and not quite in harmony with Pauline teaching. So the revisers adapted the prayer very slightly, putting in '*in lumine vitae*'. This is a slightly ambiguous phrase, but it does suggest baptism (and St Paul, Romans 6) and the consummation of the Christian life, resurrection to the light of glory.[10]

A few further examples of collects will give a notion of what I believe to be distinct improvements. It has been observed for instance[11] that the old Sunday collects of Lent never mentioned Christ. This has been rectified and each Sunday of Lent is provided with a new collect that reflects the gospel readings of Year I. Thus for the Second Sunday of Lent we have this:

O God, you commanded us to listen to your beloved Son.
May our hearts (*interius*) be fed with your word
so that our minds may be purified

---

[9] One has the impression that there have been some very fine Latinists employed in this work.

[10] It must be confessed that it is going to be a little difficult to translate. The whole of the foregoing paragraph is dependent on Jounel, *art. cit.*, pp. 37–8. How often the revisers have had recourse to this device I am unable to say. The examination of half-a-dozen sacramentaries would be a very lengthy business.

[11] Jounel, *art. cit.*

and we may rejoice at the sight of your glory.

A prayer that perfectly reflects the message of the gospel of the day. For the Fifth Sunday of Lent the message is turned in the direction of the paschal mystery soon to be celebrated in Holy Week:

Lord our God, out of love for all mankind

your Son gave himself up to death;

by his grace, may we remain in that love, readily following his example.

The Second Sunday of the Easter season (formerly 'Low Sunday') is provided with a rich and rather long prayer. It is from a Gallican source, *Missale Gothicum* (no. 305).[12] It will be best to give it in the Latin:

Deus misericordiae sempiternae

qui in ipso paschalis festi recursu

fidem sacratae tibi plebis accendis,

auge gratiam quam dedisti,

ut digna omnes intellegentia comprehendant,

quo lavacro abluti, quo spiritu regenerati,

quo sangine sunt redempti.

If the last three phrases can be translated as they demand, they will bring a note of splendid (but still prayerful) rhetoric into our liturgy.

God of unfailing love,

by their celebration of the annual feast of Easter,

you kindle the faith of the people that is dedicated to you;

increase in them the grace you have given

that they may grasp with their minds and hearts

the richness of the baptism wherewith they have been washed,

the depth of their inward renewal

and the price by which they have been redeemed, the blood of your Son,

Jesus Christ our Lord. . . .

Another prayer, for the Ascension, breathes yet an earlier world:

Fac nos, omnipotens Deus, *sanctis exsultare gaudiis,*

et pia *gratiarum actione laetari,*

quia Christi Filii tui *ascensio est nostra provectio,*

et quo processit gloria capitis,

eo spes vocatur et corporis.

The phrases underlined are from a sermon of St Leo *De Ascens.* I (PL 54, c. 396) and in effect a passage from that sermon has been shaped into a prayer giving the essential meaning of the feast. Here is a rough translation:

Almighty God, through your goodness

we rejoice with great joy

and give thanks in gladness of heart:

the ascension of Christ your Son spells our exaltation,

---

[12] See A. Dumas, *Notitiae* 61, February 1971.

for the Body in hope aspires to the glory
which the Head now enjoys.

Of the two Masses provided for Pentecost, the first, for the Vigil (to be said in the evening), stresses that the celebration of the paschal mystery is 'contained within the fifty days', thus clearly indicating that paschaltide ends with Pentecost; and the second, for the day, emphasizes the *missionary* task of the church. The collect asks that the gifts of the Spirit may be diffused throughout the world and that what was achieved through the divine mercy by the preaching of the gospel in the beginning may now be achieved by the work of believers. For the Vigil Mass there is an alternative collect which asks that the light of God's splendour may come upon us and that 'the light in which we see your light' (*lux tuae lucis*—cf Psalm 35:10) may be strengthened by a new illumination of the Holy Spirit. The post-communion prayer of the former missal which was so difficult to translate has gone and is replaced by a much better one, directly related to holy communion.

The main corpus of collects of the old missal are distributed throughout the Sundays of the year. The best have been kept and those no longer used in paschaltide are put into commission here. But even here we see the hand of the revisers, to the benefit of the prayers. The collect for XIV Sunday, the fine *Deus, qui in Filii tui humilitate iacentem mundum erexisti*, has been edited to its advantage. In the former version we prayed to be delivered from the falls that bring eternal death (*perpetuae mortis casibus*). The revisers turn it into a more Christian prayer: may we be delivered from the slavery of sin (*a servitute peccati*). It is a small touch but well worth making. On the other hand, the collects for this time are a little colourless, and some very brief, which makes their use in the liturgical assembly somewhat questionable. They are over so quickly that the people cannot grasp them. It was a pleasure, then, to come across a collect that has taken the twofold commandment of the New Testament and turned it into a prayer: 'O God, you set the fulfilment of the law in the love of you and our neighbour; grant that we may keep your commandments and so come to eternal life.' Although very slight, the last touch suggests Mark 9:17–22 (the rich young man: 'what must I do to inherit eternal life'). This again is a prayer that has been adapted, much to its advantage, from the Verona or 'Leonine' Sacramentary where it is confused and obscure. The revisers have made it more direct and more Christian.[13]

Another collect that is improved is that for the feast of the Holy Trinity. In the old version (generally attributed to Alcuin) the confessing of the

---

[13] *Sacr. Veron.* (ed. Mohlberg), no. 493. Even so, the heavily legal language of *Veron.* remains in the new (Latin) version: *sacrae legis, constituta, praecepta*, all in four lines! The Romans seem to have had an ineradicable tendency to think of love in terms of law.

trinity and the adoration of the unity in majesty was gloriously unclear, whether in Latin or English, as the celebrant rolled it out. The new version has added the 'processions' of the Word and the Spirit, but we are still asked to confess the true faith by acknowledging the trinity (of persons) and by adoring the unity (of nature) 'in the power of majesty'. The fact that I have had to add 'persons' and 'nature' shows how obscure the text is, and I just do not know *precisely* what is meant by *'in potentia majestatis'* which must apply to all three persons and not to 'nature'. The whole prayer, I suggest, could have been dropped and something quite new excogitated. There is a strong case for dropping the whole feast.

The whole Mass for Corpus Christi (as no doubt we shall go on calling it) remains the same. Evidently no one was disposed to change it and that is a witness to the excellence of the work of St Thomas Aquinas (if, of course, he wrote it). However, the collect is the only one I have noted in the whole missal that is addressed to the second person of the Trinity and then under the appellation 'Deus'.[14] On the other hand, both the feast of the Sacred Heart and that of Christ the King retain their address to the first person of the Trinity.

The collects for the Proper of Saints are extremely interesting and for the most part entirely new. In the old missal they were among the poorest texts in the missal. Either they repeated phrases again and again, and often from the Common, or they wandered on more like a baroque sermon than a collect. What is striking about the new collection is that in almost every case the prayer is closely related to the life of the saint and singles out, usually with great perception, the distinguishing mark of his life and work. Here are two examples, interesting because, in the old missal, they were both long, weary prayers, and the first retailed the legend of St Raymund flying about on his cloak (a legend attached to a number of other saints, too): the prayer says that St Raymund was conspicuous for his compassion for sinners and for the (Christian) captives who were enslaved by the Saracens; the petition, very neatly, is that we may be released from the slavery of sin and do what is pleasing to God.

The second is for the feast of St Francis of Sales: by God's grace Francis could be all things to all men for the salvation of souls (both phrases were in the old prayer but embedded in a mass of verbiage), and

---

[14] It *could* have been changed without great difficulty:

Deus, qui nobis sub sacramento mirabili

passionis *Christi Filii tui* memoriam reliquisti,

tribue quaesumus,

ita nos Corporis et Sanginis *eius* mysteria venerari,

ut redemptionis (tuae— om.) fructum in nobis iugiter sentiamus.

Alternatively it could begin *Domine, Iesu Christe,* which would keep the trinitarian relationships in order. The text as it stands suggests that 'God' 'suffered', which to the second century church would have suggested Patripassianism!

we pray that we may imitate the charity of God (a reference to his great book *L'Amour de Dieu*) by always serving our brethren.

Even the collect for St Thomas Aquinas has been shortened, re-written and, I think, improved: he was notable for his zeal for holiness and his ardent study of doctrine; may we understand what he taught and imitate him in what he did.

Sometimes the prayers are very concrete and in translating them you have to be careful. This is illustrated by the collect for St Paul Miki and Companions, martyrs (6 February). The Latin says: '*per crucem ad vitam* vocare dignatus es' which might seem no more than a cliché drawn from stock. Then you remember they were the Martyrs of Nagasaki and that they *were* crucified, so you must translate literally: 'you called Paul and his companions to undergo crucifixion and so enter life'.

Another prayer is an example of what can be done when the long and rich tradition of the Catholic liturgy is remembered and drawn on. It is again for modern martyrs, those of Uganda, Saint Charles Lwanga and companions:

The blood of martyrs is the seed of Christians.
Lord God, we ask that the blood of your martyrs, Charles and companions,
which they poured out on the field that is your church, may continually produce an abundant harvest to the glory of your name.

This, we are told, is based on a prayer from the neo-Gallican missal of the eighteenth century,[15] but we also notice the phrase that is owed to Tertullian (an African!) c. 200: 'the blood of martyrs is the seed of Christians'. So this prayer reaches from the end of the second century right up to present times and this is surely what is meant by *tradition*. The revisers have drawn on the *whole* Christian tradition of prayer and by so doing have immeasurably enriched our euchology. We can indeed drive the origins of the prayer back even further, for the simile of the church as a field is related to the parable of Matthew 13:24–30.

In some cases the prayers seem to be entirely new. Thus the collect for Sts Perpetua and Felicity, which briefly and tellingly recalls their (authentic) *acta*: they overcame the torture of (their) death, despising the persecutor; the petition is that we always grow in the love of God. This again is another touch one notices in the collects of martyrs: they are conspicuous examples of *love*; it is love and not the tortures that made them saints. In all this one marks a return to the ancient theology of martyrdom which saw them as the supreme examples of holiness because of their *imitatio Christi*: like him they suffered death out of love of God and their fellow-men.

Poor St George, whom the world has convinced itself has been virtually

---

[15] See Jounel *art. cit.*

kicked out of heaven, has been given a new and very splendid prayer that
is from an ancient source: [16]

Magnificantes, Domine, potentiam tuam, supplices exoramus,
ut sicut sanctus Georgius dominicae fuit passionis imitator,
ita sit fragilitatis nostrae promptus adiutor.

We glorify you, Lord, in your power and we humbly ask
that as saint George imitated Christ in his passion,
so he may always be a ready helper in our weakness.

Here, quite clearly, is the *imitatio Christi* theology of martyrdom and this,
the prayer suggests, is the essential thing about St George. All legends are
left behind, but on the other hand the prayer is a great deal 'warmer' than
the one in the old missal.

The collect for St Benedict (now 11 July) is very skilfully constructed
and manages to get in two key phrases from his Rule:

Deus, qui beatum Benedictum abbatem
in schola divini servitii praeclarum constituisti magistrum,
tribue quaesumus,
ut, *amori tuo nihil praeponentes*,
viam mandatorum tuorum dilatato corde curramus.

Benedict is a Master in the school of divine service—the service of God.
Then a bold adaptation: for the *nihil operi Dei praeponatur* of the Rule
the revisers have substituted nihil *amori* praeponatur, 'that we may put
God's love before everything else' and so run in the way of the commandments with generous hearts.

What others will think of such a procedure I do not know. I find it
completely acceptable that it should be possible to turn into prayer parts
of the Rule of one of the greatest spiritual guides of the Western church.
Among other things the revisers have made of it a prayer that all Christians
can pray, and that surely is required in a liturgy that is intended for all.[17]

One or two small observations must conclude our treatment of the Proper
of Saints. It will be remembered that St Vincent of Paul had a rather long
and cliché-ridden prayer. Now it says exactly the same only in about half
the number of words: he was notable for his concern for the poor and for
the clergy: may we love what he loved and do what he taught!

Finally, the prayer for St Thérèse of Lisieux has been re-written while
retaining all its substance. God opens his kingdom to the humble and to
little children (a clear reference to the gospel) and we pray that trustfully
(like St Thérèse) we may follow the way she went and so, by her intercession, come to the revelation of God's glory (as she did). Moreover, the

---

[16] It seems to be inspired by the Verona Sacramentary no. 733, though the last
part is quite different and I do not know where it comes from.

[17] Apart from the phrases from the Rule, I do not know the source of the
prayer or even whether it has one.

prayer is now addressed to God the Father which not only makes it a better prayer but much more appropriate to the saint whose message was so very much the fatherly love of God for mankind.

One turns to the section providing texts for various occasions and needs with some interest. It is said to be the newest part of the missal and in the sense that a great many more occasions are provided for than in the old missal this is true. It is also clear that Vatican II has influenced the composition of a number of the prayers, especially those on the church, but the general picture given is still that of a largely agricultural society. Earthly rulers are provided for and even the United Nations, but there is nothing about modern technological society, nothing about the investigations of scientists who have changed the face of the earth for good and for ill, nothing about the work of doctors or nurses upon whom modern society is so dependent. That said, the provision made is generous, three Mass-formulas being given for the church, for Christian Unity and for one or two other occasions.

The collects for the church reflect Vatican II quite clearly: the first (A) sees that it is God's will that Christ's kingdom should be spread throughout the world and asks that the church should be the 'sacrament' of salvation to all, the sign of God's love for all men and the means by which the mystery (of Christ) shall be made present among them.

This last point is made very strongly in the prayer (E) for the local church which, united to its pastor, and gathered in the Spirit by the Word of the Gospel and by the Eucharist (the combination of the two reflects the Constitution on the Liturgy) is to be the sign and instrument (*instrumentum*) of Christ's presence in the world.

Another prayer (C) sees the church's union as reflecting that of the Father, Son and Holy Spirit and as, consequently, the 'sacrament' of holiness and unity in the world.

In the prayers for the pope there are references to the gospel passages about Peter. Thus in Mass A the collect sees him as the head of the apostles and the one on whom the church is built (Matthew 16:18), and the petition is that he may be the visible source and foundation of unity of faith and communion. This is a thought carried further in prayer B where there is a reminiscence of Luke 22:32 about Peter confirming the brethren, and the prayer asks that the whole church may be in communion with him and that he may be the bond of unity, love and peace. These prayers, it seems to me, have been written in an ecumenical spirit and in the event of restored unity they would still be most appropriate.

There are three (good) Mass-formulas for Christian Unity, the collect of the first asking that those who are (already) made one holy people by the same baptism may share an integral faith and be bound together by the bond of love. The collect of the third Mass is a prayer more specifically for the situation as it is now: may a love of truth grow and by effort and zeal may the perfect unity of Christians be achieved.

After a variety of prayers for the pope, for bishops, priests and other ministers there is a prayer for the laity, again echoing the Council documents. Here we note that it is the 'power of the *gospel*' that is to be the leaven of the world (rather than the church) and the petition is that the laity may restore God's kingdom precisely through their work in the world. The postcommunion prayer asks that they may make the church present and effective in the world.

There is a whole Mass-formula for persecuted Christians, the collect of which states that God has willed his church to be associated with the sufferings of his Son. This reminds us of Pascal's *Jésus sera en agonie jusqu'à la fin du monde*, a sentiment that Leo the Great gave utterance to eleven centuries earlier. In a sermon on the Passion he said: 'The Passion of the Lord is prolonged until the end of the world . . . it is he who suffers in and with all who bear adversity for righteousness'.[18] The petition goes on that those who suffer for God's name may have the spirit of patience and love and be found true and faithful witnesses of his promises.

There are prayers for the nation, for rulers and for the United Nations. This last asks that its representatives may act wisely, seek the good and peace of all and not depart from God's will. In this context there is a long prayer for the Advancement of Peoples (*Populorum progressio*, in the Latin) which unmistakably reflects both the Council document on the Church in the Modern World and the pope's encyclical of that title. It runs: all peoples have a common origin in God and it is his will that they should be one family. Fill the hearts of all with love, *enkindle in them a desire for just progress*. May the goods (of this earth) that are distributed abundantly (*affluenter*) to all, make for human dignity so that equity and justice may be established in human society.

An investigation of the prayers over the offerings and those after communion would be very lengthy. We must content ourselves with two observations. The prayers over the offerings in the old missal (and they come from traditional Roman sources for the most part) were very puzzling. Often they seemed to attribute all sorts of effects, which could only be those of the eucharistic action itself, to the bread and wine lying on the altar. The only way to interpret them was by prolepsis: they were being spoken of *as if* they were already consecrated, and this seems to have been part of the Roman (and, indeed, Byzantine) tradition. The action of the eucharistic prayer, as it were, flowed back on the offerings. It is a mentality that is very different from our own, for if we can see that the whole

---

[18] De Pass. XIX, PL, 54, c. 383: '*Passio enim Domini usque ad finem producitur mundi . . . in omnibus qui pro iustitia adversa tolerant ipse compatitur*'. Perhaps the revisers could have made use of this passage.

eucharistic prayer performs the action, we find it difficult to extend its effect outside the prayer. A cursory examination of the new prayers over the offerings seems to show that much that was difficult to understand in this respect has been removed. One example is an illustration of this. It is the prayer for the V Sunday of the year: God has given us these created things for the support of our human nature: may they become for us the *sacramentum*, the efficacious sign of eternal life. It is a prayer that sees very clearly the *symbolism* of the elements used in the eucharist and so what is their function and purpose.

The prayers after communion in the old missal were often monotonous and astonishingly medical in their language. Again and again in the new missal one finds that the prayers are asking for a whole variety of effects, usually within the context of the Mass of which they are a part.

This rich anthology of prayers does, however, raise questions. The sources have been investigated, a fine discernment has been shown in the selections made from them, the modern compositions are for the most part worthy to stand by them, the rhythms (*cursus*), so far as I can judge, have been beautifully constructed, and in *Latin* these prayers are going to be very satisfactory to say. But they remain *Latin* prayers and, quite apart from the difficulty of translating them adequately, they have a mentality that is not always that of the modern English-speaking world. It may be true[19] that we need to go to school with the great Roman writers of the past for our liturgical forms. It could indeed be said that we need to *learn* from them how to pray in public and it may be admitted that if this tradition had been ignored the results would have been calamitous. But the question remains, and it may be that we shall have to think of this euchology as a stage on the way to a more native form of prayer. It is not just a question of finding 'modern language' in which to express what we need. There are whole situations which demand a different kind of expression, and this we shall eventually have to find for ourselves. The very form of the collect is the product of a particular culture and indeed of a particular era within that culture. It is highly probable that the Roman collect began to be written in the fifth century. By the ninth century at the latest the art was lost in spite of the fact that there were a few successes later than that time. The collect is the expression of a very hieratic type of worship (the utterance of the president was thought to be *all*-important) and its literary form with its conciseness and brevity makes it a difficult prayer-medium for modern Christians whose minds do not work in that way. It is conceivable that a much looser form of prayer is required which would consist of a series of statements or invitations (rather like the General Intercessions of the Mass) and the responses of the people. Much of the essence of the

---

[19] As Jounel suggests, *art. cit.*

collects could be preserved in this form, but it would allow of a much greater flexibility, easily admit a greater variety of subjects and provide a greater participation by the people in the prayer. Rome has apparently seen that the present situation is not quite satisfactory, since the rubric in the missal for Good Friday says that local conferences of bishops may insert acclamations for the people between the invitation of the celebrant and the prayer in the great series of intercessions on that day. This form, which is almost certainly the oldest Roman form of prayer, is in itself more acceptable than the usual one, and it is all the more significant that this adaptation has been suggested for this occasion. The whole form, invitation, acclamation (petition, etc.), prayer and final response (Amen) may well provide a model for the sort of prayer that is suitable to modern Christians.

The Prefaces

If the prayers are derived from the sacramentaries, the distinguishing feature of the many new prefaces is that they echo the scriptures. Homiletically this is of great importance for it means that what has been heard in the scripture readings and expounded in the homily is now echoed in prayer. It is an old device perhaps and the Roman liturgy has done it in a variety of ways (notably in the Divine Office), but too often in the past the Sunday liturgy appeared to be no more than an haphazard miscellany of texts and sometimes was. The preface, as we have observed in speaking of the eucharistic prayer, is *proclamation*, the proclamation of the message of salvation, and may be regarded as the pivot of the ministry of the word. It picks up the themes of the gospel (or other readings) and leads the people into the celebration of the eucharist so that they are able to see that the events of salvation are here and now being actualized. Practically, it means that the people should be able to see the whole Mass-formula as a coherent whole and psychologically, if they hear the scriptures being expounded in the homily and echoed in the preface, they will both understand and remember the message of the day.

The prefaces that have already come into use, for instance, those for Advent and the Sundays of the year, have already made this point clear. In that for Advent II there is a résumé of all the gospel teaching for the last days of the season: the virgin-mother receives the Word with love beyond all telling into her womb, St John the Baptist proclaims that he was to come, points him out when he does and Christ fills us with joy as we prepare to celebrate the *mysterium nativitatis*, the saving mystery of his birth. Preface I for the Sundays of the Year is a résumé of I Peter 2:4–9, II is thoroughly Pauline and Common I puts in prayer-form the teaching of Philippians 2:6–11.

But it is with the Sundays of Lent that we find the closest relationship between the preface and the gospel. Lent I draws out (part of) the meaning of the Temptation in the Wilderness and ends by asking that 'celebrating the paschal mystery (now) we may pass to the celebration of the eternal passover', thus indicating that Lent is orientated to Easter. Lent II reflects the Transfiguration, Lent III the gospel of the Samaritan woman (which may be read every year) and takes its message from the gospel itself. Lent IV (the gospel of the man born blind) refers to baptism: we, born the slaves of sin, are made children of God by the waters of baptism. The preface of Lent V (the raising of Lazarus) naturally speaks of the new life that will be given to us by the celebration of the *sacra mysteria*. This compendious phrase includes both the celebration of baptism (and confirmation) and the celebration of the 'mysteries of our redemption' in Holy Week.

With VI Lent (Palm Sunday) there is a change. The preface takes up the theme of the Servant Song of Isaiah 52:13–53:12, and in the Latin manages to echo verse 12 *'cum sceleratis reputatus est'* (*'pro sceleratis condemnari'*): Jesus was innocent, yet suffered for the guilty and was unjustly condemned for the wicked; his death has wiped away our sins and his resurrection has reconciled us to God.

These prefaces are short, but with Maundy Thursday we get a (new) long preface for the Chrism Mass in which a vast amount—perhaps too much—of teaching is contained. It is, however, interesting for the emphasis it gives on the priestly church and the view it expresses that 'men are chosen out from this priestly community' to serve the rest. It can best be presented by a synopsis:

a)   God anointed his Son high priest of the new and eternal covenant and planned that 'this one priesthood' should continue in the church;

b)   Christ gives this royal priesthood to the people he has made his own;

c)   but he chooses men to share his ministry by the laying on of hands;

d)   in his name they are to renew the sacrifice of redemption, setting before God's family the paschal meal;

e)   they are to nourish them by the word;

f)   strengthen them by the sacraments;

g)   be leaders of the holy people in love;

h)   be ready to give their lives for them;

i)   and they are called to spiritual maturity by growing 'in likeness to Christ'.

In all this we see the influence of the documents of Vatican II, though one feels that this preface is too packed and too didactic to be successful as a prayer.[20]

As we have observed above, a new collect for the Ascension is virtually

---

[20] This synopsis and a few phrases in the previous paragraph are from my book *The Liturgy of Holy Week*, A Companion to the Revised Order of 1970 (Birmingham, 1971), pp. 14 and 19.

a passage from St Leo which has been re-worded into the form of a prayer. A new preface for the feast likewise reflects the same writer. This means that collect and preface will be delivering the same message and, with a judicious choice of prefaces for the Sunday of the Year, the same will be true on other occasions also.

There are *eight* prefaces for the Sundays of the Year and if we are to avoid monotony, all of them are necessary and all should be used. As I have indicated above, some selection will be necessary. If we look into their content we find that again they are based on scripture, that they repeat the teaching of the paschal mystery (Sunday is the Day of the Lord, a 'little Easter') but throw different lights on it. A theme that appears here and elsewhere is that of the eschatological issue of the paschal mystery. Thus Sunday Preface VI which is a closely-knit anthology of Pauline doctrine proclaims that since we live, move and have our being in God (Acts 17:28—an echo of an ancient Greek poet) and are made by him (*ibid.* v. 26), we have experienced in our lives the effects of his love and mercy and already we have the guarantee of a life that is eternal. Possessing 'the first fruits of the Spirit who raised Jesus from the dead, we hope to possess eternally the paschal mystery'.

We meet again in Sunday Preface VIII one of the underlying themes of Vatican II, that the unity of the church derives from the unity of the Trinity and it is described as the people (of God), the body of Christ and the temple of the Holy Spirit. Perhaps a little too much for one text, but it does bring before us a whole wealth of doctrine about the church which is too easily forgotten.

If we turn to other prefaces prescribed for other occasions and times and look into them for some distinctively modern note we are disappointed. There is a Sunday Preface (V) which is headed 'On creation' which sums up very skilfully, a good deal of Genesis I: God has made all the elements of the world and ordered the changing seasons; he formed man to his own likeness, subjected all the wonders (*miracula*) of creation to his power and placed him in charge over them (*vicario munere*) so that he may praise God for all the wonders of his works. The text recognizes that there are wonders of creation (and the use of the word '*miracula*' is interesting), but it says nothing about *man's* uncovering of the wonders of creation. It goes on to say that man enjoys a certain charge over them; they are to be used by him and, we may gloss, the potentialities God has put into things are to be used (and not abused) by man. But one feels that if the revisers had been in close contact with modern thought and life they would have hardly produced a prayer like this. The impression given to the sharp-minded young is that of a *Weltanschauung* that is no longer credible. 'God made all things'? Yes, but how? In the twinkling of an eye? And if man has a vicarious function in relation to created things, how far does his writ run? Does God interfere? Some may think that this is to suggest a wicked 'demythologization of God'; others that to mistake poetry for prose is just as crass an error.

In connection with prefaces there is one practical device the revisers have used that merits attention. Every preface is headed by a sentence giving the subject of the text and since this is a place where the celebrant may intervene with a brief catechesis, these headings will obviously suggest the content of his remarks. It is a matter that needs handling discreetly—the celebration can be too easily drowned in the verbiage of the celebrant, a danger that is not always avoided—but with certain congregations (e.g. children) a few remarks at this point are necessary. Very neatly the new missal has provided a useful tool.

Since these headings are of some importance and indicate in any case the subject matter of the prefaces, it will be of interest to give those for the Sundays of the Year:

I   On the Paschal Mystery and the People of God.
II   On the Mystery of Salvation.
III On the Salvation of Man by Man.
IV   On the History of Salvation (a very brief recalling of it).
V   On Creation.
VI   On the Pledge of the Eternal Passover.
VII Salvation through the Obedience of Christ.
VIII On the Unity of the Church derived from the Unity of the Trinity.

Introits and communion verses

One of the most puzzling features of the new missal is the provision it has made for introits and communion verses. For the Proper of Time they are almost exactly the same as those of the old missal. The exceptions I have noted are no more than alternatives for the Midnight Mass of Christmas and Whitsunday. There are some *additions* for the Sundays of the Year. This is so extraordinary a situation that one felt it was necessary to seek light on the subject, and it is to be found in the article of Mgr Jounel.[21] It will be best to quote from his article:

'The essence of these texts is that they should be said or read and *not sung*. It is in fact wrong to call them 'antiphons'—a more neutral term would have been better. Nor is it a question of preserving in the missal the greater part of the *Graduale Romanum* so that they can be translated into the vernacular. Hence the two books will follow a different course, as in fact they did for centuries. The *Graduale* will constantly be adapted to meet the changes imposed by the new organisation of the Proper of Time, but there has never been any question of composing neo-Gregorian melodies for new texts of the missal. Likewise, there is no point in having these antiphons sung in the vernacular: they were

---

[21] *Art. cit.*, pp. 41–4.

created to make up for the absence of song. A text destined for singing must be conceived on quite other lines.'

On the other hand the same writer goes on to say that it was out of the question to jettison altogether this great corpus of texts with their chant and, of course, where they (and the graduals) can be sung, they may continue to be sung.[22]

All this explains why these texts remain and, a smaller detail, why no references to psalms or their verses are given. They are not *meant* to be sung. How, then, are they to be used? I think we can distinguish. If the communion verses were set to music, perhaps even elaborate music, they could be suitable texts to assist the people's prayer during the time of holy communion. Obviously, this would be the work of a choir, which would have to be competent, but it would give them a role which some people say (wrongly, in fact) has been taken away from them and it would mean that the texts sung, instead of being more or less haphazard motets, would be an integral part of the liturgy of the day. This will be all the easier to achieve since on many Sundays (and all the Sundays of the Year) alternative texts are provided from the New Testament. Where they are not sung (and this will be the usual situation), the celebrant will be able to use them to lead the people in their meditation after communion.

It is apparently lawful to use the introit verses in a similar fashion, according to the opinion of Mgr Jounel:[23] 'The purpose of these antiphons is to help the people to enter into the spirit of the day. The manner of executing them will depend on the mentality of different peoples. In France, a brief address from the priest will be more helpful in creating a united and lively assembly than the reading of the text by a few of the faithful.' Since the *Ordo Missae* provides for such an intervention between the greeting and the act of penitence, the text of the introit will, quite naturally, supply the matter for such an intervention. We note in any case that on certain days the text takes this form: 'Let us all rejoice in the Lord: our Saviour has been born into the world. Today true peace has descended on us from heaven' (alternative introit for the Midnight Mass of Christmas). This is the sort of interpretation that does not easily occur to the more prosaic Anglo-Saxon mind and, coming from one who worked on the subcommission that produced the missal, it has a good deal of force. He, if anyone, is likely to know 'the mind of the legislator'. Used in this way, then, these texts can be very helpful not only on Sundays but also on other days too, such as those in paschaltide which are now provided with an extremely

---

[22] If there is a case for singing introits and communion verses, I do not see that there is one for singing the graduals. The ministry of the word is now a closely integrated whole, the psalm is a commentary on the readings, and unless the verbal text of the gradual is such a commentary, it is totally irrelevant to the day's celebration.

[23] *Art. cit.*, p. 41.

interesting series, illustrating almost every aspect of the paschal mystery. This interpretation, too, releases us from the agonizing problem of trying to devise musical settings, admitting of the participation of the people, for these texts.

CHAPTER NINE

CELEBRATION[1]

COMMUNITY, participation, the importance of the word of God, these constituents of the liturgy have received considerable emphasis in the course of this book. Another word, 'celebration', appears frequently in the new liturgical documents and it needs elucidation. Sometimes, it is true, it is used in a neutral way but at other times it seems to be saying more. Thus, Bible Services are called 'Celebrations of God's Word', the Order of Baptism speaks of 'celebrating' the sacrament and in the Order of the Mass the General Instruction opens with the heading 'The Importance and Dignity of the Celebration of the Eucharist'. What follows is an investigation into its meaning which, it is hoped, will throw light not merely on eucharistic celebration but on the celebration of the whole of the liturgy.

It is arguable, and Harvey Cox in his *Feast of Fools*[2] argues it, that modern people have forgotten how to celebrate and the reason for this he sees in the development of Western culture. The emphasis on the rational, as in medieval scholasticism, the scientific, which it prepared, and on activity, work and production in more recent times, have atrophied the sense of keeping festival and what Harvey Cox calls fantasy, which he associates with festivity and which later he shows is imagination. Proofs immediately spring to mind. The seventeenth century Puritans banished holidays and they and their descendants worshipped work. In the last fifty years the poet has appeared as a more and more peripheral character and probably no age of European culture has produced so little poetry as our own. Anglo-American society is geared to production, to the production of ever more and more goods, almost regardless of whether anyone needs them or can buy them. As the same writer remarks, we have indeed produced the monumental achievements of Western science and industrial technology but in doing so we have not only done it at the expense of millions of people in the poor nations and of the environment in which we live, but we have damaged the inner experience of man (*ibid.*, p. 12). It is a heavy indictment and I do not think it can be gainsaid.

In all this the liturgy appears as a peripheral activity, without influence on social life, indulged in by 'religious' people who indeed for the most part

[1] Part of this chapter appeared in *Life and Worship*, April 1971, and acknowledgements are gratefully made to the Society of St Gregory.
[2] Harvard University Press, 1969.

get little enough joy out of it. The term 'feast-day' has been reduced to a title in a church calendar, and perhaps the most peculiar manifestation of our mentality is the term 'holiday of *obligation*'—obligation completely obscuring the idea of holiday. It is just one more occasion for committing mortal sin, as, technically, so many millions do. In fact the only festivals worthy of the name the church still celebrates are those that the world has secularized, made its own. Christmas is the most notable example and Easter the most striking since its Christian content has almost entirely disappeared. Its symbols are not the Paschal Candle and the blessed water but the new hat and the motor car in which the family departs for the first excursion of the year. Nor is the performance of the liturgy marked by any particular joy, whether it is the old or the new that is in question. As a piece of worship the old low Mass was as dismal a liturgy as you could get and the new still lacks that note of poetry that would carry people beyond the concerns of everyday life. Partly responsible for this is its English, which betrays the typical work-a-day character of an efficient technological civilization. It is indeed a symbol of it and it is this world that has killed the religious vocabulary in which for centuries man has expressed himself in worship. No doubt in time we shall find such a language, and, more optimistically, we shall find music, movement and perhaps occasionally the dance that will express our celebration of the liturgy.

But if we are to understand celebration, we must go a little deeper and here the history of the word has something to offer. Celebrate obviously comes from *celebrare*, a word that at first sight seems somewhat negative. It is in fact quite rich in meaning. The adjective, for instance, suggests the notion of 'crowd' or 'multitude' and a famous place is one that 'contains a multitude of people'. The first meaning of the verb is 'to go in great numbers' to a place for celebration. The first element, then, of celebration is people, a crowd. One cannot celebrate alone. On Christmas Day I may be very happy reading a long and learned history of the Dark Ages, but I am not celebrating. Celebration requires community. On the other hand the Latin writers use the word in a way that is familiar to us: thus Cicero speaks of celebrating *festos dies*, Virgil of celebrating *coniugia*, weddings, and Livy of birthdays (*diem natalem*) and even of funerals (*exsequias*). These were variously national, civic and family occasions; communities large and small were involved. For Ovid there were celebrations marked by word (*sermone*) and joy (*laetitia*); he is speaking of a *convivium*, convivial meal, and thinking of the conversation and joy that accompanied it. People, conversation, joy are the elements of celebration that marked 'celebration' as it emerges from this brief historical review of the word.[3] To this may be added, according to the authors, yet another element, that of song, expressing honour and praise.

---

[3] The above details are taken from Lewis and Short, *A Latin Dictionary* (1907).

Roman (pagan) religion was at once intensely national and markedly domestic. The official liturgy was an expression of the life of the state. From Augustine onwards, although already becoming enfeebled, perhaps decadent, it enshrined the genius of the Empire more than any other activity. Roma Dea coupled with the worship of the Emperor was the object of the official celebrations. Whatever we may think of the 'theology' underlying it, worship and life were all but identified. At the same time, Rome religion was very domestic. Every home had its shrine—there were the *lares* and *penates*, the household gods—and, at least in pre-imperial days, it was the focus of family life. Roman religion was the religion of a community whether great or small. Yet, it was sober, perhaps a little grim, lacking the *élan* of the Dionysiac spirit that formed one important element in Greek worship. Roman worship failed to touch the deeper springs of man and that is why the people welcomed with an indiscretion that knew no bounds the Eastern mystery religions that carried them beyond the solemn rituals of state worship and drew them out of themselves into realms where fantasy could range free. Even so, the worship of the Roman Empire seems to have lacked joy and simple gaiety. There were bacchanalia, saturnalia, wild and unrestrained celebrations, there was a desperate seeking for some sort of salvation, a desire that the mystery religions ultimately failed to satisfy, and it was not until we come to the first accounts of Christian worship that we catch the note of a simple and unalloyed joy.

However, the Greek and Roman experience was by no means exceptional. Man has 'celebrated' or kept festival throughout the ages, and it is possible, even empirically, to discern other elements of celebration. There is a wide agreement among scholars that myth celebrated in ritual lies at the heart of celebration and that they are its ultimate source. Huizinga has seen man as *homo ludens* (man as a playing creature) and Romano Guardini saw the Christian liturgy in at least one aspect as a playing before God.[4] Harvey Cox isolates three elements that he regards as of the essence of festivity or celebration: excess, celebrative affirmation and juxtaposition.[5] By the first he means going beyond our day to day behaviour, taking 'a short vacation from convention' and doing things we do not normally do (wearing funny hats) or in a way that we do not usually do them (e.g. a festive meal). The important feature here, I think, is the breaking away from routine, the willed exclusion of daily concerns and, of course, worries, the desire carried into execution to break through the apparently inevitable round of work, production, getting on, making money and all the rest of the activities that occupy nine-tenths of man's life. In fact he links festivity with fantasy and says that man is the *homo festivus* by nature as well as the *homo fantasis*[6] and by 'excess' he seems to mean precisely this element

---

[4] *The Spirit of the Liturgy* (Eng. trans. London, 1930), pp. 171 ff.

[5] *Op. cit.*, pp. 22–6.

[6] It seems that he had not the courage to say *homo fantasticus* as the people of

of the fantastic. In his criticism of modern life, he sees culture dying for want of the spirit of festivity and fantasy, human and immensely necessary values without which man cannot live. They run counter to the values of the economy of production and in the long run, if they can be preserved, should provide the point of departure for a radical criticism of modern life and open the way to an equally radical reform.

'Celebrative affirmation' is best interpreted through Josef Pieper whom he quotes in this context.[7] The latter sees celebration or keeping festival as an affirmation of life, it is to live out 'the universal assent to the world as a whole', it is 'a special time in which we affirm all of life by saying *yes* to part of it'. Birth and marriage are the most ancient moments of celebration, birth obviously for a new life has come into the world and marriage not merely because it is the promise of a new physical life but because it marks the beginning of a new kind of life for a given couple of people. Even death, at least for the Christian, is a moment of celebration, for all the liturgy affirms that the dead have passed from death to life, from the shadows of this world into the light of reality, *ex umbris et imaginibus in veritatem.*[8]

All this may seem pompous and vague. What do the authors mean by 'life'? Is not work, earning one's living, even the rat-race, Life? Is not this in fact life for the vast majority of people on the face of the earth? A clue to their meaning can be gained from another statement of theirs: keeping festival is basically an end in itself, it produces nothing, at least nothing material, and in celebrating we are saying there are other values in life that are more important because they point us to something beyond ourselves, something beyond the material values of life and, as has been observed, they are *necessary* if man is to remain human. In the circumstances in which we live, the 'secular city', which has become not a place for civilized living as it was for the Greeks but a machine to assist the processes of production (which also are in danger of becoming an end in themselves), threatens the quality of life and perhaps endangers it altogether. But in this criticism of life, there is a danger of Manichaeism, of a flight from the 'city', of a repudiation of the very means that have made life

---

the sixteenth century did, meaning precisely that element of excess of which Harvey Cox writes. It is true that they were not thinking of celebration in any ritual sense but they wanted to celebrate Man whom they saw as capable of the wildest dreams and ideas which he might not want to realize in fact but which was the stuff of poetry. This 'fantastic' spirit was excluded from Protestant worship at the time, but do we not catch some echo of it in the exciting and often fantastic churches of the Baroque period? The Baroque artists orchestrated shapes, colour, light and sound into an affirmation of a triumphant faith which was not simply polemical. They exuberated in the possibilities of new-found media or in the new-found ways of manipulating them.

[7] *Op. cit.*, p. 22.

[8] Newman's self-chosen epitaph: from shadows and images into reality.

tolerable and easy for millions of people throughout the world. We cannot and should not want to return to 'the acre and a cow' economy but we can ask that the processes of production should themselves be humanized, as indeed they have been to some extent over the hundred and fifty years of the industrial revolution. What is more important and more radical is that we should ask: what is all this production for? Is it just to make money, and often to make more and more money for fewer and fewer people? Or should it not be regarded as a means towards the creation of the Good Life for as many people as possible? If the *purpose* of the present economic system could be changed, then it would be easier to bring into our festival-keeping the celebration of the works of man's hands and minds which are also the work of God. If primitive man celebrated the gathering in of the harvest with a feast, there is no reason why industrialized man should not celebrate the work by which his life is made humanly decent.

It is undeniable, however, that material goods do obsess people, weigh them down and blinker their vision. That is why there must be another element of festival-making. It is the all-important matter of *leisure* which Harvey Cox speaks of as *juxtaposition*. We do need a contrast with our ordinary every-day work; holidays are exceptional, and just as we cannot celebrate alone, so we cannot keep festival all the year round. We need to make a hole in time, to create a space of non-productive activity, we need leisure that is not merely a void, not just not-doing, but a time when we can go out beyond ourselves, become aware of ourselves not as productive agents but as human beings whose potential is by no means exhausted by the business of earning a living. Primitive man knew these moments of creative leisure. After the harvesting or the hunting, there was the feast, a prolonged feast lasting for several days, just as in the Middle Ages there were the Twelve Days of Christmas when the whole of society gave itself up to festivity. The Christian Sunday is an obvious example of the pause in the weekly work, a day of rest that is to be regarded as a day for the re-creation of the human forces so that we can become more fully human as well as better able to take up our work again. It is a time that should be valued as a contribution towards truly human living, and it is to be deplored that in our own country Sunday is becoming ever more filled with daily chores—all that washing hanging out on Sunday mornings—and it was observed in France shortly after the war when religious-sociological enquiries were being made that in households from which no one ever went to Mass, there was a fall in the standard of human living. There was no keeping of festival, Sunday was just like any other day and the gloom of the bitter industrial life was never lifted. Dechristianization went hand in hand with dehumanization.[9]

---

[9] No doubt things have changed. The greater availability of material goods has been the means of bringing more variety and even joy to such families, and it would seem to be a grudging, clerical attitude that would condemn people because

In the elements of celebration listed above, the most important seems to be leisure, that is, a willed and created intermission from the ordinary tasks of everyday life. Without this you cannot keep festival. You cannot do so if you are hag-ridden with the anxieties of work, weighed down by the responsibilities of decision and organization. With it, the spirit of man can begin to expand, bodily relaxation gives the senses time to open to aspects of life that at other times we give little enough attention to, the imagination will begin to work and we can begin to *enjoy*. The second important element, joy, will emerge from the leisure if there is a *causa laetitiae*, a cause for rejoicing, and traditionally man has found this in the great events of life, birth and marriage, in the cycle of natural processes, seed-time and harvest. But in a special way he has found the cause for rejoicing in the myths he conceived to lie at the heart of his experience of nature. These myths he celebrated with song and dance and prayer and sacrifice. 'Excess' was a normal feature of his celebrations, he and his community, tribe or people, lost themselves in the rejoicing and felt renewed by contact with the god. In fact the whole well-being of the community depended on the celebration of the feast. Life, worship and religion were fused into a single whole and the worship was a symbol which summed up and, in celebration, expressed the deepest things of the life of the people. A whole people could celebrate because they had a common 'theology', a common ritual and a common life, and the ritual celebration which usually required days of leisure was the means by which they broke through the often grinding round of work into the realms of joy, security and peace.

In the vocabulary of Harvey Cox[10] festivity 'helps us to keep alive to time by relating past, present and future to each other'. It is his view that festivity refers principally to the past, though not exclusively so (e.g. a wedding), and fantasy to the future if only because we dream of plans for the future, of what might be, perhaps in a different kind of social order. There is, I think, no need to make this distinction. The celebration of a feast is a nodal point drawing the past into the present and projecting the people into the future because its life lies ahead of it even if it is always being refreshed from the past. It is significant of our society that, if on the one hand it is burdened with historical experience, there is a decreasing sense of the past. There is little sense that what we have now is the fruit of past endeavours, that every society, however modern, has its roots in the past and that man himself has memories of the past that are part of his subconscious and formative of his personality even now. The restoration of 'festivity' or celebration would seem to be a necessity if he is to retain his memory of the past and ultimately his mental health.

---

they seek recreation in their cars on Sundays. The much-maligned modern Sunday has in fact meant that whole families take their leisure together and find happiness and relaxation in doing so.

[10] *Op. cit.*, p. 23.

It is here that we should be able to see the point of insertion of the Christian liturgy into the life of our time. Liturgy has too often been pursued as if it were a purely church activity. The church calendar has borne less and less relevance to secular life, the style of worship has been determinedly other-worldly in language, gesture and movement and groups of people.

Is it possible to restore the sense of celebration? It will certainly be difficult, for Catholics in particular have looked on Sunday worship rather as a duty than a festival. And we have been very coy about 'enjoying' an act of worship. It seemed to be almost immoral. What is needed is a complete change of mentality and there are signs that more and more people are looking for a style of worship that communicates joy or fellowship or something of the kind. Even a humble parish church where the Sunday liturgy is celebrated with some enthusiasm seems to attract people who do not find it elsewhere. And in spite of the gloomy jeremiads about the current English liturgy, it is possible to celebrate it with liveliness, with song and with a sense that the Good News is being conveyed.

As well as a change of mentality, it is necessary, I think, to exploit the possibilities the new liturgy offers. We will say a word about two matters, music and visual aids.

Music seems to be an indispensable element of festival-making. We lose ourselves, 'make a whole in time', more easily perhaps through singing than in any other way, and although the new Mass can be truly 'celebrated' without it, there is no doubt that it is hardly a festivity. It is interesting to note that the General Introduction (19) speaks of singing as a sign of 'exultation of heart', referring to Acts 2:46. More than anything else it secures the oneness of mind and heart that was characteristic of the apostolic church.

The situation in our churches is slowly improving. There is much more singing than there used to be (though often the quality of the music is poor) and this singing is not a mere devotional adjunct to the liturgy. Thanks to the new Order, it is part of the Mass. But much still remains to be done. Composers have been struggling hard to satisfy the demand for musical settings for the Mass that can be sung by a congregation and yet are not musically banal. If there has been too much of the latter this is because we have moved into a new world and even composers are conditioned by their past. In the interests of providing congregational music they have too often thought that a kind of syllabic chant was the only thing possible. Whether they have been over-influenced by the plain-chant tradition it is difficult to say and there are a few who have realized that the choir can be used antiphonally with a congregation. But what I feel is needed more than anything else is that composers should first reconsider the *literary* forms of the liturgy. The *Gloria* is lyrical, the creed a statement (of faith) and the *Sanctus* is a cry of exultation. Even to a non-musician, like the present writer, these forms suggest that musical settings should correspond to them and if possible enhance them.

Another tradition may have played its part. For centuries the church protested against and finally banned certain kinds of secular music, usually involving the use of soloists. This has meant that in modern times even the use of a cantor or psalmist has been suspect. Yet, as we have seen, such an officer can animate a congregation and sustain its participation from the beginning to the end of a service. Repetitions, too, came under the ban— and it was indeed necessary to ban them—but these repetitions were wrong because they were non-functional, the musically and verbally idiotic repetition of unimportant words. With a deeper understanding of the texts of the liturgy and with a realization of their function in the whole celebration it should be possible to make proper use of the cantor, who, if competent, could sing more elaborate melodies (e.g. for the Reproaches on Good Friday and the responsorial psalm regularly) and at the same time lead the people into the singing of what belongs to them. In addition, such an understanding should help composers to realize that repetition is not necessarily an evil but that the texts sometimes positively demand it. *Hosanna* is a shout of triumph and it is set at one of the high points of the eucharistic celebration: the Good News has been proclaimed and the whole assembly gathers itself up to sing with the angels and saints the eternal glory of God. *Hosanna* and possibly the phrase that goes with it needs repetition if the people are to sing it with that exultation of heart the Instruction speaks of.

These are but examples taken from the texts that conventionally are associated with 'the sung Mass'. The new Order opens up many other possibilities. The entrance chant is no longer tied to a form of words set down in the missal. It is intended to be a chant that will summon the congregation to worship and to lift them up so that they feel they are a community. For this good hymns, better than many we have got, are needed, but also different forms are needed. Refrains to be sung by the people after the verses of hymns would enable composers to devise more elaborate melodies that could be sung by the choir and which they would find more interesting. Such a device would also liberate us from the rigid 'four-square' pattern of the Victorian hymn which, good as it was, is now a little stale. For the communion procession such a device is almost a necessity. People do not want to be embarrassed with books as they approach the altar and with the increasing practice of communion in both kinds they need to have their hands free. Again, after the gospel, which is the climax to the ministry of the word, one feels that a musical response is required. This could be a sort of *kontakion*, a text taken from the gospel of the day and set to music which both choir and people could sing. In short, the new Order offers many possibilities of celebration that were formerly excluded and which, if realized, will bring that note of poetry that some complain is so lacking in the new liturgy.[11]

There is another possibility. The place of celebration must speak of festivity—even the room of the Last Supper was 'large, furnished with couches' (Mark 14:14) and, as we know, lighted up. This can be achieved in a variety of ways. On feast days it has long been the custom to decorate the church with flowers and 'best' vestments and altar-furnishings are used. It is a sound tradition but can be extended. Man does not live only by words and music. He can *see* and his sight needs to be satisfied with light and colour. He can worship through his eyes just as he can through his ears. There are those who say that we have entered an age of new Puritanism, our modern churches are stark, without colour, without statues or pictures. There is some truth in this, though the reason for it is that Catholic churches until recently were such a clutter of miscellaneous objects obscuring the basic liturgical functions of the building that priests and architects have been glad to get rid of them. There should be pictures, there should be statues, but it all depends where you want to put them. The very general regulations of the Constitution (125) indicate that there is a hierarchy of values, there is a 'right order', and in the placing of such objects the people's sense of values must not be distorted. It is generally agreed that pictures and statues should be out of the 'eucharistic room', and the Instruction of 1964 *orders* that side-altars are to be. Undoubtedly the best arrangement is that shrines with statues, pictures, prayer-desks and so on should be in chapels set apart. Here people can pray privately without distraction from movement in the main body of the church.

But, like the Victorians, we have strange notions about the fixity of pictures and such like objects. As Alice Meynell said a very long time ago, if she had enough money she would change her pictures quite frequently; and everyone knows that we do not *see* a picture that is always hanging in the same place. There is need for constant variety and one has long entertained the hope that pictures, plaques, and even statues (why not, with modern materials?) should be mobile and that on great feasts or the feasts of saints they could be put in some prominent position (e.g. in the porch) with some striking text that would both please the eye and instruct the people.[12]

Liturgical celebration is in the nature of the case an intra-mural activity

---

[11] One suspects that many who criticize the new rite have never seen it celebrated in full. They are mistaking the libretto for the opera, as Cardinal Schuster said fifty years ago.

[12] This has been done for a great number of years at the Benedictine church at Cockfosters, London, and the St Thomas More Centre for Pastoral Liturgy (also London) is preparing poster-like pictures which it will be possible to put in position whenever they are needed.

and we feel impelled to ask: what, if anything, has it to say to modern society?

In a former and famous book, *The Secular City*,[13] Harvey Cox seemed to be in danger of canonizing the values of Western industrialized—and especially American—civilization. Perhaps that danger was over-emphasized, for in his *Feast of Fools* he makes a radical criticism of it. What is more, he rejects much of ancient and modern theology as being too often but the expression, and in some cases the justification, of the Western dogmas of rationalism, progress, and a somewhat narrow religious experience. He finds 'radical theology' wanting because it is not much more than an 'apotheosis of present experience'.[14] And although he is more sympathetic to the theology of hope (Metz, Moltmann)[15] he rejects it in favour of a theology of juxtaposition which he sketches out.

He began with saying that juxtaposition is an element in keeping festival. It is something that lies alongside ordinary life and supplies a criticism of it by the very fact that it represents a temporary contracting out of production and of all the material values of the world. Harvey Cox is speaking of theology, but I think that we can translate his position into the terms of the church. In the last analysis the church has to stand over against the world, it is discordant with the world, it offers (or woe betide it if it does not) a criticism of the world; there is an inevitable hiatus between its values and those of the world. It is true that the church is traditional, it comes out of the past and cannot annihilate its past; but it must be concerned with the present, otherwise it has ceased to function; it looks on with hope to the consummation, for therein is its final end. So its theology must be at once traditional, radical ('the theology of creative negation') and 'hopeful', that is, eschatological. But 'a theology of juxtaposition plays off the tensions among the three not by neatly balancing them but by maximizing the creative friction among the three. So it focuses precisely on this discomfiting point where memory, hope and experience contradict and challenge each other. It recognizes our estrangement from much of the tradition, but it is also somewhat estranged from the ethos of today. It is unwilling to reconcile itself to either. It delights in this dis-relation.'[16]

It is that word 'dis-relation' (however inelegant) that suggests an attitude in the matter of keeping festival. Harvey Cox indeed makes a plea for the

---

[13] London, 1965.

[14] *Op. cit.*, p. 132: he is thinking of the 'Death of God' theologians.

[15] Radical Theology's mistake was to elevate *present* experience to divine status; the theology of hope comes perilously close to identifying God with the *future*. *Op. cit.*, p. 130.

[16] *Op. cit.*, p. 133. For a Catholic acceptance of the proposition 'estranged from much of the tradition' would depend on what is meant by 'tradition'. If it means 'antiquity' it is acceptable. But for Catholics, and, one finds, for many Protestants, tradition is a *living* thing and the 'return to the sources' of recent theology has spelt a renewal, not merely of theology, but of the church.

restoration of the jester even in the church—he is sufficiently in the world to know it and out of it so that he can see it in proportion—and perhaps one might add that the church is somewhat in the position of the jester in relation to the world. It sees so much that is transient, relative and unimportant on which men set their hearts and their whole lives, and it is the function of the church, while remaining involved in every human concern and deeply compassionate to those who suffer from the evils of the world, to proclaim that here man has 'no abiding city'. You can do this by the fierce denunciation of the prophet, whether ancient or modern, and this has been tried, not with any great success, in modern times. But you could also do it by 'playing before the Lord', by happily and tranquilly celebrating the feasts of the church. This is not frivolity because we are in touch with the great realities of life and death and we already glimpse, improbably perhaps, the New Testament teaching about the foolishness of God who rejected the wisdom of the wise and the strong things of this world for the folly of the cross (I Corinthians 1:18–25). One is also irresistibly reminded of St Francis of Assisi, the troubadour of God, who went about singing his songs of the beauty of God, and of the sun and water and fire that he had made. Medieval theologians solemnly debated whether Christ laughed. Perhaps St Francis is the proof that he did.

Whether the world will listen, whether it will learn from us how to celebrate and then what to celebrate are questions that must remain unanswered. If it regards us as 'fools', giving time to such wantonly unproductive activities, we perhaps need the courage to try at least to be 'fools for Christ's sake'.

CHAPTER TEN

CELEBRATION AND THE NEW ORDER OF THE MASS

IF, AS we have tried to show, celebration brings a certain spirit of festivity to an occasion, it is necessary to introduce it into the celebration of Sunday Mass.[1] This is not always an easy task. The very familiarity that everyone has with the rite, the 'ordinariness' of regular Sunday practice, and often enough the necessity to provide a large number of Masses during the day, militates against any sense of celebration. Whatever is to be done about the earlier Sunday Masses, it should be possible to organize at least one during the day where there is a sense of festivity. In countries that are traditionally regarded as Catholic, one has noticed that the people do have a sense of occasion. They foregather before the Mass and after it, meet each other, exchange the time of day and often discuss matters of common interest. Such a custom is at least a pre-condition of celebration. But on the assumption that often enough this is not possible in a large town or city, it means that the celebration begins when the people enter the church. As we have seen, a welcome and an attractive décor have their importance. But much will depend after that on the priest-celebrant, and it is his function that we must now be concerned with.

The General Instruction (10, 60) describes his function clearly enough and there is no doubt that it attributes a great importance to his role as president. Apart from the material details (what he and he alone must do and when), it underlines in a variety of ways that he is leader and that upon him will depend the success or failure of the celebration. Success will come from a proper realization of what he is about. He is there to stimulate and guide a community of people in celebrating the victory of life over death, of holiness over sin, of a life that is triumphant even now. The Mass is essentially *eucharistia* and by whatever circumstances it is conditioned, whether by private or public mourning, it remains thanksgiving. This thanksgiving is made through Jesus Christ who 'by dying destroyed our death and by rising restored our life' and continues to do so. To recall a phrase from the previous chapter, the eucharist is a celebration of life, of divine life that is triumphant in Christ and that day by day is enriching

---

[1] The case for daily Masses is rather different. They are more intimate and when celebrated with a small group in, say, a house the celebratory element will largely be found in the more intimate relationship of the participants.

the life of men on this earth. This is the essence of the celebration, which achieves a new dimension when a large number of Christians gather together to profess their faith, to give God thanks through Jesus Christ in joy of heart. The celebrant must be aware of this and if he can communicate *his* sense of occasion to the people, *his* realization that he, with the community, is keeping festival, the Mass will indeed be a 'celebration'. Moreover, *he* has something to communicate to them, he has a word to give them, the word of the gospel, and if he is really interested in that, he will bring to the celebration what one can only call a heightened interest, perhaps an element of excitement, which, if only subdued, will communicate itself to the whole assembly. For this, his first contact with the community in the (brief) address after the formal greeting is crucial. His attitude, conveyed by bearing and voice as well as word, will be apparent to all.

This remains true throughout the service, and the Instruction reminds celebrants, as well as others, that the liturgical texts have different forms, readings, prayers, acclamations, instructions, and that the voice must correspond with these different forms. A certain gravity, enhanced by the previous silence, in the reciting of collects will give them a different tonality from the attitude adopted when reading a narrative. This rule becomes particularly important when the celebrant is leading the people into the eucharistic action through the dialogue and opening passages of the eucharistic prayer. The phrase 'Let us lift up our hearts' is an urgent invitation, and a slight lifting of the voice is demanded by the text and will stimulate the people to respond with vigour. 'Let us give thanks to the Lord our God' is a summary of the whole action and the words should be said with due deliberation and emphasis. So often the familiar phrases, such as these and the noble conclusions of the collects, are rolled off as if they were no more important than a laundry list. Likewise the gospel and the first part of the eucharistic prayer (whether moveable or fixed) are the principal moments of *proclamation* during the Mass, and if the celebrant is aware of this, he will bring that *mental* attitude to them which will result in the right kind of recitation.

But the priest-celebrant is more than a president. He is a producer, he has to organize a 'performance' of the central act of Christian worship and nothing can be left to chance. This is the sense of the Instruction (GI 313, and compare 10, 60). It speaks of pastoral effectiveness, of the need to *plan* a celebration, of consultation with ministers (if any), with other officials (readers, choir, etc.) and with the people. The president has to co-ordinate and harmonize the activities of all the individuals and groups who are to celebrate the service. In practice this has to be done by training (choir and servers), by discussion (particularly important with the choir), and finally by information so that all concerned know what texts are to be used, what sung, and, of course, who is to undertake the different ministries. At the time of celebration the president must have a clear picture of the whole organization of the service; then *as president* he will be able to guide it effectively towards its desired end.

It may be thought that special gifts are required for this sort of ministry and it is true that qualities of imagination and efficiency will be important. But much will depend on the structure and organization of the parish outside worship. If the clergy and people normally conduct their affairs by consultation, they will do the same quite naturally for their worship. Nor is there any reason to suppose that if a priest has not the necessary qualities he cannot delegate much of the work to others. A choir director or a master of ceremonies who are competent and who have the right attitude towards the worshipping community can relieve him of much of the burden. Even then constant consultation is necessary as the condition of a satisfactory celebration. Experience shows that only constant consultation between all who are concerned in the worship of a given place will ensure its worthy celebration. It is also clear that even if the priest is not musical or is not particularly gifted in organization, his role throughout is the formation of his people, and especially those who take more important parts in the services, in an understanding of the liturgy.

During celebration he has a number of different things to do:

1. The eucharistic prayer, the collect, offertory and postcommunion prayers are presidential and belong to him alone: 'Representing Christ, he addresses them to God in the name of the whole people' (GI 10).

2. He proclaims the gospel and preaches the homily.

3. He may intervene at certain points with brief statements to assist the congregation to renew their desire and intention to participate.

4. He is responsible for a number of significant gestures.

5. There is the question of silences that will be under his control.

Of the first group we have already observed that they demand a sense of their importance and nothing further need be said. But here, as in his function as reader of the gospel and preacher, he has to give an example of clear diction, of unhurried, intelligent reading and of a reverence for the words that are symbols of holy things. This will mean that the texts, both scriptural and liturgical, will need to be studied, prepared and understood. The Lectionary in particular demands a competent knowledge of holy scripture and some acquaintance with modern exegesis. Failing this he will be in danger both of misunderstanding the texts and of conveying faulty doctrine to his people.[2]

The third group, what is sometimes called catechesis, is a very delicate instrument to manipulate. On the one hand, there is the danger of an intolerable verbosity that does no more than obscure the pattern of the

---

[2] To take a crude example, if he gave people the impression that the account of the creation of the world in Genesis 1 were a scientific description of what happened in the beginning, he would be positively misleading them. But once he realizes that it is not, then he has got to find out exactly what the text is saying.

eucharist (as well as exasperating the people) and on the other, the mistake of using them as occasions for giving mere factual information. They are intended to introduce the people into different parts of the service, help their participation and stimulate their devotion. The Instruction says that the president may intervene at the beginning of the service (of which we have already spoken), before the readings, before the preface and before the dismissal at the end.

The purpose of catechesis before the readings is to help the people to see the connection between them. This is not always clear and needs to be pointed up, but in doing so the celebrant should be able to elucidate any difficult expression or to draw out an allusion. This is often necessary since in the course of a homily lasting about ten minutes he has insufficient time to refer to details. In any case, he has the more important task of conveying the *whole* message of the day to his people. Such catecheses must, of course, be prepared beforehand, preferably written down, and then there would seem to be no reason why the reader should not read them between the announcing of the passage and the reading of the text itself.[3]

In an integrally Catholic congregation it might seem unnecessary to intervene before the eucharistic prayer. Everyone, it is thought, knows what is going to happen. But how many of our congregations nowadays are integrally Catholic? Members of other churches or of none are frequently to be found among us on Sundays and on other occasions and they need help. It *is* a good thing to recall at this moment that the community is now going to do what Christ did at the Last Supper and that the power of his redeeming love is going to be made present among the congregation. For marriages, funerals, for public occasions, for children's Masses, it is certainly necessary. As we have seen in an earlier chapter, the headings to the prefaces are given to guide such catechesis at this point. Where, as on great feasts, the preface is a proclamation of the mystery being celebrated, a 'nuclear' statement at this point will help the people to enter into the eucharistic action with the right sentiments.

The liturgy, as we have seen, is a complexus of symbols and these are more frequently gestures than things. The president has to make the most significant of them and his manner of doing them can enhance or mar the

---

[3] There seems to be a tendency for priests to be rooted to the lectern as formerly they were to the altar. There are now three places of celebration: the president's chair, the lectern and the altar. But there would seem to be no reason why the gospel should have to be proclaimed from the lectern. It is meant to be preceded by a procession with lights (and, if desired, incense) and for this reason it will sometimes be better to leave the sanctuary and proclaim the gospel in the midst of the people. The word of Christ is proclaimed to them and for them, the gospel is the climax of the ministry of the word and it would be well to make the point by movement and position. It is true we still need a gospel book, less bulky than the lectionary, that can be laid on the altar at the beginning of Mass and carried in procession for the gospel. But no doubt such will be provided before long.

celebration. If he is directed to open his arms to invite the people to pray, as at the 'Lord be with you', it should be a large welcoming gesture, in fact significant.[4] When he is directed to spread his hands over the offerings, he should do so in a generous gesture, stretching out his arms so that people can *see* what he is doing. When he takes the bread, they should be able to see him taking it (it was a gesture of the Lord at the Last Supper which he is re-enacting) and he should hold it before him so that again they can see it. Nowadays, chalices are changing their shapes and he is no longer required to hold the cup in some complicated pattern of fingers. He can take it with both hands and the modern kind demands that he should do so.[5] It goes without saying that gestures like bowing, genuflecting, making the sign of the cross should be made unhurriedly and with dignity.[6]

There is, too, the question of singing and our record in this matter is not impressive. In the old days, when we could use the lovely plainsong recitatives (some of them surely the best in the world), the celebrant's effort was usually the worst in the whole assembly. It would seem to be basic that if the celebrant is to sing texts, he should rehearse them beforehand and with the choir. Even a wrong pitch can throw a whole choir (and congregation) into confusion.[7]

Finally, there is the matter of silence. Very difficult to obtain in a large church (and even in a small one where there are a number of young children), it is an essential element of any satisfactory celebration. But it is not a silence that just happens. It is created and it is created by the celebrant. First, his own bearing, which should be one of recollection (though not abstraction—a different thing altogether) and inner quiet, will induce a sense of recollection in the assembly. Then he will look for the right moments. After the readings, he may say a word and invite the people to reflection. After communion, he will take the words or the sentiment of the communion verse and suggest thoughts and prayers to the people. After the *Sanctus* (especially if it has been a lively one—and why not?) he will make a short pause until the whole assembly has become quiet.[8]

---

[4] Actors tells us that a mere turning of the hand on the stage is *in*significant. It does not convey what it is intended to convey and is all-but invisible. The *arm* must move.

[5] It is to be hoped that the habit of breathing into the chalice has gone.

[6] As television reveals, most priests move far too quickly. On the other hand Eastern priests seem to be able to move with a natural grace—and sing! Witness the funeral of Igor Stravinsky.

[7] The limitations of the clergy are—at last—recognized. In the directives for Holy Week, we find that the choir can assist the celebrant with the chant for the veneration of the cross and that a layman can sing the *Exsultet*.

[8] It should be hardly necessary to have to say that people need to be given time to move, to sit, to stand and the rest. In a large church it is essential to give them time. But how often, alas, does not the recitation of a text begin while there is all the noise of a large congregation settling down.

All these details may seem to be matters of no importance and there are many apparently who refuse to give them any attention. They fail to realize that they are all ways of conveying the meaning of the act of worship and ultimately the grace of God. An indifference to them witnesses to another and deeper failure. It is a failure to recognize that we worship God with our bodies or, rather, in the wholeness of our personalities.

There are one or two other matters that usually fall under the control of the clergy. They are concerned with the objects to be used in worship. In all the movement for the betterment of liturgical practice there has been a constant desire for authenticity or genuineness. If rites must be comprehensible and gestures significant, objects must be genuine and not fake. Mercifully, there has been a considerable improvement in recent years, though one still sees vestments that are badly designed, badly made and adorned (if that is the word) with various kinds of metal 'lace'. All that glisters is *not* gold, but some still seem to want it. This is not the place to discourse at length on liturgical art. I will merely remark that an insensitivity to the quality of what is used in worship witnessses to an indifference to the quality of life.

In the new liturgy there are two places where authenticity becomes liturgically important. With the increased number of communicants, with communion in both kinds and the practice of concelebration, a multiplicity of vessels on the altar at the offertory obscures the truth that all are made one in Christ by the taking of the one bread and drinking from a single cup. Ideally, there should be but one communion dish and one cup. Perhaps this will not always be possible, though if the dish is large enough (and in seventh century Rome it seems to have been very large) it is always possible to consecrate in it and distribute the hosts into other vessels for the administration of the Sacrament. Chalices also need to undergo a radical re-designing. Those in use are, for the most part, based on late medieval or baroque models when communion in both kinds was unthinkable. On the Continent much larger cups have been made, some of them of great beauty, and whole communities can receive communion from them.

Secondly, there is the rite of fraction. If the symbolism of the New Testament (I Corinthians 10:17) is to be evident, it is highly desirable that there should be one large altar-bread so that a credible fraction can be made and the people communicated from the one host. Clearly not all can receive from the one Bread and there will be special difficulties when there is a very large number of communicants, but the principle should be as far as possible maintained and it would seem desirable that calculations should be made about their optimum size.[9]

---

[9] In *Nelle Vostre Assemblee*, p. 556, Père Gelineau has calculated that an altar-bread of twenty centimetres diameter and 'a few millimetres thick' can communicate more than a hundred people. He suggests that such breads should be marked beforehand to make calculation easier.

A liturgical assembly is a group of people engaged upon the common task of giving glory to God and receiving Christ into their hearts and lives. It is not too much to ask that there should be a certain uniformity of bodily attitudes (GI 21) though it is often resisted. It seems to be regarded as dictatorship on the part of the clergy, leading to a regimentation of the people. Since the General Instruction rationalized this matter, protests have been less and it must be admitted that the pattern suggested is a reasonable one. Catholics had become conditioned by four centuries of custom that required them to kneel almost throughout the Mass and it is not surprising that they should have resisted (resented) the suggestion that it is right to stand for the entrance of the clergy and at their departure as well as at other moments during the rite. Habits were indeed very untidy and there were those who sat while others were kneeling and fell to their knees, if at all, only for the words of consecration. Yet surely the Instruction is right when it says that 'common bodily attitudes are a sign of the community and unity of the assembly'.

Of this unity the 'sign of peace' that is to be exchanged between the people before communion is intended to be the most significant sign. There has been, and no doubt will continue to be, resistance to the notion, precisely because people at worship do not recognize that they are a community. They have not yet caught up with the notion that they are a celebrating community, or in the phrase of Père Congar, 'the subject of celebration'.[10] No doubt much depends on how the matter is put to them and what gesture is suggested.[11] What above all is important is that they should realize that it is a gesture expressive of the horizontal relationship within the worshipping community through which all can manifest the church as a community of reconciliation. It has taken a long time to persuade people that they should be vocal at Mass, that they are in fact offering it, and it will take more time presumably to help them to see that actions and gestures and words are all so many signs through which they enter into the mystery of Christ and construct the great sign of the church.

The Use of the Missal and the Lectionary

As we have seen above, the new missal is rich in content and, as we already know by experience, the same is true of the lectionary. But it is necessary to have a thorough knowledge of both and a willingness to use what is to be found in them if a liturgical celebration is to be what the church intends it to be. The material breaks down into the Mass-formulas of the missal, the readings from the lectionary and the

---

[10] See Chapter three.
[11] The handshake or the double-handshake has been found generally acceptable, but other signs of mutual recognition will serve.

eucharistic prayers. Before considering these in detail, it will be as well to resume briefly the directions of the General Instruction on the principles of selection.

1.   Where liberty is given, the celebrant is to remember that he is the servant of the community and that 'he is not to follow his own inclinations but to have a care for the spiritual good of the community' (GI 316). This is particularly important when he departs from the scripture readings of the day, and if he does so the people have a right to know what texts he is going to use and why. Masses for the Dead, for instance, are not to be said frequently, 'for all Masses are offered for the living and the dead' (ibid.). It is the church's intention that the people should be nourished by the scriptures which are set out in course so that they can come to a knowledge of the whole Bible.

2.   Where several texts are given, notably in the 'Common' of saints, selection should be made in the light of what is known of the saint whose day is being kept. This diversity is *intended* and should be made use of. In the old system nothing was more deadening than the use of the small collection of passages the old missal provided for the saints' feasts that occurred almost every day of the week. The church does not wish to perpetuate that system.

3.   A different principle comes into play when Ritual Masses or those for Various Occasions are used. There is a diversity of texts precisely so that the celebration may be adapted to a given congregation. Not all are as familiar with the scriptures as perhaps they should be and certain passages will not only *not* communicate God's word to them but may repel them. Thus, I am not at all sure what would be the impact of the 'Grand Assize' passage from Matthew 25 on an uninstructed audience gathered for a funeral. To take a different situation, experience shows that even the adapted version of Ephesians 5:25-32 is not the best reading for weddings when a number of non-church people are present. For such occasions the Mass-formula has to be 'composed' (of course from the official books) and it is in such circumstances that the priest's pastoral *savoir-faire* comes into play. Where, on the other hand, practising Christians are celebrating a wedding Mass or a Mass for other occasions, they should be allowed to choose those passages from the missal and the lectionary that they think are most appropriate to the situation. They may need guidance, but usually they readily respond to the invitation.

Choosing the Mass-formula

When a priest is celebrating Mass with a community of people (the position we adopt here), he must follow the calendar. One or two *modifications* of the rule may be made on certain occasions, as e.g. a wedding on a Sunday when *one* reading from the collection for marriages may replace one of the readings of the day.[12] There is one exception even on days of obligatory commemorations and those of the Advent, Christmas and Easter seasons. If there is 'true necessity or pastoral need' other texts may be chosen. This is a clear example of the church's pastoral sense and evidence of her compassion. Such occasions would be when the local community has suffered, perhaps overnight, a calamity that has plunged everyone into distress. Or, as it seems to me, it might be an occasion of more intimate distress as when a child is 'missing' and the parents are distracted by grief. It is for the parish priest or even the celebrant to make a (pastoral) judgement on the situation and to find texts that will bring consolation (GI 333).

When optional commemorations (*memoriae*) occur, there is a very wide choice: the Mass of the feria, of the saint, or of another saint whose feast occurs the same day or of a saint who is mentioned in the martyrology for the same day. He may do the same when it is a feria (GI 316). On these same occasions, he may use one of the Mass-formulas for various occasions or a votive Mass. For the latter, the rule about serving the people is particularly important: they are not to be deprived of the word of God contained in the daily course. On the other hand, where there is a particular devotion, say, to Our Lady, then the priest should have regard for the people's desires (*ibid.*).

Even where there occurs an obligatory commemoration a certain choice remains (GI 323). The collect must be that of the saint but the prayer over the offerings and that after communion may be either from the Common or from the weekdays of the current season. In Lent the collect of an occurring commemoration may replace that of the day. In view, however, of the importance of the Lenten observance and the fact that the corpus of prayers for Lent has been renewed, one would think that there would have to be a very good reason for substituting the prayer of the day with another.

On 'ordinary' days throughout the year the choice is even wider, and evidently the reason is that there shall be as great a variety as possible so that the Mass shall become really prayerful and adapted to the needs of 'the people, the church and the world' (*ibid.*). As we have seen, there is copious provision for the principal seasons of the year, and for the rest the celebrant may choose either the prayers of the previous Sunday or of any Sunday of the year or from those provided 'for various occasions'. If this is to be possible, it will be necessary to arrange and print missals so that it can easily be done. The new missal is a bulky volume and if it is published in two parts it will not be possible to use prayers from the 'Various Occasions' section unless this is printed out twice. Naturally, alternative texts will have to be looked up beforehand and could very well

---

[12] On the greatest days of the year (e.g. Easter) this may not be done.

form the subject-matter of prayer before Mass. The same of course is true of the readings.

The use of the lectionary

An adequate treatment of the lectionary would occupy several volumes and here we can give only one or two indications as to its nature and use.

It should be sufficiently known by now (but apparently is not) that in the Sunday lectionary the first reading usually goes with the third, the gospel. Wherever in the Old Testament a text has some parallel with the gospel, this is inserted in the Mass of the day. Recent scripture scholarship has shown how embedded the gospels are in the Old Testament and for any effective treatment of the texts in the homily this fact needs to be known. Almost always the responsorial psalm binds together the Old Testament reading and the gospel and provides a clue to the right interpretation of the readings for the day. The second reading is to all intents and purposes a *lectio continua* of the epistles and non-gospel material of the New Testament, though on the greater feasts and seasons (e.g. Sundays of Lent) all three readings form a pattern. The second reading, then, must be thought of as giving that kind of instruction or as bringing before the people certain aspects of the Christian faith and life that do not need comment. In the homily, it is lawful to use it rather than the other readings, though to do this permanently, or even frequently, would be to frustrate the whole purpose of the lectionary.

Normally all three lessons are to be read and only pastoral reasons and a decree of the local conference of bishops make it permissible to omit one of them (GI 318). The criterion of omission of one of them is neither brevity nor ease of understanding (the homilist is required to do his homework!) but the message intended by the church for the day. In these circumstances it will usually be the first and third (which must always be read) and not the second and third. As the introduction to the Lectionary observes (13), the readings form part of the whole presentation of the liturgical year and the fundamental purpose of the lectionary is that the people shall be familiarized with the history of salvation (GI 317). For Sundays, for solemnities and the great feasts, there is then no choice and this surely is the best way to have it. Liturgical services are not private celebrations. They are the principal proclamation by the church of the Good News of salvation, and private preconceptions (supposing they are of any value) must give way to the public mission of the church.

The rules governing the use of the lectionary may seem unduly restricting and some would prefer a freer system. To this it must be replied that, left to our own devices, we are all inclined to choose the same parts of the Bible or even the same passages again and again. It needs a vast knowledge of the whole Bible to be able to choose passages at will that are suitable for liturgical celebration. This, quite apart from the fact that most of us are likely to take the line of least resistance and make no very great effort to select. On the other hand, the opinion has been expressed that the pattern of the lectionary is too vague and that it would have been better if the selection had conformed to the theological text-book or catechism so that really 'solid' instruction could be given. In fact, the church has opted for a *biblical* catechesis which is concrete, using a symbolic, poetic kind of language that is now generally agreed to be a better way of communication than the old abstract kind. It was on this, too, that the liturgy was constructed, and it is only this kind of catechesis that is consonant with it. As between freedom and restriction the church has chosen a middle way, giving the preacher all that is necessary for the communication of God's message and leaving him very free in his treatment of it.[13]

In other parts of the missal there is in any case a considerable range of choice, namely for 'Ritual Masses' and for those on 'Various Occasions'.[14] *If* such Masses are to be as rich in scriptural content as they should be, it will be necessary to explore all that is there and to select what is most appropriate for the situation. As a matter of practical pastoral politics, it is very helpful to make up *libelli* or booklets for different occasions in which readings, psalms and prayers will be combined in certain patterns suitable to different situations. Skeletons of these will provide the people with the texts (e.g. responsorial psalms) they need to have.

In principle, the choice of readings during the week is very wide. If there are 'various occasions', particular needs or devotional *desideranda*, these can all be met by a judicious use of the missal and lectionary. But it is the desire of the church that the daily course should normally be used. Where this is interrupted by a greater feast or some other lawful celebration, the priest may combine the omitted readings with those of the day or may use them instead of those of the day (GI 319).

In short, pastoral needs and liturgical suitability are the main criteria for the selection of readings (cf GI 319).

Choosing the Eucharistic Prayer

The use of the four eucharistic prayers is now sufficiently understood and we already have enough experience to know which of them are suitable for different occasions. But perhaps the principle that they are alternatives still needs to be emphasized. Although the General Instruction says that the Roman Canon may always be used (GI 322, a), and especially on Sundays, this, if done, would frustrate their purpose. They have been provided to illustrate the different aspects of the eucharistic mystery and this

---

[13] For further considerations on this point see A. Nocent, in *Nelle Vostre Assemblee, op. cit.*, p. 236.

[14] As also for special groups. The readings (from the Lectionary) may be chosen in the light of special circumstances (GI 319).

cannot be done if only one is used on Sundays. In practice E.P. III seems to be used mostly on Sundays and the Roman Canon is reserved for the greater festivals. E.P. IV is unfortunately rather long for Sunday worship and although it is a fine prayer, in the English translation, it gives an impression of verbosity. E.P. II can sometimes be used to advantage on Sundays, especially where another sacramental act is inserted into the Mass, e.g. baptism. It *is* shorter, and in spite of severe re-editing it remains a splendid prayer. As I have observed above, it seems a pity, however, to combine it with a proper preface. The first part of it says almost everything that most such prefaces say.

With the eucharistic prayers go the acclamations after the consecration. They do not appear to be tied to any particular prayer and can be used with any of them. *How* they are to be used on Sundays is another question. The people will in any case need to be informed and this can be done either by the provision of texts or by an announcement before the service. Some musical settings have been written and where these are in use, the sung version will be most appropriate to the principal Mass of the day. It would be better not to use the last one (the weakest of the collection) with the Roman Canon as it has no eschatological reference which is also wanting in the *anamnesis* of that prayer.

Ritual Masses and Masses for Various Occasions

Of the first group which, among other things, covers Christian Initiation, Holy Orders and Marriage, it is worth pointing out that there are two Mass-formulas for the celebration of baptism and that these may be used (whenever the rubrics allow) for the baptism of infants when this is given during the Mass. The first is a splendid text, with a collect asking that the infant may share in the paschal mystery of Christ's passion and resurrection, a special *Hanc igitur* (that for Easter time) and other special insertions for the other eucharistic prayers. The Mass for confirmation may be used in similar circumstances, that is, for almost all the Sundays of the year outside Lent, Easter time and Advent.

There are three formulas for marriage, too, with insertions for the eucharistic prayer, and three for anniversaries, including the twenty-fifth and fiftieth.

It is for Masses such as these that care is needed in selecting readings from the copious provision of the lectionary.

The second group provides, as we have observed, for very many occasions and will be useful when special groups come together for particular purposes, e.g. ecumenism, peace and justice and so on. Here it is simply a matter of knowing what is in the missal and for this some (brief) research is necessary.

With these may be grouped Masses for the Dead. For these a generous provision is made. There are *three* Mass-formulas (one for Easter time) for funerals and three for anniversaries, as well as prayers for almost every category. These formulas and the readings given in the lectionary must be carefully chosen if the Mass is going to be of that pastoral help to the people the church intends that it should be. There is no longer any excuse for repeating the same texts over and over again.

CHAPTER ELEVEN

LITURGY AND THE WORLD

LITURGY, as we have observed often enough in this book, is the sacrament of the church that manifests it to the world. Whatever happens in the church concerns liturgy in one way or another, but it is becoming clearer every day that what happens in the world affects the church. This new situation has been summed up in the phrase 'the world sets the agenda' which, of course, is only a half-truth. The agenda of the church was set by Christ in the beginning and what the phrase indicates is that the saving work of Christ has to be inserted into the world as it is here and now. For that the church has to listen to the world; in the words of Pope John, Christians have to be able to discern the signs of the times, and this has two aspects. The church not only has to discern the signs of the times so as to be able to adapt her mission to men and women at a given time, but also to be able to proclaim the truths of the gospel so that they can hear it.

The church has a prophetic role to play in the world and the ability to say the word, a word the world can understand (even if it rejects it), can come only from a reflection on the course of affairs in the light of the gospel. In the last analysis, the church has nothing but the word of the gospel to utter, but she cannot always understand that word unless and until it is reflected on. God is not locked up in the church, he is at work over the whole range of human activity, and man's search into the secrets of nature, his invention and *his* reflection on reality have in one way or another revealed certain truths that would otherwise never have been known. All who are engaged in the explicitation of natural processes, all who have sought and are seeking to improve the human condition, all who are seeking to establish peace and justice and the good life on earth are fellow-workers with God.

First, then, the church must understand and only after that is she in a position to evaluate. Evaluation in turn is no more than the precondition of the prophetic function which has two aspects:

1. The accusation has been made in recent years that the church's concern for the well-being of man and especially her involvement in action to improve the lot of man is a betrayal of the gospel which is wholly concerned with other-worldly things. It has been said that certain thinkers and writers are teaching or implying that the end-purpose of the church

is merely the well-being of mankind in this world. If this is true, then such people would have been betraying the gospel. It is more likely that they have been misunderstood. If God is at work in history, that history itself is not comprehensible without revelation whose transmission is, as we believe, entrusted to the church. The first part, then, of the church's prophetic function is to reveal, within the limits of her situation at any given time, the meaning of the whole process in which men are involved. Above all, she has to point to the end-purpose of the whole of human history. This is the light she has to hold up to the world, and since the world has not been disposed to listen for a very long time (and perhaps has had reasons for not doing so), it is not surprising that there are many who have developed a philosophy of the absurd.

But, apart from the nucleus of divine teaching, the church has no special knowledge, no special charisma to discern the meaning of things at a given moment. That is why the church has to put herself humbly to school with the world and try and enter into its mind and discover what it is doing and where it is trying to go. Out of this knowledge, which will not be mere information, the church will discover her ability to say the word that is necessary and illuminating to the contemporary situation. The proposition 'God is the final purpose of all things' is useless because it just does not seem true to people. It suggests a short-circuit. Not only will the hearer ask 'How do you know?' but he will go on to expostulate 'How can this and this and that have God for their end'. In a word, we have over-simplified a vast and complicated problem and positively *mis*-led people. Aquinas had a word, 'con-naturality', by which he meant an inner appreciation and understanding of a subject, born of an affinity that suggests the sharing in a common nature. It is this sort of knowledge, this sort of affinity, the church needs if she is to say a credible word to the modern world.

2.   With the prophetic function is usually associated the task of judgement. The world (and the church) is under divine judgement and it has often been thought that the denunciations of the prophet are a necessary part of that task. Prophecy is, in fact, a very delicate instrument to wield, and unhappily such prophets, usually self-appointed, have too often denounced the world as an essentially wicked place from which Christians should withdraw.[1]

'World' in holy scripture is an ambivalent term and means on the one hand the created universe (cosmos) or on the other the world that is still alienated from God by *sin*. Sin alone is at enmity with God and it is this that comes under the judgement. But we ourselves, who are responsible for this world, are only imperfectly redeemed, large parts of our personalities

---

[1] Such an impression might have been gathered from some of the prayers in the missal and it is interesting to observe that they have been corrected. Cf II Advent, postcommunion, where we ask that we may set a right value on earthly things (*sapienter perpendere*) instead of 'despising' (*despicere*) them.

and lives are still alienated from God and the good we do is mixed with evil, sometimes through our fault and sometimes through lack of wisdom. Once again, then, the church needs the gift of discernment and it is only when she can see that certain courses of action are hindering the establishment of the reign of God that she has the right and the duty to point out that they are condemned by the gospel. Whether and how often this is to be done is another matter, as is the way it is to be done. Mere denunciation has long ago been shown to suffer from the law of diminishing returns. The church has to find the moment and the words to intervene and this, too, is part of the reading of the 'signs of the times'. But the prophetic role does not rest only with authority and in the modern world the undramatic witness of ordinary Christians, both clergy and laity by their daily living, to the gospel truths is as effective as any other method.[2]

By nature and vocation the church is, then, the sacrament of God's word, which reveals his purpose for mankind and the sacrament of his love by which 'the scattered children of God may be gathered together until there is one sheepfold and one shepherd' (CL 2). God is present to the world and working in it and the church reveals his presence; she is, as the Second Vatican Council liked to say, 'a sign lifted up among the nations',[3] showing the over-riding purpose of all that man does.

The picture of the church, thus suggested, still bears traces of triumphalism, of the 'two societies' theology which set the church over against the world. The final thought of the Council suggests that the church is concorporate with the world. The church is not separate from human history but is affected by it and works out her own salvation in the world and finds herself involved in the vicissitudes of the historic process. 'The joys and the hopes, the griefs and the anxieties of the men of this age, especially those who are poor or in any way afflicted' are the joys and hopes, the griefs and anxieties of the followers of Christ who are the church.[4] If the church is the sign of salvation, she is also the sign of a salvation gained by suffering and death, the sign of a divine love that still suffers in the sufferings of mankind: *Jésus sera en agonie jusqu'à la fin du monde*. The tragedies of the human race are the tragedies of the church: 'The Council focuses its attention on the world of men, the whole human family along with the sum of those realities in the midst of which the human family lives. It gazes upon the world which is the theatre of man's history, and carries the marks of his energies, his tragedies, and his triumphs; that world which the Christian sees as created and sustained by its Maker's love, fallen indeed into the bondage of sin, yet emancipated now by Christ. He was crucified and rose again to break the stranglehold of

---

[2] And sometimes it is a very dramatic witness. Mother Teresa probably reveals God's love to people far more effectively than all the speeches of popes and bishops.

[3] Isaiah 11:12 (perhaps in a slightly accommodated sense).

[4] Constitution on the Church in the Modern World, introduction.

personified Evil, so that this world might be fashioned anew according to God's design and reach its fulfilment' (*ibid.*).

Underlying this passage and much more of the Constitution on the Church in the Modern World is a theology of what Continental theologians have called 'earthly realities'. God is present to the world· which is *both* the theatre of God's salvation and the theatre of man's endeavour. There are not two worlds, one sacred and the other profane. In the present order of things there is no such thing as a created world which, *ex hypothesi*, is outside the saving purpose of God. Men are called to be the collaborators with God in the very process of exploring and using the God-given world in which we live. The unfolding of its mysteries, the harnessing of its power and all the investigation of the world and its resources is also the unfolding of God's purpose for man. *All* is under God's saving grace, and the natural and supernatural, the sacred and the profane, existentially are one.[5] They can be distinguished mentally, and for certain purposes it may be necessary to do so, but in fact they are one. The Spirit of God is everywhere, guiding into good the efforts of all men who do not shut their minds and hearts to him: 'Undergoing death itself for us sinners Christ taught us by example that we, too, must shoulder that cross which the world and the flesh inflict upon those who search after peace and justice. Appointed Lord by his resurrection and given plenary power in heaven and on earth, *Christ is now at work in the hearts of men through the energy of his Spirit.* He arouses not only a desire for the age to come, but, by that very fact, he animates, purifies, and strengthens those *noble longings too by which the human family strives to make its life more human* and to render the whole earth submissive to this goal' (*ibid.*, p. 236).

Perhaps the Council document does not quite make the leap from the church to the world and even though showing a deep compassion for men, its outlook is a shade optimistic. If the Council hesitated at the first fence, Professor Karl Rahner takes two or three in his stride. He goes straight to the eucharist and sees this as the sacrament-sign of the world's death and resurrection. Man experiences in the terrestrial process all the agony of suffering, of disease and death, and it is this experience he brings to the celebration of the eucharist which thus becomes the sacrament not merely of his own experience of suffering, but of the tragic experience of the world. He does not move from the sacred to the profane.[6] He is 'profane', part of the profane world, concorporate with it, *its* experience is *his* experience, that of an engraced man who would give himself in all his 'profanity' to God in encounter with Christ through the eucharist. The barriers between 'church' and 'world', between the sacred and the profane, are irrelevant. In this sense they do not exist and the eucharist is the

---

[5] Karl Rahner, *Mission and Grace* (London, 1963), pp. 71–85.

[6] See Karl Rahner, 'Secular Life and the Sacraments', in *The Tablet*, 13 March, 1971, pp. 267–8.

sacrament-sign that God is present in the world, the sign of the tragic situation of the world, but also the means by which the world here and now can, through participation in the passion and death of Christ, overcome that part of the world that is alienated from God by sin and gradually, painfully, shape itself for the purpose God intends. The world is to be conformed to Christ who at the end will be all in all things, but meanwhile the end to be achieved is exerting its dynamic pull in the situation here and now. The whole of creation is straining towards the consummation, the final revelation (Romans 8:19) but that is *now* being realized in the celebration of the eucharist and in the lives of all who do not refuse God's invitation.

For Rahner, the Christian has first (not necessarily in time) an experience of life and it is this that he brings to the eucharist. This he sees as the sacramental expression of that same life now concretized in the re-enactment of the passion, death and resurrection of Christ. It is thus that the eucharist gathers into itself the whole worldly, secular experience of man and draws it into the process of redemption. At this level, there is no distinction between the sacred and the profane: the world of which man is part is brought into the eucharist which both declares the meaning of life and enables the Christian to offer it to God. In the eucharist, the world is achieving its purpose and through the power of Christ present in it is being carried along to the final purpose, the consummation, the *eschaton*, for which it was made.

It is a noble vision, but it assumes an understanding of the immanence of God in the world process that some may shrink from and a realization that this must be balanced by the divine transcendence in which the process finds its meaning and purpose. It assumes, too, a tragic sense of life which will not always be that of the ordinary worshipper. To this it will be said that this is the understanding he *ought* to have and it is one that can be suggested to him by opening his eyes to what is going on around him. What may be questioned is whether the very close association (almost an identity) between the saving work of Christ in death and resurrection and the 'death' and 'resurrection' of the world does not obliterate the analogous relation between the two. *People* die (spiritually) and rise again (spiritually) in baptism and the eucharist, people suffer and in as far as they are 'in Christ', he is suffering in them. But can all this be applied to nations, cultures and civilizations and if it is, are we not using the terms in a highly analogous and perhaps even romantic sense?

With these reservations, we may accept the view as valid and then we realize that there are one or two consequences to be drawn from it. The first concerns the mentality that modern people bring to worship and the second with the style of liturgy that will express such a view.

1. If people are to bring their world into the eucharist, they need to see it not as a 'magical' world nor yet as a completely secularized world, alienated from God by its very nature and constitution. Not a magical world, the victim of mysterious 'supernatural' forces, which it is the business of religion and worship to placate and manipulate so that they can be bent to the desires of the worshipper. Modern man no longer thinks of God as a celestial tyrant who sends plague, famine and war to punish a disobedient mankind. If there is plague and famine we try to find the bug that causes the one and provide the material resources to end the other. War, alas, which is a moral problem, is more intractable, but we do know that it is no good *merely* praying for peace. We have to work for it. Worship and all prayer are means by which we seek enlightenment about God's purposes and through which we harmonize our wills with his and work along with him to establish his reign. Our world is substantially a rational world, even if it is rifted by tragedy and even if there remains a penumbra of mystery connected with it. We live in a post-Copernican, post-Einsteinian, post-atomic world and it is in *this* world that God, however improbably, is present. It is this world that young Christians bring to their worship and it is the new insights into its nature that must in one way or another be reflected in the liturgical forms that are offered to them for their use.

2. But for the Christian, if this world is a rational world with a real autonomy, it is not a secularized world, a symbol of the *absence* of God. It came from him in the beginning, it is a sign of love, communicated love, and is evidence, or can be, of his wisdom and beauty. Into this complex earthly reality God inserted the whole incarnational and redeeming process of which the church and its liturgy are the continuation and the sacrament. Earthly realities cannot be indifferent to God, as we see in marriage, where the very material union of man and woman is the stuff of the sacrament which it takes up into itself so that the union expresses the creative love of God among men. The eucharist itself begins in the experience of man, in his desire for self-giving, which he expresses in the humble elements of bread and wine. These by the power of Christ become the bearers of the divine, reconciling love by which man is carried into union with God. Earthly and heavenly interpenetrate in a dynamic come-and-go between God and man. Of this meeting the liturgy is the privileged moment (*kairos*) which manifests and makes concrete the unceasing process.

This, it seems to me, is the context in which desacralization ought to be discussed. As we saw in the first chapter of this book, for primitive man the sacred was the *real* and worship, the re-enactment of the myth, was the way in which he got into contact with the real. We have seen, too, that transposed into the Christian scheme of things, this is a valuable insight. But we cannot return to the world of primitive man. If there is talk of desacralization, it is because modern man, and I include the modern Christian, has moved away from that world and has a different understanding of the world and of its relation to God. Desacralization is not iconoclasm, it is not a wanton desire to destroy an ancient heritage. It is a demand, springing out of a new understanding, for a God and a worship of him that is compatible with new insights and that makes both credible to him as he is here and now. The word 'sacred' is indeed polyvalent. It can mean the divine reality that is at the heart of the liturgy, it can mean the world seen as coming from God and consecrated by Christian work and worship, but it can also mean the envelope, heavily conditioned by a particular culture, of the liturgy that modern people are asked to use in this latter half of the twentieth century. Desacralization for many means the stripping off of this envelope and not the vulgarization of public worship.

Much of the Roman liturgy emerged in what is called a 'sacral' civilization. The Roman pagan civilization was originally such a civilization and its language is still discernible in many of the prayers of the Roman rite. Later, during the formative period of the Roman liturgy, which was, of course, pre-Copernican, with little or no understanding of the operation of secondary causes, the sacralization continued. The emperor was a sacred person, *the* sacred person, and at Constantinople there grew up around him a highly elaborate court ceremonial that is best described as a liturgy. He was approached with awe, as were other great personages, and the language used in addressing them seems to us the ultimate in adulation. Some of this 'sacredness' overflowed on to the bishops, who were given senatorial rank, and especially on to the bishop of Rome. It was in the fourth and fifth centuries that the liturgy was ceremonialized and it is not surprising that the language accompanying it was equally affected. If emperors and bishops were sacred persons and had to be addressed in a special kind of language, God, who was the Super-Sacred, had to be addressed in even more impressive language. Although neither Eastern nor Western liturgies ever lost a deep sense of the reality of God present and available to man in Christ, in both there was an obscuring of the fact that God is our Father and not a heavenly potentate made in the image of the emperor.

This sort of sacredness is no more than a contingent adjunct to the liturgy coming from the culture in which it was formed, and there is no reason at all why it should not be replaced with other forms that are more consonant with our age. Pointers in the direction of a radical change in this matter are the procedures of adaptation going forward in the countries like Africa and India which have not been formed, or only very superficially, by Western culture. They are evolving rites and gestures that are expressive of their mentality, rites and gestures that will, incidentally, 'incarnate' the liturgy in their own culture and that will speak to those who are not yet part of the Christian community.[7] Such adaptation leaves intact the inner zone of the sacred which for Christians is the mystery of Christ. Desacralization in these terms seems not so much to be reprehensible as inevitable.

The problem in industrialized countries is greater. As we observed in the first chapter, modern man has been cut off from his origins, he has a disregard for the past and symbols apparently no longer move him. He has a certain harshness of touch, he is direct, abrupt and unfeeling about modes of speech or ways of acting. The church's answer to this in recent years is to aim at simplicity, even austerity, and most modern Christians demand genuineness, authenticity. The danger, which some say we have not avoided, is that we should cultivate a dull philistinism whether in language, music or the visual arts. How far we have fallen into the danger is anyone's guess, and one suspects that those who bring the accusation are generalizing from a somewhat narrow experience. There are modern churches that are good (and I think beautiful), that are good because they are adapted to the celebration of the liturgy as the church now understands it. And there are more good objects—crucifixes, statues, pictures, frescoes, chalices and a dozen other things—in churches now than there ever were forty years ago. One of the most gratifying aspects of our situation is that architects and their clients are commissioning artists of all kinds to decorate and furnish the churches they are designing. There are churches where the 'new' liturgy is celebrated with all the resources of music and (the right kind of) ceremonial, showing that the liturgy can still be an aesthetic experience. But not everything can be achieved all at once and if the new liturgy is often celebrated inadequately, so was the old. The only difference is that the bad celebration of the old was too often taken for granted.

Is it possible to say, in the light of the foregoing considerations, what a modern liturgy should be? Should it be made plain, practical and completely functional so that only those things should be said and done that are absolutely necessary for, say, a eucharist? Are we to deceremonialize it to the point where people behave as if they were at a board meeting, wearing the secular clothes of modern secular life? Is the language to be that of a report on the new sewage farm of Little Muddleton-on-the-Ouse? Are we to banish poetry and music and the plastic arts from our worship and leave the worshippers with nothing but a read word and the staccato gestures of a modern business man? Would all this and much more make the liturgy more available and acceptable to modern man? It is more than doubtful and efforts in the past to reduce the celebration of the eucharist

---

[7] It said, too, that in some parts of Africa, *Eastern* liturgies are proving to be more acceptable to the various peoples there rather than even an adapted Roman liturgy.

to what was thought to be 'primitive' practice have shown their bankruptcy. In any case, even industrialized man is not going to be satisfied with anything as pedestrian as that. Nor is he impressed with desperate efforts to be 'with it'. Even in worship the church exercises a prophetic function. There she is engaged upon expressing, within the limits of what is possible, values that the (alienated) world does not accept. In worship the church is witnessing to the transcendence of God who if through his Son he has involved himself in it, remains the purpose, outside it, towards which it is destined. Moreover, God is not a scientist nor yet an industrialist. He is the source of beauty, of a beauty that is reflected in the created world and whose meaning is to be discerned in the 'consecration' of the material universe that was initiated by the incarnation.

What is in fact necessary is a liturgy which over the whole range of its words, gestures and symbols makes available to modern man the mystery of Christ. *Anything* that obscures this purpose must be abolished or kept away from it. Music that obscures the words and hinders the people's response to them, archaic and highly ceremonialized gesture, a symbolism that is piled on the basic Christian symbolism of the liturgy and that needs a key to understand it, all these have no place in common public worship.

There would in fact seem to be three areas where it might be useful to discuss desacralization: language, symbolic gestures and liturgical clothing and buildings.

1. How should we address God? The central revelation of the New Testament is that God is our Father and modern man will have nothing to do with the ogre God, the policeman God, the punishing God, or even the manipulating God who is always tinkering with his universe. As Christians we are the redeemed, adopted children of God and we were taught, as we do at every eucharist, to address him as 'Our Father'. Especially in the English translations of the new rites this point is made again and again. Prayers that in Latin begin *Deus*, in the English begin 'Father' and it is to be supposed that the reason for this is not simply that it is almost impossible to begin an English sentence with 'God' but that the translators felt this better expressed the sense of the prayer for modern Christians.[8] We are, it is true, infinitely less than God and we must approach him humbly, but the filial relationship remains and we did not have to wait for a revision of the liturgy to be told that. For centuries the theologians have told us that we must *not* have a servile fear of God but a filial 'fear' which I suppose we should translate as 'reverence'.

For this reason one could wish that a word like 'placate' was banned from our liturgy. It seems to derive from a pre-Christian stratum of prayer and we find it hardly tolerable to say that God was 'placated' by

---

[8] If it is said that they were doing a spot of demythologizing on the side, it can be answered that the New Testament did a fairly extensive job of demythologizing the Old.

the death of his own Son. 'Propitiation' is also tricky and when it is applied, as in some prayers over the offerings, to a piece of bread, we feel that if it is to be used at all, it should be used in the context of the eucharistic prayer itself. However, an inspection of the new missal indicates that many of such prayers no longer appear.

As to the *style* of prayers, almost all modern Christians demand that they should be direct, simple in structure and *un*rhetorical. The tone of public speech nowadays is conversational, unemphatic. Rhetoric of the old style suggests insincerity and no longer moves people. Modern written style is for the most part paratactic, one statement is added to another and Latinized forms have almost disappeared. This may seem to some regrettable, it may be indeed that our language is becoming impoverished, but it seems inevitable that the 'secular' style should be used on 'sacred' occasions. Certainly, this is one way, if a small one, that modern liturgy can be made acceptable to modern people who do not want to have to put on a special culture to worship God.

In fact, much of this has been achieved already in the English translations which have been offered to us in recent years. This does not mean that they have always been as good as they might be, even taking into account the convention the translators have adopted. But complete success is too much to ask for all at once and it remains to be proved that any other style is satisfactory. In the early days of turning liturgical Latin into English, the experiments then made were far from happy.

There is, too, the question of the *literary form* of certain prayers, notably the collects and the eucharistic prayers. The former have been much extolled for their concision and brevity. But these are precisely the qualities that provide difficulties. In practice, they are over almost before the people have been able to take in their content. It is true that they are presidential prayers and there is no question here of the validity and appropriateness of the presidential role. But the form does need thinking about and there would seem to be some official evidence that it is not always thought to be as satisfactory as it might be. In the revised liturgy of the Holy Week we learn that local conferences of bishops may *add* acclamations to the General Intercession on Good Friday. This is a pointer in the right direction. The collect-form needs teasing out and possibly it should approximate to that of the prayer of the faithful in the Mass. That is, it would be perfectly possible to state the main theme of the prayer in an invitation, give time for reflection and then sum up the whole petition in one or two short phrases to which responses for the people could be attached.

As we have observed elsewhere, much the same could be done for the eucharistic prayer. Interventions, in addition to the acclamation after the consecration, could be arranged at other points too, as has in fact been done with the two alternative prayers of blessing in the baptismal rite.

Granted that the eucharistic prayer is the supremely presidential prayer, it does not follow that it should be a monologue.

There is another matter related to this. While I would insist that any public liturgy must have a fixed pattern (otherwise all is confusion), it does not follow that you have to have fixed forms.[9] Improvised prayers, especially when there is nothing else in a service, have their dangers that are well known, but our liturgy is still too rigid in this respect. Might there not be room for *extempore* prayer? For instance, the postcommunion prayers often seem remote from the concerns of the local congregation. Why should we always have a fixed text at this point? It is true, as we have observed, that the celebrant may use the communion verse to lead the people to prayer at this point. But then, why have to say a fixed text as well? This is perhaps a small matter, but sometimes our worship seems *over*-hieratic and a little freedom would do much to humanize it.

2. The church has now recognized that gestures may have different meanings in different parts of the world and does not insist that they should always be the same everywhere. It is said that the hand-clasp in the marriage service is unacceptable in certain parts of Africa. It may be replaced by something else. The celebrant no longer has to *kiss* the book after the gospel: he may reverence the book in some other way, by bowing for instance (GI 232). Genuflexions to bishops and such like personages have, mercifully, been abolished (a nice piece of desacralization!) and on the positive side, the Hindu sign of greeting (the closing of the hands before the breast) has now been introduced into the liturgy in India.

These are but indications that there is still much to be done to work out acceptable gestures in the Western world. It will have to be done by experiment for we have lost the art of using our bodies, and it would seem to be a task the church could very usefully perform. Fundamentally, it means not that someone should devise beautiful gestures but that the Christian community should ask itself: what is the *meaning* of, say, the sign of peace? Why do we stand or kneel for certain parts of the service and are there other ways in which we can express what we discover to be the meaning of these attitudes? Is it quite beyond the bounds of possibility that the congregation should approach the sanctuary and gather round it for the eucharistic action and thus learn the meaning of being together? This in fact happens quite spontaneously in smaller and less formal groups, so it *is* natural. What stands in its way is the large amorphous congregations that have been forced on us by circumstances and which now have come to be regarded as normal. Whatever can be done about that situation, it is interesting to observe that the smaller community finds the postures and gestures that are appropriate to the occasion. Again, it is worth emphasizing that these gestures are found in a natural 'secular' situation and the mem-

---

[9] For further discussion, see J. D. Crichton, in 'Liturgical Forms', *The Way*, supplement, Autumn 1970.

bers of the community bring into their worship certain 'worldly' attitudes.

When we come to the clothing of the liturgy we have to apply a rather different set of criteria. Special clothes are part of 'celebration', part of the décor that we saw was a necessary part of celebration. There is, then, nothing particularly 'sacred' about putting on such clothes. On the other hand, if we are to judge by what is now being designed and made, there is considerable dissatisfaction with the style of liturgical clothes, even those of better quality, that have been common in recent centuries. The trend has definitively set towards flowing simplicity and austerity of decoration. Yet, such clothes are 'unworldly' and we have to ask whether they are necessary.

The question must be asked first of the president. In recent years, some priests have been seen to celebrate in the more intimate assembly in their ordinary clothes upon which, frequently, they have laid a stole. A piece of ecclesiastical embroidery added to jacket and trousers was so incongruous as to be risible, and one wonders what mystical significance the former added to the latter.

It may be said, I think, that all liturgical celebrations have a focal point. For the building it is the altar;[10] of the whole service it is the president. That does not mean that he should or even may absorb all the ministerial functions of the rite but he has to direct them and should be visibly in control of them. He has a special relationship to Christ the Priest and a special relationship to the people he is there to serve. Just as the former is externalized by a sacrament, so the latter may fittingly be marked by a special dress. The necessity is first psychological and secondly, in the broad sense, sacramental. At the same time, what is required in one kind of assembly, as, for instance, in a large church where his role needs to be emphasized, is not necessarily right for another. One can but regret that the Instruction on House Masses[11] rigidly insisted that the celebrant should wear everything he does in church. In fact, a certain simplification of liturgical vesture is already apparent. One garment, with a stole worn outside it, is becoming common and this, one would have thought, was sufficient for celebration wherever it takes place.

If it be said that this is to sacralize a perfectly normal function, it can only be replied that just as with the notion of community, as with the need to find suitable gestures for worship, so here, it may very well be the task of the church to discover appropriate signs for a liturgy which cannot do without them. In so doing, she may well teach the 'world' a lesson about old, far-off, forgotten things which are only old and far-off because the world has forgotten that they enshrined certain human values.[12]

---

[10] See the Instruction, *Inter Oecumenici*, of 1964, 91.

[11] 15 May 1969, *Notitiae*, February 1970, no. 51, pp. 50–5.

[12] The young at any rate are abandoning the dull 'business-like' dress of their elders and are indulging in the fantastic. Perhaps they do not succeed very well, but they *are* trying to 'celebrate'.

Should other members of the assembly be vested? This is more problematical and the consensus seems to be that readers should not. They come from the assembly and should visibly remain members of it even when performing their function. If, however, one of them carries the Book of the Gospels in a procession whose participants are vested, it would seem better that he were also. The vesting of others, servers and choir, seems to be a matter of aesthetics. A collection of bejeaned or short-trousered males on the sanctuary is usually not a pretty sight and their sartorial idiosyncrasies are better disguised. But there is no case at all for dressing them up as 'little clergymen'.[13] A single, well-made garment is both more practical and better to look at.

There are those who will say that all this is unnecessary. Perhaps so, but I wish I could be persuaded that modern dress is beautiful. Objectively it is quite bizarre. However, much will depend on the mood of the assembly, on its intimacy or otherwise, and on the very building in which it meets.

3. In recent years there has been a vast debate, which continues, about, first, the kind of building that is needed for the celebration of the liturgy and then, whether there should be church-buildings at all, set apart exclusively for worship.[14]

As to the first, the guide-lines were laid down in the Instruction *Inter Oecumenici* of 1964[15] and repeated in the General Instruction now included in the *Missale Romanum* of 1970. There are three principles: the shape of the church must be such as to allow the people to act as the celebrating community, the altar is the focal point of the whole building and all other elements, side-altars, shrines, statues and the rest must be subordinated to the first two. Most newly-built churches have conformed with some degree of success to these principles, but there remain the vast numbers of traditional churches throughout the world. Adaptation has sometimes been possible, though not always. In any case, there is the continuing problem of providing for the needs of great numbers of people of the vast industrial parishes and the consequence, that in these circumstances anything like a community cannot be established. The main solution to this has been the search for and animation of sub-groups within the parish which can be brought together for what one must call celebration with a human dimension. But, where the church does by its shape suggest community, where the hard and fast divisions made by screens and receding sanctuaries no longer exist, where it is possible to establish a real *rapport* between president and people, some sense of community, at least during the time of worship, can be fostered. In this *ambiance* attitudes, gestures, vestments

---

[13] The Italian word '*chierichetti*' is a bit of a give-away.

[14] See, *inter alia*, the many publications of the Institute for Liturgy and Architecture, Birmingham University.

[15] For commentary, see J. D. Crichton, in *Changes in the Liturgy* (London, 1965), pp. 86–104.

can play their part without ever turning the worship into a hieratic performance.

The second question is much more complex and differing points of view are hotly contested.

One view is that to set up churches, sacred buildings that are never used for anything except worship, is to take religion, worship and so the people, *away* from secular life. It is to suggest to them that 'world' and 'church' are opposites, that the world is not merely secular but secularized, that God is absent from it and can only be found 'in church'. It may be so, though much will depend on the mentality people bring with them to church. Buildings as such, and divorced from community, can do very little, and the promoters of the 'secular' church may themselves be suffering from a certain historically conditioned hang-over. In the nineteenth century, churches appear to have been purposely disfunctional; they were a protest or even a defiance of a style of worship and by implication of the religion and society that supported it. There was much of this in Pugin's attitude. But most modern churches no longer point a finger of defiance to the world. They settle into its background and visibly emerge from its culture—for good and for ill! The important question is whether even modern churches are expressions of a community or merely religious service-stations for a number of people who happen to live near it. In other words, the crucial test is the quality of the service that the community the building is supposed to express is giving to the wider community which surrounds it. To this matter we shall return.

The difficulties on a practical level are greater and more important. A conventional church-building is used for a single purpose and for a limited number of hours per week. The cost of such buildings is enormous and their maintenance in heating, lighting and other necessary services is considerable. The question is pressed whether Christians are justified in this sort of expenditure in a world that suffers want on a very considerable scale. Are not such buildings not so much the sign of the serving church as its contradiction? Is it a good thing for the pilgrim church to weigh itself down with property? Should we give the impression that Christians are very well installed in this world order and will not its witness to unworldly values be obscured? Then there are the needs of the Christian people, whether they may be described as a community or not, needs that go far beyond worship. Should not the parish buildings be such that they can foster a spirit of community, perhaps even create community where otherwise it does not exist? If they can, then buildings do become important, and so we are brought to the question of the multi-purpose church.

This is being strongly urged but it is necessary to insist that there is no inherent virtue in a building of whatever sort. The question that has to be asked—and answered—is whether a multi-purpose building is going to serve a community already existing or that can be brought into existence.

If around the church-complex there is a natural community—and such still exist—with sufficient provision to enable people to meet, to know each other and to engage in the activities that people normally seek, there would seem to be very little case for the multi-purpose church. But where there is nothing but a church-building, where you have new areas and people are alienated from their surroundings, which they have not chosen, and where many if not most have only the most tenuous attachment to any kind of church, there is a very strong case for the multi-purpose building.

The first thing necessary is that these people should be able to make a *human* contact with the Christian community and this the right kind of building can very powerfully assist. It will be a place into which flow the normal activities of human life, at least in its leisure moments. Ideally it will be placed at the centre of local life, easily accessible to people who come to shop, to conduct whatever business they have with the local authorities, where in fact they naturally meet. Where a new community is forming the church may be able to offer certain facilities to the public authorities who have not yet set up their organizations. In any case, there will be other needs that are not officially catered for at all: the care of the old, nursery provision for children of pre-school age and facilities for youth. If at the heart of this complex there is a 'worship room' which is known and preferably visible and if the clergy or laity are known to be available to people whatever their needs, the building will help in the work that waits to be done and it will be justified by the work it makes possible. But all depends on the *people*, both those who are trying to serve and those who come seeking various kinds of service.

To this extent, but to this extent only, a building can be said to be 'missionary'. It is positive, turned towards the world instead of away from it, it is welcoming rather than repelling, it *can* become a centre of ordinary life and through the ministry of its servants it can do something to reach out to those to whom the gospel is to be proclaimed. For it needs to be emphasized that 'the church' is people and as we have learned from Vatican II, the church is by nature missionary and the whole people bear the responsibility and burden of mission. Buildings can help or hinder, but if the most perfect multi-purpose church ever thought up were run as a conventional church, if the community were concerned with no more than its own worship and its own affairs, it would be no more missionary than a neo-Gothic structure beautifully arranged for medieval usage.

Nor should it be thought that such a building is without its difficulties. Anyone who has had to preside over a parish where the only building was a parish hall will know the daunting tasks that present themselves. There are those who argue that the 'worship room' should be used for secular activities to emphasize (such is the argument) that there are no divisions between the sacred and the secular. But, in practice, such activities are likely to take place on Saturday evening, but may go on to a late hour, and then who is going to clear up the mess? How can the building be ventilated and prepared for worship the next day? There are other problems of supervision and maintenance which may be even greater. There is a case for the multi-purpose building and in many areas it is a strong one, but it is probable that experience will show that if it is to serve the Christian mission successfully, the 'worship room' will have to be reserved for worship.

The discussion could be continued and whatever may be decided in detail, there is one over-riding consideration. The Christian community exists to serve others and it should be as close to them as possible, showing a solidarity with them in their needs, their sufferings and their joys. It is then that the 'others' will discover that 'church' can be part of ordinary life and may become part of theirs. If the buildings can become in some way the sign of this concern, they will be an authentic expression of the church's mission.

The purpose of the foregoing considerations is to show that the liturgy, without detriment to its essential structure, can be made more accessible to modern people, that it can be brought closer to their mentality and meet their needs more effectively. The result of such a mild desacralization is that the life of our society could more easily flow into and affect the celebration of the liturgy, making it visibly the expression of people of this generation. The young in particular would not feel alienated and it would be much more possible to celebrate life (in the sense of Rahner), the life of the world as we know it and experience it. At present the gap between worship and world is too wide. Liturgy still looks too much like the cultic preoccupation of a minority grouping, and although it has been transformed beyond the dreams of even the most progressive in five years, it still bears too many marks of its past.

We should be clear, however, that liturgy is not a missionary device and attempts to make the liturgy more accessible to people of our time should not be mistaken for propaganda efforts to 'bring them in', to capture the unbelieving multitudes. There is indeed a regrettable tendency to expose the eucharist to those without Christian faith. The eucharist is the sign of the believing, Christian community and whenever the faith of the community is diluted the credibility of the sign is diminished.[16] Once again, it is for the members of the community to take the gospel to others who must be prepared for participation in the worship of the community.

But the liturgy, and in a particular way the eucharist, remains the sign of the missionary, pilgrim church, and if we are to take the Constitution on the Church in the Modern World seriously, the liturgy of the church must be relevant to the world, must be accessible to the world, if it is to

---

[16] I am thinking of certain weddings and funerals where the congregation may largely be made up of non-believers. Are we right in exposing the 'sacred mysteries' to them? With funerals certainly the Mass can take place either beforehand or at some other time altogether.

become the authentic sign of both the church and the world. But it must become more than sign. It must be the means by which this world can be lifted up to God, drawn into his continuing creative purpose so that in the end it can be transfigured, bearing the image of the Risen Christ who triumphed over sin, evil, pain, suffering and death.

This is the final message of the Second Vatican Council. The pilgrim church is moving towards the consummation and it and the whole world are destined to be transformed so that there will be a new heaven and a new earth: 'We do not know the time of the consummation of the earth and all humanity. Nor do we know how all things will be transformed. . . . But we are taught that God is preparing a new dwelling place and a new earth where justice will abide and whose blessedness will answer and surpass all the longings for peace which spring up in the human heart.' But the end is now, is being realized in the processes of human history: 'For here grows the body of a new human family, a body which even now is able to give some kind of foreshadowing of the new age.' It is through the liturgy, 'the source of all the church's power', that this is being achieved now—or can be, if men can bring to it the whole of their living. Earth and heaven co-inhere, the 'sacred' and the 'profane' find their point of juncture in the worship that Christian people offer to God and 'if earthly progress must be carefully distinguished from the growth of God's kingdom', it is nevertheless true that 'the former can contribute to the better ordering of human society' and is consequently a matter of vital concern to the Christian church.

But this human society which is now being painfully shaped towards God's purpose, is destined to be transformed: 'After we have obeyed the Lord, and in his Spirit nurtured on earth the values of human dignity, brotherhood and freedom, and indeed all the good fruits of our nature and enterprise, *we will find them again*, but freed of stain, burnished and *transfigured*. This will be so when Christ hands over to the Father "a kingdom eternal and universal: a kingdom of truth and life, of holiness and grace, of justice, love and peace".[17] On this earth *that kingdom is already present in mystery*. When the Lord returns, it will be brought to full flower' (Church in Modern World, 39).

This teaching suggests the final importance of a liturgy that will welcome and embrace all earthly values. For it is this liturgy that lies at the heart of the process by which men and things are being slowly transformed until they bear the image of Christ. In the eucharist there is that same power of reconciliation, union and restoration that was present in the redeeming work of Christ on the cross and this power is made available to mankind now. It is God's intention that all things should be brought under Christ as head and that all things should be offered through him, should be purified, renewed, and their hidden potentialities revealed. But the daily

[17] Preface of the Feast of Christ the King.

offering of the world is but a preparation for the final eucharist when Christ, the Second Adam and the High Priest of the human race, will offer everything to his Father, handing them over to him so that he may be all in all.[18]

---

[18] Ephesians 1:10; I Corinthians 15:25-8.

INDEX

Acclamation, element of, in eucharistic prayer, 84, 87

Acclamations:
after the consecration, 67, 90–1, and n, 117, 157
in reformed Ministry of the Word, 68, 74, 75
power to add, to General Intercession, 168

Activism, dangers of, 13

Address, the, in entrance rites, 69, 70–1, 105

Administration *see* Communion

Advancement of peoples, prayer for, 127

Advent:
in revised Calendar, 111 and n
mass formulas, 116
prefaces, 129

Agnus Dei, breaking of bread during, 97, 105–6

Altar-bread, size of, 98, 151 and n

Altar-vessels, choice of, 151

Alcuin, 122

All Saints, formula for votive masses, 118

Alleluia, provision for, in reformed liturgy, 68, 74, 75

Anamnesis:
element of, in eucharistic prayer, 84, 91–2
interpretation of term, 58–61 and n, 64

Angels, formulas for votive masses, 118

Annunciation, Feast of the, 107n

Anointing with oil, symbolism of, 20, 22, 23, 29

Apostles, formulas for votive masses, 118

Apostolic Constitution, 1970, 47, 48–9

Ascension, Feast of the:
collect for, 121–2, 130–1
mass formula, 116
precedence among feast days, 109
preface for, 131

Ash Wednesday, in revised Calendar, 110

Ashes, symbolic function of, 29

Ashworth, Henry, 53n

Baptism, Sacrament and rite of:
alternative prayers of blessing in, 168
consultation with families on choice of texts, 43–4
mass formulas for, 117
misunderstanding of nature of, 17 and n
responsibilities of celebrant in choice of formulas, 157
significance of consecration of oils used in, 42
signs and symbols in, 21–2
ultimate purpose of, 30, 35

Baptism of the Lord, Feast of, 109, 111, 116

Bible services for Rogation and Ember days, 112

Birth, ancient monument of celebration, 138, 140

Bishops:
intercessions for, in eucharistic prayer, 95
relationship with priests and people, 41–2
theology on responsibilities of, 61

Blessing of the bread and wine, in origins of eucharistic prayer, 85–7 and n, 118

Blessings:
in the dismissal, 68
Solemn, 117

Bodily postures, gestures, significance of, 21, 40, 149–50 and n, 152, 169–70

Body and Blood of Christ, Feast of, *see* Corpus Christi

Botte, Dom, 88n, 92n, 99n

Bread, eucharistic:
breaking of, a sign of unity of faithful, 63, 65
eucharistic use corresponding to action of Christ, 63–4
mingling with wine after consecration, 98 and n, 106
misunderstanding of symbolism, 17–9 and n
presentation during offertory rite, 82–3

Bread, eucharistic—contd.
  proper management of, by celebrant, 150
  size of, 98, 151 and n
Buber, Martin, 4, 6

Calendar:
  precedence among feast days, 109, 113–4 and n
  principles underlying revision, 107–114
Cantors:
  opportunities in new liturgy, 142
  significance of liturgical functions, 42
Casel, Odo, 23–4, 27
Catechesis, responsibilities of celebrant in, 148–9
Catechumenate:
  mass formulas for, 117
  restoration of, 110
  significance of episcopal participation in initiation rites, 42
Celebration:
  and trend to secularization in modern times, 135–6, 138–9
  birth, marriage, death, ancient monuments of, 138, 140
  essential elements of, 136, 137–40
  need to restore sense of, in Christian worship, 141
  traditions in Greece and Rome, 136–7
Chalice:
  design of, 151
  proper management by celebrant, 150
  significance of elevation of, 56
Choirs, significance of liturgical functions, 42;
  see also Music, Singing
Chrism:
  mass formulas for, 117
  oil of, 29, 42
  preface for, 130
  responsibilities of celebrant in choice of texts for, 157
Christ the King, Feast of:
  in 1970 missal, 117
  precedence among feast days, 109
  preface for, 175n
Christian unity, collects for, 126–7
Christianity:
  community nature of, 8, 9–10, 13–4, 31, 32–6, 56–7, 60–1, 136
  sacramental nature of, 7–8, 9–10
Christmas:
  in revised Calendar, 110–1
  introits and communion verses, 132
  mass formulas, 116
  secularization of, 136

Church, the:
  co-inherence of earthly and heavenly, 14–5, 30, 57
  collects for, 126
  community nature, 31, 33–6, 56–7
  concept of, as body of Christ, 10–1, 30, 57
  concept of liturgy as sign of real nature of, 58–9
  concept of priesthood of, 34–6
  implications of decentralization, 43–4
  prophetic function in modern world, 159–63
Churches:
  building, furnishing, to suit modern times, 171–4
  decoration, furnishing, to aid sense of celebration, 143 and n
  mass formulas for dedication of, 117
Church-going, decline of, 1–2
Clergy, intercessions for, in eucharistic prayer, 95
Clothing see Vestments
Cockfosters, Benedictine church at, 143n
Collection:
  presentation during offertory rite, 82–3 and n
  significance of taking up, by laity, 42–3
Collects:
  in entrance rites, 69 and n, 72, 105
  origins, adaptation to modern needs, 119–27 and n
  principles underlying selection for 1970 missal, 118–9, 128–9
  reform to meet modern needs, 168–9
  see also Prayers
Commons, the, in 1970 missal, 117
Communion:
  concept of, as community action, 39–40, 98–9
  eschatological perspective in reformed rite, 66–7
  manner of receiving, 100–3 and n
  place in new Order of Mass, 63–4, 68
  principles underlying reform of rite, 96–7
  proper understanding of term, 64–5
  purpose, conduct of procession, 65, 98–9, 142
  restoration of frequent reception, 18, 56, 65–6
  restoration of reception in both kinds, 18, 100–3
  rite of administration, 99–100
  rubrics concerning priestly functions during, 50n
  singing during 103, 142

Communion—contd.
value of silence during, 103
Communion verses:
alternatives in 1970 missal, 116, 132–3
singing of, 133–4 and n
Community:
creation of sense of, in entrance rites, 69–70
evidence of, in conduct of offertory rites, 82–3
in essential nature of Christian worship, 8, 9–10, 13–4, 31, 32–6, 55–7, 60–1, 136
preservation of sense of, in design of churches, 171–4
significance of ministries of laity, 42–3
symbolized by communion procession, 98–9
Concelebration, altar-bread for, 98
Confession and absolution:
alternative version in 1970 missal, 117
in entrance rite, 71–2 and n, 105
Confirmation:
mass formulas for, 117
oil of chrism used at, 29, 42
preface for, 130
responsibilities of celebrant in choice of texts for, 157
Congar, Père, 32
Congregation for Worship, establishment of, 45
Consecration, moment of, 83–4, 94n
Corpus Christi, Feast of:
collect for, 123 and n
mass formula, 117, 123
precedence among feast days, 109
significance, 55
Corpus Christi hymn, 102 and n
Council of Trent, 52n, 60, 66, 76
Cox, Harvey, 135, 137 and n, 139, 140, 144–5
Creed, the:
constituent of reformed Ministry of the Word, 68, 74, 75
significance of recitation by all, 39, 78–9
Cross, signs of the:
conduct of, 150
in reformed entrance rites, 105
Cross, Veneration of the, 150n

Dead, the:
commemoration in eucharistic prayer, 94, 95
mass formulas for, 118
responsibilities of celebrant in choice

of formulas for masses for, 157–8
Death, ancient moment of celebration, 138
Der-Balyzeh, prayer and doxology of, 96
Desacralization of the liturgy to meet modern needs, 163–6, 167–74 and n
Dioceses:
functions in adaptation of liturgy to local needs, 41
liturgical celebrations in, a sign of the great church, 57
Dismissal rites:
form and content of blessings, 104 and n
place in 1970 missal, 68
Divine Office, priestly functions in prayer during, 54
Dix, Gregory, 92n
Doctors, mass formulas for commemoration of, 117
Doxology, at end of eucharistic prayer, 84, 95–6

Easter:
collect for, 120
in revised Calendar, 108–9 and n
mass formulas, 116
secularization of, 136
Eastertide:
collect for second Sunday of, 121
in revised Calendar, 109–10
mass formulas, 116
Eastern churches, emphasis on co-inherence of earthly and heavenly churches, 15
Ecumenism, in intercessions in eucharis-in prayer, 95
Educators, mass formulas for, 117
Elevation of the host and chalice:
rubrics, traditions concerning, 50n, 56, 84
significance of, 55, 150
Eliade, Mircea, 24, 25, 27
Ember days, in revised Calendar, 111–2
Embolism, in reformed communion rite, 97
Encounter theology, 4, 6, 24–5
Entrance chant, 69 and n, 70, 142
Entrance rites:
composition, structure, in 1970 missal, 69–72, 105
constituent of the mass, 68
ultimate purpose of, 33
Epiclesis (invocation), element of, in eucharistic prayer, 84, 87–8, 92–3 and n

Epiphany, element of, in liturgy, 23–4, 25–6, 31–2, 38–9

Epiphany, Feast of the:
in revised Calendar, 111
mass formulas, 116
precedence among feast days, 109

Episcopal conferences, duties in reform of liturgy, 46

Eschatology, in reformed eucharistic rites, 66–7

Eucharist:
community nature of, 13–4, 34, 38–9, 55–7, 60–1, 62
connection between word and sacrament in, 23, 62
constituent parts, 68
eschatological perspective in reformed rites, 66–7
misunderstanding of symbolism in, 17–9 and n
relation of liturgy to institution by Christ, 63–4
relationship of priest and laity in, 36–40
sacrament signifying love, 35, 39–40
theology of, 51–3, 55–68
transforming nature of, 10–1, 30

Eucharistic prayer:
acclamation in, 84, 87
anamnesis (memorial) in, 84, 91–2
critical observations on, 105
description of reformed versions, 63–4, 68, 117
doxology, 84, 95–6
elements in alternative versions, 90, 92–3
intercessions in, 84, 93–5 and n
invocation (epiclesis) in, 84, 87–8, 92–3 and n
proclamation in, 84–5
reform of language and form to meet modern needs, 168–9
responsibilities of celebrant in choice of, 156–7
significance in context of eucharist, 83–4
thanksgiving in, 84, 85–7, 91
words of institution in, 84, 88–91 and n

Eucharistic sacrifice, interpretation of term, 52–5 and n; see also Memorial of the Lord

Existentialist philosophy, 3–7, 9, 24–5

Experimentation, principles underlying scope of, 40–4, and n

Exsultet, singing of, 150n

Faith, relation to mystical experience, 12–3

Fantasy, element of, in celebration, 137–8 and n

Feast days, determination of precedence, 109, 113–4 and n; see also Celebration, and individual feasts

Fifty Days see Eastertide

Fraction:
conduct of, 151 and n
place in reformed communion rite, 97–8, 105–6
purpose, 63–4 and n, 65

Gelineau, Père, 151n

General Instruction:
provisions concerning holy communion, 64–7
provisions concerning the eucharistic action, 62–4
provisions concerning the mass, 51–3, 55–61
provisions concerning the role of the priest, 54–5, 61–2
purpose, theological basis of, 47–8, 50–5

Genuflection:
conduct of, 150
restriction on use of, 169

Gestures:
in liturgy suited to modern times, 169–70
responsibilities of celebrant in use of, 149–50 and n
significance, symbolism of, 21, 40

Gifts, preparation and offering of:
flexibility of provisions concerning procession, 58
integration into eucharistic sacrifice, 87–8
nature, form, content of rites, 63–4, 82–3 and n
prayers during rites, 82–3, 84 and n, 105
responses during rites, 83n

Gloria, in entrance rites, 72, 105

Gospel, the:
conduct of proclamation of, 149 and n
in reformed Ministry of the Word, 74
linking of preface with, 129–30
link with Old Testament readings, 155

Graduals, singing of, 133–4 and n

Greetings:
alternatives in 1970 missal, 117
in entrance rites, 69, 70, 105
signs and gestures of, 169

Guardini, Romano, 137

Guéranger, Abbot, 107n

Handshake, symbolic functions, 21, 152n
Harvest, ancient moment of celebration, 139, 140
Heidegger, 3–4
Hippolytus, 64n, 92, 93, 95–6
Holy Family, Feast of, 109, 111, 116
Holy Spirit:
  exercise of gifts of, through participation in liturgy, 34–6, 39–40
  invocation of, in eucharistic prayer, 84, 87–8, 92–3 and n
Holy Trinity, Feast of:
  collect for, 122–3
  place in 1970 missal, 117, 118
  precedence among feast days, 109
Holy Week:
  chant for Veneration of the Cross, 150n
  in revised Calendar, 108–9
  mass formulas, 116
  power to add acclamations to General Intercession during, 168
Homily:
  constituent of reformed Ministry of the Word, 68, 75, 76
  form, content, functions of, 76–9 and n, 148 and n, 149, 155
Host, elevation of:
  rubrics, traditions concerning, 50n, 56, 84
  significance of, 55
House-groups:
  principles underlying work of, 40–1
  vestments appropriate to masses in, 170
Huizinga, 137
Hymns, need for new forms, 142; see also Music

Incense, control of use, 58
Indexes, in 1970 missal, 118
Initiation, Christian, mass formulas for, 117
Innocent I, Pope, 94 and n
Institute for Liturgy and Architecture, Birmingham University, 171n
Institution narrative, in eucharistic prayer, 84, 88–91 and n
Intentions, distinguished from prayers, 81
Intercession, element of, in eucharistic prayer, 84, 93–5 and n
Intercessions, General:
  adaptation of form to local circumstances, 129
  constituent of reformed Ministry of the Word, 68, 74, 80
  formulas for, in 1970 missal, 118

participation of laity in conduct of, 80, 81
principles underlying form and content, 80–1 and n, 82 and n
responses during, 81 and n, 168
International Committee on English in the Liturgy, 46n, 91n
Intinction, communion by, 101–3 and n
Introits, 132–3, 133–4 and n
Invocation (epiclesis), element of, in eucharistic prayer, 84, 87–8, 92–3 and n

Jounel, Mgr., 119, 132–3
Joy, essential element in celebration, 140

Keble, John, 113
Kerygma, elements of, in homily, 78
Kirk, K. E., 9–10 and n
Kirkegaard, 27
Kiss, the symbolic functions, 21
Koinonia, interpretation of, 64–5, 99
Kyries, in entrance rites, 71–2, 105

Laity:
  functions at presentation of gifts, 82–3 and n
  importance of establishment of contact between celebrant and, 69–71
  intercessions for, in eucharistic prayer, 95
  prayers for, in 1970 missal, 127
  relationship with ordained priesthood, 36–40, 61–2, 69–71
  restoration of active participation in liturgy, 31–2, 37–40, 47 and n, 56–7, 58, 68–9, 80–1
  restoration of frequent reception of communion during mass, 18, 65–6
  significance of particular ministries of, 42–3
  to be consulted about implementation of renewed liturgy, 43–4
  tradition of exclusion from active participation in liturgy, 5, 55–6 and n
  ultimate purpose of active participation in liturgy, 37–40
Language, in liturgy suited to modern times, 167–9
Larkin, Ernest E., 11–2
Latin, preservation in communion chants, 103

Lectionaries:
consultation with laity on choice of texts, 43–4
principles underlying reform of, 74–6 and n
responsibilities of celebrant in use of, 155–6 and n
Leeuw, G. van der, 24
Leisure, man's need for creative, 139–40
Lent:
collects for Sundays of, 120–1
mass formulas for, 116
prefaces for, 129–30
responsibilities of celebrant in choice of texts, formulas for, 154
restoration of proper observance of, 107 and n, 110
Ligier, Louis, 59n, 86 and n, 87n
Liturgical year, and the revised Calendar, 107–14
Liturgy:
allocation to laity of ministries in, 42
community nature of, 13–4, 34, 55–7, 60–1, 62
concept of, as celebration of Christian mystery, 26–30
concept of, as meeting place of earth and heaven, 14–5, 30, 66–7, 164–5
contribution to modern society, 143–5
different priestly functions in, 38, 40
exercise of gifts of the Spirit through, 35
function of symbolism in, 19–21, 29, 65, 66
function of word in, 23
implications of decentralization of the Church, 43–4
importance of consultation in preparation of, 147–8
modern man's difficulties in acceptance of, 2, 164
modern trend towards desacralization, 164–6
opportunities for celebration provided by, 141–3
principles underlying adaptation to local conditions, 40–4, 45–6, 57–8, 113, 114, 117, 165–6 and n
reasons for resistance to new, 5
reform of, procedures for, 45–9
relation to mystical experience, 10–4
relationship of priests and people in celebration of, 36–40
requirements for modern times, 167–74

restoration of active lay participation in, 31–2, 37–40, 47 and n, 56–7, 58, 68–9, 80–1
scandal of particularity, 8–9
significance of 'epiphanic' element in, 23–4, 25–6, 31–2, 38–9
significance of proclamation of the word in, 39
tradition of exclusion of laity from active participation in, 5, 55–6 and n
ultimate purpose and potential of, 174–6
Lord's Prayer, in reformed communion rite, 97

Manichaeism, danger of, in trend towards secularization, 138–9
Marcel, Gabriel, 4, 6
Marriage, sacrament and rite of:
ancient moment of celebration, 138, 140
consultation with families on choice of texts, 43–4
mass formulas for, 117
mass formulas for anniversaries, 117
responsibilities of celebrant in choice of texts for, 153–4, 157
Martyrs, mass formulas for commemoration of, 117
Mary, Blessed Virgin:
feast of, as the Mother of God, 111, 116
inclusion of prayer of, in eucharistic prayer, 95
mass formulas for feasts of, 117
votive masses, 118
Mass see Eucharist
Mass formulas:
provided in 1970 missal, 116–8
responsibilities of celebrant in choice of, 153–5, 156, 157–8
Masses and prayers for various occasions:
collects for, 126–7
formulas for, 117
Masure, E., 18
Material goods:
attitudes towards, 138–9 and n
search for alternatives to dependence on, 2–3
Maundy Thursday:
in the revised Calendar, 109, 110
preface for, 130
significance of consecration of holy oils on, 42
significance of Washing of Feet on, 39–40
Meditation, modern reaction against, 13

Memoria-anamnesis, interpretation of, 59n

Memorial (*anamnesis*), element of, in eucharistic prayer, 84, 91–2

'Memorial of the Lord':
in eucharistic theology, 58–61 and n, 62–4, 101
interpretation of term, 52–5 and n

Mercy, works of, mass formulas commemorating those conspicuous for, 117

Mimesis, in primitive religion, 19

Music:
exercise of gifts of the Spirit through, 34
problems, opportunities, in revised liturgy, 70, 71–2, 73, 79–80, 103, 141–2

Mysterium, concept of, 28–9 and n

Mysterium fidei, omission in institution narrative of reformed Roman canon, 90

Mystery, Christian, essential nature of, 21, 24–30

Mysticism, Christian, ecclesial nature of, 9–11 and n

Myth:
function of, 19, 24
relation to mystery, 24, 25–6

Newman, Cardinal, 113, 138n

Offertory *see* Gifts

Offertory verses, omission from 1970 missal, 116n

Oils, Holy:
consecration of, 42, 110
symbolic functions, 20, 22, 23, 29

Old Testament:
readings from, linked with gospel, 155
restoration of reading from, to Ministry of the Word, 75–6 and n

Order of the Mass, New, purpose, scope of, 47–8, 50–2, 57–8, 105–6, 117

Ordination:
mass formulas, 117
significance of conferment in parish churches, 42
ultimate purpose of, 36–7

Organ-playing, exercise of gifts of the Spirit through, 34

Origen, 18

Palm Sunday:
combination with Passion Sunday, 110 and n

mass formula, 116
preface for, 130

Parishes:
implications of decentralization of the Church for liturgical life of, 43–4
liturgical celebrations in, a sign of the great church, 57
need for consultation and organization on preparation of the liturgy, 147–8
principles underlying adaptation of liturgy to needs of, 40–4 an n

Paschal candle, symbolic function, 22–3, 29

Paschal mystery:
at heart of liturgy, 26, 29–30, 55, 59, 60
observance in revised Calendar, 108–9 and n, 110

Paschaltide, forms for dismissal rite during, 104

Paschal Vigil, in revised Calendar, 109

Passion Sunday, combination with Palm Sunday, 110 and n

Pastors, mass formulas for, 117

Peace, Sign of:
conduct, significance of, 64–5, 152, 169
place in reformed liturgy, 71, 97–8

Penance, Sacrament of:
community nature of, 38
ultimate purpose of, 35

Penitential rites *see* Confession and absolution

Pentecost:
collects for, 122
in revised Calendar, 110
introits and communion verses for, 132
mass formulas for, 116

Persecuted, the, collects for, 127

Piédagnel, 93n

Pieper, Josef, 138

Pius V, edition of missal, 48–9, 55–6

Pius X, restoration of celebration of Sundays in Lent, 107

Plainsong, 118

Poor, apostolic nature of priestly care for, 54

Pope, prayers for, 95, 126

Prayers:
adaptation of General Intercessions for local needs, 129
after communion, 128
combination of public and private, 74
during offertory rite, 82–3 and n, 84 and n, 105
extempore, 169

Prayers—contd.
  form and content of intercessory, 80–1 and n, 82 and n
  importance of community, 9–10
  intentions distinguished from, 81
  modern reaction against tradition, 13–4
  of preparation, 97
  over the offerings, 127–8
  over the people, 117
  participation of laity in conduct of, 80, 81
  priestly functions in, 34, 54, 61–2
  reform to meet modern needs, 167–9
  responses during intercessions, 81 and n
  see also Eucharistic Prayer, Intercessions, General
Precious Blood, Feast of, 118
Prefaces:
  alternative beginnings and conclusions, 117
  character, scope of, in 1970 missal, 117, 129–32
Preparation before mass, formulas for, 118
Priesthood:
  apostolic nature of care for poor, 54
  concept of, as attribute of whole Church, 34–6, 40
  concept of functions in Pius V missal, 55–6
  primary obligations of ordained, 36–40, 54, 61–2
  relationship of ordained to laity, in celebration of liturgy, 36–40
  relationship with bishops, 41–2
  responsibilities in conduct of liturgy, 54–5, 61–2, 69–72, 146–58
Proclamation:
  element of, in eucharistic prayer, 84–5
  element of, in prefaces, 129
  see also Gospel, Word, Ministry of
Proemium, on reform of the liturgy, 47–8, 55
Proper of the Time, mass formulas for, 116–7
Psalmists, opportunities in reformed liturgy, 142
Pugin, 172

Radical theology, 144 and n
Rahner, Karl, 162–3
Readers, liturgical dress appropriate for, 171
Readings:
  constituent of Ministry of the Word, 68

principles underlying reform of, 74–6 and n, 155
  relationship of homily to, 76–9 and n
  responsibilities of celebrant in choice, presentation of, 155–6 and n
Real Presence of Christ:
  respect for, in manner of receiving communion, 102–3 and n
  theology of, 58, 89–91 and n
Recitation, responsibilities of celebrant in, 147, 148, 150n
Reconciliation, theme in reformed communion rite, 97–8
Religious:
  mass formulas for, 117
  mass formulas for renewal of vows, 117
Reproaches on Good Friday, singing of, 142
Reserved Sacrament, communication from, 66
Responses:
  after the gospel, need for, 142
  during intercessory prayer, 81 and n
  during offertory rite, 83n
  to doxology of eucharistic prayer, 96 and n
  to words of administration of communion, 99–100
Responsorial psalm:
  constituent of Ministry of the Word, 68, 74, 75
  singing of, 142
Revelation, and Christian mystery, 24–30
Ritual masses:
  formulas for, 117
  responsibilities of celebrant in choice of formulas, texts for, 153, 156, 157–8
Rogation days, 111–2
Roman Missal of 1970:
  character, scope, content of collects, 118–29
  format, 115
  illustrations, 115n
  responsibilities of celebrant in use of, 152–5
  see also individual parts, services

Sacred Heart, Feast of, 117, 118
Sacramental theology, dangers of intellectualizing signs, 16–7
Sacraments see Liturgy and under individual sacraments
Saints:
  collects for Proper of, 123–6
  insertion into intercessions in eucharistic prayer, 94–5

Saints—contd.
mass formulas for feast days, 117
responsibilities of celebrant in selection of texts for feast days, 153–4
revised feast days in Calendar, 107–8 and n, 109, 112–4 and n
St Ambrose, 18, 99–100
St Athanasius, 109
St Augustine, 37, 39n
St Bede, 112, 113
St Benedict, 125 and n
St Boniface, 112
St Cecily, 112
St Charles Borromeo, 113
St Charles Lwanga and companions, 124
St Cyril of Jerusalem, 93–4 and n, 99
St Felicity, 124
St Francis of Assisi, 145
St Francis of Sales, 123–4
St George, 124–5
St Gertrude, 11 and n
St Gregory the Great, 71–2, 94, 106, 120
St Irenaeus, 25
St John Chrysostom, 91 and n, 93n, 94n
St John Fisher, 112
St John Vianney, 113
St Joseph, 107n, 118
St Justin the Martyr, 63–4 and n, 93
St Leo the Great, 11, 28–9 and n, 121, 127, 130–1
St Maria Goretti, 112
St Martin of Porres, 112
St Paul, 118
St Paul Miki and companions, 124
St Perpetua, 124
St Peter, 118
St Raymund of Penyafort, 123
St Rose, 112
St Thérèse of Lisieux, 125–6
St Thomas Aquinas, 5, 7, 12, 13, 15 and n, 17, 39n, 52n, 60, 99, 102 and n, 123, 124, 160
St Thomas More, 112
St Thomas More Centre for Pastoral Liturgy, 143n
St Turibius, 112
St Vincent of Paul, 125
Sanctus, place in eucharistic prayer, 87
Sarapion, 96
Schillebeeckx, E., 53
Schuster, Cardinal, 143n
Scriptures see Readings
Secularization, danger to celebration in, 136, 138–9 and n
Separatism, dangers, avoidance of, 40–1
Sergius I, 97

Sermon, and homily, difficulty in distinguishing, 77 and n
Servers, liturgical functions, 42
Signs:
community nature of, 38–9, 56–7
concept of bread and wine as, 102
dangers in intellectualizing, 16–7
relation to symbols, 21–3
ultimate purpose of, 19–20, 25, 29
Silence:
creation by celebrant, 150 and n
value during communion rite, 103
Sin, and essence of baptism, 17 and n
Singing:
by the celebrant, 150 and n
during communion rite, 103
exercise of gifts of the Spirit through, 34
flexibility of provisions in reformed liturgy, 58
increase in quantity and quality, 141–2
Stolz, Alban, 10–1 and n
Sunday:
and opportunities for creative leisure, 139 and n
restoration of proper observance, 107, 108, 109
Sundays of the Year:
collects for, 122
mass formulas for, 116
prefaces for, 131–2
Symbols:
and myth and mystery, 24
concept of bread and wine as, 102
dangers, 20
essential element in liturgy, 2, 9
functions in liturgy, 19–21, 29, 65, 66
in administration of communion, 101
misunderstanding of nature of, 17–9 and n
origins in liturgy, 19, 24
relation of signs to, 21–3

Taboos, Christian abandonment of traditions of Israel, 35 and n
Taille, Maurice de la, 89 and n
Teresa, Mother, 161n
Tertullian, 93, 124
Thanksgiving:
after mass, formulas for, 118
element of, in eucharistic prayer, 84, 85–7, 91
Theology of hope, 144
Thurian, Max, 58–9n, 67 and n

United Nations Organization, prayers for, 127

Vann, Gerald, 6

Vasquez, 52n

Various occasions, masses and prayers for:
collects for, 126–7
formulas for, 117
responsibilities of celebrant in choice of formulas and texts for, 153, 156, 157–8

Vernacular, procedure for translation of liturgy into, 46

Vestments:
choice of, 151
for liturgy suited to modern times, 170–1 and n

Viaticum, formulas for administration of, 117

Virgins:
mass formulas for consecration of, 117
mass formulas for commemoration of, 117

Visual aids, to stimulate sense of celebration, 143 and n

Votive masses, formulas for, 118

Washing of the Feet, significance of rite, 39–40

Water:
formulas for blessing of, 118
eucharistic use corresponding to action of Christ, 63–4
presentation by people during offertory rite, 82–3

Wesley, John, 113

Wine:
eucharistic use corresponding to action of Christ, 63–4
mingling with bread after consecration, 98 and n, 106
presentation by people during offertory rite, 82–3

Women:
encouragement of active participation in liturgy, 31–2
mass formulas for commemoration of holy, 117

Word:
connection between eucharistic sacrament and, 23, 62
significance of proclamation of, in community worship, 39

Word, Ministry of the:
constituent parts, 68
grounds for resistance to reform, 72–3 and n
principles underlying reform of, 72–6 and n

Worship, symbol of celebration of deepest things, 140

Worship, Christian:
community nature, 8, 9–10, 13–4, 31, 32–6, 56–7, 60–1, 136
modern decline in, 1–2
need for wholeness in approach to, 5
significance of ministries allocated to laity, 42–3
ultimate purpose of, 7–8, 10–5

Index prepared by Brenda Hall, M.A.
Registered Indexer of the Society of Indexers

CHRISTIAN CELEBRATION:
THE SACRAMENTS

CONTENTS

Preface   v

Preface to the Second Edition   v

A List of Documents   vii

Abbreviations etc   ix

    I The Sacraments and Life   1

   II The Symbolism of the Sacraments   16

  III Baptism in the Context of Christian Initiation   29

  IV The Christian Initiation of Adults   40

   V Infant Baptism   65

  VI The Sacrament of Confirmation   88

 VII The Sacrament of Marriage   114

VIII Holy Order   137

  IX The Anointing and Care of the Sick   168

   X The Rite of Funerals   192

  XI The Sacrament of Penance   210

 XII Pastoral Opportunities   247

     Index   265

PREFACE

THE SUBJECT-MATTER of this volume of *Christian Celebration* is the revised liturgy of the sacraments of baptism, confirmation, matrimony holy order and the Anointing of the Sick. To this has been added a consideration of the revised funeral rites.

After a prolonged study of these documents I have become conscious of the wide range and variety of knowledge that is necessary for an adequate treatment of them. What is to be found here is only an introduction. Even so, in covering so wide a range I cannot hope that the book is free of errors. For this I must beg the indulgence of the reader and express the hope that when he finds them he will let me know and I will correct them if a second edition should become possible.

There are other texts, notably that new breviary or 'Liturgy of the Hours' which I have not been able to deal with in this volume. Whether it will be possible to write yet another volume I do not know but for me the main work has been done and it is my hope that what I have written here will be of use to those who wish to celebrate the Roman liturgy in its present form.

I wish to record my sincere thanks to Mrs Olive Yeo who has typed the whole of this book.

Lent,   J.D.C.
1973

PREFACE TO THE SECOND EDITION

WHEN I was writing the first edition of this book the Order of Penance had not appeared and in Chapter XI I speculated on what it might contain. The Constitution on the Liturgy (n. 72) had said that the rite and formulae of the sacrament were to be revised so that they might the more clearly express both its nature and its effect. In addition there were the general injunctions of the Constitution concerning the requirements for any liturgical service: it is an act of the church, not a 'private function'; there must be a proclamation of God's word; the service must have a certain visibility and must be such that the people can take an active part in it. At the time it was not possible to see how the principles would be applied. With the promulgation of the *Ordo Paenitentiae* in 1973 all became clear. As expected, the rite of private penance was retained (though revised) and the corporate and ecclesial nature of the sacrament was expressed more fully in the second and third rites.

To provide some considerations on the new Order of Penance I wrote *The Ministry of Reconciliation* which first appeared in 1974. A second edition appeared with one or two corrections in 1976. This book is now out of print (though at the time of writing is still obtainable) and my publishers have thought that the usefulness of *Christian Celebration: The Sacraments* would be increased and its life extended if the chapter on Penance were re-written and, in view of all that has happened in the liturgical field since 1973, if some additions were made to the last chapter of the book, 'Pastoral Opportunities'. This I have done. Other changes are minor. One or two errors were corrected in the reprint of 1974 and misprints that escaped my notice have also been put right.

For the rest the book remains what it was. No doubt if I were writing it now some emphases would be different but I have seen no need to make any substantial changes. The book seems to have served its purpose as an introduction to the revised liturgy of the sacraments other than that of the eucharist which is dealt with in *Christian Celebration: the Mass.* Comments and correspondence from various parts of the world seem to support such a view and I wish to express my thanks to those who were sufficiently interested to send observations and corrections.

I did a good deal of the revision in France et ici je voudrais exprimer ma profonde reconnaissance aux membres de la Communauté de Notre Dame de la Pépiole qui m'ont toujours accueilli avec une grande bonté et gentillesse. Ils ont contribué plus qu'ils ne s'imaginent à cet ouvrage et à d'autres en me ménageant une locale et une ambiance où je pouvais étudier et écrire.

Notre Dame de la Pépiole   J.D.C.
1979

A LIST OF DOCUMENTS

SINCE THE number of new Orders is now considerable, I have thought it would be convenient to list in one place those used in this book. They have appeared at various times but the order given here is that in which they are considered in this volume.

Ordo Initiationis Christianae Adultorum (Catechumenate, Adult Baptism, Confirmation and Communion), 1972;

Ordo Baptismi Parvulorum (Infant Baptism with General Introduction on Baptism), 1969;

Ordo Confirmationis, 1971;

Ordo Celebrandi Matrimonium, 1969;

Pontificale Romanum: *De Ordinatione Diaconi, Presbyteri et Episcopi*, 1968;

De Institutione Lectorum et Acolythorum; *de Admissione inter candidatos ad Diaconatum et Presbyteratum. De Sacro Caelibatu amplectendo* (Ministries of Reader and Acolyte with the Admission to the Clerical State and the Declaration on Celibacy), 1972;

Ordo Unctionis Infirmorum eorumque Pastoralis Curae (Anointing and Care of the Sick), 1972;

Ordo Exsequiarum (Funeral Rites), 1969;

Ordo Benedicendi Oleum Catechumenorum et Infirmorum et Conficiendi Chrisma, 1971 (referred to in chapters II and IX);

Ordo Paenitentiae, 1973; English edition, with official ICEL translation, *The Rite of Penance*, 1976.

Their contents are as follows:
Decree of promulgation; *Praenotanda*, pastoral-theological notes, here called 'Introduction'; the rite; permitted variations; a collection of alternative texts (when not included in the rite); a collection of scripture readings which may be used in the celebration of the rites. With the exception of the Order of Adult Initiation and the Ordination rites, these orders are numbered throughout from the first paragraph of the introduction to the end of the book, including the rites themselves. Each part of the rite thus has its own number. Three, the Orders of Confirmation, Ordination and the Anointing of the Sick, where matters of importance for sacramental

theology are concerned, were promulgated by an Apostolic Constitution of the pope. Two, the lesser ministries and the admission
to the clerical state etc, were promulgated by *Motu proprio* (*Ministeria quaedam* and *Ad Pascendum* respectively). The juridical status
of these documents will be of interest primarily to canonists. The
Apostolic Constitutions are the most important as they fully engage
the papal authority.

The official texts, in Latin, of all these documents are published
by the Vatican Press.

ABBREVIATIONS

CL = Constitution on the Liturgy (1963), in the translation of Rev Clifford Howell, SJ (Whitegate Publications, Cirencester, 1963).
Titles of other council documents are given in full.
CI = Christian Initiation to be found in *Ordo Baptismi Parvulorum.*
BP = *Ordo Baptismi Parvulorum* (infant baptism).
Occasional references to the General Instruction of the *Ordo Missae* (1969/1970) will be found under GI followed by the number of the paragraph.
LMD = La Maison-Dieu.
ST = *Summa Theologica* (St Thomas Aquinas).
PL = *Praise the Lord,* revised and enlarged, ed. Ainslie, Dean and Inwood (Geoffrey Chapman, 1972).
AAS = *Acta Apostolicae Sedis* ('Acts of the Apostolic See').
Denz. = *Enchiridion Symbolorum, Definitionum et Declarationum de Rebus Fidei et Morum,* comp. H. Denzinger (1854) and others subsequently to the 31st edition (Barcelona, 1960) inclusive.
Denz.-Schön. = *Enchiridion . . .* (as above), 32nd edition with new numeration (ed. Schönmetzer, Barcelona, 1963) and subsequent editions.
LXX = Septuagint (Greek).
Vulg. = Vulgate (Latin).

TRANSLATIONS

For the Council documents (other than the Constitution on the Liturgy) I have used the translations in *The Documents of Vatican II*, ed. Walter Abbott, SJ (Geoffrey Chapman, 1966).
Translations of the texts of the Orders are generally my own though I have made much use of the ICEL version for marriage. Thanks

are due to the International Committee on English in the Liturgy for permission to use it here and in one or two other places. For scripture versions I have generally used the Jerusalem Bible (Darton, Longman and Todd, 1966) and occasionally the Revised Standard Version (Thomas Nelson and Sons, 1966).

EDITIONS

Editions of the Sacramentaries are as follows:
  Verona (Leonine): ed. Mohlberg, Rome, 1956.
  Gelasian: ed. Mohlberg, Rome, 1960.
  Gregorian: ed. Lietzmann, Münster, 1921 (reprint of 1967).
For patristic texts details of editions are given in the text.

To

CONRAD PEPLER, O.P.

πολλῶν ἕνεκα

CHAPTER ONE

The Sacraments and Life

THE PLACE of the sacraments in the Christian life has varied a good deal in the history of the church. In the Middle Ages the sacraments were above all the sacred actions performed by the priest who alone had their secret. Including the eucharist, they were celebrated almost wholly without a ministry of the word which in any case was unintelligible to the people. They indeed brought a certain faith to the celebration and the sacraments existed in a society permeated by the Christian faith. This is some justification of the procedure. But the situation was not a happy one. It was all too easy to think that by going through certain ritual actions one was saved. With the Reformers' heavy emphasis on the word the sacraments ceased to play a dominant role in the Protestant world and came to be disregarded. On the Catholic side, the emphasis on the *ex opere operato* effect of the sacraments served to continue medieval tradition though, with the gradual renewal of the Christian life, they came to be celebrated in a new atmosphere of devotion. The realisation grew that the reception of the sacraments required certain conditions and had consequences in Christian living though the notion that people should be prepared, 'evangelised', for them remained weak. The famous Mère Angélique Arnauld who, with papal permission, was made Abbess of Port-Royal in the first decade of the seventeenth century had no formal instruction for her confirmation and first communion and *she* was from an orthodox and devout family.[1] Detestable as Jansenist doctrines were and regrettable as were the unending controversies that ensued, the demand of Saint-Cyran, Mère Angélique herself and others of this period, some of whom were hardly formal Jansenists at all, that the sacraments, especially penance and the eucharist, required serious

---

[1] If a servant of the convent had not put a book of devotion into her hands, she would have had no instruction at all.

preparation and sincerity of heart, was right and reasonable.

In the eighteenth century, the age of the 'Enlightenment', sacramental practice waned. The *philosophes* and the Encyclopedists saw in sacramental worship hardly more than the relics of primitive religions which were now becoming known in an elementary way. Religion—if there was to be religion—was to be based on a rather superficial rationalism. What could not be explained or justified on the shallow criteria of the time must be rejected. Religion was the non-worship of an inoperative Deity combined with a tedious moralism and an emphasis on duty. In this atmosphere the sacraments had no place. Nor was all well within the church. In France especially, in Germany, the home of the Aufklärung, and even in Italy (eg the Synod of Pistoia), the clergy and many of the laity were affected by the rationalist ideas of the time. The sober, sacramental piety of a Challoner in the apparently dying Catholic Church in England was not too common in Europe. The people, especially those of the rural parts of Europe, remained attached to the traditional rites, few infants remained unbaptised, but there was already a suggestion of folklore about the whole business.[2]

As is well known, the Romantic Movement that began to affect ordinary life and thinking after the French Revolution created an atmosphere that made possible the beginnings of the liturgical renewal. Not everything that was mysterious and inexplicable by the pedestrian principles of a rationalist philosophy was to be rejected. The poets and writers indeed exalted the irrational and there were a few theologians, the fideists, who would cheerfully have fallen into the trap of irrationality if they had not been called to order. There were those who would have cried with Tertullian *'Credo quia impossibile'*. The early liturgical movement was not wholly free from such notions and when its leader, Guéranger, decided to throw in his lot with the Ultramontanes, the danger of a papalist fideism was real. At the same time the sacraments were still seen as the religion of duty. Young ladies were prepared for their 'duties' which did not mean the married state but confirmation, confession and communion.

In the twentieth century, with the admission of young children to communion, with its ever more frequent reception and with the gathering impetus of the liturgical movement, sacramental practice

---

[2] For a not wholly satisfactory treatment of the period see Préclin et Jarry, *Hist. de l'Eglise* (Fliche et Martin), t.19, pt I (Paris 1955).

has steadily improved. But until the Second Vatican Council we were still burdened with fossilised medieval rites; even those sacraments which theologians commonly called the 'sacraments of the living' (confirmation, the eucharist, etc) were administered in a dead language. In spite of and no doubt because of this, efforts were made to secure a more lively celebration of the sacraments. The clergy resorted to 'commentaries', 'catechesis', the value of the symbols (candle, white garment) was enhanced and attempts were made to gather the local community for baptism. But the ritual remained unbendable,[3] as did the danger that sacraments would be seen to be divorced from ordinary living. The people were still almost wholly passive: a sacrament was valid provided the recipient put no '*obex*' in the way. They had little or no part to play except their physical presence and of course, in the case of baptism, to provide the baby!

Vatican II changed most of this but, what is more important, it consecrated a theology of the sacraments that had long been forgotten. This change can be summed up under three heads:

1. We are saved by faith and the sacraments of faith[4] which means that apart from the single exception of infant baptism, the participant must have a real, living faith in Christ before he can receive a sacrament;

2. As a result of this the sacrament is seen as the place of encounter with Christ in the fulness of his redeeming activity, called the paschal mystery;[5]

3. The people are not merely receivers of the sacraments, nor only participants. They are the celebrants (with the appointed minister) of the sacraments. This is marked by the constant appeal for their participation and by the emphasis laid in all the revised rites on the presence of the community.

If we are saved by faith, then we must have the faith preached to us (cf Romans 10:14–17). Whether this 'preaching' is called 'evangelisation', as seems to be the fashion now, or 'instruction' with all its daunting associations, does not for the moment matter. The axiom postulates and demands a living conscious faith which

---

[3] Even the placing of the Paschal Candle in the baptistery was regarded as 'odd' or even fanatical. It is now the rule!

[4] CL 59.

[5] CL 5.

has often been *assumed* in the past but which cannot be assumed now. That is why the new rites require that there shall be no celebration of the sacraments without a proclamation of the word.[6] But faith is not to be regarded merely as a pre-requisite of sacramental celebration. It needs to be expressed, and indeed is, in the celebration. Nor is this just a psychological device, though it has the immense value of enabling people to realise the truth of the axiom. The faith of the celebrants is manifested and concretised in the sacramental action itself. When a Christian engages in the celebration of a sacrament he is saying both by word and action that he believes in God and in his redeeming love made available to him in the sacrament. On the other hand, the rite of the sacrament expresses the faith of the whole church. *This* is what the church believes of, say, baptism or the eucharist and the new rites have this great virtue that they have spelt out more clearly than before what is the faith of the church as far as the sacraments are concerned. This is the meaning of St Thomas's phrase[7] that the celebration of a sacrament is a *protestatio fidei*, a profession of faith, first of the faith of the church and then of those who here and now are proclaiming it.

Further, it is because of the deep reverence for God and his saving purpose this faith witnesses to that the sacrament can be said 'to give worship to God'.[8] Through our 'faithful' approach to the sacraments we are showing our complete dependence on God, on God the Saviour, and when in the sacramental action this faith is manifested and externalised, then Christians at least can see that they are glorifying God. We are reminded once again of the phrase of Irenaeus: *Gloria Dei, vivens homo*. It is the man of faith who out of the depths of his being recognises his need of God who gives him the glory.

But man approaches the Father only through the Son and he wishes to meet God, to enter into union with him so that he can live *in* God. In the sacraments, then, we approach Christ who has taught us that in these actions we call sacraments and which are the signs of his covenanted love, he is present. In them he takes up our faith, our love and whatever devotion we can bring to them

---

[6] Infant baptism and the administration of certain sacraments to the dying or unconscious must be regarded as abnormal situations, however common the former. As we shall see later, the principle is saved by the obligation parents have to educate their own children in the faith.

[7] *ST* III, 72, V, ad 2.

[8] CL 59 and St Thomas *ST* III, 63, i.

and infuses into that faith and love and devotion his own divine life and love so that we can be united to the Father. The sacraments are not to be seen simply as adjuncts of the Christian life, sanctified lifts or elevators that transfer us to the supernatural order, nor merely as so many 'helps' (though they are that) to enable us to do those things we ought to do and avoid those things we ought not to do. They are the high moments of the Christian life when it achieves its most authentic expression. They are the most concrete signs of our faith our love and our life, of what we really *are*—if of course we are at least trying to lead the Christian life.

Sacraments, then, are not isolated ecclesiastical rites but events in the flowing life of the church and in the life of man. It is the vocation of the church to go out to man, to preach the Gospel, to 'evangelise', to spread abroad a knowledge of Christ, to confront men with the life, passion, death and resurrection of Christ so that they may accept him by faith. But the faith they profess is not something extraneous to the sacraments. These are, as we have said, concrete expressions of the faith that has come from hearing and the grace of God. There is a continuity between the faith in the heart and the faith expressed in the sacraments. When the convert is 'received', he is incorporated into a community of faith which by its very existence is the sign of faith in the world, the sacrament of Christ, as we have learnt to say, present in the world. Once incorporated, the convert then has to take up his task of proclaiming the faith to others and this, in the teaching of the new confirmation rite, he does by virtue of that sacrament. This too is the teaching of the Second Vatican Council: 'As members of the living Christ, all the faithful have been incorporated into him and made like him through baptism, confirmation and the eucharist. Hence all are duty-bound to cooperate in the expansion and growth of his Body, so that they can bring it to fulness as swiftly as possible (Ephesians 4:13).'[9]

Evangelisation, then, liturgy and mission are all of a piece and the first and the third of these elements has for its purpose the drawing of men into an encounter with Christ in the liturgy. This is the perspective even of the Constitution on the Liturgy (9): the church has to proclaim the good news of salvation so that men may be converted and meet Christ. Even to believers the church must

---

[9] Decree on the Missionary Activity of the Church, 36 (Abbott, *Documents*, p. 623) and cf General Introduction to *The Rite of the Baptism for Children*, p. 7 (Geoffrey Chapman, 1970).

preach faith and repentance, must prepare them for the sacraments and 'invite them to all the works of charity, piety and the aposto-late'. The sacramental community must be a missionary community, drawing its strength from Christ who makes himself present in the liturgy and leading men into it. Hence we get the saying 'The liturgy is the summit towards which the activity of the church is directed and at the same time the source from which all her power flows' (ibid. 10).

So far then it is clear that the sacraments have been fully inte-grated into the Christian life, even if practice still limps behind theory, as it probably always will. There remains the question of the integration of the sacraments into life simply.

This is a more complex problem, the elements of which we have sketched out in a previous volume[10] and we do not intend to repeat what we said there. However, what we have to say about the sacra-ments should be regarded as particular examples of the view sug-gested there.

In the phrase 'the integration of the sacraments into life' life has a twofold connotation. It means first the life of the celebrants, neces-sarily therefore of Christians; secondly, it means the secular life of the world. Not that these can be taken in fact as entirely separate, for Christians live in the world and secular, non-Christian people inevitably witness Christian celebrations. Witnessing them they pose certain questions or experience a certain bewilderment. What are these curious actions with their peculiar use of certain material objects? What do they mean? Are they just survival-taboos of the Christian tribe which derive from the pre-scientific culture? If inadvertently they are administered in a mechanical way, if the emphasis is on the sacraments as objects, as things, or on the quasi-automatic effect (You do this and that happens), then the modern secular man may be excused if he sees them as no more than sub-limated magic. So, as far as the Christian celebrants are concerned, it is of primary importance that their faith, their acceptance of all that the sacraments imply (Christ and his redeeming work), should be made explicit even in the celebration. In a word, the sacraments must be seen as part of their life, as expressions of it, and secular man is perfectly justified in looking for the consequences of the celebration of the sacraments in the lives of Christians. This would seem to indicate that we should be much more demanding about

----

[10] Christian Celebration: The Mass, Chapter I.

who are fit candidates for the Christian sacraments.

But have the sacraments a deeper relationship to ordinary life? Or are they pieces of ritual imposed on life? An adequate answer to these questions would require what the theologians call a Christian anthropology, that is an examination of the nature of man as he exists in the concrete circumstances of his life.[11] Meanwhile it is possible to make some suggestions. Every human being is born and although in eyes of modern human beings the wonder of a new birth is no longer the event it used to be—with the exception of the mother to whom it is always wonderful[12]—in the history of mankind it has usually been marked by some rite, such as circumcision. One of the most constant features of the life of man in the earlier stages of his development are the 'rites of passage'. People are born, are initiated, marry and die and all these events are marked by rites celebrated in common. The rites and the events of human living go together and the former are the expression and, I suppose it would be said, the sacralisation of the latter. However that may be, these are all intensely human situations and even in these days, when so much of the natural rhythm of human life has been shattered, they remain to give pattern and direction to human living.

On even a superficial view the sacraments and other rites of the church, closely connected with them, correspond to these human situations. To birth corresponds baptism and there are those who would see confirmation as the counterpart of the rites of initiation in more primitive societies, though I do not think their point of view can be justified. To the 'natural' marriage of man and woman corresponds the sacrament that is simply called after it; to illness, the anointing of the sick and to the final 'passage' of death, the rites that concern it. In this perspective the life-events and the rites are not mere juxtapositions. They witness to the need of man to refer the major events of life to a higher power, on whom he feels dependent, and implicitly he is asking that they should be taken up into the sphere of the divine, however he may conceive it.

It will be obvious that the Christian sacraments cover a wider field than that of the 'rites of passage'. Apart from the problematical

---

[11] Not therefeore the study of primitive man or even of the behaviour of modern man, though both can throw light on the subject.

[12] One mother, whose faith had been wavering, once said to me that after the carrying and birth of her child, not only did she herself believe more strongly in God but she found it difficult to understand others who did not.

sacrament of confirmation, there is the question of repentance as expressed in the sacrament of penance and there is that of Holy Order which, if it has parallels in primitive religions, is so far away from them in meaning as to make comparison misleading. Through these considerations we are brought to the question of the *seven* sacraments. It is well known that it was not until the twelfth century and largely under the influence of Canon Law that the present system of seven sacraments was established. For a St Augustine and a St Ambrose there were many more '*sacramenta*' (eg the foot-washing in the baptismal liturgy) as there are to this day in the Orthodox church. In western Catholic terminology these are called 'sacramentals' and while this may be useful for theological categorisation, there is a certain liturgical incongruity in the whole business. There are highly significant rites like that of the solemn profession of a monk (a second 'baptism'), the consecration of a virgin,[13] which have their interest precisely in as much as they are consecrations of particular ways of *life*. There is also the rite of the blessing of the holy oils[14] on Maundy Thursday. This is a specifically *paschal* rite looking forward as it does to the celebration of Easter which includes the administration of baptism and confirmation. That the primitive baptism/confirmation liturgy included a rite of anointing with oil is improbable but, against the biblical background, it was seen that oil was a significant symbol of the Holy Spirit and it was used as such. What is important is that the blessing of oil was not separated from the sacramental administration. In the Apostolic Tradition of Hippolytus the 'Oil of Thanksgiving' was blessed during the Easter liturgy and it was not until later (sixth century) that they were separated. The primitive arrangement, then, shows the close link between what later was called the 'matter' of the sacrament and the sacrament itself. Both the blessing and the sacrament were part of the one liturgical celebration. To put the matter in another way, the blessing and use of oil was a means by which the liturgical celebration could be made to meet the life-situation of the participants, for in the Mediterranean world olive oil was (and is) one of the staples of life.

The use of these '*sacramenta*' was then a way of reaching out into the life of the people and they should not be dismissed as mere ceremonial or a retrograde hanging-on to outmoded symbols.

---

[13] Vatican Press, 1970.
[14] Ordo Benedicendi ..., Vatican Press, 1971.

But on the assumption that the seven sacrament scheme exists (which is accepted though with nuances of difference by the Orthodox) it will be useful to ask whether it has something useful to offer from our point of view in this chapter.

If you ask the question: why seven sacraments? you can, as a recent author has remarked, look at the question from two sides, from the point of view of revelation (what Christ willed) and from the point of view of man.[15] With the first we are not concerned for the moment, but the same author goes on to say that the material principle of the diversity of the sacraments (which convey the power of the paschal mystery in different ways) must appeal to the anthropological constituents of man:

'The seven sacraments do not come from arbitrary decisions of Christ (and much less from a church which would dominate Christ). This diversity comes from the fact that the actions of Christ lay hold of or take up fundamental human situations to make them Christian situations.[16] The sacramental organism is an adapted organism. To be born, to pass to adult life, to review one's life with a view to a new start, to marry, to fall ill, are so many situations taken up by the sacraments and thus shown to be and established as divine-human situations. This constituent principle of the seven sacraments shows that the Christian life is the opposite of a life that is simply juxtaposed to human life. It is in fact the life of God penetrating to the anthropological roots of human existence. There are no sacraments that are not sacraments of Christ living his paschal mystery in man. But also, there are no sacraments that do not draw from the world and from man the "materiality" of their sign. The seven sacraments can be thought of as the great and fundamental lines or the strong points or even the great axes by which the Lord Jesus reaches into the depths of our human nature and transfigures it.'

There are two points here worth pondering on. The first is that by the sacraments Christ reaches down to the deepest level of human life, not merely and superficially, as might be concluded from the above statement, to acquire the right kind of material

---

[15] Henri Denis, *Les sacrements ont-ils un avenir?*, Paris, 1971, pp. 48–9.
[16] Literally, 'situations in Christ'.

signs (water, bread, wine, etc). That is not the whole meaning of the writer. Christ who 'knows what is in man', reaches down to human nature, to the very 'materiality' of human nature (eg sexual love) because man is like this and because it is only in this way that he can grasp existentially the divine reality Christ wishes to convey. This is why 'the sacramental organism is an adapted organism'. One could say that it is a conditioned organism, an organism that is conditioned by the exigencies of human nature. Sacraments are, then, profoundly human and not just something 'stuck on' to ordinary human living. They touch the deepest springs of human existence and, to use the terminology of Karl Rahner,[17] they make it possible for man in Christ to live out the human tragedy of birth and life and death and suffering.[18]

But the sacraments do not just go down to the roots of the human condition. They transform it. They are not to be thought of as actions, even actions of Christ, that reach our human condition and leave it where it is and as it is. The materiality of the human condition is the very stuff of the Christian life. It is not merely a means, sanctified by grace, by which we go to God. It is *in this* that we go to God. As we have said elsewhere, it is in the wholeness of our human personality that we need to go to God and in the sacraments Christ takes over these human situations and makes them specifically Christian 'grace-ful' situations, directing them and us to God. Here is an interpenetration of the divine and the human that at least in principle makes it possible for us to live in God. All is now taken up into him and through the enrichment he gives, we are able to carry these riches, which are both his and ours, to the world.

If redemption is to be thought of as something more than an abstract noun, as something deeper than a legalistic 'substitution' of Christ for ourselves, it is here in the sacraments that we can see what it really is: the penetration by Christ into human situations from which he removes, if we will, *self*-centredness and gives them a Godward direction. In this way, we are able to establish or enter into the interpersonal relationship with God in which salvation ultimately consists. Certain situations are sin-situations, such

---

[17] See *Christian Celebration*, Vol. I, pp. 162–3.
[18] They also make it possible for man to live out the joy of life because the sacraments are life-bearing and life-enhancing. The 'christened' man, while aware of death and suffering and indeed experiencing it himself, is also able to rejoice in the Lord and in his goodness to men.

as that that involves the sacrament of penance, and here the redemptive, reconciling aspect of the work of salvation is to the fore. But in every human situation there is the danger of the movement towards self, eg marriage and sickness, and here it is precisely the *re*-direction the sacraments give that is important. Examples will make clearer what we mean.

1. The sacrament of penance is the sign in the here and now of the reconciliation we read of in 2 Corinthians 5:19 'God was in Christ reconciling the world to himself'. This he did in principle on the cross; this he, with the Christian community, continues to do in the eucharist, for all the power that was to be found in the cross is to be found in the Mass. Indeed, the whole liturgy, including therefore the eucharist and penance, is the sacrament-sign of the redeeming, reconciling work of Christ in the world and for the world. The church as a community of reconciliation and penance is in a special way the sacrament-sign of that reconciliation by which it is conveyed to the world. Men and women bring precisely their 'broken-ness' (contrition) to the sacrament and there seek encounter with the reconciling Christ. They have experienced the tragedy of (spiritual) death and alienation and now seek life and reconciliation. It is a normal human experience which in the sacramental situation is 'redeemed' and one which enables them to insert their lives into the reconciliation of Christ. There is more to be said and to it we shall return later.

2. It may sound pompous and perhaps heartless to say that illness and suffering, which are so personal, are part of the world's tragic experience, since suffering turns us in on ourselves so that at times, and even against our will, our whole personality is shrunk to not much more than a consciousness of pain. Yet it is so and when the pain has abated we are aware that we are involved in something that exists outside us in all the suffering of whatever kind that the human race experiences. We may indeed think of illness and suffering as an assault on our personalities that is quite unaccountable and if we do, we may find a clue to an understanding of it in the Old Testament view that illness, whether mental or physical, is related to sin. Not in the crude sense that our suffering is a punishment for our wrong-doing (though we can bring disease on ourselves) but in the sense that just as sin, at least for the Christian, is a symptom of the disorientation of the world as we know it, so is illness. It throws our life out of gear and we sense a rift in the harmony of things. The good, health, is struggling with evil, disease,

it is a conflict we now experience in our own personalities and not just something 'out there'. It is this maimed condition that Christ in his church invites us to bring to him and into this condition he inserts his healing, his comfort and his peace. Here you have an encounter between something that of itself is purely secular and the healing of Christ. And it is not unimportant to realise that healing means wholeness. The broken is repaired, the forces making for the disintegration of the human personality are turned towards integration. What has fallen into dis-ease and conflict is harmonised and the personality, now made whole, can once again turn itself out to Christ and to the world of men where its true vocation lies, even if the sick person is still confined to bed. Of all this restoration the sacraments of the sick are the sign, the sacrament-sign of Christ's healing, who is thus shown to be present in the world of suffering and pain.

3. Marriage may be regarded as the archetypal case of the co-inherence of the natural and the supernatural, the sacred and the profane, of the divine and the human. Here is a human love, earthy, warm and rich with every kind of fleshly association which yet reaches beyond itself to a total self-giving. It is this love that two people bring to God and in the encounter that ensues God's love meets theirs and transfuses it so that henceforth they are able to love each other with a love in which God is creatively present. None the less, their love remains fully human and yet at the same time is the sacrament-sign of their covenanted love as it is also the means by which they and their love are sanctified. Furthermore, this love is not restricted to murmured words or affectionate gestures. It is expressed in the very ordinary events of everyday life so that the very life-together-in-married-love also becomes the permanent sacrament-sign of the presence of God's love in their life. Here can be seen the involvement of God in the ordinary life of human beings, here we can see that God is not locked up in an ecclesiastical box but is to be found in human lives in all their ordinariness.

These situations are indications that the sacraments are not alien to human life. They celebrate it, they enhance it and are witnesses to the 'human-ness' of God who thus enters into it. It should not be supposed however that these situations (and others) are *proof* of the seven sacraments. First, not all the sacraments are so clearly connected with the human condition as those mentioned. If we give the impression that confirmation is the sacrament of adolescence *because* it corresponds to natural growth we are in danger of distorting its true nature. It is to be thought of as the perfecting of what is begun in baptism and this can be done at any age. We are so accustomed to think of baptism in the terms of infant baptism that it does not occur to us that a person baptised later in life has no possibility of 'growth' in the physical sense. Yet since confirmation has something to add to baptism it is perfectly right and proper that they should be confirmed. In other words, if we press the analogy between natural life and the Christian life too far we shall distort the sacramental organism. It is also difficult to find a credible analogy for the sacrament of holy orders. We no longer live in a sacral order and the notion of the 'sacralisation' of a human person is either unacceptable or meaningless. On the other hand, the dedication of a human being to a particular way of life, for instance monasticism, is covered by the rites of religious profession.[19]

All we can show, then, by this kind of investigation is that the sacraments are congruous with the human condition. We are thus brought to the consideration which is fundamental that the sacraments are 'given', they are part of Christ's revelation and in every sense of the word they are 'mysteries'. They are mysteries because they embody the mysterious presence of God active in human situations and are the signs of it. They are mysteries because they declare the faith of the church and that of the participants. They are mysteries because however well we think we understand them, their ultimate nature and effect lie beyond us. They are in fact part of the whole history of salvation which is a *datum*, something given, the pure gift of God, and we can only understand the sacraments as we understand the history of salvation. We look at it, we ponder on it, we 'see' that it is the divinely given way God willed to save us and that the sacraments are so many ways by which we are saved, justified and united through Christ in the Holy Spirit with the Father. Other ways would have been possible. A man could be saved by turning to God in wordless repentance or lifting up his heart in the wordless prayer of praise. But then we reflect, man himself is 'given', he is made by God, and the way of salvation is in accordance with the nature of the radical gift. In effect, so long as we do not see the sacraments as 'emerging' from the needs of human nature and thus finding their justification, it is safe to

---

[19] It is significant (to me at least) that the new rite of ordination no longer speaks of the consecration of a bishop but of his 'ordering': he is incorporated into the *ordo episcoporum*. In the rite, the word 'consecration' *is* used but the title is 'The Ordination of a Bishop'.

say that they meet the needs of human nature because God has arranged the matter that way.

There remains the question of the relationship of the sacraments with the world. It will be agreed that the celebration of the sacraments is not a missionary device but it does not follow that Christians can be indifferent to what the world thinks of them or indeed of the way we celebrate them. The sacraments are not only signs of a particular intervention of God in a particular situation, for instance baptism. As the Constitution on the Liturgy (2) made clear, they are signs of the church, revealing its nature, and when the Christian community celebrates the sacraments, it is constructing a sign of the church which may be read by others even if for lack of faith they cannot have a full understanding of it. What the church *is*, the sacraments declare; what the church believes, that the sacraments profess in word and action. It follows, then, as the same document teaches (34), that the liturgy of the sacraments, as of the whole liturgy, must be simple and understandable to ordinary people. It is a matter of experience that the sacraments, when celebrated as they should be by a believing community, draw the non-believer towards the church and dispose him to listen or to come again. We also know that a bad celebration of the sacraments can repel people, sometimes for ever. We know too that in the new situation in which we are, the quality of the celebration depends on both clergy and people and sometimes, even when the former do all that is required of them, the people are reluctant to play the part that belongs to them. However, what is important is that it is the community that celebrates and it is the impression created by the whole community that will make an impact on others.

But the Constitution on the Liturgy[20] makes clear that the celebration of the sacraments is a beginning and not an end. Members of the church, by virtue of their status as Christians, have the obligation of carrying the Good News to the world. Nor is there any need to expound at length the truth that the mission of the church belongs to all the members of the church. It is however worth repeating that, according to the Constitution on the Church (31, 33), the mission of the people flows directly from their baptism and confirmation: 'These faithful are by baptism made one body with Christ and are established among the people of God. They are in their own way made sharers in the priestly, prophetic and kingly

---

[20] CL 8, third paragraph.

functions of Christ. They carry out their own part in the mission of the whole Christian people with respect to the Church and the world.' More concretely still: 'The lay apostolate is a participation in the saving mission of the Church itself. Through their baptism and confirmation, all are commissioned to that apostolate by the Lord himself' and since the heart of mission is love, a love that urges us on (2 Corinthians 5:14), it is in the sacraments but especially in the eucharist that they will find the source of that love.[21]

How all this is to be carried out is a large question but the Constitution on the Liturgy (2), which from this point of view might seem to be a less practical document, has an interesting emphasis. It sees the liturgy as the outstanding means by which the people may *express in their lives* and manifest to others the mystery of Christ and the nature of the church. It is the daily living of Christians that manifests the great mystery of Christ which is the mystery of salvation. It is in this daily living that the non-believer will (or will not) find, as it were incarnated, the love God has shown to men. Clearly this puts a very heavy responsibility on all of us who *dare* to celebrate the liturgy and perhaps we have not always thought of it this way. But at least we can say, however unsuccessful we may be, that the notion of the liturgy as simply a ritual operation is banished. As it must be approached with a living faith, involving the whole personality, so its consequence and, in a sense, its validity must be seen in the life of Christians. The liturgy lives and moves and has its being in the flowing life of Christian people who through it, through the mystery of Christ with which they come in contact, reach out to the world around them and strive by example and word to carry Christ to it.

---

[21] Const. Ch. 33. There is much more to the same effect in other conciliar documents, notably in that exclusively concerned with the laity.

CHAPTER TWO

The Symbolism of the Sacraments

SINCE THE sacraments use a number of gestures and objects combined with gestures that are in fact constituent elements of the sacraments, it will be useful to say something about them at this point.

As we have attempted to show in a previous volume, the liturgy is by nature symbolical.[1] It lives in the world of symbols through which it manifests and conveys the mystery of Christ. Leaving out of account the eucharist, which we have already considered, we can see that the liturgy of the sacraments is particularly rich in symbolic objects and gestures. Water is used in baptism, oil in baptism, confirmation, holy order and the sacrament of the sick. Then there are certain gestures that are constitutive of the sacramental action, such as pouring the water or immersion in baptism, and others that are secondary, the signing with the cross, the laying-on of hands (essential in confirmation and holy order), the wearing of the white garment, the carrying of the candle in baptism, the assemblies that gather for the celebration of various sacraments, themselves symbolic since they represent a greater and wider reality, the whole church. Of these symbols it seems necessary to say something about water, oil and the laying-on of hands for they are the most important of all and their deeper significance is often unknown. The practice of anointing with olive oil, for instance, instead of being a sign that conveys a meaning, is in some parts of the world, including Northern Europe, a barrier to understanding.

Symbolism of Water

Until comparatively recently, water was an element whose significance was understood by everyone. But since it has been tamed, tanked and tapped and is available at will, people treat it as they do

---

[1] *Christian Celebration: The Mass*, Chapter II.

electric power. It is always there: you just turn on the tap and it comes. Few have looked down into the mysterious depths of a well, and those who have seen a rushing torrent think of it as no more than a piece of scenery. A fountain throwing up its water in all directions is just a show-piece erected by some more imaginative town council or by a tycoon of yesteryear who had nothing better to do with his money. In spite of the efforts of scientists and lunar-nauts to find water on the moon, we do not readily see water as the *source of life*. Yet this is how it was seen for untold thousands of years and especially in the dry East where it became sacred because men knew how they depended on it.[2] As is well enough known, in Egypt the whole economy was dependent on the flooding of the Nile and 'in Egyptian belief ... the *divine* waters could give life in every form in which the mind could conceive it'.[3] The same was true of India: an old text apostrophises water 'Water, you are the source of everything and of all existence'.[4] Further, it was an ancient and widely prevalent belief that water flowed from the womb of the earth or of paradise, a notion that, transformed, found a place in the old text of the Blessing of the Font at the Easter Vigil. There the font (spring, source) is the womb of the church from which the waters flow 'for the renewal of the nations' and new births come forth to the enrichment of the church:

'Look with kindness on the face of your church and increase in her the number of your children. She is that city of yours which you refresh with *flowing streams* of grace and there *you open up a spring to water the whole earth, her fountain of baptism for the renewal of the nations* .... May he (God) make this a life-giving water—this water prepared for man's new birth—secretly im-buing it with his own divine power, *that sons of heaven may be conceived and emerge from the spotless womb of this divine font reborn...*'.

Later, the ancient symbolism of water as flowing forth from the womb of the world appears along with the theme of water as a necessity of life for a desert people:

---

[2] See F. W. Dillistone, *Christianity and Symbolism*, London, 1955, pp. 185 ff. The author points out that for Arabs water is so much the source of life that the same word is used for water and the male semen.

[3] *Op. cit.* citing the *Journal of the American Oriental Society*, 56, p. 158.

[4] L. Beirnaert, *ibid.*, p. 185.

'In his (God's) name (I bless you) who bade you well forth from a *spring in Paradise* and branch into four streams and *water all the earth*. In the desert, when you were gall to taste, he gave you sweetness and made you fit to drink. When his people were parched with thirst he brought you from a rock ...'.

According to some[5]—and it seems difficult to resist their view—the symbolism is carried through to its logical conclusion. The water is seen as being fecundated (*foecundet*) by the plunging in it of the phallic symbol, the lighted candle, itself seen as a symbol of the Holy Spirit: 'May the power of the Holy Spirit come down into this water ... and charge it (*foecundet*) through and through with power to give new life.'

It is surely a pity that nothing of this pregnant symbolism has been retained in the new prayers of the blessing of baptismal water. Whether we accept Jung's theory of archetypes or not, here is a symbolism that at once goes back to the folk memory of people and yet is immeasurably enriched by being transmuted into a specifically Christian symbolism. Even if the reference to the early memories of mankind are lost, the figure of the church as *mater ecclesia*, a mother of life and the bride of Christ, is something that would countervail the all too prevalent notion of the church as an institution whose embraces have not always been as tender as they might have been. It may be agreed that the prayer was too long but either there was, somewhere along the line, a failure to see what was symbolically important in the prayer or the symbolism was deliberately rejected. One wonders if it was thought to be too realistic: even the word *foecundet* is removed from the text at the moment of plunging the candle into the water, though the gesture is kept at least for the Easter Vigil.

The new rite has however retained another aspect of water-symbolism. In many different cultures the passage through water has been seen as the symbol of regeneration and new life. The water could be the sacred river, Lethe, or a spring or even the sacred bath (cf Ephesians 5:26, 27). By its cleansing and purifying power the candidate entered into a new life. This is the symbolism of St Paul in Romans 6 which assumes baptism by immersion. In the prayer of

---

[5] C. Jung, and Gerald Vann in *The Water and the Fire*, London, 1953, pp. 90–3. Gerald Vann also pointed out that the celebrant (in the then rite) breathed on the water making the form of *psi*, the first letter of the Greek word for life or life-principle (*psyche*).

the Blessing of the Water, in both the old and the new editions, this symbolism is given in the terms of the history of salvation. The Flood is a symbol of regeneration (*speciem regenerationis*[6]), marking as it did the end of sin and the beginning of the virtuous life. The waters of the Red Sea, through which the Israelites passed, is in the first place a figure of deliverance; they moved from the slavery of Egypt into the freedom of the desert and there through the covenant and its accompanying sacrifice they became the people of God. *This*, says the prayer, is the symbol of the new people of God who are delivered from sin by baptism. By its connection with baptism the water thus becomes in the second place the symbol of regeneration.

But the symbolism of water is ambivalent. If it is the source of life and is necessary to sustain life, it can also stifle it. In the ancient world the sea at least was much feared on account of its mysterious, incontrollable strength and its power to kill. Water generally was seen as the abode of demons, of fearsome monsters like Leviathan (cf Job 40:25) which God alone could master. When the baptismal liturgies were coming into existence from the second to the fourth centuries these memories were still vivid. The candidate had to be exorcised several times and the last time immediately before baptism. Turned towards the West, the abode of demons, he renounced the devil, even in some rites spitting at him, and then, turned towards the East, he professed his adherence to Christ. Then, before entering the water, he must strip not wearing 'any alien object'[7] for fear, it would seem, that the devil should get a foothold. He was anointed all over with oil, prepared as it were for the *agon*, the struggle with the powers of evil. This notion is always implicit, as the symbolism itself shows, but occasionally it becomes explicit as in the Homilies of Narsai: 'The three Names (of the Trinity) he (the priest) recites, together with the rubbing of the oil upon the whole man: that hostile demons and vexing passions may not harm him.' It is not, the preacher goes on, that power resides in the oil itself but in God, the oil proclaiming [being a symbol] of the divine power: 'By his power body and soul acquire power; and they no more dread the injuries of death. As athletes they descend (and)

---

[6] The ICEL translation virtually eliminates this phrase.
[7] *Apostolic Tradition* XXI, 5 (ed. G. Dix), p. 33.

stand in the arena, and they close in battle with the cowardly suggestions that are in them.'[8]

Not only, however, was the candidate exorcised, the water also had to be and the reason was precisely because it was regarded as the abode of demons. Once exorcised, the water could become the source of life and in it the candidate met not the devil but Christ. The first statement is amply illustrated by the (old) text for the Blessing of the Font, which, though edited, derives from the prayer in the Gelasian Sacramentary, dating, as far as this text goes, from the sixth century: 'Command, then, Lord, every evil spirit to be banished from this element, banished be the whole malice of diabolical deceit. No room here for this water to be imbued with an opposing power, flitting watchfully about it, insinuating itself by stealth and tainting it with poison.'[9] Nor is this exceptional. The Ambrosian prayer[10] is particularly vigorous: God is asked to exorcise the water so that it will have the power to put to flight every 'infestation' of the devil and 'to root out the devil himself' from those who are to be baptised. If these and other prayers[11] do not speak of the presence of demons in the water and indeed in some instances envisage the struggle as *beginning* with baptism, it is because the water has been exorcised and the demons have given place to the presence of Christ. For Narsai, the power of God dwells in the visible waters and destroys the might of the Evil One and of death.[12]

In most of the prayers this divine presence is given a more concrete expression. One of the constant features of these baptismal prayers, as of the patristic literature on the point, is the reference to the baptism of Christ. This is seen as the archetype of Christian baptism and also as its source. For Cyril of Jerusalem the water was 'consecrated' by contact with the divinity of Christ.[13] According to John Chrysostom, Christ 'cleansed' the waters and left them as a now 'sanctified' element for the sacrament of baptism.[14] Gregory of Nazianzen brings a new richness and depth to the matter. He

---

[8] Hom. 20. See E. C. Whitaker, *Documents of the Baptismal Liturgy*, 2nd ed, London, 1970, p. 54. From this invaluable work other information about the baptismal liturgies is taken.
[9] Trans. *Layman's Missal*, London, 1962.
[10] *Missale Ambrosianum*, 1949.
[11] See Whitaker, *passim*.
[12] Whitaker, *op. cit.*, p. 55.
[13] *Myst. Cat.* III, i (ed. Piédagnel, p. 122).
[14] Both passages quoted in Aquinas, *ST* III, Q.39, i.

sees the baptism of Christ as a 'mystery', still effective: 'Christ is enlightened and at the same time, we are; Christ is baptised and we, at the same time, go down [into the water] and rise from it. John is baptising, Jesus approaches, perhaps sanctifying the baptiser, but without any doubt burying the Old Adam in the waters, before us and on our account sanctifying them ... Coming up out of the waters Jesus raises the whole world with him and cleaves open the heavens which Adam and his posterity and the fiery sword had closed.'[15] Christ is here very conspicuously the second Adam who is enacting in his own person the whole drama of salvation. Indeed the dimensions of Gregory's view are cosmic: the whole of creation is renewed and raised up by the baptism of Christ in the Jordan. The power of Christ in the baptismal water is very clear.

These ancient symbolisms perhaps make little appeal to modern man or to modern Christians though their transposition into the Christian register should make them meaningful to the latter. But can we be so sure? It was Jung's contention that modern man needs these symbols and periodical confrontation with them if he is to retain his psychological health. If this is so, it means that the way we use them becomes crucial. Baptism in the West (though not in the Eastern Churches) has for centuries been by 'infusion', the pouring of water on the head of the candidate. Even the casuists said it must *flow* and it is a practice that retains one elementary symbolism, that of cleansing, though this was reduced to a 'washing away of original sin'. The difficulty is in presenting in celebration the deeper and more extensive symbolism of water, for if its effect is to be achieved on Jungian terms, it must make an impact of some force. Clearly, baptism by immersion does this and it is interesting to observe that in the baptismal Orders of 1969 and 1972 immersion is suggested, not merely because it is given as an alternative but because it is the method suggested in the first place.[16] The question is: how is it to be done? That baptism by immersion is not wholly impracticable can be seen from the practice of the Baptist Church though it is probable that in an individual Baptist church baptisms are not very numerous in the course of a year. This suggests the direction in which we should look. Baptism by immersion, quite apart from people's reluctance to undergo it, would have to be an

---

[15] *Orat.* 39 in *Sancta Lumina*, 14–16, 20, the patristic lesson for the feast of the Baptism of the Lord in *Breviarium Romanum*, 1971.

[16] *Ordo Baptismi Parvulorum*, no. 60, Vatican, 1969; *Ordo Initiationis Christianae Adultorum*, 220, Vatican, 1972.

occasional event, and in fact, if it were, it would make all the greater an impact. The plunging of the candidate into the water would recall not merely that it is the life-giving element in the natural order but the theology of St Paul in Romans 6:3, 4 that we are buried with Christ in the waters of baptism and raised from them by the power of his resurrection to a new kind of life, would be strongly suggested. This text, with its great depth of meaning, would thus come alive.

There are of course many difficulties, both psychological and physical, that stand in the way of restoring this practice and to these we shall return in our discussion of baptism.[17]

Symbolism of Oil

While olive oil in the Mediterranean world is still a normal constituent of human living, in most parts of the world, including Northern Europe, it is not; and even in the Mediterranean world it is more likely to be thought of as the accompaniment of food than as anything else. In spite of its rich symbolism in the Old and the New Testaments, it remains difficult for us to use.[18] In industrial society it is thought of as a lubricant and those bold enough to examine the sumps of their cars know that it is a nasty, black mess. It does not help very much to be told that Greek athletes anointed themselves with olive oil to give strength and suppleness to their limbs. For as soon as you have to be told that this 'signifies' that, you are being told at the same time that the symbol is dead. Symbols are either significant or they do not exist. What then is to be done? Is the use of oil to be abolished altogether? There would seem to be no reason why it should not be for it is not necessary for the validity of any sacrament except that of the anointing of the sick.[19]

The question then resolves itself into this: is it desirable that we should try to keep alive a symbol that has lost almost all its

---

[17] As to practical difficulties, baptisteries and fonts would have to be constructed on quite different lines and would require piped warm water. Some new baptisteries in recent years have at least provided *flowing* water, which suggests life, and only a slight adaptation would be required to make immersion possible. See eg that at Our Lady of the Wayside, Shirley, Solihull, Warwickshire and St John's Abbey, Collegeville, Minn., U.S.A., the best I have seen.

[18] Gen. 28:18; Ex. 31:25 ff.; 1 Sam. 10:1 ff.; James 5:14-15, etc.

[19] Not for baptism for both anointings may be omitted, not for ordination for the anointings in the orders of presbyter and bishop are now visibly secondary rites. Confirmation remains doubtful. It is still required (*Ordo Confirmationis*, 9, 27) though doing duty for the laying-on of hands. But in different times and places the laying-on of hands has been sufficient.

significance? An answer in favour of its continued use can be given if we consider the biblical background and exploit its symbolism more adequately. If we look at the use of oil in the ancient world we find that it has certain parallels in our world. It is well known that the sun, especially in hot countries, dries up the skin and that over-exposure to it burns. In Egypt, it would seem, the high conical hair-styles, which are to be seen on bas-reliefs, were drenched with a perfumed oil which flowed down on the (bare) shoulders keeping the skin supple and giving off what was regarded as a pleasant odour.[20] Sunbathers of today do exactly the same with their various oils and lotions and for the same purpose. The perfume may be more delicate nowadays but the ancients had stronger stomachs. If this is true, we can the better understand the daunting picture of Aaron with his beard flowing with oil which runs down onto his vestments (Ps 133 (132):2). For the psalmist it is a symbol of Yahweh's blessing, given copiously like the dew of Hermon, falling on the heights of Zion. Nor is it difficult to understand that oil has certain healing properties. It soothes pain, even if sometimes it will ultimately increase it if poured on a broken skin that then suppurates. But the ancients at any rate thought of it as healing and soothing. Hence its association with the sacrament of the sick (cf Mark 6:13 and the parable of the Good Samaritan, Luke 10: 29–37).

In the Bible, and in the ancient world from which in this matter it did not differ, oil has an even wider register of significance. It is used copiously, it is *poured*, it is mixed with perfume and on the human level it is the sign of love (Song of Songs 1:3), of honour (Luke 7:46 and Matthew 26:7) and of joy (Pss 104 (103):15; 45 (44):8) and it is clear that it received its significance from a generous use of it in a festive atmosphere. Water for the feet, oil for the head and wine that makes glad the face of man were ingredients of eastern hospitality and feasting. But from another point of view it was a sign of election and consecration (1 Sam 10:1–6; 16:13), accompanied by the giving of the Spirit. It was this combination of unction and Spirit, we are told, that was the origin of the fundamental symbolism of oil.[21]

---

[20] See H. Lubienska de Lenval, *Liturgie du Geste* (Paris, Tournai, 1956), p. 47.

[21] The above is taken from X. Léon-Dufour, *Dictionary of Biblical Theology*, London, 1967, s.v. 'Oil' and 'Anointing'. The length of the latter article indicates the richness of the material on this subject in the Bible.

Although in the New Testament there is no reference to physical anointing (apart from Mark 6:13; Luke 10:34; James 5:14), the notion of a spiritual anointing is frequently found and it is possible to discern in the early centuries of the church the combination of the physical gesture of the laying-on of hands with various anointings. These are always associated with the giving or outpouring of the Spirit in baptism, in what later was called confirmation, and in other rites too. These Christians seem to have felt a compelling need to externalise what they believed to be happening in the soul because for them unction did mean joy and richness and, in the end, the bounty of God. Nor was this—as happened later on in the Middle Ages—a mere copying of the Old Testament customs. The first Christians were filled with the sense of their union with Jesus, the Anointed of God, the Messiah, the Son of God.[22] He was supremely the Anointed and he was the source of the unction, the symbol of the manifold grace of the Holy Spirit, whom the sacraments communicated to them.[23]

The Church Fathers took over almost all this symbolism without difficulty. For those writing in Greek the relation of 'chrism' to 'Christ' was obvious, both coming from the same word, though it was more usually called 'myron'. For Hippolytus the bishop anointed the baptised with the 'oil of thanksgiving'[24] and St Cyril of Jerusalem exploits almost every aspect of the symbolism, though he remains very close to the scriptures. Chrism is the exact image (antitypon) of that with which Christ was anointed who was filled with the Holy Spirit. The references to Luke 4:18 and Isaiah 62:1 are given. Anointing with the myron is compared by way of Psalm 44 (45):8 with the oil of joy with which Christ was chrismated in the incarnation because 'he is the author of spiritual joy'. Again, the oil is perfumed and the inevitable reference to 2 Corinthians 2:15 occurs, though Cyril is careful to point out that the perfume itself, no doubt on account of its richness, is a sign of the gift of Christ which has by the presence of the Holy Spirit become efficacious of his divine power: 'It is with this perfume that symbolically your forehead and other senses are chrismated; your body is chris-

---

[22] Hebrews 1:9 and cf Ps 45 (44):8.
[23] Cf *Dictionary of Biblical Theology*, 'Oil'.
[24] *Ap. Trad.* XXI 6, 18.

mated with this perfume; your soul is sanctified by the holy and life-giving Spirit.'[25]

This is as far as we need go in the examination of the biblical and patristic literature. Subsequent writers will add little or nothing of importance. Abundance, joy, the self-giving of God in the 'anointing' of the Son, and healing properties seem to give the essential symbolism of unction. If its use is to be continued, this understanding of it is necessary, but how is it to be acquired? Since the Bible itself gives so rich a symbolism of unction, it is to this in the first place that we must go. Quite apart from the liturgy, if people are to understand the Bible message, they will have to learn what the Bible is saying about it. We may well need to put off certain western preconceptions, it may be a painful experience to enter into another culture for which oil was of considerable significance, but this is the cost we must pay if we are to understand it and incidentally to widen our understanding of how other people think and act. Once this is done and the symbolism of unction is firmly attached to Christ, the archetype of all anointing, the spiritual significance of the use of the oil in the sacraments should be apparent. This, as we have seen, is the approach that Cyril of Jerusalem made to the matter.

But present practice also needs to be improved. First of all, the quality of the chrism needs to be improved. For all the tradition, it was a perfumed oil and the perfume was supposed to be, on the human level, part of its charm and, on the religious-symbolic level, a sign of spiritual joy. In the patristic period it was thought of as perfuming not merely the candidate but the whole building where the sacramental rite was being celebrated. In the new rite (1970)[26] for the Blessing of Oils, the introduction (4) says that chrism is made of oil and aromatic or perfume-bearing substances (*ex aromatibus, seu materia oderifera*), leaving the rest to the imagination. How we are to get such a chrism is beyond the competence of the present writer to say and such is the corruption of one's taste in these matters that one can only think of brilliantine. But something obviously ought to be done to improve the present condition of a chrism that is called 'sacred'. If olive oil is difficult to obtain or if (as one may suppose) there is another oil that has significance for a certain region or culture, the chrism may now be made of it (3)

[25] *Cat Myst.* III, 1, 2, 3, 4. The 'other senses' were the ears, the nostrils, the breast, for such was the Jerusalem custom.
[26] *Notitiae*, 62, March, 1971, pp. 89–91.

and this may well facilitate a better understanding of the symbolism of oil.[27]

Secondly, the cautious dabbings of oil which are immediately rubbed off should give way to a more generous administration. In the early centuries the minister took it in his hand and rubbed it on or, in the case of confirmation, simply placed it on the head and one must suppose that sometimes it did run down on the neck. In the scriptural imagery the Holy Spirit is constantly said to be *poured out* on people and although the mixture of metaphors may not be to our taste, the sense of the gesture is clear: an abundant pouring that is a symbol of the abundant giving of the Spirit. Where the head is anointed, as in baptism and confirmation, there would seem to be a case for the revival of the chrism cap which might be worn at least until the end of the service.

As for the continued use of the anointing before baptism, it is difficult to see any justification for it. As we have seen, originally it meant an anointing for the struggle against Satan and the whole body was anointed. What significance can a dab of oil on the chest of a wriggling infant have? And has anyone with equanimity thought of the impression an anointing of this kind would have on an adult candidate and his friends? It might just as well be given up.

The Laying-on of Hands
The hand, along with the word, is one of the most expressive means of language that man has.[28] It has various significances but the gesture of the laying-on of hands is the most important. In the Old Testament it could mean consecration, the setting apart of certain men, eg the Levites, for the service of God (Numbers 8:10) and the giving of the Spirit of wisdom (Deuteronomy 34:9). In the gospels there are many examples of Jesus laying his hands on the sick to heal them but it is in the rest of the New Testament that the notion of the transmission of the Holy Spirit is principally found. Peter and John lay hands on the Samaritans and they receive the Holy Spirit, and Paul does likewise for the people of Ephesus (Acts

---

[27] The same is true of the oils of catechumens and of the sick, though the introduction does not say so. In neither of the prayers is the olive mentioned though it is in that for the Blessing of Chrism. It may be noted here too that the bishop may mix the chrism during the course of the service (5) and if this were done with really aromatic herbs the whole church would be scented with them.

[28] X. Léon-Dufour, *Dictionary of Biblical Theology*, London, 1967, s.v. 'Imposition of hands'.

8:17; 19:6). Elsewhere, the laying-on of hands signifies the transmission of authority (Acts 6:6; 13:3) and in the Pastoral Epistles the giving of a *charisma* for a minstry or function in the church (1 Timothy 4:14; 2 Timothy 1:6, 7). In the liturgical tradition, the laying-on of hands is so constantly accompanied by the anointing with chrism that we must suppose that the former attracted the latter to itself because the anointing was seen as a more explicit symbol of the giving of the Spirit.

In the early church it was used far more frequently than now. During the course of the catechumenate hands were laid on the candidates; in the *Apostolic Tradition* the bishop laid hands on them after baptism and anointed them with 'the oil of thanksgiving'; and when people were reconciled to the church, either after apostasy or sin, hands were laid on them again. In all these situations the gesture signified the giving of the Spirit and perhaps it is worth reflecting on the implied doctrine that reconciliation after penitence is the work of the Spirit. A vestige of this once significant gesture remains even in the present ritual of penance where the confessor is instructed to raise his hand while pronouncing the words of absolution.

The gesture is seen at its most significant in the ordination of a bishop. The chief celebrant lays hands on the elect and the concelebrants then do likewise, all in silence. The gesture itself is a pleading that the Holy Spirit may come upon the elect and incorporate him into the episcopal order. This is then made explicit in the ancient prayer, that of Hippolytus (now happily restored to the rite), which asks that the *Spiritus principalis*, the sovereign Spirit, given first to Christ and then to the apostles, may fill his being so that he may rule the flock of Christ according to God's will.[29]

It needs perhaps to be emphasised that the laying-on of hands is a very ancient gesture, probably older than anointing, and evidently it is still significant. It needs little if any explanation. Hence, we can say that the antiquity of a symbol is no argument that it is no longer relevant. It may also however be significant that it is a human gesture, an action and not a thing, and it may be that this is the direction we shall have to move if we are to keep symbols alive. In the Middle Ages the anointings of the bishop and priest were re-

---

[29] There is of course a laying-on of hands for the presbyter and the deacon and to this we shall return when dealing with Holy Orders. Neither however is as impressive as that in the ordination of a bishop.

garded as all-important and it is interesting to note that they have become distinctly secondary rites in the revised liturgy of Holy Orders.

CHAPTER THREE

Baptism in the Context of Christian Initiation

WHEN LITURGICAL rites are reformed people usually concentrate on matters of detail. This or that familiar feature has disappeared or has undergone a transformation and they feel upset or affronted. Until all the documents concerning Christian Initiation are translated and published in English and until they have entered into the ordinary practice of the church, it is possible that their broad significance will be overlooked. Infant baptism still remains the practical norm, the position of confirmation in the initiation process is still unclear and First Communion is hardly seen as part, the climax in fact, of Christian Initiation. The deeper significance of the promulgation of the Orders of Baptism (1969) and the Order for the Christian Initiation of Adults (1972)[1] is that people become Christian by a whole process that involves their life as well as the community of the church. Christian Initiation is not (except very exceptionally) the pouring of a drop of water on the head of an infant but the total adherence of an adult person to Christ by faith and incorporation into him by baptism, confirmation and holy communion. It involves the Christian community which undertakes a certain responsibility for him, which must be present and which must receive him into itself.

Nor is initiation a purely mental (if engraced) operation. The candidate adheres to Christ with his whole personality. He is drawn into Christ by word, by rite and by symbol which 'speak' to his personality and enable him to engage both body and mind in the process of his becoming a Christian. In this sense the new order of initiation marks a return to a more fundamental and more organic view both of nature and grace. For as long as we have records of religion, man has approached God gradually through rite and sym-

---

[1] *Ordo Baptismi Parvulorum, Ordo Initiationis Christianae Adultorum* (Vatican Press).

bol and his liturgy moved according to the rhythms of his natural life. His birth was marked by certain rites and at puberty he underwent (and in some places still undergoes) the ritual of initiation into the full life of the tribe and participation in the ancestral religion. These have proved to be the strongest bond binding him to his people. In the Christian order there was the approach by faith in response to the proclamation of the word, the establishment of that faith and initiation into Christian living through the catechumenate, and finally climactic experience of sacramental incorporation into the community by baptism, confirmation and holy communion.

It is this vision that the new Orders have restored to the church and whatever the difficulties of adaptation, it is this that should be kept in mind. For far too long our sacramental practice has moved away from life. It has not even been parallel to it. The dislocation of the sacraments of initiation has been complete and, apart from baptism, the various sacramental acts bore no relation to the life-rhythm of the candidates. It may be thought that this is one reason why Christian practice has suffered such difficulties in recent years. A religion, a worship, that is not integrated with life can easily be shed and often is.

A further consequence of this restoration is that it provides the basis for a more coherent theology of the sacraments of initiation and it is to this that we must now turn.[2]

The organisation of the material to be found in the Order of Baptism of 1969, which contains a general introduction to baptism, a special one on the baptism of infants and the rite for the baptism of infants and the Order of Adult Initiation, presents some difficulty. There is further the Order of Confirmation (1971) which is an integral part of initiation but which, owing to the complexities of the subject, must be dealt with separately. The order we follow here will then be: the general introduction to baptism, the Order of Adult Initiation, the baptism of infants and finally in a separate chapter, confirmation.

In view of what has already been said, it is not surprising that baptism is firmly set in the context of the sacraments of initiation but the matter is not left vague. Nor, on the other hand, does it unduly separate the different sacraments of initiation. All *three*

---

[2] As already observed, the General Introduction falls into two parts, the first called 'Christian Initiation' with which we shall be dealing first. Its paragraphs or articles are numbered from 1 to 35 and will be referred to as CI 1, 2, 3 and so on.

sacraments of baptism, confirmation and holy communion combine
to bring Christians to the full stature of Christ. This doctrine, which
is wholly traditional, eliminates the need to examine too closely
the respective effects of the different sacraments though, against
this background, this may properly be done. As the Order says,
baptism makes people members of the body of Christ and of the
people of God. It takes away their sins, makes them a new creation
and the adopted children of Christ, and it is important to notice
that all this is effected 'by water and the Holy Spirit'. The Spirit
is given in baptism too. But people are also sealed by the Spirit in
confirmation, the more perfectly to conform them to Christ and
to enable them to bear witness to him for the building up to its
fullness of his body. In the eucharist, as well as receiving the bread
of eternal life, they manifest, make the sign of, the unity of the
people of God and 'by offering themselves with Christ, they share
in his universal sacrifice: the entire community of the redeemed
is offered by their high priest' (Christ).[3]

Such is the comprehensive vision of this document which it will
be profitable to keep in mind when we have to examine the sacraments of initiation in greater detail. But at once two further elements
may be noted. The first is that the newly baptised join with the
Christian community to pray for the outpouring of the Holy Spirit
'so that the whole human race may be brought into the unity of
God's family'. The vision is broad, as broad as the human race,
and the church sees the eucharist as the dynamic centre of the redeeming love of Christ which goes out to the whole world, invisibly
but surely gathering men and women everywhere into communion
with Christ. The second thing is this: Christ is indeed working out
his purpose for the salvation of mankind but through all three sacraments of initiation he calls his people to be his ambassadors, his
fellow-workers to collaborate in that work (2 Corinthians 5:20;
6:1). By baptism, confirmation and the eucharist Christians are
committed to mission in the church and for the world.

The Nature of Baptism

In recent years it has become ever clearer that baptism is the
basic sacrament, with an importance that can hardly be measured.
Ecumenically it is the sacrament of Christian unity. All who are
baptised are members of Christ even if, as the *Decree on Ecumen-*

---

[3] This last phrase from St Augustine, *De Civ. Dei*, X, 6.

ism says, those outside the visible unity of the Catholic Church have a less than full or perfect relation to it. But it is also basic in the life of the individual Christian who is called to live out throughout his days what he receives in baptism. In a phrase much used by the late Dom Gregory Dix, we have to become what we are and this is true whether we are baptised in infancy or later in life. It is not surprising, then, that the Order in the section called 'On the dignity of baptism' (CI 3–6) should offer a statement on the meaning of baptism, a statement that provides a very condensed theology of the whole sacrament. We can do no more than take up some of its points.

Faith

Throughout the whole series of documents on initiation and in the rites themselves the church shows a dominant concern for faith. This has always been explicit in the teaching and practice of the church but not since the early centuries have faith and sacraments been so closely integrated as they are now. Baptism, according to the Order (CI 2), is the sacrament of that faith by which, through the enlightenment of the Holy Spirit, we respond to the gospel of Christ; and the church believes it to be her fundamental duty to inspire all, catechumens, parents of children still to be baptised and god-parents, to that true and living faith by which they adhere to Christ and enter into or confirm their commitment to the new covenant (CI 3). Even the language is remarkable, so different from the stale language of the catechism and the text-book. But if we turn to the New Testament we see that this teaching is no more than a re-statement of what is to be found there, though the evidence is so vast that one can do no more than cite one or two texts. Thus, in St Mark (16:16), a statement that seems to sum up so much of New Testament teaching on the point: 'He who believes and is baptised will be saved.' Of this Matthew 28:19 is no more than an elaborate echo: 'Go and make disciples of all nations, baptising them in the name of the Father and of the Son and of the Holy Spirit.'[4]

When we come to the action of the apostles there is no doubt at all. First, there is the preaching, then there is the first conversion

---

[4] The first comes from the 'longer' ending of Mark and the scripture experts seem to think that Matthew 28:18–20 is a summary of a floating piece of catechesis. If so, it means that both passages became anchored at the end of the two gospels.

and in response to the question 'What shall we do?' Peter answers 'Be baptised in the name of Jesus Christ' (Acts 2:37–41). Faith comes from hearing, says St Paul, and for the hearing and the faith a preacher is necessary (Romans 10:14–17). The apostles first preached, men conceived faith in their hearts and then they proceeded to baptism. From Acts 2:42 we may conclude that the new converts then joined the eucharistic assembly. The pattern is constant and did not vary for the next five hundred years.[5]

Faith, then, is an indispensable necessity for baptism and it will be as well to see what kind of faith is in question. There has been a tendency to think of faith as static, as merely an assent, which could and should be protected by prayer but which once given remained much as it was. The Order speaks of a true and living faith by which people adhere to Christ and enter into a commitment to the new covenant which he brought into existence. So the faith here spoken of is not merely an assent to the articles of the creed nor is it simply a minimal guarantee of orthodoxy. It is a faith that is the act of our whole personality going out to the person of Christ to whom we commit ourselves totally. At least, we do this in intention though we know that such a total giving is impossible in one act and that it takes years, perhaps a whole lifetime, to bring that commitment anywhere near perfection. The Christian life is a living out of this faith received in baptism, a faith that it enriches but always presupposes.

All this is to say no more than is said in the *Constitution on the Liturgy* (59): '(The sacraments) not only presuppose faith, but by words and objects they also nourish, strengthen and express it; that is why they are called "sacraments of faith". They have indeed the power to impart grace, but, in addition, the very act of celebrating them effectively disposes the faithful to receive this grace fruitfully ...'. Certainly in 'the very act of celebrating', according to the Orders of Initiation and Baptism, there is no doubt at all that faith is expressed and professed as well as witnessed to by the whole assembly. As the former shows very clearly, faith is presupposed, is deepened during the catechumenate, is professed in the 'giving back of the creed' and expounded in the several services of the word that make up so much of the catechumenate. In the latter, and just before the service reaches its climax in the act of baptism, the

---

[5] The only exception is the baptism of infants who in the third, fourth and fifth centuries were baptised with their parents. It was not until later, as we shall see, that the pattern was broken.

candidate is required to make a public profession of the faith in the presence of the assembly when he adheres to God, Father, Son and Holy Spirit. In the baptism of infants, there is understandably an even greater emphasis on the need for faith, a faith which the parents who are undertaking the Christian education of their children (BP 39) must profess. This faith is proclaimed in the word of God and the homily (44, 45), is prayed for in the intercessions and again is professed before the act of baptism and summed up by the celebrant in the words: 'This is our faith. This is the faith of the Church. We are proud to profess it, in Christ Jesus our Lord' (58, 60 and cf 64).

Participation in the Mystery of Christ

By faith and baptism, then, we come to Christ; but is he just a generalised figure, the *object* of faith, or even the teacher of faith? For the Order (CI 6), baptism 'recalls and effects the paschal mystery itself', it is a celebration of the passion, death and resurrection of Christ and through it men and women are able to pass from death to life, are engrafted into his death and rise with him by the power of his resurrection.

This teaching raises the whole question of participation in the mystery of Christ which is central to Christian living. We are perhaps more accustomed to think of the matter in the context of the eucharist which in a unique way recalls and makes present the passion and resurrection of Christ. None the less baptism is a celebration of the paschal mystery and by it we are first made like Christ in his passion and resurrection. It is here, in Pauline language, that we first put on Christ, the Christ who suffered, died and rose again so that the barrier of sin might be destroyed and mankind could be reconciled to the Father. The similarity of the effects of baptism to those of the eucharist (or for that matter, to those of Penance) has given theologians some little trouble. Perhaps it was precisely the separation and eventual categorisation of the sacraments that produced the problem. In the sacraments, in the whole of the liturgy, we are celebrating the one mystery of Christ. It is contact with that mystery (a contact that may be and is initially made by faith also) that spells salvation, though we may approach it in several (God-given) ways and share in it in different ways. Baptism is the first way in which we are enabled to make our own and enter into the mystery, and the commitment spoken of earlier is necessarily a commitment to the suffering and glorified Christ. Our life as

Christians is meant to bear the marks of both: 'If in union with Christ, we have imitated his death, we shall also imitate him in his resurrection',[6] not merely at the resurrection of the dead but here in our earthly life when, as we hope and pray, the power of the risen Christ is overcoming the deathward tendencies of the body.

Here again we are involved in a process. As St Paul says in the same place, we have to live a new kind of life that looks towards God through the risen Christ. Clearly this is a life-long process and it is at this point that we can see the connection between baptism and the eucharist. The latter, in all the early liturgies, is the culmination of the former; but at a level even deeper than that, we can see that if the Christian life is a dying and rising with Christ, then it is in the eucharist where we meet him week by week that we are able to appropriate the power of his death and resurrection. In the simplest language, by baptism we *begin* to be Christians; and to go on being Christians, to grow as Christians, to become the perfect man 'fully mature with the fullness of Christ himself' we need to be conformed again and again to the Christ of the passion and resurrection through celebration of the holy eucharist. At this deeper level, the Christian life is all of a piece and the truth underlying the old system of the sacraments of initiation was a fundamental one. It may be thought that this is a sufficient reason to return to an ancient custom (retained by the Eastern Churches) of communicating even infants after baptism. This would make sense especially when infants are baptised during the eucharist. In the Order of Infant Baptism the eventual communion of the infants is at least mentioned (67).

Incorporation into the community of the church
After all the writing and preaching in the 1930s and 1940s about the church as the mystical body of Christ as well as all the emphasis the Liturgical Movement laid on the people's share in Christ's priesthood, it was to have been expected that people generally would have come to realise that baptism effects the incorporation of the individual into the community of the church. But apparently the 'hang-over' from former times has not yet been dispelled. For many, baptism is still merely a rescue operation to save a child from the effects of Original Sin—which only shows that an inadequate and unintelligible rite helps to propagate false views. The thinking of

[6] Romans 6:3-5.

the introduction and of the whole rite of baptism is quite different. The former says *tout court* 'Through baptism men and women are incorporated into Christ' (CI 2) and again they 'are incorporated into the church' (CI 4) which is the house of the Spirit and they become members of the holy nation and the royal priesthood.[7] In the rite this is symbolised by the anointing on the head after baptism and the words which accompany the action. The candidates have been freed from sin, regenerated by water and the Spirit, 'added' to the Lord's holy people and made members of Christ who is prophet, priest and king. Thus, they are incorporated into the people of whom Christ is the head and high priest. It is through baptism that they become sharers in the priesthood of Christ and therefore, in the words of St Peter (1 Peter 2:5), have for their task and vocation the offering of spiritual sacrifices which belong to the spiritual house of which they are living stones. As is now well known, in the liturgy and in the eucharist in a special way they exercise that priesthood by offering themselves in and through Christ.[8] Here again the eucharist appears as the completion and culmination of baptism.

Two further points may be noted here, both of which are relevant to confirmation, which we treat below. The first is that the above prayer affirms that regeneration is effected by both water and the Holy Spirit, thus clearly indicating that the Spirit is given in baptism. Popular writing and preaching on confirmation has frequently overlooked this matter and the impression has been given that the Holy Spirit is given for the first time in that sacrament. It is an untenable point of view for how can regeneration, with all it implies, be effected without the intervention of the Holy Spirit? The second point is this: by the introduction into the same prayer of the teaching that the baptised Christian shares in the priestly, royal and prophetic qualities of Christ, thus implicitly quoting 1 Peter 2:5, 9 (not to mention other New Testament texts), the church is affirming that mission, the proclamation of the saving deeds of God, is part of the vocation of the Christian. The Christian is 'sent' by baptism and he does not have to wait until he is confirmed to exercise his ministry.

---

[7] The texts referred to are Ephesians 2:22 ('the house where God dwells, in the Spirit') and 1 Peter 2:9.

[8] Cf *Mediator Dei*, 92, CL 14 and the author's *Christian Celebration*, Vol. I, pp. 36–8 (London, 1971).

Fellowship with the Holy Trinity

The teaching on incorporation is carried through to its ultimate conclusion by another passage in the introduction. Incorporation into the church means entrance into fellowship with the Holy Trinity. Perhaps we do not even reflect on what the so frequently repeated teaching of the New Testament on the 'adoption of sons' means. It means adoption into the divine family: 'The blessed Trinity is invoked over those who are to be baptised. Signed in this name, they are consecrated to the Trinity and enter into fellowship with the Father, Son and Holy Spirit' (CI 5). This may be regarded as a most useful commentary on the significance of baptism in the name of the Trinity but it will be worthwhile to draw out its implications. The climax of the baptism rite, as the same texts says, is the baptism in the Triune name, and we may add that it is also its final purpose. Incorporation into the church is but a step, normally a necessary step, to union with God. But he is Father, Son and Holy Spirit and it is into the life of the Trinity that we are introduced by baptism. We are initiated into the divine life and that life is essentially the lived relationship between Father, Son and Holy Spirit. Ceaselessly, without loss or diminution the Persons of the Trinity give themselves to each other and in the love they communicate to one another they enfold the baptised Christian who is thus able to participate in that creative love. As in the sacrament he receives the new life from Christ by the operation of the Holy Spirit, he is able to breathe out his love for the Father, a love that is transfused with the divine love and so acceptable to him. By baptism, then, the Christian begins to live the Christian life as from its centre and this, once again, is clearly a life-long task. Lastly, since the eucharist is pre-eminently the sacrament of love, it provides the principal means by which the Christian is able to live the divine life. This too makes it clear that the eucharist is the culmination of baptism.

Celebration

Liturgical documents are practical documents and if they are rightly concerned with theological ideas it is only so that they may be translated into action. It is not surprising, then, that the baptism Orders speak of celebration, though it is gratifying that they have chosen this word. It has been more common to speak of 'administering' or 'conferring' sacraments as if the laity were solely recipients. Celebration, which involves community and participation, is a much more significant word. If the sacraments are in the phrase of St Thomas Aquinas 'protestations of faith',[9] they are also the recognition of God's saving love which reached its culmination in the passion, resurrection and ascension of Christ, and the Order sees baptism as the celebration of the paschal mystery: 'Those who are baptised are engrafted into the likeness of Christ's death. They are buried with him, they are given life with him again and with him they rise again. For baptism recalls and effects the paschal mystery itself, because by means of it men and women pass from the death of sin into life' and the Order draws the practical consequences. The joy of the Christian community through its recognition of the paschal mystery should be reflected in the celebration itself (CI 6) and this is why the sacrament is to be celebrated during the Easter Vigil or on Sundays, and, as often as pastorally desirable, within the eucharist. All through the Orders we find this relationship between baptism and the paschal mystery being established, sometimes in quite small matters as when it urges that the Paschal Candle shall stand in the baptistery throughout the year.

How this sense of celebration is to be expressed is another matter. For adult baptism there is no difficulty. It is to be celebrated either during the Paschal Vigil or during a Sunday eucharist when the joy that belongs to celebration finds its natural expression.[10] With infant baptism there is a greater difficulty. Celebration at the Sunday eucharist is desirable but it is not always possible. However, what is probably necessary is that both clergy and laity should change their views about baptism and see it as a community action in which as many as possible should be involved. This is certainly the thinking of the Order for Infant Baptism (BP, 4, 9) and some pattern needs to be established and become customary. In recent decades Catholics have been accustomed to going to only one service a Sunday, the Mass. Perhaps with the restoration of the Prayer of the Church to our Sunday worship, the baptism of infants could take place in conjunction with that service. If so, the texts provided by the Order, chants, hymns and acclamations could, on the assumption that they are set to music, be sung by all present and turn the service from being an 'administration' into a celebration. To achieve anything like this it must be admitted that we have a long way to go.

---

[9] *ST* III Q. LXXII, 5, ad 2.
[10] It is to be supposed that adult baptism may be celebrated privately in very special circumstances though the Order does not envisage such a procedure.

Community

As is immediately obvious, you cannot have celebration without community.[11] It is *people* who celebrate, it is they who are the church, it is they who profess the faith of the church and it is they who sing God's praises. One of the more striking features of the Order of Christian Initiation for Adults is that it requires in no uncertain terms the help and presence of the Christian community not only at the liturgy but also throughout the whole process. In the case of infant baptism this is particularly important since the Order expressly teaches that infants are, in the traditional phrase, baptised 'in the faith of the church', the faith which is declared and professed throughout the rite. If it is *theologically* true that baptism incorporates into the Christian community, it must be made liturgically plain that this is what is happening. For this clearly some representation of the local community is necessary. Pastorally speaking, their presence is going to be of the greatest help to the candidates. They will realise that they are being incorporated into the great church of which the local community is an expression and they will be encouraged in their profession of faith by the faith of the surrounding community. Where infant baptism is being celebrated, the weaker Catholic will feel strengthened and supported by the presence of the same community and will no doubt rid themselves of a certain feeling of isolation or even alienation that often overtakes them.

The above teaching is expressed in the liturgies of initiation, as we have attempted in part to indicate, but it seemed necessary to give it at this point. We are now in a position to consider the Order of Christian Initiation for Adults and the liturgy of adult baptism which is included in it.

---

[11] Cf *Christian Celebration*, Vol. I, pp. 136 ff.

CHAPTER FOUR

The Christian Initiation of Adults[1]

IT MAY be thought surprising that the church has found it necessary to restore the catechumenate. It may seem to deserve the charge of irrelevancy which has become almost a new mortal sin. If we think that way it means that we have become more conditioned by our situation than perhaps we like to think. Without reflection we have come to assume that infant baptism is the norm and that any other system of Christian Initiation is abnormal. For a very long time, perhaps for too long, we have assumed that we were living in a Christian society, however broad the connotation of 'Christian'. We readily deplore the unchristian spirit of our age but we do not realise that the arrangement we regard as traditional is breaking down. The baptism of infants of families of no apparent faith is already posing more or less acute problems and we must expect that the situation will get worse rather than better. Yet a mere refusal to baptise such children solves nothing and we are faced or soon will be with the prospect of pastoral action in their regard. If the requirements of the new Order for the Baptism of Infants are to be met, it seems inevitable that as the years go by there will be an increasing number of people who are not baptised. Instead of being brushed aside as an irredeemable residue, it will be necessary to think out pastoral approaches and techniques by which they can be drawn to the church and eventually incorporated into it.

---

[1] For the purposes of this chapter this term covers all that is to be found in the *Order of Christian Initiation for Adults* (1972) from the first approach of a seeker to the church to mystagogy which is the final stage. In the Order the various items, including the *praenotanda* or introductions, are numbered from 1 to 239. Whether they refer to these or parts of the rites it is these numbers that will be given in what follows. In this chapter it will also be necessary to include sundry variations of the Order and the rite of admission of a baptised Christian into the Catholic Church. This rite is to be found in an Appendix and is separately numbered.

Adult baptism is not so much on the horizon as with us already.[2]

For some parts of the church this situation is not new and since the experience gathered there has led to the restoration of the catechumenate some account of its previous history will be in place here.

The 'homelands' of Europe, notably France, have been faced with a dechristianised society for some long time. Considerable numbers of children are not baptised and yet in adulthood, either through the pastoral action of Christians or on the occasion of marriage, they approach the church and often wish to be received into it. The existing structures proved inadequate to meet the situation and over ten years ago the French bishops set up an official catechumenate. In missionary areas adult baptisms of course remain common, but here again and although there were elements of a catechumenate in existence, those engaged in the work felt it was inadequate. It was something outside the liturgy and running alongside it. It was thanks to the pressure from these two sources that in 1962 Rome issued a document restoring the catechumenate. It was not much more than a re-arrangement of the material to be found in the *Rituale Romanum*[3] of that time and with its rigidity and multiplicity of minor rites that could not be varied from one culture to another it proved to be unsatisfactory.

There was another factor of even greater importance. The bishops, whether in the homelands or in the missionary areas, asked that the catechetical formation of those approaching the church should be 'sanctified by the sacred rites of the catechumenate'. The word 'formation', which in the document is distinguished from 'instruction', points to a deeper understanding of initiation. The bishops were asking that potential converts should be not merely instructed but *initiated* into the Christian life and into the community of the church. Nowadays people who approach the church are usually not just 'changing churches', as was common in the nineteenth century. They are coming out of a world that is almost wholly pagan, a world that imposes considerable pressures on Christian and catechumen alike, a world that either does not know or rejects prayer, worship and all the moral effort that goes with the

---

[2] In one parish known to the present writer at least three people received adult baptism during the Easter Vigil in 1971.

[3] Text in *ASS*, Vol. LIV, num. 6, pp. 310 foll., 30 May 1962. Cf also for French translation *Documentation Catholique*, t. lix, num. 1, 380.

Christian life. Catechumens need to do a great deal more than to accept doctrines. They need to realise that they have to begin a new way of life that will involve a new outlook on life in general and probably a change of habits. And since Christianity is itself a life they need to be initiated into it. They need to learn how to live in the Christian community before ever they make a commitment that is definitive.

This is the background of the Second Vatican Council's decision that the rites of adult baptism should be revised and that the revision should take into account the (already) restored catechumenate (CL 66). This revision has now been completed with the promulgation of the *Ordo Initiationis Christianae Adultorum* which includes the rite of adult baptism. Since it is a very long document, the longest in fact to appear so far from the Congregation of Divine Worship,[4] it is necessary to give a summary of it.

At first sight the most surprising feature of the new Order is that it is a restoration, one might almost say, a resurrection of the Roman catechumenate of the last century of its existence, when in fact it was beginning to be obsolescent since by the end of the fifth century society had become largely Christian. The reasons for this choice seem to be fairly obvious. Instead of thinking up an entirely new system the revisers examined the tradition, as they have in all their work, and saw that it provided the necessary pattern even for today. It provided for the first approach to the church, it was progressive, it already contained the rites that were needed and it incorporated the whole process of initiation, baptism, confirmation and holy communion. Even so, a first reading of this document with its rites, so numerous and apparently complex, will tempt some to say that the whole thing is impracticable and irrelevant to the situation in which the church has to work today. This objection is foreseen and answered: pastors of the church will find here material from which they can construct a system suitable to their own circumstances (3) and in fact they are required to do so. But there is something more important still: the Order endorses the view set out briefly above that approach to the church and eventual incorporation into it is a gradual process that must be concretised in liturgical services and rites so that the candidate may grasp, with the whole of his personality, Christian faith and life and so be truly initiated into Christian living. In face of the complexity of the

---

[4] Longer by thirteen pages than the *Ordo Missae*.

material and the evident difficulties of implementation these factors should always be kept in mind.

The first part of the Order (1–239) may be divided as follows:

1. Evangelisation and Pre-Catechumenate.
2. The Catechumenate.
3. The Time of Purification and Enlightenment.
4. Sacramental Initiation.
5. Mystagogy.

Evangelisation and the Pre-Catechumenate

This is the stage with which most will be familiar. People approach the church out of interest, through contact with Catholics, out of a desire to make some sense of life and so on. After preliminary interviews they will ask for and be given some instructions, usually by a priest or some other person delegated for the purpose. Under the old system (still in force), they were in due course received into the church either by baptism if they had not been baptised or by the rite devised for the purpose,[5] both being private ceremonies, and then admitted to holy communion. In this system evangelisation, the pre-catechumenate stage and the catechumenate were so telescoped as to disappear from view.

The outlook of the Order is totally different. It assumes evangelisation and in another context it would be relevant to ask what is meant by that and how we go about it.[6] However, the Order requires that before admission to the catechumenate candidates should be in possession of the elements of Christian doctrine, that they should have formed their intention to change their life and conceived the beginnings of repentance (15). On the part of the 'applicant' this stage is meant to be a time of questioning (7, a) so that all major doubts are cleared up to make way for the proclamation on the part of the church of the Good News about the living God and his Son, Jesus Christ, whom his Father sent into the world to redeem it (9). The first conversion is to be the response to this proclamation of the gospel and at the same time help is to be

---

[5] Involving abjuration of and absolution from heresies they were totally innocent of!

[6] On the improbable assumption that the much vaunted media of social communication were open to the church (which they are not), how should we go about the matter? My only contribution to the discussion would be that we should make a serious and prolonged study of the advertisements. If you can sell soap by advertisement, presumably you can sell the Good News in the same way.

given the applicants to purify their intentions and clarify their motives. Even at this stage the Order is concerned with Christian living and with what I suppose can be called an existential grasp of the faith (10, 11).

At this first stage too, the Order emphasises the importance of community, as it does throughout. According to circumstances and individual dispositions, candidates should be enabled to experience the spirit of the Christian life as lived within the community or, if they are not in a position eventually to be incorporated into the catechumenate, to make at least external contacts with Christians (12 (2)). The Christian life is not a communion of the alone with the Alone but a corporate life and of this life the church even as local community is the sacrament-sign. Therefore, the implication is, potential converts should experience this from the beginning.

All this may seem to be very foreign to the conventional notions of 'conversion' but the Order, which in any case is taking a world-view of things, is concerned to emphasise that there are people who are drawn to Christianity but who are as yet undecided or who on account of their situation, moral or otherwise, are unable and perhaps unwilling to take steps that will commit them to ultimate incorporation into the church. The Order calls them 'sympathisers' and no doubt in missionary areas they are numerous, but in the industrialised regions of the modern world they are to be found too. Among these people will be those who have been involved in divorce or other irregular situations and the question as to what can be done for them when they approach the church is becoming acute. It is something for the clergy or members of the parish to show sympathy for them but it is not enough. On the other hand, they cannot (at least for the time being) be incorporated even into a catechumenate. Hence the remarks of the Order, as given above, and its further recommendations that they and others whose situation is regular should be received at gatherings of the local community when there will be opportunity for conversation and the formation of friendships. Whether or not there is to be some external sign or rite marking their approach to the Christian community is left to local conferences of bishops to determine (12, 13).

In some ways, of course, there is nothing new here. In England, and no doubt elsewhere, what are called Enquiry Classes are held where potential converts hear about the elements of the Christian faith and are able to meet Christians and form friendships with them. But the *spirit* of the Order is rather different. It seems to suggest that the atmosphere should be really warm and one may doubt whether the authors of it envisage the somewhat bleak setting of a schoolroom. And they add one or two details that are important: the 'friend', who will become the sponsor accompanying the seeker throughout the period of initiation, introduces him and there will be some gesture, however informal, that the community is accepting him. He will thus not remain simply an 'outsider' who happens to be enquiring about the faith but will contract a relationship with the Christian community. He will feel that he 'belongs', however tenuous the relationship may have to be for some time to come. There is considerable pastoral wisdom behind this point of view. The process of converting a nation or an individual is a long one and often in the past it has been too hurried. It is a common complaint that the children of those who become converts lapse and in the history of the church the partial collapse of a recently converted community is a commonplace. It will be better to move slowly and build up an outer circle of 'sympathisers' who are won to the Christian faith and life by their experience of the Christian living of a community (cf 12 (2)).

The Catechumenate

It is during this stage and the next ('purification') that the whole richness of the church's mind on the formation of a Christian is revealed. By word and human contact, by symbol, rite and gesture which correspond with deep human needs, the catechumen is led from an incipient faith into the fullness of the Christian life. It is important to realise this since the organisation of these two stages of Christian Initiation will be difficult and in the text it looks over-complicated, even ritualistic, although off-setting this is the considerable faculty of adaptation that is assumed and enjoined by the Order. At any rate it would be a gross misunderstanding of the restored catechumenate to see it as no more than the ritualisation of what might, mistakenly, be thought a very simple matter. Conviction about the Christian faith is one thing, practice is another and since Christianity is rather a life to be lived than a doctrine to be believed, it is absolutely necessary that people, especially modern people, should be initiated into Christian living during the time of their preparation.

For this stage the Order assumes that the candidates have an initial faith, have undergone the first (moral) conversion, have been familiarised with prayer and have made contact with the Christian community. That granted, the catechumenate is 'of the highest importance' for it is at this point that the candidates *publicly* declare their desire to be incorporated into the church and the church, performing her apostolic function, publicly admits them as potential members (14). In addition, there are certain social consequences. Now they belong 'to the household of Christ', they are fed by God's word in the Christian assembly, they are strengthened by liturgical rites and they may receive certain liturgical blessings. There is a special marriage rite for them[7] and if they die during their catechumenate they are buried with the Christian funeral rite (18).

The content and style of the catechumenate are indicated (19, (1), (2), (3), (4)). They consist of a suitable catechesis integrated with the liturgical year and supported by Bible Services. Teaching on the church's doctrines and the Christian precepts is to be given but above all the candidates are to be led to a deeper understanding of the mystery of salvation. They are to be assisted to live the Christian life and, even while catechumens, they are to learn to bear witness to Christ. Finally, there are the liturgical rites which we describe below. However, it is necessary to say a word about a suggestion that is contained in 19 (3).

It raises a quite big question whether catechumens are to be admitted to the eucharistic assembly proper. The Order urges that catechumens should take part in the ministry of the word along with the faithful, and therefore at public Masses, but it also says that they are to be 'kindly dismissed' unless there are difficulties 'for they should await baptism, by which they are incorporated into the priestly people when they will acquire their right to celebrate the new worship of Christ'. An unpopular suggestion, one imagines, for it has been the custom to 'get them to Mass' for fear they will not acquire the habit. This fear is dispelled by the Order which provides the means to teach people how to worship and the question remains: how far is it right to allow and even invite people to the eucharist when they cannot communicate and must in the nature of the case appear to be 'outsiders'? It is a large question, as yet without an answer.[8]

---

[7] *Ordo Matrimonii*, 55–6.

[8] J. Gelineau in *Nelle Vostre Assemblee* (Brescia, 1970), pp. 72–3 raises the question not only in connection with catechumens but with those public ceremonies and certain marriages and funerals where most of the congregation are

The Liturgy of the Catechumenate (106–31)

The first rite is naturally that which admits people to the cate-chumenate. Candidates with their friends and members of the local community meet in the place designated, preferably the narthex of the church which will thus return to its ancient function. The celebrant greets them, expresses the joy of the church at their coming, reminds them of the significance of the event and invites the whole company to take up the places allocated to them. During this Psalm 62:1–9 may be sung. There follow the questions ('What do you ask of the church of God? Faith ...') and the first commit-ment.[9] This is preceded by a brief address of the celebrant who reminds them that since they have followed the light 'the way of the gospel is now open' to them. He concludes by asking the can-didates if they are willing to take the way of Christ in faith and each replies 'I am ready'. The sponsor and the others present are asked for their support which they promise in the same terms.

According to different situations and needs (eg where certain kinds of 'magical' religions are prevalent), there may follow a brief exorcism and renunciation of evil. Otherwise the celebrant con-cludes this part of the rite with a collect and an expression of thanksgiving.

There follows the signing with the cross which signifies the new status of the candidates and the protection of Christ: 'Receive the cross on your forehead. Christ himself protects you with the sign of his love. Learn to know and follow him.' There is a second signing on all the senses which however may be wholly or partially omitted. The celebrant recites the formulas while others sign the candidates: 'Receive the sign of the cross on your ears that you may hear the voice of God ... on your eyes that you may see the glory of God ... on your lips that you may respond to the word of God ...'[10] This signing is an example of a symbolic-Christian ges-

---

not Christians in any real sense. What right have we to expose the holy mysteries to them? Are we not laying ourselves open to radical misunder-standing? And here and elsewhere he suggests that catechumens should be dismissed before the eucharist proper: 'The restoration of the catechumenate invites us to ensure a certain pedagogy to assist the approach to the sign of the Christian mystery ... *It is not normal* that a catechumen should be present at the eucharist in which he is not permitted to receive holy communion.'

[9] No. 76; in the Latin, *Prima adhaesio*.

[10] I am unable to find the source of this manifold signing. The rite may be omitted either in whole or in part (85). There is a similar rite, though *after* baptism, in Cyril of Jerusalem, cited above, p. 25.

ture that may in certain circumstances be very appropriate and its use could well be extended to other situations: eg the appointment of a lay-reader.

This part concludes with a collect which is the old prayer of the catechumenate, now slightly re-edited: the church prays that now the candidates have been signed with the cross, they may be protected by its power and that, keeping the commandments, they may come to the glory of the new life.[11] The catechumens are now led into church with the old formula revised and enriched: 'Come into the church that you may have part with us at the table of God's word.' There follows a Bible Service during which there may be a giving of the gospel text and general intercessions for the catechumens. Finally, there is the dismissal with a reminder to the candidates to be assiduous in coming to church to hear the word of God. If Mass follows, they may stay but clearly the Order thinks it is better they should not.

During the period of the catechumenate, which may last for several years, giving time for the candidates' faith and conversion to 'mature' (98), the Order provides for a series of Bible Services, Exorcisms and Blessings. It is here perhaps more than anywhere else in the restored catechumenate that the nature of the process by which people become Christians is made clear. Yes, there is instruction in the doctrines of the Catholic faith; yes, they are to be encouraged to practise the precepts of the Christian life and to join in worship so far as that is possible for them; but all this is taken out of the realm of the merely intellectual or exhortatory. These things are inculcated in the context of liturgical rites which are intended to be *formative*. In the Bible Services, for instance, the catechumens will not merely hear the word of God, they will pray about it and in their endeavours to live the Christian life, they will be supported by the exorcisms and blessings provided for them.

As to the exorcisms, the Order (101) says they are intended to be positive and deprecatory and the six prayers for this purpose amply prove that this is so (113-18). The emphasis on the devil is very light (113 '*spiritum malignum*' without a capital 'S') and they are much more requests that the catechumens will grow in virtue and will resist the evil that comes from their own nature or from the surrounding world.

---

[11] There is an alternative.

The blessings are prayers, which may be used at the dismissal of the catechumens, even more positive, intended to encourage the catechumens on their way to the church, to show the care of the church for them and, as the texts of the prayer show, direct their minds and hearts to the re-birth that is to be the conclusion of the whole process.[12]

The Time of Purification and Enlightenment (152–207)

The Order sees this as the really decisive stage. The catechumens make a deliberate and final decision to proceed to the reception of the sacraments of initiation and, for its part the Christian community, after consultation between the clergy, sponsors and catechists determines to admit them to full membership (135). The part to be played by the community is striking and very demanding and one wonders how far it will be practicable in the circumstances of the modern urban parish. In urban parishes people hardly know each other sufficiently to be able to offer opinions about the fitness of candidates for baptism and there is of course in any case all the danger of petty dislikes playing their part. Unless and until urban parishes can be organised on rather different lines it will be for those who have been responsible for the formation of the catechumens to make the necessary decisions and the local community will at the liturgical service endorse them. This is in fact provided for in the Order (144).[13]

The nature and purpose of this stage of Purification and Enlightenment (wholly traditional terms though others may be used) can be gathered from the following. It coincides with Lent when, with the Christian community, who recall and renew the grace of baptism at this time, the catechumens will be helped to ponder on the meaning of the paschal mystery which the sacraments of initiation communicate to each of them (21). This in fact explains the nature of the liturgical arrangements for this stage. At this time it is conceived that there will be a period of more intense spiritual recollection and formation. The hearts and minds of the candidates are to be purified by an education of the conscience and by penitence and it is these elements that are insisted on rather than further instruction. It is to this end that 'scrutinies', which form part of

---

[12] Certain features of the next stage may be anticipated in this (119).
[13] The decision-making does not of course exclude the bishop. There will be previous consultation with him and at the service either he or his delegate will announce the decision (23).

this stage, are enjoined. Their purpose is first to reveal what is still weak or perverse in the candidates' conduct so that this may be put right (*ut sanetur*) but secondly to show what is good, strong and holy that it may be established in them. The enlightenment comes with the exposition and 'giving' (*traditio*) of the creed and the Lord's Prayer. The first is seen as a summary of the Good News of salvation, which they will accept with joy, and by the latter they will learn to recognise the deeper significance of their being children of God, an acknowledgement they will make when (eventually) they recite it 'in the midst of the eucharistic assembly' (25, (1), (2)).

At this stage, too, they become the 'elect' (another traditional term)[14] not simply because they are enrolled and their names entered in a register but because, says the Order (23), the church's act of calling and choosing them is founded on the choice God has made of them (22). This statement, based no doubt on texts like Ephesians 1:4, restores to currency a certain theology of vocation in the sense of calling and of the conversion, which is its consequence not merely for those usually called converts but for all Christians. It is evidence of how serious the church considers this matter of becoming a Christian. Conversion is not a sociological or psychological accident; it is evidence of God's call, indicated perhaps by the conditions of one's life, but manifested in the call and election of the church and sealed by the sacraments of baptism, confirmation and the holy eucharist.

The Liturgy of this Stage

First, it is to be noted that this liturgy is firmly integrated into that of Lent, the rite of admission taking place on the First Sunday of Lent (140). This links it with the preparation of the whole Christian community for the celebration of the paschal mystery at Easter.

The liturgy consists of the following: the rite of admission, the scrutinies with exorcisms and the giving ('tradition') and the rendering of the creed and the Lord's Prayer.

First, the catechumens are presented and then in terms that remind one of the ordination service, they are invited to come forward and their sponsors are questioned about their fitness. In

---

[14] In different parts of the church and at different times various terms were used for catechumens: 'elect' was a Roman term; 'photismenoi', 'those to be enlightened' a Greek term.

their turn, the catechumens are asked about their intentions: do they wish to be initiated into the sacraments of Christ, baptism, confirmation and the eucharist? and they answer that they do. They are then formally elected: 'You are now chosen that you may be initiated into the sacred mysteries at the coming celebration of Easter.' There follow intercessions for them, concluded with a collect and the dismissal.

There are three scrutinies which are to take place on the Third, Fourth and Fifth Sundays of Lent after the homily. These are not 'examinations' nor are they enquiries into the moral fitness of the candidates. They are prayers for their spiritual strengthening and they take the place of the General Intercession of the Mass (154). After the prayers there is what is called an exorcism for which three collects are provided, each of which echoes the theme of the respective Sunday gospel, thus restoring the sense of these gospel passages for Lent.[15]

On appointed week-days during Lent there is the 'tradition' of the creed and the Lord's Prayer. The celebrant addresses the candidates, and leads them in the recitation of either the Apostles' Creed (which thus returns to our liturgy!) or, at choice, the Niceno-Constantinopolitan Creed which we use at Mass. There follow a prayer for the elect and a laying-on of hands with a prayer. The service of the 'tradition' of the Lord's prayer follows the same pattern and naturally includes the gospel passage (Matthew 6:9–13) in which the Lord taught it to his disciples.

At an appointed hour on Holy Saturday the elect are assembled, if possible, and then 'give back' the creed and the Lord's prayer. The rite of the *Ephpheta* (the opening of the ears and mouths of the candidates to hear and speak the word of God) may be performed as may the anointing with the oil of catechumens. The candidates are to be anointed on the breast and the hands and other parts of the body, if desired. Presumably there are parts of the world where these rites are still acceptable but they present considerable difficulties for modern western man. Local conferences of bishops may allow their omission and it is to be hoped that they will.

The Order gives the impression that these week-day rites are not so important as the others and there will be practical diffi-

---

[15] In the early Middle Ages they were in fact the 'scrutiny' gospels and when the catechumenate fell into disuse they were moved to certain week-days. They have now been restored to their original places.

culties in finding suitable times for them. *Ephpheta* and anointings apart, there is however a case for them. The Order, with sound psychological insight, sees the value of active participation here as elsewhere in the liturgy and the ritualisation of the giving back of the creed and the Lord's Prayer should help the candidates to feel more personally committed to what they are undertaking. Simple gestures involving personal choice should not be undervalued.

The Initiation: Baptism, Confirmation and the Holy Eucharist (208-34)

Since confirmation demands separate treatment and since there are few special features of the eucharist on this occasion, this section will deal principally with what is now in effect the rite of adult baptism.

Three aspects of the new liturgy of Christian Initiation stand out and deserve attention.

1. These sacraments are now normally to be celebrated within the Easter Vigil. This is not to be regarded as merely a good liturgical arrangement. It indicates that baptism, confirmation and the eucharist are all means by which the Christian participates in the paschal mystery, the passion, death and resurrection of Christ. This more than preaching or lectures will teach the Christian people that these sacraments are so related.[16]

2. The ancient relationship between baptism, confirmation and the eucharist is visibly restored. The candidates proceed from one sacrament to another in an ordered sequence for, even if a bishop is not present, they may be confirmed.[17] This will do more than anything to inculcate in the Christian people (including the clergy) that this is the right order of events and pastoral practice will, presumably, eventually be affected by it.

3. Adult baptism appears in its 'pure' state, totally different from the complex and obscure rite of the now-obsolete *Rituale Romanum*. The reason for this is that the old rite had telescoped the whole of the catechumenate into a series of prayers and gestures which in that context were meaningless.[18] Since the catechumenate has been

---

[16] For sound pastoral reasons this liturgy may be celebrated at Whitsuntide or on Sundays.

[17] *Ord. Confirm.* 7b.

[18] And even then managed to make no reference to confirmation and the eucharist!

restored and everything belonging to it has already been done, there is nothing left but to baptise the candidate. This means that it is a very simple rite, simpler now than that of infant baptism which has retained certain features of the catechumenate, and its description can be brief.

The Liturgy of Adult Baptism

The service of baptism begins after the homily of the Mass. Either before or during the singing of the Litany of Saints, the candidates are gathered in the baptistery. Before the Litany begins the celebrant addresses them: 'Let us beseech our God and Father for these his servants who ask for baptism. He has called them and led them to this moment to give them light and strength so that courageously they may adhere to Christ and profess the faith of the church. May he renew them through the Holy Spirit whom in a few moments we are going to call down on this water.'

Although this is not a fixed text (213) it is very important. It is at baptism that the Christian commits himself to Christ and undertakes to profess the faith and is regenerated by water and the Holy Spirit. This text has, as we shall see, interesting implications for confirmation.

The Litany, during which there is a special petition for the catechumens, is sung and is immediately followed by the Blessing of the Font. The three prayers to be found in the Order of Infant Baptism may be used at choice, the first being a shortened and unfortunately emasculated version of that in the old Roman Missal.

The renunciation of evil and the profession of faith follow.[19]

It may be thought that since the catechumen during the time of preparation has renounced evil, has been exorcised and professed the faith in one way or another, a repetition here is superfluous. The Order takes up this point explicitly (211). The renunciation of evil and the profession of faith, it says, here have their full force: 'Since baptism is a sacrament of faith by which catechumens adhere to God and at the same time are re-born, these acts by which they now renounce sin and Satan fittingly precede the act of baptism itself. By these acts, which were pre-figured in the covenant with the patriarchs of the Old Testament,[20] the candidates

---

[19] If the pre-baptismal anointing has taken place earlier on Holy Saturday morning, it will of course be omitted here.

[20] Entry into the covenant involved the repudiation of idolatry, with all its attendant immorality, and adherence to God. It was the constant cry of the prophets.

adhere for ever to the promise of the Saviour and the mystery of the Trinity. By their profession, which they make before the celebrant and in presence of the community, they signify their will, matured in the time of the catechumenate, to enter into the new covenant with Christ. In this faith, handed on to them by the church, a faith they have already embraced, they are (now) baptised.' It is to be seen then as a summing up and declaration in the presence of the community, of all they have already undertaken. The text invites commentary, which however would take us too far. It may be said *en passant* that the covenant-language, thus brought back into currency in an official document, throws light on the whole of Christian living. We are a covenanted people, enjoying, if we will, the benefits of God's fidelity to his promises but we in turn are required to be faithful to God who has shown us his mercy in Christ. We note too that the existing faith of the candidates is an active element in their baptism and we recall the 'form' of baptism in the Apostolic Tradition of Hippolytus.[21] The minister asked if the candidate believed and it was the candidate who professed the faith, upon which and without further ado he was plunged into the water. It is difficult to think of a more striking example of active participation than this and it is a pity that the church has not restored this mode of baptism at least for adults.[22]

After this, there remains only the act of baptism, which may be by immersion (which is put first in the text) or by affusion. In the first case the celebrant immerses either the head or the whole body under the water; in the second he pours the water on the head in the way with which we are familiar. Acclamations or other chants to accompany the acts of baptism are recommended.

The post-baptismal rites remain, the clothing in the white robe and the lighting of a candle (done by the sponsor from the paschal candle). There is also the question of the post-baptismal anointing about which we say a word below. There is a minor difficulty about the white robe. What sort should it be? Presumably the modern sort of alb, shaped and held together with a linen girdle, would be suitable to both men and women but some experimentation is needed. Sponsors could perhaps provide it and it could be worn

---

[21] XXI (ed. Dix, 1937, p. 33).
[22] It would not necessarily involve baptism by immersion.

throughout the following Mass. The formula for the handing of the candle to the newly-baptised is eloquent:

'You have been made light in Christ.
Ever walk as children of light.
So persevering in faith,
May you meet Christ when he comes again
with all the saints in the court of heaven.'

The omission of the post-baptismal anointing if, as will usually be the case, confirmation immediately follows, is puzzling. The introduction offers no commentary and yet if the chrismation is to take place it is grouped with the '*ritus explanativi*' (white garment and candle) which surely means rites that unfold the meaning of baptism. The text of the prayer accompanying the chrismation teaches that the neophyte is 'joined' to the people of God and made a member of Christ who is priest, prophet and king. Neither the rite of baptism nor that of confirmation has this teaching elsewhere and the implication seems to be that all that is conveyed by chrismation is conveyed by confirmation. Could the alternative also be true, as it was assumed to be true in pre-Carolingian Gaul when presbyters chrismated and this was regarded as confirmation? It would seem more probable that chrismation is regarded as an expendable extra (in spite of Hippolytus who has both chrismation and confirmation) especially as, according to the Order of Infant Baptism (24, (4)), if the number of candidates is very great, it may be omitted. The conclusion must be that in spite of the long (western) tradition, chrismation is not to be regarded as important.

Of confirmation itself all we need say at this point is that it is to be regarded as normal, almost *de rigueur*. It is only '*peculiari de causa*' (and one wonders what *that* could be) that it is to be omitted (244).

There are few special features of the Mass. The creed is naturally omitted; the neophytes are to take their part in the General Intercession; there are special inserts into the eucharist prayers, not merely for I but also for II, III and IV; communion, it is recommended, should be given in both kinds to the neophytes, their sponsors, relations and any concerned in their instruction. Before the *Ecce, Agnus Dei* the celebrant may speak briefly of the greatness of the eucharistic mystery which is the culmination of initiation and the centre of the Christian life (234).

The Conclusion or Mystagogy[23]

A word must be said about this phase with its ill-sounding name, 'mystagogy'. It is well known that in the classical period of the catechumenate there was a final stage in Easter week when the neophytes were initiated into an understanding of the mysteries of baptism and the eucharist which they had received at the Vigil. The catechetical instructions of a Cyril of Jerusalem and an Ambrose of Milan, to mention no others, remain to show what was done at this time. The candidates met daily in church and the bishop led them into a deeper understanding of what they had done and received. During this week they wore the white garments with which they had been clothed after baptism. The Order has kept the general sense of this phase but has not thought good to ritualise it.

Its purpose is to deepen the neophytes' understanding and appreciation of the paschal mystery and to help them to harmonise their daily living with it (37). This is to be achieved by hearing the word of God, by a particularly frequent celebration of the sacraments[24] and by an ever closer association with the Christian community (38, 39). The Order urges that the neophytes should be particularly careful to gather with their friends for the celebration of the Sunday Masses of Eastertide of which the readings of Year A are especially appropriate to their condition (39, 40).

What it all comes to is that the newly-baptised should, with their sponsors, friends and the local community, celebrate the Sunday eucharist at this time with a special joy and appreciation.

Simpler and Abbreviated Forms of Initiation

The first (240–77) is intended for 'extraordinary circumstances' when the candidate cannot undertake all the stages of the catechumenate or when the Ordinary is satisfied with his sincerity and maturity (240). Three things are assumed: a) sufficient knowledge of the faith; b) the assistance of a sponsor; c) familiarity with the local Christian community. The last two emphasise, as the Order does throughout, the need for the support of the community in the person of the sponsor and the presence of the community into which the candidate is to be incorporated. The rite itself is

---

[23] 'Mystagogy' simply means 'an introduction to the mysteries'.
[24] 'Sacramentorum' is the word used but since the eucharist can be the only one in view, it must be that the word is used in the sense of 'mysteries', the 'sacred mysteries' of the new Order of the Mass.

again intended to emphasise that conversion and incorporation into the church are public acts, manifesting the assent of the candidate, his desire for initiation and the acceptance of him by the local community (241-4).

The rite, which is to be celebrated at Mass, may be done as one action and consists of the questions (to both candidate and sponsor), a collect and the ceremony of introduction to the community. The ministry of the word follows with intercessions, exorcism and the first anointing. The act of baptism follows with confirmation and holy communion and their attendant rites as in the longer form.

However, directives are given (274-7) for the incorporation of certain rites from the longer form and for their distribution over an appointed period of time. Unless circumstances (envisaged by the Order (274)), make it necessary to abbreviate the whole rite, this will surely be the better way. Further, if the intentions of the church are not to be frustrated in this matter, this catechumenate is a quasi-necessity. In fact, this shorter form, properly used, will be the one that is most practical in the circumstances of the large urban parish.

The Abbreviated Order (278-94) is intended for those in danger of death whether a catechumen or not. In the latter case, he must give certain signs that he wishes to turn to Christ and that he is willing to take up the full catechumenate on recovery. The rite is simple and impressive. There are the questions ('This is eternal life; that we may know the true God and Jesus Christ whom he sent. This is the faith of Christians. Do you know this? I do'), there is the support of a sponsor or witness who promise to help him; there are intercessions, renunciation of evil and profession of faith, the baptism, confirmation and the administering of holy communion.

On Those Baptised in Infancy but not Instructed (295-305)
If the elaborate catechumenate seems impracticable, it cannot be said that the revisers lack pastoral sense. They have provided for almost every pastoral situation that is likely to be met with in normal parish work and in this section (Chapter IV) they give certain 'pastoral persuasions' as to how to deal with those who were baptised Catholics in infancy and have never been confirmed or received holy communion. Their remarks are deliberately called 'persuasions' (*suasiones*) and might be translated as 'suggestions'. What they come to is an adapted catechumenate, though the Order insists that such

people are in an entirely different situation from that of catechumens (295). Sponsors and the local community are again in the picture and the text suggests that incorporation into the Christian community through liturgical rites such as those of the 'giving' of the creed, the Lord's Prayer and the gospels, is the method by which they should be initiated into the sacraments they have not yet received. No Order, however, is given and the pastoral clergy are thus left with wide possibilities of adaptation. It is however insisted that these people should be adequately prepared by instruction and attendance at liturgical services.

The injunction (296), however, that the instruction should be protracted may or may not be practicable. Sometimes it is true that people approach the church and it is only after many conversations that it is revealed that they were baptised Catholics in infancy. The more usual case is of those who wish to get married and then there is little enough time to initiate them into the faith and prepare them for confession, communion and confirmation (which last will not be possible unless they can approach a bishop).[25] However, even in these cases the general outlook of the Order should be regarded as helpful. The 'giving' of the creed, the Lord's Prayer and the gospels suggest where the emphasis should lie in whatever instruction can be given and if these 'traditions' are done as simple rites in church, the instructions are more likely to be effective. In addition, preparation for the sacraments through the use of the liturgical texts will make the whole process concrete and meaningful to them.

The Initiation of Unbaptised Children

A quite common situation in parish life is the need to receive into the church children who were not baptised in infancy. Their parents may wish to become Catholics or have already done so, or the parents, though Catholics, were for one reason or another unable to have their children baptised when they were born. There is also the phenomenon of families who through pastoral effort have been 'reclaimed' for the church. Whatever the situation, the question of initiating such children has posed certain problems. Often enough, for want of documents, they have been baptised conditionally in a miserable little ceremony, that made little or no impact. This Order

---

[25] In view of the now very extensive permission to priests to confirm, there is a case for the further extension of this faculty both for this category and the one that follows.

caters for this situation and offers a most attractive way of initiating such children.

The Order is based on the lines of the classical catechumenate, set out above, but there is an important observation on the need for a very considerable adaptation (312). The local bishops' conferences are to see to this adaptation not merely of the rites but, and this is of immense importance, of the *language* of the texts: 'When this Order is turned into vernacular languages, care must be taken to accommodate the addresses, the intercessions and the prayers to the capacity of the children.' For this work the bishops will obviously have to invoke the aid of skilled catechists and it is clear that this process of adaptation could lead to a harmonisation of the instruction given in the classroom and the liturgy performed in the church. It is also clear that at least one or two versions will have to be made to adapt the Order to different age-ranges. What is suitable to a child of eleven will not be suitable to a child of seven.[26]

Quite properly the Order sees the initiation of such children against the background of the family, who have a decisive part to play, and in the context of what it calls 'the catechetical community' of which the child is a member. These two groups are the immediate community in the presence of which all the acts of initiation are to be performed though the larger, parish, community is also to play its part at certain moments of the initiation.

The Order begins with a rite of entry consisting of a few simple questions (eg 'Why do you wish to be a Christian?'), and a dialogue between the celebrant and the parents and/or sponsors during which the children go to their parents and ask their consent to be made Christians, a consent which the parents are required to give *viva voce* to the celebrant. He then signs the children with the cross, enrolling them among the members of the church, and invites their parents to do likewise. The children are then led into the church where a simple Bible Service is celebrated[27] during which a copy of the gospels may be handed to the child. The service ends with intercessions and a collect. After this, the children, now called catechumens, are dismissed. It is taken for granted that if the

---

[26] It is difficult to discern from the Order what age the compilers had in mind. They speak of 'several years' in one place (307). For young children this is far too long. Experience shows that it is a matter of months rather than years and even months seem an eternity to an eight-year-old. We may suppose that this question of age is one that the bishops should consider.

[27] Scripture passages are suggested (326), some of which do not seem very appropriate.

eucharist is to be celebrated they will not be present for it.

In the event of this catechumenate being prolonged some of the rites of the adult catechumenate may be used, scrutinies, exorcisms and the pre-baptismal anointing. All are to be adapted to the situation.

The last stage is the sacramental initiation, baptism, confirmation and the celebration of the eucharist. It does not appear from the Order (349) that the prayer of blessing of the baptismal water may be adapted and no doubt it is supposed that one or other of the alternative blessings in the Order of Baptism, which are rather simpler, will be used. However, just as in the case of eucharistic prayers there is need for texts written for young children, so is there here. The best people to *initiate* the composition of such prayers would be the bishops' conferences themselves.

The Admission of the Validly Baptised into Full Communion

This Order, tucked away in an Appendix at the end of the book, has an importance much greater than the simple little rite it encloses would seem to indicate. The thirteen articles of its introduction set out a whole ecumenical theology on the admission of members of other churches to full communion with the Roman Catholic Church. The desire not to give offence whether by language or practice is very evident. Such converts are to be sharply distinguished from catechumens (5), no abjuration of heresy is required and the rite is drawn up so that the candidate may enter into the unity and (full) communion of the church (1). For this reason nothing other than what is necessary is to be imposed (*ibid.*, with a reference to Acts 15:28).

The rite of reception, which normally is to take place within the Mass, again strikes the same ecumenical note. It is an action that should be seen as a celebration of the church which finds its culmination in communion in the eucharist (3, a). Thus are brought together communion with the church in the sense of membership and communion in the sacrament which is both creative of union and its chief expression. But the Mass is to be celebrated simply and without any suggestion of 'triumphalism' (*magnificentiae*) and the Order enjoins that two factors shall decide the style of celebration: ecumenical propriety (*boni*) and the bond with the parish community. According to the Order, then, most often a Mass with a small community will be best though the circumstances of each case are to be taken into account (3, b).

The preparation, which includes instruction of the candidate, is apparently to be private, ie without any liturgical acts. He is to have a full knowledge of the faith but his spiritual formation is also to be attended to. He is to see that his adherence to the church is the fulfilment of all he has received in baptism (5).[28]

The conditions for reception no longer include, as we have seen, the abjuration of heresy and the Order repeats the instructions to be found in the Ecumenical Directory (14, 15) on the subject of conditional baptism which is *never* to be given as a matter of course but only after the necessary investigation if there is any reason to doubt the validity or existence of the first baptism (7). In any case, it is to be given privately. The local Ordinary is to decide exactly what is to be done (*ibid.*). Confession of sin is to be made beforehand to a confessor who is to be warned that the candidate is to be admitted into full communion with the church (10).

The rite is very simple. It takes place after the homily in which the celebrant gives thanks for the event, points out that baptism, which the candidate originally received, is the foundation and ultimate justification of what is happening. He continues with references to the sacraments of confirmation and communion which the candidate is to receive. The celebrant then invites him to make his act of faith either in the terms of the Apostles' Creed or of the Niceno-Constantinopolitan Creed. At the end and at the prompting of the celebrant the candidate then says: 'I believe and profess all that the holy Catholic Church believes, teaches and proclaims as revealed by God.' The celebrant then pronounces the formula of admission ('You have full communion with us in the faith which you have professed') and confirms the candidate. He with his sponsor(s), friends and others will go to holy communion and all may receive it in both kinds (11).

Finally, it remains for local conferences of bishops to adapt the rite according to circumstances, if they think fit, and to add to or subtract from it (12). It is difficult to suppose that anyone will want to abbreviate it.

After the liturgically jejune rite of former times with its heavy

---

[28] We also read that during the time of preparation he may communicate in certain sacred acts and a reference is given to the Directory of Ecumenism, 19, 20. These will include blessings, 'sacramentals' and presumably attendance, though obviously not communion, at the eucharist. He is *not* a catechumen so may attend 'the sacred mysteries'. Here again however circumstances will alter cases and it will often be necessary to initiate a candidate gradually into a kind of worship with which he may be quite unfamiliar.

legalistic flavour this new rite must be welcomed on every ground.

Pastoral Reflections

No great powers of discernment are required to predict that when this Order is translated and presented to the clergy, it will be rejected as both unnecessary and impracticable. Unnecessary, because most of the people we receive into the church are already baptised and because all this ritualisation of what is fundamentally a very simple act is unacceptable to modern people. Impracticable, because it would involve a vast amount of work on the part of an already overburdened clergy.

As to the first, we have already suggested that the situation is already changing and may be changing more rapidly than most of us realise. It may be doubted too whether the rites would be unacceptable to modern people. Many priests have for some long time felt that something more than mere 'instruction' was required and some at least have done what they could to temper the wind of doctrine by giving the instruction a more practical turn, by taking their candidates round the church and explaining what goes on in it and why certain objects are there. Others have felt that their candidates had certain psychological needs, that they wanted to see the instruction incarnated in certain actions. It has been clear that the candidate goes through certain stages quite rapidly and soon has but one desire and that is to be a participant in the life of the church. Candidates are often ready for reception long before they are able, say, to go to confession and yet all the sacramental acts are heaped up at the end. The general pattern of the catechumenate provides precisely the ritual-symbolic supports that the candidate needs and, as we have already said, gradually initiate him into the Christian life.

On the assumption, then, that the catechumenate is at least becoming necessary and is a suitable way to initiate people into the church, we have to ask whether it is practically possible.

The Order assumes two things: community and a sufficient number of intelligent and active Christians from whom can be drawn the sponsors who are going to accompany the candidates throughout the time of initiation. Community, it is widely agreed, is what is lacking in the urban parish and if the catechumenate is to be operated, a considerable change will have to take place. Indications of such a change are already apparent where parishes have made some attempt at decentralisation through the establishment of house groups which may or may not be representative of a sector within the parish. If they are not, then the principle will have to be carried further, the area of a parish will have to be examined and, wherever possible, sectors will have to be formed in which there will be certain lay-people with a responsibility for their sector. From among the parish clergy individuals will have a special care for these areas. This is not just a matter of organisation. It is necessary if 'sympathisers', seekers, are to make contact with a community at a human level. It is here that they will be able to enter into dialogue, examine their own assumptions about life and see if they can commit themselves to the Christian community, the church.

There will be the further task of forming lay-Christians both intellectually and spiritually so that they can become leaders of their communities and it is from such people that the sponsors required by the Order will be recruited. The Order evidently envisages that the laity are going to take a considerable part in the formation of future Christians and this is the natural order of things. Children are formed as Christians within the community of the family and normally adults in most areas of human living are supported by a community. There are exceptions and vast numbers of people have become Christians without the help or support of the local Christian community. If there are those who want it that way, there is no good reason to disturb them though it should be at least pointed out that being a Christian means being a member of a community in which the relationship between the members is visibly expressed and symbolised by liturgical acts.

Given this situation, there is no reason why some of the ritual actions of the catechumenate should not be performed in these communities. They may not require the intervention of the priest since the Order frequently speaks of catechists presiding at such gatherings. Only the greater actions of the catechumenate need then be done in church, eg the scrutinies at the Lenten Masses. The sacramental initiation will of course be celebrated with as full a gathering of the community as possible which will support and endorse all that has gone before. Circumstances alter cases, however, and other ways of dealing with the matter remain open.

The Order is strongly in favour of the last part of the catechumenate (The Time of Purification and Enlightenment) taking place in Lent and the liturgy of the catechumenate and that of the eucharist have been harmonised with this end in view. Such an arrangement is clearly appropriate; the catechumenate will be *seen* to reach its climax in the celebration of the paschal mystery at Easter. But there are difficulties and the Order is aware of them. Other arrangements are feasible but the final initiation must always take place at the Sunday eucharist with the maximum presence of the local community. In the circumstances of the 'ordinary' parish what seems necessary is that a system be set up and made public. On the assumption that normally the catechumenate will take months rather than years, the parish could be informed that the first acts of the catechumenate are to take place in the autumn. Candidates with their friends will be assembled wherever is judged suitable and the rite of enrolment and entry will be performed. According to the needs of the situation the whole or parts of the catechumenate can be gone through in the subsequent months. The final part would take place in Lent and the whole process of initiation would culminate in the celebration of the sacraments of initiation at the Easter Vigil.

It will be evident, however, that all the foregoing is a matter of supposition. The notion of a catechumenate and the principles it assumes will have to be accepted before there is any likelihood of its being organised. A considerable task of education lies before us before this can be achieved.

On reflection, one feels that two things need immediate attention. The first is an adaptation of these new rites of Christian Initiation to those baptised in infancy and never brought up as Christians. While they are to be distinguished from what may be called the theological catechumens, practically they are in the same situation. Their *psychological* needs are the same and mere 'instruction' cannot be regarded as satisfactory or sufficient. They have to become *conscious* believers and appropriate, make their own, the faith they received in baptism. They need to be taught not only the importance of worship but how to worship and this cannot be done just by giving them instructions. Even for these people, then, it would seem that elements of the catechumenate should form part of their approach to full church practice. Secondly, the whole question of the incidence of adult baptism even now should be statistically examined and some prognosis for the near future established. It may be that in this particular case we have time to plan and in view of the change the institution of catechumenate will make to pastoral attitudes and habits, the sooner this planning is done the better.

CHAPTER FIVE

Infant Baptism

THIS IS not the place to go into the vexed question of infant baptism. Even the recent bibliography on the subject is enormous, for theologians of almost every denomination have been discussing it very vigorously for some years. The Catholic Church (Roman and Orthodox) has accepted the practice from a very early age (though the New Testament evidence is indecisive) and still accepts it. It will be as well, however, to spell out what the church means by it. As the whole of the new Order of Baptism makes clear, it means *the baptism of the infants of believing and practising parents* (even if the question of belief is sometimes a matter of discussion) *who intend to bring up their children in the faith of Christ.* This is fundamental to an understanding of the new Order and it is regrettable that while the rite has proved to be very acceptable to both clergy and people, its implications and the plain teaching of the introduction have not been so welcome. If that teaching is not accepted, it is very difficult, if not impossible, to find any justification for infant baptism. In recent years the church has reiterated again and again that we are saved by faith and the sacraments of faith. Both are necessary and yet there seems to be an ineradicable tendency in certain quarters to act as if the former were unnecessary. The indiscriminate baptism of infants (because otherwise they cannot be saved?) leads only the multiplication of nominal Christians who have no real attachment to the church and yet who are held by certain juridical requirements of the church.[1] If the new rite of infant baptism is approved of, it is equally important that its implications should be accepted and put into practice. Anything less is sheer ritualism.

---

[1] In marriage, for instance. A Roman Catholic baptised in infancy and with no knowledge of the church cannot contract a valid marriage outside the church, unless, improbably, he or she is granted a dispensation from the 'form'.

Faith

The first of these implications is in fact faith and since, in the view of the Order, faith on the part of the parents is an indispensable necessity for the admission of a child to baptism, it is necessary to say something further about it here. It is to be noted that throughout the introduction and the rite, it is the faith of the *parents* that is in question and, to anticipate for a moment, it would be quite intolerable to use this service unless the parents can give evidence of a credible faith. It would be to perpetuate precisely that insincerity and inauthenticity with which our liturgy has been afflicted for so long. It is not surprising, then, that no less than seven times during the service, the faith of the parents is called into play or mentioned (39, 44 (45), 47, 56, 58, 60, 64). Particularly important are the following: the parents undertaking to bring their child up in the faith (39), the scripture readings and homily (44, 45) whose purpose is to evoke and renew their faith, the address before the profession of faith when they are reminded that it is by faith they are led to undertake the Christian upbringing of their children (56), the profession of faith itself (58) and perhaps most important of all, the assent they make just before the act of baptism (60): 'Do you wish your child to receive baptism in the faith of the church which we have just professed together?' This faith has been made sufficiently explicit and indeed inclusive in the ancient formula of profession which, with slight alteration, goes back to the time of Hippolytus in the early third century.

This teaching, which has always been implicit in the rite of infant baptism and explicit in the documents of the church, is further unfolded in the introduction. Since infants have not a personal faith (*fidem propriam*) they are baptised in the faith of the church (*in fide ipsius Ecclesiae*, a phrase found at least as early as St Augustine) and 'church' here is not left as an abstraction. It is represented by the parents, godparents and members of the local community who during the course of baptism profess it (BP 1, 2). It is obvious that the parents too must have a 'personal faith' and the profession in the rite is not to be regarded as a mere form of words that may be uttered without conviction.

Nor of course does the Order leave the matter there. Both before and after the celebration there is something to be done. Beforehand the parents are to be prepared and if necessary instructed in the faith (5 (1), 8) and afterwards means are to be found to help parents to fulfil the obligations they have undertaken (BP 7 (1)). But the over-riding importance of faith both for the parents and the child is underlined. The Order uses a remarkable phrase to introduce the subject: 'To fulfil the true meaning of the sacrament'[2] the children are later to be formed in the faith in which they have been baptised. As the Latin has it, '*Ad veritatem sacramenti complendam*' which might be translated 'to achieve the authenticity of the sign' (which of course is the sacrament), as if to suggest that without this subsequent formation the sign is not authentic.[3] Baptism is one of the sacraments which, in the ancient phrase,[4] *significando causant* and in the case of baptism if the subsequent formation is not given the significance of the sacrament is prevented from having its full effect. Furthermore, the introduction goes on to state that baptism is the basis of Christian education in the course of which the child will gradually be led to understand God's plan of salvation effected in Christ so that ultimately he will affirm and ratify the faith in which he has been baptised.

Infant baptism is theologically not without its difficulties. As is clear from the general teaching of the New Testament, normally faith comes before sacrament. But against the background as given in the new Order it is justifiable. An analogy may help to show this. The child lives in its mother's womb for nine months and is totally dependent on her for life and nourishment. After birth it remains dependent on her and on the family group, a dependence that becomes increasingly important as it grows. It is from the family it receives the stimuli to discern the outline of its world, to speak and to become conscious of belonging to a community. Psychologically, the child lives in the womb of the family until about the age of twelve and only then begins to become independent, a person. What is true in the natural order is largely true in the supernatural order. During childhood parents have the responsibility (now made very clear in the Order) of seeing that the child does grow in faith and, if all is well, he does so grow, making ever more explicit and personal assents to the faith given in baptism. During this time Christ will become a person to him. In short, the parents and the family group communicate the faith to the child or perhaps actualise the faith given as a potentiality in baptism. In any case, baptism is to lead on to confirmation and the eucharist (in that order), as the introduction

---

[2] Thus far ICEL translation.
[3] Though of course valid!
[4] Cf *ST* III, Q LXII, i, ad 1. St Thomas's phrase is '*efficiunt quod figurant*'.

(BP 5 (5)) and the final address of the rite make clear (BP 68).

In all this teaching there is clearly a whole programme of Christian education suggested and the pre-supposition is that it is the parents who will do it though with the assistance of bishops, clergy and (unspecified) lay-people (BP 7 (1)). There is much to be done on this field and, as we suggest elsewhere, one of the most fruitful developments in the contemporary church would be the training of lay-catechists among whom it is to be wished that large numbers of parents would be included. Not only are there great numbers of children who cannot get to Catholic schools but it is a fact of experience that schools in this all-important matter of Christian education are well-nigh powerless to bring up children as Christians without the active cooperation of their parents.

Community

In infant baptism the community has a role of peculiar importance. As we have observed, by baptism people are incorporated into Christ and made living members of his body the church. As the Constitution on the Liturgy (41, 42) and the new Order of the Mass (GI 7) have it, the local community, normally the parish, is in its liturgical celebrations the sign or 'sacrament' of the whole church throughout the world and although it is into the one, holy, Catholic and apostolic church that we are admitted by baptism, it is through the local church that this is achieved. Further, it is in the faith of the church that children are baptised and therefore, says the Order of Infant Baptism, the local community should be represented when the sacrament is celebrated. 'The people of God, represented by the local church', it says, 'have a large part to play in the baptism of both adults and children' (BP 4) and as far as the children are concerned, 'they have a right to the love of the community both before and after baptism'. This love will be shown by their presence, by the prayers in which they join for the child and the family and above all by giving their assent of faith with the celebrant after the parents have made their profession of it (ibid.). Parents, community and celebrant all join in making the profession of a faith that is common to all, and thus is made very concrete the saying that the child is baptised 'in the faith of the church'.

This of course represents a change of emphasis in the practice of baptism that has been typical in recent centuries. It was for the most part a *private* celebration, and there are those who would still have it so. But just as the full significance of the eucharist cannot be seen unless it is a community celebration, so with baptism. Psychologically the family group will feel strengthened in its faith by the presence of the community and where weaker parents are concerned, they will be encouraged by the presence of a believing community ready to support them in their undertakings.

Celebration

There is little to add to what we have said about this matter in connection with adult baptism. Here the presence of the community will make it possible, however improbable it may seem at the present time, that 'sung baptisms' will become the custom. The Order lays down (BP 9) that baptisms are to be celebrated on Sundays (and only once a day) or at the Easter Vigil and that they take place within the Sunday eucharist, though this should not be done too frequently. Experience however is showing that, in modern pastoral conditions, celebration within the Sunday eucharist is the only way in which the community dimension and a note of joy can be obtained. Since there are in most churches several Masses on a Sunday any one of these can be chosen and thus it would not be more or less the same people who every time witness the baptism. On the assumption that some form of afternoon or evening service can be maintained (and it is more and more difficult to do so) baptism should be celebrated then.

Pastoral Preparation

The introduction to the Order of Infant Baptism is a strongly pastoral document showing an awareness of the importance of the matter and also of the difficulties encountered in its practice. It can no longer be said, if it ever could, that the church takes infant baptism as a matter of routine. As we have seen, baptism requires a follow-up, the further Christian education of the child. But it also requires preparation which conditions the time when baptism is to take place.

When should baptism be celebrated?

To the question when should a child be baptised, canon law said as soon as possible after birth. The new Order of Baptism has a quite elaborate answer which is based on the great principles that run throughout it: namely, faith, the role of the parents, community and celebration. All these factors are to be taken into account in fixing the time when a child should be baptised and the conclusion must be that baptisms may be less frequent than they used to be but that more children will be baptised on a single occasion. But here again, it will be *local* conditions that dictate the best course of action. In a very populous parish, there may already be many baptisms every Sunday and to group them, say, once a month would impose a burden on both parents and priests. What is desired is that baptism shall be a celebration and not just an administrative act.

In detail, then, the Order says that the following factors should be taken into account in arranging the baptism of a child. (i) The health of the child: if there is any danger then baptism must be given as soon as possible; (ii) the health of the mother, that is, it will be necessary to wait until she has got up or returned from hospital, for the Order is emphatic that the parents of the child should be present (BP 4 (2)); (iii) sufficient time to make the necessary preparation of the parents and (iv) to organise the celebration, not merely in church, one would say, but also in the home. Relatives, friends and others will want to come and time should be given to invite them. These indeed are envisaged as taking some part, if necessary, in the preparation of the parents before baptism (BP 5 (1)). This is but another illustration of the importance of community in the whole celebration of the sacrament.

The Preparation of the Parents

Normally, then, the child is to be baptised in the first weeks after birth (BP 8 (3)) but the parents are asked to let the parish clergy know, either before birth or immediately after it, that they wish their child to be baptised. Granted this and the circumstances being normal, the parish priest or one of his assistants will visit the family and give them such instruction as may be necessary. No doubt this will not be necessary for every child of the same family nor need the instruction be lengthy or heavy-handed. The text of the rite is the best basis for such instruction for it expresses in concrete form the content of the introduction and at the same time covers matters of ceremonial which concern the parents. It is not possible to celebrate this rite without some preparation and where parents of weak faith are concerned, it would be intolerable that they should be required to undertake serious obligations both on their own behalf and on that of the child without being given time to reflect on them.

Even if a house-visit should prove impossible (and in the circumstances of the large urban parish this may well be so), an interview

with one or both of the parents before baptism is indispensable.
There are several matters (eg the insertion of the child's name(s)
in the litany) that need discussion before the baptism and make
contact with the parents necessary if the rite is to be celebrated with
conviction and in the spirit the church now demands. As far as
the minister of the sacrament is concerned, this is a matter of obligation but one which he cannot carry out properly without the collaboration of the parents: 'Every celebration of baptism should be
done with dignity and accommodated so far as may be necessary to
the conditions and desires of the family' (BP 6 (2)).

The Question of Delay

If all were for the best in the best possible of worlds, the above
arrangements would provide no difficulty. But we know this is not so
and the Order envisages the situation where parents have insufficient
faith to make the promises or have shown by past experience that
they do not in fact bring up their children as Christians (BP 25).
Here the Order sees that some delay is necessary and requires local
conferences of bishops to lay down guide-lines for their clergy in
the matter. They, in the light of such instructions, are to make a
judgment *when* a child of such parents be baptised (BP 8 (4)). The
Order does not in fact contemplate the possibility of *refusal*. Such
refusal may well come from the parents when they have been confronted with their obligations. But, as everyone knows, the whole
situation is a very delicate one, calling for considerable tact and
prudence. On the one hand, it is intolerable that a sacrament of
faith should be administered without faith and that its normal
effects should be frustrated by a lack of Christian education and, on
the other, it is extremely hard even to *seem* to refuse a sacrament which normally is necessary for salvation. Rigid rules however in one direction or another are not likely to solve the problem,
which is an essentially human one and therefore untidy.

First, then, since the Order does not speak of refusal it would
be a mistake, perhaps because one has *a priori* notions about the
problem of those who have been baptised though lapsed, to indulge
in talk about refusing baptism. The Order speaks of *delay* and even
a suggestion of this may cause trouble.[5] If a parish has been able
to establish the custom that baptisms are only administered after

---

[5] There are those who like to insist on their 'rights' and who never perform
their duties.

interview (and this seems to be the situation in most places), it is highly likely that the difficulties of a case can be solved, one way or the other, at this point. It is the priest's duty to help the parents to understand what they are undertaking and if at this point they feel they cannot undertake their obligations, it is they who will withdraw perhaps for further reflection. On the other hand, it is not for the priest to be too demanding. Some may have difficulties about this or that point of Christian teaching. This does not mean they have no faith[6] or even an insufficient faith. This, we have indicated above, is to be thought of as a global faith which can be expressed in the terms of the creed professed in baptism. Again, an insistence on regular Sunday worship or even 'Easter duties' as a condition of the admission of the child to baptism would be too rigid a rule. If, however, parents of a weak or wavering faith (and there seem to be quite a number of the latter nowadays) make the first approach, this should be regarded as a positive sign that they have some desire to do what the church wants them to do. They may of course have all sorts of folk-lore notions in their heads (and it may be as well to discover what part the grandmother is playing behind the scenes) but their very approach offers something on which to build. Once baptism and the other sacraments are seen as something more than pieces of isolated ritual, their celebration is seen to offer pastoral opportunities. Finally, there will always be a greater or smaller residue of cases where it will be impossible to admit a child to baptism at once but the Order does not see this as the end of the affair. It is but a beginning of a new pastoral effort which will seek to bring back the parents to a true faith when they will be able to have their children baptised. If this new Order of Infant baptism suggests a whole programme of Christian education it also suggests a whole programme of pastoral care to which a good deal of thought needs to be given.

In the event of one parent not being able to make the profession of faith, the Order shows a wide comprehension and a great respect for the human conscience. This will often be the case where there is a mixed marriage. In interview one finds often enough that though the non-Catholic partner is not a practising Christian he or she is able and willing to make the profession of faith with the Catholic. Where this is so, they should be invited to do so and to take as full

---

[6] Whatever may be the truth of the old tag 'if you doubt in one matter of faith, you doubt the lot', it is of no use in pastoral work and any insistence on it can only do harm.

a part in the rite as possible. Where however one or other of them cannot do this but is willing to allow the child to be brought up a Christian, he (or she) may remain silent (5 (4)).

Godparents

The most significant change in the new Order is that the parents occupy the central place in its celebration. They ask publicly for the baptism of their child, they sign him on the forehead at the rite of admission, they renounce evil and profess the faith, the mother holds the child at the font, the father holds the lighted candle and at the end there is a blessing for each of them (BP 5 (3)). They are active participants in bringing their child to the new birth by water and the Holy Spirit. Nevertheless they can and should be supported by godparents who represent both the extended family, which can be of such support to parents and children in a world that is increasingly impersonal, and the Christian community which should be the first to show their care for them. The primary role of the godparents is to assist the parents to fulfil their obligations and they seem to have no direct relationship with the child. This is what they undertake to do in the rite (BP 40). In practice of course the two go together. The minimum requirements for godparents are that they should be 'sufficiently mature' (not children therefore), and must have been baptised, confirmed and have received holy communion. They must be Catholics. But it is possible to admit members of the Orthodox Church as godparents and members of other churches as witnesses to Christian baptism (C 10).[7]

The Ministers of Baptism

According to the Code of Canon Law (738 (1)) the ordinary minister of solemn baptism is a priest though the right to celebrate it is reserved to the parish priest or his assistants duly appointed.[8] The outlook of the Order (CI 11) is rather different. The ordinary

---

[7] In an earlier booklet *Companion to the New Order of Baptism* (1970), p. 16, basing myself on the text of the Order, I gave it as my opinion that Christians of other denominations, as well as the Orthodox, could be admitted as godparents. It seemed to be a modification of the instructions of the Ecumenical Directory (Eng. trans., 1967, no. 57, p. 23). Such an interpretation is however ruled out by a reply from the Secretariat for Christian Unity which states that the directive in BP is not to be regarded as an extension of the Directory. Cf *Notitiae*, 62, March, 1971, pp. 92-3. One can only comment that the Latin of the Order should have been more precise.

[8] By cn. 744 the bishop is urged to be the minister of adult baptism.

ministers of the sacrament are bishops, priests and deacons. The first are no longer to be thought of as 'extraordinary' ministers, intervening only on very important occasions, nor yet are the deacons. Nor is all this a matter of rights and duties. Bishops, says the Order, are the dispensers of the mysteries of God and presidents of the whole liturgical life of the diocese (12) and, in accordance with the principles of the Constitution on the Liturgy, their role has to be made visible. There would seem to be a strong case therefore for bishops to celebrate baptism when for instance they come for confirmation. If in addition certain children could be admitted to first communion on the same occasion, the bishop would visibly appear as the president of the whole process of Christian Initiation. The objection that this would mean a very long service can be answered by providing that there are only small numbers of children involved.[9] As for deacons, they are now able to administer baptism as a matter of course but in a large parish they will also usefully concelebrate the sacrament with the other clergy (BP 61). In this way the presbyteral community will match the community of the people.

The Place of Baptism

For centuries the place of baptism has been the parish church and many were the bitter battles fought over this issue in the Middle Ages. Battles apart, this is still the situation with the Order (BP 10, 11), though the bishop may permit other places if there is real need. Again, the reason for this is not just the protection of the rights of parish priests but that the parish church is the normal place of assembly for the Christian people and since they have a role of considerable importance to play in the celebration of the sacrament, it should be in the normal place of assembly. Modern conditions may however modify this and a *real* community may well be able to meet in some other place than the church. A link with the wider parish could be established by prayer at the eucharist both before and after the event for the candidates and their parents.

The Baptistery and the Font (CI 18–28)

The new Order of Baptism changes many things and makes

---

[9] This too of course raises the vexed question of the size of dioceses but does not the bishop's liturgical (and pastoral) role provide one criterion, and a fundamental one, for the division of dioceses?

almost superfluous some of its own injunctions. It says for instance that the water must be clean, a very difficult matter under the old regime where the water was changed only one or twice a year and was infused with holy oil into the bargain. With the strong recommendation (*optandum est*) that the water should be blessed every time (which implies that it must be fresh for every baptism), even in Paschaltide if it seems opportune, there is little danger that it will be anything but clean. In the light of the remarks of the Order itself (21) and of the structure of the service the recommendation could have been much stronger. It is in the prayer(s) of blessing that the symbolism of the water is expounded and much of its precise sacramental significance is made plain. It is an integral part of the rite and its omission would be regrettable.

As has already been provided for in many new churches, the water may be flowing and in this case it is the flowing water that is blessed and not a certain quantity of it. Finally, an echo of the *Didache*, it may, when necessary, be warmed—a humane provision in winter.

It was hardly to have been expected that baptism by immersion would be recommended but so it is (22) and both here and in the rite (60) it is put first, even if in the former place it would seem to be restricted to places where it is customary. Whether or not this is so (and the two ways are distinguished by the lightest Latin disjunctive, '*vel*'), it is hardly a live issue in most western countries as yet.[10] Mothers will be understandably reluctant to allow it though if the font looked more like a 'bath of regeneration' and was filled with warm water, some of their reluctance would no doubt disappear. It is the view of the introduction, at any rate, that immersion better expresses the meaning of baptism in which we die with Christ in the waters and rise from them with him to the new life of the resurrection.

The font should not only be kept clean (and not used as the repository for miscellaneous and forgotten objects) but is also to be beautiful, worthy of its purpose. Which is but another way of saying that just as the altar is a symbol of the eucharist, expressing something of its nature, so the font and the baptistery should express by their form something of the meaning of baptism. However, it is not just a question of having a beautiful font and baptistery. Both are the focus of a community action and their arrangement is

---

[10] It is course the normal way of baptism in the Orthodox Church.

conditioned by that fact. The thinking of the Order marks a considerable break with more recent tradition. The baptistery has too often been an obscure and undistinguished part of the church which gave the impression that infant baptism was a private action in which the smallest number of people possible would be involved. The first principle then that now comes into play is that baptism, like the eucharist, is an action of the Christian community and the baptistery must be such that the people can gather there and take part in the celebration of the sacrament. Even the pattern of the rite is to be taken into account: it requires a ministry of the word and that too must be provided for. Given current conditions, then, it is not surprising that a considerable freedom is left to the local clergy in arranging the place of baptism. Where the baptistery is small and possibly dark, cut off from the body of the church, a font may be set up wherever it is found most convenient and that means a place where a community celebration can take place. As in all the recent liturgical reform, the role of the people is paramount. Generally speaking, where it is not possible to devise a large compartment of the church for baptism, a place with seats and big enough to hold twenty, thirty or even more people, it would seem best not to have a fixed font at all. A large bowl of silver or copper will meet the requirement of the Order that the font should be beautiful.[11]

In fact, four places can be envisaged for the celebration of the sacrament: (1) somewhere near the main entrance where the minister will welcome the baptismal party and ask the first questions; (2) a place for the ministry of the word during which the people will no doubt like to sit down; (3) the place for 'the celebration of the sacrament' which could be the conventional baptistery or some other place in the church, eg near the sanctuary; (4) before the sanctuary for the conclusion of the rite.

The Liturgy of Infant Baptism
This already lengthy account of baptism is significant of the

---

[11] In some modern churches the font is placed on the sanctuary balancing, as it is said, the lectern. Perhaps too formal an arrangement and there is the danger that having cleared our sanctuaries of a lot of unnecessary furniture we are now replacing with 'liturgical' objects which lead to a new kind of clutter. However a baptistery that is off-sanctuary but at the sanctuary end has much to be said for it. It would also be the most convenient place for the Paschal Candle, even in paschaltide. The transporting of the Candle from one place to another is far from convenient.

great change in the church's thinking on the subject. Compared with the baptism of infants, that for adults is quite simple if only because the issues are so much clearer. Since however we are in a situation that is still new and indeed since for the first time in the history of the church we have a rite for infants that is truly adapted to their condition, some examination of the rite is necessary.

A Summary of the Rite

i) The reception of the baptismal party whom the minister welcomes. The first questions establishing that the parents undertake to bring up their children in the Catholic faith. The signing of the child by the minister, parents and godparents.

ii) The celebration of God's word. One or two scripture readings, the homily, the intercessions.

iii) The prayer of exorcism (two texts provided) and the anointing with the oil of catechumens.

iv) The celebration of the sacrament: the blessing of the water, the parents' renunciation of evil and profession of faith, the baptism, the anointing with chrism, the clothing with the white garment, the giving of the candle (the Ephphata, if retained).

v) The conclusion: the procession to the sanctuary, the final address with the Lord's prayer and the blessings.

Commentary

It may be said at once that though the rite is new, it discreetly incorporates (and adapts) much that was to be found in the old liturgy of initiation. The first questions include the old 'naming' rite (which has persisted through the centuries in almost every baptismal rite) and the signing with the cross represents the former rite of the enrolment of catechumens. The ministry of the word corresponds to the former and lengthy instruction given during the catechumenate and the intercessions and brief litany take the place of the great prayer sung by the assembled community while the baptisms were taking place. The exorcism and the anointing with the oil of catechumens were also part of the catechumenate and the renunciation of evil was associated with the latter. The profession of faith has its parallel in the candidates' profession of faith both before and during the act of baptism. The post-baptismal chrismation is at least as old as Hippolytus (died c. 235) and the clothing with the white robe is of equally ancient date. The giving of the candle is a medieval rite and appears for the first

time in the eleventh century.[12] The conclusion of the rite is new.
The first thing to be said about this liturgy is that it is so much
more than a piece of ritual. It is addressed to people, it constantly
engages their attention and requires their very active collaboration.
The celebrant too is required to act in a human and welcoming
fashion (BP 36, 41) and throughout the rite he delivers various
(brief) addresses to them to arouse their faith and to lead them to a
fuller understanding of the paschal mystery of which baptism is a
celebration. At the same time, the rite leads them into the praise
of God whom, through chants and hymns, they thank for the
continuing work of salvation made present by the celebration of
the sacrament. In short, it is an act of worship and not merely an
'administration'. All this is expressed in detail and in various ways
throughout the rite.

Thus the *first questions* emphasise the importance of the parent's
faith and inculcate the commitment they are required to make on
behalf of their child.

The signing with the cross is to be regarded (BP 41) as the sign
that the child is admitted to the Christian community.

The celebration of God's word, which is the newest feature of
the rite, has a peculiar importance. It is a practical application of the
axiom which underlies the whole of the revised liturgy: no sacramental celebration without a proclamation of the word. In infant
baptism it is intended to renew and deepen the faith of the parents
and god-parents and of all who are assembled for the celebration and
it is the function of the homily in particular to draw out the meaning
of whatever readings are chosen and to lead the people onto an
understanding of the baptismal mystery. It is not desirable that
the homily should be lengthy but it should aim at achieving at
least this. In the event of infants being over-vocal the Order recommends that they should be taken to another place, though this
should be done by someone other than the parents or godparents
to whom in a special way the word is proclaimed (BP 43).

As for the readings, the Lectionary offers a rich anthology which
it would be difficult to improve on. The following, all from the
New Testament, carry a fundamental message: Romans 6:35 (we
die with Christ in baptism and by him are raised to a new life);
1 Corinthians 12:12, 13 (we are all baptised in one spirit and form
one body); Ephesians 4:1–4 (one Lord, one faith, one baptism); 1

---

[12] For the foregoing see A. G. Martimont, *L'Eglise en Prière,* 1961, pp. 517–36.

Peter 2:4-5, 9-10 (a royal priesthood); Matthew 22:35-40 (the
law of love); Matthew 28:18-20 (go and make disciples of all
nations); Mark 1:9-11 (the baptism of Jesus); Mark 10:13-16
(let the little children come to me, a text used in the Sarum Manual
and retained by the Book of Common Prayer); John 3:1-6 (unless
a man is born again ...). This is but a selection and leaves out the
Old Testament readings provided, since they offer special difficulties and will be used only for groups whose knowledge of the
Bible is rather deeper than is usual. The celebrant is left a wide
choice though it would seem that he should use at least one gospel
passage; the Baptism of Jesus provides most valuable material for
the homily. It should be noted too that between the readings,
psalms or hymns may be sung and though the latter are very scarce,
this will be the right place to introduce some singing.[13]

The *intercessions* speak for themselves but it should be noted
that in the short litany the patron(s) and other saints may be
invoked.

The sense of the exorcism is not, as in the former rite, that
devils should be cast out of the candidate but that when we are
born and whether we like it or not we enter upon the struggle
between good and evil which is part of the human condition and
which will go on to the end of time. The prayer is for the protection of the child in that struggle. The second (alternative) makes
this clearer than the first: May these children who are going to
experience the wickedness of the world and the power of Satan be
protected by the power and grace of the passion and resurrection
of Christ. Incidentally, the first of these prayers is the only text in
the whole rite that mentions original sin.

With the exorcism is combined *the anointing with the oil of
catechumens* which in the earlier rites of baptism was called the
oil of exorcism. Its sense is the same as that of the prayer. This
is one of the rites that local conferences of bishops may, 'for grave
reasons' allow to be omitted, and the reason is pretty obvious.
If everything else in the rite is perspicuous in meaning this is not,
and for an explanation of it one has to go back to a much earlier
age of the church's history. This rite seems to derive from the
anointing that took place just before the baptism.[14] The candidate

---

[13] See *Praise the Lord* (ed. 1972) nos. 1-5 (and cf also certain Easter hymns).

[14] I say 'seems' because there were exorcisms and anointings during the catechumenate, but in the Order this anointing is put in the traditional place immediately before the blessing of the water.

was stripped, anointed all over with oil and invited to renounce Satan and all his works. Even if one could find a suitable opportunity to give this explanation, it is hardly likely to seem relevant to the modern parent. A prayer for the protection of the child against evil is comprehensible and welcome but a dab of oil on the breast seems to mean precisely nothing, especially since, as we have observed above, the use of oil is one of the most opaque symbols for modern people of industrial society. By the decision of the bishops it has to be retained in England and no doubt some other places. It would have been better to leave its use to the discretion of the parish clergy. However, for them there seems to be an escape route in CI 35 which says that in preparing and celebrating the rite the minister of the sacrament is to take account of 'the desires of the faithful'.

The first element of the celebration of the sacrament is *the blessing* of the water for which three prayers (to be used at choice) are provided. The first of these includes all the great types of baptism of the Old Testament (the creation of water, the rescuing of Noah and his family from the destruction of the flood, the passage of the Red Sea 'a figure of the baptised') and much of the doctrine of the New (the baptism of Christ, the piercing of his side on the cross and right at the end, the Pauline teaching on burial and resurrection in Christ). Perhaps too much is packed in here though something can be done to interpret the text by using as readings Romans 6 and the incident of Christ's baptism. The prayer is based on the ancient text found in the Gelasian Sacramentary and, as we have observed above, it is a pity that in the revision the vivid symbolism speaking of the font as the womb of life fecundated by the Holy Spirit has been eliminated. The two other prayers given are much simpler and will often if not usually be more appropriate. The first of these has, in its first part, the literary form of Jewish prayer of blessing *(berakah)* 'Blessed be God, the only Son, Jesus Christ. From your side flowed blood and water that by your death and resurrection your church might be born' and the people's acclamation may be in similarly Jewish form: 'Blessed be God.' The second half of the prayer consists of petitions responded to by the people asking for the blessing of the water. Among other things, these two texts suggest interesting possibilities for new eucharistic prayers.

The renunciation of evil and *the profession of faith* come *after* the prayer of blessing and this is a little odd. The renunciation was traditionally associated with exorcism. The candidate was anointed with the oil of exorcism, turned to the North (the supposed abode of evil spirits) and then turned to profess his faith in baptism. In this rite a much more appropriate place for the renunciation would be before the prayer of exorcism. Presumably the revisers had before their minds the ancient pattern where the renunciation was immediately followed by baptism.

There are two formulas for renunciation, the second of which may in many circumstances be more appropriate: it begins with a general renunciation of evil and Satan appears lower down the list. It is foolish not to recognise that some people, while they are fully conscious that there is much evil in our world, have difficulties about Satan and a baptismal service does not seem to be the occasion to rub their noses in a difficult doctrine. In any case, local conferences of bishops may vary these formulas (BP 24 (3)) and the criterion will be the different levels of culture and knowledge of the Christian message. There is however a good case for making them more concrete and to specify what people are being required to renounce. No doubt there is no need to go as far as mentioning pornography though the fourth century Christians knew that when they rejected the devil's *pompa*, they were rejecting the sadistic-sexual excitements of the arena.[15] This was not a vague expression.

Of the profession of faith there is little need to say more than a word. It is the old Roman baptismal creed almost exactly in the form of Hippolytus's *Apostolic Tradition* used in the act of baptism itself. To the profession of faith are attached two formulas which are worth noting. The first (BP 59) said by the celebrant and community together runs: 'This is our faith, this is the faith of the church which we are proud to profess in Christ Jesus our Lord'; and the second (60) is this: 'Do you wish N to receive baptism in the faith of the church which together we have all professed?' Thus written into the rite is the doctrine that has been laid out in the introduction.

The chrismation, one of the oldest baptismal rites of the western church, has always signified the incorporation of the baptised into the church which is the body of Christ who is priest, prophet and king. This is now spelt out clear in the text of the prayer that precedes the anointing. The best commentary on it is 1 Peter

---

[15] See for example St Augustine, *Confess.*, L.6, 13, the incident of Alypius at the games drunk '*cruenta voluptate*'.

2:2–10. The Christian people by baptism are made priests who through Christ can offer 'spiritual sacrifices' to the Father. They are 'prophets' sharing in the church's mission to bear witness to Christ in the world and they are 'kings' in that they collaborate with him in making the world a better place until it reaches that fulfilment appointed by God and can be offered by Christ to his Father (1 Corinthians 15:25–8). All this, and it is important to note that it includes mission and witness, is effected by baptism and the Christian does not have to wait for confirmation to be 'sent'.

In view of the former undesirable practice of putting a square of linen on the head of the child, it is necessary to emphasise that the *white robe* is meant to be a real garment, in fact the traditional christening robe which for long enough it has been the custom to clothe the child with before baptism. It is the desire of the church that it should be put on after the chrismation (though immediately after the baptism would be the more logical and traditional place). Mothers need to be told of this and experience shows that when they understand the purpose and significance of the gesture they readily accept the new way of doing it. Unless local custom indicates otherwise, its colour must be white. This no doubt is for traditional reasons (in the early church the candidates were clothed in white) but, although the formula accompanying the gesture does not say so, it is as well to reflect that white is the messianic colour in both the Old and the New Testaments.[16] As the formula does say, the candidates by baptism have been clothed in Christ and the colour of the robe indicates that they share in the 'lordship' of the Messiah who will come at the end 'with great power and majesty' to 'gather his chosen ones from the four winds, from one end of heaven to the other' (Matthew 24:30, 31).

In practice, the church desires the family to give the robe and this is usually done, but there is a good case for the parish, or a society in the parish, to give it. If this were generally done, it would be possible to design a garment rather more convenient than the Victorian-style things with narrow sleeves which are so difficult to put on.

The father (or a godparent) is to light *the candle* from the Paschal Candle, the purpose of the rite being to indicate the connection between the celebration of baptism and the paschal mystery.

The conclusion of the whole service takes place before the altar.

---

[16] The texts are well known and too numerous to cite.

The parents are reminded that baptism leads to confirmation and holy communion and that the children, as are all Christians, are children of one common Father and to express their sonship all join in the recitation of the Lord's prayer. Then come the blessings, one for the mother, one for the father and one for the whole assembly. The first of these replaces the old Churching ceremony and is readily acceptable to the young mothers of today.[17]

Some Critical Observations

If the supreme test of a rite is that it 'works', then the new Order must be said to be good. Again and again parents have expressed their satisfaction, even their delight, with it and if it is celebrated in a relaxed and friendly fashion, it becomes the occasion of a real meeting with people. There are however one or two points that could be improved.

The formula which the celebrant addresses to the parents at the beginning asking if they are ready to bring up their children as Christians is complicated and unwieldy: 'You have come to ask that your children should be baptised. Are you aware of your duty to bring them up in the faith so that, as Christ taught, they may keep the commandments of God, that is love the Lord and their neighbour?' The ICEL translation does nothing to improve the Latin. At first, they had 'raising' children but evidently the English-speakers of Great Britain objected. We speak of 'raising' crops, not children. But ICEL then opted for 'training them in the practice of the faith'. Then they go on 'It will be your duty to bring them up to keep God's commandments as Christ taught us *by* loving God....' The awkwardness of the translation indicates the awkwardness of the Latin. It is merely an inexpert re-writing of the old formula. Is the 'faith' here spoken identical with keeping the commandments? In fact, the phrase is far too condensed. *Two* questions are needed: 1) are you willing to bring the children up in the (Christian) faith? 2) Are you willing to bring them up to *live* as Christians keeping God's commandments ...? It may be objected that this is to perpetuate the old notion that you can be brought up 'in the faith' and remain uncommitted to Christian living. There may be some truth in this but you can distinguish the two and parents ought not to have to do a vast amount of

---

[17] But this too needs explaining to them in the instruction given before the baptism.

ratiocination before making this answer.

As we have observed above, the anointing with the oil of cate-chumens provides difficulties to some parents and it is difficult to understand why it was retained.[18] The prayer of exorcism and the brief formula to be used *without* anointing sufficiently make the point of the whole rite.

As we have also indicated above, it would have been better to attach the renunciation of evil to this rite for whatever historical precedent the revisers had in mind (whether they deliberately con-flated the renunciation that occurred in the catechumenate with the profession of faith or were thinking of the renunciation that occurred almost immediately before the act of baptism), in this rite the position of the renunciation next to the prayer of exorcism would have been much more comprehensible to modern people. It is the *parents* who will have the primary task of shielding their children from evil.

A small practical improvement in the second and third prayers of the blessing of the water would make it easier to use them. The people do not readily respond 'Blessed be God' after each para-graph. They need a phrase to 'lead them in'.

In spite of the revision of the prayer, chrismation remains ambiguous. If the number of children to be baptised is exceptionally large it may be omitted (BP 61) though one has to suppose the Order has something like dozens of children in mind. And in the adult form when confirmation follows, it may be omitted altogether. This does not seem very satisfactory. Chrismation either has some meaning or it has not. If the latter, it should be omitted altogether. If the former, why omit it on any occasion? On the principle, written into the official documents themselves, which place this among the '*ritus explanativi*', its purpose is to unfold or explicitate certain aspects of baptism. The prayer now says explicitly that it signifies the candidates' incorporation into the people of God. It seems to be worth saying since this meaning is given nowhere else.

One notes that the new Order continues the old and undesirable custom of addressing the unconscious child in at least one place, ie for the giving of the white garment. It would have been better to devise another form of words addressed to the parents and the assembly.

---

[18] It has been said that it was retained because the Orthodox still have it and there was a desire to keep a link with their practice.

The *Ephpheta* rite has been retained for optional use and in England it is not normally to be used. If it is, it is to be explained. It once formed part of the last exorcism done shortly before the baptism and in imitation of what Christ did (Mark 7 : 32–5). It was itself regarded as an exorcism. The old gesture, involving the touching of the ears and nose of the candidate, was a deviation from the gospel incident it was supposed to repeat. This at least has now been put right and the formula interprets it as meaning that the ears are to hear the word of God and the mouth is to proclaim the faith. Understandable enough, but the rite is in a very curious place (it would have come better in connection with the ministry of the word) just before the blessings and it is difficult to understand why it was retained at all. It is no more than an archaeological remain.

The Problem of Infant Baptism

It is undeniable that the question of infant baptism is a matter of concern both for Catholics and those of the reformed tradition. The New Testament has been scrutinised anew to see whether the practice is justifiable or whether some firmer authority can be found for a practice that is very ancient. This is not the place nor is it within the writer's power to add anything to theological discussion. But one or two things may be said to help a pastoral orientation on the subject. First, the New Testament certainly makes it clear that *normally* people approach Christ by faith and then by the sacraments, even if in the New Testament there were one or two occasions (eg Acts 16 : 30–3[19]) when children may have been baptised. Secondly, neither the introduction to the Order of Baptism nor the service itself give any emphasis to Original Sin. What conclusions, if any, are to be drawn from this it is impossible to say but it is worth noting that, as we have shown above, the positive side of the sacrament receives very great emphasis. Again, the possibility of delaying infant baptism is written into the introduction with the obvious implication that some infants will not in fact be baptised. It is not for a document like this to say how such children may be saved but at the practical level it does mean that a whole new policy of pastoral practice in their regard needs to be worked out.

It can, I think, be said that this document represents a change of

---

[19] The gaoler 'and all those belonging to him' (*kai hoi autou apantes*) were baptised after his 'household' (*oikos*) had believed.

emphasis in the church's teaching and this reflects a change of mentality among the people too. Even good Christians no longer feel the urge to rush the child to the font at the earliest possible moment and some are seriously questioning the advisability of baptising infants at all. Since they are being brought up in a Christian community, first the family and then the parish, would it not be better to wait until they can give their assent to this all-important event in their lives with the enormous consequences that follow from it? If, on the other hand, infant baptism continues to be the custom, as seems most likely, what view does the church take of the baptised at a later age refusing to endorse what has been done in infancy on his behalf or being unable, through loss of faith, to ratify what has been done? Does the subject remain free to choose or not to choose? How is such a person to be regarded in his relationship to the official church? Is he an apostate or just 'lapsed'? Does he remain bound by the church's laws? These questions are already being asked and it is well enough known that a considerable number of young adults are rejecting (not merely slipping away from) the faith of their baptism.

If these questions were satisfactorily answered, we could continue the practice of infant baptism with greater tranquillity. It must be said too that the consequences of *not* baptising infants would be incalculable. Not only would the whole system of sacramental initiation (first communion and the rest) be over-turned but the very pattern of Christian education would be wrecked. Even more important, the child would not be living in Christ in the way it does from baptism onwards. The best way to meet this problem of infant baptism would seem to be to insist on its positive side, on what is *given*. This, regeneration, life in Christ and in the Trinity, may only be germinal and the seeds have to grow to become the full flower of the Christian life. But there is a *datum* and if we think there is not, we are in danger of thinking that God can only do what man permits.[20] It can be said, that if we take in the *whole* teaching of the new baptismal Order and *if it is put into practice*, infant baptism remains theologically credible and practically of the greatest importance. Perhaps we have got too individualistic and tend to forget the organic relationships that are the stuff of family, with the consequence that we do not see as clearly as we ought that it is perfectly natural that Christian parents should

---

[20] See L. Brockett, *The Theology of Baptism*, Cork, 1971, pp. 78-9.

want their children, who by blood belong to the Christian community of the family, to be incorporated into the greater family of the church by which they themselves live. After that, all will depend on the love, intelligence and skill of the family to bring up children as lovers of God.

This in turn suggests or reminds us of what the Order (BP 4, 5 (5)) has to say about the help to be given by the Christian community in the upbringing of children. For this a vast programme of adult Christian education, directed to parents as well as to others, should be initiated if we are to have the sort of Christians that the church so badly needs and that the sacrament of baptism envisages.

Since the promulgation of the Order of Infant baptism there has been a good deal of discussion in some places of the possibility of an enrolment service for those children whose parents are unable to undertake the obligations required by baptism. Such a practice would certainly mitigate the difficulties involved in the delay of baptism, would ensure that the children were registered and provide a tangible link between the family and the church. A service, perhaps adapted from the enrolment rite of the Order of the Christian Initiation of Adults (75–87) including some expression on the part of the parents to receive further instruction, would seem to be appropriate.

CHAPTER SIX

The Sacrament of Confirmation

THE RESTORATION of the liturgy of Christian Initiation has now firmly established that confirmation is part of that process and already the separate celebration of confirmation has a certain air of anomaly. Given current practice, the Order[1] had perforce to appear as a separate rite though there are signs that the practice of a thousand years is coming to an end. All the new documents on Christian Initiation constantly speak of baptism, confirmation and the eucharist as being the sacraments by which people are made Christians and assume that that is the order in which they are going to be received. Further, the permissions granted to non-episcopal ministers to confer the sacrament mean that quite normally confirmation can precede holy communion, whatever other problems, concerning for instance, the age for the reception of confirmation, such a practice may seem to raise. In all discussion on confirmation it would seem to be essential to keep the above perspective in mind. Those in favour of a later age for confirmation will have to come to terms with the theological implications of the ancient and traditional order of the sacraments of initiation and those who favour an early age, ie before communion, will have to produce convincing arguments for the 'sacramentalisation' of infants and young children.

Since almost all the problems concerning confirmation have come from its peculiar history, it is necessary to give some account, necessarily summary, of its practice through the ages. History may not be determinative of truth but in liturgical practice it plays a role of peculiar importance.

Confirmation does not appear as an identifiable rite until the beginning of the third century and whatever may be the meaning of Acts 8:15–17 and 19:5 foll., these texts seem to have played no

---

[1] Vatican Press, 1971.

part in establishing confirmation in the first three centuries. The first text in which confirmation (though not under that name) can be identified is the Apostolic Tradition of Hippolytus.[2] Before baptism the bishop blesses the 'Oil of Thanksgiving', the baptism and profession of faith follow and then a presbyter anoints the candidate with that same oil. After putting on his clothes, he goes to the bishop in church ('in the assembly') who lays his hand on him while saying a prayer. The bishop then pours out the 'Oil of Thanksgiving' on his hand and lays the latter on the head of the candidate saying 'I anoint thee with holy oil in God the Father Almighty, and Christ Jesus and the Holy Ghost'. After this, he 'seals' or signs the candidate on the forehead and gives him the kiss of peace. He then joins the assembly for the prayers after which the members of the assembly exchange with him the kiss of peace. The eucharist follows.

For so early a document this is an elaborate ritual and is carefully described by the writer. The second anointing by the bishop seems to be clearly identifiable as 'confirmation' though it receives no great emphasis. The prayer asks that the candidates may be filled with the Holy Spirit that they may serve God. There is no question of the candidate being committed to the church or sent on 'mission' and, what is more important, the action of the bishop is part of a continuing process that begins with the rites before baptism and ends with the eucharist. It was in fact a true concelebration of the local church, presided over by the bishop and performed by him, the presbyters and deacons with the participation of the assembly.

A similar picture is given by the well-known passage of Tertullian, of about the same date, quoted in the papal constitution placed at the beginning of the Order (p. 7). The flesh is washed, he wrote, that the soul may be cleansed; the flesh is anointed that the soul may be consecrated; the flesh is signed that the soul may be protected; the flesh is overshadowed by the laying-on of the hand that the soul may be enlightened by the spirit; the flesh is fed with the body and blood of Christ that the soul may be nourished by God.[3] Tertullian seems to be saying the same thing as Hippolytus though, writing, as was his habit, vividly and rhetorically, it is difficult to say. Was there a post-baptismal anointing, a signing of the head (*De Baptismo*) and a laying-on of the hand? Scholars are not

---

[2] About 215 AD, ed. G. Dix, XXI, 6, 19; XXII, 1–6.
[3] *De Resurrect. Mort.* VIII, 3.

certain of the *precise* meaning of the passage. The post-baptismal anointing is probably to be associated with baptism and not confirmation. The hand-laying was the traditional gesture for the giving of the Spirit. For Tertullian no doubt the whole effect was to be attributed to the four actions he details, including the holy eucharist.

This Roman and Western rite has been taken as the paradigm of the sacraments of initiation but in the face of history this can hardly be maintained. In the fourth century St Cyril of Jerusalem knows a post-baptismal anointing but only one. In the area of the Syrian church (*Didascalia*, Narsai, St John Chrysostom) there is no post-baptismal anointing of any kind and these writers show that they believed that initiation, including the giving of the Spirit, was achieved by baptism and the eucharist. A curious passage from the compiler of the Apostolic Constitutions (also most probably Syrian), who knew the Apostolic Tradition very well, is worth repeating. After giving a conventional description of the post-baptismal anointing he writes, 'But if there be neither oil nor chrism, *the water is sufficient for both the anointing and the seal*'.[4] The compiler certainly believed the Spirit was given but evidently he did not see either hand-laying or anointing as essential. For him, both 'anointing' and 'seal', which he regarded as important, did not need physical gestures for them to take place.

All this may be thought to be a 'primitive' theology and liturgy which would have to be 'developed', or merely the aberration of a local church, though the practice was widespread and lasted for some long time. In any case, it is very close to what we can discern in the New Testament on the subject of baptism. Again and again we find there that in baptism the Spirit is given in contexts where there is no mention of 'confirmation'. The *whole* effect of initiation was achieved by baptism and the eucharist.

In addition to all this, the Eastern Church took a different way from the Roman. To preserve the integrity and order of the sacraments of initiation the Eastern Church preferred to allow the presbyter to confirm candidates immediately after baptism and even in the case of infants to communicate them. This is still the custom and the link between the bishop and the celebration of the sacrament is maintained by the requirement that the chrism or *muron* must always be consecrated by the bishop.

---

[4] E. C. Whitaker, *Documents of the Baptismal Liturgy*, 2nd ed., London, 1970, p. xxxi.

To return to the West, the witness of St Ambrose is particularly important. He was in the Roman tradition but, as we know, he could be independent of it[5] and he witnessed to a post-baptismal anointing, the washing of the feet (in which consciously he differed from Rome), the clothing with the white garment and the signing of the forehead which was the gesture for the giving of the seal of the Spirit which he calls *signaculum spiritale*. After the font, he wrote, 'it remains for the "perfecting" to take place, when at the invocation of the priest (*sacerdos*=bishop) the Holy Spirit is bestowed, the spirit of wisdom and understanding, the spirit of counsel and strength, the spirit of knowledge of godliness, the spirit of holy fear, as it were the seven virtues of the Spirit'.[6] Whether this text from Isaiah 11 : 2 foll. was already part of a prayer of invocation or whether it suggested to the compilers of the Roman Sacramentaries the theme of a prayer, it was destined to have a long history before it. Coming as this rite does at the end of the elaborate rite of baptism, it witnesses to a quite developed notion of confirmation.

Rome, too, always remained faithful to its own tradition, even when adult baptism with its catechumenate had disappeared.[7] The pope presided at the Easter Vigil at the Lateran, a liturgy which included the sacraments of initiation and in the stational or regional churches of Rome the same liturgy took place, assistant bishops in Rome conferring confirmation.[8] In the Gelasian Sacramentary the prayer accompanying the bishop's hand-laying and consignation takes up the text of Isaiah mentioned by St Ambrose and is practically identical with the prayer now said towards the beginning of the confirmation rite when the bishop extends his hands over all the candidates. It is certainly an ancient prayer and may be older than the sacramentary itself.[9] Its sense is made clear not only by the content of the prayer but by the rubric which says that 'the

---

[5] *De Sacr.* III : 5.

[6] Text and trans. E. C. Whitaker, *Documents*, p. 130.

[7] The rites of the catechumenate remained, somewhat adapted, and were 'practised' on infants for centuries and provided the basis for the rite of baptism in the old *Rituale Romanum*.

[8] See J. D. C. Fisher, *Christian Initiation in the Medieval West*, pp. 22–3. The evidence is not perhaps completely cogent but given Rome's age-old insistence on the order of the sacraments of initiation and the right of the bishop to confirm, any other arrangement is hardly conceivable.

[9] See J. D. C. Fisher, *op. cit.*, p. 22. For the Latin text, see Gelasian Sacramentary, ed. Mohlberg, no. 451. For the text in English see Whitaker, *Documents*, p. 188.

sevenfold Spirit' is given to the candidates by the bishop.

However, in other parts of the West, confirmation by a bishop was by no means the invariable practice. In Rome and no doubt in big city centres like Milan it was possible to conform to the Hippolytan model but even in rural Italy (until Innocent I put a stop to it) and certainly in Gaul and Spain, presbyters were authorised by synods and bishops to confer confirmation. The reason was that by the fifth century, especially in the two latter countries, the structure of the church was beginning to change. As the church moved into the great rural areas of Europe (and we recall the continual journeyings of St Martin in Gaul before the end of the fourth century), it became increasingly difficult to maintain the pattern of the city church organisation with the clergy of various degrees gathered round the bishop. Priests, with perhaps the assistance of a deacon and a reader, were taking charge of groups of Christians, later called parishes, geographically distant from the episcopal see, and it became difficult if not impossible for parents to approach the bishop for the confirmation of their children. Yet Christians were so convinced that the integrity of the sacraments of initiation should be preserved that the Gallic and Spanish churches authorised priests to administer these sacraments. Infants were baptised, confirmed and communicated in one service, though the rite that did duty for confirmation was the *first* post-baptismal anointing, a fact which caused some confusion when later on the Roman system was introduced into the Carolingian church. But efforts were made at this time and throughout the ensuing centuries to secure that people should present their children to bishops for confirmation; and bishops and synods, mostly in vain it would seem, constantly enjoined on the faithful the duty of presenting their children either within a week of baptism or at the Easter celebration or during Easter week.

In this same region, about the middle of the fifth century, appeared a document that would have an extraordinary influence on the theology of confirmation, and a word must be said about it here. It was a sermon preached by Faustus, first a monk of Lérins then bishop of Riez. In it he tries to tackle the problem raised by the apparently growing custom of priestly confirmation and to answer the question: what does the bishop's hand-laying effect? In the course of his answer he says that it gives an *augmentum gratiae* and strengthens the Christian for the struggle of the Christian life. In one place he even uses the military metaphor though not quite in the sense that it has been used more recently. This teaching that was eventually condensed in the Scholastic *augmentum gratiae ad pugnam* had its extraordinary influence because it was incorporated into the False Decretals (which were concerned to exalt episcopal power) and from them passed into the *Decretum* of Gratian and finally into the Scholastics of the twelfth century whence St Thomas took it. On the way it acquired a bogus authority through its attribution to a non-existent pope (Melchiades—there was one called Miltiades). Medieval theologians were in no position to check the matter.

The text which, I think, is unique is so out of line with the western tradition of the time that one is prompted to ask if there were special reasons for its peculiar character. Faustus had been an earnest monk of Lérins, he was a zealous bishop, but he also moved in the semi-Pelagian circles of Southern Gaul. He was suspected and eventually accused of heresy in this respect.[10] Given this background, it is not surprising that he put what was regarded as undue emphasis on the role of the human will in salvation and the spiritual life. It was with this last that he was most concerned, he was thinking of the combat of the spiritual life and to do him justice his teaching went a good deal deeper than the soldier-of-Christ view that was later based on it. It cannot, I think, be regarded as an authentic addition to the theology of confirmation.

When in the ninth century the liturgy of the Roman books was being imposed by Charlemagne we note a further step in the disintegration of the pattern. Chrismation by the presbyter was regarded as the sign of the giving of the Spirit. What then was to be made of the episcopal hand-laying and anointing? Alcuin and later Rabanus Maurus introduced a new notion. For both of these writers the laying-on of the bishop's hand meant that the candidate receives the Spirit 'to preach to others'. A somewhat *ad hoc* interpretation it must be admitted because both Alcuin and Rabanus Maurus were convinced that the Spirit had already been given, though the latter made no difficulty about that. From a liturgical point of view, what is even more curious is that candidates were baptised, chrismated by the presbyter and communicated and only after that was confirmation given by the bishop, usually at a separate

---

[10] See J. Tixeront, *Histoire des Dogmes*, Paris, 4th ed., 1919, t. III, pp. 293 foll.

service, a favourite time being seven days after Easter.[11]

By the tenth century the ancient order of Christian Initiation had broken down. Baptism, which was given almost immediately after birth, was no longer celebrated within the Easter Vigil. If the bishop was not available, as was usually the case, confirmation was delayed indefinitely and the whole complex of notions and phobias that militated at this time against frequent communion militated also against the communication of infants at baptism. So you have three separate celebrations: baptism given within a day or two of birth, confirmation at some unpredictable moment and communion.

This separation of the sacraments of initiation received a certain, if unwitting, sanction when the Fourth Lateran Council (1215) decreed that those who had reached 'the age of discretion' must receive holy communion at least once a year. This suggested that communion now had to be received separately from baptism and, given the circumstances of the medieval church, it meant in practice that most would receive communion before confirmation. It is true that synods and individual bishops made strenuous efforts to see that children were confirmed even as early as the age of one and in synodal law at least the age was usually not more than seven. This witnesses to a realisation that confirmation should be both near in time to baptism and should come before communion, but the facts were against the legislation and that it had to be repeated again and again shows that it was not effective.[12]

By the end of the Middle Ages the age of confirmation seems to have risen to ten or twelve or even fourteen and it is this situation the Church of England seems to have inherited. The continental Reformers retained what is best described as a para-liturgy, a profession of faith and commitment to Christ, which was performed (of course by a non-episcopal minister) at about the age of fourteen.[13] Rome held to the tradition from which it has never wavered: confirmation must precede communion and it is worth noting that the 1595 edition of the *Pontificale Romanum* still envisages infants being presented for confirmation.[14] It may be remarked too that

---

[11] For all this see J. D. C. Fisher, *Christian Initiation: Baptism in the Medieval West*, London, 1965, pp. 59–65. It is interesting to note that Alcuin refers to holy communion given at the end of the (Gallican) rite as 'confirmation': 'he is confirmed with the Lord's body and blood', p. 61.

[12] See Fisher, *op. cit.*, pp. 120 foll.

[13] See J. D. C. Fisher, *Christian Initiation: The Reformation Period*, London, 1970, pp. 159 foll.

[14] Fisher, *Christian Initiation: Bapt. in Med. West*, p. 137.

Rome never endorsed the practices of the churches beyond the Alps.

The last stages of the history are familiar. As long as the age of First Communion remained at ten or twelve confirmation beforehand was a possibility and in certain countries, like Spain and South America, confirmation has always been given before communion. But when Pius X decreed that children of seven years or less could be admitted to communion that possibility became remote. Hence what seems to be the prevalent custom; communion at seven or so and confirmation at any age thereafter until about twelve. This system seems to make the worst of all possible worlds. It should be noted however that the current Canon Law (788) still speaks of 'seven years', a requirement that is modified by the new Order (11).[15]

It will have been seen that the factors making for the present position were almost wholly non-theological and confirmation after communion or even a late age for confirmation were not endorsed by the Roman tradition.[16]

In recent years there has been a vast debate about confirmation in its every aspect, all sorts of questions have been asked, some of which still lack a definitive answer. The tradition has been re-scrutinised and the history revealed. It is this untidy situation with which the revisers were faced when they came to re-write the confirmation rite and it is both practice and theology they have had to take into account.

As a preliminary to a further consideration of the Order, we may note the following:

1. It is a separate service though in the liturgy of Christian Initiation it appears as part of it.

2. There is an insistence on the *order* of the sacraments of initiation: 'The faithful who have been re-born in baptism are streng-

---

[15] The language of the canon is remarkable: in the Latin church confirmation may be 'conveniently deferred' until seven, which would seem to indicate the confirmation at baptism is not ruled out. Moreover, it may be conferred even earlier, not merely on danger of death but 'for just and grave reasons', the judgment to be made by the minister.

[16] A comparatively recent example of Roman thinking can be found in the reply of Leo XIII to the Bishop of Marseilles who sought guidance about the order of confirmation and communion. The pope replied that confirmation *after* communion was not in harmony either with the ancient and constant tradition of the church or with the good of the faithful (see A. Hamman, *Baptême et Confirmation*, Paris, 1969, p. 224).

thened by the sacrament of confirmation and finally fed by the bread of life in the eucharist, that by these sacraments of Christian Initiation they may receive more of the treasures of the divine life and be brought to perfect charity.'[17] The Introduction (1) sees confirmation as a stage through which baptised Christians must pass though here it does not mention the eucharist, as the Order of Baptism does (1) and of course the Order of Adult Initiation.[18] However, the point is made in another way: normally confirmation is to be conferred during the eucharist (13).

3. Although the Order refers to adult catechumens and children who have not been baptised in infancy as receiving baptism, confirmation and the eucharist at one service, it goes on to say that 'in the Latin Church confirmation is generally *delayed* until the age of seven'. This clearly echoes the Code of Canon Law and expresses the Roman tradition. Like the Code, it seems to leave the way open for infant confirmation.

4. Local conferences of bishops however may, for pastoral reasons, decide on a later age *(aetate maturiore)*.[19] These reasons are indicated: the purpose of the delay should be a) to form people in a more perfect obedience to Christ so that b) they may bear more effective witness to him. Dom Bernard Botte, however, who was a member of the original commission on confirmation points out that the papal constitution 'which engages the pope's doctrinal authority' has nothing to say about this and, as we have seen, affirms that it is the second stage of Christian Initiation. The matter of age was deliberately left to the local conferences of bishops, a decision that Dom Botte thinks wise, given the practical difficulties of the administration of the sacrament. While expressing his trust in the bishops' wisdom, he ends with a *mot* from an experienced bishop which Dom Botte begs the bishops to reflect on: 'You cannot build a sound pastoral action on bad theology.'[20] With which sentiment one cannot but agree. The above 'pastoral reasons' are an aspect of the theology adopted by the Order of which we will now give some account.

---

[17] *Constitutio Apostolica* of Paul VI, prefixed to the *Ordo Confirmationis* (1971), p. 8.
[18] See above.
[19] Hardly eight, nine or ten, one would think.
[20] See *Questions Liturgiques*, Mont-César, Louvain, no. 1, 1972, pp. 5–8.

The Theology of Confirmation

This is to be found in three places, the Apostolic Constitution that prefaces the Order, in the rite itself and, to a lesser extent, in the Introduction (1, 2).

The main feature of the teaching of the Constitution is the wide scriptural context in which it places the sacrament. Christ was baptised and the Spirit came upon him (Mark 1:10 and par.) and he began his mission under the impulse of the same spirit (Luke 4:17-21). He promised the Spirit to his apostles that they might bear witness to the faith before persecutors (Luke 12:12) and before he suffered he announced that they were to receive the Spirit of truth who would remain with them for ever (John 15:26, 14:16). Then at Pentecost they and Mary and the company of the disciples received the Spirit. The proclamation of the new messianic age followed and those who believed were baptised and received the gift of the Spirit (Acts 2:38).[21]

Christians, continues the text, are incorporated into Christ and conformed to him, made his living members, by baptism, confirmation and the eucharist. In baptism they receive the remission of sin, the adoption of sons and the 'character' by which they share in the priesthood of Christ.[22] In confirmation they receive the Holy Spirit himself 'by whom they are endowed with a special strength',[23] signed with the 'character', are bound more perfectly to the church and contract a stricter obligation to be witnesses to Christ and to propagate and defend the faith. Finally, confirmation is so bound to the eucharist that confirmed Christians are fully *(plene)* inserted into Christ by the eucharist.[24]

It is remarkable that in the above account no reference is made to the action of the Holy Spirit in baptism, though the baptismal texts always do so, as indeed does this Order (24, 25). The theology of the Constitution is in some ways more conventional than that of the Order. Secondly, though 1 Peter 2:5 and 9 is used to show that Christians receive a share in the priesthood of Christ at baptism no reference is made to the fact that the same text says that Christians have a vocation to proclaim the saving works of God (verse

---

[21] The text of the Constitution seems to take the giving of the Spirit in Acts 2:38 as something separate from the baptism.

[22] Reference is made to 1 Peter 2:5 and 9.

[23] Cf Const. on Church, 11.

[24] Throughout references are made to the Council documents. This Constitution reflects the theology of the Council.

9 precisely[25]). In fact, the exegesis of the scriptural texts is a great deal less simple than the Constitution indicates.[26]

There follows a treatment of the 'matter' and 'form' of the sacrament which recognises a pluralism of practice in the past but opts for chrismation as the 'matter'. The 'form', which has been changed, is (literally) 'Receive the seal of the gift of the Holy Spirit', a text borrowed from the East where it has been used since the fourth or fifth century. This, we are told,[27] is a decision that engages the pope's teaching authority and so is of great consequence. The extension of the hands over all the candidates together is not essential to the rite but is an integral part of it and retained as explicitating its meaning. The gesture, combined with its accompanying prayer, clearly expresses the giving of the fulness of the Spirit.

When we turn to the rite itself and, to some extent, to the introduction we find this doctrine expressed rather more subtly and there is other teaching that does not appear in the Constitution. The latter says that in confirmation the baptised receive the Spirit poured out on the Apostles at Pentecost and by this gift they are a) more perfectly conformed to Christ and are b) strengthened (here the medieval teaching appears) so that they may bear witness to Christ for the building up of the church in faith and love.[28]

The homily suggested for the use of the celebrant, while setting confirmation in the context of the Pentecost event, deepens the notion of both conformity and witness. The gift of the Spirit the baptised receive in confirmation is a spiritual seal (an expression used by St Ambrose)[28] which will conform them more perfectly to Christ and make them more perfectly members of his church.[29] Conformity to Christ as the effect of the post-baptismal anointing is much emphasised by Cyril of Jerusalem whom the homily seems to be following here. For him candidates are conformed to Christ (*summorphoi*) and by the symbolic act of anointing (*eikonikōs*)

---

[25] The translation in JB 'sing the praise of God' is not generally endorsed by the versions: eg RSV 'that you may declare the wonderful deeds' of God, which seems to us the more accurate translation.

[26] See below p. 105.

[27] B. Botte, *Questions Liturgiques*, I, 1972, p. 7.

[28] *De Sacr.*, III, 8; Whitaker, *Documents*, p. 131.

[29] The text does not say exactly 'more perfect members' though it may be thought that this is what it means, nor yet does it say that they are made 'fuller' members of the church. As we have seen, the Constitution says they are made 'fully' members of the church by the eucharist.

they are made images (*eikones*) of Christ.[30] But the context of Cyril and of the homily is first the baptism of Christ, when he received the Spirit, and secondly the beginning of his preaching (Luke 4:17–21). The Holy Spirit is operative on *both* occasions and the second is seen as the fulfilment or working out of the first. The candidates have a mission because they are conformed to Christ who was 'sent', who had a mission. How far Cyril thought of this as a separate 'effect' from those of baptism is very doubtful. For him the supreme model was the *baptism* of Christ in which he saw concentrated all that was unfolded in the liturgical rite. Conformity to Christ is mentioned again (24) and this, with the emphasis on incorporation and service of the mystical church, provides a theological basis for confirmation as understood by the Order. It must be admitted that it is very much more satisfactory than the teaching current since the thirteenth century and then later hardened and narrowed to a defence of the institution.

Conformity to Christ or imitation of Christ, always according to the homily, is to be found in two ways. The sign of the cross with chrism signifies the power of the Spirit enabling the candidates to bear witness by their lives to the passion and resurrection of Christ, that is to the paschal mystery and, it is hinted, the living out of the paschal mystery is the consequence of confirmation. This is a deeply traditional teaching though it must be confessed that in the earliest centuries it was associated with baptism and the eucharist. Secondly, Christ is the head of the body, the church of which Christians are living members and like him who came to serve and not to be served, the confirmed are to be the servants of all. But this service is raised above the level of mere moral exhortation. It is a service that springs from a *datum* which is nothing other than the *donum Spiritus Sancti*, the Spirit who gives himself and who at the same time gives to each, again according to the homily, the charismatic graces meant for the building-up of the Body in unity and love. Here too the teaching of Vatican II is discernible.[31] All receive the gifts for service inside and outside the church, revealing it as the Spirit-filled body of Christ. Given this teaching and the fact that confirmation is set in the context of the Pentecost event, we can see emerging in this rite a pneumatology which has long been wanting in the western church. For a very long time the church was

---

[30] *Cat Myst.*, III, i (ed. Piédagnel, p. 121).
[31] *Constitution on the Church*, 12.

seen as institution and even when new emphasis came to be made, as in the theology of the mystical body, the church was attached to Christology. It was the body of *Christ* and by the use of terms like 'the extension or prolongation of the incarnation' it was seen almost wholly in relation to the latter. As some eastern Catholics said even as late as Vatican II, western ecclesiology was wanting in emphasis on the Spirit in the church in general and in the liturgy in particular.

This teaching is carried forward and given, as I think, a different *nuance*, first in the rite of the laying-on of the hands and then in the new 'form'. In the invitatory to the prayer for the Holy Spirit the celebrant asks that the Spirit may come to 'confirm' the candidates (who have already been born by water and the Holy Spirit) with the abundance of his gifts and by the anointing to conform them to Christ. Perhaps the Greek Fathers would have put the matter a little differently though the use of 'confirm' here in conjunction with the giving of the gifts suggests the view held earlier in both East and West that the second giving of the Spirit was to *establish* his indwelling in the candidate (unless of course rejected by sin). As we shall see, the earlier notion in the West is that 'confirmation' has the sense of 'establishing' and completing what is done in baptism. The 'sealing' is a sort of guarantee that the Spirit will always be present. If this is so, then it is merely the echo of a text which though not about 'confirmation' understood in the modern sense is often in the background of patristic teaching.[32] 'But it is God who *establishes* us with you in Christ and has commissioned us; *he has put his seal upon us* and *given us his Spirit* in our hearts as a *guarantee*' (2 Corinthians 1:21, 22).

More significant still is the new 'form' which marks a conscious change from the past. But to be understood it needs to be put back in its context. St Ambrose, an assiduous student of the Greek writers of his time, speaks of the *signaculum spiritale* which takes place after baptism and, interpreting the gesture, he writes, 'After the font, it remains for the "perfecting" to take place'.[33] The word *'perfectio'* (and its cognate forms) corresponds to the Greek word *'teleiosis'*, so much used by the Greek Fathers, and it too means 'perfecting', 'accomplishing', 'achieving' something that has been begun. Confirmation is a perfecting or completing of the work of God begun in baptism. It is not primarily a perfecting or strength-

---

[32] Eg St Ambrose, text quoted above.
[33] See Whitaker, *Documents*, p. 131.

ening of the candidates in the moral or psychological order though, as in baptism and the eucharist, that is on the horizon. This, I believe, is the sense of the words 'Receive the seal of the gift of the Holy Spirit'. The anointing with chrism or *muron* seals, makes safe, establishes the candidate in the Spirit who gives himself to him and who, as the prayer for the Spirit over the candidates indicates, 'completes' the process of initiation in which the Spirit has been active from the first conception of faith until now.[34] As all the texts of the New Testament and of the liturgies show, we are regenerated 'by water and the Holy Spirit'. The Greek Fathers and St Ambrose, whose *signaculum spiritale* could be translated 'the seal of the Spirit', say that the gift of the Spirit is now 'sealed' by the post-baptismal rite whether it is the laying-on of the hand or anointing or both.

This too seems to have been the teaching in earlier times in the West. To leave Hippolytus aside for the moment, we find that the earliest form of the sacrament, as given in the Gelasian Sacramentary, is *'Signum Christi in vitam aeternam'* (the sign of Christ for eternal life). This is laconic enough and its interpretation must remain doubtful but it says nothing about being 'confirmed' (as the twelfth century form does), and it seems to hark back to the *signaculum spiritale* of St Ambrose. When in fifth-century Gaul the word *'confirmare'* began to come into use, it did not mean 'confirm' in the modern sense. An examination of the semantics of the word shows that it meant 'to establish', 'to complete' or 'to perfect'.[35] And this sealing, ratifying or completing referred directly not to the candidate but to the gift. In the same context it is also interesting to learn that the eucharist is spoken of occasionally as the *confirmatio* of the whole process of initiation. This witnesses to a profound insight into the nature of the eucharist in which the Spirit is present and gives himself so that the church may be built up ('it is the eucharist that makes the church') and become *koinonia*, com-

---

[34] Perhaps the failure to realise that the Spirit is active wherever there is faith and sacrament has created difficulties for an understanding of confirmation. The Spirit is active in the holy eucharist. Too frequently, popular catechesis has given the impression that at confirmation the Spirit is given 'for the first time'!

[35] J. D. C. Fisher, *Christian Initiation in Med. West*, Appendix I. He points out that in Ambrose *'confirmavit'* is related to *bebaiōn* of 2 Cor. 1:21-2 which Ambrose refers to: 'It is God who *establishes* us' (RSV). The same use is found in John Chrysostom, in the *Apostolic Constitutions*, III, 117, and VII, 22, 'where it is clear that the editor of the *Apostolic Constitutions* understood *bebaiōsis* to mean sealing, or ratifying or completing', pp. 142-3.

munion, indwelt by the Holy Spirit. What is begun in the first conception of faith and is carried forward by the catechumenate, baptism and confirmation reaches its climax, its *confirmatio* in the holy eucharist.

All this teaching should have important pastoral consequences. In this perspective, confirmation *after* first communion does not make much sense. Confirmation is related both to baptism which it completes or perfects and to holy communion in which the whole of Christian initiation reaches its achievement. One of the enormous disadvantages of the separation of these three sacraments is that the organic relationship between them is almost totally obscured. We may rightly try to distinguish 'moments' in the whole process of initiation when this or that effect is achieved but we are not going to make much sense of them if they occur in the wrong order. In this matter the paradigm case of Hippolytus still seems to have validity, especially if we understand his liturgy as *a continuing action* in which the effect or effects are to be attributed to the *whole* action, including the eucharist which immediately followed the liturgy of baptism and 'confirmation'.

Whether and how far this teaching can be harmonised with the missionary-witness theme, so strongly emphasised in the Order, is another matter.[36] It is worth noting that in the renewal of baptismal promises there is no reference to witness or mission and it cannot therefore be regarded as a commitment of the candidate to witness or mission.[37] An attentive study of the texts however shows that they do not directly relate the missionary element in the Pentecost event to the candidates. As we have seen above, the giving of the Spirit is directly related to the imitation of Christ in his passion and resurrection and to service. But since it is into the church, the body of Christ, that they are incorporated and since the church has from Christ the mission to preach the gospel to every creature, confirmation can be seen as the sacrament-sign of that mission. Further, if we can see the setting of confirmation in the context of the Pentecost event as evidence of a certain pneumatology, we can also see that confirmation represents a deepened relationship to the church as the Spirit-filled body of Christ in which the Christian lives and moves and has his being. It is through the

---

[36] It seems to me that there are *two* theologies in this rite which are only imperfectly harmonised, if at all.

[37] Though there is nothing to stop local conferences of bishops from inserting such a commitment (cf 17 (a)).

Christian that the Spirit, working through faith and the sacraments, and especially those of initiation, shows the church to be the 'pneumatic' body, a body permeated by him.

As for the act of confirmation proper, the controversy whether it is effected by the laying-on of the hand[38] or by anointing no longer seems to be an urgent one. The new Order sees the signing of the forehead with chrism *as* the imposition of the hand and commentators make it clear that the celebrant is no longer required to perform the awkward gesture of laying-on the hand (which in practice meant four fingers) and at the same time anointing the forehead with the thumb:[39] 'The sacrament of confirmation is conferred by the anointing with chrism on the forehead *which is done by the imposition of the hand* and the words ...'.[40] This really marks a return to early medieval custom, witnessed to by Innocent III, the second Council of Lyons and the Decree for the Armenians that was drawn up after the Council of Florence. The hand-laying rubric was absent from the revised Roman Pontifical of 1595 and was inserted into the rite as late as the time of Benedict XIV (died 1753). In practice it will mean that the gesture is much easier to make.[41] The laying-on of hands (no longer called 'the extension of the hands') at the beginning of the rite is regarded in its proper role as a liturgical gesture explicitating the meaning of chrismation.[42]

There remains the question of the translation of the formula. 'Receive the seal of the gift of the Holy Spirit', which is its literal translation, by its complete lack of emphasis and, as one may think, a failure to ask what it means, conveys almost nothing. The French have adopted the translation 'Receive the mark (seal?) of the Holy Spirit who is given to you'[43] which is very close to the version first suggested in the commission by Dom Bernard Botte,[44] *'Accipe signaculum Spiritus sancti qui tibi datur'*—and it is a pity it was not

---

[38] Always 'hand' in the early and even the later liturgical documents.

[39] B. Botte, *Questions Liturgiques*, I, 1972, pp. 3–4 who emphasises the importance of retaining the anointing since it is a gesture common to both the Eastern and the Western church. B. Kleinheyer, *LMD*, 110, 1972, pp. 68–70. Cf also the reply to this effect, *Notitiae*, 76 (Sept.-Oct. 1972), p. 281.

[40] *Constitution*, p. 14.

[41] It may be that the hand-laying plus chrismation was brought back because the theologians used Acts 8:15–17 and 19:5, 6, as 'proof-texts' for the existence of confirmation. As we shall see below these texts are not so straightforward as they might seem.

[42] Cf *Constitution*, p. 14.

[43] '... reçois la marque de l'Esprit-Saint qui t'est donné'.

[44] *Art. Cit.*, p. 5.

adopted. He insists that the central truth of the formula is that it is the Holy Spirit who is given and that it is this that must be emphasised in vernacular versions. With this we can agree though one asks: but what then is the force of 'seal'? The translators of the ICEL text have investigated the scriptural background of the text and point to 'seal' (cf Ephesians 1:13), 'gift' (Acts 2:38 'you shall receive the gift of the Holy Spirit') and 'Gift' in the sense of the Holy Spirit himself (cf Luke 24:29; Acts 1:4; John 14:26, etc) which must all be taken into account. Their version is 'Receive the seal of the Holy Spirit, the Gift of the Father' which seems to do justice to the scriptural contexts.[45] It makes clear 'the personal nature of the Gift', suggests its origin (the Father) and since the action of the Son is evident throughout the rite there was no need to attempt to bring in this element explicitly. This version has now been confirmed by the Roman Congregation for Worship.

Some Critical Observations

The theology of the Order offers a grand vision and is an infinite improvement on the etiolated theology so long associated with confirmation. But should all this richness be associated with it? Are not the effects of confirmation also those of baptism? According to the New Testament it is by baptism that we are made members of Christ (1 Corinthians 12:12, 13 etc), are conformed to Christ in his passion and resurrection (Romans 6:3, 4), and receive the Spirit, for we cannot be regenerated without the Spirit (Galatians 3:26, 27; 4:6, 7; cf Romans 8:14-16; Titus 3:5). By baptism too we are called to service (1 Corinthians 12:12 foll.) and receive a mission to proclaim the saving deeds of God (1 Peter 2:4-9). The Order seems to leave us with the dilemma: if these functions are given in baptism, what is confirmation for? And if it is said that it is *for* all these functions, what becomes of New Testament teaching?

My own view, for what it is worth, is that in the New Testament all the effects of baptism and confirmation were concentrated in the former sacrament and confirmation, as subsequent centuries have come to know it, is an unfolding of the content of baptism. This view would seem to be supported by the witness of the Syrian church

---

[45] They remark that the *Filioque* is not in question since we are here dealing with the external mission of the Holy Spirit and not the intra-trinitarian relationships.

whose theology may be said to be undeveloped but where we find the deep conviction that the Spirit is given in a rite which had no elements of confirmation. Such a view would also help towards an explanation of the situation in Europe where for centuries millions of Christians must have died without confirmation as we have come to know it. Confirmation by the presbyter with the *first* post-baptismal anointing is a solution that had something to be said for it. There is however another way of looking at the matter. It would appear that there is more than one theology of Christian initiation in the New Testament, the Pauline one which saw 'baptism' with the giving of the Spirit as complete in itself, and the Lucan one which saw the church as 'endowed with a special outpouring of the Spirit for the promulgation of the gospel'.[46] This is to be distinguished from the gift of the Spirit at baptism for regeneration and cannot be 'harmonised' with it in the context of the New Testament. It was the Jerusalem church, presided over by the apostles, which had so conspicuously received the gift of the Spirit. The consequence of this was the spread of the gospel. When we come to texts like Acts 8:14–17 and 19:5, 6 which have been used as 'proof-texts' of confirmation, they are to be seen as acts of the Jerusalem church to establish the unity of the church. For this purpose the emergent local churches like that of Samaria, Antioch and others must receive the Spirit both to show their unity with the mother-church and to guarantee that they would play their part in the spreading of the gospel. Since it was on the apostles that the Spirit had come at Pentecost, it was their function to communicate the Spirit to these churches. But the main point was to maintain the unity of the church. Perhaps we could add that in one sense it was an act of 'authority' but it is significant that authority meant the communication of the Spirit. The whole church had to become visibly the living, breathing, Spirit-filled body of Christ.

The two texts from Acts are cited in the papal constitution and the second (only) in the homily and it is a question whether in the former document they are to be seen rather as an argument *ex traditione* than as one *ex sacra scriptura*. Such is often the style of papal documents. It does however seem possible to discern the above Lucan theology in the homily where it is said that the Spirit

---

[46] For an excellent study of the various theologies of the Spirit in the New Testament see Austin P. Milner, *The Theology of Confirmation*, Cork, 1972, pp. 90–9.

is given for the building up of the church and for its unity in love.[47]

The Rite (20–32)

Like all the other sacramental actions of the reformed liturgy, confirmation is normally to be celebrated within the Mass after the ministry of the word. The bishop sits and the candidates are presented to him by the parish priest or others concerned in their instruction. If they are children, they are to be presented by their parents or sponsors. Unless they are very numerous they are to be called by name.

The homily follows in which the celebrant takes up the themes of the readings and uses them to lead the candidates to a deeper understanding of 'the mystery of confirmation'.

The homily ends with the invitation to renounce evil and profess the faith: 'Before you receive the Spirit, be mindful of the faith which you or your parents or godparents professed with the church.' The renunciation consists of but one sentence and the profession of faith makes special mention of the Holy Spirit: 'Do you believe in the Holy Spirit, Lord and giver of life, who today in a special way is given to you by the sacrament of confirmation as he was to the apostles on the day of Pentecost?'

After concluding the profession of faith the celebrant, standing, pronounces an invitatory, there is silence and then the prayer for the coming of the Spirit with the sevenfold gifts on the candidates.

For the chrismation either the candidates approach the celebrant or he them while the sponsor places his right hand on the shoulder of the candidate. The celebrant anoints the forehead with his thumb (nothing is said about his laying the hand on the top of the head) while he pronounces the formula. To this the candidate replies *Amen*.

The Order then says that the sign of peace is to be given. The General Intercession (replacing that of the Mass) follows. The formula is given as a model only but it is good and might well be used regularly. It prays for the candidates, for the parents and sponsors, for the whole church and for the world.

---

[47] A. Hamman in *Baptême et Confirmation*, p. 194, takes the same view as Milner though he deals with the matter much more summarily. Milner has made a contribution to the theology of confirmation of great importance. There does however remain the text of 1 Peter 2:4–9 which is presumably neither Pauline nor Lucan and attaches the preaching of the gospel to baptism and (probably) the eucharist. See Y. Congar, *Le Mystère du Temple*, Paris, 1958, pp. 208–15. All is not yet clear in this complicated matter.

The rest of the Mass follows (there is a special *Hanc igitur* for use in the Roman Canon) and candidates may receive communion in both kinds. The Mass concludes either with the solemn form of blessing or with the special 'prayer over the people' which incorporates the old phrase (originally an introit) 'Confirm, Lord, what you have effected in us ...'

Commentary

While the organisation of the presentation of the candidates may present some practical difficulties, it is evidently intended to express the desire of the parents to have their children confirmed or, in the case of adults, to express the intention of the local community to do likewise. It is a significant gesture and should be kept wherever possible. It is another reason for keeping the number of candidates small.

At first sight, there is an anomaly in asking the candidates to renew their baptismal promises. In the new baptismal Order children do not make any and the situation is only saved by the clause 'which you or your parents .... have professed'. We may suppose that there was some compromise at this point. The revisers did not want to give way to the pressure of certain powerful groups to turn confirmation into a 'sacrament of Catholic Action' or of commitment.[48] Confirmation is not the sacrament either of childhood or of adulthood and where grown-ups who have just been baptised are concerned further acts of commitment are out of the question. It is because some have thought confirmation had something to do with adolescence that this notion has been prevalent.

We have already spoken of the invitatory. Its underlying theology is very balanced. Neither it nor the prayer itself speak of commitment, mission or anything of the kind.

The prayer for the giving of the Spirit is ancient, coming from the Gelasian Sacramentary and reaching back perhaps to the time of St Ambrose. The intrusive *Amens*, a later feature, have been eliminated. It should be noted too that the gesture of the hands during the prayer is no longer spoken of as 'extending' them over the candidates, as the former pontifical did, but as of a 'laying-on of hands' (*manus imponunt*—the rubric assumes that presbyters are going to concelebrate the sacrament with the bishop).

The Introduction (8) foresees that confirmation is going to be a concelebration of other non-episcopal ministers (vicars-general and

---

[48] See B. Botte, *art. cit.*, pp. 6–7.

other dignitaries but notably parish priests and those who have been concerned in the preparation of the candidates) with the bishop and while the clause in (8) seems restrictive, the ritual seems to envisage the concelebration of other ministers as normal. We may imagine that this will become usual practice. They are true concelebrants: with the bishop they lay hands on all the candidates together, they receive the chrism from the bishop (a sign of their delegation) and with him anoint those candidates allotted to them. The theological implications are interesting. Here is a concelebration for the giving of a sacrament that at least in the West has already been regarded as an episcopal prerogative; but more than that, the unity of the priesthood is made very plain. Presbyters are visibly, liturgically and sacramentally sharing in the one priesthood that ultimately is Christ's and of which the episcopate is the primary but by no means exclusive manifestation. It comes close to the vision of the *Constitution on the Liturgy* (41, 42) which sees the bishop as the president of the liturgy of the whole diocese which in turn 'manifests' the church. Given this experience, the people will understand all the more easily the role of the presbyter when, as in certain circumstances he may (7), he confirms alone in his own church.

Finally, a word must be said about the kiss of peace that concludes the administration. The *alapa*, that thirteenth century 'interpretation' of the gesture, has gone. It is no longer to be found in the rubrics and local conferences of bishops may decide how it is to be done. As the ancient texts show very clearly it was originally the kiss of peace exchanged in the eucharistic community and was given to the neophytes for the first time to show that they were now members of the community.[49] With the unique exception of the Roman rite this was the moment, ie just before the eucharistic action, when the kiss of peace was always given.

How and indeed when is it to be done? There is the practical difficulty that the celebrant, whose hand is covered with chrism, can hardly give the peace in the form of the handshake which is now widely accepted. And we may ask: is it necessary to give it precisely at this moment? It would seem best to delay it until the time of communion when the candidates could be brought before the celebrant to receive it. It would then be linked with the eucharist as it originally was. To save a further movement, there they could remain until they receive communion.

---

[49] Hippolytus *forbids* the exchange of the kiss of peace between catechumens and Christians until this moment (*Ap. Trad.* XVIII, 3).

Where confirmation is given outside the Mass, candidates could be assembled after the Lord's prayer when the sign of peace could appropriately be given.

Confirmation outside the Mass

There are few changes. There is an opening collect, the ministry of the word, the homily, the renewal of baptismal promises, the administration, the General Intercession, ending with the Lord's prayer. There is finally the solemn blessing or the 'prayer over the people'.

Practical Pastoral Directives

These are to be found in the *Praenotanda* (here called the Introduction) (1–19).

Parents: As in the Order of Infant Baptism, the role of the parents is much enhanced. 'For the most part it is for the *parents* to see that their children are prepared for confirmation' and this they are to do 'by forming them gradually in the spirit of faith' and by supporting others who may instruct them. This duty will receive its proper liturgical expression by their active participation in the ceremony and notably when they present their own children to the bishop. The parents are naturally to be helped by others, the clergy and catechists, but 'the preparation of the baptised for confirmation concerns the whole people of God' though how this is to be carried out in practice is a question. However, the community at least can be asked to pray about the event and petitions can be inserted *before* the day of confirmation in the General Intercession of the Mass.

Sponsors: These are retained but the background of their function is again community. They are not Christians who merely lay a hand on the candidates. They are supposed to assist them before, during and after the celebration. That is, they are to have something to do with leading the candidates to confirmation, presumably by associating with them and giving informal instruction. In the course of the celebration, if the parents do not do so, they are to present the candidate to the bishop and, in doing so, they represent the local community. Afterwards they 'will help the candidates to keep the promises they have made in baptism' (5).[50]

---

[50] If this is meant to refer to children it is a little odd, for they have made no promises in baptism. One has to suppose that the revisers had adults in mind —or that Homer nodded. If for 'baptism' one read 'confirmation' the injunction would be comprehensible.

To signify the link between baptism and confirmation the sponsors of the former may continue their function for confirmation and for the latter parents may stand.[51] This may well be the best way to deal with the matter. Where parents are practising, they will be the children's best instructors and support and where they are weak, confirmation may well provide (another) occasion when their faith and practice may be strengthened.[52] Sponsors must be mature, must be Catholics, themselves have received the three sacraments of initiation and be free from canonical impediments.

No doubt it is a good and desirable thing that there should be sponsors and that they should have some part in the preparation of the candidates and continue to support them after confirmation. But this pre-supposes a parish that is a community where people know each other and that there is a large number capable of sustaining the role. Once again we meet the problem of community and also the need to form parents and other adults in a mature Christianity. As with so many matters that seem at first purely liturgical, here also we find that wider issues come into play. Until there is some recognised form of adult Christian education, it is improbable that the sort of sponsors envisaged by the Order will be found.

The Minister(s) of Confirmation: Taking up a term invented by Vatican II[53] the Introduction (7) states that the *minister originarius* of confirmation is a bishop and in the context of the Council document this can only mean the diocesan bishop with a pastoral charge. The term would seem to mean that the source of power for conferring confirmation resides in the bishop and the theological basis for this, to be found in the *Constitution on the Church* (28), is that bishop and priest share in the one priesthood of Jesus Christ. The 'power' therefore is not merely a legal one but a sacramental one. In the Eastern Churches the bishop is clearly the 'originating minister' since it is he who blesses the chrism and the priest who regularly confirms. In the West this is true also though the priest receives a special delegation to confirm. According to the Introduction, the bishop is to be regarded as the *normal* minister of the

---

[51] Canon 796, says the text, is abrogated.

[52] If of course they have receded from the church so far that they can hardly be said to be members of it at all, other remedies will have to be sought and the question of the confirmation of the candidate, if very young, may have to be reviewed. It is the problem of infant baptism all over again.

[53] *Constitution on the Church*, 26.

sacrament since he is the successor of the apostles who received the Spirit at Pentecost and the power to transmit him.[54] Yet, it is a marked feature of this Order, as well as that of adult initiation, that a variety of non-episcopal ministers may now, with proper authorisation, confer the sacrament. The reason for this is undoubtedly the inability of the diocesan bishop to be present wherever and whenever he is needed. With this recognition of the practical difficulties, as well as an enhanced esteem of the importance of confirmation, western practice is now beginning to approach that of eastern Christians. If the plain implications of the Orders of confirmation and adult initiation are to be reduced to practice, that is, if the order of baptism, confirmation and the eucharist is to be observed *as a norm*, it will be necessary for priests to be regularly delegated to administer confirmation.

Apart from those who hold a special charge yet without the episcopal order (7a), priests who *ex officio* baptise an adult or a child not baptised in infancy or, as we have seen, admit a baptised person into the full communion of the church, may confirm and the power to do so is granted by this Order. The permission to confirm in danger of death, first restricted to parish priests and then to some others, is now extended to a wide variety of them (7c).

The cooperation of priests in the celebration of confirmation is expressed sacramentally in the rite itself. The bishop associates them with himself. With him they lay hands on the candidates and from him receive the chrism. The whole liturgy is a true sacramental concelebration.

The Age of Confirmation: We have already said something about this above. The Order practically repeats the canon that confirmation is to be delayed (*differtur*) until about the age of seven. This, as we have seen, represents the ancient Roman tradition which has never varied: confirmation is to take place before communion. Yet there are practical problems which the Order recognises and leaves to local conferences of bishops the responsibility for setting a later age. There must be (good) pastoral reasons and these are suggested: they are to train the faithful to a fuller and enthusiastic devotion (*obtemperantiam*: lit. 'obedience') to Christ and to a greater capability to bear witness to him.

---

[54] It is this last phrase that, presumably, in the mind of the Order distinguishes the apostles from the other Christians who were present in some numbers on the same occasion. They received the Spirit but not the power to transmit him.

What age is this to be? The Order speaks of an *aetas maturior* and this could hardly be said to be eight, nine, ten or eleven. On the other hand there are few who would admit the age of early adolescence as suitable. Is anything as late as eighteen or nineteen envisaged? It seems bizarre. By that time some people are married. The question has been debated for over twenty-five years and it is pretty safe to say that no satisfactory conclusion has been reached.

The whole problem has come from a) the separation of confirmation from baptism, which, as we have seen, was due to non-theological factors and b) to the consequent association of this sacrament with adolescence. The notion too that confirmation was concerned with commitment to the work of the church ('mission', and in some places 'Catholic Action') also had much to do with the controversy which has raged until now.

If we look at the theology of confirmation as it is set out or is discernible in the liturgy, it is clear that it has nothing to do with adolescence. If it had, there would be no point in confirming an adult convert. Secondly, if it speaks of the mission of the church, it does so in a very special way, as we have observed above. Thirdly, as we have also tried to show, there is a logic in the order of the three sacraments of initiation which carries its own weight. In the early church, even for children, the holy eucharist was seen as the perfecting of baptism and confirmation and to confer the latter after communion is to pervert the right order of things. We are forced or, before long, will be forced to re-unite confirmation with baptism and then the problem will be not the age at which confirmation is given but whether or not we baptise and confirm certain children at all. Infant confirmation or at least confirmation before communion will become the custom.

There is one qualification to this view. The theology of the sacraments of initiation has been built on the tradition and practice of the early church. We have to ask: is this *mere* tradition? Adult baptism was the norm and the order of the sacraments seemed inevitable. If we are to change this system, then theologically convincing arguments will have to be found to justify the change. That is to say, different relationships will have to be discovered between baptism and confirmation and between confirmation and the eucharist. It will have to be shown that confirmation has so little connection with baptism that it may be conferred independently of it and at a much later age than has usually been envisaged. It will have to be shown that communion may be received normally and properly before confirmation and not merely as now as a 'practical' necessity. Many changes have occurred in sacramental practice in the course of centuries, notably in the sacrament of penance, and an official change in the order of the sacraments of initiation may be possible though such a possibility seems remote. But before any such change can be made a sound theological basis will have to be provided for it. Sound pastoral practice cannot be built on bad theology.

Celebration and Community: There are the usual recommendations that the celebration should be festive, that normally it is to take place within the Mass and that the local community should be assembled for it. Since confirmation has always been a community celebration and usually sufficiently festive, there is no need to insist on these matters here.

Adaptation: Local conferences of bishops may adapt the formulas of the promises and profession of faith, as in baptism, and it is to be hoped that they will not be adapted in the direction of the soldier-of-Christ-defence-of-the-church mentality which is quite unsupported by the texts of the liturgy. Such conferences may however adapt the texts to the mentality of the candidates and this will be particularly important in the case of children.

As we have observed, the manner of giving the kiss of peace is to be determined by the same local conferences of bishops.

The *celebrant* may adapt the address according to the psychological needs of the candidates as well as the invitatory to the prayer for the laying-on of hands and may insert brief commentaries (*'monitiones'*) where he thinks they may be needed. If he is not a bishop, he should mention that the bishop is the normal minister of the sacrament.

CHAPTER SEVEN

The Sacrament of Marriage[1]

THE DEVELOPMENT in more recent years of the theology of marriage, in which secular factors (changing attitudes to sex and love, the equality of women, etc) have played their part, has revealed or re-discovered new aspects of Christian marriage. The Second Vatican Council both summarised and carried forward this development, principally in its document, *The Constitution on the Church in the Modern World* (47–52).[2]

Christian marriage is a union of *persons*: one is not the servant of the other. Marriage which is entered into by the irrevocable consent of the partners is a covenant in which they give themselves to each other and their union becomes the sacrament-sign of the love with which God has loved his people throughout the ages: 'Christ our Lord abundantly blesses this manifold love which springs from the source of divine charity and forms a union on the model of his own union with the Church. For just as God once encountered his people in a covenant of trust and love, so now, as the Saviour of the world and Spouse of the Church, he encounters the faithful spouses in the sacrament of Christian marriage.' Their love is taken up into the divine love and enriched by the love of Christ (50). There is much more on the same subject which it would be impossible to summarise here. Sufficient to say that the Council teaches a deep and rich doctrine of marriage, much of which is incorporated into the new marriage rite.

---

[1] The new Order was promulgated 19 March 1969. The rite for England and Wales was approved in 1970. Editions: *The Rite of Marriage* (Geoffrey Chapman, 1971); *The Marriage Rite* (Goodliffe Neale, 1970). There are others, more or less complete. As is usual with these documents, the Order is numbered throughout, the Introduction running from 1–18 and the rite from 19–66. In the English editions there is an Appendix on 'The Celebration of Marriage in England and Wales'.

[2] Extracts from this and other Council documents will be found conveniently arranged in Clifford Howell, SJ, *Companion to the New Order of Marriage*, Alcester and Dublin, 1970, pp. 29–40.

This doctrine was largely in possession before the Council opened and although the *Constitution on the Church in the Modern World* came along after the *Constitution on the Liturgy*, it is not surprising that the Council Fathers decreed that 'the marriage rite now found in the Roman Ritual is to be revised and enriched in such a way that the grace of the sacrament is more clearly signified and the duties of spouses are impressed on them' (77). If the last phrase seems a little over moralistic and perhaps a bit condescending, one needs to remember that the liturgy constitution was the first to be debated in the Council and that later documents show a deeper understanding of the sacrament. The 'duties' and responsibilities are shown to arise from the nature of marriage itself and are not something externally imposed on the laity, unfortunately married, by a clerical church.

From a liturgical and even a human point of view, the marriage rite that was to be found in the then Roman Ritual was jejune in the extreme. In the deepest sense of the word it was an *insignificant* rite that hardly expressed the theology of marriage even as it was then known. Unless there was a wedding Mass (and until comparatively recently wedding Masses were rare) there was no ministry of the word, sometimes not even a sermon.[3] There were simply the expression of consent, a prayer for the blessing of the ring, a few versicles and responses and a not very inspiring collect. There was not even a blessing at the end.[4] The reason for this strange state of affairs was that when the rite was drawn up in the early seventeenth century, the compilers assumed that different countries and regions had their own rites and customs which it was intended should continue in use. In Europe this was indeed the case and some of them were rich and embedded in the national culture. Unfortunately no provision was made for the church in the new countries and since they could not plead customs of their own, they had perforce to use the austere rite of the Roman Ritual. Here in England we were protected from the rigours of that rite since both the Roman Catholic and the Anglican Churches (with

---

[3] In the *Ordo Administrandi Sacramenta*, originally edited by Bishop Richard Challoner, there was a homily written by him for use at the service. It survived until this century.

[4] *Rituale Romanum*, tit. VII, cap.ii. Was it merely an accident that the service was placed in the book immediately after the funeral rites? Certain it is that about a hundred years ago on the occasion of an uncle's wedding the celebrant—an ancient canon—began reading the funeral service over the bewildered pair until the bridegroom protested!

one or two differences) retained the rite of Sarum. This, especially in the texts of the exchange of promises, has a warmth that is totally lacking in the Roman rite and, as is now well known, these texts, with but few changes, have been incorporated into the rite of the church.[5]

An examination of the texts of the marriage service, both those in the Order and those in the missal, shows that the church is now emphasising two truths that have always been implicit in Christian marriage but which have never been so clearly expressed in the liturgy as they are in the new rite. The first is the importance of the human love of those about to be married, and the second is covenant.

The first must be said to be principally a contribution from modern society which very generally has repudiated arranged marriages and has come to a deeper understanding of what love can be between a man and a woman. The church's part in this matter has been largely one of reflection on the experience of married Christians, though an increasing tendency to put love (charity) at the centre of theological concerns has also helped Christians to integrate their sexual love into an authentic Christianity. None the less it may be said to be an interesting example of the influence of the laity on clerical thinking.[6] This development has a very great importance for, as we have said above,[7] marriage is a paradigm case of the interpenetration of the divine love with the human.

In the secularised, non-religious and non-sacral civilisation in which we live, worship and religious practice seem to be a fringe activity indulged in either by the frightened to whom religion is a sort of fire-insurance or by others for even less accountable reasons.

---

[5] That is of course with the exception of the Eastern Churches which retain their own. In medieval England (and in other countries too) the liturgy of marriage was a gay and friendly affair. After the *Pax* in the Wedding Mass the bridegroom kissed the bride. The Mass-formula was that of the votive Mass of the Holy Trinity with 'proper' readings and if it was not a very satisfactory text, it was one used in England for occasions of rejoicing and thanksgiving (see *L'Eglise en Prière*, ed. 1961, pp. 601, 604; F. Proctor and W. H. Frere, *The Book of Common Prayer*, ed. 1965, p. 611).

[6] There has almost certainly been an inter-reaction of both on each other though the literature on the subject, which is vast, going back to the early thirties, seems at first to have been purely clerical. One remembers H. Dom's fruitful book which however authority suppressed at the time, at least *donec corrigatur*. In more recent years the laity have written a good deal on the subject. No attempt is made here to give a bibliography: it is too great.

[7] Chapter I.

Even Christians constantly experience the difficulty of relating their life to their worship and too often they are kept in separate compartments. There is no need to give examples, we are all aware of it and we all suffer from it. Marriage is important not merely for its own sake but because it involves a meeting of what is most ordinary and 'worldly' with Christ who gives it a divine dimension and depth.

Two young people love each other and, however imperfect their understanding of what love implies, however little they may know of its depths, its richness and its complexity, they also realise that it involves a mutual self-giving that is total. They are aware, of course, that their love becomes enfleshed in the union of bodies, that in a sense there is nothing more earthy than sexual union. But they realise in one way or another that this giving and even this giving-in-the-flesh transcends itself. There is a plus-value to their love and it is only the cynic who would say that they are not seeking it. It is *this* human love that 'becomes' the sacrament of marriage through which God transfuses it with his love. It is not merely that the human love of a couple is 'sanctified' as if it were left intact in all its secularity, much less is it just a 'blessing' that remains external to the 'real thing'. It is not even that this love is 'consecrated' so that in marriage it is redeemed from its earthiness. Sanctification and consecration do occur and both enable the partners to direct love away from self to the other for, as everyone knows, human love can be marred by selfishness and lust, even in marriage. The deepest truth seems to be that two people jointly bring their love to God in a spirit of self-giving to each other and to him and in the encounter that ensues, God's love meets theirs. As we have said, he transfuses it with his own. Henceforth they are able to love each other with a love in which God is present and active. Their love however remains human, it is not 'angelised', and is always limited by what the two personalities are and by what they will be throughout their lives. Their love for each other will undergo various vicissitudes, it will often be less than generous, sometimes self-seeking, but whenever they are truly loving each other, God is present to them and in their love. For *ubi caritas et amor, Deus ibi est* (Where is love and lovingkindness, there is God).

This view is at least implied in the first address of the minister of the sacrament: 'You have come together in this church so that the Lord may seal and strengthen your love ... Christ abundantly

blesses' it. The love already exists and will remain intact but it
is going to be 'strengthened' by God, turning it, we may suppose,
from the radical self-centredness that is in everyone to an other-
centredness, precisely the partner who is the 'other'. And while
'blesses' is a rather vague word it would seem to indicate that the
love is going to be transformed, as we can see from the texts that
occur later in the rite.

But this love is not restricted in its expression to the exchange
of promises before the altar nor yet to the more private and purely
inter-personal relationships of the husband and wife. Young people
today, with the recession of the high tide of romantic love, know
very well that neither love nor marriage consists of murmured
words or gestures of affection. They know that it is expressed in
the most ordinary actions of human life, that marriage is not a
romantic affair but that it is marked by a daunting ordinariness,
by all the anxieties of forming a home, by the bringing up of
children and the caring for each other in illness, depression and
times of tension. All these vicissitudes offer opportunities of self-
giving, of mutual love, and God is present to them in the stress
and anxiety of their lives as well as in their joys. In all of them
they meet God or rather God comes to them anew, animating their
dedicated love and supporting them so that the process of mutual
self-giving can continue. In this way, life in all its drabness and
stress and joy is lifted up to God so that it is transformed. One is
inclined to echo: *imma summis iunguntur*; the lowly is united with
the Highest. Thus Christian marriage is able to play its part in
the perfecting of this world until it too bears the image of Christ
and at the end will be lifted up to the Father.

If the first address implies this view of love, other texts teach it
explicitly and carry it further. Thus the second nuptial blessing
asks that husband and wife 'may share the gifts of *your* (God's)
love and become one in mind and heart'. Here it is clear that
human and divine love are intended to interpenetrate one another
and that the partners are meant to grow in a love which they share
with God. In the same sense we read in the third group of blessings
at the end of the services: 'May Jesus, who loved his church to
the end, *always fill your hearts with his love.*' A collect, that of
the third wedding Mass, shows the appropriateness of celebrating
marriage within the eucharist: 'May the mystery of Christ's un-
selfish love, which we celebrate in the eucharist, *increase their love
for you and for each other.*' But perhaps the most striking text is

to be found in one of the prefaces which may be used for the
wedding Mass. It sees the whole plan of salvation in the terms of
love and marriage:

'You created man in love to share your divine life.
We see his high destiny in the love of husband and wife,
which bears the imprint of your own divine love.
Love is man's origin,
love is his constant calling, love is his fulfilment in heaven.
The love of man and woman
is made holy in the sacrament of marriage,
and becomes the mirror of your everlasting love.'[8]

The message these and other texts of the rite convey is a simple
if profound one and there is no reason to suppose that it will not
be clear to the participants. The somewhat bleak injunction of the
Constitution on the Liturgy has been surpassed and in the new
marriage rite we have a liturgy that will teach what Christian
love is and indeed what love *tout court* is. In the world in which
we live this is a very important matter. If romantic love has brought
with it certain gifts of tenderness, of sensibility, or perceptiveness
and *innerlichkeit* so that modern people have been able to love
each other with an intensity and awareness that seems to be foreign
to civilisations that have not known it, it has too often been debased.
Love has become *mere* emotion, mere feeling so that people can
say, when this emotional love has disappeared, that the marriage
has come to an end. What the new marriage rite is saying is that
love is above all self-giving whose supreme model is the self-giving
of the Persons of the Trinity. They give love to each other and
then pour out that same love upon all mankind: 'love is man's
origin.' God created man because he wanted him to share his love
and it is with love that God throughout the ages has called man
to himself. This calling and this divine self-giving, to man, reached
its climax in Christ who 'gave himself up' to death (Ephesians
5:1) so that he might call into existence a people who, in covenant,

---

[8] ICEL translation. The Latin, in the last sentence, speaks of the 'mystery'
of holy matrimony which is the *signum* of God's love. The ICEL translation is,
I think, very good indeed and these two words give great difficulty in translation. You cannot say 'the mystery of marriage'! Nor I think would 'sacrament'
for *signum* have conveyed that marriage is the 'sacrament-sign' of God's love.
But perhaps it is worthwhile pointing out what the Latin actually says.

would be bound to him by love. Of this union, achieved by a sacrificial love, marriage is the sacrament showing forth and making that love present to husband and wife. Love is self-giving not self-seeking and it is in the self-giving that marriage has its origin and the sacrament provides the guarantee of its continuance. This is expressed at the high point of the whole marriage service when the partners give themselves to each other 'to have and to hold from this day forward, for better for worse, for richer for poorer, in sickness and in health, to love and to cherish, till death do us part'. Nothing could be more inclusive and nothing could better express in concrete fashion the truth of the scriptures that marriage is the sacrament of divine love.

If married love, as we have described it, binds husband and wife together and is a sharing in the love God has shown for mankind through the ages, that means that it is a sharing in the *covenanted* love of God for mankind and this is why in the new rite marriage is spoken of in terms of covenant. It has been pointed out[9] that the *Constitution on the Church in the Modern World* never speaks of the marriage *contract* but prefers the more biblical term 'covenant' *(foedus matrimonialis)*. This is reflected in the new texts. The Introduction (2) refers to marriage as arising 'in the *covenant* of marriage or irrevocable consent' of the partners, the consent evidently being the means by which the pact or covenant is formed. But this covenant is not merely a legal thing, a contract in secular terms. The contract is no more than an external sign, one among others even if an indispensable one, of the more fundamental thing, namely the covenant. This in turn is a sacrament sign of *the* Covenant. Thus in the second preface of the wedding Mass we read: '... through Jesus Christ our Lord ... you entered into a new covenant with your people ... This outpouring of love in the new covenant of grace is symbolised in the marriage covenant that seals the love of husband and wife and reflects the divine plan of love.'[10]

As the whole history of salvation shows, the covenant is the expression both in the Old and the New Testaments of God's steadfast love for man. In the Old Testament two words are always associated: mercy and faithfulness. God is faithful to his promises to rescue and redeem, he will not go back on his promises, he is

---

[9] See D. O'Callaghan, 'Marriage as Sacrament' in *Concilium* (vol. 5, n. 6, pp. 101–10), quoted by R. L. Stewart, 'Marriage: the New Rite' in *Life and Worship*, October 1970, p. 13.

[10] ICEL translation.

always *there* offering his love. This saving love and faithfulness reached its supreme expression in the obedience of Christ to his Father, an obedience that carried him to the self-giving and death of the cross. The faithful love of Christ was also supremely creative; it brought into existence 'the wonderful sacrament of the church', the people of God, and it is of this love that marriage is the sacrament-sign, declaring in all the ordinariness of married life the mystery of God's unfailing love for man. It is this love that the partners are pledging to each other and to God and the fidelity of marriage is not simply something imposed by law for the good of the partners and society. It is an exigency that arises from the very nature of the love they pledge to each other and insofar as they live in faithful love, they will be making the sign to the world of God's steadfast love present and active among the men and women of today. It is not surprising then that the Introduction (1), quoting the *Constitution on the Church* (11), can say that married people have their own special gift (*charisma*) among the people of God and it is a matter of experience that the devoted life of a Christian family bears constant witness to the reality of God's love at work in mankind.

But if it is of this kind of love that marriage is the sacrament-sign, it is also clear that it is a sign of a love that gives itself to the point of sacrifice. This is the plain teaching of the Letter to the Ephesians,[11] part of which has for so long formed part of the formula of the wedding Mass. But though this passage, taken by itself, gives important teaching on Christian marriage, that teaching is greatly deepened if it is put into its context. The chapter begins with a statement about divine love and its issue: 'Try, then, to imitate God, as children of his that he loves, and *follow Christ by loving as he loved you, giving himself up* in our place as a fragrant offering and a *sacrifice* to God.'[12] The self-giving of Christ was total and issued into the suffering and death of the cross. It is with this sort of love that husbands are required to love their wives and we may add, that wives are required to love their husbands. It implies a giving that is self-sacrificial. Put this way, it may sound dramatic, or even over-dramatic, and married people may say that they do not recognise their marriage in it. Maybe that is because

---

[11] 5:21–33. It is still one of the readings that may be used though it needs to be used with discretion. In a 'mixed' congregation there will be many who cannot understand its relevance since they have not the background to do so.

[12] Ephesians 5:1, 2. This passage has been inserted into the Lectionary.

they are right in the situation and since self-giving involves self-forgetfulness, they do not remember the innumerable occasions, great and small, when they have given themselves to each other. The outsider can often see this, especially as husband and wife grow old together and are moved, it would seem, by but a single spirit. In any case, it is of this self-sacrificial love that marriage is the sacrament as the partners themselves declare when they say that they take each other for better for worse, in sickness and in health, until death shall part them. And as they declare it, God comes and makes that love possible and fruitful in their lives. For the sacrament is not merely a sign of this love; it is the efficacious sign of this love.

Married love, then, is a covenanted, pledged love involving self-sacrifice. But this immediately suggests permanence. Marriage is not simply a consent but a commitment to a way of life and the emphasis is now not merely on consent or contract but on relationship which has its origin in consent and is protected by contract: 'The Council's teaching is not concerned with the contract as such, but rather with the whole institution of marriage, the *communitas* (the common life) of man and woman that is initiated by the contract. Many theologians therefore see the whole marriage *relationship* as the grace-giving sign or sacrament, which is initiated by the marriage consent.' This fits in with what has been said above that marriage and married love is a life of which the consent and the contract are but the initiating signs. The 'graces of state' are not just so many *consequences* of the once-for-all contract. Rather, 'the key to the sacramental nature of marriage is to see it as a man-and-woman partnership directed to integrate and perfect the partners as persons and as Christians, and eventually to civilise and Christianise the world at large'.[13]

Relationship means not only the more intimate and inter-personal life of the partners but also their whole way of life and it is not new doctrine to call marriage a permanent sacrament. Pius XI, in *Casti Connubii* (116), citing a passage from the sixteenth-century Bellarmine, could state that the sacrament of marriage can be considered in the moment of its accomplishment and in its permanency afterwards: 'This sacrament, in fact, is similar to the eucharist, which, likewise, is a sacrament not only in the moment of its accomplishment but also as long as it remains. For as long

---

[13] *Art cit.*, p. 14, the second quotation being from O'Callaghan, *Marriage as Sacrament*, p. 104.

as husband and wife live, their fellowship is always the sacrament of Christ and his church.' This means that no less than the sacrament of baptism that manifests and effects the regeneration of man through the passion and resurrection of Christ, marriage reveals and makes present Christ's redeeming power and love in the most ordinary life of the most ordinary Christians living in the world. For the eye of faith, Christ with his love is here present and active showing that life in all its secularity or 'profaneness', with all its tragedy, its sufferings, its needs and its joys, is taken up into the loving purpose of God who, through it, works out his saving purpose for mankind and first of all for the men and women who in this way enter into his covenanted love.

If contract is less emphasised in the church's current teaching on marriage, it none the less remains essential to it because of the greater realities of marriage of which we have spoken. It is the necessary sign of what is inwardly intended and since marriage is a union that brings into existence a new community, both church and state need to take cognizance of it. Normally, marriage implies community, the family, and communities affect the life of society generally. As the church has said tirelessly in modern times, the well-being of the state as of the Christian community itself is dependent on the well-being of the institution of marriage and of the family that arises from it. Contract remains important since in the days in which we live, when marriage is becoming a temporary union, sometimes entered into with little thought or preparation and dissolved, it would seem, almost at will, it is necessary to emphasise the binding nature of marriage of which the public contract is the sign and evidence. By it the partners declare their intention before church and state to enter into a life-long union.

Contract too is the guarantee of freedom of consent: all contracts to be binding and valid must be freely entered into and the law of the church has always insisted on this freedom. Since marriages in our society are no longer 'arranged' it might seem that this is an unimportant element. Yet people are getting married nowadays at a very early age and it is necessary to ensure that they are fully aware that they are entering into a life-long contract and that they are doing so with a fully free consent. Perhaps young people are no longer carried away by emotion as they were (or were alleged to be) in the great days of romantic love. We may think that they are highly sophisticated about the whole business of love and marriage. They may be so about sex, but what do

they know of love and indeed what experience have they had of
life? How the gravity of the affair is to be brought home to them
is another matter and there is at least one celibate priest who feels
himself not a little handicapped in trying to do so.

All these—fidelity, contract and freedom of consent—are clearly
set out in the new marriage rite.

In the first address the celebrant reminds the bride and bridegroom that Christ has provided them with a special sacrament
which enables them to take up 'the duties of marriage in mutual
and lasting fidelity'. This is put with more force in vows they
make when they promise 'to love and to cherish each other' until
death shall part them. Then, as the prayers for the blessing of the
ring(s) and the formula for putting it on reveal, the ring is the
outward sign of the partners' fidelity: 'the ring which you give' is
'a sign of your love and fidelity'; and, 'Take this ring as a sign of
my love and fidelity' (27, 28). Finally, in the collect of the first
formulary of the wedding Mass this doctrine is combined with
that of the co-inherence of the divine love with the human:

'Father,
you have made the bond of marriage
a holy mystery,
a symbol of Christ's love for his church.
Hear our prayers for N. and N.
With faith in you and in each other
they pledge their love today.
May their lives bear witness to the reality of that love.'[14]

Contract and consent are inseparably bound up together in the
various declarations and promises the partners make at the beginning
of the marriage service (24, 25). They freely undertake the obligations of marriage, they declare themselves ready to give themselves
to each other without reserve and to accept lovingly such children
as God may send them. Freedom is declared in the formula which
has been taken over from the civil marriage rite and it and the
contractual element can be seen in the questions and answers (25)
which (for England) have been retained from the former rite. The
combination here (24, 25) of the civil and ecclesiastical formulas
is a valuable indication of the importance that both church and
state attribute to free consent and the permanence of the union.
Likewise, it is a further sign that in marriage the 'sacred' and

---

[14] ICEL translation.

the 'secular', religion and life, are more closely associated than perhaps in any other area of Christian practice.

In the institution of marriage it has been realised very acutely in recent times that there is always the possibility of tension between the different ends of marriage. In the past the emphasis was rather that marriage was 'for' the procreation of children, what used to be called 'the primary end of marriage'. The *Constitution on the Church in the Modern World* refused to endorse this way of thinking and its views are found also in the new marriage rite. Both documents teach that marriage is for the human and spiritual perfection of the husband and wife *and also* for the procreation of children and their education. Thus in the Introduction (3) there is the statement which is very close to a passage in the *Constitution on the Church in the Modern World* (48, 49): 'Christian couples nourish and develop their marriage by undivided affection, which wells up from the fountain of divine love, while in the merging of human and divine love, they remain faithful in body and mind, in good times and in bad.'[15] But married love, while destined for the perfecting and indeed salvation of the partners, is intended to issue into the procreation of children which is the sign not only of the human fruitfulness of the marriage but of God's love which in this way is revealed to be present in the marriage. As the Council put it: 'Authentic married love is caught up into divine love and is governed and enriched by Christ's redeeming power and the saving activity of the Church. Thus this love can lead the spouses to God with powerful effect and can aid and strengthen them in the sublime office of being a father or a mother.'[16]

But the Introduction (4) carefully repeats the teaching of the *Constitution on the Church in the Modern World* (50)[17] that procreation and the education of the children *together* constitute an end of marriage. The married couple are instructed (4) that 'by their very nature, the institution of matrimony and wedded love are ordained for the procreation and education of children and find in them their ultimate crown. Therefore, married Christians, while not considering the other purposes of marriage of less account,

---

[15] ICEL translation. 'Merging' comes from the translation of the Constitution in *Documents of Vatican II*, ed. W. Abbott, p. 253 and is perhaps a little strong for 'sociantes'. A *socius* is one who 'goes with' another and is hardly 'merged' in the other. However, Lewis and Short s.v. '*sociare*' indicate that it can mean 'united', at least for abstract things.

[16] *Constitution of the Church in the Modern World*, 48, ed. cit., p. 251.

[17] ed. cit., p. 254.

should be steadfast and ready to cooperate with the love of the Creator and Saviour, who through them will constantly enrich and enlarge his own family'.[18] Much has been written about this tension and there is no need to go into it here. The documents however do suggest that irresponsible procreation is not what is meant by this 'end of marriage' and that the sincere concern of husband and wife to produce a balanced family in which all the children will have their due meed of love and attention is also the sign of God's creative love in the marriage.

The acceptance of children is, as we have remarked, found in the first undertaking of the bride and bridegroom (23) and while the doctrine mentioned above can hardly form the subject of a prayer, we find that three nuptial blessings (33, 34) pray that the marriage will be blessed with children and their function as parents is underlined.

There is a final teaching which receives great emphasis in several parts of the service. The love of husband and wife, a love that is concretised in the gift of children, must be turned out from themselves and even from the family, first to the church and then to the world:

'You are the loving Father of the world of nature;
you are the loving Father of the new creation of grace.
In Christian marriage you bring together the two orders of
    creation:
nature's gift of children enriches the world
and your grace enriches also your church.'[19]

Elsewhere it is emphasised that Christian marriage is a witness in the world and to the world of God's ever-present love for mankind and the Christian community is conceived of as a community that is going to transmit that love to society around it. The theme is found in various places but notably in a blessing that will in fact be the last words the bride and bridegroom will hear before they leave the church:

'May you always bear witness to the love of God in this world
so that the afflicted and the needy
will find in you generous friends,
and welcome you into the joys of heaven.'[20]

[18] ICEL translation.
[19] 115; first Preface of the wedding Mass; ICEL translation.
[20] 37; ICEL translation.

The Liturgy of Marriage

Though profoundly rooted in the experience and customs of mankind, marriage has always had a rite that is basically simple, namely the exchange of consent and the giving of one partner to the other. This had been elaborated in the Catholic tradition by its association with the eucharist and in the Byzantine rite by the crowning of the spouses. Yet its simplicity remains. This is true, in spite of an appearance of complexity, in the new Order.

Like other sacramental rites, it takes place within the Mass, after the homily, and not before it as it was throughout the Middle Ages and until recently. Since marriage is now described as a covenant and a sign of the covenant between God and man and since the eucharist is supremely the renewal of that covenant among men today, the appropriateness of this arrangement is obvious.

The first part of the marriage rite proper (23–26) is concerned to secure an understanding of the obligations of marriage, the freedom of the partners and their mutual self-giving. Freedom to marry and intention to do so will already have been obtained before the marriage ceremony and these statements are to be seen as *public* declarations of the interior sentiments of the couple. In this sense they are sacramental signs.

It is worth pointing out that these texts are conflated from various sources. The declaration of freedom, to be used only in England and Wales, beginning 'I do solemnly declare ...' is taken from the civil rite and the words are always to be recited exactly as they are with the full names of the bride and bridegroom. The words of consent 'A.B. will you take C.D. here present ...' are from the former Roman Ritual[21] and were part of the rite of marriage in use in England until the new Order. The formula for the exchange of promises comes from three sources: 'I call upon these persons present ...' (which must always be repeated exactly and with full names) comes from the civil rite: 'I A.B. do take thee, C.D. to be my lawful wedded wife, to have and to hold ...' comes from the old Sarum rite and the phrase 'to love and to cherish' comes apparently from the Book of Common Prayer.[22] The sentence by which the celebrant receives the consent of the bride and bridegroom replaces

---

[21] Tit. VII, cap. ii.

[22] The text from the Sarum Manual is given accessibly in F. Proctor and W. H. Frere, *A New History of the Book of Common Prayer* (ed. 1905, reprint 1965), p. 614. The phrase 'to love and to cherish' seems to replace the bride's 'to be bonere and buxum in bed and at board' of the Sarum text.

the very contentious one 'I join you together in matrimony, in the name of the Father ...' It does not appear in marriage rites before the fifteenth century but made a deep impression and its meaning was fiercely debated at the Council of Trent.[23] Some thought it was the 'form' of the sacrament and that the priest was the sacramental minister—a view which has been held since, but which in the West seems now to be abandoned.[24] Instead of this equivocal text a more general one is substituted in which the intervention of God is underlined. The last phrase, from the gospel (Matthew 19:6), which likewise does not seem to have been in marriage rites generally in the Middle Ages until the fifteenth century, has been retained.[25]

The Blessing of the Ring(s): The handing over of the ring(s) and its blessing ultimately derives from the *sponsalia* or engagement ceremony of the Middle Ages. It has long lost connection with it and the new Order merely recognises the now age-long custom of giving a ring or rings during the marriage service. The first blessing (27), given in the text of the rite is the shortest and is apparently new. The second (110) is from the old rite and dates from as early as the eleventh century.[26] The third (111) is notable for the fact that it is a blessing of the bride and bridegroom rather than of the ring. It may be seen as a text unfolding the meaning of the blessing of a ring or any other object. It is really a blessing of the people who will wear it or use it. The symbolism of the ring is again underlined in the formula for putting it on the finger of the bride: it is a sign of both love and fidelity.[27]

The intercessions ('Bidding Prayers'), the prayer of nuptial blessing and the final blessings follow at this point in all marriages.

---

[23] See A. Duval, 'La Formule "Ego vos coniungo" ... au concile de Trente', *La Maison-Dieu*, 99, 1969.

[24] Père Gy, *LMD*, 99, p. 134 thinks that the expression 'ministers of the sacrament' as applied to the spouses is not very happy. He would prefer to say 'the spouses themselves form the sacrament'. The difficulty seems to lie in an understanding of what is meant by 'minister'. In a sense and whatever may be held as to who are the 'makers' of matrimony, the priest, apart from the most exceptional circumstances, is the indispensable minister and with the couple does celebrate the sacrament.

[25] R. Mouret, 'Le Rituel français du Mariage', in *LMD*, 99, p. 190.

[26] See P. Gy, *art. cit.*, p. 135.

[27] The French word for the wedding ring, *'alliance'*, expresses this and also recalls the covenant which marriage is. The same word is used in French for the covenant between God and his people.

The Wedding Mass: From very early times marriage has been associated with the eucharist. Tertullian saw the 'offering' (of the eucharist) as 'confirming' the marriage of Christians,[28] and the Roman tradition, as represented by the sacramentaries,[29] had a wedding Mass formula in which are to be found three separate versions of the Nuptial Blessing as it was in the former Roman Missal. But a church wedding was not, it seems, obligatory[30] and it was not until the social order in Europe had broken down in the seventh and eighth centuries that the Church, to protect freedom and prevent clandestine marriages, felt the need to intervene in an authoritative manner. Then the marriage came to be performed (literally) *in facie ecclesiae*, before the church doors, and in the presence of the parish priest and witnesses. From there the whole party moved into church for the Mass.[31] The last stage has been reached by the new Order which requires the marriage to be celebrated *within* the Mass.

In the new missal there are three formulas for the wedding Mass all of which are new and all the texts emphasise love and covenant.

The Lectionary: This too provides a whole new range of texts for use at the wedding Mass and their selection for different marriages is a matter requiring tact and discernment. Most of the Old Testament readings will be appropriate only to a congregation that is sufficiently instructed in the Bible. It is not difficult to guess the effect of reading 'I hear my Beloved ... leaping on the mountains ...' though one supposes that the last part could be used: 'Love is strong as death...'. Genesis 1:26–28, 31 and 2:18–24 can be used in conjunction with Ephesians 5:2, 21–33 and Matthew 19:3–6. Jeremiah (31:31–34) with his reference to the covenant is usable and it is perhaps a pity that room was not found somewhere in the Mass-formulas for Jeremiah 31:3: 'I have loved you with an everlasting love...'.

---

[28] Cited in P. Gy, *art. cit.*, p. 135, n. 29. He refers to *Ad Uxorem*, II, 8. Tixeront sees in the *oblatio* of the text a reference to the eucharist (*Hist. des Dogmes*, I, p. 452).

[29] Verona, 1105–1110 (pp. 139–40), Gelasian, 1443–1455 (pp. 208–10) (both ed. Mohlberg), the Gregorian, 200 (ed. Lietzmann, pp. 110–12).

[30] Cf E. Schillebeeckx, *Marriage, Secular Reality and Saving Mystery*, 1965, pp. 18–56.

[31] The introit, sung during the procession, was the well known psalm 127 (128), for long and for obvious reasons used on the occasion of marriage.

Of the non-gospel New Testament readings the most appropriate will be Romans 12:1–2, 9–18, 1 Corinthians 12:31–13:8 (the song of love), Ephesians 5 and the two passages from 1 John 3:18–24 and 4:7–12. These, with the reading from 1 Corinthians, give the doctrine of love which in the marriage rite receives its particular and telling application. Of the psalms provided, 32, 33, 102, 127 and 144 combine most easily with texts speaking of love.

The gospel material is very various going from the beatitudes according to Matthew to the texts on love from St John. Experience shows that the Johannine texts make the deepest impact (15:9–12, perhaps the best of all with its reference to joy, 15:12–16, 17:20–26). All the scripture texts give plenty of scope but perhaps their chief contribution is the emphasis they give to love, thus echoing the marriage rite itself.

The intercessions ('Bidding Prayers') are a new element (coming from the Mass) and are to be used even when the marriage is celebrated apart from the Mass. The celebrant may compose them and it would be highly appropriate to work them out with the bride and bridegroom. To keep the marriage rite intact the creed, if it is to be said, should be recited *after* the intercessions.

As full a participation as is possible in the circumstances is urged for the bride and bridegroom and consequently the Order recommends that they should bring the offerings to the altar. This is not only the restoration of an ancient custom but is meant to be a symbol of their joint self-offering to God. In practice, it will mean that the bread and wine and other offerings they and the assembly may care to make will have to be placed near the sanctuary. Otherwise, the bride and bridegroom will have a long walk up and down the church.

For the eucharist proper three prefaces are provided (from one of which we have quoted above) which again give much the same teaching as is to be found elsewhere. There is one special insertion (*Hanc igitur*) which unfortunately may only be used with the Roman Canon. Others are required like the one given which emphasises the self-offering of the bride and bridegroom. It is apparently adapted from the Hanc igitur of the Roman sacramentaries.[32]

The Nuptial Blessing: A small change in the Order of Mass brings this prayer nearer communion and thus more clearly indicates that the covenant of marriage is sealed by the covenant of the eucharist.

---

[32] P. Gy, *art. cit.*, p. 135.

After the Lord's prayer, the embolism is omitted, the nuptial bless-ing is said and then follow immediately the prayer for peace, the giving of the 'peace', which the bride and bridegroom exchange, and communion, usually in both kinds.

Of the three prayers said at this point and usually known as the nuptial blessing, the first has its origins in the old sacramentaries. The version in use until recently is to be found in the Gregorian Sacramentary. It is a fine prayer but, as the Fathers of Vatican II observed, it needed to be changed since it was addressed exclusively to the bride.[33] Occasion was taken to revise or rather re-write the prayer, some questionable remarks have been removed, the models of conjugal fidelity are subsumed under a general phrase and a blessing for the bridegroom is included. The substance of the prayer has been retained but some difficulties remain[34] and it is in any case a little long. It has had to be changed to include the blessing of the husband and has thus turned the prayer from its original sense. It was, as is well known, a blessing of the *bride* and it was *she* who figured the church. Adjustments have been made to show that it is the marriage of husband and wife that is the symbol of the union of Christ with his church. However, towards the end passages have been added concerning the witness that marriage should give and family life.

Of the two new texts, which are more specifically blessings, the second is the simpler, more moralistic in tone and makes no attempt to convey the symbolism of Christian marriage. The first expresses quite adequately that symbolism. Marriage has its origin in the beginning of the human race and it was God's plan to reveal his love through it for it is 'an image of the covenant between you and your people' and so, in the Christian dispensation, becomes 'a sign of the marriage between Christ and his Church'. Love, covenant, people, Christ and church, that is the order of the thought and though it is not without difficulty for catechetical purposes, it is clear and can be handled if care is given to the matter. This prayer, as well as speaking of witness and family, is much more concrete in its language: it asks in simple language all can understand that the bride may be a good wife and mother and that the bridegroom

---

[33] CL 78.

[34] eg '(Marriage) ... symbolises the marriage of Christ and his Church.' Put like that it will not be understood by those unfamiliar with the scriptures. The same teaching in more assimilable form is given elsewhere.

may be a faithful husband and father. When couples are helped to choose the texts of their own marriage liturgy, they almost always go for this one.[35]

The Concluding Blessings: These are particular examples of the more solemn blessings that may now be given at the end of every Mass, are for the most part good in quality[36] and in one way or another sum up most of the themes which have been prominent throughout the rite. For England and Wales there is an alternative taken from the Book of Common Prayer and seems to be remotely related to the final blessing of the Sarum rite.[37]

Pastoral Considerations

That the pastoral care of couples before and after marriage is one of the primary duties of the parish clergy goes without saying but it is a subject that goes beyond the scope of this book. We must restrict ourselves to the immediate preparation before marriage.

In more recent years, thanks to a deepening understanding of the importance of marriage both on the part of the clergy and the laity, interviews before marriage have become *de rigueur*. And the purpose of these interviews is not simply instruction to ensure that the couples understand that they cannot get divorced 'because the church says so' nor yet to dispel unacceptable notions of birth prevention. They are to be prepared mentally and spiritually for the marriage they have already decided to undertake. Where both partners are Catholics, they should be encouraged to intensify their prayer-life, to make a particularly thorough confession and, if they do not already do so, to receive communion as often as possible. Mentally, they need to be led to a deeper understanding of the sacrament of marriage and for this purpose far the best material is the texts of the marriage liturgy itself. Copies of the marriage rite should be made available to them and the talks will take the texts as the point of departure. In the course of such instruction, it seems important to deepen their understanding of

---

[35] It should be noted that local conferences of bishops may have others composed (cf Introduction, 17).

[36] In the second set it is a pity that ICEL could think of nothing better than the phrase 'in good times and in bad'.

[37] Cf Proctor and Frere, *op. cit.*, p. 617, n. 1.

human love for it is this, as the texts say, that is taken up by and into the love of God.

On the other hand, there are difficulties for a celibate priest in giving such instruction. Since he has had no experience of married life, it ill becomes him to be heavily moralistic about its duties. With people of normal intelligence, an exposition of the meaning of marriage will enable the couple to draw their own conclusions. Where there is serious intent and goodwill—and experience shows that this is nearly always present—they will readily take up points themselves and apply them to their own situation.[38]

Where one or both of the partners is of weak faith, there is of course more to be done but experience shows that on the occasion of marriage, people in this condition can be brought back to religious practice—at least for a time—and their faith can be revived. The attitude of the priest here is of the greatest importance. Such people need to be encouraged, they may need a little elementary instruction on certain aspects of religious practice which they have forgotten and the duties of worship and prayer will have to be brought before them. They too of course will need to go to confession and here great tact is necessary. It may well be that they choose not to have a wedding Mass and if they do so choose, it would seem to be unwise to press them. The congregation may be largely non-Christian and it does not seem wise to expose the 'holy mysteries' to them. The marriage service with its scripture readings, prayers, hymns and blessings is more than adequate to meet the situation.[39]

The situation is sometimes more difficult. People of little or apparently no faith present themselves for marriage and while this situation is fraught with difficulties of one sort or another, it seems necessary to confront such people with the fact that marriage, like all the sacraments, is a sacrament of faith, both requiring faith and, in its celebration, expressing it. The problem is similar to that of 'delaying' baptism and the possible unpleasantness is as acute. But the question has to be asked: is it right to admit to a sacrament of faith those without the latter even if long ago they were bap-

---

[38] Where it is a question of what has been conventionally called 'the use of marriage', lay help would seem to be a necessity. This can often be got at Marriage Guidance Centres but there are far too few Catholic ones and more ought to be founded in every part of every diocese.

[39] Clerics sometimes have an exaggerated notion of what the laity, especially those of weaker faith or none, look for in a church service. Provided it is done well and with sincerity, they do not look for any elaborate ceremonial.

tised?[40] The spiritual preparation of such people of course is immensely difficult and often little enough can be done.

Then of course there are the Mixed (religious) Marriages. Some of the 'myth' that has surrounded such marriages in the past has disappeared. They no longer appear to be the 'evil' some thought them and the *Motu proprio* of 31 March 1970 has done much to ease the situation. However, it needs to be used in a human and pastoral and not a rigidly canonical way. In interview the attitude of the priest should be warm and welcoming and he should realise that often for the non-Catholic partner it will be the first time that he (or she) has ever had personal contact with a clergyman of any kind. The impressions such people carry away will be important in determining their attitude to religious practice (baptism of children, their first communion, etc) in the future. But here too there is often, one would say usually, a chance to revive religious faith and to encourage a re-thinking of attitudes.[41] It goes without saying that the *celebration* of these marriages is a matter of the greatest importance. The non-Catholic partner must be made to feel at home in the church and the ceremony must be done with all the care that is possible. It should strike a note of joy and not gloom and the clergy should realise that it offers an opportunity to proclaim the gospel to people who hear it all too rarely.[42]

In the preparation of the marriage liturgy there are a number of matters to be attended to. In going over the texts the bride and bridegroom should be encouraged (and guided) to choose the texts, readings, collects, prefaces, nuptial blessing and final blessing that they think best meets their own case. Likewise, the hymns to be sung and where in the service they are to be sung will be a matter of discussion and again guidance. Not all that is wanted is appropriate.[43] Finally, there will be the rehearsal which (rightly) almost

---

[40] In practice one will have recourse to the bishop, but, objectively and without rigorism, it is surely a bad thing to admit such marriages.

[41] Inter-church marriages are in a different category. For the preparation they present fewer difficulties though the subsequent pastoral care is both necessary and a matter calling for great tact. See *The Joint Care of Inter-Church Marriages*, the Joint Working Group of the British Council of Churches and the Roman Catholic Church (B.C.C. London).

[42] Needless to say, denunciations of divorce will hardly strike the right note and in the past some preachers have not been able to restrain themselves.

[43] Like the mother who insisted on a hymn paraphrase of the *De profundis* because, as the event proved, she was the only one who could sing it. Which she did in an ageing contralto. But this was years ago when things were less well ordered.

all people of today demand. In any case, it is the best tranquilliser in the world.

The Organisation of the Rite

Customs differ in different places and the Order has some regard for this factor. The celebrant, vested, may either welcome the bride at the church door or at the altar. The former custom is much favoured by some but in other places it is regarded as the *bride's* procession and a portly cleric preceding her is not likely to enhance the occasion. In any case the celebrant will welcome the bride and bridegroom and the assembly and the right moment to do this will will be after the liturgical greeting.

The Mass proceeds normally and it is to be noted that in all weddings, whether inside the Mass or outside it, whether of Catholics or non-Catholics, there is *always* to be a homily when the celebrant will speak about 'the mystery of Christian marriage, the dignity of wedded love, the grace of the sacrament and the res- ponsibilities of married people' (22).[44] The marriage rite proper follows and, given rehearsal, will present no difficulty. Where two rings are used it seems advisable to ask the bride and bridegroom to face each other, otherwise the putting on of the bridegroom's ring presents some difficulty.

In the intercessions that follow it would seem right that the bride and bridegroom should have some part in their composition.

After the Lord's prayer and before the embolism (which is omitted) comes the nuptial blessing.

The bride and bridegroom give the 'peace' to each other, as in the Sarum rite, and together they will receive holy communion in both kinds, if they so wish.

The Mass ends with the blessings and the departure of the bride, bridegroom and party.

The Order (for England and Wales) enjoins that the signing of the civil register shall take place after the intercessions and it is convenient if a table for it is placed somewhere near the sanctuary. There the bride and bridegroom with the witnesses can go with- out making yet another procession.

---

[44] The 'mystery of marriage' is not perhaps the happiest of phrases and, if used, might raise an unwelcome smile. It means of course the sacrament as related to the saving work of Christ.

Marriage outside the Mass

The rite is exactly the same as within the Mass and no difference is made between fully Catholic marriages and Mixed Marriages. Both take place within a ministry of the word, including the homily. There is a greeting, prayer (one of the collects from the Mass-formulas will be appropriate), the scripture readings with a psalm or a hymn and the homily which is to be 'drawn from the sacred text' (42).

The rest is as above. 'The entire rite may be concluded with the Lord's prayer' and with the blessings (51).

In the case of marriage between a Catholic and an unbaptised person there is a modified service which however does not differ in pattern from the one given above (55–66).

Some Critical Observations

As has been observed above, many of the Old Testament readings are difficult to use. Old Testament notions of marriages were quite different from ours, the position of women was almost totally different and there has of course been a considerable theological development. Here would seem to be a case where Old Testament texts could be dispensed with and the positive content of Genesis 1 or 2 could be brought into the homily if that were appropriate to the occasion.

In the rite for England and Wales there is an uncomfortable duplication at the beginning. The partners are asked (24) to state that they are free to marry and willing to take each other for husband and wife and then they do it all over again (25). In celebration this proves to be very clumsy. In 23 and 24 there is some wording that is hardly happy. The couple are asked to state their intentions. This phrase has certain overtones in English life, rather old-fashioned but now mock-humorous. In 24 it would have been more idiomatic to say 'I now ask you ...' instead of 'I *shall* ask you ...'

These are perhaps small matters and if one is to judge by the reactions of the people, the rite is a very successful one.

CHAPTER EIGHT

Holy Order[1]

SINCE THE liturgy of holy orders was revised and simplified in 1968 it is difficult to recall its former complexity. As you climbed up the sacred ladder so the complexity increased: vestings, anointings and the delivery of various cultic articles occurred at one point or another with a bewildering abandon. And if twenty or thirty years ago you had asked lay people what was the essential rite they would almost certainly have answered that it was the anointing of the hands for the priest and of the head for the bishop. Likewise it was commonly thought by both priests and laity that the priest-hood was the highest dignity or 'power' that could be given to a human being with the consequence that bishops appeared as a sort of sacramental afterthought. No doubt theology at this time was beginning to change or rather return to an older tradition but popular views remained the same. In other words the liturgy was putting the emphasis in the wrong place and popular theology and sentiment had got the proportions wrong. The Second Vatican Council, notably in the *Constitution on the Church*, reversed these notions and, taking up the theology that had been developing for some years, taught that the episcopate is the *primary* participation in the priesthood of Christ and that by it is conferred the full-ness of the priesthood. The key passages are the following:

'In bishops, therefore, for whom priest are assistants, our Lord Jesus Christ, the supreme High Priest, is present in the midst of those who believe. For sitting at the right hand of God the Father, he is not absent from the gathering of his high priests,

---

[1] The revision of the liturgy of holy order, episcopate, presbyterate and diaconate, appeared in 1968: *Pontificale Romanum: De Ordinatione Diaconi, Presbyteri et Episcopi*, Vatican Press. The institution of the minor ministries with the rites, the form of admission to the clerical state and the declaration in celibacy was promulgated by a *Motu proprio* of Paul VI, *Ministeria quaedam*, Vatican Press, 1972.

but above all through their excellent service he is preaching the word of God to all nations, and constantly administering the sacraments of faith to those who believe.' They are shepherds of the Lord's flock, they are servants of Christ, stewards of the mysteries of Christ and witnesses to the ministration of the Spirit to make men just. Thus 'For the discharging of such great duties, the apostles were enriched by Christ with a special out-pouring of the Holy Spirit, who came upon them. This spiritual gift they passed on to their helpers by the imposition of hands, and it has been transmitted down to us in episcopal consecration. This sacred synod teaches that by episcopal consecration is conferred the *fulness of the sacrament of orders,* that fulness which in the Church's liturgical practice and in the language of the holy Fathers of the Church is undoubtedly called the high priesthood, the apex of the sacred ministry.'[2]

This decisively restored the episcopate to its ancient place in the hierarchy of holy order and presumably settles once for all this particular controversy. No doubt the council does not solve all problems connected with papacy, episcopate and priesthood for the relationships at least in practical terms between the papacy and the episcopate on the one hand and between the episcopate and the priesthood or presbyterate on the other still remain partially unde-fined. This much at least is clear: bishops are not delegates of the pope nor are they, in the rude language used by some at one time or another, 'pope's curates'. Their order is of divine institution and with him they share a common pastoral care over the whole church.[3] *Vis-à-vis* his clergy the bishop is not an overlord. With them he shares a community of sacrament and presbyters asume their role, with their liturgical and pastoral functions enhanced, as his coun-sellors, as his *consilium* of the sort we discern in the *Apostolic Tradition* of Hippolytus.[4] The episcopate and the presbyterate form a sacramental communion of which brotherly cooperation is the

---

[2] *Constitution on the Church,* 21 (*Documents of Vatican II,* ed. W. Abbott, London, 1966), pp. 40–1.

[3] This settles in principle the long and sometimes unpleasant controversy that raged in the centuries after the Council of Trent. See J. D. Crichton, 'Church and Ministry from the Council of Trent to the First Vatican Council', in *The Christian Priesthood,* ed. N. Lash and J. Rhymer, London, 1970, pp. 117–39.

[4] VIII, ed. G. Dix (1937), pp. 13 foll.

consequence, that is, it is not merely in the moral order. It is an exigency of what both *are*.[5]

A third change brought about by the Council is that the diaconate has been restored as a permanent ministry in the church.[6] For centuries merely a stage on the way to the priesthood, it can now once again play its part in the life of the church. It is for this reason that the functions of the deacon have been somewhat extended and although there has not yet been time to see exactly what his work is likely to be, there is no doubt that in principle he could be a most valuable aid to the pastoral clergy. The restored diaconate also envisages married deacons (there are some already at work in parishes) and these two factors, permanence and marriage, have made it necessary to modify the ordination rite.

In addition, the four minor orders, now to be called 'ministries' have been reduced to two; tonsure and the subdiaconate have been suppressed and two new elements have been added: admission to the clerical state and the public declaration of intention to observe celibacy for all but married deacons.

With the promulgation of the documents on 'ministries' and the other two rites, the revision of this part of the Roman Pontifical is now complete.

Ordination to the Episcopate: the Liturgy

The order of events as given in the Pontificale Romanum of 1968 is as follows: the ordination of deacons, secondly of priests and finally of bishops. But since the Council re-established the primacy of the episcopate it will be best to reverse the order of the pontifical. Secondly, since the liturgy of Holy Orders is less familiar to the laity, a synopsis of the liturgy of each order will be given first and commentary on them will follow.

Like other sacramental acts, the ordination of a bishop takes place at the end of the ministry of the word.

1. Immediately after the gospel the *Veni, Creator Spiritus* or a similar hymn is sung.

---

[5] There remain certain anomalies, eg religious priests carrying out important pastoral work and yet having an ill-defined relationship to the episcopate. For useful reflections on this see David N. Power, *Ministers of Christ and his Church*, London, 1969. One can hardly forget that England was without Roman Catholic diocesan bishops for three hundred years (1559–1850) and this apparently by the desire of Rome.

[6] See *Constitution on the Church*, 29, ed. Abbott, pp. 55–6.

2. The bishop-elect approaches the principal consecrator and is presented.

3. The homily by the principal consecrator.

4. The interrogatory, that is, the traditional questions concerning a bishop's obligations and duties.

5. Prayer of the assembly in the form of the Litany of the Saints.

6. The bishop-elect kneels before the principal consecrator who in silence lays hands on his head. The co-consecrators do likewise after him.

7. The principal consecrator places the gospel-book on the elect's head and two deacons hold it there.

8. There follows the consecration prayer.

9. The principal consecrator anoints the elect's head with chrism.

10. He then gives him the gospel-book, the ring, places the mitre on his head (without formula) and puts the staff (crozier) in his hand.

11. If the elect is in his own cathedral he is now led to the episcopal chair (cathedra) and he and the consecrating bishops exchange the kiss of peace.

12. For the end of the Mass a special blessing is provided.

The Theology of the Episcopate

Perhaps 'theology' is too grand a word for what follows but, as is agreed by most scholars, it is possible to deduce a theology from a liturgy and the picture of the episcopate is clear in the new formulas for the ordination of a bishop.[7] There are two places where this theology may be discerned, first in the homily, the themes of which are suggested by the pontifical, and second, the consecration prayer.

The homily is not a fixed text of the rite. It is no more than a suggestion to the consecrating bishop and it is difficult to determine what 'external' authority it may have. But here, and in most of the other Orders, the text is heavily dependent on the documents of Vatican II whose authority it will naturally enjoy. The homily is in fact not much more than a catena of texts from the *Constitution on*

---

[7] This is the term the pontifical, in accordance with ancient usage, uses for the rite in general though it speaks of the 'consecration' of a bishop in the texts. Its significance is that a bishop is raised to or incorporated into the 'rank' or 'order' of bishops who together form the 'college'. The notions underlying these terms go back to Hippolytus and probably beyond.

the Church which, as we have observed above, restored the episcopate to its earlier place in the sacrament of Holy Orders. The main
lines of the homily then will be fairly familiar but it will be worthwhile to give a synopsis here.

Christ, sent by the Father into the world to redeem it, appointed
the apostles to continue his work of preaching, sanctifying and
ruling the flock entrusted to them. The bishops, who are the successors of the apostles, receive the gift of the Holy Spirit by
the imposition of hands and thereby receive also 'the fulness of the
sacrament of Order'. This 'tradition' has come down through the
succession of bishops from the time of the apostles until now so
that the redeeming work of Christ may be continued. Thus is
expressed the Council teaching on the place of the episcopate in
the structure of the ministry and it is interesting to observe that
the order is spoken of in terms of 'gift', presumably *charisma*,
which at once removes the whole notion of Holy Order out of the
legal and juridical sphere. The term 'power' is nowhere used in
the whole rite and yet it was largely in terms of power that the
episcopate-presbyterate was discussed for many centuries.

In the next paragraph we have a strong suggestion of a mystery-
theology of the sacrament. Christ, the high priest, is *present* in the
bishop with his presbyters. The *presbyterium* or the *consilium*, as
in the days of Hippolytus, is the *locus* of Christ. It is he who
preaches in the bishop, he who is present in him when he celebrates
the mysteries of faith and dispenses them to the people[8] and it
is he who through the bishop adds new members to his body.
Through him Christ leads the people in their earthly pilgrimage to
their home in heaven. This teaching seems to be a particular application of the Council's teaching that Christ is present in the liturgy
which is 'an exercise of the priestly office of Jesus Christ'.[9] It is
however a little surprising that the homily does not give expression
to another truth of the Council that there is only one priesthood,
that of Christ, of which holy orders are ministries.

Concluding the first part of the homily the consecrating bishop
addresses the people and asks them to receive among them him
'whom we are co-opting (*cooptamus*) into our college'.

Then he turns to address the bishop-elect personally. He is taken

---

[8] It is not quite clear whether '*mysteria fidei*' refers to teaching, *expounding*
the mysteries of faith, or as above, celebrating them in the liturgy. I think the
latter.

[9] *Constitution on the Liturgy*, 7.

from among men and is appointed to act for men in their relations with God (Hebrew 5 : 1). He is to be their servant, for the episcopate is not an honour but a responsibility (*nomen est operis non honoris*)[10] and his service is to be both liturgical and pastoral. Of the liturgy he is the president (*moderator*),[11] the minister (*dispensator*) and the guardian (*custos*). He is to preach and teach and in prayer and sacrifice he is to seek grace from God for the people. In his pastoral work the Good Shepherd is to be his model. He is to work *with* his fellows in the ministry (*in ministerio consortes*) and he is to have a special care for the poor, the oppressed and the stranger or exile. Those not of the flock also have claim on his care. But, a member of the college of bishops, he shares with them 'the care of all the churches', especially of those in need. 'Give your care to the whole flock in which the Holy Spirit has set you to rule the church of God[12] in the name of the Father whose image you show forth in the church,[13] in the name of his Son, Jesus Christ whose function of teacher, priest and pastor you perform and in the name of the Holy Spirit who gives life to the church and strength to you in your weakness.' A noble ending and a remarkable summary of the bishop's role in the church.

The second text that claims our attention is the consecration prayer itself. As is now well known, this is the prayer that is to be found in the *Apostolic Tradition* of Hippolytus dated about 215 AD.[14] Just as few imagined that we should ever be able to use his eucharistic prayer, there were probably fewer who thought that his prayer for the consecration of bishops would oust the text that is found in the Leonine (or Verona) Sacramentary and that was the consecration prayer of the Roman rite from at least the sixth century. Yet this has now been done and we may adopt the view of a recent writer that in the whole history of the liturgy of ordination there has never been a reform comparable to this.[15]

Dom Bernard Botte, who played a principal part in the revision of the liturgy of ordination, reveals the motives that led to this change.[15a] The former prayer was long and even so, as he says, 'short' on theology. To make up for its deficiencies, to the sacramentary

---

[10] An ancient phrase.
[11] Cf CL 41.
[12] Cf Acts 20:28.
[13] Cf St Ignatius of Antioch, Ep. ad Trall., 3.
[14] Ed. G. Dix (1937), I, iii, pp. 4–6.
[15] B. Kleinheyer, 'L'ordination des prêtres', *LMD*, 98, 1969, p. 94.
[15a] *LMD*, 98, pp. 113 ff.

texts a series of hortatory passages were added at a later date. These did little to relieve the essential poverty of the principal text and when the anointing of the head was introduced in the tenth century the prayer was divided into two parts. This threw the emphasis on the anointing, making it look more important than the laying-on of hands which in the earliest tradition of both East and West was always *the* rite of episcopal as of priestly ordination. Further, since the prayer of Hippolytus underlies all the rites of ordination of the Eastern Church, it was clear that its restoration to the Roman rite would be a notable ecumenical gesture. So it was done and the prayer appears in the Roman Pontifical of 1968 with only quite minor verbal changes. It is clear, simple and significant and its restoration to use must be regarded with satisfaction.

After a preliminary recalling of Old Testament arrangements the prayer goes on: 'Pour out now on this your Elect that strength (*virtutem*) which is from you, the sovereign Spirit, whom you gave to your beloved Son (Child=Servant) Jesus Christ, the Spirit he himself gave to the holy apostles who established the church in different places to the unceasing praise and glory of your name.' Although Dom Botte did not think it necessary or even desirable, the decision was made that all the consecrating bishops should pronounce this part together. It is to be regarded as the 'form', though such notions were foreign to the church of the time, as Dom Botte states. The whole prayer is consecratory. However, it was a compromise which some judged to be necessary.

The last part of the prayer lays out the functions of the bishop and in so doing reveals what he is. He is the shepherd of the holy flock of God, he exercises the high priesthood (*summum sacer-dotium*), serving God night and day and by 'offering the gifts of your holy church' he is to propitiate God unceasingly. By the power of the Holy Spirit he has the authority of the high priesthood to remit sins. Likewise he enjoys the authority once given to the apostles to order the offices concerning pastoral care. He is to be gentle and clean of heart, offering (by his life) a sweet savour (to the Father) through the Son 'through whom is given glory and power and honour, with the Holy Spirit in holy church, now and throughout endless ages'.

Short though this prayer is, expert commentary[16] reveals the depth and richness of its content. Among other things it consists

---

[16] A. Rose, 'Le Prière consécratoire de l'évêque', *LMD*, 98, 1969, pp. 127 ff.

of a tissue of scripture texts and references that it would take too long to draw out here. We can give no more than the main lines of interpretation. There is a very close correlation between the baptism of Christ with the illapse of the Spirit on him, the Pentecost event and the liturgical celebration when that same Spirit who came upon Christ and through him was given to the apostles, is, now by the laying-on of hands, conceived to be given to the bishop: 'Pour out *now* the power of that Spirit whom *you* (the Father) gave to your Son and whom *he* gave to his apostles.' This Spirit is the sovereign Spirit *(pneuma hēgemonikon)*, the *spiritus principalis* of psalm 50:14 (LXX and Vulg.) and signifies the 'power of ruling' or government though the style of government is given in the rest of the prayer (eg *mansuetudine et mundo corde*). But it is important to realise that this is the *specific* gift of the Holy Spirit for the bishop whose office is *primarily* pastoral though not exclusive of liturgical functions through which he in fact exercises the 'high priesthood'.[17] The liturgy itself, the offering of the eucharist, the forgiving of sins, prayer, is a pastoral service of God's people.

It is this realisation that the episcopate is a pastoral charge, in this sense, that made it possible for Vatican II to get rid of the topsy-turvy theology of orders which had been current since the early Middle Ages and re-establish the right relationship between the episcopate and the presbyterate. No longer is it a question of the presbyter possessing certain 'powers', eg that of consecrating the eucharist ('than which there is no higher') and, as it was said, making him 'equal' to the bishop so that the latter appeared as some sort of sacred appendage. The bishop is the chief pastor of his diocese and in him principally are vested all the functions, both the purely pastoral and the liturgical, that belong to the priestly office.[18]

The next part of the prayer that merits some commentary is that which speaks of the functions of the bishop. 'Father, *knower of hearts*, grant to this your servant whom you *have chosen* for the

---

[17] As Rose points out, *art. cit.*, p. 133, the prayers for the ordination of priests and deacons ask for 'the Spirit of grace and counsel' for the presbyters and 'the Spirit of grace and zeal (in service)' for the deacons.

[18] This at least is the vision of Vatican II and of Hippolytus. It is another question whether this is all to be said and the New Testament experts seem to endorse nowadays the high likelihood of a plurality of ministries, on a rather different pattern, in New Testament times. Still, holy order in the terms of bishop-presbyter-deacon goes back beyond Hippolytus to Ignatius of Antioch and, probably, to Clement of Rome.

episcopate'; this recalls the context of Acts 1:15–26 when Matthias was elected to the apostolic body and thus relates the election of a bishop to the election of an apostle.[19] All this is a much more profound way of expressing the notion of apostolic succession than that of a merely tactile continuity by the laying-on of hands from the beginning till now. The apostolic succession, as was made clear as early as Irenaeus,[20] is wider and deeper than that. To understand episcopacy we have to see it as existing in the apostolic context which involves a succession of *doctrine*, the preservation of the unity of the faith and the *koinonia* of the local church which in turn is an indispensable link in the *communion* of the great church. The bishop's liturgy, that is, the liturgy he presides over, surrounded by the *presbyterium* or counsel of priests and the deacons, who are his and the community's servants, a celebration at which he proclaims the word of God for the building up of the body of Christ, is the sacrament-sign of this *koinonia* or communion. This in miniature *is* the church and the bishop's key position in its structure and his necessary role in its action are very clear.

Even in the statements defining the functions of the bishop the background of the prayer remains richly scriptural. He is to be the Good Shepherd and the whole world of the biblical teaching on shepherd is immediately evoked. Peter was given the supreme pastorate over the flock of Christ (John 21:12), the heads of the local communities are called shepherds (Ephesians 4:11), in Acts (20:28) Paul tells the *episcopoi* that they are to 'shepherd' the church of God and in 1 Peter 5:2 the 'elders', whoever they were, are exhorted to 'be shepherds of the flock of God that is entrusted to you'.[21]

He is 'to exercise the high priesthood'. The Latin is odd: '*exhibeat* tibi summum sacerdotium'; presumably the translator had difficulty in rendering the Greek which means precisely 'to act as high priest' (*archierateuein*). But what is surprising is that the office is called a 'priesthood' and even a 'high priesthood', terms restricted in the New Testament and in sub-apostolic literature generally, to Christ himself. However, if we are to judge by Cyprian's use of them, they had become general less than fifty years

---

[19] Rose, *art. cit.*, p. 135. This is Lécuyer's view too.
[20] *Adv. Haer.*, III, ii–iii (Eng. trans. Bettenson, *The Early Church Fathers*, 1956, pp. 122–6).
[21] Cf A. Rose, *art. cit.*, p. 137.

after Hippolytus.[22] At any rate, if the prayer of Hippolytus seems to be less 'sacerdotal' than subsequent prayers and theological statements, this term is sufficient to show that he thought of the bishop as not only a priest but the chief priest of his diocese.

This priest serves (*leitourgounta*) God night and day, and presumably prayer is intended here, but it is also his function 'to offer the gifts of your holy church' (*prospherein dora*) and thus gain God's favour for his people. This is clearly a eucharistic expression and refers to the bishop's role as the (principal) offerer of the eucharist and it is interesting to recall that the 'prayer of offering', that appears in the *Apostolic Tradition* and has now (with additions) become the second Eucharistic Prayer, follows on immediately after the ordination of the bishop as a model for his use. Thus, while there is but this single reference to the eucharist in the whole prayer, it says all that is necessary and if the whole liturgy is taken together, as it is in the *Apostolic Tradition*, the bishop's function in this regard is made amply clear.

In the perspective of the prayer, the function of remitting sins is an action of this same priesthood and here again, as the Greek text makes clearer, these few phrases recall the New Testament at almost every step (cf Matthew 9:6; John 20:23 and for the giving of the Spirit, the same place, verse 21).[23]

In the same way, what might be called the administrative duties of the bishop, the supervision of the clergy, and the quality of his own life which is to be marked by gentleness and purity of heart, are exercises of his priestly function and the latter, in accordance with New Testament teaching, is to be a sacrifice (*offerens tibi odorem suavitatis*) which is combined with the offering of the eucharist.[24] Even this brief examination of the prayer will have revealed its depths and scriptural richness and we may conclude with A. Rose that 'a comparison of the vocabulary and style of this prayer with the New Testament and the writings of the earliest Fathers reveals the profound unity that exists between it and the sources of revelation'.

The other texts, eg the interrogatory, and rites add nothing of substance to what is contained in the homily and the prayer and

---

[22] See P. Gy, 'Vocabulaire antique du sacerdoce', pp. 141–4 in *Etudes sur le Sacrement de l'Ordre*, Paris, 1957; (Eng. trans. 1962, pp. 98–115).

[23] Cf A. Rose, *art. cit.*, p. 138.

[24] Further scriptural references will be found in A. Rose, *art. cit.*, pp. 139–41.

this is all as it should be. The prayer is the climax of the rite and all that follows are what they should be, namely *ritus explicativi*, gestures and accompanying texts which unfold the meaning of the prayer. In the questions we need here note only the one that clearly reflects Vatican II theology: 'Is it your will to build up the body of Christ, his church and to remain united with it along with the order of bishops under the authority of the successor of blessed Peter, the apostle?' To this of course he answers that it is.

Among the rites subsequent to the prayer, the formula for the anointing of the head deserves brief attention. In the former liturgy this rite appeared as the climax and the formula was 'Let your head be anointed and consecrated with heavenly blessing (to incorporate you) into the pontifical order.'[25] The new formula clearly indicates that the anointing is no more than the explicitation of what has already been done in and by the consecration prayer: 'May God who *has* made you a sharer in the high priesthood of Christ, fill you with the grace of (this) mystical anointing and by the richness of (his) spiritual blessing make you fruitful.' The gesture and the substance (chrism) are a symbol of the fulness of the Spirit which has been given by the laying-on of hands. Here symbolism is performing its proper role.

The Rite: a Brief Commentary

The former rite of consecration was one of the most complicated of the Roman liturgy and except to the connoisseur of ceremonial (and there were such), wearisome and largely incomprehensible. It will already have been noticed that the new rite is comparatively simple. Of course even this can be 'built up' if anyone is disposed to do so but in structure it is simple and all the signs are that it is meant to be presented as such. In what follows we attempt to isolate the most significant moments and to indicate some of the changes.

First, it will be as well to dispel an illusion that is still common. It has been thought for a long time that two assistant bishops to the principal consecrator were necessary for validity. As we see in the early centuries of the church, it was the bishops of a province or region who presided at the election of a bishop and who proceeded to 'order' him, that is incorporate him into the episcopal

---

[25] The Latin is odd and needs interpretation! '*Ungatur et consecretur caput tuum, caelesti benedictione, in ordine pontificali.*'

order. In the course of time and as the collegiality of the episcopate began to be forgotten, they were reduced to two, the smallest number to express the notion that a man *was* added to the episcopal college. Validity is a quite modern notion. The new Order returns to the older custom: at least two bishops must assist and lay-on hands but it is recommended that *all* the bishops present (and these will normally be the bishops of the province at least) 'ordain' *(sic)* the elect.

Formerly, two bishops introduced the elect—as if only bishops could introduce a bishop even if he was only *in fieri*. Now two priests *(presbyteri)* present him to the principal consecrator. There follows the reading of the Apostolic Commission and the homily.

Formerly the interrogatory (which took place at the beginning of the Mass) was a formidable affair. There was a long oath-formula in which the elect promised among other things to 'pursue' *(persequar!)* and fight *(impugnabo)* heretics, schismatics and those who had rebelled against the Lord. For all its bloodcurdling solemnity, bishops seem to have taken little notice of the content of this oath for several hundreds of years. There followed a long interrogatory in which the elect was required to profess his faith in detail and to reject an amazing number of heresies. All of course was in Latin, no doubt to the edification of the admiring multitudes who heard their bishops talking Latin for the first and only time in their lives.[26] In the new rite, in response to the questions (nine), the elect promises to proclaim the gospel, to guard the faith handed down from the apostles, to act in union with the college of bishops, to give due obedience to the successor of St Peter, to care for the people and clergy *(comministris)* entrusted to him and to exercise the pastoral ministry for the good of all. All very reasonable and simple.

The Litany of Saints that follows calls for no special mention though we may note that the collect concluding it has been salvaged from the former rite where it appeared as the introductory prayer to the prayer of consecration.

The *ceremonial* of the central part of the rite that comes next deserves more attention. The bishops stand together with the principal consecrator in the midst of them; the elect comes forward

---

[26] In my edition of the *Pontificale Romanum* this procedure occupies six pages, not counting the rubrics!

and kneels before them. The principal consecrator then in silence lays hands on the elect's head and then the other bishops do likewise. So far this is exactly the ceremonial of the *Apostolic Tradition* and its symbolism is as rich as it is profound. Here the gesture of the laying-on of hands, which always means the giving of the Spirit, appears in its most significant form: the gesture alone, without words, is sufficiently strong to convey its message.

Then comes a rite that is first found in the East (fourth century?), the imposition of the gospel book on the head of the elect. Formerly it was held by two bishops (no less!); now by two deacons who were the original ministers. What is its meaning? It is not wholly clear. One view is that it signifies the giving of the fulness of the Spirit and one could point to Luke 4:16–21 as its possible source. The other is that it signifies that the bishop is to live under the yoke of the gospel and this view finds support in the gesture itself: the book is laid on and then held over the elect's head (not as formerly on his neck). Of the two I prefer the former though the second is better supported by the documents.[27]

The consecration prayer proceeds and apart from the section 'Effunde super hunc electum ... nominis tui' is said (sung) by the principal consecrator alone. The book is now removed and the anointing of the head follows immediately. Once that is finished, the principal consecrator delivers the book of the gospel to the new bishop with the charge to preach the word of God. He then receives the ring, symbol of his 'marriage' (a very ancient notion) to his diocese. The mitre is placed on his head without formula and the pastoral staff, with its obvious significance, is delivered to him. As Dom Botte drily remarks, since the mitre is no more than a *couvre-chef*, a head-cover, it was not thought that there was any need for a formula. The revisers rejected the bizarre symbolism of the old Order.[28] It has been remarked that since the mitre has no symbolism and is in fact no more than a head-cover, it would have been better to delay investiture with it until after the delivery of the staff. It would make better sense and, if anyone is still 'gone on' mitres, would make a nice aesthetic climax. It may be noted that if any-

---

[27] See *Etudes sur le sacrement de l'Ordre* (Paris, 1957), discussion between B. Botte and J. Lècuyer, pp. 36–7; Botte holds for the first view and Lécuyer for the second. Apparently the original meaning was already lost by the time of St John Chrysostom (died 407).

[28] The origin of the mitre seems to have been the Phrygian cap—no very respectable *couvre-chef* at any time in history: it begins with the priests of Cybele and ends with the French revolution!

one wishes to bless these insignia, this is to be done before the service. The rite concludes with the kiss of peace exchanged between the new bishop and the other bishops. This has the special significance on this occasion that the new bishop is welcomed among the bishops as one of them. Finally, if the new bishop is consecrated in his own cathedral it is he who is the principal celebrant of the eucharist that follows.

The Priesthood or Presbyterate[29]

If the revision of the liturgy of the episcopate is the greatest reformation of it since the third century, that of the presbyterate is hardly less so though the revision has taken a rather different line. The former liturgy of the presbyterate, which has been described as a 'maquis presque impénétrable',[30] has been very considerably simplified and it would serve no good purpose either to detail the rite as it was or to note every change in the new one. The first thing that is important is that the revisers have adopted the same pattern for all three orders: laying-on of hands and prayer of consecration/ordination, the subsidiary rites (anointing) and the delivery of insignia. This alone shows, as it has been observed,[31] that they are three degrees of one and the same sacrament. It is a point worth making since people have been asking: 'Is, then, the episcopate an eighth sacrament?'

Ordination to the Presbyterate: the Liturgy

1. After the gospel the candidates are called by a deacon (not by a bogus archdeacon).
2. They are presented by a priest delegated for the purpose.
3. The homily.
4. The interrogatory (new).
5. Litany of Saints.
6. The act of ordination. The candidates approach the bishop one by one who lays hands on them in silence. The priests who are present do likewise and then form a half circle round the

---

[29] There is a question of terminology. 'Priesthood' applies primarily to Christ, second to the episcopate which is the primary participation in it and for centuries *sacerdos* meant 'bishop'. On the other hand, the term priest has become so common for the one who has the second rank in the priesthood that it seems somewhat artificial to use the term 'presbyter'. I have used it whenever I have wished to point the contrast between the episcopate and the presbyterate.

[30] An 'almost impenetrable thicket'; cf B. Kleinheyer in *LMD*, 98, 1968, p. 95.

[31] *LMD, num. cit.*, p. 68.

bishop though the rubrics do not say that they continue to hold their hands raised. The prayer of ordination follows.

7. The anointing of the hands. First, priests, without ceremony or formula, arrange the candidates' stoles and invest them with chasubles. (Formerly this was a more elaborate ceremony done by the bishop.) The bishop then anoints the hands of each (on the palms) with *chrism* (formerly oil of catechumens!) while either the *Veni, Creator Spiritus* or psalm 109 with the antiphon 'Christ the Lord, high priest for ever in the line of Melchisedek offered break and wine', may be sung.[32]

8. The delivery of the bread and wine (not chalice) while psalm 99 or *Iam non dicam* or other chants may be sung.

9. The kiss of peace ends the ordination rite and the ordained concelebrate Mass with the bishop. The Order urges that other priests should be invited to celebrate with them.

Commentary

From this brief synopsis of the rite it is clear that it is simple and straightforward. There is the laying-on of hands, the ordination prayer and the anointing of the candidates' hands which clearly appears as a subsidiary rite. The 'tradition of the instruments' which played so large a part in the ordination of priest for so many centuries has been transformed and the heavy emphasis on the priesthood as a cult-ministry has disappeared. Likewise, other subsidiary rites such as the commissioning of the priest to forgive sins after communion (which got there by accident) have been suppressed.[33] It is however on the quality of the ordination prayer that the whole rite must be judged and it is this that we will consider in a moment. As in the liturgy of the ordination of a bishop, so here the prayer is preceded by a specimen homily which merits consideration.

It must be emphasised that it is no more than a specimen and the ordaining bishop will want to adapt it to the circumstances of the time and place and speak more directly to the people than this

---

[32] Other *suitable* chants may be used.

[33] The explanation is that in the Romano-German Pontifical of the tenth century the rite ended with the mention of the participation of the new priests in the eucharist. When in the twelfth-thirteenth century a formula for the laying-on of hands was added a copyist finding a space at the end of the rite inserted the phrase 'Whose sins you shall forgive ...' in that place. Hence the rite after communion! See Kleinheyer, *LMD*, 98, 1968, p. 102 and also his long study *Die Priesterweihe im römischen Ritus* (Trier, 1962), pp. 208–11.

sample indicates. It is not without importance however since it is heavily dependent on the documents of Vatican II.[34]

The whole people of God is a royal priesthood,[35] but Christ, the high priest, chose disciples to perform the priestly office for the people. As the Father sent the Son, so are they sent into the world to continue Christ's work. These are the bishops who share the teaching, priestly and pastoral functions of Christ. Presbyters are their cooperators sharing with them those same functions in the service of the people. More particularly, they are ministers of Christ's priesthood (*inserviant*) and through their ministry the church, that is the people of God, is built up and grows.

Here the total dependence of the earthly ministry on the priesthood of Christ is made very plain, as is also the truth that the priesthood is *for* the service of the people.

The image of Christ is to be formed in them (*configurandi*), they are to be united to the priesthood of bishops (so there is a *sacramental* and not merely a juridical union between priest and bishop) and they will be consecrated to preach the gospel, to care for the people and to celebrate the Lord's sacrifice. The order of the functions is noteworthy and their implications are then spelt out. They are to meditate on the word of God, to believe what they read, to teach what they believe and to imitate in their lives what they preach. In this way their word and their lives will help to build up the people of God.

Likewise, their liturgical ministry is not to be that of a mere functionary. Christ's sacrifice which they celebrate is to be the pattern of their lives which will be the expression of the paschal mystery of Christ's passion and resurrection. Their personal lives will be fused with their liturgical function: they are to realise what they are doing and to imitate (in their lives) what they celebrate. Thus is salvaged the phrase found in the address of Durandus of Mende in the thirteenth century Pontifical. But this liturgical function too must be orientated to the service of the people: it is through it that the people are able effectively to make their 'spiritual sacrifice',[36] now united with Christ's, to the Father.

The ministry of the other sacraments, baptism, penance and the anointing of the sick is recalled and the candidates are reminded that

---

[34] Especially that on the Church and the *Decree on the Ministry and Life of Priests* (ed. Abbott, pp. 532–76).

[35] Cf 1 Peter 2:9; Rev. 1:6; 5:10.

[36] 1 Peter 2:5 and cf Rom. 12:1. This teaching is from the Decree on Priests.

prayer too is a ministry. They are to praise and thank God in the Divine Office and pray not only for the people of God but for the whole world.

Finally, there is the pastoral care of the people committed to their charge and here their model is to be the Good Shepherd who came to seek and save that which was lost, to serve and not to be served. Caring for their people in all these ways, priests are to lead them 'through Christ in the Holy Spirit to God the Father'.

Of its nature a model address like this can hardly be very specific or concrete though it may be thought to mention at least all that is important. The priest's liturgical role which was so heavily emphasised for so many centuries is at least put in the context of life and service. It is to be seen as the sacramental expression of *both* and the demands that view of the priesthood makes are very great. But perhaps there is still not sufficient emphasis on mission. There are few, if any, countries in the world where the church is not in a missionary posture and vast numbers of priests are looking for inspiration and help to enable them to carry out the mission they believe is theirs. Here above all the episcopal celebrant of the sacrament will need to speak out of his knowledge and experience of his local church and see ordination as a unique occasion to give both priests and people a new vision of their missionary role.

The Ordination Prayer

This is of course the key text of the whole rite and the revisers had difficult decisions to make. Having adopted the Hippolytus text for the ordination of bishops, they will naturally have thought about his text for the ordination of priests. But first, it is rather short and *at first sight* remarkably unexplicit about the nature and role of the presbyterate. Secondly, in the *Apostolic Tradition* the prayer runs straight on from that for the ordination of a bishop and one gathers the impression that in the mind of the author the ordination of presbyters regularly took place on the occasion of the ordination of bishops. Since presbyters share in the priestly office of the bishop, the specifically priestly roles are indicated in the prayer for the ordination of bishops. Nowadays however a presbyter is rarely ordained at the same time as a bishop and the prayer would be evidently inadequate. The revisers, then, chose the old Roman prayer[37] in a slightly shortened and revised edition.

---

[37] *Sacram. Veron.* (ed. Mohlberg), pp. 121–2.

A brief summary of the Hippolytus prayer will provide a useful term of comparison with the present text.

The prayer asks that as God of old looked on his chosen people and commanded Moses to appoint 'elders', whom he filled with the Spirit which he had given to Moses, so may God look upon this servant (here present) and grant him the Spirit of grace and of counsel that belongs to the *presbyterium*. By the Spirit may he help and govern the people of God with a pure heart. The prayer ends with petitions that 'we' (bishops and priests) may, by the gift of God, never lose this Spirit and may serve him, praising him through his Child Jesus Christ through whom is glory and power with the Holy Spirit in the Church now and for endless ages. That is all. There is no mention of the presbyters' liturgical function if only perhaps because at this time they did not celebrate the eucharist independently but always celebrated with the bishop.[38] The proper functions of the presbyter are counsel and government and this is wholly in accord with the thinking of the ancient world on the 'council of elders'.[39] Hippolytus seems to witness to a very primitive arrangement, close to the New Testament, and suggests the situation thought by many scholars to be that of the famour First Letter of Clement to the Corinthians: it was sent by the Roman presbytery. We note however that it is the *same* Spirit that is given to both bishop and presbyter and, as the theology of orders developed, it was seen that the presbyter shared certain functions with the bishop. The reference to Moses makes this certain.[40] In Numbers 11:16, 17 we read 'I will take some of the spirit which is on you and put it on them', that is the seventy elders whom Moses appointed to help him in ruling the people. The Hippolytus prayer interprets this 'spirit' as the Holy Spirit of the New Testament and it is this same spirit who is given to both bishops and priests. But the ruling function, and we may add the counselling and judging functions, of the presbyterate are also made clear.

This exegesis helps us to understand the Moses-typology which is retained in the Roman prayer which we will now consider. The pattern of the prayer is similar to the Hippolytan one though more explicit even if by later medieval standards insufficiently so. After

---

[38] Text of *Ap. Trad.* (ed. Dix), pp. 13–14.

[39] Cf A. Lemaire, *Les Ministères aux origines de l'Eglise*, Paris, 1971.

[40] The reference to Moses is interesting not only as testimony of a quite advanced typology but because it is found in the later Roman prayer and has remained throughout.

an introduction which speaks of hierarchy, and growth and order in nature, the prayer speaks of the growth of the degrees of the priesthood and of sacramental institutions. God has set bishops (here called *pontifices*, a Roman pagan word) in the church to rule over the people and *they* have elected others 'of second rank' to help them. At this point Moses is evoked and also the institution of the seventy elders through whom God 'propagated the spirit' (a curious phrase) and who were the helpers of Moses in ruling the people. But to this is added at this point mention of the Aaronic priesthood which is a foreshadowing of the Christian priesthood. Priests are ordained so that there may be a sufficiency to 'offer saving sacrifices and to provide a more frequent celebration of the sacraments'. The prayer has become more 'sacerdotal'. Yet, as the text goes on to indicate, presbyters share with the bishop in the government of the people and in his teaching office and as a recent commentator has observed,[41] the spirit of the bishop animates the whole *presbyterium*. The prayer ends with a passage which has been re-written in the interests of mission: 'May they (the presbyters) prove to be honest cooperators with our order so that the word of the gospel may reach the ends of the earth and all the peoples of the world may be gathered to Christ and made one holy people of God.'

Priests, then, are clearly subordinate to the bishop but they are also his co-workers enjoying, as we have observed, a sacramental union with him. They share in his work, whether that is liturgical or pastoral or teaching. It is not for a liturgical text to give a theological elaboration of its themes but there is sufficient here to show that the *lex orandi* (the rule of prayer) provides a sound basis for the *lex credendi* (the rule of faith). *This* is what the priest is even if it is not all that he is.

This prayer with the laying-on of hands by bishop and presbyters is the climax of the rite and in the revised liturgy stands out as such. In the old rite it was overshadowed by the anointing of the hands which was solemnly inaugurated with the singing of the *Veni, Creator Spiritus*. At this point everyone felt that the real business was beginning. In the new rite the anointing is clearly explicative: it unfolds the meaning of the ordination prayer and of the laying-on of hands, which is the principal sign of the giving of the Spirit, that precedes it. The formula used for the anointing shows that the

---

[41] P. Jounel, *L'Eglise en Prière*, p. 495.

rite is the continuation of the thought in the prayer: 'May our Lord Jesus Christ whom the Father anointed with the power and the Holy Spirit keep you that you may sanctify the Christian people and offer sacrifice to God.' It is in this way that 'the portion of the spirit' who descended on the seventy elders from Moses now descends through Christ, the Anointed of God, on the presbyter by the laying-on of hands. And his function to sanctify, or as I suppose we should say, to be the means of sanctification of the people and of offering sacrifices, is also made plain.[42]

While the anointing takes place either the *Veni, Creator* or some other chant or psalm 109 with the antiphon 'Christ the Lord, priest in the line of Melchisedek, offered bread and wine' may be sung. It may be thought that the use of the *Veni, Creator* at this point perpetuates the misunderstanding of the old rite. Yet it is traditional and it is not easy to suggest any other place in the rite for this hymn which is otherwise wholly appropriate to the occasion. A possible place was at the end of the Litany of Saints though this has been provided with an ancient collect that formerly preceded the prayer of ordination. Since it prays for 'the blessing of the Holy Spirit and the grace of the priesthood' the hymn would have looked too much like a duplicate.

The cultic function of the priesthood has been sufficiently emphasised by the foregoing gestures and texts and for this reason it was possible to modify others. The solemn clothing with the sacerdotal vestments by the bishop has given way to a simpler action: members of the clergy present re-arrange the stole and put on the chasuble. The famous *traditio instrumentorum* (the giving of the paten and chalice) with its emphatic formula 'Receive the power to offer sacrifice to God for both the living and the dead' and which in all the later Middle Ages was regarded as essential to the rite, has been reduced to a giving of the *people's* offering of bread and wine (in paten and chalice) which are to be used in the Mass that follows. This is made plain by the accompanying formula: 'Receive the offering of the holy people which is to be offered to God. Realise what you are to do, imitate the mystery you are going to handle and conform your life to the mystery of the Lord's cross.' Apart from other considerations, the reason for the change is that the priest

---

[42] The Latin word *'custodiat'* 'keep' or 'guard' you is a little odd. Something like 'appoint' would have been more to be expected. Perhaps, however, the revisers see the 'appointing' as done in the ordination prayer itself. Anyway, it is difficult to translate *custodiat* in this place!

has *already*, by virtue of the ordination prayer, received the power to offer the eucharist.

The ordination rite concludes with the giving of the kiss of peace by the bishop and the attendant priests to the newly ordained. Meanwhile, during the giving of the offering and the kiss of peace either the well known *Iam non dicam servos* ('I will no longer call you servants ...') or the thanksgiving psalm (99) *Iubilate*, with the antiphon 'You are my friends ...', may be sung. The newly ordained then concelebrate with the bishop. The giving of the kiss of peace is of course, as in the ordination of the bishop, the sign that the newly ordained are incorporated into the *presbyterium*.

One or two other matters call for comment. After the homily and before the Litany there comes an interrogatory, which is new, and the promise of obedience which has been moved from the end of the ordination Mass to this place. Obviously a great improvement. The four questions the bishop asks the candidates sum up the four great themes of this new ordination rite. Put positively they run like this: The priest, as co-worker with the bishop and under the guidance of the Holy Spirit, has a pastoral care over the people of God. He is commissioned to celebrate the mysteries of Christ in praise of God and for the sanctification of the people. He has a ministry of the word, the proclamation of the gospel and the teaching of the Catholic faith. Finally, he promises with the help of God to enter day by day into an ever closer union with Christ and with him to consecrate himself to God for the salvation of the people. The union of personal life with pastoral function is emphasised throughout the rite and an attempt is thus made to close the gap between truly priestly work, whether in liturgy, preaching or care of people, and the *fonctionnairisme* which was the plague of the priesthood for so long.

The promise of obedience formerly came at the end of the ordination Mass along with a clutter of other rites, the final unfolding of the chasuble, the commissioning to forgive sins and the famous 'penance' which was imposed for being ordained! The promise looked very much like an afterthought and yet it is one of the most important and difficult duties of the priest's life. It is wholly appropriate that it should be brought forward and placed with the undertakings which we have considered above. It should be noted that the gesture of laying the hands in the bishop's folded hands, comes from feudal custom and the church does not wish any longer to insist on it. Bishops' conferences may decide on some other gesture.

It is curious that the text of the Order makes no provision for priests of religious orders. No doubt provision *will* be made but why not write it into the text?

The Diaconate

Along with the episcopate and the presbyterate the diaconate is one of the primitive ministries of the church. It is the first degree of the sacrament of holy order and its importance has always been realised even if the addition of the subdiaconate to major orders by Innocent III in the thirteenth century did something to overshadow it. Since the early Middle Ages it has too been no more *in fact* than a stage on the way to the priesthood. Recently the church has made two changes of considerable importance. The Second Vatican Council envisaged the setting up of a *permanent* diaconate and the subdiaconate has finally been suppressed.[43]

The first change is of considerable pastoral importance and has brought with it some minor modifications of the rite. Canonically speaking, it means that the obligations of celibacy and recitation of the Divine Office have now been attached to the diaconate. Furthermore, admission to the clergy is now delayed until the diaconate, the rite of tonsure being abolished, and a special rite of commitment to celibacy for non-married candidates is attached to the diaconate. These changes hardly affect the rite of the diaconate and something will be said about them lower down.

A Synopsis of the Rite

1. After the gospel of the Mass the candidates are presented to the bishop by a priest appointed for the purpose.
2. The homily.
3. The interrogatory and promise of obedience.
4. Prayer, the Litany of Saints.
5. The bishop (alone) lays on hands in silence.
There follows the ordination prayer.
6. The vesting with stole and dalmatic by other deacons or presbyters.
7. The delivery of the book of the gospels.

Fundamentally, it is a very simple rite and like that for the episcopate and the presbyterate has been pruned of much later medieval accretion.

---

[43] *Constitution on the Church*, 29; *Motu proprio, Ministeria quaedam*, of Paul VI, 1972.

The Theology of the Diaconate

This is to be found principally in the homily and the prayer of ordination.

The homily is largely an extract from the Constitution on the Church but like those proposed for the ordination of bishops and priests, it is in no way obligatory and the celebrant may compose his own. However, it does provide a useful summary.

The deacon has a threefold ministry, of liturgy, of the word and of charity. In the liturgy he assists the bishop and/or presbyter in the eucharist, reading the gospel, preparing the offerings and administering communion. In addition, he administers baptism, assists at and blesses marriages, takes communion to the sick and dying and presides at funeral services. As for the ministry of the word, he preaches at liturgical and non-liturgical services and he teaches the faithful and unfaithful alike. All these are by no means radical changes though there is some extension of their powers both in what they may do and in the source of their power. As we have observed in the matter of baptism, they are now no longer 'extraordinary' ministers of it and their presiding at marriages and funerals is new. Evidently the giving of blessings, at marriages for instance, is not (or no longer) a sacerdotal privilege.

While his liturgical ministry is clear, the ministry of charity he is said to have for the assistance of bishop and priest remains vague. Emphasis on it no doubt represents an attempt to restore this ancient function. Deacons, who in Rome became archdeacons and often eventually popes, were very important persons at a time when the church had large numbers of dependants, widows, virgins, the sick, on its 'pay roll' and they came to control considerable amounts of property. Presumably this situation is not envisaged! Even where in the modern church priests are often administrators of diocesan charities of some size, there would seem to be but a poor case for making deacons such administrators. In any case, it would seem that only permanent deacons are envisaged here. Where they are married and remain substantially members of the lay community, they might well become useful ministers of the less fortunate members of society and through the knowledge and experience gained in this work, they could bring to bishop and priest valuable information about the needs of people who do not normally come across the notice of the parish clergy. Perhaps it will be a case of *solvitur ambulando* but it does mean that permanent deacons should not be looked on as just clerical assistants.

Charity is a broad term and almost anything might be brought under its umbrella but the deacon's function as teacher might well be thought of in this light. Given the widespread need for instruction to various groups of Christians both young and older ones, it would seem that the permanent deacon could offer most valuable assistance if he were trained in catechetics. With this knowledge and expertise he could instruct groups here and there and become the means of forming them into authentic Christian communities who in turn would help the neighbourhoods in which they live.

The last part of the address is directed to the candidates themselves and they are bidden to live a sincere Christian life, to be strong in faith and to reproduce in their living the lessons they teach to others.

Of the questions and promise that follow, which do not add anything of substance to the above, we need to note that there are two new elements of the rite. The first is evidence of the church's concern that candidates for major orders should have a clear and firm determination about what they are doing. They are left in no doubt about this and, even without the new rite of commitment to celibacy, they are being asked to consecrate themselves to the ministry. This will take different forms with the permanent and married deacon and with the 'temporary' deacon but the reality remains the same. The promise of obedience too has a new importance since deacons are now for the first time entering the clerical state, a moment when it is opportune to declare the necessary obedience publicly. In fact it high-lights an aspect of the diaconate that elsewhere in the rite is not emphasised. In all the early literature the deacon is the assistant of the *bishop*: he serves him at the eucharist and he acts at his bequest. Things have changed somewhat since then and his work will in fact be with the presbyter but his primary relationship will be to the bishop.

The Prayer of Ordination

The first change here is in line with the ordination of bishops and priests. Formerly, the bishop simply began reciting the prayer of ordination at the end of which he laid his right hand on the candidate saying, 'Receive the Holy Spirit for strength to resist the devil and his temptations'—not a very inspiring thought anyway! The laying-on of one hand only was presumably a childish medieval way of showing that the deacon was not quite a priest. Now the bishop lays both hands on the candidate, in silence and before the beginning of the prayer. The ancient order is thus restored and the symbolism of the hands-laying is given full prominence.

The prayer itself, basically the old Roman one, has been corrected and considerably changed in the last part. The long exordium remains: God the giver of honours, arranges orders and distributes functions, renews all things and through Jesus Christ his Son who is Word, Power and Wisdom, dispenses everything harmoniously in time and place. This variety is reflected in the church, which is his body, by the variety of graces which all make for the unity and growth of the body and by the threefold ministry of bishop, priest and deacon. Of this last the ministry of the Levites in the Old Testament who served in the tabernacle is a foreshadowing. Up to this point the text is corrected only in minor ways. Then comes an almost entirely new section that runs on to the end and gives a much more Christian and a fuller notion of the diaconate.

The text recalls the institution of the seven deacons of Acts 6:1-6: in the beginning of the church the apostles of the Son chose out seven men who were to help them in their daily ministry so that they (the apostles) could give themselves more effectively to prayer and the ministry of the word. By prayer and the laying-on of hands they committed them to the 'ministry of tables'. While this emphasis on service is to be welcomed, it should be said that by no means all scripture experts regard this incident of Acts 6 as the institution of the diaconate.[44] However it does connect the diaconate with the New Testament ministry, which the old version failed to do, and by its reference to 'the service of tables', even if that is not a very happy phrase in the context, relates the diaconate to the ministry of charity, also wanting in the old rather clerical version.

The next part of the prayer was given over to more or less appropriate common-places and ended with the unsatisfactory formula 'Receive the Holy Spirit ...' which had been interpolated into the text. That formula, which formed a duplicate with what followed is now suppressed and the prayer runs on asking God

---

[44] Cf *inter alios* J. Colson, *La fonction diaconale*, pp. 39–46 (quoted in *Le Sacrement de l'Ordre*, Ludwig Ott, Paris, 1971, p. 24). Colson writes: 'If the "Seven" were not perhaps the first deacons, they were at least probably at the origin of the diaconate in the church.' He sees the event as an early case of differentiation of function in what he calls 'la fonction episcopo-presbyterale'.

to look graciously on the candidates whom the bishop is dedicating
to the ministry of the altar. Then comes the solemn invocation of
the Holy Spirit: 'Send, Lord, your Holy Spirit on these (candidates)
that they may be strengthened by the gift of your sevenfold grace
for the faithful execution of their ministry.' This is not only more
pertinent but emphasises that the diaconate like the other orders
confers a *charisma* (and not merely a 'power' to do something) for
the building up of the body of Christ. The theme of the prayer is
now quite consistent.

The last part of the prayer which, as in the other rites, is addressed
to the candidates, is only slightly revised. The deacon is to be
conspicuous by his sincere love and care for the sick and the poor
(there is the ministry of charity), he is to bear himself modestly (and
we remember the acid comments of St Jerome on the Roman
deacons who gave themselves airs) and he is to lead a life of
innocence and purity. The attachment of celibacy to the diaconate,
though it was mentioned in the old version, becomes particularly
important and, in the case of married deacons, one must suppose
that the phrase refers to married chastity. The prayer ends on the
note of service: the deacon is to be like Christ who came not to be
served but to serve.

Whatever may be the difficulties of working out the implications
of the diaconate in the terms of pastoral action, the prayer makes
abundantly clear what it is.

The Explanatory Rites

In the former rite there was at this point the solemn 'delivery'
(*traditio*) of the diaconal vestments, stole and dalmatic, and the
clothing of the candidates with them to the accompaniment of
formulae. Deacons (or presbyters) now put them on without formulae while psalm 83 or some other chant is sung. The delivery
of the gospel book which follows was formerly made with the formula: 'Receive the *power* to read the Gospel in (the) church for
both the living and the dead'! This was obviously an imitation of
the 'power' given to the priest by the tradition of the paten and
chalice. The formula now says: 'Receive the *Gospel of Christ*
whose herald you now are; believe what you read, teach what you
believe and imitate (in your life) what you teach.' A concise phrase
that sums up much of the meaning of the order the candidate has
received. While this is being done psalm 145 which speaks of the
service of the poor and sick may be sung and its significance for the

rite is underlined by the antiphon: 'If anyone serves me, my Father who is in heaven will honour him.' These simple rites do in fact unfold the meaning of the diaconate as a ministry: the deacon is a minister of the liturgy, of the word and of charity.

Commentary

The revised order for the diaconate is so clear that it hardly calls for further commentary. As with the other orders one feels that it would have been better if the homily followed immediately upon the gospel. The rite would then continue in unbroken succession: the introduction of the candidates, the questions, the homily, the prayer of the assembled community, the ordination prayer and the performance of the explanatory rites.

It is questionable too whether the psalms or other chants provided to accompany these rites are really necessary. Presumably the revisers envisaged a large number of deacons and the continual repetition of the same formula would be boring. However, it would seem highly desirable that the people should hear the formula for the giving of the gospel more than once. The words are worth pondering on. True, these psalms remain optional and those in charge of the celebration will arrange for their singing or the singing of other chants as they think best. What 'other chants' are to be used is a problem. In the English language at least none as yet exist and there is a case for composing some though the authors and the composers will have to be filled with a sense of what holy orders are if they are going to be appropriate. One does not envisage with equanimity the singing of 'Sweet sacrament Divine' or of anything from the epoch to which it belongs.

The Lesser Ministries

Since the *Motu proprio, Ministeria quaedam,* of 15 August 1972 made a number of changes in what used to be called 'Minor Orders', it will be as well to set them out here.

1. Tonsure has been suppressed and replaced by 'Admission to the Clerical' which is an action to be combined with the diaconate. A man becomes a cleric with all the consequences (eg incardination into a diocese) only on receiving the diaconate.

2. Only two Minor Orders remain now, to be called 'ministries', the offices of Reader or Lector and Acolyte.

3. The subdiaconate is suppressed, the obligations of this ministry (celibacy and the recitation of the Divine Office) being

attached to the diaconate. Other functions are divided between the ministries of Reader and Acolyte.[45]

4. These ministries may be committed *(committi possunt)* to laymen but, 'in accordance with the venerable tradition of the church' not to women.

We are not concerned here with the canonical side of institution to these ministries. It is sufficient to note that candidates must ask in writing for institution and it rests with the Ordinary to accept the petition or not. They must have a firm purpose to serve God and the Christian people and must be endowed with the right qualities of personality.

The reason for the change of name is not merely negative—to distinguish more adequately major or sacred orders from minor—but is positive. These ministries are means of *serving* the people whether within or outside the liturgy and as the needs of the people change, so can the ministries.[46] The institution of these ministries brings to mind such passages as Romans 12:6–8 and 1 Corinthians 12:4–11 and they may not unfairly be described as more or less permanent *charismata* for the building up of the body, the church. The *Motu proprio* even envisages that these ministries may be multiplied if the needs of the people require and local conferences of bishops so ordain. The ministry of catechists is among those mentioned.

The Functions of the Lesser Ministries

The Reader

Quite obviously his function is to read the lessons, except the gospel, whether at Mass or at any other service, but the document remarks that he may perform the duties of cantor *(psalmista)* mentioned in the *Ordo Missae* of 1969 (64). He is to support and lead the people in singing and in general participation in the liturgy. If trained, he could render valuable service. In the absence of a deacon he will lead the people in the General Intercessions of the Mass.

According to the *Motu proprio* (V), the reader may be given other duties too though the document is remarkably laconic: 'He

---

[45] The document says that if local conferences of bishops wish, the acolyte can be called a subdeacon!

[46] *Motu proprio*, p. 8.

may instruct the faithful in the worthy reception of the sacraments.'
He evidently has a teaching function and it is for the local church
to make as much of his function as possible. He may also train
those who 'temporarily' act as readers at the liturgy, though some
of these will perform for life!

For his personal life the reader is exhorted to meditate on the
scriptures and live by their message.

The Rite: The rite, which is short and simple, begins after the
gospel of the Mass (or a Bible Service). There is the homily and,
in the sample given, we note that the reader has an additional
function: to proclaim the good news of salvation to those who are
ignorant of it. There follows an invitatory, the collect by which the
Reader is blessed and then the delivery of the Bible with the charge
to hand on the word of God faithfully 'so that it may be active in
men's hearts'.

The Acolyte[47]

His function is essentially liturgical. He is appointed for the
service of the altar, in particular of the presbyter and deacon in
the eucharist. However, his function has been extended and in
cases of necessity he may assist in the giving of communion 'even
to the sick'. In the liturgy he will make administration of holy
communion a great deal easier and since he may take it to the sick,
he could be of considerable assistance to the parish clergy. If he
intends to proceed to holy orders this would be valuable experience
and if not, he could become a regular 'minister' of the parish. In
addition, he may expose the Blessed Sacrament (but not give the
blessing) and instruct those who serve at the altar.

The Rite: This is the same as for the Reader: homily, invitatory,
prayer of blessing and the delivery of the sign of office, namely
a vessel containing bread or wine. Acolytes receive communion immediately after the deacon and may be allowed to assist in the
distribution of communion.

Pastoral Observations

Even if it is agreed that the whole business of 'minor orders'
needed reform, it is unlikely that anyone will get very excited

---

[47] A Greek word meaning 'follower'. We could do with an English one.

about the institution of these new 'ministries'. Yet, one of the effects of the reform is to smudge the distinctions between clergy and laity and since laymen may be instituted to these ministries, it will be here that their value will chiefly lie. Much will depend on what local conferences of bishops choose to make of these ministers but they could be very useful assistants in the parish. It may be asked whether it was necessary to institutionalise such functions. There is a case for it. A recognised body of lay-readers, who could also be authorised as 'acolytes', would mean that structures could be set up for their training and parishes would have available sufficiently educated men to carry out a great variety of tasks.

When young men who are candidates for the priesthood receive these ministries, they should be authorised to exercise them in parishes as often as possible. Not only should they read at the liturgy but they should, we think, be regularly authorised to give communion to the sick during vacations. In this way the whole purpose of the document would be realised.

Admission to the Clerical State

Formerly tonsure admitted men to the clergy and we remember the bitter battles that were fought over the issue in the Middle Ages. Then there was a 'clerisy' which had become a separate caste. With the abolition of the tonsure which had become almost meaningless and the reformation of the 'minor orders' whose members are *not* clerics, it was thought necessary to transfer the admission to the clerical state to the time when men are ordained. It could very well have been dispensed with altogether but the church authorities have an understandable anxiety about the determination and good will of candidates for major orders. Admission to the Clerical State is then to be seen primarily as a commitment to the service of the church whether in the diaconate or the priesthood.

The Rite: It may take place at a time to be determined by local authority but in connection with the diaconate.

There is the homily after the gospel which is followed by a short interrogatory to secure the candidates' commitment. This is followed by an invitatory, intercessions and the collect which asks that the candidates may persevere in their vocation.

The Public Declaration on Celibacy

Celibacy, formerly attached to the subdiaconate, was never mentioned in the ordination rite. With the growing concern about this matter, the church authorities have for years sought to secure from candidates an understanding of what they were taking on themselves. It has been thought good to make the whole matter explicit at a liturgical and public level and a rite is now provided which is to be inserted into the ordination service of deacons. The words of commitment take their place among the other promises the candidate makes.

Celibacy is seen as a sign of charity which enables a man to give himself to the pastoral ministry with freedom and 'undivided heart'. Accordingly the question put to him is: 'Is it your intention to keep perpetual celibacy on account of the kingdom of heaven, as a sign of your dedication and for the service of God and man?' To which he replies 'Yes'.

Married candidates then come forward and to both groups is committed the obligation of reciting the Divine Office.

CHAPTER NINE

The Anointing and Care of the Sick[1]

SINCE THIS Order contains a great deal more than the rite of the Anointing of the Sick it is necessary to detail its contents.

Apart from the decree of promulgation, there is first the Apostolic Constitution *Sacram Unctionem* which gives the official background to the revision. This is followed, as usual, by the *Praenotanda*, divided into 41 paragraphs and referred to hereafter as the 'introduction'. The Order is divided into seven chapters:

I   Visitation and Communion of the Sick, comprising recommendations (a) for the care of the sick and (b) the rite of communion.

II   The Order of Anointing, the 'ordinary' one, the one as celebrated within the Mass and a third for celebration with a great gathering of people.

III   *Viaticum* both within and outside the Mass.

IV   The Order for the administration of these sacraments to people in proximate danger of death, the Continuous Rite (penance, anointing and *Viaticum*); anointing without communion.

V   Confirmation in the danger of death.

VI   The Order for the Commendation of the Dying.

VII   A collection of texts, prayers, suggested lists of scripture readings for use *ad libitum*.

In view of the importance of the Anointing of the Sick from many points of view, it will receive first consideration here.[2]

---

[1] *Ordo Unctionis Infirmorum eorumque Pastoralis Curae*, Vatican Press, 1972. It was actually promulgated on 7 December 1972 but was not available until 1973.

[2] In what follows, the sacrament will be referred to as 'the anointing' as the whole phrase is cumbersome and 'unction', apart from being very Latin, has unhappy associations.

With it we shall of course consider the various styles of celebrating it (chapters two and four), then the visitation and communion of the sick which will be followed by a commentary on *Viaticum*. Confirmation in danger of death calls for no special comment and the whole treatment will end with the Commendation of the Dying.

The Anointing of the Sick

In view of what has been said in Chapter I of this book[3] it is interesting to note that the introduction sets the sacrament firmly in the life-situation of ordinary people, envisaging at first non-Christians. Disease, suffering are part of the experience of every man and present peculiar difficulties for all. The Christian faith however does help those who believe. It enables them to understand something of the mystery of suffering and to bear it more bravely. But illness is (for the most part) not to be thought of as a punishment for sin;[4] it is a *natural* phenomenon as is also, under divine providence, man's struggle against it and his desire for healing. To this the introduction adds that doctors, nurses and all who serve the sick are cooperating with the divine order of things. They are fulfilling Christ's command that we should visit the sick and, the text goes on, it is as if Christ committed the whole man (*totum hominem*) to their care so that they may restore the sick person by means of both physical and spiritual remedies. We may add, that this is true even if the doctors and nurses do not know Christ but are striving according to the rules and art of their profession to restore health.

All this, it seems to us, is a sane, realistic and ultimately Christian view and, although the text does not refer to it, it reflects teaching to be found in the *Constitution on the Church in the Modern World* (18, 22). Illness and the suffering that comes with it are purely natural phenomena and it is wholly right and proper that we should have recourse to medical science to be healed. Although there is a mystery of suffering which we can never hope fully to understand, our first approach to it must be realistic and practical even if the mysteriousness with which doctors sometimes like to surround their craft does not always make this easy.

Yet this approach is not the end of the matter. It is little more than a beginning and it is a common experience that serious illness

[3] p. 11.
[4] The Order refers to John 9:3 though not all scripture experts interpret the passage in so simple a way.

and suffering, especially when prolonged, can almost destroy a personality. Not only is there the erosion of the body by disease, there is all the mental and psychological stress that goes with it. There is the difficulty of understanding the mystery of suffering experienced in one's own personality and there are the questionings that inevitably arise. It is well known that some people do experience temptation in illness. They lack, they say, trust in God's goodness and as their mind gets weary, they may have temptations against faith in God altogether.

It is not surprising, then, that the introduction sketches out a spiritual theology of suffering. It will be best to make an approach to the matter rather different from that of the introduction which puts the difficult text of Colossians 1:24 in the forefront of its thought.[5] The best approach is through the great baptismal text of Romans 6:3-5. By baptism we are committed to a life of 'imitation' of Christ. Interiorly we have to be conformed to him in his passion as well as in his resurrection; his life has to become the pattern of our own and even if we feel we shall never achieve 'crucifixion' with Christ so that we are able to say 'I live no longer I but Christ in me' (Galatians 2:19, 20), yet this must be our aim. Without succumbing to fatalism (even of a Christian kind) or passivity, our attitude must be one of acceptance of what life brings which includes illness and pain. Granted this, illness and suffering can become participations in the sufferings of Christ for the sake and the good of 'the church which is his body'.[6]

Mysteriously in Christ there is a communion in sufferings as there is in faith and love and it is this that it is possible for us to experience in illness. Possible, because for most it is very difficult to rise to this height when we are in pain. Our ability to 'handle' suffering is conditioned by our whole life and if we live outside Christ instead of in him, we cannot hope to rise to the mystical heights of consciously suffering with him.

This is in line with the use the introduction makes of Isaiah 53:4, 5 first to show that illness is not a punishment for sin but, secondly and more importantly, to indicate the solidarity there is between Christ and those who suffer: 'Christ, who is without sin,

---

[5] Difficult for many reasons but among others because there can be no 'addition' or 'making up for' (JB) the sufferings of Christ which in verses 19, 20 St Paul has already made clear are all-sufficient.

[6] For an excellent treatment of Col. 1:24 see J. H. Houlden, *Paul's Letters from Prison* (Penguin, 1970), pp. 176-8.

took upon himself all our "sickness and pains"[7] and shared the sufferings of all men. Indeed, in those of his members who are conformed to him he is crucified and suffers (*angitur*) when we suffer pain.'[8] We are reminded of St Leo's saying: 'The passion of Christ is prolonged until the end of the world ... it is he who suffers in and with all who bear adversity for righteousness.'[8]

This, broadly, is the Christian teaching on illness and suffering. Both remain ultimately mysteries but for the Christian there is here light and help. Light, because he is better able to see suffering in the whole context of Christianity and help, because Christ comes to our aid. If suffering, whether our own or that of others, is a puzzle, at least we can see that God has not left us to ourselves. He in Christ has taken upon himself all the suffering of mankind, he has involved himself in the human condition at its weakest and most anguished, and by his love and his power he redeems this condition, at least for those who believe in him. In all the sacraments we meet the suffering and the risen Christ, that is, we are able to share in his paschal mystery, but in illness we are called in a special way to share in the sufferings of Christ and through the sacrament of anointing, as well as in communion, he reaches out to us, or rather reaches into the innermost places of our being, to raise us up in hope, to dispel anxiety and despair and to heal that condition so that we can return to the community of men and the community of the church, there to serve our fellow-men and to give praise to God.

Another element the introduction sees in the experience of illness is a sense of proportion about the meaning of life. It helps us to see that this life is not everything, that our sufferings, compared to the glory to come, seem light and of little weight and the text refers to 2 Corinthians 4:17. If this consideration seems a little light-hearted to one who is weighed down by pain, later on the text refers to Romans 8:19-21 and sees illness and pain as part of the whole process which the world is undergoing until it achieves deliverance. The world 'groans' and we literally groan with it. We experience something of the tragedy of things and we bring that experience to Christ in the sacrament where he works 'alleviation'. As the introduction says further on (5), in the sacrament of anointing Christ brings to his faithful ones who suffer a most certain help.

---

[7] RSV, *in loc.* margin.
[8] *De Pass.*, XIX, *Patrologia Latina* 54, c. 383.

The Existence of the Sacrament and its Effect[9]

Although there is in the Letter of St James (5:14-16) what seems to be a clear enough reference to the sacrament, it is not in fact heard of again until the beginning of the third century. It is one of the many puzzles of the history of sacramental theology. In James there are already all the elements of the sacrament. There is the assembly of the presbyters (as still in the Byzantine rite), prayer, the anointing with oil and the twofold effect, the 'raising up' of the sick man and, if necessary, the forgiveness of sins. The introduction sees in this passage the 'promulgation' of the sacrament which was 'instituted' in the gospels (the Apostolic Constitution refers to Mark 6:13).[10] The introduction goes on, 'From that time it has been the custom of the church to celebrate the sacrament with the anointing and prayer of the presbyters, commending the sick to the suffering and glorified Lord that he may raise them up and save them' (5). The reference to 'the suffering and glorified Lord' is interesting: the sacrament is a means of sharing in the paschal mystery. The words 'save' and 'raise up' however need a little further explanation especially as both now come in the new formula of anointing.

The text of James 5:14-16 is not at all as clear as our traditional understanding of it has made it seem. What does 'save' mean? In contexts referring to judgment and eternal death, it can mean 'salvation' which consists in eternal life. But, apparently in contexts concerning sickness (Matthew 9:21, Mark 5:28, etc) this is not so. Similarly, 'raise up', *egeirein*, 'which occurs only here in James' can refer both to resurrection from the dead (which is not in question here) or to 'raising up from sickness' (Matthew 9:5-7; Mark 1:31, etc). A modern Catholic exegete writes, 'Here in the present context the most obvious meaning of the words seems to be that the sick man will be "saved" from death and "raised up" to life and health'.[11] If this exegesis is sound, then anointing is certainly a sacrament of healing and not a preparation for death. It also follows

---

[9] A recent study is that of B. Sesboüé, *L'Onction des Malades*, Lyon, 1971.

[10] A modern exegete has this to say about the Marcan text: 'The fact that healing by unction was practised by the early Church (James 5:14 f.) is no ground for denying that the disciples, or even Jesus himself, may have practised it.' D. E. Nineham, *Saint Mark* (Penguin Books, 1963), p. 171.

[11] Kevin Condon, 'The Sacrament of Healing', pp. 179-82 in *Sacraments in Scripture*, ed. T. Worden, London, 1966. The same author goes on to say that if this is not the right interpretation of the words, we are involved in insuperable difficulties. The above paragraph is dependent on this essay.

that the words in the formula of administration must be translated 'save' and 'raise up' though one hopes that someone will have the courage to translate the latter as 'raise you up to health' or even 'restore your health'.

After the text in St James we hear nothing about an anointing of the sick until the *Apostolic Tradition* (V) of Hippolytus. There the oil is blessed after the eucharistic prayer and is clearly intended for healing whether by external application or by drinking. In the Sacramentary of Serapion (c. 350) oil for healing is blessed in much the same place.[12] There is the well known letter (28) of Pope Innocent I (died 417) who, interpreting the James text, says that there is no doubt that the faithful who are sick can be anointed and the oil used is chrism.[13] Not to take the matter any further, there is the prayer of blessing, found in the Gelasian Sacramentary,[14] later in the Roman Pontifical, where it still is, though in slightly revised form. All these texts, referred to in a general way in the Apostolic Constitution (pp. 7, 8), stress the healing property of the sacrament but nowhere more strongly than in the prayer of the Gelasian book. Since it may be used, in cases of necessity, in the administration of the rite itself, it will be useful to give a translation of it.

God, Father of all consolation,
it was your will that the sick in their weakness should be healed
    by your Son;
hear the prayer of faith;
send from heaven your Holy Spirit, our advocate, upon the
    richness of this oil
which by your kindly providence is produced by the olive tree
for the restoration of the body.
Through your blessing may it be
a source of strength for the body, mind and spirit
of all who are anointed with it.
May it dispel all their pains, weakness and sickness.
May it be a holy oil, Lord, blessed by you in the name of our
    Lord

---

[12] *Sacramentarium Serapionis*, XVII, ed. Funk, *Constitutiones Apostolicae*, Vol. II, pp. 178–81.

[13] Text in Denzinger, 17th ed. (1928), no. 99.

[14] Ed. Mohlberg, no. 382, p. 61 where the oil is again called chrism. For a brief summary of the history of the sacrament see the present writer's article 'Unction' in *A Dictionary of Liturgy and Worship*, ed. J. G. Davies, London, 1972.

Jesus Christ who lives and reigns with you through endless ages.[15]

The first thing that is notable is the heavy emphasis on healing. What is more, it is a healing of the whole personality, body, mind and spirit, and in this sense the prayer is astonishingly modern. We note too that the forgiveness of sin is not mentioned, nor is it in the letter of Innocent. What the formula was in the fifth and sixth centuries we simply do not know though we do know that 'patients' drank the oil and, a little later, we find that it was applied to those places where the pain was greatest. What is clear is that the symbolism of oil as a healing element was dominant, and as far as we can discern, gave the 'tone' to the whole sacrament. It was later, in the tenth century, that it came to be associated with penitence and death.[16]

When we turn to the statement of the introduction on the effect of the sacrament we find that it is very elaborate.[17] In the sacrament of anointing the grace of the Holy Spirit brings help to the sick person for the salvation of his whole personality (qua *totus homo* ad salutem adiuvatur); his trust in God is raised up, he is strengthened against temptations and the anxiety that the thought of death brings; he is enabled to bear his sufferings more patiently and, if it is expedient for his spiritual salvation, his health is restored. Finally, if he is in need of forgiveness, his sins will be pardoned and the sacrament is described as the consummation of penance (6). In the next article the sacrament is spoken of as 'a pledge of the kingdom to come'.

There is a great deal here, too much perhaps, and the statement is to be regarded rather as a description of the effects of the sacrament than as a definition. On the one hand, the revisers seem to have been practising a certain theological concordism taking up into their description all that has been said by theologians since about the time of St Thomas who saw anointing as the sacrament that '*immediately* disposes a man for glory *since it is given to those who*

---

[15] The last sentence is new.

[16] For a convenient summary of Chavasse's research on this sacrament see Dom Placid Murray's article 'The Liturgical History of Extreme Unction', in *Studies in Pastoral Liturgy*, 2, Dublin, 1963, pp. 18–38. The revised text of the prayer of blessing does not differ substantially from that in the Gelasian sacramentary. The reference to drinking the oil is removed and the famous phrase about the oil being a chrism with which priests, kings, prophets and martyrs were anointed (a phrase that has its origins in the Apostolic Tradition of Hippolytus) has been removed.

[17] It is heavily dependent on the Council of Trent, Denz., 909.

are dying'.[18] Hence we get the statements that the sacrament is a 'consummation of penance' and 'a pledge of the kingdom to come'. They also make rather too much of the *'tentationes maligni'*, the temptations of the Evil One, and the struggle against illness or pain (it is not clear which) which psychologically may be a bad thing. And 'health' is slipped in as if it were unimportant. This is odd since the rite itself is much more emphatic.[19] On the other hand, the great positive contribution of this statement is that it refuses to accept any sharp division between body and soul. In this it is in line with the psychosomatic views of modern medicine. The dispelling of anxieties can help physical health and alleviation of pain can bring a more tranquil state of mind to the patient. This view is also in accordance with biblical teaching which did not distinguish body and soul as they have been since Scholasticism became the prevalent philosophy of the church. The Bible, especially the Old Testament, saw sickness and sin as closely connected.[20] 'And just as the miraculous healing by Jesus (in Matt. 9:1–8 and par.) operated first on the body and then on the soul, so here the ritual of the priests works not only on the body but, when necessary, on the soul.' The object of the sacrament is the whole personality *(totus homo)* which it seeks to heal. It is against this background that we should see the apparently difficult statement that in this sacrament 'the grace of the Holy Spirit brings help to the sick person for the salvation of his whole personality'. Here *'salutem'* is, I think, to be taken in its widest possible sense : health for the body and salvation for the soul, or rather, a salvation that means health, the reintegration of the vital forces which are disorientated by disease for the body, and a spiritual renewal of the whole personality.

The forgiveness of sin of course assumes repentance on the part of the patient and the introduction on the point is laconic, much less explicit than the Council of Trent whose doctrine it is summarising throughout this paragraph (6). Trent put the taking away of sin first (in line with Aquinas's teaching) and speaks (again in the language of St Thomas) of the removing of the 'remains (reliquiae) of sin'. The introduction simply uses the expression *'veniam pec-*

---

[18] *ST* III (Supp.) xxix, a.1, ad 2. His theology (which may not have been his final thought) is clearly conditioned by the practice of his time.

[19] One hopes that the reasons for this are not that introductions matter and the liturgical texts do not.

[20] See K. Condon, *art. cit.*, p. 184, in *Sacraments in Scripture*, ed. T. Worden, and other articles in the same book on 'Sin'.

cati', pardon of sin, which the sacrament can effect.[21] It is more difficult to understand why anointing is called 'the consummation of penance' (or perhaps, as the text has it, 'Christian penitence'). This seems to be a relic of the medieval situation when the sacrament was all mixed up with the discipline of penance. As we have seen, in the fifth and sixth centuries this was not so though we can see from the letter of Innocent that the recipient of the sacrament must be repentant. One must suppose then the phrase means that if patients accept their illnesses and the sufferings they involve as reparation for sin and in union with the passion of Christ, such acceptance will be a significant expression of their life-long penitence.

As we have observed often enough, we are saved by faith and the sacraments of faith and the introduction underlines this (7), as well as connecting faith with prayer. As in St James, it is the prayer of faith that will save the sick man. So, says the introduction, *both* the celebrant and the patient must have faith and it is a faith that is at once the faith of the individual and the faith of the church. It looks to the person of Christ in his passion and resurrection, the Christ who shared human suffering, who by his resurrection radically overcame death, sin and disease, and whose power is the source of the sacrament. It is a faith too that looks to his second coming (*futurum prospicit regnum*) when all tears and mourning and suffering will be done away. Anointing is both a participation in the paschal mystery of Christ and an anticipation of the final consummation.

Who may be anointed?

This too has been a contentious matter in the past, especially when the sacrament was associated with death. The priest felt that there must be some grounded expectation of death before he was justified in administering it. In more recent years practice has tended to be more flexible and now the Order comes along to say that it is not danger of death that is the condition of reception but '*a serious illness*' (8) and judgment on its gravity need only be

---

[21] Aquinas saw the sacrament as principally aimed at spiritual infirmity brought about by the sin-ridden condition of mankind and the *reliquiae peccati* are 'the defects (or weaknesses) left in man' by sin. It is *these* that the sacrament is concerned with, strengthening the patient against their consequences. Cf *ST* III (Supp.) xxx, a. 1. The revisers evidently did not wish to concern themselves with this theology which must be regarded as coming out of a now obsolete situation.

'probable' though doctors may usefully be consulted. No doubt the casuists, as they have done in the past, will try to define more closely what 'gravity' is but it would seem that it is hardly necessary. The introduction is speaking of the normal judgment priest or patient will make on the matter. Once the emphasis on death is removed, judgment becomes all the easier.

Anointing may be given to the same person as often as there is serious illness and also during the *same* illness when there is a new and more serious crisis, as is usually the case. A monthly anointing in cases of prolonged illness, as some expected, is not allowed for. On the other hand, where an operation becomes necessary on account of a dangerous disease (*morbus*), the patient may be anointed beforehand. This has long been requested and is now officially granted. Again, the old, even if not dangerously ill, but suffering the debility that often accompanies old age, may be anointed. This too is new but in practice it is not at all an easy matter to find the right moment for this, especially as it is often the old who think of anointing as a prelude to death.[22] Likewise, children who have a sufficient use of reason to understand the sacrament and 'to receive comfort from it' may also be anointed. This is a rather more liberal permission than the former *Rituale Romanum* (V, i, 8) which seems to say that the use of reason must already have been achieved. In practice, young children seem rarely to have been anointed though after they have made their first communion, however young they may be, they can certainly 'appreciate' the sacrament of anointing. As before, the unconscious may be anointed on the assumption that they have had a desire for it. If a person is dead, however, the priest is to pray that God may forgive him his sins and admit him to his kingdom. If there is doubt about the actuality of death, he may anoint conditionally. There is nothing new here although surprisingly the text does not mention conditional absolution which is common practice in these circumstances.

Finally (13), the laity are to be instructed to ask for the sacrament and, it goes without saying, receive it devoutly 'and with full faith'. They are not to conform to 'the bad custom' of procrastination. In the new atmosphere created by this Order, an atmosphere that in fact is already widely prevalent, it will be all the easier to

---

[22] However, I find that the old when they are unwell, even if not seriously, are willing to ask for the sacrament if the priest is attentive to them.

persuade people to ask to be anointed. The death-nexus has certainly done ill service to pastoral work in the matter.

The Ministers of the Sacrament

Little need be said here. Everyone from bishops to parish priests, their assistants and hospital chaplains are the ordinary ministers of this sacrament and in cases of necessity, all priests with the presumed permission of the parish priest.

The Oil of the Sick

As we have seen, the oil used in the anointing of the sick in the fifth and sixth centuries was called chrism which on account of its richness and perfume was regarded as the symbol of the Holy Spirit. But since at this time and until much later it was the custom for the people to bring oil for the use of the sick to Mass to be blessed, it will have been the ordinary oil used in the house. Either *chrisma* in the texts means simply 'holy oil' or perhaps it means oil blessed by the bishop more solemnly. However, no distinction seems to have been made between chrism and the oil of the sick until the ninth century.[23] However that may be, until now the oil to be used in the sacrament has always been olive oil but the Order (20) now says that it may be any oil so long as it comes from a plant. The Apostolic Constitution (p. 10) explains that this has been allowed at the request of many bishops who have made known that olive oil cannot be obtained in certain regions or only with difficulty. It is a plain example of the 'adaptations' mentioned in the *Constitution on the Liturgy* (40) and witnesses to a gratifying flexibility about symbolism. It is to be the oil of a plant since it is 'more like' that of the olive and can, as easily, carry its symbolism.

The oil must still be blessed by a diocesan bishop (or by one who is 'equiparated' to him) unless, for urgent reasons, it is blessed by a priest. This he will do during the administration of the sacrament. The reasons for this are fairly obvious: on account of distance he may not be able to renew his supply, communication lines may have been broken down by flood or some other natural disaster. The regulation witnesses to a right sense of proportion: it is more important for a sick man to be anointed than it is that the bishop should bless the oil.

---

[23] See B. Poschmann, *Penance and the Anointing of the Sick*, Eng. trans. London, 1964, p. 247.

The Manner of Administration

This too has been changed. Only the forehead and the hands are anointed though more numerous anointings may be allowed if local custom requires (24). The first part of the formula is said while the forehead is anointed and the second part while the hands are anointed. A rather complicated affair! In cases of necessity only one place need be anointed, as in the former rite.

The Liturgy of the Sacrament

1. The greeting and the blessing of the patient and the room (with holy water, if desired).

2. Brief introductory remarks which include the recitation of James 5:14–16.

3. The penitential act or sacramental confession of the patient if this has not been done beforehand.

4. A scripture reading and brief homily if possible.

5. Intercessions for the patient and his attendants.

6. The laying-on of hands in silence.

7. The blessing of the oil (in case of necessity); otherwise a prayer of Jewish pattern, blessing God for his compassion shown in this sacrament.

8. The administration. The formula is said once, the patient is anointed in two places, the forehead and the hands.

9. The rite ends with the saying of a collect (a selection is given to be used according to circumstances), the Lord's prayer, and a special form of blessing.

Commentary

Those who are familiar with the former rite will see that there are considerable differences. The first three prayers of that rite were really a blessing of the house and those in it with no special mention of the patient. There was not even a proper laying-on of hands. The rubric instructed the celebrant to 'extend' his right hand over the patient while he said a long and unmanageable prayer. After the anointing there were three collects, the first of which mentioned the James text for the first time, all asking for the restoration of health even when the patient was visibly dying. The new rite conforms to what is now the set pattern for sacramental celebration. There is first a ministry of the word, prayer and finally the administration of the sacrament. The whole rite is visibly more personal, directed to the patient and engaging his and the attendants' participation. Finally, it may be noted here that for almost every part of the rite alternative texts are given which together build up a powerful impression of the healing power of the sacrament.

The Preliminary Rites: The blessing with holy water is interpreted by a formula saying that the sprinkling is a reminder of baptism and recalls Christ who by his passion and resurrection redeemed us. Anointing is a celebration of the paschal mystery which for the Christian begins with his baptism.

The address (or invitatory), which may be replaced by a collect, again emphasises that we have to do with a sacrament of healing: in the gospel the people approached Jesus asking for health and he is amongst the company now commanding (present tense) that 'if any one is sick among you, let him call in the priests of the church' and the rest.

The penitential rite may be the same as that in the Mass but the second alternative is worth looking at: 'By your paschal mystery you gained for us salvation; By the wonderful works of your passion, you do not cease to renew us; By our partaking of your Body you make us sharers in your paschal sacrifice' and to all these sentences the people reply either *Kyrie eleison* or *Christe eleison*. There is liveliness and sound teaching in all this.

The Ministry of the Word: A very large selection of scripture readings is provided for the sick and the dying and they are to be used at the discretion of the minister. They are intended to be used in *all* the eventualities of ministering to the sick and the dying both in church and at home and they provide material for the construction of services of the sick. They are drawn from the Old Testament, the epistles and the gospels and their content is so various that it would be impossible even to summarise them here. The reading in the text of the rite is Matthew 8:5-10, 13, the incident of the centurion's servant with the words 'Lord, I am not worthy ...'. When the time comes for providing texts for the clergy it will be necessary to print out at least a selection of these texts. One cannot go round with a Bible under one's arm.

The intercessions that come normally after the reading (though they may be said after the anointing or even in some other place (73)) represent one of the oldest and most important elements of the rite: 'The prayer of faith shall save the sick man ...' and there was much praying in the medieval rites. This situation is summed up in the former Roman Ritual (V, ii, 7) where the attendants were enjoined to recite the Litany of the Saints, the seven penitential psalms (a relic of the connection with penance) or other prayers *while* the minister anointed the patient. Apart from the undesirability of having a paraliturgy going on, it in fact never worked. The family was too concerned to indulge in a self-directed liturgy. Still, the principle was preserved and, as we have remarked elsewhere, the prayer-element in the celebration of sacraments in all the early church was seen to be most important. If it has been adequately maintained, the charge of sacramental automatism or even magic would never had been made.

The style of the intercessions, of which three forms are given, is litanaic, of the kind we have become used to. They ask that God will come to the patient and strengthen him with the anointing, that the sufferings of all the sick may be alleviated and that those in charge of the patient may receive help from God. The response is 'Hear us (Lord), we beseech you'. Two further points may be noted: 1) the introduction explicitly takes up the James' text: the assembly is praying the prayer of faith; 2) the last petition leads to the laying-on of hands: 'May he in whose name we lay on our hands give life and salvation (*salutem*=health?) to the patient.'

The other two forms are worth looking at. The second (240) is shorter and more scriptural: (The Lord) took upon himself our sickness and bore our sufferings; he had compassion on the multitude and went about doing good and healing the sick; and (finally) he sent out the apostles and bade them lay hands on the sick, a petition that leads to the laying-on of hands. The response is *Kyrie eleison* (al. *Christe*). The third form (241) has shorter petitions but are rather more numerous though covering the same ground. It ends with the petition about the laying-on of hands as the first form does. In certain circumstances, eg when the patient is in pain, this will be the best form to use. The petitions are short and are likely to be more easily grasped by the patient.

The rite, though simple, moves to an impressive climax from the readings and through the prayers to the laying-on of hands and the anointing. The restoration of a proper laying-on of hands is welcome not merely for its liturgical appropriateness but for its theological implications. The sacramental action is now visibly the extension in time of Christ's gestures of healing in the gospel. In recent years we have heard often enough the Augustinian tag 'When the church baptises, it is Christ who baptises' and we are justified in saying 'When the church anoints, it is Christ who anoints'. As so many of the texts of the rite say, Christ is present with his power of healing and comfort.

After the hand-laying there is either the blessing of the oil or the 'blessing' of God for his compassion shown in the sacrament. Clearly it draws attention to the oil and this is no doubt intended. It is a Jewish form of prayer, blessing God for his gifts: 'Blessed be God, Father almighty, for us and for our salvation you sent your Son into the world'. The response is 'Blessed be God'. The second is addressed to the Son and the third to the Holy Spirit. The litany ends 'May your servant who is in pain, Lord, be restored (to health), may your power strengthen him (*confortari*) in his weakness (or illness) as in faith he is anointed with this holy oil'. It might have been the 'form' of the sacrament!

The Administration

The 'form' of the sacrament is much changed. The chief change is that while the former one (no older than the tenth century) seemed to be wholly concerned with *sin* ('May the Lord forgive you whatever sins you have committed by sight'),[24] the new one suggests by its position that it is the secondary effect of the sacrament. Since the Latin, which is very packed, provides some difficulties of translation, it will be best to give it in Latin:

Per istam sanctam unctionem
et suam piissimam misericordiam,
adiuvet te Dominus gratia Spiritus Sancti; (℞ Amen)
ut a peccatis liberatum
te salvet atque *propitius* allevet (℞ Amen).[25]

The first two lines are from the old formula and the last three

---

[24] Perhaps this English translation was rather more explicit than the Latin: '*indulgeat ... deliquisti*' which might be turned 'your delinquencies'. Still, the meaning was plain.

[25] In a hand-out to recommend the new Order by no less a body than the Secretariat of State a translation is given: 'Through this holy anointing and his most loving mercy, may the Lord assist you by the grace of the Holy Spirit, so that when you have been freed from your sins he may save you and in his goodness raise you up.' The purpose of the hand-out is to undercut the critics of the revised liturgy. The full weight of the church's authority that is behind the Order is indicated.

are new. It is the last three that require commentary and provide difficulties in translation.

(a) *Adiuvet* (help). This is rather vague. Presumably it was chosen rather than 'Heal' (*sanet*) because the revisers had the *whole* effect of the sacrament in view.[26]

(b) *Gratia Spiritus Sancti*. This phrase directly refers back to the prayer of blessing of the oil and is intended to do so. Once again we note the link between *prayer* and the action of the sacrament. This phrase, then, introduced into the formula of administration, reminds us that the effect of the sacrament is the work of the Holy Spirit, as the prayer of blessing says it is, and if the Roman Church in the past could be accused of neglecting the Holy Spirit in its liturgy, this can no longer be said!

(c) The last two lines echo the James text with its message of 'deliverance from sin' and the healing effect (*salvet ... allevet*) though precisely what the former word means is not clear. In verb or noun form it occurs elsewhere in the service (intercessions, blessing) and yet its meaning remains unclear. If it means 'save' or 'salvation' it is odd for we never speak in that way of the effect of any other sacrament. It is a deliberate reference to the 'save' (*sosei*) of James 5:15 and will have the same interpretation as that text bears.[27] '*Raise up*' can only mean 'raise up to health', restoration to health, as the collect after the administration says: 'Restore to him full health, interiorly and externally'.[28]

The Conclusion

Six collects in all (243-6) are provided for use after the anointing, the last four adapted to the condition of the patient: for one weak from old age, for one in great danger, for use when anointing and *Viaticum* are given together and for one in his (last) agony. This directly responds to the request of the Council Fathers in the *Constitution on the Liturgy* (75) and relieves one of having to pray for the recovery of one who is certainly dying. The first collect (77), phrases of which are to be found in the Gelasian Sacramentary (1539), is ancient.[29] An examination of all these collects would be

---

[26] Cf *Constitution*, p. 9.

[27] See above, p. 172.

[28] The provenance of the second part of the formula is unknown to me. Up to the thirteenth century, many were in circulation but there is nothing comparable to this. See *L'Eglise en Prière*, ed. Martimort, Paris, 1961, pp. 584-7; M. Righetti, *Storia Liturgica*, Milan, 2nd ed. 1959, Vol. IV, pp. 333-4.

[29] The second collect of the former Ritual is not repeated though it is found in so respectable a source as the Gregorian Sacramentary (208).

profitable. They underline the healing properties of the sacrament very strongly. Thus the alternative under no. 77: (grant that) by this anointing his strength may be restored, he may be consoled by (your) help, his powers be renewed (*vires erigat*) and all evil be dispelled. In addition, these prayers are filled with a truly Christian compassion which one hopes will not be smudged out in translation.

Even the blessing deserves mention. It runs:

'May God our Father bless you (℟ Amen, and so throughout).
May the Son of God heal you.
May the Holy Spirit shed his light on you.
May he guard your body and save your soul.
May he enlighten your heart and bring you everlasting life'.

And then the usual form of blessing follows.

The Communal Celebration of the Sacrament

In recent years there has been a growing practice of anointing people at Mass, sometimes in considerable numbers, as at Lourdes. This is the direct result of separating anointing from death and it is certain if that this sacrament is to appear for what it is in the eyes of ordinary people, such public celebrations are necessary. They will do more than any instruction to show them that anointing is a sacrament of healing and they will readily ask for it.

Anointing then may be celebrated within the Mass for one or two sick people (80–82), for a large number of the sick (83–85) and outside the Mass in a service that takes the form of the ministry of the word.

There is no variation in the rite itself which is fitted into the structure of the Mass (or the service) in what is now the accustomed place, namely after the homily. The minister(s) will receive the sick at the beginning of the Mass immediately after the greeting, and except for days of the highest liturgical rank (81), the readings may be taken from those provided for the sick in the lectionary and the other texts are to be taken from the Mass-formula 'For the Sick'. Thus after centuries is united the sacrament of the sick with the eucharist. The vestments, it is interesting to note, are no longer to be violet (a sign of penitence) but white.

The sacrament is administered after the gospel and its homily which is to take the scripture texts as its basis (82), showing the significance of human suffering and disease in the divine plan of salvation though the celebrant is to have regard for the condition of the sick. Brevity will be the keynote. There follow the intercessions (which however may be deferred until after the administration), the blessing of the oil (if necessary) or the 'blessing prayer' for the oil and finally the anointing itself. If many priests are taking part each one lays hands on one of the sick persons and then anoints (19).[30] Otherwise, the various actions of the Mass may be distributed among the ministers (*ibid.*) What is evidently to be avoided is the administration of the anointing by two ministers. The intercessions may take place at this point and if they do, they conclude with the collect of the rite. The Mass then proceeds as usual though we note that the sick and their attendants may receive communion in both kinds (82, c).

Celebration of the sacrament outside the Mass hardly differs though the arrangements may be more flexible. The sick are to be given opportunity to confess beforehand, they are received at the beginning, there is an act of penitence. There may be one or more readings, there is to be a homily after which silence may be kept. During the administration suitable chants may be sung though the text (90) says that the words of administration should be heard at least once. After the administration, either a collect from the rite or the Lord's prayer may be used, and the latter may suitably be sung. The service concludes with the blessing.

These communal celebrations may take place not only in churches but in hospitals or other suitable places though the bishop remains the judge and is in any case responsible for their proper organisation.

The Visitation of the Sick

Probably the least used part of the former *Rituale Romanum* was that called 'The Visitation and Care of the Sick' (V, iv). The reasons for this were that it was very long and rarely translated into English. The Irish *Collectio Rituum* (1960) showed what could be done. The compilers, as well as translating the text into English (and Irish), divided the material into three parts which could be used on successive visits.

The revisers of the new Order have taken a different way. They have subsumed under the heading 'Visitation' the Communion of the Sick and other pastoral care, including of course confession. But

---

[30] The text says '*possunt*'. The individual hand-laying is not obligatory but seems highly appropriate.

they have not seen fit to provide a service. They recommend however a pattern which follows the now familiar lines. There will be
a reading of the scriptures 'which will be prepared with the patient
in a friendly and informal way' (45). This will lead to prayer from
the psalms or other sources and the visit will conclude, if circumstances indicate, with a blessing and a laying-on of hands. This
latter was an important feature of the previous form and is very
important. It continues the gesture of Christ and, without being a
sacrament in the strict sense, must be conceived of as at least a prayer
for Christ's healing. The alternative blessing after the anointing
(237) would seem to be an appropriate text to use: 'The Lord Jesus
Christ be present with you and defend you/; May he go before
you and lead you and follow you and protect you/; May he look
upon you, preserve you and bless you.'

It is probably a very good thing that the pattern has been left
free. Sick people differ enormously and if they are really ill, they
cannot manage formal services. It is the familiar and very simple
prayers that count at this time and the priest has to find out what
they know and like. But this does not exclude other material and
as the people are becoming more familiar with the psalms, phrases
from these too, as the introduction suggests, will be helpful. Certainly passages from the gospels about Christ's healing and compassion are acceptable. And the 'sentences' provided for the
Commendation of the Dying offer another suggestion for those who
are sick. No doubt each priest will make up his own anthology and
use it according to circumstances.

But there is something else of even greater practical importance.
Right at the beginning the Order establishes that it is not just the
clergy who are to visit the sick. It is a duty incumbent upon all
the faithful (42). They are to 'share the care and love of Christ for
the sick, they are to visit them, to comfort them and where there
is necessity, to provide for their material needs'.[31] Everyone knows,
and this goes for the clergy too, that a 'sick visit' can be nothing
much more than an enquiry after the patient's health, a brief prayer
and a blessing. The bunch of grapes (rarely eaten by the patient)
and the glossy magazine (on the assumption that you can get one
that is respectable) are hardly adequate to express one's Christian
care for the patient. What, then, is required is small booklets with

---

[31] This is an echo of the *Rituale Romanum* in its excellent pastoral notes
before the Visitation of the Sick but there the obligation of material help is laid
on the clergy!

collections of texts (including the most familiar prayers) for use by the laity and by the sick. Alongside the scripture texts there should be short, simple and direct prayers that will 'speak to the condition' of the sick person. Given a new outlook and this simple instrument, the visitation of the sick by the laity could become a permanent activity. One of the 'seven corporal works of mercy' *and* the fulfilment of the gospel injunction would become a reality in the lives of many Christians.

Communion of the Sick

In the former Ritual this was a very jejune rite which one felt compelled to 'nourish'. The new rite follows the now familiar pattern: introduction, blessing of the house and sick person, the penitential rite, the reading of the scriptures, the Lord's prayer, the administration, the final collect and blessing.

Even this is not a great deal and the scripture passages could well be extended. The revisers did not think to include 1 Corinthians 10:15, 16, nor 1 Corinthians 11:23–26, nor any of the narratives of the Last Supper from the synoptists. Yet the sick often need to be reminded where the communion they are receiving originated. Likewise, the administration of communion could have been enriched by one or two prayers before receiving. After communion the minister will be free to add prayers in the space before the concluding collect. Intercessions too after the scripture might have been inserted as it is standard pastoral practice to ask the sick to pray for others and such intercessions would give them the opportunity to do so.

Viaticum

This follows the same pattern as that of the Communion of the Sick though there are one or two differences. a) The 'Last Blessing' is neatly included in the penitential rite. b) After the reading of scripture there is a profession of faith (in the terms of the Apostles' Creed). This is a restoration of an old practice which survived, I believe, only in the administration of *Viaticum* to a bishop. It is a valuable feature. c) Intercessions, of very good quality, are provided. d) The problem of pronouncing the old and rather frightening formula at communion has been eliminated. The minister says 'The Body (or Blood) of Christ', the patient says 'Amen' and the minister continues 'May he guard you and bring you to everlasting life'. Discreet but sufficient.

The 'Ritus Continuus' for those near to Death

There is no fundamental change here. The omissions are predictable: duplications are eliminated. What *is* important is that *Viaticum* has been restored to its original place, the *last* sacrament before dying. It was ousted from this place when anointing came to be regarded as a preparation for death and in the twelfth century acquired the name of 'Extreme Unction', the last anointing—before death. It was in fact restored to its original place in some of the vernacular rituals of the pre-conciliar days, notably in the German *Collectio Rituum* (1950), which here and elsewhere has exercised a certain influence on this new Order.[32]

It should be noted that *Viaticum* may be given during the Mass and the Order (26) recommends this on account of the special significance of the eucharist as a participation in 'the death of the Lord and his passage *(transitus)* to his Father'. This means in practice that bishops should readily give permission for the Mass to be celebrated in the homes of the dying. It should be noted too that where there is a lack of priests, authorised lay-people, whether men or women, may give *Viaticum* to the dying (29), as indeed they may do to the sick once they have received authorisation. The extension of this permission is much desired, especially in parishes where there is only one priest. Finally, both the sick and the dying may receive communion in the form of wine if they cannot take it in the form of bread.

The Commendation of the Dying

Assistance of the dying is one of the greatest, and at the same time, one of the most difficult, of charities. The Order is aware of this and urges both clergy and laity to do all they can to help the dying. The aim should be to help the patient to overcome the natural fear of death by arousing his hope in the power of the resurrection of Christ through whom he will enter into eternal life (139). He is to be led to accept his death in imitation of the suffering and dying Christ.

The Order is to be seen as a collection of 'sentences', scripture readings and prayers of various kinds which may be freely used

---

[32] Which is not surprising as Dr Baltasar Fischer of Trier has been concerned with both. It is also a good example of how liturgical reform has been going on since the late forties, and represents work on which the Council was able to build. Unhappily, there were some in this country who were either indifferent or hostile to such efforts. It was a case of 'those dotty foreigners'.

according to circumstances. The condition of the dying is to be closely observed and the minister is to recite slowly and in such a voice as may help him (140). As well as the texts suggested, others may be used and short prayers ('ejaculations'), which as is well known are most acceptable at such a time, should be used. Simple gestures, like signing the patient with the cross, are also recommended. The minister should also remember that those present will also profit from the prayers and other texts used on this occasion. They will strengthen them for what is always a very great ordeal and they will learn to see death as a participation in the paschal mystery of Christ (139).

The 'order' breaks down into four parts: a) 'sentences' all from holy scripture and of course to be used at choice; b) scripture readings (some obviously from the passion narratives); c) prayers of various kinds; d) the commendation proper which includes the famous *Proficiscere* (shorter and much improved), another similar prayer, a litany (similar to the one in the former ritual though much shorter and better) and another commendation. Immediately after the expiry the *Subvenite* is said. The text suggests that before the *Subvenite* the *Salve Regina* may be *sung*. A lot will depend on circumstances but one recalls the Canadian chaplain who on the death of Maurice Baring stood up and recited the *Magnificat*.[33]

Pastoral Considerations

Further comment is almost superfluous. The new Order is a thoroughly pastoral document and has only to be read to be appreciated. In all the discussion about the role of the priest in modern society it rarely seems to be understood that, apart from him, there is no one else always available to give the spiritual help and comfort that are necessary to the dying. It is true that, as the Order urges, the laity too must play their part. Care of the sick and dying is not the exclusive duty of the clergy but it is he who will be the leader if others are to take it up.

It is however very arduous work and both clergy and, when they take it up, the laity need a good deal of help if it is to be done effectively. There are four categories of patient one can think of right away:

a) those ill at home, perhaps seriously but not fatally; b) there are those who are terminally ill and most likely in hospital; c) there is the problem of the old; d) finally, there are the mentally ill.

---

[33] Laura Lovat, *Maurice Baring*, A Memoir, 1947, p. 33.

a) It is easier to minister to those ill at home than to anyone else. There is time and there is privacy. Although illness can have devastating effects it often provides time for reflection and the patient becomes open to God and to his word. Much can be done but much more could be done with the informed and willing help of the laity. Authorisation of lay-people to give holy communion so that patients receive it *frequently* is now necessary. At the very least texts of the new Order must be published in such forms as to be usable (and obtainable) by ordinary Christians. In these booklets the introduction or at least a summary of its main teaching should be printed. With this material familiar prayers (even the Hail Mary which some have forgotten!) should be included.

b) The difficulties of the care of *the sick in hospitals* are considerable and the greatest is lack of privacy. Chaplains overcome this difficulty and others in a remarkable way but it would seem that some formal approach to hospital authorities is sometimes necessary to secure the necessary conditions. For the terminally ill, both clergy and laity are in need of information and help from doctors and psychiatrists though even here the situation is improving. Courses of one sort or another are being made available.[34]

c) *The old.* Perhaps a good deal is known on the subject but it has hardly filtered down to parish level. How do you give spiritual comfort to those who are 'hard of hearing' in a hospital ward or an old people's home common room? How do you get people to return to Christ after forty or more years of lapsation? What are the phases through which old people go? Are they better off in a 'home' or at home and if the latter (which seems more desirable), could not something more be done to look after them? These are some of the questions that need asking. There is here a whole new and very difficult field for which the pastoral clergy need help. If sight is faint and hearing all but gone, no amount of new 'orders' will help them. The clergy of course must play their part, but it is here one feels that laity, trained in some measure for the task and with leisure to talk to the old for quite long periods, would be of the greatest assistance. A small but practical and very important 'instrument' would be a booklet for communion and the other rite printed in large type. I do not know of even a New Testament so printed.

d) The greatest defect of the new Order is that nowhere does it

---

[34] For literature see H. Guntrip, *Psychology for Social Workers*, 1971; Heije Faber, *Pastoral Care in the Modern Hospital*, 1971, with review in *Clergy Review*, February, 1973, by Peter Hocken.

mention those who are *mentally ill*. At times they can be very ill indeed and the mental illness can affect their physical health.[35] Even apart from that, it is now recognised that mental trouble is an *illness*. In this condition people suffer from great anxieties, apparent denial of the faith and a whole range of troubles which anointing, in the terms of the Order (6), could alleviate. Yet the matter is not mentioned. This is inconsistent with the general line of the introduction and the rite which makes no sharp distinction between body and soul. In the opinion of the present writer, the clergy would be justified in making up their own minds on the matter though it would be better if the church authorities recognised that this situation exists and that the remedy of the sacrament is readily available. The pastoral care of such patients is extremely difficult and a great deal of help and information is necessary if the pastoral clergy are to perform their task adequately. It is yet another field which, from the standpoint of pastoral care, is insufficiently explored.

---

[35] Years ago I anointed a woman (who had to be held down) who was very seriously ill from mental trouble which eventually killed her.

CHAPTER TEN

The Rite of Funerals

IN RECENT years it has become a common-place to say that the modern world no longer believes in death. It is the supreme non-event. Before its onset it is disguised in certain ways and after it the corpse is swept away to be buried or cremated as soon as possible. Even expressions of grief are for the most part suppressed for it is not regarded as the proper thing to indulge them. It is indeed difficult to discern what people, sometimes even Christians, believe about death and what, if anything, is to come after it. Among others, Catholics are affected by this attitude though they have at their disposal a more clearly articulated belief in heaven, hell and purgatory than any others. But this belief is often held in an almost crudely materialistic form and we can agree with a recent writer that 'perhaps no area of Christian theology is in more need of a responsible *demythologisation* than eschatology, that is, the theology of the last things, of death, judgment, heaven and hell'.[1] The demythologisation should cover the whole range of events that concern both the individual and the end of the cosmos but for our purposes here it will be sufficient to concentrate on death, judgment and the time-model that most of us use to think of the other world.

For Christians death should not be the mere cessation of biological life even though with them the ending and the severance are usually uppermost in their minds and sentiments. However paradoxical it may seem, death is a part of life. All through our lives we are dying. We die to childhood or if we do not, we remain infantile. We die to youth as the price of maturity. We die to family that we may enter into a totally committed love for another or for another kind of life, the priesthood, the religious life or some form of dedication to the service of others. But all these dyings are the seed of a newer, richer kind of life. You could say that we die *into*

---

[1] Michael Simpson, SJ, *Death and Eternal Life*, Cork, Theology Today Series, no. 42, 1971, p. 9.

a new life and the condition of entry into it is the death.

This means that we are continually making assents to life, and however obscurely, we are saying that life has a purpose that is worth living for. If we are Christians it means that we are continually assenting to Christ, doing what he wants of us. Work, an avocation, a vocation—and that covers almost every human activity —and all the effort that goes into them, all the strivings, all the prayer, every kind of service we do for others, are so many attempts to say Yes to God—in conventional language, to do his will.

Or, to put it another way, God has made himself known to us in his Word who has given us his word in the gospels. He calls us to accept it—and him—and this we do or try to do throughout our lives. Whether we celebrate the sacraments, whether we pray, listen to God's word in the Bible, we are responding to the call of God, we are trying to give ourselves to him. Then comes the final call of death. Is all that self-giving that has gone before, no doubt imperfectly, throughout our lives of no account when we come to die? The conventional answer, which is true but insufficient, is that we shall be 'rewarded' though often enough the implication is that the 'reward' has nothing to do with what has gone before—like giving a boy a book on mathematics for winning the cross-country race. If it is true that we are constantly 'dying into' a new and richer kind of life here below, it is at least intelligible that our death at the end of our life is a dying into eternal life which is promised to us by the word of God. It is at least intelligible that death, instead of being the supreme negative, is the supreme and all-embracing affirmation of our life by which, with all our being, we are able, through the mercy of God, to say Yes to his love.

All this may seem a little speculative and *a priori* but if we turn to the death of Christ we find the same pattern. And the first thing we notice is that the death is not the end. As the liturgy has always had it and as a renewed reflection on holy scripture has shown, the passion-death-resurrection are *together* the saving work of Christ. As he himself made clear (John 13 : 1 foll.), his death was a passing over from this world through the suffering and the supreme self-giving it involved to the glory that was his before the world began. He 'died into' the resurrection and the glory. As St Paul would say, he 'emptied' himself and the results of that emptying were seen in the mysterious cry of abandonment on the cross : 'My God, my God, why have you forsaken me?' He gave all and the self-giving that went on all through his life reached its culmination in the Last Supper when he said 'I dedicate myself for their sake' (John 17:19), I am giving myself over to sacrifice for them and all who shall believe in me through them. Further, St John uses the strong and rich word *tetelestai* to describe the final and complete giving of Jesus on the cross: 'It is finished, it is accomplished', the whole life of obedience, the life of self-giving here reaches its supreme expression and because that self-giving was borne up by and permeated with Jesus' love for his Father, his saving work could be redemptive of the whole human race. In the terms we used above, the death of Jesus was the supreme affirmation of his life.

There was the giving, the affirmation, and this was 'answered' by the resurrection, the exaltation and the glory: 'Therefore God has highly exalted him and bestowed on him the name which is above every name' (Phil. 2:9). Through his death Jesus acceded to the full life of the resurrection when his human nature became totally permeated by the Holy Spirit and became total gift to the Father.

It is in this sense that the death of Jesus is the model or type of all human dying. Always we are dying, that is trying to give ourselves, so that we may live more fully, and then comes the final death through which we enter into a new and richer kind of life. It is at this point that the words St John records of Jesus speaking of his own death become relevant: 'Unless a grain of wheat falls into the earth and dies, it remains alone; but if it dies, it bears much fruit.'[2] Jesus is the grain of wheat and by dying he became 'the source of life to all who believe in him'. All proportions kept, if we die into the Lord, if we make our passage through death, accepting it, we too shall pass into the fuller life that is called eternal and shall become, under Christ, a channel of life to others. For that is what the communion of saints means.

Understandably, then, the church sets the funeral rite in the framework of the paschal mystery, thus emphasising the truth that in death the faithful Christian shares in the death of Christ and passes over into eternal life. Thus in the first collect of the funeral Mass we ask that as in this life the deceased has believed in the death and resurrection of Christ, so by that same mystery (the paschal mystery) he may be brought to the resurrection. This is typical of a great number of other texts, prayers, antiphons and readings which we will examine later.

---

[2] John 12:24. The words that follow give the teaching of dying to life so that we may come to a richer one: 'He who loves his life, loses it, and he who hates his life *in this world* will keep it for eternal life.'

There is, I think, a change of emphasis of another sort. Catholic funeral rites were for a very long time dominated by the thought of purgatory and while there is no reason to believe that we are in less need of purgation than our forefathers were, the reason for that point of view is probably a defective understanding of the next world. Here almost all is mysterious but at least we can say that clock-time does not apply there. To recall the adage of Aristotle, time is the measure of motion, itself thought of as a measurable quantity. Clearly it belongs only to this material world and can have no place in the next. Likewise, eternity is thought of as unending duration and understandably people think of it as rather boring. Admittedly, the matter is difficult, not least because the industrial-ised world lives by clock-time as the condition of its continued exis-tence. Yet, we are not wholly conditioned by it. We experience moments of *intensity* when we are unconscious of the passage of time and the more intense the experience the less relevant measured time becomes. The lover takes no account of time. As he says, the world stands still. The saint who is caught up in prayer is even less conscious of the passage of time but the intensity is the greater as it is less time-conditioned.

This would seem to provide a basis for understanding a world that is without clock-time. What happens when we die is a mystery, we can have no experience of it but it is credible that at that moment when, in Christ and by the power of Christ, we sum up our life, we make the supreme affirmation, we are also 'living' at the greatest moment of intensity. Its only parallel is the highest mystical experi-ence. At this same moment we are confronted with God *for* whom we make the final choice and yet at the same time in our personalities there remains much that has resisted him in this life. In this en-counter and in the intensity of the experience, all that is imperfect is purged away and we are able to enter into the joy of the Lord. Whatever may have been Newman's picture-world of purgatory, judgment and heaven, he seems to have a glimpse of this notion in his *Dream of Gerontius* where the Angel speaking to the Soul just dead says, 'Learn that the flame of Everlasting Love/Doth burn ere it transform'. Death is an encounter with the Everlasting Love and we have no need to look elsewhere for a cleansing or a means of purgation. But it is a Love that transforms and must be thought of in terms of intensity rather than time.

This view also provides a background for a consideration of judg-ment. The 'Grand Assize' parable has sometimes been interpreted as literal fact and medieval people seem to have thought of God as some sort of earthly judge, only more terrible. Yet the whole point of the parable is in the words 'As you did it to one of the least of these my brethren, you did it to me' (Matthew 25:40). In so far as we have responded in life to Christ in his and our brethren, we have been responding to him and the contrary is also true. Then there is all the sense of St John's gospel that judgment, *krisis*, decision and so separation are *now* (2:19; 9:39; 12:31; 16:11). The responses whether positive or negative we make in life are going to be of literally supreme importance in the moment of death. We hope and strive to respond positively to Christ in life, we pray that these responses are constantly cancelling out the negative ones and that the main thrust of our life is ever Godward. The judgment will simply be a confrontation with God when by his grace we shall be able to embrace his will for us with all the energy of our being or, on the other hand, there remains the awful possibility of the final refusal. But because our responses have often been feeble, because there have been refusals in our life and our motives have often been impure, there is the need for cleansing, for being perfected so that we may come to the vision of God.

But it does not seem possible to postulate time for that cleansing and perfecting process. We must think of it then in terms of intensity and it is a matter of experience that a person can undergo a spiritual growth that is quite incommensurable with time. Why then should we pray for the dead, why go on praying for them perhaps and indeed usually for years? The reason again is that there is no time with God. Our prayers are necessarily spread out in time but with him they exist in a single undivided moment and he, at the death of an individual, takes account, so to say, of all the prayer that has been made or will be made for him.

These considerations may well be elementary but there seem to be people almost hopelessly puzzled about death and the after-life and perhaps for this reason they turn away from it with dismay. In any case, in one way or another these notions underlie much of the new liturgy of the dead which we must now consider in detail.

The Funeral Rite[3]

It would not be difficult to show from the actual liturgical texts

---

[3] *Exsequiarum Ordo* (Vatican Press), promulgated 15 August 1969. Cf *Notitiae*, 49, 1969, pp. 423–30 for the Latin text of the Introduction or *Praenotanda* which is the one used here.

of the new rite that the paschal mystery of Christ, Christian hope, and the meaning and necessity of prayer for the departed are the three foundations on which the whole rite is built. This teaching is summarised in the Introduction and of this we give an account first.

In the death of a Christian the church celebrates the paschal mystery of Christ. This is the primary sense of the celebration. But the paschal mystery is not simply a past event or something existing 'out there'. The Christian shares in it in life—and in death. 'By baptism they have died in Christ and been raised up in him, they have become members of his body and with him they pass through death to life' (1). The funeral liturgy is a celebration of the paschal mystery as it has been enacted in the life of the Christian. This is the reason that it is now recommended that the paschal candle should stand at the head of the coffin (38).

But the departed, as we may suppose for most of us, are not yet perfect and there is the process of purification to take place so that they may be prepared to enter the company of the saints and await the blessed hope of the coming of Christ and the resurrection of the dead.[4] It is this hope that Christians express in the liturgy of the dead (2) and it is because the departed still need perfecting, in ways known to God alone, that the living plead the sacrifice of Christ in his eucharist and pray for them in various ways and on different occasions (1). This prayer of the members of Christ's body is part of the divine economy of salvation and an expression of the communion of saints (ibid.).

It will be useful to single out a few texts of the rite that illustrate these points.

The collect of the first formula (A) of the Mass for the dead clearly expresses the paschal nature of Christian death:

Lord God, almighty Father,
we believe that your Son died and rose again;
may our brother (sister) N who has gone to his rest in him,
be raised up to eternal life
by the power of that same mystery of Our Lord Jesus Christ....

---

[4] The document here is simply repeating the scriptural and credal statements on the subject of estchatology and the resurrection of the dead. Rightly, it refuses to speculate but many theologians are now saying that the resurrection of the body is not in some far distant future but in a way not wholly explicable the dead are united with their bodies after death. Even so conservative a theologian as L. Billot held that the union of the soul with any 'matter' was sufficient to constitute it as a person.

In the collect for an anniversary we pray that God whose Son redeemed us all by his death and resurrection may have mercy on the deceased who believed in the mystery of resurrection. Thus believing, may he come to the joys of eternal life. Here very evidently the death and resurrection of Christ are the exemplar of the Christian's.

The fourth preface for the dead recalls that all are redeemed by the death of Christ and prays that we may be raised up to the glory of the resurrection. The fifth prefers to emphasise the victory of Christ: we are redeemed by his victory (on the cross and in the resurrection); may we be called back to life with him.

In another way, the familiar preface of the dead (1) expresses the paschal mystery combining it with hope: in Christ the hope of resurrection shone forth and if we are dismayed at the thought of our mortal condition, we are buoyed up by the promise of eternal life. Death is not an ending: it is transformation: *vita mutatur, non tollitur*, and to this earthly way of life will succeed the unending life of heaven.

To these could be added numerous other liturgical texts both old and new. Perhaps we have not always reflected that the *Requiem aeternam*, part of the older stratum of the funeral liturgy, was a hymn of hope and even joy (*et lux aeterna luceat eis*), as the very chant emphasised. The 'eternal light' that we pray the departed may have is the completion but also the extension of the 'light' they have received in baptism. The communion verse too, with its exultant chant, carries the same message. This is the spirit of what is probably one of the oldest texts for the dead in the Roman rite, the *Memento* of the Dead. It recalls that Christians are marked 'with the sign of faith', the mark of the cross they received in baptism when they were 'enlightened', and goes on to ask that what was done then may now be completed: may they have light, happiness and peace. In fact, what has happened *textually* in the revision of the funeral liturgy is that all the later medieval elements have simply dropped away and we have a funeral service that expresses an earlier, but purer, sense of Christian death.[5]

As however the Introduction points out (11), it is the readings that deliver the full teaching on the paschal nature of Christian death: 'they proclaim the paschal mystery, they hold out the hope

---

[5] The famous—or infamous—*Libera me*, such a 'popular' feature at clerical funerals and sung *fortissimo* throughout, was redolent of the medieval notions of judgment with all its mythological scenario.

that we shall come into God's kingdom, they teach the people the right attitude (*pietatem*) to the departed and they exhort all to give the witness of a Christian life.' The range of selection offered by the Lectionary is very wide and understandably the Introduction urges the clergy to be careful in their choice of the readings (18) and where possible to consult with the relatives of the deceased in doing so (23, 24 (1)).

It is of course the New Testament readings that convey the teaching of the paschal mystery. In the non-gospel material, it is found most clearly in Romans 6:3–9 and it is not at all fortuitous that this is also a reading for baptism. 1 Corinthians 15:20–8 and 15:51–7 of the same epistle proclaim the same message though both need careful handling in the homily. In the gospel readings John 11:17–27 ('I am the resurrection and the life'), 12:23–8 ('if the grain of wheat ...'), 14:1–6 and 17:24–6 all teach in one way or another that the Christian in death is making his passover in Christ. John 6:51–9 with its reference to the bread of life can easily be turned into an effective homily that moves from the death of the deceased to the celebration of the paschal mystery that is taking place. Likewise, the 'passion texts' Mark 15:33–9, Luke 23:44–9 with 24:1–6 (a resurrection narrative) directly relate the death of the Christian to that of Christ.

The principal contribution that the Old Testament texts make is to raise hope in the goodness of God who takes the deceased into his care. See, for example, Wisdom 3:1–9, which already seems to have become a favourite and, it is interesting to recall, *used* to be applied exclusively to the saints. Isaiah 25:5–9 with great finality declares that God has destroyed death for ever. The New Testament texts mentioned above also of course emphasise the Christian hope, giving the ground for it in the resurrection of Christ himself. The same is true of the better known reading from 1 Thessalonians 4:13–18. That from Philippians 3:20–1, though short, suggests the process, the transformation we shall undergo at death if we have been faithful: his own glorious, risen body is the model of our own transformation. The responsorial psalms too give a message that is at once full of hope and expressive of a tender regard for the departed. Nor should the importance of the *Alleluia*, now happily restored to the funeral rite, be forgotten. With its joy and its Easter associations, it decisively changes the whole atmosphere of the Christian burial service. It suggests that the Christian has fought the good fight and is now entering into his reward and incidentally that 'time-in-purgatory' is no longer in the church's perspective.

Other readings bring another emphasis, that of judgment, Acts 10:34–43 and notably Matthew 25:31–46. The latter particularly needs delicate handling and with some less instructed congregations it might give a counter-message. The notion of God as a sort of super-policeman is far from dead and it will be best to expound the judgment as the confrontation with God when we, as it were, through his eyes see ourselves as we have been. It is the moment when we shall learn the meaning of 'The flame of Everlasting Love (that) doth burn ere it transform'.

A last element of the new funeral liturgy that marks a very great change is the rite of Final Commendation. As the Introduction teaches (10), it is not a rite of purification nor yet, we may say, is it a sort of rehearsal of the final judgment as the old Absolution so brutally suggested. It is, as the document continues, the last farewell of the Christian community to a departed member and, as the texts of the rite show, there is a spirit of calm and confident hope and yet a realistic sense that when we die we are far from perfect. The church gently commends the deceased to the mercy of God for she believes that those who have died in Christ will be raised to life at the last day. The question of judgment is not burked and the celebrant's address and the collect that concludes the rite underline by their very content that the church is praying for the departed. In other words, all the traditional elements are here though, cast as they are in the context of the paschal mystery and Christian hope, the whole atmosphere of this rite, as of the whole liturgy of the dead, is considerably changed.

Planning the Rite

Funeral rites and customs are as old as the recorded history of mankind and until recent times death has always been seen as a religious moment when the unseen world, however envisaged, impinges upon this world. It was a moment when people became conscious of the divinity, the *numen*, as present in their affairs and death, with its funeral customs, was seen as one of the 'rites of passage', the final one, when the spirit, hardly if at all distinguished from the body, passed into another and mysterious world. Again and again the funeral customs of various peoples of various epochs bore witness to a belief in a life beyond this and this belief underlay the many different ways in which people celebrated, if the word be allowed, the moment of death, or rather the moment of passage. For these reasons even Christian customs have and do differ a great deal. In the earliest Christian days the funeral followed quite closely the customs of the Greco-Roman world. There was the preparation of the body, the *toilette* of the corpse, the vigil with its meal and then the procession to the place of burial. There was at first no funeral Mass. But soon the abuses connected with the meal both at the vigil and later at the tomb led to a change. Funeral meals were discouraged and the Mass came to form part, the central part, of the funeral liturgy.[6]

In the Middle Ages, when the social economy was largely rural, it was easy to organise the rite round the local church. The clergy went to the house of the deceased and from there led the body and the mourners to the church for the *Requiem* and from there to the surrounding churchyard where the deceased was buried. This is still possible in some parts of the world but social conditions have changed so much that the greatest flexibility in the organisation of the funeral liturgy is necessary.

To accommodate the very various customs of different cultures and the conditions of modern industrial life, the revisers have accordingly made possible the greatest liberty within certain fixed patterns. As well as allowing for considerable adaptation within the liturgy, they have suggested alternatives which the local conferences of bishops may adapt to the circumstances of their countries or regions. The revisers accordingly give three 'models' (*typi*):

1. According to the first the funeral rites take place (a) in the home of the deceased, (b) in church, usually with the funeral Mass and (c) in the cemetery. This, which differs but little from what has been customary for a very long time, is to be regarded as the normal model.

2. The funeral takes place in the cemetery chapel and at the grave. With this model too many are familiar though it is usually a rather sad affair because the deceased and the relatives are usually only loosely attached to the church. There may however be some countries where nothing more is possible and the Order enjoins that the funeral Mass should be said on some other occasion (7).

3. Even more exceptional circumstances are envisaged by the third model. The funeral will take place in the home of the deceased,

---

6 See *L'Eglise en Prière*, ed. A. G. Martimort, Paris, 1961, pp. 623–4.

when, with the permission of the bishop, the funeral Mass will also be celebrated.[7]

Here, after a word or two about the second and third models, we will take the first as the subject of our commentary. In both the second and the third (if there is no Mass) there is to be a ministry of the word, consisting of scripture readings, homily and prayers. The Final Commendation will be used and certain prayers that normally will be said at the grave-side may be said in the home. If the second model is used it would seem to be important that the relatives should be given the opportunity for a funeral Mass either before or after the cemetery service (cf 7). There may well be good reasons why there should not be a full funeral service (the deceased has had no connection with the church for years, has led a 'scandalous' life (which however may not be of such sort as to exclude Christian burial altogether) but the need to offer the Mass and prayer for the dead may be all the greater for the exceptional circumstances. In addition, a quiet 'family' Mass (which is envisaged by the *Missale Romanum* for certain occasions) will help the mourners both emotionally and in an understanding of Christian death.

The Order (8) refuses to speculate on the circumstances necessitating a funeral in the home, even with Mass, but it will not be difficult to imagine such circumstances. The reason for this arrangement is that the deceased may have a fully Christian burial service that would otherwise be impossible. The argument is that these circumstances do exist and it is better to give some indications of what should be done than to leave the whole matter vague. In any case, it is one of the many cases which local conferences of bishops must provide for.

The First Model
Although this model is close to what has been customary, there are one or two new features. The first is the provision of a vigil either in the home or in church. This is interesting as a very definite christianisation or perhaps re-christianisation of the 'Wake' which in some countries has survived but for which no liturgical provision was made. It is really a popular 'office for the dead', one that will most probably be used instead of the more complicated form to be found in the new breviary.

---

[7] *Ord. Exsequiarum* (4, a, b, c.).

The priest or an authorised lay-person will go to the house of the deceased, will offer sympathy, using words from holy scripture (Matthew 11:28 'Come to me all you that labour ...'; Ecclesiasticus 2:6; 2 Corinthians 1:3–4) and after a few words of explanation, will recite a psalm: 129 (the *De profundis*) or 22 (The Lord is my shepherd) or 113 (the *In exitu*, one of the psalms associated with Christian death from a very early age). Then he will say a collect for the deceased and one of consolation for the mourners. A reading or readings from scripture will follow and the celebrant may deliver a homily, obviously based on the readings. The service will conclude with prayers of intercession and either the Lord's Prayer or one of the collects provided. If there is a custom of religious rites when the body is placed in the coffin these or some other texts (which are indicated) may be used. This latter would not appear to be a custom that is often met with nowadays but perhaps we should try and do something to re-introduce it.[8]

This vigil is separate from the first action of the funeral rite proper which envisages the clergy with servers going to the home and conducting the body and the mourners back to church. This will not be possible in most places and what would seem to be indicated is either that the vigil should be kept as above in the home and the body received with a short service (one or two prayers from the above service) or that the visit to the home should be omitted and the whole vigil service done in church.[9] There is a case for this as people usually feel deeply about death, even when the deceased is not a relative and they need some means of expressing what they feel. Centuries ago the Office of the Dead was no mere clerical affair. The people came together for the Dirge (from the Latin word *Dirige*, the first three of the Mattins psalms—in the

---

[8] The practical difficulties are considerable. Bodies cannot be kept in the modern home for the most part and usually lie in the funeral director's 'chapel of rest'. This may well be a considerable distance from the home of the relatives but where it is not, efforts should be made to visit it and funeral directors, one has found, are usually very accommodating in this matter. The advantage of the new Order is that it provides suitable texts for such occasions, gives people in fact a prayer-vocabulary they badly need at such times as these.

[9] At the same time, there would seem to be no reason why the vigil service should not be conducted both in the home and in church if two or three days have elapsed between the two events. The second way does give the local community an opportunity to come and pray with the mourners and for the departed. However, the feelings and sentiments of the mourners must be taken into account. Funerals are ordeals for many and church services, other than the funeral Mass, may be too much for them.

old breviary) and for the *Requiem* the next morning. Wherever circumstances indicate, it would seem to be a good thing to restore this practice which is now so eminently feasible.

A wide-spread custom is to bring the body into church the evening before the funeral Mass which is to take place next day. People attach a great deal of importance to this though their reasons are often obscure. All the more reason to conduct a vigil service, even if it is short. The next day the funeral Mass will take place and this offers no very great difference from the former rite. We know of course that the *Dies irae* has no longer to be sung or said and if it was lugubrious enough when sung (apart from the beauty of the chant), it is impossible when said. We also know that the strange offertory antiphon, which seems redolent of only a half-Christian world, has been suppressed. And the new Roman Missal provides a series of Mass-formulas some of which do not involve even the introit, *Requiem aeternam*. We are under no obligation to *sing* any of these texts.[10] In point of fact, it is pastorally impossible to do so. In parish life, even if it is possible to assemble some of the community, including a few members of the choir, the musical programme must necessarily be limited. An entrance hymn which can be sung by all is much better than a feebly sung psalm and the hymnals now provide material for this.[11] If there is difficulty in singing the responsorial psalm the metrical version of Ps 22 'The king of love my Shepherd is' will do very well. The importance of singing the *Alleluia* should not be overlooked. The preparation of the gifts is best done without singing and if the custom still survives in some places of making money offerings on the occasion, they would be best brought up with the bread and wine and, with the agreement of the relatives, given to a named charity. During communion, if singing is possible, the hymn 'Jesus, Son of Mary' (PL 119) is suitable. Whatever may be the details, the mind of the church now is that funerals should be marked by a buoyant hope and even a certain subdued joy. Both are present in the verbal texts and are best expressed by song. Normally, the mourners appreciate the element of song and if the musical texts are well chosen, they more than anything else convey the new spirit of the funeral liturgy.

---

[10] See *Christian Celebration*, vol. I, p. 132.

[11] The new edition (1972) of *Praise the Lord* has a small selection which could be extended by the use of Easter hymns (197, 203) and one or two others, though unfortunately the editors do not refer to the former.

The Final Commendation, a carefully articulated piece of work, restores an accent that was common in the fourth century and is therefore wholly traditional.[12] The texts are calm and without being anodyne, compassionate. The address (which may be varied) speaks of the imperfection of the deceased who is awaiting the resurrection. May God's judgment be merciful, the text goes on, and may the Good Shepherd lead the departed safely to the peace of his Father's home. The body is sprinkled with holy water, a reminder of the baptism which made the departed a child of God, and censed because the body was the temple of the Holy Spirit. Meanwhile the *Subvenite* is said or sung[13] and the celebrant finally commends the deceased to God, expressing the hope that he (or she) will be 'raised to life on the last day'. The procession with the body to the hearse may be accompanied by the singing of the *In Paradisum* and the *Chorus angelorum* and these are restored to their original function as antiphons to psalms. Suitable ones are suggested.[14]

On the assumption that the funeral party can go directly to the graveyard, psalms can be sung on the way but this is hardly possible nowadays except in the most rural of settings. The celebrant or another will meet the party at the cemetery and there a brief service of committal follows. This may include further prayers of intercession but experience shows that at this point they are hardly necessary. A prolonged station at the graveside is a hang-over from the days when the 'poor' were not normally buried with a funeral Mass.

A word may be said about the homily during the Mass (or for that matter at the service of the word outside Mass). The documents are emphatic that it is to be an exposition of the texts of the day and its purpose is to proclaim the meaning of the paschal mystery, to strengthen the faith of the community and arouse its hope in the power of Christ to gather all to himself in eternal life. The preacher will also underline the need for prayer and the purpose of celebrating the Mass. But all this does not mean that it is

---

[12] The *Libera me* was at one time only one of *four* texts to be sung at this point and the others (which in one way or another remain in the new rite) did much to mitigate the piled-on horror of that text. It is odd that, except for the funerals of bishops and the like, the others should have fallen away and only the *Libera* remained to give an exaggerated emphasis. For the history, see *L'Eglise en Prière*, pp. 628–9.

[13] A good musical setting for this is needed.

[14] The setting at PL 121 may well do for this though it is a pity that the composer did not think to make the two texts antiphons to be sung with psalms.

an 'objective' and unfeeling discourse. It is perfectly right and proper that he should refer to the deceased, drawing on his knowledge of him to illustrate his points. A mention however brief of what he was or what he did is sufficient to earn the gratitude of the relatives and little more is needed. In any case, the homily is not to be a panegyric (45) and there are occasions when the preacher must exercise great tact. People in any case do not expect insincerities on the occasion. But the Order (46) does allow, with the permission of the local bishop, lay-people to speak briefly after the period of silent prayer. This is often done quite effectively though the best place for it would be a service taking place sometime after the funeral.

Finally, as for the Marriage service (5–7), so for the funeral service, the Order (17, 18) urges upon the clergy an awareness of the pastoral opportunity offered by a proper celebration. It bids him be mindful of the sorrow and needs of the mourners *and also* of those, whether Catholics or not, who can be described as 'occasional worshippers' or who have apparently no religious faith. In practice, this means a careful selection of texts both scriptural and liturgical. One of the reasons for rejoicing at the disappearance of the *Libera me* is that its message was no longer credible to modern people, whether Christians or not. The scripture reading, 1 Thessalonians 4:13–18, may also deliver a counter-message. The first two verses are a clear statement of the paschal mystery but verses 16 and 17, which speak of the trumpet call of the angel and of our being carried up into the clouds to meet the Lord, impose a certain strain on those who are unfamiliar with the eschatological scenario. A careful use of texts which shall not put off those of weaker or no faith is not a case of 'How much will Jones swallow' but a true pastoral concern to persuade them that the central message of life in the risen Christ is true.

Pastoral Recommendations

The whole attitude and pastoral policy (if that is the right word) of the priest towards sickness, death and its consequences is summed up at the end of the Order. He will administer to the sick and the dying, being present with them at this time. He is to teach right notions on the meaning of Christian death and, after death has occurred, he will comfort the relatives in their sorrow and help them in whatever way he can. Furthermore, the celebration of the funeral rites, adapted as necessary to the condition of the relatives, is seen as part of the whole programme of consoling and helping them. This is in fact what is usually done, as the gratitude of so many towards their clergy bears witness, but the injunction underlines the importance of seeing the liturgy itself not merely as something that is done or has to be done in abstraction from human need but as something that expresses that need.

Adaptation

As we have said above, funeral customs vary greatly from one part of the world to another and the Order gives considerable liberty of adaptation though imposing on local conferences of bishops the duty of doing so (21). They are to consider existing customs which may not necessarily be specifically Christian and to adopt those that are considered to be 'useful or necessary'. If there are regions with their own rituals and if the rites harmonise with the requirements of the Constitution on the Liturgy (37, 38), they may be retained. These options are hardly likely to concern English-speaking countries. If we ever had any peculiar funeral customs they have long ago disappeared and the medieval rituals ceased to be used in the first two or three decades of the seventeenth century.[15] But clearly in regions and cultures which have retained certain customs this permission for adaptation is of the greatest importance. If people become Christianised it is now agreed that they have not also to be 'Romanised' or 'Europeanised'; they have a natural right to their own culture and its religious manifestations, provided they are not 'indissolubly bound up with superstition and error' (CL 37).

In addition, local conferences of bishops are to organise for their own regions the pattern of funerals according to the three models (8).

The Funerals of Children

The old funeral rite for children, consisting as it did principally of psalms that were supposed to express the joy of the Christian community on the death of a child because he had immediately entered heaven, was very unsatisfactory. Its compilers can never have been in contact with parents who had lost a child. In pastoral

---

[15] If I remember rightly, there is a Sarum *Manuale*, (i.e. *rituale*) dated 1612, in the Downside Library. The *Rituale Romanum* was not issued until 1614.

life, the death of a child provides one of the most difficult and heart-rending tasks. It is all very well to say that he is happy in heaven. The fact is he is fruit of the womb, the object of indescribable affection and the centre of hopes. The rending is terrible. Perhaps later on it is possible to say that the child is happy in heaven and that he will be praying for his parents and brothers and sisters but the chief task at this time is to console the parents and to strengthen their faith—no easy task. This point is made in the Order (13) where we read that children by virtue of their baptism are the adopted sons of God and so enter at once into glory but the church prays at this time for the *parents* that in their sorrow they may have consolation.

For the first time, then, Mass-formulas are provided for the burial of infants, and are full of compassion. The introit, for instance, runs: 'Come, blessed of my Father; inherit the kingdom prepared for you from the beginning of the world.' It is in God's providence, mysterious as it may be, that the child has been taken from the world. It is not just an 'accident'; this death is foreseen in his merciful love and he takes him to himself. This too is the sense of the collect (Mass A): God in his wisdom has *called* this child to himself in the very beginning of his existence and the church prays that since he has been made a child of God by baptism and, as we believe, is even now dwelling in heaven, we may some day share with him the joy of eternal life. The prayer over the offerings is even more significant: the parents received the child from God and are now thought of as giving him back; in God's kingdom they will one day again take him into their arms. If parents in this situation are or become able to say this prayer with faith and conviction it can be said to sum up a totally Christian view of the death of a child. The communion verse again recalls baptism and expresses the Christian faith that we shall live with Christ to whom the child is now united (Romans 6:4, 8). The prayer after communion prays for the consolation of the parents.

In the second formula (B) there is a direct reference to the sorrow of the parents—they are oppressed by the loss of their child—and it asks for faith to believe that he is in heaven. The prayer over the offerings asks that the parents may have the grace of submission to the divine will and that after communion sees the child already 'making his communion' at the heavenly banquets you have granted him to sit at the table of the heavenly kingdom; may we also share it with him.

The final commendation is naturally adapted and expresses the sentiments of the above texts.

The readings suggested for these funerals are simply selected from the larger collection provided for the funerals of adults. Revelation 7:9–10, 15–17 (God will wipe away all tears) may be thought particularly appropriate as is the passage Matthew 11:25–30 (I thank you, Father, that you have revealed these things to the little ones).

Finally, there is a formula even for children who have not been baptised and this alone witnesses to new thinking on the subject in the church. One collect asks that the parent may have comfort in the knowledge that God has taken the child into his care and the commendation which is very short begins: 'Let us commend this child to the Lord....' There is little more to be said but this is all that need be said. The fact that these texts exist in the official liturgy of the church is calculated to arouse the faith and hope of the mourning parents.[16]

---

[16] Understandably the Order (82) warns against minimising the necessity of baptism in any homily that is preached.

CHAPTER ELEVEN

The Sacrament of Penance

IN THE course of this book I have tried to relate the sacraments and their liturgy first to ordinary human living and then to the Christian life. When I came to consider the new Order of Penance in *The Ministry of Reconciliation* (London, 1974) it seemed unlikely that this formula would work. Some reflection and reference to other documents and articles showed however that it was possible to relate penance to the religious experience of non-Christian religions and so to the life of those who make no profession of the Christian faith.

A link between the practices of non-Christian religions and Christian penance is established by Pope Paul VI in his letter *Paenitemini* (E.T. *Penitence*, published by C.T.S., London). He addressed it to men of goodwill and says that the church has noted that 'almost everywhere and at all times penitence has held a place of great importance in non-Christian religions and is closely linked with the intimate sense of religion which pervades the life of most ancient peoples as well as with the more advanced expressions of the great religions connected with the progress of culture' (p. 5). Judaism and Islam are examples that spring to mind. The final teaching of the Old Testament on repentance is so profound and important that it has been taken over almost wholly by the church. But in its earlier stages sin was often seen as the breaking of a taboo and 'repentance' was thought of as a ritual cleansing. The externalism of this phase had to be rejected by the prophets and they and the psalmists came to a deep understanding of the holiness of God and of the need for a total conversion if God was to forgive the sin. In non-Judaic religions, expiation—again perhaps for an external, ritual fault—seems to have played a great part and if it is unsatisfactory in that it leaves the personality unchanged, it is at least testimony of the sacredness of life presided over by the Supreme Being. Such an understanding of things brought with it the penitential practices of prayer and fasting which can be seen as medicinal in that they deliver man from slavery to his instincts and from the domination of material forces over his life. There is something beyond it, Someone whom man acknowledges, Someone whom he can offend and whom therefore he must placate.

If all this seems very 'primitive' it provides some release from the anguish that man experiences in the face of wrong-doing, whether his own or someone else's. Modern man has denied himself this way out and yet he experiences the agony of right-doing in conflict with wrong-doing which St Paul described in Romans 7 : 14–25. Though writing in the context of law and sin, Paul is witnessing to the drama that goes on in every human being, a drama which he himself experienced: 'I do not understand my own actions. For I do not do what I want, but I do the very thing I hate. . . . I do not do the good I want, but the evil I do not want is what I do. . . . Who will deliver me from this body of death?' And the answer is 'Jesus Christ our Lord', 'who was put to death for our trespasses and raised for our justification' (Romans 4 : 25).

This teaching of course brings us right within the Christian context where sin is an ever-present reality and repentance a necessary accompaniment of the Christian life. This theme, too, Pope Paul took up in his Letter: ' "Repent and believe in the Gospel" . . . constitutes, in a way, a compendium of the whole Christian life' (p. 5), and since it is the mission and vocation of the church to preach the gospel to every creature, in that proclamation it must also announce the gospel of repentance for otherwise it would be unfaithful to its mission. But further, since all the members of the church bear the burden of that mission, there must be a penitential element in their lives, rejection of all that is evil and adherence to all that is good, restraint and abstinence even in those things that are good. In all this Christians may well experience in their own lives that drama of which St Paul wrote. Yet it is but a beginning. The Stoic could reject evil and adhere to the good but he was far from the kingdom of heaven. The whole process must be lifted into the sphere of the redeeming work of Christ. In him alone is salvation and through him alone can come forgiveness of sins. The living out of the passion, death and resurrection is central to the life of the church and to that of the individual Christian and it was to this that Paul VI pointed when he said that we are committed to the living out of the paschal mystery in our own experience: 'The sacrament of baptism configures him [the Christian] to the passion, death and resurrection of the Lord and places the whole future life of the baptised under the seal of the mystery' (p. 7). But this can come only through a constant turning in repentance to Christ, i.e. by conversion, *metanoia*.

The Order of Penance (2) carries the matter further and shows the relationship between baptism and penance, thus returning to currency a notion that was prominent in the early liturgy and in the teaching of the Fathers: 'The first victory over sin is shown in baptism when we are crucified with Christ that "this sinful body" may be destroyed and we may be delivered from slavery to sin (Rom. 6 : 6). Risen however with Christ, we can henceforth live for God. . . . But further, Christ committed a ministry of penance to his church, so that Christians who have fallen into sin after baptism may be renewed in grace and be reconciled with God.' As St Ambrose put it, 'The church has water and tears, the water of baptism and the tears of repentance', a theme that is expressed magnificently though in a more liturgical way in the great Maundy Thursday text for the Reconciliation of Penitents that is to be found in the Gelasian Sacramentary: 'Now has arrived, Venerable Pontiff, the accepted time, the day of divine propitiation and the salvation of mankind when death was destroyed and eternal life had its beginning, the day when a new plantation is to be made and all that is old cleansed and healed. . . . Our number is increased by the accession of those to be re-born and *we grow by the return of the repentant*. Water washes, tears wash, whence comes joy over the accession of those who have been called and rejoicing over the penitent who are absolved . . .'[1] These few phrases formed part of the public liturgy of reconciliation of penitent sinners which was a sacrament-sign of the repentant church. As the Second Vatican Council said, the church is *semper purificanda* and the other face of purification is repentance.

---

[1] *Gelasian Sacramentary*, ed. Mohlberg, nos. 353–9.

Reconciliation

Both the texts cited above, and the Order, use the term reconciliation and this is a notion that dominates throughout. The term is used again and again and quite deliberately. If there had not been a pastoral need to maintain a certain continuity with past usage one suspects that the document might well have been called 'The Order of Reconciliation'.[2] It is necessary then to give some attention to this term.

Reconciliation means the reunion of two persons or two communities by the removal of whatever has separated them. Thus in Matthew 5 : 23, dissension between two members of the Christian community is a barrier to making an acceptable offering to God. Their differences must be resolved, the two must be reconciled before the offering can be made. In Ephesians 2 : 14–18, Jesus is spoken of as 'the peace' that has thrown down the barrier between Jew and Gentile, and this truth is driven home in a series of powerful phrases: by the blood of the cross Jesus has made peace, has created one single new Man in himself, and in his own person has killed hostility, so that both communities have the one Spirit through whom we have access to the Father. In penance the barrier we have set up by sin is removed by the reconciling power of the cross. But if this is to take place we must first respond to the word of God who indeed takes the initiative, who calls us and who by his grace makes our repentance possible. Nevertheless, the term repentance (and *a fortiori* 'penance') emphasises the human response. If the sinner is to be re-united to God, the barrier of sin must be removed and repentance alone cannot do this. When we were in sin, God made us alive with him (Christ), forgiving our trespasses, cancelling the bond (*cheirographon*) that stood against us, setting it aside and nailing it to the cross (Colossians 2 : 14). Thus was the barrier removed and the sinner reconciled to God. In reconciliation there is not only the divine initiative to repentance, there is the second intervention through Christ through whom and in the Holy Spirit we are united to God.

---

[2] See Austin Flannery, *Doctrine and Life*, 24 (April 1974), who refers to an issue of the *Osservatore Romano* (8 February 1974) in which it is said that the terms 'reconcile' and 'reconciliation' were deliberately chosen instead of 'absolve', 'absolution' and 'confession'.

Reconciliation then emphasises both man's approach to God and God's to man and the reunion effected by the passion, death and resurrection of Christ.

But the ministry of reconciliation is not separated from, nor merely exists alongside, the church or community that is the people of God—no more than the eucharistic memorial or *anamnesis* of the passion, death and resurrection of the Lord can be divorced from the church that celebrates it. As the new Order says (2), echoing St Paul, Christ committed the ministry of penance to his church: 'God was in Christ reconciling the world to himself . . . entrusting to us the message of reconciliation. So we are ambassadors for Christ, God making his appeal through us.' Therefore, continues St Paul, 'We beseech you on behalf of Christ, be reconciled to God. For our sake he made him to be sin who knew no sin, so that in him we might become the righteousness of God' (2 Corinthians 5 : 19–21). No doubt Paul had in mind the divisions of the church at Corinth but his teaching is applicable to the whole church. And as the church is the repentant church, the assembly of sinners who have repented, so it must be the church of reconciliation first among its own members and then as the instrument of the reconciliation of the world with God and of man with man. The eucharist is the sacrament-sign of the church that came into existence by the passion, death and resurrection of Christ and is sustained in its unity by the continual celebration of the paschal mystery. The sacrament of penance in all its breadth and depth is the sacrament-sign of the reconciliation effected on the cross and made present by the proclamation of the gospel of repentance, by the prayer of the church and above all in the continual celebration of the ministry of reconciliation in the sacrament of penance.

In this teaching will be found the fundamental reason why the church has turned the sacrament from being a purely private transaction (or so it seemed) into a public ministry in which the church in the name of Christ can call all men to repentance and through the power of the reconciling Christ bring all into union with God. Not surprisingly therefore the whole of the new Order is built on the two foundations of repentance and reconciliation and these two themes are expressed throughout the three forms that the celebration of the sacrament may take. If this 'reform' seems to be an innovation a brief glance at the history of penance will show that it is a return to tradition though that return is not a mere piece of archaism.

Penance in the Past

Like many other parts of the liturgy Penance has undergone considerable changes in the past and it could be said that from being one of the most public rites of the early centuries of the church it became the most private. Once a public acknowledgement of sin on the part of both the sinner and the church, it became the private avowal of personal sin in the darkness of a confessional.

The church began its life on the day of Pentecost with the proclamation of the gospel of repentance: 'Repent and be baptised every one of you in the name of Jesus Christ for the forgiveness of sins' (Acts 2 : 38) and we may observe *en passant* that this is the faithful echo of our Lord's own ministry, 'Repent and believe the gospel', words with which he opened his mission (Mark 1 : 15). Although in New Testament times the converted were not expected to sin, some undoubtedly did. There was the public sinner of 1 Corinthians 5 whom the local church was required to reject though the rejection was not definitive (cf 2 Corinthians 2 : 5–11). St Paul tells the community to receive back the sinner, to forgive him and comfort him lest he 'be overwhelmed by excessive sorrow'. For St John there was always prayer, if the sin was not 'deadly', and the powerful advocacy of Jesus Christ the righteous (1 John 2 : 1 and 5 : 16–17).[3] Above and beyond all this was the figure of the merciful Saviour who was a vivid reality to the first Christians and not a person in a book.

It seemed necessary to recall, however briefly, the spirit of New Testament repentance, forgiveness and reconciliation since in the second century a period of rigorism set in whose ultimate effects were not always happy.

Canonical Penance

By the end of the second century the discipline called canonical penance was in full force and was very rigorous— though less so than, in the opinion of some writers, in the early

---

[3] The 'deadly' or 'mortal' sin seems to have been apostasy, for which an intervention of the church was necessary (see JB *in loco*).

part of the century (e.g. Hermas). The question was asked: Could great sins, that is, public sins, be forgiven? Some said no but others (and this was the Roman practice) said that after a long period of penance, usually lasting a life-time, such sinners could be reconciled and re-integrated into the full life of the church. Reconciliation, however, could only take place once. A second sin meant exclusion for ever from the sacramental life of the church.

The pattern of the 'sacrament' was approximately this. There was one who had committed a public sin, either apostasy (frequent enough in times of persecution), homicide or adultery and in the small communities of the time such sins would be known. Through the church's preaching of repentance he was invited to repent and if he did repent this meant that he voluntarily submitted himself to public penance. By the time of St Augustine he approached the bishop and from him received the *correptio*, i.e. the bishop confronted him with the demands of the gospel and urged him to take upon himself the discipline of penance. This involved many years of fasting, abstinence from the use of marriage and in fact the living of the life of an ascetic or monk. Although the penance was rigorous it was not thought of simply as 'punishment' for sins committed, but rather as medicinal, a means by which the sinner could renew his spiritual life.

This can be understood the more readily when we see that along with the penance went the prayer of the church for sinners which formed a regular element of the intercessions or 'prayers of the faithful' at every celebration of the eucharist. This was regarded as of the highest importance, for it was by the prayer of the church that the ultimate and complete conversion of the sinner would be obtained.

By the sixth century in Rome (if the Gelasian Sacramentary reflects the practice of that time) the sinner, after penance, was reconciled in the public service of reconciliation that took place on Maundy Thursday. The rite in the Gelasian Sacramentary envisages several penitents. They are led into church by the archdeacon who bids them prostrate on the floor of the church. He then addresses the pope, who presides, in very moving terms, one or two of which we have quoted above. In reply the pope pronounces in a long prayer the reconciliation of the penitents, their re-integration into the life of the church and their re-admission to holy communion. As the texts indicate the church is renewed and made whole again by the return of the penitents who can now begin a new life.

Whatever may have been the disadvantages of the discipline of penance it kept before the people the great themes of repentance, of prayer, of reconciliation and of the ministry of reconciliation committed to the church by Christ. Moreover the whole process remained profoundly ecclesial: the sense of the church both in respect of sin and respect of the reconciliation was acute. As St Ambrose wrote, 'by us the church is wounded (*in nobis ecclesia vulneratur*)' and again 'Let us take care lest our falls wound the church'.[4] Without slavish imitation of earlier models of penance, the church has now restored the ecclesial dimension to the sacrament.

Tariffed Penance

Whatever mitigations the system of penance underwent it remained too severe for the generality of Christians many of whom (including Ambrose and Augustine) preferred to remain catechumens in all the stormy days of their youth. Others who had sinned put off reconciliation until their death-beds with the result that they would go without communion for most of their lives.

For the daily faults of the Christian and no doubt for bigger ones that were not public the means of forgiveness were prayer (the Lord's prayer was especially important in this regard), fasting and almsgiving: in the sermons of Leo the Great for Lent and the Ember days these can be clearly seen as reparatory. Whatever is to be said about this system, it did at least keep before the people the notion that penitence is a normal part of the Christian life.

Whether or not the people of Northern Europe found this system unsatisfactory or whether they acquired a deeper sense of sin is a matter for further investigation; for it was from there—from Ireland in particular—that a change came. There the church was organised on a monastic basis. The abbot was the all-important man and if there was a bishop in the community he was not necessarily its head. The rule was rigorous, the chapter of faults occurred frequently and the monks had to

---

[4] See H. de Lubac, *Méditations sur l'Eglise*, Paris, 1953, p. 99.

declare their faults to the abbot. No doubt they did not make much distinction between faults of breaking the rule and more serious faults that we should call sins. It is out of this situation that the notion of frequent confession came. In addition, what was regarded as an appropriate penance was allocated for the faults committed. As one writer has put it, 'ten years on bread and water for homicide and six blows for coughing during a psalm'.[5] The notion was that the punishment should fit the crime and when the system was transferred to the secular sphere, as it was very quickly, tariffs were drawn up that were conceived to meet the needs of the often violent society of the time. Then they were published in Penitentials of which examples remain from Ireland, England (the Penitential of Theodore of Canterbury), from Gaul and Spain, and whether with or without interacting influences, there were very similar penitentials in the eastern church.[6]

How this system worked for ordinary Christians who never committed any sin of great consequence must remain a matter of speculation. If 'tariffed penance' opened the door to more frequent confession, it would be some time before it affected general practice. Penances in any case remained severe and the custom of postponing reconciliation to the end of one's life continued. Meanwhile the whole of social life was affected by tribal and feudal customs which are clearly marked in the Penitentials. Lords and other great people did indeed submit themselves to penance after a notable crime or sin but the tendency grew to get others to perform the very heavy penances. Sometimes the priest employed on their lands was made to do penance in their stead and many were the monasteries founded to pray for and make expiation for the sins of their founders. Again, penances were commuted; a long period of penance was replaced by a short sharp one, e.g. severe fasting for a number of days, or a payment, i.e. charitable alms, were substituted. All this led to obvious abuses and was undesirable in itself. Tariffed penance did however lead to the practice of more frequent confession.

[5] K. Donovan in *Music and Liturgy*, 1 (Autumn 1974), p. 11, to which article this section owes a good deal.
[6] See B. Dunne, OSB, 'The Sacrament of Penance in the Eastern Churches', *Doctrine and Life*, Supplement for January–February, 1977.

There was however a further development. In tariffed penance the old order of events was kept: presentation to the bishop (or priest), some form of confession, the acceptance of penance, its performance (however done), reconciliation and finally re-admission to holy communion. But gradually this order was changed: reconciliation (now called more and more frequently absolution) was granted immediately after the confession and *before* the penance had been performed. Except for notorious sins, when something of the old discipline was retained, the penitent was immediately admitted to communion.

Private Penance

This form of penance, which we have come to regard as typical, was little used before the Fourth Lateran Council (1215) which decreed that all should go to confession at least once a year before making their Easter communion. This is not to be seen as penal legislation; its intent was pastoral. The council desired that people should approach communion worthily and that the custom of infrequent communions (once or twice in a lifetime!) should cease. From the thirteenth century onwards the custom of frequent confession and communion became customary, at least among the devout. For most, however, annual confession and communion remained the norm.

It was this tradition that the Council of Trent took up and sought to improve. It urged more frequent communion and, again to ensure worthiness, laid down that normally it should be preceded by confession. When in the last decades of the nineteenth century, and especially after the decree on frequent communion of Pius X in this century, great numbers went to communion at least once a week, they felt a certain obligation to go to confession as often. This led to a situation that we can see now was more than a little odd: considerable numbers of devout souls with little if anything to confess besieging confessionals every Saturday evening. What had happened is that church legislation, which had quite different circumstances in view, was transferred unthinkingly to a new situation. The same thing happened, I believe, in the matter of children's first confession and as one views the past it is difficult to see that there was any worked-out theology underpinning this practice. There was indeed an ideal of spiritual perfection that the church authorities wished to put before the people but this hardly adds up to a theology and one has to ask whether what was intended by the use of the sacrament of penance could not have been achieved by spiritual counsel.

In any case the people themselves have seen that there is no essential connection between confession and holy communion and current practice is that people go to confession more rarely but very often make a better use of the sacrament. Its celebration is more relaxed, more human, the 'confession' is often more like a dialogue than the mere listing of sins and the existence of 'confessional rooms' (replacing the 'box') witnesses to the desire of many for spiritual counsel.

This, in very general terms, is the situation in which the new Order of Penance has appeared, and if it is in some sense a restoration of the past, only the exploitation of its *whole* content will show whether it meets the needs of people today and of future generations. At the time of writing the results that might have been expected from the new Order are hardly apparent. Most people use the sacrament very much as they did formerly and some, both clergy and people, are irritated by the greater elaboration of the rite of 'private confession'. As in the eucharist and the other sacraments, *speed* is the enemy of a devout celebration of penance. For those who have appreciated the corporate nature of the revised liturgy generally, the public service of penance is found to be helpful, though the individual and private absolutions seem to be somewhat anomalous and in practice are not easy to organise. Finally, the doubts about when and in what circumstances the third form that includes public reconciliation and absolution may be used have largely inhibited its use in the life of the church. No doubt, as with the eucharist, a new understanding and use of penance will take time. If this is to be achieved three things would seem to be necessary.

1. The importance of the proclamation of the word of God calling Christians to repentance must be appreciated.

2. In no sacrament are the acts of the participant so important as in this. They are part of its very substance and a deeper understanding is necessary of all three elements, contrition, confession and satisfaction.

3. There is a need to understand the communal or corporate nature of the sacrament. It is an act of the church, involving

the whole church both in its awareness of sin, in the corporate nature of reparation for sin and in the reconciliation it effects.

These points will now be taken up in the context of what the Order calls 'The Parts of the Sacrament' (6, 7).

The Parts of the Sacrament

As we have indicated above, these include the acts of the penitent, which have a special importance in this sacrament. Negatively the matter can be put in this way: without repentance there is no sacrament and, in the present discipline of the church, confession or avowal of sin committed is an integral part of the sacrament. Positively, with the absolution of the confessor they constitute the sacrament and if we look for the sign of the sacrament it is here that we shall find it. In other words, when the penitent declares his sorrow, confesses his sins and accepts the 'penance' imposed by the confessor he is making the sacrament. As Karl Rahner has put it somewhat bluntly, 'The confessing sinner celebrates a part of the Church's liturgy and does not receive the effect of someone else's liturgy.'[7]

Contrition

The Order retains the term and the definition of the Council of Trent:[8] 'Contrition is heartfelt sorrow for sin committed and detestation of it, together with the resolve not to sin in the future.' But, taking a lead from Pope Paul VI's Letter (p. 6), the Order broadens and deepens its meaning. The wider perspective sets it in the context of the Christian life as a whole: 'We may only approach the kingdom of Christ by *metanoia*, that is, by an inner change of the whole human personality (*totius hominis mutatione*), and in repentance we begin to examine and judge our lives and seek to put them in order.' This is undoubtedly the meaning of the gospel term and it might seem to make very great demands on us. This is true, but it is not for us to water down the truth of the gospel. Perhaps if we had been confronted with it earlier in life we should have taken

---

[7] *Theological Investigations*, Vol. II, London, 1963, p. 160. Elsewhere (p. 156) he says that 'within the totality of the sign (and only then) the priestly absolution is for St Thomas the decisive element as the causal effect'.

[8] Denz.-Schön. 1676 (as given in the *Ordo*).

'conversion' more seriously: repentance in this sense would have been a more profound and permanent element in our lives. But precisely because repentance is so far-reaching it must be the matter of a life-time and one of the purposes of the *sacrament* of penance is to maintain and make effective the spirit of repentance. The sacrament can be seen—and it is one of the great virtues of the Order that it so sees it—as part of the continuing process of being or becoming a Christian. 'Conversion,' says the Order, 'must affect man interiorly if he is to be progressively enlightened and become more and more like Christ.'

The Order continues with the traditional doctrine that sorrow for sin must be prompted by the love of God but the way it expresses it is more in accord with modern biblical considerations than the old formulation of it. The penitent is to be moved by the *holiness of God* and *his love as revealed in Jesus Christ*, in whom the fulness of God dwelt and through whom God reconciled to himself all things whether on earth or in heaven, making peace by the blood of the cross. Reference is made to Colossians 1 : 19, to the general teaching of the first part of that epistle and to the parallel passages in Ephesians. Thus the reconciling power of Christ is seen as the supreme motive of repentance. It would not be too much to say that the whole paschal mystery, concretely the passion, death and resurrection of Christ, is to be the motive of repentance: '[Give thanks to the Father] who has qualified us to share in the inheritance of the saints in light. He has delivered us from the dominion of darkness and transferred us to the kingdom of his beloved Son, in whom we have redemption, the forgiveness of sins' (Colossians 1 : 13–14). The paschal mystery is celebrated in the rite but it must be a reality in the interior life of each repentant Christian. As the Order says, on this heartfelt contrition depends the reality of the sacrament.

No doubt it is not the intention of a liturgical document to decide disputes between theologians—in this case that concerning contrition and attrition—but it must be said that attrition does not enter into the thinking of the Order. This may be because the Order regards repentance as a continuing process. At the beginning it may indeed be imperfect but, according to the mind of the Order, it should be deepened and grow towards 'perfect' contrition day by day. It would not seem however to be the implication that the confessor should make exorbitant demands of the penitent. He must meet him where he is and, by presenting to him the love of God as revealed in the passion, death and resurrection of Christ, seek to vitalise his repentance to the point where there is a response of love, however imperfectly formulated, to the love of God. On the other hand, all preaching and instruction about the sacrament of penance should put before people the whole doctrine of the Order in this respect, a doctrine that can be said to be that of the church. In this context services of penance have a very important role to perform.

Confession

In the time of Tertullian the avowal of faults was known as *exomologesis* which meant a great deal more than a detailing of sins. The word, a noun coming from the same verb used in some of the praising psalms (e.g. *Confitemini Domino*, 135), implied an act of worship, a recognition of the holiness of God and of what he demands of us. The Order seems to look back to this tradition rather than to the more recent one: 'examination of conscience and the verbal declaration are to be done in the light of the God of mercy'. Confession is the expression of what we *are* before God as well as of the contrition we have conceived in our hearts. Indeed as almost all penitents know (though they may not reflect on the matter), confession is a mode of contrition; it is penitential and sometimes painful because humiliating. If then we see confession as a humble avowal of what we are and of the faults that indicate what we are, then we shall see it not so much as a strict accounting of sins but as a way of putting ourselves before God as sinners seeking his forgiveness. If justification is sought for auricular confession of sins, it is to be found along these lines rather than in the sphere of providing 'matter' for judgement.

But, as we have seen above, confession is part of the sacramental sign and that is not just a theological statement. It expresses a profound human need. We can and do conceive sorrow for sin in our hearts but we also feel the need to express it in words or in some external action. An apology that is never externalised is simply not an apology. As many have borne witness, the need to confess, especially to one who, as the Order says, acts *in persona Christi*, is deeply rooted in human nature and releases many from what would be an intolerable burden. The apparent indifference of many modern Christians to this aspect of the sacrament is disturbing and may well be a symptom of the loss of the sense of sin which in turn may mean a loss of the sense of God.

The penitent, then, submits his sin to the 'spiritual judgement' of the confessor for absolution—or not, as the case (very rarely) may be. The Order is repeating the well-known doctrine of the Council of Trent but, as we shall see, when we come to consider the role of the confessor, the emphasis is a little different from what has been common in manuals of theology. He acts '*in persona Christi*' and the compassion of Christ must condition his 'judgement'; he shares in 'the power of the keys' but this is rather to authenticate his role as representative of the church than as some secular judge pronouncing sentence. The whole process is different. Karl Rahner has noted that from the beginning the church has bound only that she may loose: 'Binding and loosing are not two sides of an alternative, but two phases of the one reaction whereby the Holy Church answers the sin of one of her members'. The purpose of the binding is to uncover the anomalous situation of the sinner *vis-à-vis* the church which is holy and of which he is an unholy member. His belonging to the church is a contradiction of her holiness and 'this has to be brought to light on the visible plane of the church' and only then can the guilt towards God and the church be lifted or 'loosed, again on the same plane, i.e. on the sacramental plane'. As Rahner goes on to say, this is how the early church always understood the matter. The 'binding' is essentially an act of mercy, not a condemnation with punishment attached.[9]

How the examination of conscience and subsequent confession are to be made will be considered later but meanwhile we may take into account some considerations of L. Monden.[10] The confession of the penitent is much more a sign of his repentance than a piece of criminal accounting. In practice, he often confesses more than he expresses in words and, on the other hand, sometimes and unwittingly less. As for the priest's

---

[9] *Op. cit.*, p. 142.
[10] *Sin, Liberty and Law*, New York, 1965, p. 47.

judgement, 'his human meeting with sinfulness is only (again) a *sign*—often a very imperfect and shadowy sign—of the merciful salvific judgement of God'. The priest is the *minister* (servant) of Christ, not his substitute.

Satisfaction

'Satisfaction' is not a happy term. The human being can never make 'satisfaction' to God whom he has offended by sin. If satisfaction was to be made there was need of a Redeemer to make it. Moreover, it is difficult to find in the New Testament any basis for the distinction between sin and 'the punishment due to sin'. When God forgives, he forgives all. The *word* is first found in Tertullian (*De Paenitentia*, 8) and, according to A. Blaise, it refers there to the avowal of sin that in itself indicates an intention to do penance.[11] According to the same author, it means generally an action to make satisfaction to God by *penitence* or, more generally still, amendment of life by contrition, prayer and mortification. This puts us on the right way to an understanding of the term and the action as they existed in the time of public penitence. The time of penitence was not so much the making of satisfaction—even to the church—but a time for the deepening of repentance and the acceptance of a whole way of life that would restore the sinner to his former condition. Perhaps it would be an over-simplification to say that for the Fathers and the Christian writers of the time the purpose of the penance was medicinal rather than punitive but that is the general impression one takes away from them. This view is supported by the continual prayer that was made for the penitents in the liturgy: to repeat what has been said above, the ban, the 'binding', was essentially an act of mercy for it is not an act of mercy to allow a sinner to continue in his sin or in the notion that what he has done is not sinful.

Broadly speaking, this is the view of the new Order. It is both reserved and positive on the subject. It nowhere uses the phrase 'temporal punishment due to sin' and is content to speak of 'reparation for the damage caused by sin' (which of course in cases of theft or calumny is a kind of satisfaction),

---

[11] A. Blaise, *Dictionnaire Latin-Français des Auteurs Chrétiens*, Strasbourg–Paris, 1954, *s.v.* 'satisfactio'.

of 'the order injured by sin' and of the 'disease' (*morbus*) which is to be cured by the appropriate remedy. In this paragraph the Order speaks of 'restoration', 'cure' and 'renewal of life', all of which it sees as the positive values of 'penance' (satisfaction) in the narrower sense. There is no suggestion of legalism anywhere, and in one sentence the Order goes to the heart of the matter. The penance is to be a remedy for sin and a means for the renewal of life so that the penitent 'forgetting those things that are behind' (Philippians 3 : 13) may *once more be inserted into the mystery of salvation.* That indeed is the whole purpose of the sacrament: re-integration into the saving mystery of Christ's passion, death and resurrection. We naturally think of the insertion of the individual into the mystery of Christ first through baptism and then in the eucharist. But if Christ came to take away 'the sin of the world' (John 1 : 29), it is here in the sacrament of penance that the penitent meets the saving, forgiving Christ, is reconciled with him so that he may take up the 'following of Christ' which, in Pauline terms, (referred to in the Order) means sharing in his death and resurrection: 'All I want is to know Christ and the power of his resurrection and to share his sufferings by reproducing the pattern of his death . . .' (Philippians 3 : 10–11).

On this view 'penance' is the bridge between the sacrament and daily living, and it is the intention of the Order that it should be seen as such. It is also wholly in accord with the teaching of Paul VI in his letter *Paenitemini* (E.T. p. 7): 'Following the Master, every Christian must renounce himself, take up his cross, and participate in the sufferings of Christ. Thus, transformed into the image of Christ's death, he is capable of meditating on the glory of the resurrection. Furthermore, following the Master, he can live no longer for himself but must live for him who loves him and gave himself up for him. He will have to live for his brethren . . .'[12] The question of 'penance' is thus opened out to Christian living. It will

---

[12] The number of texts given shows that the pope's teaching is wholly biblical: Phil. 3 : 10–11; Rom. 6 : 10; Gal. 2 : 20; Col. 1 : 24, though this last citation has a rather different sense from that given by spiritual writers. The 'sufferings of Christ' are intimately connected with the completion of *the preaching of the gospel*, so they would be the apostolic sufferings endured as the gospel is continually brought to new places until a certain quota is reached. Thus R. E. Brown, J. A. Fitzmyer and R. E. Murphy (eds.), *The Jerome Biblical Commentary*, London, 1969, p. 338, *in loco*.

consist first in the faithful performance of the duties of one's daily life and acceptance of the difficulties of one's daily work and existence. But 'living for the brethren' in current terms means serving one's neighbour and in this light 'penance' takes on a wholly new dimension which indeed is a main concern of the Order: sin, reparation, re-integration into the life of the church and a concern for others. It is what the Order calls the 'social dimension of the sacrament of penance'.

Absolution (6d)

Faithful to the sacramental theology of the Constitution on the Liturgy (7) the revisers describe absolution 'as the sign by which God grants pardon to the sinner who manifests his conversion to a minister of the church and thus the sacrament is brought to completion'. But as we have said above, the acts of the penitent are parts of the sacramental sign and with the absolution constitute the sacrament. We need to be aware that there is here a process (which in the earlier ages of the church took quite a long time) and absolution is the definitive moment when the whole process is brought to completion by the power of Christ working through the church and his minister. But the Order is not content with this; it goes on: 'By the divine economy, as God willed that the kindness and love (*philanthropia*, in the Greek) of God our Saviour appeared visibly to mankind (Titus 3 : 4–5), so it was his will to grant us salvation by visible signs and thus to renew the covenant broken by sin.' This puts the whole sacrament in the context of the history of salvation which reached its culmination in the passion, death and resurrection of Christ by which we are reconciled.

The profoundly scriptural teaching of the Order is reinforced by its own commentary on the meaning of absolution which in itself seems so cold a word: 'By the sacrament of penance, therefore, the Father welcomes the repentant son who comes back to him, Christ puts the lost sheep on his shoulder and brings him back to the fold, and the Holy Spirit sanctifies once more the one who is the temple of the Holy Spirit. . . . Finally, all this is manifested (one might almost say, "celebrated") through a renewed and more fervent participation in the table of the Lord's eucharist in which, now that the son has returned from a distant land, there is great joy in the banquet of the church of God.' This passage, perhaps more than any other, gives the church's view of this sacrament, reminding us as it does of the formula of absolution. There is the saving mercy of God, Father, Son and Holy Spirit, who are each active in the return of the sinner, and the eucharist is revealed as the culmination of pardon and absolution, as it is of all the sacraments. The way to it has been barred by sin but now the barrier is removed, pardon and reconciliation are achieved by encounter with the redeeming Christ.

The Role of the Confessor (9, 10)

In the mind of the Order the confessor is not just someone who 'hears confessions' or 'judges' the condition of his penitents in human fashion. Whether bishop or priest, he is a minister of *conversion*. Nor does he exercise this ministry simply in the sacrament. He 'preaches conversion and calls people to repentance'. This echoes the Constitution on the Liturgy (9): 'To believers also the Church must ever preach faith and penance' and it is especially in services of penitence, organised from time to time, that the church is able to preach the gospel of repentance. In the administration of the sacrament 'in the name of Christ and by the power of the Holy Spirit', confessors 'bear witness to the remission of sins and impart it'. The constant recalling in the Order of the operation of the Holy Spirit is quite remarkable and puts us in touch both with the thinking of the Eastern Churches and with the practice of the early church when the laying-on of hands was the symbol of the communication of the Holy Spirit in the reconciliation of the sinner to the church.[13] Against such a background are set the qualities and function of the confessor. He is to have the necessary knowledge, acquired by study, which he will use with prudence 'under the guidance of the church' and he must pray for further guidance. But, given this, he will be able to discern the illnesses of the soul, provide apt remedies and 'exercise the function of judge'. But this power of

---

[13] This emphasis on the work of the Holy Spirit in the new Order seems to be quite deliberate. Père Ligier, who was a member of the first commission on the rite of penance, wrote in *LMD* (90, 1967, p. 161): 'In the eastern perspective the administration of this sacrament requires not simply the *power* of the Holy Spirit but also a familiarity with divine things which is possessed by those who live in the Spirit and know the things of God and the secrets of hearts.' He refers to Origen, *De Oratione*, 28. The whole article seems to have influenced the redaction of the Order.

judgement is of a quite special kind, as the Order makes clear: judgement in the sacrament of penance is an exercise of the 'discernment of spirits which is a gift of the Holy Spirit giving an intimate knowledge of the workings of God in the human heart and in itself the fruit of charity' (10). It is a teaching that once again emphasises the work of the Holy Spirit in the sacrament of penance and reflects at once John 20 : 22–3 and the formula of absolution. Moreover, it extends what has been for long a traditional notion. 'Discernment of spirits' has usually been thought of as a special gift of special people who can guide those in the higher reaches of the spiritual life—or alternatively those who could discern diabolical from benign spirits at work in the heart. Now it is said that every confessor who has prepared himself by study and prayer has this gift and in the administration of the sacrament he is exercising it. He is not *just* a spiritual psychiatrist (though a knowledge of psychiatry is helpful), much less is he merely an earthly judge handing out sentence according to some code of law. He is a spiritual man— in the old medieval term, a 'ghostly fader'—who is operating under the influence of the Holy Spirit and bringing to birth in a soul the effects of repentance and amendment of life.

As if this were not enough, the Order adds that in the sacrament he is essentially 'father', bearing in himself the image of Christ and revealing to the penitent whom he welcomes 'the heart of the Father' who is ever ready to forgive. In himself he is a sign of the Father's love shown forth in the Son and by consequence he is exercising a function of Christ himself 'who in mercy effected the work of redemption and by his power is present in the sacraments' (cf CL7).

All this represents a high doctrine of the role of the confessor and if this role may be difficult always to live up to, it is as well to be aware that this is what a confessor is. The work of preparation for this ministry by study and prayer is seen to be all the more important.

Before speaking of the role of the confessor, the Order (8) has dealt with an aspect of the ministry of penance which has rarely been seen in modern times. 'The *whole* church as the priestly people', it says, is involved in different ways in this ministry of reconciliation. The church, the local community for instance, does this by calling sinners to repentance through the proclamation of God's word, by praying for them and by showing a maternal care and concern for them and by coming to their aid.

There is much that could be said about this. Few parishes seem to have any great concern for those who are called lapsed or the indifferent and all of us are a little self-conscious about calling other people 'sinners' since we are so conscious that we are sinners ourselves. But evidently there is here a whole pastoral policy to be thought out for the reclamation of those members of our communities who for one reason or another have fallen away. The phrase 'the priestly people' is very striking and since the Christian people are such they share in some way in the more strictly priestly ministry of reconciliation. Perhaps 'reconciliation' is the key-word. There is much that the laity can do in parish communities to reconcile those who are divided or to draw them back gently to the church from which they have become alienated. In any case, there is the whole ministry of *prayer* for 'sinners' which the early church practised with such vigour and conviction. At least in Lent then there should be constant and discreetly-worded petitions for sinners and if a portion of the Divine Office is celebrated in parishes there is room there for the same intention.

The Penitent (11)

Little enough is said here about the role of the penitent because the matter has already been dealt with (6a, b, c) and because there is more to be said in a practical way later on (17–20). What the Order does do is to emphasise the importance of the acts of the penitent and in doing so echoes the teaching of Rahner given above. Through his acts the penitent is playing his (necessary) part in the celebration of the sacrament: 'Thus the Christian, while experiencing God's mercy and proclaiming it by his life, celebrates with the priest the liturgy of the church which constantly renews itself. The renewal of the penitent is part of the constant renewal of the church itself.'

Practical Matters

Section 9a, b is concerned with the canonical aspect of ministry. The ordinary ministers of the sacrament are *bishops* and priests 'who are in communion with their bishop and act by his authority'. Priests must be willing to hear people's confessions whenever they reasonably ask. Lent is a particularly favourable time for the celebration of the sacrament and communal services of penitence should be celebrated at this time to give opportunities to the faithful 'to be reconciled with God and their neighbours so that, spiritually renewed, they may celebrate the paschal mystery at the end of Lent'. This is but one of the many touches that relate penance to the paschal mystery.

The Place of Confession

Since the sixteenth century confession has been made in a structure called the confessional and the Code of Canon Law (1918) laid down that it must be in a conspicuous place and that there must be a grille between the confessor and the penitent. Local conferences of bishops may now make other arrangements (38b). Two considerations come into play here.

1. For some time now many people have made known their desire to have what they call a more human situation for confession. To kneel in front of a veiled grille and to speak to an unseen person the other side of it some find inhibiting. Accordingly in many churches 'confessional rooms' have been provided where penitent and priest can sit facing each other and enter into a dialogue. There is also the problem of what to do when there is a service of penitence and many confessors are engaged to hear confessions. 'Boxes' cannot be provided for them all. Clearly different arrangements in different situations are necessary and it would be detrimental to the celebration of this sacrament if hard and fast rules were laid down, *ne varientur*. Provided that the secrecy of the confession can be preserved there would seem to be no reason why confessions should not be heard on the sanctuary (as in the Middle Ages) or in a side chapel.

2. This is all the more necessary as the one symbolic gesture of this sacrament is the laying-on of hands, which should be seen by the penitent and others. This gesture, in somewhat vestigial form, has been preserved throughout the centuries and the new Order insists on it; 'After the prayer (act of sorrow) of the penitent the priest extends his hands over his head (or at least his right hand) and pronounces the essential words of absolution' (19). The importance of this gesture is that in all the early practice of penance and reconciliation it was seen as the sign of re-integration into the church of the sinner effected by the power of the Holy Spirit. Since it is a sign or symbol it should be seen. But that is usually impossible in the conven-

tional confessional. Other arrangements then need to be made if this symbol is to retain its importance and since this sacrament is weak in symbolism, there is all the more reason to see that it is made visible.

Likewise, conferences of bishops are to suggest appropriate gesture or gestures to be used in services of public reconciliation on the part of those who wish to receive the general absolution (35). This may be either a bowing of the head or kneeling down. Since this part of the service follows on the homily, the people will be sitting and it will be for the celebrant to invite those who wish to be absolved to kneel. There is no difficulty about this since the whole assembly usually wish to receive the absolution. In other cultures than our own there may well be other signs of repentance that will be appropriate.

The Three Liturgies of Penance

1. The Reconciliation of Individual Penitents (41–7)

Since the Order has been in use for some five years there is no need to give any elaborate account of this liturgy. There is the welcome by the confessor, the words he addresses to the penitent to stimulate trust in God's goodness, the proclamation of God's word (read either by the penitent or the confessor), the confession and the giving of spiritual counsel, the prayer of repentance, the absolution, a brief thanksgiving and the dismissal. Commentary on one or two of these points may be useful.

Before confessing the penitent is encouraged to make known to the confessor the conditions and circumstances of his life, the difficulties he may find in leading the Christian life 'and whatever may be useful for the confessor to know for the exercise of his ministry' (16). This is not laid down as an obligation and it is for the penitent to take the initiative but it does suggest that confession is to be seen as at least partly a dialogue and not just a listing of sins.

The reading of a passage of scripture is an expression of the axiom that we are saved by faith and the sacraments of faith but here in particular it is intended to confront the penitent with the demands of God that are made known in his word. Unhappily, it seems already to have become a formality and many if not most penitents seem quite happy to have it omitted. Old habits die hard. After confession the confessor exhorts the penitent to true repentance and will provide appropriate counsel for the living of the Christian life. If necessary he will instruct the penitent in the duties of Christian living and in the case of damage, whether material (theft) or spiritual (calumny), he will 'lead the penitent to make fitting restitution'.

Closely connected with the counsel is the 'penance'. This is to be thought of not merely as expiation for past sins but as a remedy for weakness and a help towards amendment of life. It may consist of prayers, acts of self-denial but especially of 'service of neighbour and works of mercy which will throw light on *the social nature of sin and its remission*' (18). In a word, the new way of life that the penitent now undertakes is the real 'penance' and it will be seen that it is the link between the sacrament and life. It also extends the vision of the penitent far beyond his own private concerns and reminds him that he is part of a living body which is injured by his sins and which can be enriched by the quality of his Christian life.

Of the prayer, or 'act of contrition', which the penitent recites after receiving the 'penance', the Order says that it should be largely in scriptural terms. However, this is hardly verified in the formula it gives and the reader should note the many alternatives to be found under nos. 85–92. The shortest is one of the most effective: 'Lord Jesus, Son of God, have mercy on me a sinner' (cf Luke 18 : 13).

Something has been said already about the formula of absolution but a few further remarks will be in place here since, apart from the public form of penitence, it is always used.

It should be noted first that, apart from the last sentence 'I absolve you. . . .', it is in deprecatory form: i.e. it is a prayer, a fact that is disguised by the exigencies of English translation. In Latin it is in the subjunctive mood and is a petition to God the Father that through the paschal mystery of his Son who reconciled the world, and through the Holy Spirit who was sent for the forgiveness of sins, the penitent sinner may receive pardon and peace, which are the effects of reconciliation. This form reflects the church's usage of the time before the twelfth century when absolution and reconciliation were wholly in the form of prayer (cf the Gelasian Sacramentary referred to above). The last sentence, in the indicative mood, comes from that same century when the canonists, who greatly influenced the theologians of their time as of subsequent ages, thought that the indicative was the appropriate mood for sacramental formulas.[14] The whole formula in English is this:

> God, Father of mercies,
> through the death and resurrection of his Son,
> has reconciled the world to himself
> and sent the Holy Spirit among us
> for the forgiveness of sins:
> through the ministry of the church
> may God give you pardon and peace,
> and I absolve you from your sins
> in the name of the Father, and of the Son,
> and of the Holy Spirit.
> *Resp.* Amen.

The prayer 'The passion of our Lord Jesus Christ. . . .' which always concluded the old rite of penance has been retained as an alternative text but it may be noted that whereas the old edition spoke of the penitential deeds of the penitent as 'taking away the sins', the revised version is altered to 'for a remedy for sin'. This confirms the view of the 'penance' given above.[15]

Pastoral Considerations

After four years' experience it must be said that this rite is not working as it should. In spite of instruction and the provision of books and cards setting out the rite, almost all make their confession in the old fashion and so many seem to be in a hurry to get it over. The reading of the scripture passage, however brief, seems to them an irrelevancy and the old lists of sins make it difficult for the confessor to give that counsel which not only the Order recommends but which every book on the subject recommended long before it. In addition, some priests find the whole procedure tedious and go on much as before. And it must be admitted that when there are great numbers of people to be confessed it is a very fatiguing business. An

---

[14] Though they overlooked the formulas of the anointing of the sick which were always in the subjunctive. The same could be said of the sacrament of ordination, though the formulas here were overlaid with the more peremptory phrases accompanying the 'tradition of the instruments'.

[15] For further information about this prayer and its meaning see my book, *The Ministry of Reconciliation*, pp. 40–1.

enquiry into the stress and fatigue symptoms of confessors would produce interesting results, among others perhaps that no one should be *allowed* to hear more than a given number of confessions.

The remedy for this unhappy state of affairs can only be a determined and intelligent catechesis. This is particularly important in schools of all kinds for it is only there that the young can be initiated into new ways of using the sacrament and indeed into a whole new vision of its meaning and what it could do for them. It is widely known that the young, in the majority, do not in fact use this sacrament any more and if the necessary effort is not made now the danger is that a whole generation of Catholics will grow up without any knowledge or experience of the sacrament of penance. This would mean a very considerable spiritual impoverishment and eventually some very acute crises of conscience.

2. The Reconciliation of Several Penitents with Individual Absolution (48–59)

In this service and in the one that follows the church has met the often-repeated request for a public liturgy of penance.

The case for it can be summed up like this:

1. All sacramental celebrations, by the terms of the Constitution on the Liturgy, demand a proclamation of God's word.

2. For penance it is particularly important that we should hear the urgent message of the Bible to repent.

3. The Order recognises explicitly that penance is an ecclesial and communal sacrament, that sin has effects on the community and that the sinner's reparation must be assisted by the community. We sin not simply as individuals but as members of a community and indeed as a community: some expression of that common sinfulness is demanded by the nature of the sacrament.

4. Prayer once formed a very important element of the sacrament and in this rite the Order provides for common prayer for our own sins and those of others.

5. Confrontation with the word of God and in particular with the demands of the gospel assists 'examination of conscience', deepening our understanding of sin and widening our horizons about what is sinful and what is not. Psychologically this is of

particular help to those who find reflection on themselves difficult.

6. The making of 'satisfaction' will be more realistic, for the whole community can be invited to take up 'the works of mercy' the Order refers to.

The Rite

1. Entrance chant, greeting, brief address and collect.
2. The proclamation of the Word of God with psalm.
3. The homily.
4. Examination of conscience.
5. The general confession (as in Penitential Rite I of the Order of Mass).
6. Prayer in litanic form always ending with the Lord's prayer.
7. Private confession and absolution.
8. Thanksgiving, blessing and dismissal.

The form of the service is the now conventional one for Bible Services and does not call for extended commentary.

We may note that in the reading of the scriptures we are hearing *God's* word (cf CL7), in this case calling us to repentance and amendment of life. But, as the Order also says, the readings show forth the mystery of reconciliation effected by the death and resurrection of Christ and by the giving of the Holy Spirit. Finally, they give the message of divine judgement on good and evil in the life of mankind and thus enlighten the conscience.

As elsewhere in the new liturgy the homily is to be based on the readings (they are not meant to be vague moralising extravaganzas). The preacher is to remember that the readings convey the voice of God calling to repentance, conversion and renewal of life. He is to remind his hearers that sin is committed against God, the community, their neighbours and themselves and he is to recall to them that God's mercy is infinite and exhort them to true, interior repentance, such that they will make reparation for any harm they have caused to others: the *social aspect* of sin is to be brought to their attention. They will have to practise love of neighbour if their satisfaction is to be adequate (24, 52). Naturally it will not be necessary to include all these considerations every time and what the preacher says will of course be conditioned by the nature of his audience.

The homily is part of, and leads into, the examination of conscience: if these two things are done well they are two of the most valuable parts of this rite. Most of us are very limited in our outlook on what sin is and what sins we ourselves have committed. The 'social aspect of sin', so heavily emphasised by the Order, is often completely overlooked. How far, for instance, are we responsible for at least some of the evils of our society? Do we accept evil situations simply because everyone else does and because if you lift up your voice you will get disliked? The texts and the homily can also help us to deepen our understanding of sin. Have we lost a sense of sin as something opposed to the holiness of God and the dignity of human beings? In the more private sector of morals is there not a need to point out that reconciliation between individuals, however effected, is a central requirement of the gospel? People can get all steamed up about sexual sins while at the same time failing to realise that their lives are full of bitterness and hatred. Within families it is sometimes necessary for their members to realise that forgiveness and reconciliation are the very condition of their lives as Christians.

These are some of the questions prompted by the scripture texts and the words of the homilist and while the shaping of such questions is a matter of some delicacy, they need to be presented. Knowledge of the laity on the part of the preacher will help him to frame the questions and during Lent, for instance, a consultation with them on the sins of the society in which they are immersed will be very profitable to both. As the community becomes aware or more aware of the evils of their society, the greater is the likelihood that they will be able to do something about them. This again relates the sacrament and the 'penance' to ordinary human living, for the community as such can be asked to correct those evils within the limits of its power.

(It should be noted that the scheme for the examination of conscience in Appendix III of the Order is optional and need not be used. It is no more than an up-dated version of the forms to be found in old-fashioned prayer books. It is better to 'search the scriptures' and find passages that meet particular occasions; there is general provision made for this in the Order itself. It means more work but the results are more profitable.)

The next section, significantly called 'the Rite of Reconcilia-

tion', consists entirely of prayer. First, there is a litany of intercession and then the Lord's prayer which must always be included and said at this point. A study of the two samples given
(and they are only samples) shows that the whole range of the
new vision of the sacrament is conveyed by them, but the most
important point to note here is that this is the prayer of the
church for sinners and represents that element of the life of the
church in the early centuries when sinners were conceived to
be converted by prayer. One of the purposes of the long periods
of canonical penance was that the penitent sinners might be
converted by the prayer of the church and, as we have noted
above, the Lord's prayer was regarded as peculiarly effective
in the remission of sins of the ordinary Christian. Private confession and absolution follow and the rite concludes with the
thanksgiving and dismissal. The text leaves open wide possibilities: 'The celebrant surrounded by the other priests who
have heard confessions invites the people to make a thanksgiving and exhorts them to good works *whereby the grace of
penance may be manifested in the life of each of them and in the
life of the community*' (56). This gives scope for the appointing
of tasks to the whole community, which might be invited to
accept them as visible signs of their repentance and thus relate
the sacrament to life, the life of the society in which the community exists.

Pastoral Considerations

This form of the celebration of penance is undoubtedly rich
in content and can be effective in practice, as least as far as the
awakening of conscience is concerned. Experience shows that if
the service is carefully prepared and if the homilist is adequate
to his task, subsequent confessions do benefit from it. There
are two difficulties. Several priests are necessary for the
private confessions and these are not always easy to come by.
Even so, the confessions tend to take up a good deal of time
(and that is as it should be) but the final act of thanksgiving can
hardly take place because people are not willing to stay for it.
The circumstances in which the rite is best used is a day or
half-day of recollection for a parish or other community. A
time can be appointed for the conclusion of the service, and
if there are grounds or any other suitable place, the people can
go there and await the concluding prayers for which they will

return to the church. But after the very communal nature of the service the private confessions and absolutions do seem to be something of an anomaly and people have remarked on this.

As to how often these services are held, experience also shows that they are profitable in Advent and Lent though these seasons do not exhaust the possibilities. Parish 'missions' are somewhat rare events nowadays but if they do occur, this form of service could very properly be used though it is to be hoped that those responsible will respect the spirit of the Order and draw on its considerable resources. Another occasion is the dedication of a church which used to be preceded by a day of fasting. Its sense, in the new Order of Dedication (1977), is that it is a sign of the spiritual renewal of the whole parish or community. A day of penitence could be appointed some convenient time before the dedication.

3. The Order for the Reconciliation of Penitents with General Confession and Absolution (31–5; 60–3)

From a liturgical viewpoint, the third rite of Penance is the type or exemplar on which the other two may be said to be based. It is visibly a public service of the church, it involves the community, there is a public proclamation of God's word, there is a general confession of sin and the absolution and reconciliation are also public. But as everyone knows there are theological and what I would call administrative difficulties about which something will be said below.

First then let us look at the rite (60–6).

Let us consider the language with which it is introduced. As one writer has observed, the thought behind this rite is very different from what we have conventionally understood as a 'general absolution'.[16] It is a service of reconciliation with God and the church, it is a liturgical service and not just the utterance of a formula, and by its very texts and structure demands the repentance and conversion of the participants. Moreover, it retains all the features of classical penance (whether ancient or modern) with the sole exception of the *private* confession of sins for the occasion. The service differs but little from the former and may be summarised like this:

---

[16] Austin Flannery, OP, in *Doctrine and Life*, 24, April 1974, p. 206n.

1. There is the usual introduction and the reading of the scriptures.

2. The homily.

3. The general confession made by all those who wish to receive absolution, according to the formulas used in other services or at Mass.

4. There is prayer, as above in the previous service, always ending with the Lord's prayer.

5. Finally, there is absolution in very solemn form.

(The conclusion of the service is the same as in the second rite.)

Commentary

The fact that the reconciliation/absolution is embedded in a service of the word and prayer gives it a different complexion. Confrontation with the word of God and prayer provide the context for the whole service and they lead naturally and one would say inevitably into the reconciliation and absolution that follow. First, confrontation with the word of God enables the participants to realise more clearly the evil of sin. This is carried forward by the homily that leads into examination of conscience and repentance, on which the Order so strongly insists. The general confession here acquires its full force: the whole gathered community expresses its sinfulness *with a view to* reconciliation and absolution that appear as the climax of the service. There is no break: proclamation of the word, prayer, confession and reconciliation follow one after another. This, one feels, is as it should be and the hiatus of the second rite is no longer apparent.

The formula of absolution is in itself a remarkable piece of writing. It invokes the Father, the Son and the Holy Spirit. The Father, who desires not the death but the life of the sinner and who first loved us and sent his Son to save us, is asked to show his mercy to us. The Son who was delivered up on account of our sins to make us righteous, gave the Holy Spirit to the apostles to forgive sins. The prayer continues: 'May he (Christ) through our ministry free you from sin and fill you with the Holy Spirit'. In the Holy Spirit, given for the remission of sins, we have access to the Father and he is asked to purify our hearts, to shed his radiance on us that we may proclaim the saving deeds of him who has called us out of darkness into light. The usual formula: 'I absolve you. . . .' concludes the form of reconciliation.

We note that, apart from the last sentence, the whole text is a *prayer* that by means of a catena of scripture quotations expresses the great effect of the sacrament, reconciliation with God and his church. Secondly, the emphasis on the work of the Holy Spirit is strong. He is operative in all the work of reconciliation, he 'fills' the penitent, purifies his heart and radiates his whole being. Thirdly, while the formula of reconciliation is being pronounced the celebrant holds his hands over the penitents and the meaning of that ancient rite is made clear: the Holy Spirit is being given *for* reconciliation with the church, as it was in the early centuries of the church when the lapsed, the heretic and schismatic were regarded as having put themselves outside the ambit of the Holy Spirit's operation. For if he is the Spirit of Christ he is also the Spirit of his body which is the church.

The Conditions of its Use

All Catholics are aware of the practice in times of danger of death, e.g. shipwreck or fire, of absolving a number of people at once and after exhorting them to repentance. The Order takes this for granted as a permissible practice but it extends the occasions when such absolution may be given and lays down the conditions when it may be given. They can be summarised as follows:

1. There is a large number of penitents.

2. There is not a sufficient number of confessors to hear and absolve them.

3. Without their fault they would be deprived of the grace of the sacrament or of holy communion for some long time (*diu*).

4. This can happen in missionary territories but also elsewhere when there is a gathering of people and it can be established (*constat*) that the necessity (for confession and communion) exists (31).

All this seems clear enough and these conditions are found in a vast number of parish churches in Holy Week and at Christmas. There are large numbers of people to be confessed, and it is now in most places morally impossible to find a sufficient number of confessors, and the people have to wait an inordinate length of time. True, they are not sent away, but the quality of the celebration of the sacrament suffers considerably. After a certain number of penitents the confessor inevitably tires and the penitents themselves, feeling the pressure of all who are waiting, wish to get their confessions over as quickly as possible. In other words, all the evils of the old way of doing the sacrament remain, yet the Order is concerned that it should not continue! There is in fact a limiting clause in the Order: 'This (the use of general absolution) is not lawful simply on account of a large number of penitents since confessors can be made available (*cum confessores praesto esse possunt*)'. This is a statement of fact and a very extraordinary one. How can the authorities in Rome know when and where confessors can be made available? Not only in missionary territories but in vast areas of the so-called civilised world confessors in sufficient numbers simply cannot be obtained at times like Christmas and Easter. Almost all the parish clergy have had experience of the lack of confessors even for the second rite and all of them know what a burden is put on themselves and the people by the great number of confessions at the great seasons of the year. The Roman authorities have however insisted on the letter of the Order, greatly to the detriment of its operation and to the good of the people.

It is for diocesan bishops, in consultation with the conference of bishops, to determine when the rite may be used but some at least have been rebuked for giving what seemed to Rome over-liberal permissions. Even so, it is difficult to imagine that bishops can know the circumstances of all their parishes and so the Order gives permission to the local priest to decide if there is a necessity for this rite either after consulting his bishop, or if that is impossible, informing him afterwards.

Further clarification of this whole matter is necessary. One can only speculate on the reasons for the rigidity hitherto shown but the reason for it may be the fear that the practice of private and individual confession will disappear. But it may also be that the ruling of the Council of Trent that all mortal sins must be confessed in number, kind and circumstances is regarded as absolutely binding. Certainly much of the underlying theology of the Instruction is based on the teaching of that council. There arises then the question of the confessing of mortal sins and the further question of what is mortal sin.

As to the reception of general absolution it should be noted that the Instruction incorporates the 'norms' of an Instruction issued by the Congregation for the Doctrine of Faith issued eighteen months before the Order.[17] The general view is that the Order in this place is to be interpreted by that document. The Order (33) gives the conditions required for a fruitful reception of the general absolution:

1. The penitent must be truly repentant and have a true sorrow for sins committed.

2. He must have the intention to refrain from sin.

3. He must be willing to make reparation for any scandal or injury he has done.

4. He must have the intention to confess all mortal sins privately 'in due time (*debito tempore*)' and in any case before benefiting from another general absolution. Short of moral impossibility, he is to make a private confession within the year, for the obligation of confessing all sins, especially mortal sins once a year, still stands (34).

At the end of paragraph 33 the Order says that these conditions are necessary '*ad valorem sacramenti*'. There has been some debate about this last phrase.[18] What does this term mean? It has been argued that it does not necessarily mean 'for validity' yet on the other hand the ICEL translators have 'for validity'. If the whole paragraph is taken together it can be seen as simply stating traditional teaching and therefore 'for validity' is probably correct. But the crux of the matter is the confessing of mortal sins and in the context of the rite of general absolution, within a reasonable length of time, a year at most. The question then arises: is the penitent absolved? Is the absolution effective (i.e. valid)? Probably the answer to the question turns on the *intention* of the penitent to confess in due time. If that were lacking, he would be putting an obstacle (*obex*) in the way of the effect of the sacrament. On the other hand, if he has the intention, but for one reason or another does not confess his mortal sins privately, the absolution is

---

[17] 'Normae pastorales circa absolutionem sacramentalem generali modo impertiendam' (dated 16 June 1972), *AAS* 64, 1972, p. 511.

[18] See *Clergy Review*, 60, May 1975, p. 334; *The Month*, 236, July 1975, p. 218; *Clergy Review*, 60, August 1975, p. 542 and the preliminary note to the second edition of *The Ministry of Reconciliation* (1976).

probably valid. A deliberate intention not to confess would, in the present discipline, invalidate the sacrament for the penitent. That would seem to be the sense of the Order.

So we come to the second question which concerns first the obligation of confessing mortal sins. It is noteworthy that the terms of the Order are not on the whole restrictive. It simply says that the obligation to confess all sins, including mortal sins, once a year to a confessor is still in force. It does indeed refer in a footnote to the document of the Congregation for the Doctrine of the Faith which states that auricular confession is of 'divine precept'. But the meaning of this term is not beyond dispute. Thus Louis Monden states that though confession of mortal sins is said by the Council of Trent to be *iure divino*, this term 'had not yet acquired the meaning we assign to it to-day and was often used for ecclesiastical or even for civil law'.[19] This chimes with what Père Tillard has to say about a long debate at the Council of Trent. The debate was in fact inconclusive and Tillard goes on to say that the Council of Trent in its declaration '*Statuit et declarat*' was merely affirming '*the customary law of the church*'. He also cites the opinion of a modern moralist that confession before communion and after mortal sin is to be regarded rather as an ecclesiastical precept.[20]

The question may seem to be of not much more than academic interest and we must take into account that a Roman document of 1972 may well be interpreting earlier statements. Auricular confession has certainly been the custom for a very long time though it is a long step from 'custom' to 'divine law'. In any case, there remains the problem of reconciling this teaching with the practice of all the early centuries when people received communion at every eucharist they attended and, apart from the notorious and public sinners, never 'went to confession'. However, there is no doubt about the present discipline of the church, and there can be no question here of inviting people to ignore it. On the other hand, theologians might well turn their attention to the matter for in the long run it is the good of the people that is at stake.

---

[19] *Op. cit.*, pp. 47–8.
[20] *LMD*, 90, 1967, pp. 117–24. For a summary account of the debate, see J. Fitzsimons (ed.), *Penance: Virtue and Sacrament*, London, 1969, pp. 45–6.

This question is obviously connected with another: what is mortal sin? In recent years there has been a great deal of discussion about it.[21] Theologians are distinguishing between sin that is a complete turning away from God and the sort of sin that is by no means a rejection of God but rather a falling short of the dominant direction of a life which is towards God. This has been called the 'fundamental option'. People whether consciously or not have chosen God and his demands but from time to time fall away. There is a failure of response to the demands of God whom they wish with all their hearts to serve and, it is argued, the relationship with God is not broken. The notion that anyone after breaking the law of God on a single occasion could be 'sent to hell' for all eternity is no longer acceptable and is indeed regarded as bizarre. What sort of God would that be? The new notion (if it is new) also contains a fundamental psychological truth: the whole personality is rarely involved in one single act and yet we find it quite conceivable that a long series of wrong acts do produce a state that can be said to result in an alienation from God.

All is not clear in this theology but it does seem to get nearer the truth of human actions than the old quasi-automatic notion which has weighed on the consciences of people for too long. No doubt, too, much more needs to be said and further theological reflection is necessary. Conclusions in the direction indicated above would make the operation of the third rite all the easier.

Pastoral Considerations

Confusion over the conditions when this rite may be used and what seems to have been a genuine misunderstanding on the part of several bishops in different parts of the world have rendered the use of this rite very difficult. This is the greatest of pities because it has affected the whole presentation of the new rite of penance. It is hardly honest to present the new Order to people while holding back on the third rite. And it is absurd to tell them about it and then say (more or less) 'but of course it cannot be used in our circumstances'.

---

[21] See, for instance, D. O'Callaghan, 'What is Mortal Sin?', *The Furrow*, 25, February 1974, p. 82 and L. Orsy, 'Common Sense about Sin', *The Tablet*, 9 February 1974, pp. 125–8.

In the Order there is a progression from 'private penance' to the second rite of which only a part is public and on to the third rite where all is. As the Order itself lays out the pattern the third rite seems to be what I have called the exemplar of the others. In practice there is a reverse tendency. It is a matter of experience that, where people have been able to benefit from a celebration of the third rite, after being long away from the sacraments, they have readily confessed their sins privately some few days later. It is a fact of psychology, known to most of the pastoral clergy (though hidden apparently from the wise and prudent), that when the weight of *guilt* is lifted people feel able to confess their sins in the confessional. The service itself leads them to a true repentance unlikely to be attained if left to themselves. The experience of being part of a congregation that as a whole confesses its sinfulness helps them to repent and amend their lives. And this is the plain teaching of the Order, namely that we all share a solidarity in sin and all can contribute to its reparation.

The fear has been expressed that the third rite might eventually eliminate private confession. This fear is exaggerated, to say the least. The Order envisages that its celebration will be infrequent in the course of a year and it maintains the obligation to confess mortal sins afterwards. What still needs doing is that the whole of the Order, doctrine and practice, should be put before the people so that they know what is available to them and what is required of them. A vast catechetical programme is needed if this is to be achieved and it is particularly important that this should be done in schools at all levels. It is to be feared that this has hardly begun though where permission has been granted for the use of the third rite in secondary and comprehensive schools the result has been spiritually very satisfactory. The need in parishes is equally great and now that discussion and prayer groups are a normal part of parish life it is here that the teaching should be given, but for this people need a well-planned programme that will cover the whole of the Order. Given in an atmosphere of prayer, such teaching would be peculiarly effective for the spiritual doctrine of the Order is deep and rich.

CHAPTER TWELVE

Pastoral Opportunities

PROLONGED STUDY of the new liturgical documents on the sacraments prompts certain reflections. In spite of the fact that the new
rites are basically traditional, they have opened up a whole new
world. The meaning of sacramental actions has been greatly clarified
and for the Christian at any rate they are easy enough to understand. Pastorally speaking, this is of immense importance and in
this the revisers have been completely faithful to the *Constitution
on the Liturgy*. In addition they have clarified sacramental theology
in many respects, notably in holy order and the anointing of the
sick. The old organic system of the sacraments of Christian Initiation has, at least in principle, been restored. The non-sacramental
rite of funerals breathes the air of the early church. But there are
other aspects of this considerable work of reform that deserve
attention.

One dominant impression left by a study of these rites is that
they are so much more *personal* than those they have replaced. For
centuries priests poured streams of Latin over half-comprehending
people and the words were inevitably directed to no one in particular. But the change has not come from merely translating Latin
texts into the vernacular. While translated texts would have been
more understandable, they would still have lacked that personal
emphasis that is to be found throughout the new rites. Words now
are always directed to real people who are present and they in turn
are required to be actively involved. If there is one calculable effect
of the reform it is that people do feel so involved. This is a gain
whose value can hardly be estimated and it does mean that the
liturgy is doing that for which it was devised: to convey God's redeeming power to the people in a way that is in accordance with
their nature and to enable them to respond with the whole of their
personalities. No doubt something still remains to be done by way
of adaptation to make the rites even more effective. There is too

the still troublesome business of symbolism which may or may not be viable in the world of today. No doubt many of the clergy need to learn that liturgy is personal and not formal. They too must feel involved. It none the less remains true that the church has put into the hands of clergy and laity alike an invaluable means of approaching God and of being united with him.

Another inescapable impression is that the new rites are essentially *communal*. Their celebration demands the presence and co-operation of the local community and often their help before and afterwards. *Normally*, there is no such thing as a private celebration of the sacraments and in this too the revisers have been very faithful to the Constitution (26). This does not mean that we have to agonise over the notion of 'community', and ask whether parishes are or not communities Wherever two or three are gathered in the name of Christ, he is in the midst of them. The important thing is that the principle is stated and again that normally a community will be present. Often, as in the case of confirmation and ordination, the absence of community is hardly conceivable and would make nonsense of a good deal of the rites. Here too a change of mentality is required, especially among those laity who seem to think that *their* baptisms, weddings and funerals are purely private affairs. This principle of community is in fact carried so far that no one in 1963 would have thought that there could ever be such a celebration as a public anointing of the sick. And this has come from the rediscovery of an ancient truth that that sacrament is primarily a sacrament of healing.

As we have observed in the first chapter, the sacraments have once again been firmly set in the context of *life*. They are no longer isolated bits of ritual. This, it seems to me, has vast consequences for the pastoral life. Over twenty years ago the French began discussing the possibilities of a *liturgie pastorale*. In more recent years they have been talking about a *pastorale liturgique*, a term almost impossible to translate into English. By it they mean at least that pastoral action should be centred on the liturgy and especially on the sacraments. For far too long pastoral life and practice have moved parallel with the liturgy when they did not cut across it (as in the case of those famous 'mission' services) or ignore it altogether. The new rites have now opened the door to a pastoral action that will be on the one hand rooted in the liturgy and on the other leading people to it. Here the emphasis on *faith* in all the new orders is the key factor. We proceed from faith to sacrament. We believe and then we are baptised. From baptism we move to the eucharist by which we live and from the eucharist we go to the world to carry to it the message of Christ.

Once we have got used to the new rites, it would seem that there should be a complete re-thinking of pastoral practice. This becomes more and more difficult year by year. There are all sorts of factors in play here which it would be impossible to deal with adequately. We may mention one only: the intense mobility of population. The pastoral clergy are constantly exhorted to 'instruct' their people; they are asked to do this or that with them or for them and yet as far as the people are concerned, it is often a case of 'here today and gone tomorrow'. The chances of any consecutive work are slim. Yet, most of these people require the sacraments at one time or another. They want their children baptised, they wish them to be confirmed. They want them to receive their first communion and so on. The young want to get married (distressingly young sometimes) and people fall ill and all die—even the clergy. All these are crucial moments of *life*, people's lives are patterned by these events, it is at times like these that they are most open to the word of God and it is of these occasions that the greatest possible use should be made. The clergy may or may not be able to visit house-to-house, they may or may not be able to organise parish councils, bazaars and/or football pools, but one thing they have to do by professional and vocational commitment is to celebrate the sacraments with and for their people.

Perhaps however it is not a case of either/or. It *is* a case of putting the liturgical-sacramental element, which is central to the Christian life, in the centre of the picture. If we look at the matter from a coldly practical point of view, it will be seen that once you refuse to accept sacraments as merely pieces of ritual, you are inevitably involved in people and their life.

Let us start at the beginning of the life-cycle with marriage. Nowadays and for some years past it has been common practice to see prospective couples several times before marriage. This is pastorally speaking a *tempus opportunum*. Almost invariably they want to make a good marriage. Often enough they feel that the event offers them an opportunity to deepen their spiritual life. They are interested in marriage! Here the priest has a golden opportunity to deepen their faith, to help them to see the implications of Christian marriage and often to change their whole outlook. Through these meetings he usually builds up a friendship with them and if they stay in his district afterwards, he has a ready entrée to their home. But even if they do not, in due course they will have a child whom they will want baptised and, according to the new order of baptism, the clergy are required to see them, to talk about the meaning of the sacrament and to show them what their commitments are. Without anyone realising it, their faith is being deepened. As the sacramental events go by there will be further contact with the parents in eg the matter of first communion and it is a reasonable estimate that for about ten years people will be in contact with the clergy and one may suppose growing as Christians. This is quite a long time in the life of anyone and if in that time the clergy have not managed to inculcate the essentials of Christian faith and practice, then there is something wrong with the presentation.[1]

In addition, there is all the care of the sick that is so constant a feature of the pastoral life, the ministry to the dying and all the attention that must be given to the bereaved on the occasion of death. Whatever may be the difficulties—and one is that it is often difficult to give as *much* time to the dying as one would like— all these events require constant contact with people who are in great need of help. It may be thought that there is a large time gap between the age of ten or twelve when there are no special sacraments to give and that of old age when illness and all its handicapping consequences set in. But parents and grandparents get involved in the younger members of the family and they too benefit from what is done for them. Baptism, confirmation and first communion are all or can be truly *family* events and have the great advantage of assembling the family around a sacramental celebration. It is in this way that worship becomes embedded in life, their life.

The above is no more than a sketch of possibilities. The contention that lies behind it is that the sacramental-liturgical system offers a framework for pastoral action. Life, instruction and liturgy will move together and it may be said that if the clergy were exploiting this situation for all it was worth, they would be exercising a pastoral ministry that would touch a very large proportion of the people committed to their charge. Nearly all these events require house visitation and on these terms it proves to be profitable. Without any

---

[1] It is my personal view that there is. One straw in the wind is that even now people still seem to be 'instructed' in the sacraments without any reference to the liturgical texts. And yet these are supposed to teach!

beating about the bush, it is possible to approach people directly and talk to them about God and the things of God. It is a manner of 'preaching the gospel', unobtrusive if you will, but none the less fundamental.

No doubt there are other people with other needs. There are the lapsed to be regained, there are the non-Christians to be converted and for these other methods need to be worked out. One could wish that more thought was being given to the enormous problem that lies before us: hardly ten per cent of the population attached to any church. There is in addition the problem of the young who are receding from worship and church-membership and who are completely allergic to injunctions and commands even of the highest authority. We must take account too of the increasing number of people in this country who are not baptised and even among Roman Catholics this number is likely to increase if the requirements of infant baptism are to be met. Whatever may be thought of the details of the Order for the Christian Initiation of Adults, it is important as showing a way by which the non-baptised, when once they approach the church, may be gradually incorporated into it. The day may not be far distant when there will be, as in the fourth century, a large section of the Christian community who are in one sense or another 'catechumens', people drawn to Christianity, full of good will and desirous of associating with Christians, but who are not yet ready to commit themselves to the whole of the Christian life. Many of the semi-lapsed are really in this position: unfortunately they have the *dis*advantage of being baptised!

But study of these documents prompts other reflections. In spite of all their flexibility, of the alternatives offered and the suggestions for adaptation, they seem a little rigid, perhaps because they bear a certain stamp. True, they have been drawn up by international groups of experts but the texts have a certain European and indeed Latin flavour. It is true that the needs of missionary territories with other cultures are constantly in the background and at least *opportunities* are given to adapt the rites as and where necessary. But still, the rites often say and require us to do things that we should have said and done rather differently. The question is then whether these rites are to be regarded as definitive or whether they can and should be used as points of departure for the construction of other rites that will more adequately express the needs of other peoples and cultures? Such long range adaptation, which seems to be in accordance with the *Constitution on the Liturgy* (40), would seem to be on the horizon. The events covered by these rites are the great life-moments of ordinary people and if they are to become part of their lives, they will have to be so adapted as to express *their* way of life, *their* sentiments and *their* needs. How this is to be done is another matter and there is no need to be in any great hurry about it. With the use of the rites people will begin to discover their needs and since liturgy at its best is a matter of natural growth rather than authoritative dictation, it will be best to allow people to discover their needs. What is necessary is to see the rites as 'open-ended', offering opportunities of quite radical adaptation for such adaptation is the very condition of their continued effectiveness.

When I wrote this book in 1972/3 most of the new rites had been issued though the anointing of the sick which came in 1971 had not come into use and the Order of Penance had not been issued at all. By the end of 1972 most people were familiar enough with the new rite of the Mass though some did not like it and moaned and complained in the Catholic press at great length. The new rites of baptism and marriage were in use by 1970 and have generally been pronounced a success. Although the anointing of the sick with its attendant rites has had a shorter life this too has proved to be very acceptable to the people. Of the Order of Penance I have spoken above. In a sense, then, the new liturgy has been absorbed into the current life of the church without too much difficulty and this must be said to be great gain. But in a sense only. What has become apparent in the last ten years or so is that *celebration*, the meaning of celebration and the manner of celebration is a key issue.[2] Even good rites cannot wholly mitigate bad celebration though the worst features of the old way of doing things are a thing of the past. One does indeed hear of Masses said 'at speed' and of administrations of infant baptism that are scrambled affairs. On the part of some of the clergy there seems to be an indifference to the importance of symbolic actions like the sign of the cross, genuflexions, the laying-on of hands and one's general bearing during liturgical celebration. What is more important is a disregard for the *word* whether that is the word

---

[2] See *Christian Celebration: the Mass*, chapters 9 and 10.

of God in the Bible or the words of the liturgy. The truth that
we are saved by faith and by the sacraments of faith (and faith
comes by hearing, said St Paul) does not seem to have sunk in.
All the new rites insist on the proclamation of the word before
the sacramental action itself takes place though theologically
speaking it is difficult to separate the one from the other. No
doubt it is difficult to achieve a balance between the formal
utterance that the liturgy demands and that personal dimension
which makes it possible for the ministry of the word to appear
as a message from person to person. But it is not impossible
and the remedy is to be found in a respect for the word and in
a conviction that the word in the liturgy is not simply man's
word but God's (cf CL33).

On the part of the laity, too, there seems to be an impatience
about the word. Lay-readers often read too quickly as if the
point of the exercise was to get it over as quickly as possible,
or they mumble and so make an absurdity of the whole procedure. These defects can be cured by training but what is
more difficult to cure is their indifference to the word as it is
proclaimed to them in the course of various rites.[3] Here the
need seems to be an educational one: a better initiation into the
Bible and an ability to attend to words whether they are those
of the scriptures or the liturgy. We seem to be moving into an
un-literate age in which noises are taking the place of words,
i.e. sounds that have meaning. If this is so, it is vital that the
church should keep alive the importance of the word for without it the church cannot exist.

Another reason for this unhappy state of affairs is *haste*.
Both laity and clergy, or large numbers of them, seem to want
to get their worship done as quickly as possible. Why this
should be so it is difficult to understand though it is probably the result, at least in part, of those quick 'silent' Masses of
half-an-hour and those rapid administrations of sacraments to
which so many were accustomed for so long. Here again, education in the meaning of worship would seem to be the remedy.
But 'education' does not mean simply 'instruction' of the
academic kind. People need to be initiated into the ways of
worship largely through participating in liturgies well done.

---

[3] Cf. *The Lector's Handbook*, C.T.S., London, 1978.

Then the *personal* dimension of the new rites, mentioned above, will be able to make its full impact.

As the experience of the last few years has shown, this has become ever more important. It is this that many, perhaps most, are seeking, and oddly enough it is connected with the matter of community. This has been a bogey to some who still wish to preserve their splendid isolation in worship. What many are seeking, and not only in Great Britain, is a truly communal worship that is at the same time personal, one in which they feel personally engaged and in which the celebrant is someone who cares for them and is a great deal more than a hieratic figure. In the course of these years, then, the desire for *smaller* worshipping communities has made itself felt. The smaller parish with a living community is attracting many and the large church without any visible community is less and less popular. This would seem to bear out what I have written elsewhere in a rather different context.[4]

What can be done about this at the practical level is another matter: large parishes exist and large churches exist and they cannot just be wished away. One of the striking features of the Catholic Church is that vast numbers of people still go to Mass in spite of all that has been said about the dwindling faith and feeble practice of modern Catholics. This situation does pose problems but they are not insuperable. There are ways of creating community both within and outside the liturgy. If a parish, even a large one, has a genuine community life, this will show in worship and there are simple and unpretentious ways of making this apparent. If there is a welcome, the provision of the necessary book or books and a general sense of caring among the more active members of the congregation, the impersonality of so much worship in large churches would be removed. In fact, it is now a matter of experience that the new liturgy has done much to foster the sense of community in the church. The many 'good works' of the modern church, both intra- and extra-mural, witness to it.

It has been said above that 'the sacraments have once again been firmly set in the context of life', though whether the potentialities of the new rites have been exploited in parish life

---

[4] *The Once and Future Liturgy*, Dublin, 1977, pp. 75 ff.

is not clear. Parishes seem to go on much as before: sacraments are 'administered', social events are organised and people are visited (though less and less). Prayer and discussion groups have indeed appeared and are doing valuable work. But all this activity still lacks a centre. It is still not seen as proceeding from the liturgy and leading back to it. In other words we still lack a *pastorale liturgique*. Although new problems are already on the horizon, e.g. the continuing shortage of priests, no effort at serious pastoral planning is being made—or if there is, it is local and perhaps temporary. The hesitation and even reluctance in some places to institute lay ministers of holy communion or to ordain married men to the permanent diaconate are symptoms of a deep rooted refusal to change, whatever the situation in which the church has now to live and act. Too many are content to go on doing what they have always done with just a top dressing of 'new liturgy'.

Nor are these simply domestic matters. The Roman Catholic church in Great Britain has moved into a position where it is seen to be an important element, perhaps an irreplaceable element, in the national life. This is not a position of honour but one of responsibility but we need to show more effectively than we do that we have responsibilities to the whole country. All that we do and say has repercussions far outside our own community with the consequence that we need constantly to weigh our words and examine our modes of action. We need to realise more vividly that we are under scrutiny by vast numbers of people, many of whom are 'searching for God'. As far as liturgy is concerned, this situation raises two questions, that of adaptation and that of evangelisation.

To take the second first. Evangelisation, though having one over-riding aim, namely to proclaim the Good News of Salvation and to bring men and women into contact with Christ, is specified by the situation in which the word has to be proclaimed. This for us is Great Britain and even within that area there are considerable differences between England and Scotland, between England and Wales and between England and Northern Ireland. Even more specifically, localities differ from one another and what can be done in a small town cannot (often) be done in a large industrialised city. This is no more than a long way round of speaking of those 'basic communities' which are given such emphasis in *Evangelii nuntiandi* of Paul

VI. Communities that belong to a given district, that reflect
the concerns of the district and that know or come to know
what are the needs of the district, are the places where in one
way or another the Good News is going to be made known.
It is in these communities, where people know each other as
persons, that the word of God can be effectively proclaimed
and where people can be brought to Christ.

This is of course an enormous question that cannot be dealt
with adequately here. I cannot, even were I competent, suggest ways and means although I believe that the vitalisation of
'basic communities' is fundamental to the whole matter. But
one or two more questions may help towards finding the right
answers. What is the stance of the church in this country to the
community in which we live and by which we live? Or have
we any stance at all? Are we content simply to preserve (and
more and more precariously, some would say) what we have
got and so conduct our diocesan and parish affairs, including
the liturgy, as if we had nothing to say to the world and the
world has nothing to say to us? Do not some parishes seem to
exist in what I would call a sociological void? To give one
example: in most places the arrival of a new parish priest
arouses a certain interest. People, and not only Catholics, wish
to meet him and, among other things, want to know if he is the
sort of man who will have a concern for the community in
which he is going to work. And yet his induction is often a
purely domestic affair. Only Catholics are invited and the ceremony usually takes place in the context of the eucharist. Implicitly the local community is excluded and even if they are
invited, they cannot take part in the eucharist by receiving
holy communion. Here a change of attitude brings with it a
realisation that there must be a certain adaptation (the organisation of a non-eucharistic service) to meet the needs of those
whom we call our brothers and sisters in Christ even if they do
not belong to our church.

Again, many parishes have a potential in manpower, buildings and sometimes money, not to mention the undoubted *devotion* of many of the laity within their parishes. Could not
some of this potential be actualised for the good of the surrounding community? Ought not this to be regarded as the
normal and necessary use of parish resources? The church does
not exist for itself, we do not exist for ourselves—or, to put the

matter in the positive terms of Vatican II, the church is essentially missionary and all its members everywhere are responsible
for that mission. Perhaps we are victims of conventional expressions. When we say 'mission' we think of preaching the gospel
to 'natives' of other countries. Perhaps we think we have to
'talk religion', that we have to expound the Bible or instruct
others in the doctrines of the church. We must *convert* them or
all our work is in vain. In spite of Vatican II, which spoke of
the servant church, we do not seem to have realised that the
gospel can be preached, and very effectively, by *service*—and
that is pretty close to the heart of the gospel. The simple,
humble, psychological truth that you cannot reach anyone, even
with God's word, unless you have won his or her confidence
and perhaps affection, still seems to be largely unknown. Service is a mode of loving and only when we love, whether as
individuals or communities, can we reach others.

This attitude, too, affects the tonality of our worship. Nowadays there are many who have no formal attachment to our
church but who come to attend services. If the local assembly
is welcoming, they will at least feel that we are trying to be
Christians, loving our neighbours even when they are anonymous. This of course is particularly important for baptisms,
confirmations (when non-Catholic parents are happy to attend),
marriages and funerals. On all these occasions nowadays there
are considerable numbers of those we call loosely non-Catholics, and through the liturgy, through the way we celebrate it,
we are—or are not—serving them, trying to convey to them
something of the gospel truth, the saving word of God that is
made known to people in the ordinary circumstances of life of
which these events are an inevitable part. Surely it does not
need to be repeated that the celebration of marriage is one of
the most effective ways of 'preaching' the Christian doctrine of
marriage and the care and attention that the parish clergy take
over preparation for baptism is usually a lesson in itself to the
family. The bearing and the words of the bishop at confirmations and his willingness to meet the parents afterwards and
talk with them are what is now expected and everyone knows
that such encounters can be very fruitful. Likewise, the attentive care of the sick and dying which the Order so greatly
facilitates, and the celebration of the funeral rites for the dead,
coupled with comfort for the bereaved are so many sermons in

words and action that reach the hearts of many. Viewed in this light the revised liturgy has been of immense *pastoral* benefit to great numbers of people. In this sense a *pastorale liturgique* is in existence, at least where the possibilities of the new liturgy are being realised.

For that is the point. As I have said above, the new liturgy is open-ended but it is so in two senses. It is open-ended first for those with the necessary understanding and imagination to arrange a service for a particular occasion or a particular group of people. The rubrics of the revised liturgy are not blueprints or working-drawings that dictate every word and action to be done. They are directives or guide-lines that make it possible for a celebrant, in consultation with the laity (who are also celebrants), to produce a liturgy that over the whole range of its action will communicate the message of Christ. Some few years ago there was a good deal of discussion about 'creativity' in liturgical matters and too many thought that this meant creating new liturgies but it was made clear that quite apart from such (unlawful) procedure there was considerable room for 'creativity' in the manner of arranging, organising and celebrating the liturgy.[5] The *same* rite celebrated with the requisite qualities of knowledge, understanding and imagination can appear to be very different from one where those qualities are lacking. As Cardinal Schuster said more than fifty years ago, the written liturgy as found in the books is no more than a libretto. It has to be brought to life and that happens only in celebration. It has to be clothed with sound (music—of the right sort), light and movement, and it is only then that it begins to make an impact or, more importantly, communicate the divine message of which it is the medium. This is as true of the sacraments as it is of the Mass. The baptism and confirmation of an unbaptised convert within the celebration of the Easter Vigil is a very different thing from a private event which can hardly be called a celebration at all. No doubt there are occasions when a more domestic kind of treatment is appropriate. Some baptisms have to be celebrated with the minimum of ceremonial and when there is great grief it is often a kindness to the bereaved to make the funeral as simple as possible. Pub-

---

[5] See (among other places) *Notitiae*, 73, May 1972, pp. 151 ff and 157 ff.

lic anointings of the sick, too, call for a previous psychological preparation and an initiation into the meaning of the sacrament. But granted that, such a celebration can bring comfort to the sick and show the sacrament for what it is. It is strange that there has been no official encouragement in this country of public celebrations of the anointing of the sick.

Much then still remains to be done within the limits of the existing liturgy if its potential is to be realised.

Those however who have done their best to 'make the most of the liturgy' have come up against problems and difficulties and they as well as others have come to realise that the new rites are sometimes defective. I have remarked above that the texts have a European and inevitably, since they were drawn up in the language of the western church, a Latin flavour. They in turn have been translated into what someone has unkindly called 'mid-Atlantic' English. Yet, while granting that it was hardly possible to achieve perfection (if it ever can be achieved) in rites and language, it is necessary to say that those committed to the use of the Roman rite are now very numerous in many countries and continents that know little or nothing of European culture. Thus the question of *adaptation* is raised, adaptation that goes far beyond the permitted adaptations that are available in the official books to conferences of bishops and pastors. It is highly likely that this will be the great question of the future. Fortunately both the Constitution (37–40) and the official books, in numerous places, allow of such development.

What then will happen? No one, I imagine, would be so rash as to predict anything in detail but it may well be that in India, in the very different countries of Africa and perhaps (who knows?) in China, Christians will examine the traditions of their own cultures and will find in them insights and ways of doing things that are consonant with the liturgy but which are expressive of *their* culture, their ways of thinking and their ways of acting. As a recent writer has pointed out, in the early formative period of the liturgy there was not only adaptation but there were two ways of doing it: by assimilation and by substitution.[6] The Roman liturgy in the course of centuries

---

[6] A. J. Chapungco, 'Greco-Roman Culture and Liturgical Adaptation', *Notitiae*, 153, April 1979, pp. 202 ff.

took over certain cultural elements and added them to the rites, sometimes to their detriment. But the church also *replaced* certain symbols with others. Thus the rite of anointing the forehead in confirmation has ousted what was almost certainly the primitive rite of the laying-on of the hand. Both procedures are fraught with danger, for the first can clutter up a liturgy and the second can obscure its original features as did the anointings in ordination. Historically speaking, then, adaptation has sometimes been a mixed blessing, and in our own time, when there is often a misunderstanding of or a disregard for the meaning of symbols, we should be duly cautious. The new and unwarranted breaking of the bread at the words of institution distorts the shape of the eucharist as we have known it from the beginning. Both assimilation then and substitution need to be carefully watched in the process of adaptation that will certainly go ahead in years to come.

None the less there is a strong case for adaptation. The church is Catholic and it must be able to incorporate into its life and worship as many elements as are necessary to show that it is. Already and for centuries there are the Eastern liturgies which differ widely not only from the Roman liturgy but also often from each other. There is no reason why Africa, Asia and India should not gradually evolve liturgies that are comparable to the eastern rites but that also express their cultures. One can see three areas where such adaptation might take place.

1. Symbols

Though there is a strong case for the retention of the basic symbols of the liturgy that derive from the Bible, bread and wine, anointings with oil and the laying-on of hands, there are others that could be changed though even the use of oil has not quite the same importance as the others. It does indeed seem to be a pretty universal symbol of abundance though apart from the anointing of the sick (where it need no longer be olive oil) and in the present discipline of confirmation, its use is no longer necessary for the validity of any sacrament. In regions then where it has no significance—perhaps in the far North— it might be dispensed with. Again, the rigid system of liturgical colours which in the West is not attested before the thirteenth century (Innocent III) is no longer imposed. In China (and apparently in sixteenth century France, if we are to trust the portrait of Mary, Queen of Scots *en deuil* for the death of her young husband, François II) white is the colour of mourning.

2. Gestures

The ancient Christian and indeed Jewish gesture of holding the hands raised with the palms upturned as a sign of supplication may not be expressive to some peoples and even in the West it has been largely replaced by the gesture of holding the hands joined. This derived from feudal custom in the Middle Ages and for the laity it has to all intents and purposes ousted the more ancient custom. The Indian gesture of joining the hands together as a sign of welcome is already in use in the liturgy of that country. In the West the genuflexion, a Byzantine gesture apparently, largely replaced the bow as an act of obeisance (except in secular ceremonial). No doubt in different parts of the world there are other ways of expressing the same thing. One would ask also whether kneeling, which is really a sign of repentance and to which western Christians are so much attached, has the same or any significance in other parts of the world. In many cultures it would seem the dance plays an important role in worship; if that is so, there would seem to be no reason why it should not be introduced into Christian worship. The Constitution (37) speaks of 'the genius and talents' and 'the way of life' (i.e. cultures) of different peoples and these are very various, perhaps more so than the fathers of the council knew. Different peoples express their sentiments and emotions in different ways and these, with the precautions laid down by the Constitution, may be allowed to have a formative influence on worship. There is really nothing new in this. A liturgy according to the Byzantine rite which gradually received its form from the culture of the Byzantine empire *looks* very different from a celebration of the Roman rite but its content is exactly the same. It is simply a different way of doing the eucharist that the church received from Christ. Yet it can reach the hearts of its participants and speak to them in a way that the Roman rite cannot. In years to come we should expect that the peoples of Africa, India, Asia and elsewhere should construct liturgies that are as eloquent as those of the Eastern Churches and as authentic.

3. Language

As everyone knows, the Roman liturgy since the council has been translated into dozens of vernaculars of almost all the peoples of the world. What has not been sufficiently noticed is that this has been the first and major adaptation that has taken place in the last fifteen years or so. For translation, if it is to be authentic, is an attempt to transfer the *thought* of one language into the thought of another. It was and remains a major task and the opinion is widespread that, with some exceptions, the English translations have not been very successful. Perhaps it is significant that the French and Italian translations are generally judged to have been more successful though the French has been criticised.[7] The reason for it may be that they are more closely related to Latin than English is. However that may be, what English-speaking peoples have yet to learn is how to express in a language that is really their own what needs to be expressed in the different rites of a liturgy that is Roman but not necessarily Latin. As has been observed above, some texts of the marriage rite are very unhappy and could without much difficulty be improved. Other unfortunate translations have been mentioned in the course of this book and there is no need to repeat them here. No doubt the translations we now have will undergo revision sooner or later but when that does occur, it is to be hoped that the translators will cease to use the chopped-up style that presumably they think is modern.

A further development that we can look for is more important. It should be possible for different regions and even different countries to re-shape the rites according to native genius. English people do think and express themselves differently from Americans and what might seem starchy or over-dignified to the latter may well be the natural way of expression for the former. What may seem to be to English people a proper and natural way to handle the marriage rite may be unacceptable to Americans. This has to some extent been done. The marriage rite is proper to England but a writer in *Liturgy* (the organ of the English National Liturgical Commission) has expressed the

---

[7] The change of opinion of Julien Green, however, is interesting. In his *Journal 1966–1972* he was critical of the first attempts, but later, when the official translation had appeared, he finds in it a certain dignity and his reservations have largely disappeared (see *Ce qui reste du Jour*, 1972, the title of this volume of his *Journal*).

view that more might have been done and could still be done
to exploit the English tradition stemming from the old Sarum
rite.[8] He wishes to retain the archaic sentences 'With this ring
I thee wed; this gold and silver I thee give; with my body I
thee worship; and with all my worldly goods I thee endow'. He
finds this more expressive than the current formula. Apart from
the archaism which may not be acceptable to young couples, it
is unfortunately not wholly true. The bridegroom does not in
fact give all his worldly goods to the bride. In these days of
equality they may give whatever they have to each other or not
at all. That 'a more imaginative and suggestive' rite might have
been devised is true but if it is to be so devised it would be
better if it came out of our present understanding of marriage
and in consultation with those who are already married or are
about to be. However one cannot but agree with the writer that
'the Introduction to the *Ordo Celebrandi Matrimonium* (OCM)
gave ample encouragement to individual bishop's conferences
to adapt or even omit elements of the rite provided in OCM
and to substitute other elements which would fit in better with
the practice of the people'. This is in fact to say little more
than the rite of 1614, which envisaged the use of local rites,
very numerous at the time, and wished to insist only on what
was essential, namely, the exchange of consent before an authorised priest.

What is more important is that the recommendations of the
OCM could be more widely applied. It is not only 'missionary'
countries (which are rapidly becoming the mainstay of the
church) that have cultures and usages apt for incorporation into
the liturgy. Other, older countries have them also, and it should
be possible for them to adapt, re-shape and reform rites so that
they are expressive of their ways of thinking and their cultures.
If the fear were expressed that there would be a vast diversity
that would be either disturbing or intolerable it has to be said
that unity of faith with diversity of rite has been a mark of the
church for centuries. A wedding according to the Byzantine rite
is very different from one according to the Roman rite but
they both celebrate the same sacrament. The same can be said
of the sacraments of initiation and ordination.

---

[8] See editorial of *Liturgy*, 3, August/September 1979, by A. A. B(oylan).

Nor would this be diversity for its own sake. The great task—and opportunity—for the church today is to insert the saving message of the gospel into the lives of ordinary people. Every time we seem to distance them by rites that seem 'foreign' or difficult to lay hold of, we are making that insertion of the gospel message less likely. At this point liturgical adaptation joins mission for if liturgy is not of itself a missionary device it is largely through a liturgy that speaks to a particular people that the gospel message is communicated. Mission and liturgy march together and it is to be hoped that the days are long past when it was thought that you could 'instruct' people in the faith and then let them make their way in worship as best they could. Liturgy incarnates faith, arouses faith and communicates faith and it does so at the level of life. If the liturgy is apt, the right instrument for a given people, they will believe, live and act as Christians through their experience and celebration of it.

Whether or not such adaptation goes ahead in the years to come is a question that no one can answer at the moment. Much will depend on a real and realistic decentralisation of the church, but meanwhile it can be said that our current liturgy remains open-ended and allows of a development that can only be for the good of the people of God.

Index

Abbott, W., *ed.*, *Documents of the Church*, prelims, 5n, 138n
Adult baptism, *see* Baptism, adult
Alcuin, on communion, 93, 94n
Ambrose, of Milan on catechumenate, 56; on confirmation, 91, 98, 100, 101
Ambrosianum, Missale on baptism, 20n
America, South, 95
Anointing, 22–7
  baptism, 26, 77, 79–80, 81–2, 84
  catechumenate, 51, 55
  confirmation, 89, 101
  ordination, 22n, 27–8, 140, 149, 151
  the sick, 22, 169–71
  writings on, 23n, 25n
Aquinas, St Thomas, 4n
  on baptism, 20n, 38, 67n
  on confirmation, 93
  on the sick, 174–5, 176n
Armenians, Decree for, 103
Arnauld, Mère Angélique, 1
Augustine, St, on baptism, 31n

BCC (British Council of Churches), 134n
Baptism, 29–39
  anointing, 81–2, 84
  baptising, 74–6
  candle, 3n, 18, 76n, 77–8, 82
  Canon Law, 73
  earlier rites, 3, 16, 33, 35, 79–80, 80–1, 81–2, 94
  eucharist, 34, 35, 37, 38
  font, 20, 22n, 53
  meaning of, 31–7
  scriptures on, 22, 32–3, 35, 36, 81–2

water, 16, 18–22, 31, 60, 75, 80
  writings on, 5n, 20–1, 31n, 33, 38n, 39n, 78n, 81, 86n, 95n
Baptism, Adult, 13, 29, 30, 38, 40, 41, 53–5, 73n
  anointing, 51, 55
  candle, 55, 77
  community, 39, 64
  robe, 54–5, 77
  writings on, 42
Baptism, for older children, 5n, 58–60
Baptism, Infant, 4n, 29, 30, 33n, 34, 35, 38, 40
  community, 39, 68–9, 70, 74, 87
  godparents, 73
  parents; at the rites, 73, 77, 78, 82; preparation of, 66–8, 70–3, 232
  problem of, 85–7
  rite, the, 76–85; anointing, 26, 77, 79–80; candle, 77, 82; readings, 78–9; robe, 77, 82; water, 77
  writings on, 67n, 73n
Beirnaert, L., on water, 17n
Bettenson, *trans. Early Church Fathers*, 145n
Blaise, A., on satisfaction, 225n
Botte, Dom, on confirmation, 96, 98n, 103–4, 107n; on ordination, 142, 143, 149
Breviarium Romanum, on baptism, 21n
Brockett, L., *Theology of Baptism*, 86n

Candle, the Paschal,
  in baptism of adults, 55, 77
  in infant baptism, 77, 82

Canon Law, 7, 8
  baptism, 73
  confirmation, 95n
Catechumenate, 40–64
  candidates, 45–6
  community, 44–5, 49, 59, 62–4
  conversion, 43–5
  eucharist, 46, 47n, 52, 55, 56,
    57
  final decision, 49–50
  rite, the, 47–9, 50–6; anointing,
    51, 55; baptism, 53–5;
    candle, 55; initiation, 52–6;
    laying-on of hands, 27, 51;
    simpler forms; for the
    baptised but uninstructed,
    57–8, 64; for unbaptised
    children, 58–60; into Full
    Communion, 60–2
  Vatican Order, prelims
  writings on, 27, 41, 46n, 47n,
    54n, 56
César, Mont- Questions Liturgiques,
    96n
Challoner, 2
Churches, British Council of,
    134n
Chrysostom, John on baptism, 20;
    on confirmation, 90, 101n
Clement, of Rome on ordination,
    144n
Colson, J. Fonction diaconale,
    161n
Condon, K. see Worden
Confirmation, 12–13, 55, 88–113
  age for, 111–13
  Canon Law, 95n, 96, 110n
  celebrants, the 110–11, 113
  community, 113
  earlier rites, 88–95
  godparents, 109–10
  parents, duties of, 109, 110
  rite, the, 106–9, 113; anointing,
    22n, 89, 101, 106; family,
    106; outside Mass, 109
  scriptures on, 88, 91, 97, 98, 100,
    104, 105
  theology, 97–106, 112
  Vatican Order, prelims

writings on, 55, 89, 90, 91n, 93,
    94n, 95n, 96n, 100, 101,
    103n, 105n, 106n, 107n, 108n
Congar, Y. Mystère du Temple,
    106n
Constitution on the Church, see
    Abbott
Constitution on the Liturgy, see
    Howell
Council of Churches, Joint
    Working Group, Joint Care
    of Inter-Church Marriage,
    134n
Crichton, J. D.
  Christian Celebration: the Mass,
    6n, 10n, 16n, 36n, 39n, 204n
  Christian Priesthood, 138n
  Companion to the New Order of
    Baptism, 73n
  Ministry of Reconciliation, The,
    210, 234
  Pontificale Romanum, 148n
Cyran, Saint-, 1
Cyril, of Jerusalem, 47n
  on anointing, 90, 98
  on baptism, 20, 99; adult, 47n
  on catechumenate, 56
  Cat. Myst. III, see Piédagnel

Davies, J. G., ed., Dictionary of
    Liturgy and Worship,
    Crichton, J. D., Unction,
    173n
Denis, Henri, Les Sacrements ont-ils
    un avenir?, 9n
Dillistone, F. W. Christianity and
    Symbolism, 17n
Dix, Dom G. on baptism, 32
  ed. Hippolytus, Apostolic
    Tradition, 8, 27, 77
  baptism, 54n, 81
  confirmation, 55, 89n, 101n,
    108
  laying-on of hands, 27
  oil, 24n, 55
  ordination, 142, 143, 144n,
    146, 149, 153, 154
  sick, the, 173
  water, 19n

Donovan, K., 218n
Dunne, B., 218n
Duval, A. on marriage, *Maison-Dieu*, 128n

Ecumenical Directory, 61, 73n
Eucharist, 31, 94, 95
  baptism and, 35, 37, 38
  catechumen, for the, 46, 47n, 52, 56
  for members of other churches, 60–1
  young children admitted to, 2

Faber, H. *Pastoral Care in the Modern Hospital*, 190n
Faustus, on confirmation, 92, 93
Fisher, J. D. C.
  Christian Initiation: Baptism in the Medieval West, 94n
  Christian Initiation in the Medieval West, 91n, 101n
  Christian Initiation: Reformation Period, 94n
Fitzsimons, J. *ed. Penance, Virtue and Sacrament*, 244
Flannery, A., on reconciliation, 213n, 239
Florence, Council of, 103
Font, the, 22n
  blessing, 20, 53, 75
  significance of, 17
  the water, 75
France, 2, 41, 103, 203
Frere, W. H. *see* Proctor *and*
Funerals, 192–209, 232
  arrangement of the rite, 200–6, 207
  attitudes to life and death, 192–6
  children's, 207–8; consolation for the parents, 208; readings, 208
  earlier rites, 200–1
  priest's duty to the afflicted, 206–7
  rite, the, 196–206; commendation, 200; readings, 198–200; vigil, 202–4

scriptures on, 193, 194, 199, 200, 203, 209
writings on, 192n, 196n, 204n, 205n
Funk, *ed. Constitutiones Apostolicae*, 173n

Gaul, 92, 101
Gelasian Sacramentary, ed. Mohlberg
  on confirmation, 91, 101
  on marriage, 129n
  on penance, 212, 216
  on sick, 173, 183
Gelineau, J. *Nelle Vostre Assemblee*, 46
Germany, 2
Gregorian Sacramentary, ed. Lietzmann
  on anointing the sick, 183n
  on marriage, 129n, 131
Gregory, of Nazianzen
  on baptism, 20–1
Guéranger, 2
Guntripp, H. *Psychology for Social Workers*, 190n
Gy, P.
  on marriage, 128n, 129n, 130n
  on ordination, 146n
  on penance, 216n

Hamman, A. *Baptême et Confirmation*, 95n, 106n
Hippolytus, *Apostolic Tradition, see* Dix, G. *ed.*
Hocken, P., on care of the sick, 190n; on validity, 243n
Holy Order, *see* Ordination
Houlden, J. H., *Paul's Letters from Prison*, 170n
Howell, C. H., *Companion to the New Order of Marriage*, 114n
  trans. Constitution on the Liturgy, 4n, 5, 14, 15, 229, 233
    baptism, 33, 42
    funerals, 207
    ordination, 141n, 142n
    sick, 183

Ignatius of Antioch, on ordination, 142n 144n
Infant baptism, *see* Baptism, infant
Irenaeus, 4
Italy, 2, 92

Jansenist doctrine, 1
Jerome Biblical Commentary, The, 226n
Jounel, P. *L'Eglise en Prière*, 155n
Jung, C. and Vann, G. *Water and the Fire*, 18n, 21

Kleinheyer, B. on ordination, 142n, 150n, 151

Laying-on of hands,
   catechumenate, 27, 51
   confirmation, 22, 51, 89–90, 100
   ordination, 27; bishops, 140, 149; deacons, 158, 161; priests, 150, 155
   scriptures on, 26–7
   sick, the, 26
   significance of, 26–7
   writings on, 26n
Layman's Missal, on baptism, 20n
Lécuyer, J. on ordination, 149n
Lemaire, A. *Ministères aux Origines de l'Eglise*, 154n
Lenval, H. Lubienska de *Liturgie du Geste*, 23n
Léon-Dufour, Xavier, *Dictionary of Biblical Theology*, 23n, 24n, 26n
Lietzmann, *ed. Gregorian Sacramentary*, *see* Gregorian
Ligier, Père, on Holy Spirit, 228n
Liturgy, *see also Constitution on the Liturgy*
   adult baptism, 76–85
   anointing the sick, 179
   catechumenate, 47–9, 50–2
   funerals, 196–206
   infant baptism, 76–85
   marriage, 127–32
   ordination: bishops, 139–50; deacons, 158–63; minor orders, 163–6; priests, 150–1

penance, 210–16, 226
Lovat, L. *Maurice Baring*, 189n
Lubac, H. de *Meditation sur l'Eglise*, 217n
Lyons, Council of, 103

Marriage, 12, 65n, 114–36, 231–2
   arrangement of the rite, 134–5
   blessings: concluding, 118, 126, 128, 132; nuptial, 118, 128, 130–2; of rings, 124, 128
   earlier ritual, 115–16, 127, 129, 131
   eucharist, 127, 129, 130; Mass; with, 129–30; without, 133, 136; readings, 129–30, 136; ring, 124
   outside the church, 65n
   partners, the, 114, 116–26; preparation of, 132–5; their children, 125–6; their contract, 123–6; their love, 116–22; their offering, 130
   register, the, 135
   rite, the, 114n, 127–32; addresses, 117–19
   writings on, 114, 115, 116n, 120, 122, 125, 127n, 128n, 129, 130n, 131, 132n, 134n
Marriage Rite, 114n
Martimort, A. G., *ed. L'Eglise en Prière*
   anointing of the sick, 183n
   baptism, 78n
   funerals, 201n, 205n
Maurus, Rabanus, 93
Milner, A. P. *Theology of Confirmation*, 105n, 106n
Mitre, the, 140, 149
Mohlberg, *ed.*, *see Gelasian Sacramentary and Verona Sacramentary*
Monden, L. on confession, 224n, 244
Monks, profession of, 8
Mouret, R. on marriage, 128n
Murray, P. on anointing the sick, 174n

Nineham, D. E. *Saint Mark*, 172n
Notitiae: anointing, 103n; baptism, 73n; funerals, 196n; oil, 25n

O'Callaghan, D., *Marriage as a Sacrament*, 120n, 122n; on mortal sin, 245n
Oil, 8, 22–7
  baptism, 77, 79–80, 81–2, 84
  catechumenate, 51
  confirmation, 22n, 89, 101
  ordination, 22n, 27–8, 140, 149, 151, 155, 158
  scriptures on, 22n, 23, 24, 25
  sick, anointing of, 22, 178
  significance of, 22–6
  writings on, 23n, 24n, 25n, 55
Ordination, 8, 137–67
  Bishops, 137–8, 138–50
    earlier ritual, 147–8
    rite, the, 139–50; consecration, 13n, 148–50; consecration prayer, 142–50; homily, 140–42; laying-on of hands, 27
    theology, 140–7
  Deacons, 139, 158–63
    rite, the, 158–63; consecration prayer, 160–2; homily, 159–60
    oil, 16, 22n
  Minor Orders, 139, 163–6
    acolyte, 163–4, 165–6
    celibacy, 166–72
    reader, 163–5; duties, 164–5; lay readers, 166; the rite, 165; tonsure, 163, 166
  Priests, 150–8
    the rite, 150–1; consecration, 155–6; consecration prayer, 153–6; homily, 151–3; interrogation, 157
  scriptures on, 142
  writings on, 137n, 138n, 139n, 141n, 142, 143, 144n, 145n, 146, 148n, 149, 150n, 151n, 152n, 153, 154, 155n, 158n
Oriental Society, American, 17n
Orsy, L. on mortal sin, 245n

Parents,
  child's baptism; at the rites, 73, 77, 78, 82; preparation for, 70–3, 249
  child's communion, 109, 110
  duties of, 4n, 34, 66–8, 83, 84
  loss of a child, 208
Payl VI, on celibacy, 137n; on confirmation, 96n; on ordination, 158n, 163, 164n; on penitence, 210–11, 246
Penance, 11, 210–46
  earlier rites, 215–19
  private, 219–21
  reconciliation, 213–14
  repentance, 210–12
  rite, parts of, 221; contrition, 221–3; confession, 223–5; satisfaction, 225–7; absolution, 227–8, 234, 236, 240; confessor, 228–30; place of confession, 231–3
  services of, 232–4, 235–8, 238–45
  scriptures on, 210–12, 213–14, 222, 226
Piédagnel, *ed. Cat. Myst. III*, 99n
  on baptism, 20n
  on oil, 24–5n
Pistoia, Synod of, 2
Poschmann, B. *Penance and the Anointing of the Sick*, 178n
Power, D. N. *Ministers of Christ and His Church*, 139n
Préclin *et* Jarry, *Histoire de l'Eglise*, 2n
Procter, F. and Frere, W. H. *New History of the Book of Common Prayer*, 127n, 132n

Rahner, Karl, 10, 221n, 224
Righetti, M., *Storia Liturgica*, 183n
Rite of Marriage, 114n
Rituale Romanum, 91n, 207n
Robe, baptismal
  adults, 54–5, 77
  infants, 77, 82
Rose, A. on ordination, 143n, 144n, 145n, 146n

Sacramentaries, *see*
Gelasian, Gregorian, Verona
Sarum Manuale, 15n
Schillebeeckx, E.
Marriage, Secular Reality and Saving Mystery, 129n
Sesboüé, B. *Onction de Malades*, 172n, 216n
Sick, the, 11–12, 168–91, 232
anointing, 169–71; oil, 178; when to anoint, 176–8; who may anoint, 178
care of, 169, 175, 189–91, 232
dying, the, 187–9
mystery of suffering, 169–71, 176
rite of anointing, 179–82; anointing, 181; blessing, 182; collects, 183–4; during Mass, 184–5; scriptures on, 26, 172–3, 175; Vatican Order, prelims
visiting, 169, 185–7
writings on, 169n, 170n, 172n, 173, 174n, 175, 176n, 178n, 183, 189n, 190n
Simpson, M. *Death and Eternal Life*, 192n
Spain, 92, 95

Tertullian, on confirmation, 89–90; on confession, 223; on satisfaction, 225
Tillard, J. M. R. on penance, 244

Tixeront, J., *Histoire des Dogmes*, 93n, 129n
Trent, Council of
on anointing the sick, 174n, 175
on marriage, 128
on penance, 223n, 226

Vann, G. and Jung, C. *Water and the Fire*, 18n
Vatican,
Council, Second, 3, 5; adult baptism, 42; confirmation, 99, 100; ordination, 137–8, 144, 152, 158
publications,
on the consecration of a virgin, 8
Verona Sacramentary ed. Mohlberg
on marriage, 129n
on ordination, 142, 153n
Virgins, consecration of, 8

Water,
in baptism, 16, 18–22, 31, 60, 75, 77, 80
significance of water, 17–22
writings on, 17n, 18n, 19n
Whitaker, E. C. *Documents of the Baptismal Liturgy*, 20n, 90n, 91, 98n, 100n
Worden, T. ed. *Sacraments in Scripture*,
Condon, K. on anointing the sick, 172n, 175n

CHRISTIAN CELEBRATION:
THE PRAYER OF THE CHURCH

Contents

Preface   v

Abbreviations   vii

Texts   vii

    I The Problem of Liturgical Prayer   1

   II The Prayer of the Church   16

  III An Historical Sketch of the Divine Office   29

   IV 'The Liturgy of the Hours'   62

    V The Prayer of the Psalms   76

   VI The Lectionaries   91

  VII The Hymnary   102

 VIII The Intercessions   107

   IX The Celebration of the Divine Office   119

Index   129

Preface

This book has occupied me for many months. The material to be handled is very considerable; the office, whether that of the diocesan clergy or that of monks, is a complicated form of prayer that has grown over many centuries. The *Divine Office* of 1971 has indeed simplified matters but the fact that its contents fill three bulky volumes shows that the simplification has been somewhat relative. Again, in all this multiplicity of texts it is not always easy to see the meaning that underlies them. At a practical level, it cannot be said that the office has been a prayer that the clergy have found easy to use, much less the people who until recent years, when it was freed from the obscurity of a dead language, hardly knew what was to be found inside a 'breviary'. For these and other reasons it has seemed necessary to write at some length about certain aspects of the office. There is the question of what *sort* of prayer the office is. I have tried to say something about this. The General Introduction states that the Divine Office is the prayer of Christ in his church (3–9) but it seemed important to examine this statement and to attempt to support it with other New Testament material not found there. One long chapter is devoted to the history of the Divine Office, a difficult and complicated matter not yet fully elucidated, which is necessary for an understanding of the new form of the office. Without that understanding the work of the revisers might seem merely capricious and the history shows us that the important distinction between the 'cathedral' office and the monastic office is valid. The observations of the revisers on the crucial importance of Lauds and Vespers rest on that understanding. Other matters that seemed to call for attention are the use of the psalms, the nature of the lectionaries and the meaning of intercession now represented in the office by the 'prayers'. The first two call for expert knowledge to which I do not pretend. It is to be hoped that the efforts of a general practitioner are not hopelessly inadequate. The hymns and the collects called for a more extended treatment than I was able to give them. Books, especially nowadays, have to be confined within certain limits.

I have kept certain traditional terms. Thus, except in the historical part, I have used *Lauds* and *Vespers* for morning and evening prayer. That they are Latinised words seems to me no reason for dropping them. The Latin contribution to the English language is being jettisoned so rapidly that there is a danger that we shall soon be talking some kind of neo-Anglo-

Americano-Saxon. Likewise, I have continued to call the two principal New Testament canticles by their Latin names, the *Benedictus* and the *Magnificat*. Since the office uses the Septuagint-Vulgate numeration of the psalms I have kept it almost throughout. When discussing the scripture lectionary I have used the term Apocalypse, used by all the old lectionaries, for the Book of Revelation.

This book completes the trilogy to which I set my hand some five years ago. The three books, with the *Ministry of Reconciliation*, complete what I have to say on the revised liturgy. Not that it is all there is to be done. There is the vast corpus of the Mass-lectionary which deserves commentary, not simply of a scriptural-exegetical kind but one that would take account of the liturgical context in which the various pericopes appear. Another need is a commentary on the liturgical year as it now appears in the texts of the official books. Both call for a high degree of scriptural and liturgical knowledge. It is to be hoped that younger liturgical scholars will turn their attention to them. Meanwhile I am glad to have been able to do the work I have done and it is no small thing in these days that it has been published. I hope it will be useful to others.

Memoria of St Charles Lwanga and Companions
3 June 1975

J. D. C.

Abbreviations

CL = The Constitution on the Liturgy (1963) translated by Rev. Clifford Howell, S. J. (Whitegate Publications, Cirencester, 1963).

GI = *The General Instruction on the Liturgy of the Hours,* translated by Peter Coughlan and Peter Purdue (Geoffrey Chapman, 1971). Referred to in the text as 'The General Introduction'. It is to be found also in the *Divine Office*, Vol. I; in Latin in *Liturgia Horarum*, Vol. I.

DACL = *Dictionnaire d'Archéologie Chrétienne et de Liturgie*; ed. F. Cabrol and H. Leclercq.

F. X. Funk = *Didascalia Constitutiones Apostolorum*, Paderborn, 1905; ed. anastatica, two volumes in one, Torino, 1964.

JBC = *The Jerome Biblical Commentary,* ed. R. E. Brown, J. A. Fitzmyer, R. E. Murphy (Geoffrey Chapman, 1970).

LMD = *La Maison-Dieu* (Paris, 1945); given with number of fascicle and year.

LQF = *Liturgiewissenschaftliche Quellen and Forschungen*, Münster.

ODCC = Oxford Dictionary of the Christian Church (ed. 1974).

QLP = *Questions Liturgiques et Paroissiales* (Mont-César, Louvain). The works of Bishop Pierre Salmon present a particular difficulty for reference purposes. He has written several times on the office in different places.

OD = *L'Office Divin* (Paris, 1959; American translation: *The Breviary through the Centuries*, Liturgical Press, U.S.A., 1962).

EP = 'La Prière des Heures' (pp. 789–876) in *L'Eglise en Prière*, ed. A. G. Martimort (Paris, Tournai, etc, 1961).

ODMA = *L'Office divin au Moyen Age* (Paris, 1967).
Other works by the same author are given with the necessary details.

TEXTS

The Latin text of the office is:
Officium Divinum . . . LITURGIA HORARUM *iuxta Ritum Romanum.* Four volumes. (Vatican Press, 1971–2).
The English translation is:
The Divine Office. The Liturgy of the Hours according to the Roman Rite. Three volumes: Collins (London, Glasgow), Dwyer (Sydney, Australia), Talbot (Dublin), 1974.

For the New Testament I have used the *Jerusalem Bible* version (Darton, Longman and Todd, 1966) though with occasional reference to the Revised Standard Version and the New American Bible. For the psalms I have used the *Grail Psalter* as found in the *Divine Office* where it is slightly revised. I have also occasionally referred to *The Psalms: A New Translation* (Collins, Fontana, 1963) which is also the copyright of The Grail (England).

CHAPTER ONE

The Problem of Liturgical Prayer

What is the problem of public prayer whether we call it the Liturgy of the Hours, the Divine Office or Mattins and Evensong or by any other title? It seems to be a comparatively new problem. For more than two millenia Jews, Christians and Muslims have prayed at least twice daily according to fixed forms and traditional patterns. Up to and including the first decades of this century devout Catholics attended Vespers on Sunday evenings and, even though the office was in Latin, seemed to find satisfaction in it. Some at least attended the long office of *Tenebrae* sung in the evening of the last three days of Holy Week and it is improbable that the later medieval 'decorations', the gradual extinguishing of the brown candles after each psalm or the *strepitus* at the end (which in some choirs and places where they sang became a mini-battle of books) were what attracted them. No doubt the haunting plain-song of the responsories and the solemn polyphony had something to do with it but these could only be heard in very few churches. Again, for generations of Anglicans the offices of Mattins and Evensong have provided a vehicle for true worship and devotion.

Much of this has gone. The offices, it is true, remain, now revised, re-formed and reshaped, but the people are absent. No doubt social and sociological changes in society have had much to do with this. Evening services were a nineteenth-century invention and reflected the social patterns of the time. The gentry and the well-to-do went to Mass or Mattins in the morning and (on the whole) the servants in the evening. Hence the cold Sunday supper. Since then the patterns of social life have changed radically. There is no longer a leisured class and those who are well-to-do for the most part do not go to church at all. People are intensely mobile. Even if they are at home for the week-end they will be out in their cars most Sundays and for most of the day. Entertaining, visiting, recreation of various kinds fill up their day and even if they are Christians one church service a day is as much as is possible or desired. There is little hope of a second liturgical assembly on Sundays.

But not only has there been an abandonment of public prayer, but prayer of any kind has come to be severely questioned. Many, it is said, who formerly prayed do so no longer, though one wonders how those who say this know. For many public prayer seems to be too remote, too formal for them to find it helpful for their life. What is sought is a sense of immediacy, of intimate contact with God which can be experienced in less formal contexts, in the familiar atmosphere of the house group or the charismatic gathering. Then again, people are so *busy*, not merely about household chores or the earning of a living, but often enough about the service of others whether their immediate neighbours or the poor and deprived at home or in places far away. If it is true that there is less praying, it is also true that Christians are far more concerned and active about the welfare of others than they used to be in former times.

However, that is not the whole picture. If people nowadays do not observe the traditional times and occasions, if they do not pray regularly morning and night (though it is surprising how many admit to doing so – and not only the old either), many pray in ways that are more consonant with the rhythm of modern life. Apart from the routine (slavery, if you like) that factory and shop and office impose on people, modern life is largely unpatterned. People are forced for a variety of reasons to move about a great deal, they have to do things when they can and not always when they want to. It is into this sort of life that many fit their prayer. They will attend day or week-end recollections, they will make retreats (which even the devout did not do in the nineteenth century), they will attend conferences where there is nearly always some kind of group-prayer or they will join groups, sometimes of the pentecostal kind, where they will be drawn into prayer. It is significant too that right in the heart of the industrial racket there exist small and humble communities who pray in quiet and silence. A moving description of such a group, the Little Brothers of Charles de Foucauld, is given by Father Mark Gibbard: 'There was incessant noise outside but oddly enough this seemed to drive you to prayer rather than distract you from prayer.'[1] The well-spring of prayer has not dried up.

All this may seem to have little enough to do with liturgical prayer but not necessarily. Even small groups who take life seriously and try to live some form of community life, however loosely organised, discover empirically the need for an ordered, structured prayer. One such group was the Taena Community, who began without any formal Christian attachment, and who discovered the need for organised prayer with a predictable pattern to be said at stated times. In due course they came to the divine office or a form of it which was used every day at the appropriate hours.[2]

This experience—and it is not singular—points to an important truth. Communities discover the need for a *structured* prayer that will go beyond the needs or insights of individuals and will be the means to express the worship of the group. It is indeed surprising that so many religious congregations in the last four centuries have been able to sustain some sort of community life without a structured prayer, except the highly repetitive 'Little Office of Our Lady'. There was indeed the daily meditation but this was completely individualistic, a factor that was not mitigated by the miscellaneous 'devotions' that also formed part of the community's prayer.

It is perhaps not surprising that communities of this kind have run into crisis in recent years[3] or that on the rebound, as it were, they have taken up with enthusiasm the morning and evening prayer of the new office.

Even so, the objection is pressed that formal offices and the like restrict the movement of the Spirit. The quick answer to this is: are we always certain that it is the Spirit who is moving us? But I think that we must look at the matter in another way. Most of us are pretty self-centred, not so much in the sense that we are selfish (though that too may be true) as that we are restricted by personal experience and mental capacity. The mind and heart need to be opened to wider horizons than are normally given by our grasp of reality or by a prayer that is purely individual. We need, in other words, to be opened *out* to the reality and presence of God, of the God who transcends us and who is made known in all the breadth and length of his redeeming work in his Son, Jesus Christ. Our very desire needs to be extended for we may desire too little. For St Augustine the object of our desire is nothing other than God himself, in all the fullness of his being, and in all the blessedness he has prepared for us. This beatitude is very great, he says, and we are small and limited.[4]

But if we are to desire we must first know and this immediately suggests that the content of common prayer, or indeed prayer of any kind, must be the self-disclosure of God, in a word the Bible. But knowing is obviously not sufficient and, to continue St Augustine's thought, prayer is the expression of the desire for God who has revealed himself and that desire can continue without ceasing. It is as it were the ground-base of the Christian's life. But at certain hours and on certain occasions we use words to express that desire and these are signs that remind us how much progress we have yet to make in desiring as we should. The *words* serve to expand the desire and without them our desire would die. Not that a great many words are necessary or not always: to use many words is one thing, but a continuing desire is another (*aliud est sermo multus, aliud diuturnus affectus*).[5] But words are necessary, he goes on, and he gives a miniature commentary on the Lord's prayer with liberal quotations from the psalms. Anticipating what is to be said lower down about the words, the prayers, i.e. the psalms which the church has elected to use, let us see why St Augustine thought the prayer of the psalms was so important: 'God could give us no greater gift than that he should make the Word, through whom he created all things, our head. . . . The Saviour of the body, he prays for us and in us and we make our prayer to him. He prays for us as priest, he prays in us as head and we pray to him as our God. *Let us then discern our words in him and his in us.*'[6] For St Augustine, as for all Christian antiquity, Christ was in one way or another present in the psalms and this is the principal reason why the Church has made them the substance of her prayer.

But when we have said that the Bible as revealing the object of our desire and the psalter as the means by which we may express that desire are understandably the content of Christian prayer, we have still to see how most appropriately they may be used. Is the continuous reading of the Bible from cover to cover in a given space of time the right way to use it for *prayer*? Does the prayer of the psalms consist of the recitation of them in considerable numbers one after another? Both of these ways have been practised at one time or another. In Cluniac monasteries at one time all sixty-six chapters of Isaiah were 'dismissed' in a week and there were parallels elsewhere. The desert monks recited great numbers of psalms at once, thirty-six in some places and eighteen in others. But this was the monastic tradition and in other circumstances a different pattern was adopted.

As we shall see in greater detail later,[7] in Spain and Southern Gaul in the fifth-sixth century, the number of psalms used for morning and evening prayer, which were intended for both the clergy and the laity, was small. But there was always a reading from the Bible and in addition intercessions and the Lord's prayer. These may be said to be the essential elements of public prayer. From the Roman tradition we can gather a different but still very balanced pattern. In the somewhat fossilised Masses of Ember days in the former Roman missal we find six lessons divided by graduals, which were no doubt originally psalms, intended as meditations on the preceding reading, and collects. The scheme at its best can be seen in the existing Vigil Service of Easter Eve where there is the same pattern but where also reading and psalm (i.e. canticle) and collect are identical in theme and deliver therefore the same message in different ways. A similar scheme can be seen in the brief and informal services that accompanied Egeria's visits to the Holy Places in the fourth century:

> Prayer
> (appropriate) lesson
> (appropriate) psalm
> Prayer (and a blessing if a bishop is present)[8]

It is one of her most constant observations that the texts whether readings or psalms were always appropriate to the occasion and while this seems to have struck her as something new, she evidently did not find the *pattern* new.

From these traditions we can gather another fact about Christian prayer. As we see with particular clarity in the Easter Vigil, these forms reflect and convey a particular view of salvation history which is so much more than the recounting of facts. In these ancient forms of prayer there is in the readings the proclamation of God's approach to man offering his love and inviting man's response. What therefore is proclaimed in the readings is reflected on in the following psalm which, in the tradition recorded by Cassian, is followed by a silence. The collect sums up the prayer of the whole unit. This, as far as we can see, is the oldest form of Christian public prayer and in substance may indeed go back further to the synagogue. Mere antiquity does not of course prove that it is the right way of prayer but the fact that countless generations found it satisfactory is an indication that it is so. But there is another reason for thinking that this is the right way and this reason is to be found in the answer to the question: what is prayer?

Here of course we are thinking of Christian prayer and on reflection it is odd that sometimes it has been thought of as a straining upwards or outwards to a God who was very far away. It was very much *our* effort and because it was, the pressure had to be put on. There was tension, we screwed ourselves up, it was all so very difficult.[9] This sense of tension was, I think, greatly increased by the forms of prayer that have been common in post-Reformation times. They were a curious combination of the mental ('mental prayer') and the voluntarist. A considerable power of reflection on self was required which had to issue into constant 'resolutions' which had to be made, varied no doubt, day after day. It is not surprising that people felt discouraged. In the same period there was too an emphasis on the human individual who, often unwittingly, was the real centre of concern, and the theology of grace (Molinism and its derivatives) that emerged in the late sixteenth century did much to foster the notion that he was.[10]

This is not to say that all in that tradition was bad. Far from it. It sanctified innumerable souls—the record of sanctity, both official and unofficial, since the sixteenth century is impressive. But it is not merely a matter of totting up 'saints'. What is clear is that this tradition did something that was of the highest importance. It can be described as the interiorisation of religion. In the Middle Ages, especially before the fourteenth century, one gets the impression that the recitation of formulas was too often mistaken for prayer. There were all those additions to the office that was already long: the fifteen psalms that preceded 'mattins' in monastic houses, the seven penitential psalms that were said on certain days, and the inclusion of the 'little offices' of the Blessed Virgin and the Dead in the daily course. Furthermore, the medieval Christian, including the priest and often the monk, seem to have found reflection on self very difficult and the official prayer of the church was not seen to have an essential reference to the living of the Christian life. The post-Tridentine Christian realised that prayer must engage the mind and the heart and must have an issue in daily living if it was not to be hypocritical though the notion of daily living was not always, or as often as it should have been, extended to social life. By a roundabout route these Christians had come back to the teaching of St Benedict that in singing the psalms mind and voice should be in harmony, a phrase that was inserted into the Constitution on the Liturgy (11).[11] Unhappily the Christians of this tradition were for the most part indifferent to the public prayer of the church which in any case had become very formal and which was hardly accessible as prayer to the multitudes of religious who did not know Latin.

In the older tradition, represented by the Rule of St Benedict, the prayer of the office went forward in an atmosphere of tranquillity and private prayer was a prolongation of public prayer. As Benedict said, the prayer of the brethren 'ought to be short and pure, unless it chance to be prolonged by the impulse of divine grace'.[12] He was not indifferent to the movement of the Spirit and saw the office with its tranquillity as providing the *kairos*, the privileged moment, for the reception of the Spirit. Moreover, in the Benedictine tradition the spiritual life is the matter of a life-time—hence enclosure—and the monk and nun have time to grow spiritually.[13]

These considerations have their importance but they do not answer the question: what is prayer? The central Christian insight in this matter of prayer is, I think, that it is primarily a response to God who has revealed and given himself. In Christ he has revealed himself and through Christ we are able to learn something of the breadth and height and depths of the love of God towards us and of God who *is* love. Through Christ and in the church, he becomes accessible to us. In the liturgy 'God speaks to his people'[14] for if revelation was a once-for-all event, it has to be actualised for us here and now, it has to make its impact on us in this twentieth century. Only then can we respond to the revealing word and to the ever-present love that enfolds us in itself. Although he did not use this language of response, that great prayerful soul, Baron von Hügel, was saying the same thing in the more conventional terms of his time when he spoke, as he did so often, of 'the grand prevenience of God'. God is there, God is before us, offering himself to us—in the traditional language, prompting our thoughts and our desires (Romans 8:15, 16, 23). Again, in wholly traditional language, in the proclamation of his word in the liturgy God is offering us his grace, inviting us to open our minds and hearts to him so that in faith and love we can take his word to ourselves. This is the fundamental reason why in the liturgy, in all liturgy and especially in liturgical prayer, there must be a reading of holy scripture. It may be that it was not always so. It may be that Christians in the early centuries like the desert fathers were so God-possessed that they could recite the whole of the psalter at once or needed only phrases of psalms to sustain their contemplation though we do not know how well the system worked. At a fairly early stage Pachomius felt the need to put some order into it. In any case, these were rather special Christians, very different from those of the twentieth century. It may be too that at times in the past the scripture-reading content of the office was non-existent (as may have been the case in Jerusalem) or very small. But this cannot be regarded as a typical or a desirable situation.

It does not matter which aspect of prayer we take, response remains central to it. In the prayer of praise and thanksgiving, generally regarded as less self-interested, the individual Christian or the community is responding to God's revelation of himself. In the psalms, as indeed in the eucharistic prayer, there is a regular pattern: we praise God for what he is and what he has done. Thus 'Sing a new song to the Lord . . . Let Israel rejoice in its maker let Zion's sons exult in their king . . . *For* the Lord takes delight in his people . . .' (psalm 149). Again, in psalm 117, which is composite, the goodness of God without further definition seems to be the motive of praise: 'Give thanks to the Lord for he is good' but the text immediately goes on to say 'for his love endures for ever' and the psalm then details how that love has been expressed towards the psalmist. And even when, as in psalm 8, the opening seems to be a burst of pure praise 'How great is your name, O Lord our God, through all the earth' the psalm lower down spells out in detail what the greatness of God implies: 'When I see the heavens, the work of your hands / the moon and the stars which you arranged / what is man that you should keep him in mind. . . . You have made him little less than a god . . . .'[15] The response that issues in prayer comes from the contemplation of God who has revealed himself. It is an exulting in the greatness, the glory, the love and beauty of God and is expressed perhaps most succinctly in the phrase of the *Gloria in excelsis*: 'We give you thanks *for your great glory*.'

Evidently the response is a going out from ourselves to God and this is why some have regarded it as a 'purer' form of prayer than any other. But in fact our response will be conditioned by a number of factors. It will be conditioned by what we know of God, or more exactly by the authenticity of our knowledge of God. If we think of him as some kind of primitive, tribal deity, the inexhaustible dispenser of favours, or one who requires constant placation, the praise and thanksgiving will be coloured by self-interest. For good or for ill, prayer always raises the question of God, of who and what he is. This is one reason why we should always be praying consciously in Christ who is the revelation of the Father. But our response will also be conditioned by our own state, by our feelings of inadequacy, by our sense of sin, by our sheer need. If a sense of personal inadequacy is dominant, we shall want, in the phrase of St Augustine, to appear 'as beggars before God', displaying our moral wretchedness, the rags and tatters of our lives. If we have sinned, we shall want to 'answer' with repentance; to respond to the invitation to repentance of the gospel. If we have reason to be grateful, we shall respond with prayers of thanksgiving which merge into the prayer of praise for here the two seem to fuse and then we are at heart of the worship that is given to God by the prayer of the church. Since all these themes of prayer weave in and out of the psalter, perhaps it becomes easier for us to understand why the church has made use of the psalms from the beginning.

We shall have to consider the psalms elsewhere in this book but meanwhile there are certain truths about prayer we can learn from them. The psalter, heavily conditioned as it is by the religious culture from which it emerged, can be seen as the Prayer Book of Mankind. The psalms range over the whole gamut of human experience, from intense physical and spiritual suffering, from loneliness and a sense of helplessness, to the most exultant praise. If there are some psalms where the speaker seems to be repulsively self-righteous ('I have done everything the Law, or you, God, have asked for and yet you treat me like this . . .'), he is speaking very consciously in the presence of God. This perhaps brings us to the very heart of prayer. The psalmists had a vivid sense of the reality of God, they were extraordinarily God-conscious and even if they complain at times that he is remote, they had a sense of the immediacy of his presence. This is why on the one hand they could pour out their hearts in petition, in anguished cries and even rebukes. But on the other hand, it was this sense of the presence of God and of his holiness, power and beauty that drew from them those almost ecstatic songs of which the group 148–150 are the best known.

For a recent writer the psalms provide an answer to the anguished question of man's destiny: what is the meaning of life? And he shows how the ultimate extremity of despair can in the psalms issue into the celebration of God's glory:

> Reduced to the ultimate extremity of despair we go beyond in a hymn of praise. When the Jewish editors of the Old Testament called what we now call the Psalter or Book of Psalms, *tehillim*, 'praises', they may not have been much concerned about literary genres, but they were aware of the ultimate point of liturgical celebration and the celebration of life: the praise of God's glory, even in the abject desolation of abandonment by God. When Jesus cries out on the Cross (Mt. 27: 46), 'My God, why have you forsaken me?', he is using the opening words of Ps. 22 (21), addressed to the holy one 'enthroned on the praises of Israel' (v. 3) and which concludes with a song of praise. The desolation, the ultimate extremity of the why-question is the way of its overcoming in praise, in resurrection, in glory.[16]

It is perhaps a surprising conclusion which some may think paradoxical. But it does not seem to be entirely new. The truth it expresses in the terms of modern existential *angst* and which I think deepens our insight into the matter, is found in another register of reference in St Thomas. Working within the austere categories of a rational ethic—*religio* (worship) is a subdivision of justice—he sees man as achieving the fulfilment of his human personality through the relationship that is established by worship. Submitting himself to God his last end or, we may say, the purpose of his existence he is united to God and thus achieves beatitude.[17] Where the modern theologian speaks of explanation, a revealing of the meaning of life or a light thrown on the human predicament, St Thomas speaks of fulfilment (*perfectio*), of the fulfilment of man's destiny through union with God. His account is calm and objective and seemingly untouched by experience though we cannot forget his exclamation after his vision of God towards the end of his life: *omnia ut palea*. All he had thought and written was but straw compared with the vision he had seen. But the modern theologian has brought all this teaching to a new level of consciousness and sees man immersed in the tragedy of life, reaching out for light, explanation, the dividing of the veil through which he hopes to see the meaning of his life.

We cannot go further into this matter here but it is worth remembering that when we are engaged in prayer and the praise of God, we are not performing a merely ritual act. We are moving towards God who has called us to himself and as we express ourselves, our desire for him, in petition and praise, we are celebrating him and we are celebrating life, our life which will achieve fulfilment in him, the source of beatitude, and the resolution of the problem of human existence.

There is another aspect of the matter. As we catch some glimpse of God's wonder, greatness, and holiness, like the psalmist we feel impelled to adore, to bow down before this greatness and to acknowledge our littleness before his face. But with this comes also a longing, a desire to be united with the God who is love and who has poured out his love on ourselves. Adoration moves into love and is indeed a mode of loving. Somewhat as the lover is 'caught' by the beauty of the beloved and breathes out names that add nothing to that beauty, names that are in a sense useless and yet are necessary to sustain the love, so the Christian who has caught a glimpse of the glory and beauty and love that is God, utters his praise and adoration in 'useless' words which in fact reach the Lover through Jesus Christ, our advocate and mediator. For St Augustine we worship God by faith, hope and love. We respond to him first in faith, we trust in his goodness and the whole of our praise, thanksgiving and petition is suffused with the love that is poured into our hearts by the Holy Spirit. It is this that lifts prayer out of the category of 'duty' or obligation, out of the sphere of mere moralism ('it is good for you') and ultimately out of that sort of spiritual self-seeking which a former Bishop of Oxford called 'a self-regarding soul-culture'.[18]

It is here too that, I think, we can see a point of convergence between contemplation and public prayer. In principle they are not, as is sometimes supposed, in conflict with one another though certain temperaments may be more given to the one than the other. If we are to profit from liturgical prayer, we need times and occasions when we can stand back from it and from the ordinary tasks of life. We need time for reflection on what God is, we need to recall at greater leisure his saving works through which he has revealed himself, revealed his 'faithful love' throughout the millenia. For, to repeat, it is only this sense of God and of his presence to us and to the world that can turn our 'sayings', our words, into prayer. But at the same time, the psalms, the readings and other texts of the office are a vehicle of contemplation. They are uniquely centred upon God, they reveal a myriad of aspects of his saving love and through them the worshipper is, or can be, drawn towards him who is the source of their being and its ultimate meaning.

Obviously, if this is to happen the two kinds of prayer, contemplative and private, and official and public, must not be kept apart. If private prayer is done in abstraction from liturgical prayer, it is likely to become thin in content and will move in a very narrow circle of ideas that may become obsessive. If it is done in abstraction from community, whether the local one or that of the universal church, it tends to become unduly self-regarding and self-centred. It can be readily admitted that the balance is not always easy to maintain but if there is a deliberate exclusion of the liturgical and the communal, the results are not likely to be happy. In fact, the two kinds of prayer will enrich each other and it is one of the best features of the new office that it has made possible a contemplative prayer of the hours.

To that extent, the problem is at least in principle overcome. But there is another. In modern times we have forgotten the necessary link between the interior and the exterior, between what we think, experience and desire and what we do. In the matter of prayer, there has been the tendency to think that the more interior it was, the more genuine. Indeed, in the past some spiritual writers have had difficulty in finding a convincing justification for vocal prayer which they thought was a lower species. It is obviously true that vocal prayer which does not engage the mind and the heart is senseless but it has not always been understood that it is natural, i.e. in accord with the exigencies of the human person, that we should express in exterior ways, by words and music and gestures, what we think and feel. If the lover never tells his love, its very existence is doubted. Vocal prayer is then not so much a lower form of prayer as a necessary part of it and if with St Augustine we see it as the expression of our desire for God, if in particular we see the prayer of praise and adoration as a manner of loving God, we shall also see that it is natural to want to express our love, our praise, our adoration in words. There is in fact a double movement in prayer: the words of liturgical prayer penetrate our minds and hearts and feed them. On the other hand, our interior prayer sooner or later demands expression and this it finds both in liturgical prayer, which is a channel for so much we cannot express adequately, and also in the prayers, however inadequate, we make up ourselves. In any case, it is difficult to conceive of a prayer that never expressed itself exteriorly.

This of course is for our own sake and not for God's and it is part of the whole strange business of worship and prayer that though it is centred upon God, it ultimately turns back on ourselves. This is true, whatever kind it may be, praise, adoration, thanksgiving, repentance or petition; it is for *our* good for of course God does not need our praise and thanksgiving.[19] We do not pray to do good to God and the odd notion of giving 'external glory to God'—the grander the ceremonial, the greater the glory given— has disappeared from religious talk and writing since Vatican II showed that the glory given to God is to be found in the life and conduct of the worshippers. To quote once again the phrase of Irenaeus, *Gloria Dei, vivens homo,* it is the Christian responding to God not only in worship and prayer but also in his life who is a showing forth of the loving action of

God upon us. Once this has happened, others are drawn to respond to God in like manner and in their turn witness to the presence of God in the affairs of men.

There is then a basic human need to express our prayer in words, not to mention song and gesture. We are body-soul creatures and because we are we need to offer a two-fold worship to God, interior and exterior,[20] and once you say vocal prayer and external worship, you say community. The impression has sometimes been given that the 'purest' prayer was that of the 'alone with the Alone' or the flight of the self to the One. But this is the language of Plotinus and his circle who were not Christians and were indeed hostile to Christianity. There is no doubt, as we have said, that we need private prayer and we recall Matthew 5: 5–6, though this passage does not set private prayer in opposition to public prayer. It is thinking rather of motive.[21] Christian prayer is radically communal. It is the prayer of the *ecclesia*, the assembly that is the body of Christ and all Christian prayer is prayer in Christ and through Christ. Even the most solitary mystic is praying in Christ and if he is not, his prayer is no more than a psychological exercise. He may be more or less conscious of the fact in the time of his prayer which, it would seem, is anyway without concepts. He may during prayer not be conscious of the community of which he is a member but he none the less remains one and on return to the normal duties of life gladly accepts that he is. Nor is it accidental that so many of the mystics have felt impelled to utter in writings what they are the first to say is unutterable. They are driven by a sense of service to their fellow Christians with whom they wish to share the vision of the divine glory they have seen. Nor is it without importance that most of the mystics were members of religious orders who celebrated the liturgy day by day in community. The really solitary mystic seems to have been a rarity in the history of the church.

Vocal prayer then is a human necessity and, as I have said elsewhere, implies community which again is a fundamentally human need.[22] But perhaps it needs to be emphasised that it is as necessary to prayer as it is to sacramental worship. Sartre's 'Hell is others' is not only the complete antithesis of the Christian gospel, it is also totally inhuman. Human beings are united with each other by a whole network of relationships that extend from the closest and most intimate in the family to all the inter-connecting forces that make social life possible. For Christians these relationships are deepened and enhanced by the grace of Christ but they remain human and we do not lose the need for them just because we are Christians. It is not without significance that as it has become more and more difficult to establish and maintain these face-to-face relationships which the sociologists tell us are of the essence of community, that smaller groups, whether charismatic or not, have felt the need to meet both to foster personal relationships and to express them in prayer. In another context it has been said often enough that the very position of monks in choir expresses in concrete form the truth that they are brothers and that *together* they are turned to God by and in their prayer. But when we are considering Christian prayer, once you say 'community' you are saying 'church' and thus we come to the prayer of the church. But this is a vast subject which will be broached in the next chapter.

But one thing that follows from these notions is that as soon as you have community you discover the need for a structured prayer, one that can be shared by 'others'. If there is no recognizable pattern, a community simply cannot pray together. Hence the need of a form of prayer in which the various parts follow each other in ordered fashion to form a whole that has a discernible meaning. Mere strings of prayers and other texts that follow one another in a haphazard way simply baffle the mind and the emotions and leave the worshipper in a state of disarray. On the other hand, the very content of the prayer must be such that it can meet the varying temperaments and needs of a community. If the content is individualistic and even idiosyncratic, it is obviously unfitted for community prayer.[23] In the Bible, and particularly in the psalter, the church has found the texts that in differing arrangements at different times have provided the forms of prayer that can express the life of Christian communities. Other texts like responsories whose content is almost wholly biblical, hymns at least to some extent, and collects which are more heavily dependent on the biblical texts than is always realised, are simply extensions of the principle that the church prays out of the Bible. There is no need to repeat that it is because of this that the divine office can be and is the response of the community to God who has disclosed himself in the word of the Bible. Nor is it necessary to emphasise that that self-disclosure was made to a community, first the people of Israel and then to the new Israel which through the saving work of Christ continues while transcending the existence of the old. Further, as the proclamation of the word and salvation itself came first to the community, so it follows that community as community must respond to the saving initiative of God. This it does largely in the words in which that salvation was made available.

But if the words of the church's prayer are those of a community, it does not follow that they are impersonal and say nothing to individual members of the community. The Bible is supremely personal. It is the word of God to his people seeking their response and their commitment. As we know from an experience that stretches back from our own times to that of the desert fathers the words, the phrases of the church's prayer, can be appropriated and become our own so that they become the very breath of our prayer. As in all liturgical worship there is a nice and sometimes difficult balance to be maintained between the communal and the personal. If the first is over-emphasised, worship can become formal and even hypocritical, if the latter is given free rein it can turn to sheer idiosyncracy. Given a right understanding of the forms and patterns of the office both extremes can be avoided and it may be said at this point that the new

Liturgy of the Hours has done much to restore a balance that was not to be found in its predecessor.

Briefly, the case for common prayer seems to be exactly parallel with that for a communal rite of the eucharist. Just as the community needs a rite in which it can express itself and lift itself up in offering to God, so it needs a rite of prayer through which as community it can respond to God in praise, adoration, thanksgiving, repentance and petition.

All the foregoing is one way of putting the matter. There is another that was in vogue for a very long time and since it played an important part in the system of obligation that affected clerics for centuries, it will be useful to look at it. The line of argument ran like this. Worship, including of course public prayer, is an act of the virtue of 'religion' which regulates the activities of man in worship.[24] Further since God is the supreme being and creator and since we are totally dependent upon him, we owe him a *debt* of homage, reverence and an acknowledgement of his sovereignty. This debt we pay by 'the acts of religion' which include prayer. But since in the not very alluring phrase of Aristotle we are 'social animals' and since in as much we form society, the whole of society has a debt to pay as the community of mankind. This prayer has been organised according to times and occasions and in certain patterns so that mankind can render the debt. It is out of this thinking that emerges the notion of *obligation*. All Christians have an obligation to pray and this they should do morning and night. But this is not sufficient. The prayer should ideally go on all the time and since obviously ordinary people engaged in the necessary tasks of their daily living cannot do this, certain persons are 'deputed' (by the church) to do it for them and thus throughout the world the daily round of prayer and praise is kept up.

This view, though it cannot be said to be erroneous, is a somewhat bleak philosophy which seems to make little appeal to people today. It is more ethical or even deontological than religious and since the obligation was backed up by centuries of customary law and legal injunctions of a more formal kind, common prayer acquired a strongly juridical flavour. If for instance a priest (and the obligation bore on the clergy quite heavily) 'said his office' for the day, even without attending very much to its content, and even if it did not engage his mind and heart (as often it did not), he had satisfied his obligation and all was well.[25] The man clothed in severe black reading out of the little black book was in some mysterious fashion giving glory to God.

The trouble with this philosophy is that it not only stressed obligation but insisted on an obligation based on juridical notions which have played so large a part in the Christian thinking and practice of the western Catholic church. In the last analysis, this juridical theory turns the whole Christian order upside down. It is, as we have seen, in the nature of things that we should respond to God in prayer and worship and if we see the meaning of life and something of the reality of God, we cannot but respond to him whether or not there are any laws telling us to do so. Obligation then arises out of that situation and is only justifiable on the assumption that that is the situation. Too often in the past the divine office has been seen as simply obedience to a positive law of the church with the consequence that there seems to have been current the notion that if the law were abrogated, there would be no need for common prayer. Since in recent years not only legalism but law itself has fallen into disrepute, there are those who in former years recited the office out of a sense of duty, but have now abandoned it, sometimes, it would seem, without putting anything else in its place. Since most of us are not geniuses at prayer, there may well be the danger that there is no prayer-life at all for such people. Even a daily celebration of the eucharist, if unsupported by prayer, can easily become a formality.

It is another matter what may be demanded by law and basically what is in question is not so much law as education. But that apart, every right-thinking Christian, every right-thinking Jew (for the prayer of the church was almost certainly conditioned by and based on Jewish prayer forms) and for that matter every Muslim, recognizes the duty to approach God in prayer morning and evening and even if there were no 'office' for these times we should be obliged to pray to God. In this sense the prayer of morning and evening, organised into offices, is no more, but *no less*, than the recognition of the church that such prayer is in the nature of things and at the same time the means of fulfilling the obligation.[26]

This era now seems to have passed. Apart from urgent recommendations to say at least Lauds and Vespers and of course at the appropriate times, the Introduction to the *Liturgy of the Hours* has little to say about obligation. Perhaps it was not the business of the Congregation for Worship to do so but it is none the less the great merit of that document that it has attempted to formulate a theology of common prayer and it is on this that it has based its recommendations. The era seems to be past in another sense. The revised office seems to have met the needs of vast numbers of the clergy who have taken it up very readily. The reason may well be that the new office is by its structure and content visibly *prayer*, the prayer of Christ. His presence is made clear throughout the hours and this gives the user of the office a sense of praying in Christ. But this matter too must be explored in the next chapter.

NOTES

1. *Why Pray?* (London, 1970), pp. 12–13.
2. See George Ineson, *One Man's Journey*.
3. Though of course there are other reasons.
4. Ep. 130, 7; PL, 33, c. 500. In the background here lurks the question of disinterested love of God which gave Fénelon so much trouble. It is a complex matter but if the above seems to suggest that for St Augustine love was always self-interested there are two phrases that show he did not hold that view and they will serve to provide the solution to the problem: if we love

God, he says, we at the same time love ourselves: 'we love God for himself and we love ourselves and our neighbour for his sake'. *Ibid.*, c. 499. The two loves, if they are two, coincide. When we love God we are loving the end and purpose of our existence *even if we never think of it.*

5. *Ibid.*, c. 501.

6. *Enarrat. in psalm.* 85, i; PL 36, c. 1081. The passage is quoted in part in *Mediator Dei*, n. 152 (Eng. trans.).

7. Chapter 3.

8. See J. Wilkinson, *Egeria's Travels* (London, 1971), p. 64.

9. This is not to deny that prayer *is* difficult or that we do have to make an effort, but as it seems to me, a wrong notion of prayer produces unecessary tension that we should be glad to be rid of.

10. In the theology of grace, it has been said, 'The Tridentine teaching hardened into a position which seemed to divorce the gift of grace from the Giver'. See C. Ernst, *The Theology of Grace* (Cork, 1974) p. 6.

11. The *Rule*, chapter 19 and cf chapter 20 'Let us be sure that we shall not be heard for much speaking, but for purity of heart and tears of compunction' (Translation of Justin McCann, *The Rule of St Benedict*, London, 1951 and 1972, p. 69.)

12. See *Rule*, ch. 20, *ed. cit.*, p. 69.

13. As an abbot said to me years ago, 'It is the *life* that finds you out. If you can live it, you will find yourself being formed. We do not need special techniques.' This last may be questioned. Some modern monks have profited from the tradition of Zen Buddhism though they may be finding there what is already implicit in the Rule.

14. CL 33.

15. Surely an enormous statement for an Old Testament poet.

16. See Cornelius Ernst, *The Theology of Grace* (Dublin and Cork, 1974), pp. 70–1.

17. See *S. T.* II–II, 81, vii, 84, i, 2. In this St Thomas is saying in rather different language the same as St Augustine in his letter to Proba, Ep. 130 (see above).

18. Dr K. Kirk in his book *The Vision of God.*

19. *S. T.* 81, vii, 2.

20. John Damascene in *S.T.* 84, ii.

21. See JBC II, p. 73, J. L. Mackenzie on Mt. 6:5–15: 'Prayer said when one is not being observed is surely prompted by the proper motive. The saying does not refer to public common prayer in the temple or the synagogue'.

22. *See Christian Celebration: The Mass*, p. 32.

23. On reflection it is odd that so many modern religious communities were able to survive for so long on the public recitation of prayers that were obviously meant for private use.

24. Thus St Thomas. See references above. He had much more to say of course and his question on 'Devotion' is particularly interesting.

25. Of course the spiritual writers and various devices like the prayer *Aperi, Domine* attempted to induce the notion that the priest was engaged in prayer and should do his best to make it such, but it cannot be said that these efforts were highly successful. The instrument, the office, was faulty, and the language, Latin, was for many a real barrier.

26. Significant of a whole mentality was the practice of some clerics who, when for perfectly legitimate reasons they were unable to say the whole office on a particular day, in fact said none of it. It did not occur to them that it would have been wholly fitting to say Lauds and Vespers.

CHAPTER TWO

The Prayer of the Church

It has been stated in the previous chapter that public prayer is an exigency of community and if we are to understand what this means in the Christian context we have to explore the relationship between prayer and the church, the assembly (*ecclesia*) of God's people. But since the church is the sacrament-sign of Christ we have to examine, however briefly, his prayer which according to the Constitution on the Liturgy (83) is prolonged or continued by the church.

The Prayer of Christ

It is manifestly impossible here to deal with the whole vast question of the prayer of Christ in the gospels.[1] All we can do is select one or two points that are particularly significant for our purposes.

If we examine the three occasions in the synoptic gospels where indications are given of the content of Christ's prayer we find that they are marked by the use of the word 'Father' (Abba): 'I bless you, Father, Lord of heaven and earth . . .' (Matthew 11:25 cf Luke 10:21); in Gethsemane with the addition of 'my': 'My Father, if it is possible let this cup pass me by . . .' (Matthew 26:39, 42; Mark 14:36 ('Abba'); Luke 22:42); and on the cross in a passage peculiar to Luke: 'Father, into your hands . . .' (Luke 23:46). 'Abba' we are told, is a familiar form of address used by children to their father and though it could be thought of as 'Daddy' it conveyed a nuance of respect that is not found in the English expression. As we can see from the texts, it is this expression that Jesus always used in his prayer to his Father. There is no doubt that it is proper to Jesus for 'there is no single instance of God being addressed as Abba in the literature of Jewish prayer'.[2] Furthermore as Matthew 11:25 shows, the word is a revelation of the unique relationship between Jesus and his Father. This was the invariable undertow of his life, and the doing of his Father's will was the very meaning of his existence and mission (cf John 5:30; 6:38–40, etc.).

This relationship was *revealed* on certain occasions such as his baptism Mark 1:9–11 and his Transfiguration and in Luke on both these occasions we note that the revelation comes, as it would seem, as the result of Jesus' prayer (Luke 3:21, 22 and 9:29). At other times it was *expressed* and, it would seem, with great emotion. The utterance in Matthew 11:25–7 seems to be almost ecstatic, expressing both the depth of the relationship and the longing of Jesus, so frequently expressed in the Fourth Gospel, to be with his Father. Something of the same sort may be said of the Transfiguration. Apart from other aspects of the event, it may be seen as the breaking through into the order of this world of the sublime and intimate union that Jesus had with his Father.

Perhaps no incident reveals so clearly that this relationship was real, personal and not merely 'theological', as that of Gethsemane. In Mark the word 'Abba' is actually used (14:36), and the total dependence and submission of the Son to the Father is revealed precisely in the work of salvation that he was bringing about. Finally and more important than all else, the reality of the relationship is revealed by the struggle, in traditional language the *agony*, that submission to the will of the Father demanded of him.[3] Jesus was always Son and he realised this existentially in the experience of his life. He was *conscious* of his Sonship and it was the most precious thing in his life. Nothing must be allowed to interfere with it and when Jesus so ruthlessly repelled Peter ('Get behind me, Satan', Matthew 17:23) it was because Peter was in danger of running against the will of the Father for the salvation of mankind to be effected by his Son through suffering.

An exploration of the use of 'Father' in the Fourth Gospel would take us very far. All we can do is to note one or two passages. John 11:42 seems particularly significant for the calm assurance of Jesus and for the unaffected simplicity with which he speaks to his Father. There is nothing of the ecstatic quality of Matthew 11:25 or of the excitement of the Transfiguration. Here indeed is a revelation of the constant prayer or interior dialogue that went on all the time: 'Father, I thank you for hearing my prayer (a prayer that has been made in silence). *I knew indeed that you always hear me.*' Of this he was sure but he uttered his prayer and revealed his assurance for the benefit of those standing by.

With John 17 we move into a different world. The prayer is solemn, hieratic, and we must suppose that it bears the marks of editing and minor changes that had occurred in the process of transmission. For our purposes we may note that the prayer speaks of community, of love and unity. Jesus is addressing the apostolic body whom he envisages as being sent as his witnesses, as the men through whom others will believe in Jesus himself. The union he prays for is the reflection and consequence of the deep and intimate union that exists between himself and his Father, a union that it is his will should continue into the future. Finally, this union is the fruit of love and through it Jesus will be in them and they in him. However wary we should be in reading later notions back into first century documents, it seems clear enough that Jesus is here speaking of the church and promising that he will be present to it, that its members will be united with him and that there will be dialogue at the level of faith and love between them and himself. If this dialogue is to be apparent it will have to be voiced in prayer and it will be a prayer 'in Christ': 'Father, may they be one in us, as you are in me and I am in you' (17:21).

From this brief consideration of the prayer of Jesus in the gospels we can conclude that his was essentially a filial prayer, the prayer of Son to Father, and that it was the expression of the intimate union that exists between them. If Jesus is the model of the Christian, he is the model in this matter too, not merely in the sense of giving us 'a good example' but rather in the sense that our prayer is to be of the same kind. It is the plain teaching of the New Testament that Christians are by baptism the sons or children of God—in the phrase of a well-known theologian, we are *filii in Filio*;[4] we are sons in the Son and through his saving work that is mediated to us through the sacraments. This relationship which is established by Christ is nourished and strengthened by all the practices of the Christian life but especially by prayer and when we say the Lord's prayer we are putting ourselves in the posture of Christ who made and makes it possible for us to pray the prayer of the children of God. Nowhere is this teaching so clear as in St Paul (Romans 8:15, 16; Galatians 4:6) who using the old Aramaic word shows that we are praying as *filii in Filio*: 'The proof that you are sons is that God has sent the Spirit of his Son into our hearts: the Spirit that cries "Abba, Father" and it is this that makes you a son . . . and if God has made you son, then he has made you heir', with Christ, as Paul adds in the Letter to the Romans. The passage also shows that when we pray the Lord's prayer we are praying 'in the Spirit', who prompts us to do so, and thus it suggests the basic Trinitarian form of prayer: to the Father, through the Son, in the Holy Spirit.

The Lord's Prayer

But the Lord's prayer has another importance. It is the first prayer of the community that is the church and itself the supreme community prayer. That this was the intention of Christ and the understanding of the disciples is the conviction of Professor Jeremias: 'The request at Luke 11:1 therefore shows that Jesus' disciples recognized themselves as a community, or more exactly as the community of the age of salvation, and that they requested of Jesus a prayer which would bind them together and identify them, in that it would bring to expression their chief concern . . . *When the Lord's Prayer was given to the disciples, prayer in Jesus' name began* (John 14:13f; 15:16; 16:23).'[5]   The Lord's prayer is then not simply the model prayer in the sense that it tells us what words to say or even in what order to use them—though that is true—it is the basic prayer of the Christian community because in it we are praying as the community of Christ to Father, through the Son, who brought it into existence and holds it together in unity, and *in* the Holy Spirit who prompts our prayer and returns it to the Father. Prayer at its deepest is thus shown to be not merely a saying of words but a kind of living in God. The ultimate model of it is the Trinity itself, which is supremely life, where the Three Persons perpetually live in each other and communicate their love to each other.

But the Lord's prayer also provides the pattern of the church's prayer. It is the response of the Christian community ('our') to the Father, a response which, to repeat, is prompted by the Holy Spirit. Its members are praying consciously through the Son who has made them children of the Father. They seek first the glory of God and in total submission to the Father desire only that his reign (kingdom) may come and envelop the earth, for this is his will. Turning now as it seems to their own needs but still mindful of the coming reign, they ask for the bread that will indeed support them day by day but which is an anticipation of the eschatological banquet when God's saving will shall have been accomplished.[6] They then turn towards each other to seek forgiveness for they know, as the Lord has told them, that they must be a community of reconciliation and love. Finally, they ask that they may remain faithful to God who is always faithful so that they may withstand the final eschatological test as well as the trials of daily life which anticipate it.

At the risk of underlining the obvious, let us say that the Lord's prayer is God-centred and not man-centred and the same is true of the Divine Office especially through its use of the psalms. It is the prayer of a community that seeks to do God's will, the accomplishment of which is its sole reason for existence. In the Divine Office through the scripture readings and in the terms of the history of salvation, God's saving purpose is unfolded year by year. As in the Lord's prayer, there is petition for every kind of human need the satisfaction of which is one way or another of bringing the reign of God into the lives of ordinary men and women. At certain times of the year, notably Advent, the Divine Office puts before us the biblical teachings on the consummation and in prayer and hymn we pray that we may be delivered from destruction in the Final Test.

The Prayer of the Church

Our brief commentary on the Lord's prayer has anticipated a little the question of how the prayer of Christ is related to the prayer of the church and it must be said to contain the answer in germ. We have now to tease out the argument and exploit other evidence.

The documents of the church state that the prayer of the church is the prayer of Christ, as we see from the Constitution on the Liturgy (83) where it deals with the Divine Office: 'Christ Jesus, high priest of the new and eternal covenant, taking human nature, introduced into this earthly exile that hymn which is sung throughout all ages in the halls of heaven. *He joins the entire community to himself,* associating it with his own singing of this canticle of divine praise.

For he continues his priestly work through the agency of his church which is ceaselessly engaged in praising the Lord and interceding for the salvation of the whole world. She does this, not only by celebrating the eucharist, but also in other ways, especially by the Divine Office.' To this we may add the statement of article 7: 'He is present lastly, when the church prays and sings.' Since the same passage goes on to say that the liturgy, all the liturgy, is an exercise of the priesthood of Christ, the statement obviously means that the presence of Christ in the church's prayer is a priestly presence.[7]

The view is cosmic. It embraces the perpetual praise of heaven and sees the prayer of the church as a participation in it and as the anticipation of the eschatological fulfilment when all the redeemed in the company of Mary and the saints will sing: 'Blessing and honour and glory and power, through endless ages, to him who sits on the throne, and to the Lamb.'[8] What seems to underlie the statement of the Constitution is Hebrews 1: 1–2 which speaks of the coming of the Son into the world and in particular verses 8–9, a quotation from Psalm 44 (45), which the Christian tradition has interpreted as the anointing of Jesus for the priesthood. It is the priestly Christ who brings into the world the eternal praise of heaven and by joining the community of the church to himself makes it possible for it to take part in the same heavenly song. Behind this we catch a reference to Hebrews 12:22–25: 'But what you have come to is Mount Zion and the city of the living God, the heavenly Jerusalem where the millions of angels have gathered for a festival *with the whole church* in which everyone is a "first-born son" and citizen of heaven. You have come to God himself, the supreme Judge, and been placed with the spirits of the saints who have been made perfect and to Jesus, the mediator who brings a new covenant and a blood for purification which pleads more eloquently than Abel's.' Jesus is the mediator, supremely the priest, who by his covenant of love has joined the earthly church to the heavenly church so that, the suggestion is, the worship of both is one.

We may draw the same inference from the book of Revelation where, as will be remembered, we find several vivid pictures of heavenly worship at the centre of which is the sacrificed Lamb ('between the throne . . . and the circle of elders'). The texts of the worship are given, 'Holy, holy, holy . . .' and the voices sing of the Lamb who has 'bought men for God, from every race, language, people and nation and made them *a line of kings and priests*, to serve our God and to rule the world.[9] To the heavenly court are joined in chapter 7: 8–17 the countless multitudes of the redeemed, 'a line of kings and priests', who worship God and the Lamb: 'Victory to our God, who sits on the throne and to the Lamb!' Further on we read that the prayers 'of all the saints' are offered with incense by an archangel before the throne of God (Revelation 8: 2–5).

If the mediation of Christ precisely in prayer is not mentioned, he is present as the Lamb that was slain who is *Redeemer*. He has loved his chosen ones and washed away their sins with his blood and made them a line of kings and priests and *therefore* they are able to give praise to God: 'To God be glory and power for ever and ever' (Revelation 1: 5, 6). He is *Mediator* in the eschatological events that are unfolded throughout the book. With him are associated the vast numbers of the redeemed, those who have washed their robes white in the blood of the Lamb and who 'stand in front of God's throne and serve him (*latreuousin*—i.e. worship) day and night' (Revelation 7: 15). Whatever else heaven is, according to Revelation it is a liturgical community in which the saved are united with Christ and give continual praise and thanks to the Father.

If we are to evaluate these texts aright for our purpose here, we must understand that the writer is attempting to express as best he could what he had experienced in a mystical encounter with God. It is not a photographic record of actual happenings but, as in all such experiences, the mystic brings to his descriptions of them something of his own mentality and ideas derived from his ordinary living. Without, I think, straining the evidence we may conclude that in the writer's descriptions of heavenly worship there is reflected something of what he and his fellow-Christians experienced in their ordinary assemblies. The scenario is unimportant but we may say that they experienced *as a community* union with the Redeemer, they expressed their sense of union in praise and petition, and above all they were conscious of the interpenetration of the two kinds of worship. Through their humble weekly worship with its 'spiritual songs' and its simple eucharist they were aware of the vast cosmic worship of the celestial community in which they, through their worship, took part.

If we now go to other parts of the New Testament we can, I think, find a closer relationship with the statement of the Constitution. St Matthew's gospel, which has often been described as the most ecclesial of the gospels, has some relevant material in what is the most ecclesial of its chapters (18). There we find the well-known passage, which is in fact cited in the Constitution at the end of the statement given above: 'Where two or three are gathered together in my name, I shall be there with them.' If we add to it, the sentence that immediately precedes it. we see at once that the text has to do with *prayer*: 'I tell you solemnly once again, if two of you on earth *agree to ask* anything at all, it will be granted to you by my Father in heaven.' Clearly here we have prayer of the community, however small it may be, and the members of the community must be 'agreed', in harmony with one another.[10] We are reminded of the descriptions of the first Christian community in the Acts of the Apostles where the believers are said to be of 'one mind and heart' and showed that they were in the eucharist, in 'the prayers' and in the common sharing of all they possessed.[11] But this harmony was something more than likemindedness : the union that they have is rooted in their union in Christ for they must meet *in his name*, for that is the meaning of that phrase.[12] The meeting then in Matthew is a meeting for prayer and for a prayer that is communal; its members are united in Christ and *because of that union*, all that they ask will be granted by the Father. In one sentence we have the basis and indeed the essential meaning of the public prayer of the church which has come to be called the Divine Office.

Nor does the teaching of the Fourth Gospel go beyond that of Matthew. It is richer and its implications are spelt out at length but it is the same: 'If you remain in me and my words remain in you, you may ask what you will and get it'; or again, 'The Father will give you anything you ask in my name' (John 15: 7, 16; cf 14: 13). In both the Matthew and the John passages what is insisted on is union, the union of Christians through Christ with the Father and union through love with each other. Here indeed is the heart of Christian prayer. Just as in the eucharist we are able to offer because our offering is enfolded in Christ's, so we are able to pray and 'have access to the Father' because our prayer is incorporated into the prayer of Christ and becomes his. This, according to St Augustine, is why union with Christ in prayer, a union of *life* on which is based the union of mind and heart, is fundamental and essential to Christian prayer.[13] Finally, and to return to the Constitution, it is because of this union that Christ can be said to be present in the prayer of the church.

It may be said that these passages come rather late in the composition of the New Testament, Greek Matthew generally being regarded as late as 80 A.D. and John, as we know, is of the last decade of the first century. This however strengthens rather than weakens our case for it means that the church was now experiencing in life what Jesus had taught. The church, which had now broken away from the temple worship, had for some time been finding its own way in the matter of prayer, perhaps precisely in the process of prayer, coming to a deeper realisation of its union with Christ. However that may be, the texts are to be seen as indications of what the first Christians found there.

What is not explicit in these texts is that the prayer of the church is precisely the prayer of Christ the priest. For this we have to go elsewhere. Although the notion of Christ's priesthood is said to be 'absent from the Pauline corpus',[14] we note that his 'intercession' in Romans 8: 34 is set in a paschal context: 'He not only died for us—he rose from the dead and there at God's right hand he stands and *pleads* for us.' This seems to be the theme of the heavenly sacrifice, that is, one offered by a priest, and we note that the word for intercession here is the same as that used in the well-known passage of Hebrews, 'He is living forever to make intercession for all who come to God through him' (7: 25): '*entugchanein*'. Whatever may be the truth of the Romans text [15] (and if the *notion* of priesthood is not there the *reality* is, for Christ's redeeming work was for St Paul a sacrifice; cf I Corinthians 5: 7), the one from Hebrews is certainly priestly.

In the Letter to the Hebrews we have the fullest exposition of the priesthood of Christ in the New Testament though we cannot retail it here. We note that the above passage occurs in a priestly context; the priesthood of Christ brings into existence a new covenant, his priesthood is 'for ever', replacing and transcending the old one and because of this his 'power to save is utterly certain, since his is living . . .' This covenant he brings into existence as *mediator* (9: 15) for he is 'the high priest of the blessings to come, through the redemption, wrought by the shedding of his blood and the perfect sacrifice which he offered, namely himself'. Priest, mediator, sacrifice all come together. But as in Revelation the interpenetration of the earthly and the heavenly worship is always in the background: this high priest who offered the once-for-all sacrifice is now exalted to the right hand of the Father and is now the *leitourgos*, the 'minister' of the sanctuary presiding as it were at the heavenly liturgy and offering the worship and the prayers of the 'saints' (8: 1, 2).

It might seem that all this connected with sacrifice only but we recall that as priest (though not in the order of Aaron) during his life-time he 'offered up prayer and entreaty, aloud and in silent tears'[16] and because he submitted so humbly to the Father's will, his prayer was heard and he became the source of salvation to all who obey him (5: 7–10). Then at the end of the letter there is the curious passage (13: 15) where the writer prays that we may offer a *sacrifice of praise* to God, the fruit of lips that acknowledge his name.[17] The first phrase comes from psalm 49 (50) which is precisely about interior, genuine worship and the second, from Hosea 14: 3 which delivers a similar message. This is the main emphasis but, as one commentator says, Christian worship, disentangled from the material conditions of Old Testament worship consists of 'the praise of God, the homage of faith and adoration given to God which is happily described as "the fruit of lips" '.[18] But the phrase should not, I think, be taken merely in the sense of interior worship if by that is meant wordless worship. The ancients whether Jews or Christians felt a need to express their worship and for the writer we may safely assume (does he not quote a psalm?) that he had vocal prayers in mind also and perhaps primarily. Moreover the 'sacrifice of praise' is said to be ceaseless, which reminds one of the injunctions of the gospel and other parts of the New Testament to pray always, and sacrifice at any rate took place at fixed times. Although Bonsirven's viewpoint is a little different from ours, he ends his commentary with an enthusiastic description of the virtues of Christian prayer: 'Not only can this spiritual sacrifice [which he seems to take as wholly interior] be offered ceaselessly but it has a supreme value: presented by Jesus Christ, to whom we are intimately united and who has made himself our mediator and as it were the expression (of our prayer), our prayer becomes the prayer of the Son of God and shares in the efficacy of his intercession.'[19]

This is perhaps sufficient to show that the prayer of the church, whether it is praise or thanksgiving or petition, is the prayer of Christ and that when the Christian is engaged in public prayer, he is united in an especially intimate way with Christ the priest and the intercessor. This may explain the expressions we find in the tradition that the Office is the *Vox ecclesiae* (the Voice of the Church) or more significantly still *Vox Sponsae* (the Voice of the Bride) though the origin of these terms is to be found in the Christian use of the psalms. But whatever the origin, these phrases express very briefly the pregnant truth that the prayer of the church is the prayer of Christ. Another term, also found in the tradition, points in the same direction: *Choregos*,[20] leader of the choir, or in Latin *Magister chori*. The head and leader of the choir is Christ himself who joins their prayer to his own and offers it to the Father.

If the teaching of Hebrews is thought to be a little eccentric and perhaps without any very wide circulation in the early church, we can turn to the prayer of Christ in John 17. If it may not be properly called Christ's 'Priestly Prayer',[21] it was a prayer that in the Johannine tradition was put on the lips of Christ the evening before his death. It may indeed be said to be the paradigm of the prayer of the church. It is strongly ecclesial in character: Jesus is praying in the midst of his apostles (even if they are never called such in the whole chapter). He is praying for them and for the unity that will always be the mark of the Christian community—a theme that is found almost invariably in the liturgical prayer of the early church. His vision goes out to the future, to all who will believe in him through his disciples. He will be in them and they in him and the bonds of unity will be faith, love and prayer. Finally, he is dedicating himself to his sacrifice the next day (17:19) and if priestly language is not the language of John, (and it has often been said that John saw the 'robe without seam' as the priestly robe), Jesus seems to have his sacrifice in mind as he prays to be 'dedicated' or 'consecrated' for it. The implication of the passage is that when the Christian community prays it does so through Christ who is saviour and priest. This is but to echo the Constitution on the Liturgy which sees Christ present in the prayer of the church exercising his priestly office (7). Priesthood and sacrifice have been so closely associated (especially when sacrifice, as in the (corrupt) practice of the Old Testament, is seen as simply a ritual action) that it may seem a little odd to think of prayer as a priestly act. It will then be useful to recall that all liturgical prayer (with a few and late exceptions) is 'through Christ our Lord'.[22] That is in prayer, as in all his redeeming work, Jesus is *mediator*, he is exercising his mediatorial function [23] and as the Letter to the Hebrews has shown us, mediation was effected through the exercise of his priesthood. What perhaps we need to do is to extend our notions of sacrifice which even for the Old Testament, as prophet and psalm reiterate, was a pleading from the heart, accompanied by prayers, without which the ritual act was regarded as not merely useless but pernicious. And if we ask how the effects of Christ's redeeming work are made available to us now the answer given by the Letter to the Hebrews is that it is through the 'intercession' of Christ, as it were presenting and pleading his sacrifice before the throne of his Father. No doubt we are conscious of metaphors here but the range of expression at our command in these mysterious matters is limited. As far as Christ and his Father are concerned we cannot suppose that there is any doubt about the issue of the intercession. Christ does not intercede 'in the hope that' or 'with an expectation that' he will be heard. He intercedes in the certainty that his redeeming sacrifice and the prayer that goes with it will be efficacious for the salvation of mankind.[24] And it is on this that the efficacy of the church's prayer is based.

It looks then as if for us too prayer and sacrifice must go together and it is at this level that the prayer of the Divine Office must be seen as related to the eucharist and as a celebration of the paschal mystery. The Divine Office has often been described as the 'setting' for the eucharist or as 'a round of prayer'. But this is not sufficient if it is thought to be merely a verbal or psychological extension in the sense that it 'reminds' us of the saving events of the paschal mystery. The Divine Office is related existentially to the eucharist, it is its prolongation at the level of *life*, in its own particular manner it makes present the redeeming work of Christ throughout the day.

This is made clear by the texts of the Office itself. At the climax of the two key hours of the day, Lauds and Vespers are the songs of redemption, the *Benedictus* and the *Magnificat*. Lauds is a celebration of the Risen Christ and Vespers explicitly the 'evening sacrifice', as so many of the psalms, especially the Sunday psalms show. And in the other day-hours various phases of Christ's redeeming work are pointed up especially by the collects. The church has been conscious of this from the earliest days, before the organisation of the Divine Office, when the themes of Christian prayer can be discerned.

A further element of the prayer of the church that must not be forgotten is that it is prayer 'in the Spirit'. The church is the Spirit-filled body of Jesus Christ and prays not only through Christ but also in the Spirit. For St Paul the Spirit is at the very heart of that prayer, one might almost say, the Spirit is the breath of prayer for it is the Spirit who voices the desires, the longings, the needs of the church even when its members are less than half aware of what they are asking for: 'The Spirit too comes to help us in our weakness. For when we cannot choose words in order to pray properly, the Spirit himself expresses our plea in a way that could never be put into words, and God who knows everything in our hearts knows perfectly well what he means and that the pleas of the saints are according to the mind of God' (Romans 8.26).[25] The 'pleas of the saints' are the prayers of the members of the Church—so we have the ecclesial note again—and in these prayers the Holy Spirit is present, prompting them, inspiring them and the other Advocate [26] carries them to the throne of God. Secondly, because the Spirit is supporting and breathing out the pleas of the saints, the prayer that results is 'according to the mind of God'. Here again we have the note of union: the church united with Christ and praying in the Spirit is able to approach God with the conviction that the prayers will be heard. Thirdly, the text suggests that what we ask for is often beyond our knowledge. For St Augustine this is precisely 'the unknown reality' of God and it is the Holy Spirit who inspires in us the desire for the indescribable greatness and beauty of God, an interpretation that seems to be close to the meaning of the text. But we may also think of it as something that goes beyond our expectations *because* our petitions are 'according to the mind of God' and the church in the course of history has had this experience as have individual Christians. In our own time this was the way of it with the prayer the church made before and during the second Vatican Council. Few if any can have had any notion of what was to happen and many in the course of it felt it ought to be taking another way. But the Spirit intervened and guided the Council 'according to the mind of God' and not according to the designs of men. When then the Christian community prays, the Holy Spirit is actively present in its prayer which is taken up by Christ, priest and mediator, and becomes his own. It is here that we find the dignity and power of the church's prayer and if it must always be a fully human operation on our side, the Spirit will come to help us in our weakness and enable us to unite our prayer with Christ's and give acceptable praise and thanksgiving to God.

Such then is the prayer of the church. There is little need to elaborate the theme further though it needs to be applied to particular situations. According to Matthew 18 the 'church' can consist of as few as two or three but the prayer is always the prayer of a community. It is essentially communal prayer and this conditions its structure and forms. It must be of such sort that it can be used by a body of people. As in the eucharist, there must be dialogue, distribution of parts and hence a certain 'hierarchy'. In the course of centuries the church has evolved certain structures and forms and it is not unimportant to realise that all of them, whatever their differences, have been devised to enable a community to worship God through Christ in the Holy Spirit. The Divine Office is just as much a liturgy as the eucharist and as the latter expresses and manifests the church in its celebration, so does or should the Divine Office. It can be described as the voice of the community or, if you like, simply as the praying church with all the depth and width that the word 'prayer' implies.

If this is so, we are naturally led to enquire a little more closely into the make-up of this community. The Divine Office has been imposed on the clergy as an obligation for so many centuries that it has come to be regarded as an almost purely clerical exercise. 'Father' had to say *his* office and if it was dimly glimpsed as a peculiar form of prayer, it was one with which the laity had nothing to do. The situation was somewhat similar to that which prevailed with the eucharist about fifty years ago. The 'saying of Mass' was a clerical perquisite which the 'faithful' were allowed, indeed obliged, to witness. But whereas the Catholic world now realises that the Mass is the action of the whole community, it has not yet come to accept that the same is true of the Divine Office. Yet the principles that underlie the communal celebration of the eucharist are exactly the same for the office. The celebration of the Divine Office is not a private function and all who take part in it are exercising liturgical ministries whether it be of singing, reading or serving.[27] The theological basis for this is again the same as that for the Mass: all share in the priestly office of Christ and because this is so, all can and should exercise that priesthood in prayer and so be united with the eternal intercession of Christ. The priestly community of prayer is the correlative of the priestly Christ who is ever living to make intercession for us.

Whether and how the people can be persuaded to take their part in the prayer of the church is another matter to which we shall return.

NOTES

1. For which see A. Hamman *La Prière*, (Desclée, Tournai, 1959) pp. 78–94 and pp. 385–412 for the Fourth Gospel.
2. See J. Jeremias *The Prayers of Jesus* (SCM press, London, 1967), p. 57.
3. Cf also John 12:27, 29.
4. See E. Mersch in his posthumous work *La Théologie du Corps Mystique* (Desclée, Paris 1949).
5. See *The Prayers of Jesus*, p. 94.
6. See Jeremias, *op. cit.*, pp. 101–2 for a very rich and full commentary on this petition: e.g. 'it entreats God for the bread of life', and he goes on 'For Jesus earthly bread and the bread of life are not antithetical. In the realm of God's kingship he viewed all earthly things as hallowed.'
7. It may be remarked that the first passage (83) is practically a verbatim quotation from *Mediator Dei* (Eng. trans. CTS, no. 152) which mentions simply the incarnate Word. The Constitution has added the teaching on Christ's priesthood thus considerably strengthening the statement of *Mediator Dei*.
8. *Mediator Dei*, Eng. trans. no. 222. It is the conclusion of the whole Letter.
9. Cf Rev. 4:1–10; 5:9, 10 (the translation of JB is rather free) and also 1:6.
10. The Greek word sumphōnēsōsin = 'are in symphony'.
11. Acts 2:42–47; 4:32–35.
12. See *Jerome Biblical Commentary* on John 14:13, p. 453: ' "In the name of Jesus" implies a communion of persons.'
13. *In Ioannem, Tract.* 102, PL, 34, 1896.
14. *JBC*, in Rom. 8:34, p. 318.
15. We should note that in Rom. 8:26 the same Greek word with *huper* is used of the action of the Holy Spirit.
16. Presumably a reference to the agony in the garden.
17. 'Acknowledge' ('confess' *homologountōn*) is a worship word, used frequently in the psalms.
18. J. Bonsirven *Epître aux Hebreux* (Verbum Salutis series, 2nd ed. 1943), p. 529.
19. Op. cit. p. 530. He refers to Heb. 7:25, I John 2:1 (Jesus the advocate), John 14:13, 15:7 which we have used above. He accepts that the word 'intercede' in Heb. 7:25 (and presumably in Rom. 8:34) has the meaning of 'advocate' though he thinks its meaning can be legitimately extended (see p. 340).
20. Cf for example, Clement of Alexandria.
21. Cf Christopher Evans *Lumen Vitae*, Vol. XXIV, 1969, No. 4, p. 582. The writer states that there is no mention in it of 'sin or sacrifice'. Perhaps not of sin but 17:19 seems to refer to the sacrifice of the cross.
22. See J. A. Jungmann, *The Place of Christ in Liturgical Prayer*, (Eng. Trans. G. Chapman, 1965), *passim*.
23. Cf St Thomas, III, 22,4, ad Ium.
24. Only human beings can prevent its effect.
25. The translation of this passage is not without its difficulties and the J.B. version (above) may be said to be a maximalising one. In RSV and the New

American Bible it is the *Spirit's* intercessions 'for the saints' that the Father understands and the phrase 'in a way that could not be put into words' (the 'unutterable groanings' or 'sighs') is more closely related to the Spirit. In the Greek 'the wordless groanings' are directly related to the Spirit who however is said to 'hyper-intercede', i.e. to 'intercede over and above' our pleas (Cf JBC, *in loc.* p. 317). *Both* Spirit and 'saints' then are pleading and this may be a sufficient basis for the view we have taken in the text.

26. Cf I John 2:1.
27. Cf CL 26, 28.

CHAPTER THREE

An Historical Sketch of the Divine Office

It might be thought that the theology of the divine office which we have tried to construct in the previous chapter would be reflected in the prayer of the early church. The matter is not so simple as that and as we have learnt in the theology and liturgy of the sacraments there is not always a straight line of development as older scholars sometimes thought. Furthermore, no department of liturgical studies is so complex and in some matters so obscure as the history of the divine office. Studies like those of Batiffol and Baümer-Biron of some sixty years ago are now known to be seriously defective. Yet for an understanding of the divine office or the *Liturgy of the Hours* which is now the official prayer of the Roman church, some knowledge of its previous history is necessary. *How* did this new office come about? Was it thought up by some academic liturgists in Rome? What were the criteria they adopted for its construction? Until the proceedings of the Congregation for Worship are made known, it may not be possible to answer all these questions but a consideration of the history of the office from the beginning until now will throw light on the matter.

Origins

That the first Christian communities, whether at Jerusalem, Antioch, Corinth or elsewhere, were praying communities is clear from even a superficial acquaintance with the New Testament and there is no need to multiply references some of which have been given in the previous chapter. It is altogether another matter to discover non-eucharistic, regular and organised prayer. In the Acts of the Apostles there are, according to my count, twenty-six references to prayer but nowhere is it possible to discover a daily 'order' or course of prayer. Of these references ten are concerned with special occasions, such as prayer for Peter when he was in prison (12: 5) or the sending of Paul and Barnabas on a mission (13: 3) or the appointment of elders (14: 23). Two other references call for comment.

1. Acts 4: 21–31 records the prayer of the community on the release of Peter and John from imprisonment by the Jewish leaders. This too then is a special occasion and has no eucharistic content. It is however an instance of some interest because something of the content of the prayer is indicated.

It is strongly Jewish and we find the Christians using a psalm (2), interpreted in a Christian sense, as the theme and framework of the prayer. Evidently it would seem that the Christians had already discovered how to use the psalms not only for preaching but also for prayer.[1] Finally, it may be worth noting that it was a charismatic form of prayer-service. The community was filled with the Holy Spirit, the house is described as rocking and all began boldly to proclaim the word of God. The account gives us some indication of what an early prayer-meeting could be like.

2. In Acts 2:42 we read that the newly converted Christians 'remained faithful to the teaching of the apostles, to the brotherhood (*koinonia*), to the breaking of bread and to the prayers (*hai proseukai*)'. What were these 'prayers'? You can read the text as the description of four activities, teaching or rather listening to the teaching, being faithful to the 'koinonia' by associating with it, by celebrating the eucharist, and by prayers, understood in the sense of a prayer service. This however does not seem probable. As Professor Jeremias has pointed out the four phrases are governed by the one verbal participle: *proskarterountes* ('persevering in' or 'devoting themselves to' or 'being faithful to'). What is envisaged then is *one* action in four movements: to use modern terms, the ministry of the word, the celebration of the eucharist by the *koinonia* (and we remember Ignatius of Antioch's emphasis on being faithful to the one eucharist) and 'the prayers' which may have been psalms or intercessions during the eucharist.[2] This is a convincing interpretation of the passage and, if correct, rules out any special service of prayer.[3]

The conclusion then seems forced upon us that if the primitive church was a praying community, there was, apart from the eucharist, no organised prayer. Eucharistic celebrations were at times lengthy and included readings, sermons and prayers (cf Acts 20:7-12). There are mentions of 'vigils' (Acts 12:5; 16:25; II Corinthians 6:5; 11:27; Ephesians 6:18—these last three references give no more than the word 'vigil') but we do not know what was their content and they do not seem to have been regular hours of prayer but rather responses to particular situations. There are also of course mentions of prayer at the third, sixth and ninth hours (Acts 2:15; 3:1; 10:9; 10:30) though Acts 3:1 is a reference to *Temple* prayers and the last two occasions refer to the prayer of individuals (Peter, Cornelius). There are the hymns which modern exegetes seem agreed were once independent pieces: Phil. 2:6-11; Ephs. 5:14; I Tim 3:16 and various texts that are to be found in the Apocalypse, though apart from Ephesians 5:14, which is regarded as a baptismal hymn, we do not know when they were used or if they were used regularly. Finally there are certain semitic phrases like *Amen, Mar anatha* and others which are part of the stock of the prayer-language of Jewish worship.

These words however remind us that the first Christians were Jewish converts, conditioned as everyone is by their past, and brought up in a tradition of piety and prayer that they would not willingly have abandoned.

It is now agreed that the Christian liturgy is rooted in Jewish liturgy, especially in that of the synagogue and one writer indeed speaks of the 'genetical link' between the two liturgical traditions.[4] This line of research has been pursued for some years and efforts have been made to establish that the patterns of synagogue worship are to be found in the primitive prayer-services of the church. A recent analysis of the Jewish and New Testament material attempts to show that a prayer-service consisted of psalmody, readings from the Bible with homily, the Lord's prayer, the *Sanctus* and some of the (Jewish) 'Blessings'.[5]

The weakness of this and other similar theories is that it is difficult to establish that these hypothetical prayer-services were separate from eucharistic celebrations. The service recorded in Acts 20 seems to have gone on all through the night and will have been made up of various elements which certainly included the eucharist. Again, it seems to be agreed that a service of the word always accompanied the 'breaking of bread' and, given the sociological composition of the first Christians, it seems unrealistic to suppose that they were in a position to gather regularly for other services. There is of course the well-known letter of Pliny to the Emperor Trajan dated in the first decade of the second century but its interpretation is notoriously difficult. From Pliny's garbled account it *seems* that there were two services, the one before dawn (*ante lucem*) when the people sang 'antiphonally' (*secum invicem*) a hymn to Christ as to a god (*carmen Christi quasi deo*) and bound themselves by an 'oath' (*sacramento*) not to commit thefts, robbery or adultery, and the second later (we do not know the hour) when they met again 'to take food'. This seems to have been an ordinary meal (the Christians *said* it was) and may well have ended the *liturgical* vigil which, as in Acts 20, will have included the eucharist. There is little to our purpose, I think, that can be concluded from this text.[6]

We shall be on firmer ground if we consider the known prayer-practices of the Jews at the time of Christ. There can be little doubt that they were also used by the first Christians and can reasonably be assumed to have had a formative influence on whatever patterns of prayer eventually emerged.[7] It is known that the observant Jew at the time of Christ recited morning and evening the *Shema* ('Hear, O Israel, the Lord our God is one God. You shall love the Lord your God with all your heart . . .'), this practice probably having its origin in Deuteronomy 6: 5–7: 'These words shall be upon your hearts and (you) shall talk of them . . . *when you lie down and when you rise*.' But the *Shema* was not properly speaking a prayer—J. Jeremias calls it a creed—and for this we have to look elsewhere. In the middle of the second century B.C. Daniel is recorded as praying three times a day, the times of the principal acts of worship in the Temple towards which he looked. The two practices were eventually fused. By the end of the first century A.D. with the morning and evening *Shema* had been combined the *Tephilla*, the prayer *par excellence* (also called the Great Benediction), namely the 'Blessings' (eighteen by the end of the century) while the afternoon prayer at about 3.0 p.m. consisted simply of the *Tephilla*. There were two further elements: private petitions, 'intercessions', were added to the morning and evening prayer;[8] and those of the 'priestly course' who were not on duty in the Temple used to assemble in the synagogue at the times of Temple worship and added scripture readings to the prayers. Already then we can begin to see a certain pattern emerging: praise (in Jewish terms, the 'Blessings'), petition and scripture readings. What about psalms? The evidence does not seem so explicit. At least at the Sabbath assembly psalms 145–150 were recited and these, as is well known, formed the nucleus of the office of Lauds where however it was only the last three that were used.[9] To these we may add without hesitation the Lord's prayer which brings the specifically Christian element into the pattern.

All this is a good deal more than can be gathered from the New Testament material though we do not know in what order the various items were arranged nor how often or who used the formulas. For J. Jeremias the Greek verb *proskarterein*, used in Acts 1:14 for what is obviously a prayer-service, means 'faithfully to observe a rite' from which we *could* gather that what the author of Acts was describing was an ordered form of prayer.[10] It may be so, though it seems rather early in the life of the first Christian community to have worked out a fixed form of prayer (unless of course Luke is retrojecting his experience into the past!) and the phrase may mean simply that the disciples were observing the three traditional hours of Jewish prayer.

In the time of Christ there were three hours of prayer, in the morning, in the afternoon and in the evening. The church simply took over these by now traditional *times* of prayer but, as J. Jeremias observes, 'the new life bestowed through the gospel shatters the fixed liturgical forms, especially with regard to the content of the prayers. What is new here can be summed up in the one word "Abba" '.[11]

This is already evident from the *Didache* (8) which enjoins that the Lord's prayer, with its liturgical conclusion 'For yours is the power and the glory for ever and ever', should be said three times a day. We are left wondering whether this was the sum total of the prayer. There is a small phrase in what is regarded as the oldest part of this almost certainly first century document which seems to indicate that even so early there were meetings for prayer: 'Confess your sins *in the assembly* (*en ekklesia*) and do not come to prayer with an evil conscience.'[12] Although at this early date we must not press the *en ekklesia* phrase, it could be said that these prayer-meetings were ecclesial. Further, there was some sort of confession of sins, there was a form of prayer (*proseukē*) which will have included the Lord's prayer or perhaps ended with it. There is however no indication at all of the frequency of such meetings; it is difficult to suppose that they took place three times a day.[13] Perhaps the injunction to say the Lord's prayer three times a day was meant as a minimum for any and every Christian who would be faithful to the Lord's command.

The Development of Public Prayer: Second to Fourth Centuries

When we move into post-New Testament times the picture for long is no clearer. We can pick up references to prayer in some numbers. There is the long prayer in the Letter of Clement of Rome (c. 96 A.D.) which however seems more like a long intercession made in the eucharist (59–61). In the Dialogue with Trypho of Justin the Martyr we are told that by the cross 'and the water of purification' the people are made 'a house of prayer and adoration', which tells us nothing more.[14] In the Pastor of Hermas [15] there is a fairly complete theology of prayer but nothing about hours of prayer. It would not be difficult to continue this list but to do so would yield very little. That the early Christians prayed, that they had an ability for constructing prayers of some nobility is beyond question but we must resign ourselves to the fact that there is no evidence to show when or what was the structure of their prayer.

We have to wait until nearly the end of the second century before we can glean any further information. This is to be found in Clement of Alexandria (died c. 215) and his slightly younger contemporary Tertullian of North Africa (died c. 225). It is from them that we discover that in addition to morning and evening prayer there had come into existence prayer at the third, sixth and ninth hours which were not based on the Jewish hours of prayer but on the official Roman division of the day.[16] The basis of this scheme was the saving deeds of Christ. There is at once a break-away from the Jewish tradition and an intention to sanctify the hours of the secular day. We shall say something about this matter below but meanwhile two points are worth noting. Clement refers to prayer before meals and before sleep at night and reveals that it consisted of praise, of psalms and the reading of the scriptures.[17] The combination of psalms and readings is interesting and is perhaps the first explicit mention of such a pattern. Elsewhere he speaks of an assembly of some size which comes together to form one flock whose scattered and dissonant voices are subjected to the divine harmony so that finally they make one symphony for 'the choir, obedient to its *choregos* and master, the Logos, finds rest only in truth itself when it can say "Abba, Father". Then its voice, conformed to truth, is readily accepted by God as the first joy offered him by his children.' Whether or not this passage refers to a eucharistic assembly it is impossible to say but it is evidence of what Clement saw in the gathering. There is a sense here of an assembly whose unity is to be found in Christ who is 'the choir-leader': all are singing and praising through him and there is such an identity with Christ that together they are able to utter the words 'Abba, Father'. Clement is generally thought to be very Hellenistic and indeed Platonic and it is impressive to see the primitive Aramaic substructure coming through the elaborate and platonised description. Unpredictably Clement seems to be reflecting the early Judaeo-Christian tradition though, it would seem, through St Paul.[18]

Though Clement seems to be generally uninterested in liturgical matters, he is an important witness to the existence of Christian hymns, the texts of some of which he gives, in the prayer of this early period. He repeats the (probably) baptismal hymn of Ephesians 5: 14 and records an additional verse: '(Christ) who is the sun of resurrection, begotten before the daystar'—which may well indicate that it has become a hymn for morning prayer.[19] If the famous *Phōs hilaron* ('Hail gladdening light') is of Egyptian provenance, Clement might well have known it as a hymn for evening prayer.[20] We can conclude, then, that Clement knew prayer in the morning and evening as well as prayer at the third, sixth and ninth hours and he is not thinking simply of an interior raising of the mind and heart to God. The prayer he speaks of is vocal prayer which is often done with hands raised.[21] For him it can be said too that 'the whole of life is one long day of festival, it is a sort of continual paschal celebration'.[22] In this, as we shall see, he is completely in accord with Hippolytus of Rome.

As well as recording the practice of prayer at the third, sixth and ninth hours, Tertullian is aware of the 'customary prayers' that are said 'at the approach of day and the coming of night'. These he calls *legitimis orationibus* which are said as a matter of course (*sine ulla admonitione*).[23] In a subsequent passage he reveals something of the content of the prayer (27). At least the more devout (*diligentiores*) add the Alleluia psalms (110–113 LXX-Vulg), the rest of the community responding, presumably by singing the Alleluia. For Tertullian, like Clement, prayer is a spiritual sacrifice (28 and cf Hebrews 13: 15, 16) and Christians who are true adorers pray in the Spirit (cf John 4: 24). But unlike Clement, Tertullian knows the prayer at midnight.[24] As is well enough known, Tertullian has much else about prayer but it is not to our purpose here and we can do no more than mention the magnificent peroration to his Treatise on Prayer where he sees the whole world caught up in the worship of God even the cattle, the wild beasts and the birds 'who make a cross with their wings', giving praise to God (29).[25]

By far the most copious information about the prayer of the hours is to be found in the Apostolic Tradition of Hippolytus, a document that is usually dated about 215 A.D. and is thus roughly contemporary with Clement and Tertullian. We may conclude that in regions as different as Alexandria, North Africa and Rome a common pattern of prayer was emerging. There are several points of interest in the Hippolytus document.[26] The first and in many ways the most important is that there is prayer both at home and 'in church'.[27] Hippolytus urges the laity to pray at home the first thing in the morning but if there is a service 'in church' they are to go there to listen to readings from the Bible, to the instructions given by the clergy and to pray 'for he who prays in church will be able to avoid the evils of the day'. For Hippolytus these gatherings were important and the scripture reading and the teaching no formality. The people are to realise that they are hearing God through him who speaks and 'they will profit from what the Holy Spirit gives them through him who gives the instruction'. We note too that there were both readings and prayers, no doubt psalms.[28] The evidence for a regular evening prayer is not so clear. Hippolytus describes what is evidently an *agape*.[29] The lamp is brought in and there is a prayer of thanks for the gift of light, very obviously on the lines of a Jewish prayer of blessing (*berakah*). A deacon then takes the chalice and says one of the Alleluia psalms and 'if the presbyter so ordains' other psalms of the same kind. The bishop then offers the chalice and says one of the psalms appropriate 'to the chalice'. This may have been psalm 115 (LXX-Vulg): 'I will take the cup of salvation and I will call on the Lord's name', which in the psalter comes between the two sets of psalms that are called 'alleluiatic'. The people are to respond to the psalms with Alleluia, perhaps the oldest way of responding to the singing of the psalms. Here there is a complete ecclesial service whose roots are obviously to be found in the Jewish ceremony of the lighting of the lamps on the eve of the Sabbath. There do not appear to be any readings and most likely this was a weekly service held on the eve of Sunday. At the same time Hippolytus witnesses to the use of the Alleluia psalms which later on in the West became the psalms for Vespers.[30] But by far the most important feature of Hippolytus's evidence is his teaching on the meaning of the prayer of the hours. For him the framework is the paschal mystery with in night prayer an emphasis on Christ's second coming. Prayer at cockcrow, at the third, sixth and ninth hours and in the evening are all so many ways of participating in the redeeming work of Christ. Various writers, Clement, Tertullian and later Cyprian all give various interpretations of the third, sixth and ninth hours. Hippolytus's is firmly paschal and seems to have been particularly Roman in character. Christ was nailed to the cross at the third hour and it has been pointed out that only Mark, perhaps written at Rome, attests this.[31] At this moment Christ is, for Hippolytus, the sacrifice that fulfils and perfects the sacrifices of the Old Law 'for he is both Shepherd and the bread that comes down from heaven'. The sixth hour marks the beginning of 'the great darkness' and Christians are exhorted to make 'a strong prayer' in union with him who prayed on the cross. Here the identification of the prayer of the Christian with that of Christ is very close. The ninth hour has a double significance: from the pierced side of Christ there flowed both water and blood and with the sleep of death he introduces the next day and makes an image of the resurrection.[32] Evidently Hippolytus has both cross and resurrection in mind and with all the writers of his time he sees them as two phases of the one redeeming action. Nowhere better than here do we see that for him the prayer of the Christian community is a celebration of the paschal mystery.

Echoing the New Testament teaching that prayer, especially at night, is to be made in expectation of the coming of the Lord,[33] Hippolytus gives an eschatological emphasis to prayer at midnight. He sees it as a preparation for, and an anticipation of, the *parousia* and refers to Matthew 25:6: 'Behold a cry is heard in the middle of the night saying: Behold the bridegroom is coming; rise and go to meet him . . . That is why you should keep watch [*vigilate*] for you do not know at what hour he will come.' This sense of the Second Coming which had not faded in the time of Hippolytus, gave a peculiar intensity to the early Christian prayer at night, which has not been wholly lacking in the later vigil-prayer of the church.[34]

To complete Hippolytus's interpretation of the hours, let it be said that, as we should expect, morning prayer (at cockcrow) is related to the resurrection both of Christ and the Christian. The language is obscure though we note the phrase that 'at this moment we recognize him [Christ] by faith', which would seem to be a quite modern way of saying that it is only the eye of faith that can 'see' the Risen Christ.

Hippolytus then gives a quite complete theology of Christian prayer and his system might seem to us a very demanding one. Whether or not anyone practised it we do not know though Jungmann[35] has pointed out that prayer at midnight was not so demanding when people went to bed just after dusk and had ten or so hours of sleep before then. Nor should we think of this prayer whether of the night or the morning as a purely private and mental prayer. Non-vocalised prayer was something that people at this time found very difficult, just as reading a book silently was also something unusual.[36] The prayer was also 'ritualised'. People prayed with gestures, raising the hands like the *Orante*, or in penitence kneeling. When husband and wife were both Christians they prayed together and of course aloud and there would seem to have been a much stronger sense of family worship than is common now. Hippolytus himself is witness to it and it may well be a practice derived from Jewish worship of which in any case there are traces in the account given by Hippolytus.

Whether it is right to see in the Hippolytan scheme the 'origins' of the divine office as it came to be, is another matter. The distinction between the clergy and the laity at this time was less clearly defined than it was two centuries later and there is no reason to suppose that the intervention of the clergy was necessary to make their prayer the prayer of the church.[37] Nor can one suppose that there was any direct line of continuity between the practices of the early third century and those of the fifth. The Decian, Valerian and Diocletian persecutions intervened and a new factor, the prayer of the desert monks, came in the fourth century to modify the pattern of liturgical prayer.

Indications of public prayer do indeed occur in other places in the middle of the third century though the information to be gleaned is nothing like so complete as can be found in the *Apostolic Tradition*. Origin speaks of prayer in church, a place that is holy first because of the presence of the angelic powers and secondly and more importantly 'because of the power of our Lord and Saviour himself'.[38] Further on he gives some information about the prayer that was made in the assembly. It begins with the praise of God 'through Christ who is praised together with him in the Holy Spirit'. It continues with thanksgiving for both general and particular benefits and moves into confession of sins with a view to their remission. There is petition that those who are praying will receive the great and heavenly gifts and intercession for people generally and for relations and friends. The whole prayer ends with 'praise to God through Christ in the Holy Spirit'.[39] There is, it is true, no mention of readings though it is difficult to imagine a service which Origen had anything to do with where there was no reading of scripture and no homily. It is also difficult to discern whether or not the prayer he is describing is part of a eucharistic celebration. What is clear is Origen's well-known insistence that all prayer should go through Christ, our high priest, and not directly to Christ. If he seems unduly strict we have to remember that he was speaking specifically of public prayer and was in any case voicing a rule that was observed in all the early churches.[40]

But another change of far-reaching consequence was taking place. From the beginning of the fourth century the practices of the desert monks were affecting church life. When under men like Pachomius the hermits were gathered into communities (*coenobia*), it became necessary to organise a form of common prayer. First, there was the organisation of regular hours of prayer and then the allocation of psalms to them. Finally, there was the institution of the night office, known as vigils, and here the number of psalms varied in different places from thirty to twelve. This office took place at cockcrow and preceded the now ancient prayer of praise at dawn. The institution of the regular night office and the recitation of the whole of the psalter 'in course' in a given period of time were the two main features of the monastic office. They would have a considerable influence on the development of the divine office in the centuries that lay ahead. These monastic practices came to the church in the West and are described by Cassian (died 435). They can be seen as the basis of the arrangements of the *Regula Magistri*, which was perhaps pre-Benedictine, and had their influence on the office of St Benedict himself.[41]

Henceforth there would be two systems of prayer in existence, the first that which scholars have called the 'cathedral' office and the second that known as the monastic office. The first consisted of morning and evening prayer, both with a limited number of psalms, of 'hymns', a reading from holy scripture and prayers. The second added the night office with its recitation of the psalms 'in course', an extended use of psalms in morning and evening prayer and eventually a regular course of the reading of the Bible, the *lectio continua*. The hours of Terce, Sext and None were incorporated into the daily course and Cassian records the institution in Bethlehem of what is generally agreed to be Prime, an office that came between morning prayer and Terce.[42] The whole system was devised for a stable community and not for the generality of the people who obviously could not be present for every office every day. But through the centuries the monastic office steadily exerted its influence on the 'cathedral' office until both the daily course of offices and the regular recitation of the whole psalter within a given space of time came to be accepted as the divine office or the prayer of the church.[43]

But this development was a gradual one and the more popular offices of morning and evening prayer remained for some time. There is a description in one of St Basil's letters that seems to witness to a 'cathedral' type of morning prayer. Basil of course is the author of one of the great monastic 'rules' in which he laid down certain prescriptions for the office of his communities. The interest of the letter is that it does not seem to have such communities in view.[44] It reveals a mixed community as well as something of their form of prayer. The people (*laos*) who are with us, (evidently the clerical-lay body forming the bishop's *familia*), he writes, go to church to keep vigil. First there are prayers of a penitential kind, then psalms, sung both 'antiphonally', it would seem, and responsorially and divided by 'prayers'. There is meditation on the scriptures and so presumably the reading of them, and at dawn the morning office which included Psalm 50, one of the permanent psalms for this hour though it is sometimes difficult to discern at what point it was recited.[45] No doubt the traditional Psalms 148–150 were also sung. Basil is writing to answer the objections of a neighbouring church though it is difficult to see quite what the point of the objections was. It may be that the vigil part of the office was regarded as a monastic practice which the clergy had no intention of adopting and this would not be the last time that that objection would be heard. What is interesting is that it was the *laos* who were present both for the Vigil and the morning prayer which seems to have been of the traditional kind.

The fullest description we possess of the offices is to be found a little later in the travelogue of the loquacious nun from (probably) Southern Gaul who was perhaps called Egeria.[46] If the offices she describes were affected by monastic usages and if the nucleus of those attending were the ascetics (male and female), morning and evening prayer were definitely of the 'cathedral' type. There was a vigil service before dawn, attended principally by the ascetics. Morning prayer followed at dawn when considerable crowds were present. The assembly sang the '*matutinos hymnos*' after which the bishop with the clergy appeared to lead the prayers for different categories of people. The office ended with the dismissal which was prolonged, all coming to kiss the bishop's hand. Evening prayer, of a similar pattern, was very solemn and attended by all.

Though Egeria does not enumerate the psalms sung, we know from contemporary sources that they included psalms 62 and 148–150. Possibly the *Orthros*, the *Gloria in excelsis*, still a prayer of the Byzantine morning office, was also sung. In the evening the *psalmi lucernares*, which included psalm 140, were used though whether the *Phōs hilaron* was sung, as it seems to have been in St Basil's church, is uncertain.[47] The prayers of intercession, led by a deacon and repeatedly responded to by boys with *Kyrie eleison*, were lengthy and there was the same sort of dismissal as in the morning.

One further feature may be noted. On Sundays, after a short vigil office at cockcrow there was the solemn proclamation by the bishop of the gospel of the resurrection.[48] Apart from this there is no mention of readings for any of the offices. Some scholars see this as an indication that in the early office there were no readings at all. They hold that there were two separate kinds of service, one they call latreutic, consisting of psalms and prayers, and another they call kerygmatic which was instructional.[49] Even if this were the situation at Jerusalem, since its liturgy had many peculiarities—extreme mobility being one of them and a multiplicity of services another—we may not suppose that what was done there was done elsewhere and in fact we know that there were readings in the offices of some other churches.

By the end of the fourth century morning and evening prayer, attended by the clergy and at least the devout laity, had become customary. Augustine speaks of his mother Monica going to church twice a day in the morning and the evening that she might hear God in his word and he might hear her in her prayers. He also speaks of the devout Christian who 'like an ant' runs to church to pray, to listen to the lesson, to sing the hymn and to ruminate on what he had heard.[50] Clearly then there were readings as well as psalms and this is borne out by what we know of the office at Milan in the time of St Ambrose.[51] There was prayer in the morning and evening and Ambrose frequently exhorted the people to attend, which seems to indicate that often they did not. As was traditional, morning prayer was related to Christ's resurrection—he is called the Sun of Righteousness—and consisted of psalms and canticles as well as of 'modern' hymns when Ambrose had written them. It would seem that there was a reading of the beatitudes, which may reflect an earlier custom, though it is difficult to believe that they were used daily.[52] No doubt, as was now the custom everywhere, morning prayer included psalm 50 and psalms 148–150. Evening prayer was sung 'at the lighting of the lamps'—it was the old *lucernarium* known to Hippolytus and retained in the Ambrosian rite to this day. It was also called the 'evening sacrifice' which seems to indicate that psalm 140 was used, as in the East.[53] As in morning prayer a hymn was sung, e.g. *Deus creator omnium*, composed by Ambrose. There was also an hour of prayer at midday before the eucharist when psalm 118 seems to have been used. If this is so, it witnesses to the ancient custom, preserved by Rome even until today, of using this psalm in sections for the offices of Terce, Sext and None. Ambrose also speaks of a night office when there were readings.[54] These preceded the prayers, it would seem, and witnesses to the increasing influence of monastic practices.

That there were popular vigils or '*solemnes pernoctationes*', attended by large crowds (some of dubious character), can be gathered from Jerome who writes to Laeta and tells her to keep her daughter near her.[55] Of these vigils the greatest was that of Easter and others during the year will have been rare. They were not the monastic vigils which took place every night and had a different form.

From a different area and right at the end of the fourth century we have other evidence of an office that was attended by the people. Niceta of Remesiana, the most probable author of the *Te Deum*, wrote two small treatises, *De Vigiliis* and *De Psalmodiae bono* which yield some interesting details.[56] He was bishop of this small town, now in Yugoslavia, on the main road to the East and his congregation was made up of a very miscellaneous collection of people. There do not seem to have been any monks of any sort. He expects his people to attend week-end vigils which consist of 'prayers, hymns and readings'. From his treatise on psalmody it is not clear whether he has vigils or morning prayer in mind. No doubt by this time and at least for week-end vigils the two services had been combined. What he gives and what I think no one else of this time gives is information about the canticles used in his office. He details the following: Exodus 15:1 ff.; Deuteronomy 32:1–44; I Samuel 2:1–10; Habbakuk 3; Jonah 2:3–10; Isaiah 26:9 ff. and possibly one from Jeremiah. These, as we know, have been found in the Roman office for centuries and their number has recently been increased. Finally, he refers to the Canticle of the Three Young Men in the furnace which is also a classical text for morning prayer. In addition, he mentions a considerable number of psalms though it is difficult to discern when these or the canticles were used. In any case, he seems to record a transitional stage.

From yet another area, Spain and Southern Gaul towards the end of the fifth century, there is evidence that morning and evening prayer were still regarded as the prayer of the church. The whole of this considerable evidence is summed up by Jungmann as follows: '. . . from Spain's southern tip to the banks of the Rhone, not only were Morning Hour and Vespers regular church services but they had a form of ritual which was regarded as legitimate'.[57] The synods exhorted the clergy to attend but the services were meant for the people and were accordingly comparatively short. The psalm-content was small though morning prayer always included psalms 148–150. There was also a reading from holy scripture which came after the psalms and for Caesarius of Arles at least there was a homily. From the synod of Vaison (529) we learn that the prayer included the *Kyries*, for the use of which it invoked Roman custom. So this element existed at Rome too. The office ended with a collect and the Lord's prayer but a blessing was given only when a bishop was present. To sum up, we may say that these offices consisted of psalms, reading (sermon), hymns in some places, intercessions and the concluding prayers. Apart from a tendency to increase the psalm-content, these offices are of the genuine 'cathedral' type and show little trace of monastic influence.

The situation in Rome was, it seems, rather different. As early as the first half of the fifth century the popes (Xystus II and Leo I) had invited monastic groups to take over the office in the great basilicas though the clergy were required to take part in morning and evening prayer. There is no mention of the people being present though we could argue that from what is known of Milan and Ravenna at the same time, they were. According to Jungmann, as well as intercessions, witnessed by the presence of the *Kyries*, there was also a reading at morning prayer, and it is his view also that by the sixth century this had been incorporated into a system of readings belonging to the vigil: 'The Morning Prayer had acquired a preamble.' This is one explanation of how the night office acquired the element of Bible reading.[58]

By the end of the fifth century, then, the main lines of the prayer of the church are clear. Essentially it consisted of morning and evening prayer made up in the manner we have described above. These are what the Constitution on the Liturgy (89, a) calls the two focal points of the daily office and they almost wholly stand outside monastic influence. They are the prayer of the gathered church both clerical and lay. But alongside it there developed the office of 'vigils' which was celebrated every night and sometimes had a very large quota of psalms—36 in the *Regula Magistri*!—with a regular course of Bible reading. To this were added the offices of Prime, Terce, Sext, None and Compline so that practically the whole day was covered. Thus was achieved obedience to the gospel injunction to pray always. Even so, for long enough there remained the offices of morning and evening prayer celebrated by the bishop's *familia*, clerics of various degree, as well as by the as yet unorganised ascetics, virgins, widows and other devout laity who lived in or near the church buildings. Here we have both in content and celebration an office which, *pace* the late Dom Gregory Dix, was not the creation of monks, and which modern scholars now see as the nucleus of the prayer of the church, or, as it is now called, the Liturgy of the Hours.[59]

The Divine Office in the Early Middle Ages

The sixth century is the watershed in the development of the divine office. Until then churches everywhere celebrated the 'cathedral' office for the cathedral with the clergy gathered round the bishop was the real parish of those times. But at this time they had no sense of obligation to recite all the offices that were customary in the great basilicas of Rome, where, as we may have seen, monks had already taken over that duty. But from the sixth century onwards there was steady pressure on clerics to celebrate all the hours. In fact what we witness in the next two centuries is the monasticisation of the prayer of the church. But we must dispel two illusions. In the sixth century and for a long time to come there was no notion that there should be but one office which should be celebrated all over the western church. The great centres in Italy, Gaul and Spain all retained their own traditions, their own books and their own ordering of the office. Development there was and it was all in the direction of a monastic type of office but it was sporadic and uneven. The second fact was that it was some time before any 'secular' community felt that it ought to use all the hours that had become part of the monastic office. The clerics of Rome for instance resisted attempts to get them to celebrate vigils [60] and especially in Gaul (Auxerre, Tours), when the various hours were adopted, they were shared out among the clergy of the various churches in the same city. Finally, no one at this time thought of an individual obligation to 'say' the office. It was clearly understood that the office was the prayer of the ecclesial community which as such gave praise to God.

But when we speak of the monasticisation of the office in this period we must be clear what we mean. It is now agreed that an office of the monastic type existed in the Roman basilicas before St Benedict's time and it is this basilican office that is the origin of what became the divine office of the western church. In the course of its development it was affected by the Benedictine office but it always had an independent existence. In view of its importance it will be useful to detail its content. The whole psalter was recited every week and, with a few exceptions (to provide psalms for Lauds, for example), it was arranged in the following order psalms 1–108 were allocated to vigils and psalms 109–147 to Vespers. The daily vigil office consisted of twelve psalms and of four lessons in winter (three in the summer). On Sundays there were eighteen (or even twenty-four) psalms distributed over three nocturns, and nine lessons with nine responsories. For festal days there were only nine psalms (three to each nocturn) and nine lessons with eight responsories, the ninth being replaced by the *Te Deum*. This is a thoroughly monastic office. Lauds had four psalms, one canticle (O.T.), the 'praising' psalms, 148–150, and the *Benedictus*. For Vespers there were five psalms specially chosen to fit the hour, and the *Magnificat*. Psalm 118, divided into sections, provided the psalmody for Terce, Sext and None. Each office ended with *preces* and the Lord's prayer since in the basilicas the collect was reserved for the pope or his deputy. There were no opening versicles and responses, no hymns, and no chapter or short reading. The office of the last three days of Holy Week until the recent reform gave an adequate idea of what the ancient Roman (festal) office was like.[61]

The Office of the Rule of St Benedict

Since the Benedictine office exerted an important influence on the development of the office it is necessary to give some account of its content.

It is now generally accepted that Benedict adapted and added to the office already in possession in the Roman basilicas.[62] He grew up in Rome and was familiar with the Roman *ordo psallendi*. In spite of a few additions (the opening versicle and responses and the hymns), Benedict's office was in some ways shorter than the Roman. There were never more than twelve psalms at vigils, only four at Vespers and at Compline three. In the summer, when dawn comes early, the scripture readings were reduced (the missing portions being read in the refectory) and in the second nocturn there was no more than one short reading. On Sundays and festivals however there were in addition three canticles and four lessons from the New Testament with responsories, this last part looking rather like a vestige of the old cathedral week-end vigil. The whole was concluded with the *Te Deum* and the chanting by the abbot of a gospel passage.[63]

Lauds however, especially on Sundays, was rather long. Apart from psalm 66 (to be said every day to allow the brethren to assemble), there were three psalms (one being the classical 50), the *Benedicite* and psalms 148–150. On weekdays there were two psalms, an Old Testament canticle (after the Roman custom) and psalms 148–150. We note too that there was a reading (short, for it was to be said by heart), the responsory, the versicle, the *Benedictus*, the *Kyrie eleison* and the conclusion which consisted of the Lord's prayer and possibly the collect though the Rule does not say so.[64] In all this the reading, perhaps the responsory and the hymn seem to be additions to the Roman office which apart from ferial days seems to have lost the *Kyries* and the Lord's prayer which together formed what Benedict called the *supplicatio litaniae.*

Though Benedict kept the distribution of the psalter over the week, he had to modify the Roman *cursus.* He needed psalms for Prime (a monastic office) and to this he allocated psalms 1–19 (with the exception of three used elsewhere). Psalm 118 was used for Terce, Sext and None on Sundays and Mondays and for the rest of the week he took psalms 119–127, used in the Roman system for Vespers. Benedict too seems to have been the first to make a systematic use of psalms for certain hours on account of their appropriateness. Thus he allocated psalms 117 (a resurrection psalm), 62 (long traditional for this hour), 5, 35, etc. to Lauds.[65]

Such in broad outline was the office that Benedict provided for his monks. For a community that lived by the rhythm of an agricultural society it was a reasonable and manageable form of prayer, much more reasonable than that of the *Regula Magistri* or the later one of Columbanus, both of which Benedict's office gradually ousted.

There were now two models of the divine office in existence, the Roman-basilican and that of St Benedict's Rule. But it does not follow that either was in *use* everywhere. Not to mention the East, the Roman office was in use in certain churches in Rome but other great centres in Italy, Gaul and Spain had their own traditions. The Benedictine office was confined to the Benedictine family and that family developed slowly. Monte Cassino itself was destroyed in 580–1 and Benedict's work had to be begun all over again. Here St Gregory the Great played an important role for it was from refugee monks from Monte Cassino that he learnt the Rule and it must have been the office of the Rule that St Augustine brought to

England. Another centre from which the Benedictine office was propagated was the monastery of Fleury-sur-Loire in the seventh century.[66]

Where however the Benedictine office exerted its influence was on *celebration*. Benedict gave the example of a community which made itself responsible for the recitation of all the hours from vigils to Compline in one day. This, if not a new idea, was a practice that stable communities of monks could undertake and gradually their example affected practice in other and different places. Thus in Gaul, notably in Auxerre, an ancient centre where there were several churches, the bishop arranged that the clerics of different churches should recite in turn different parts of the office. The episcopal city was still regarded as the nuclear community of the diocese and it was this whole community that undertook the daily course of prayer. When and wherever the Benedictine rule was established, its influence on single communities to undertake the whole course of daily prayer was powerful.

In this respect England, thanks to St Gregory and the mission of St Augustine, played a significant role. As is well known he and his monks brought the Roman tradition of liturgy to England [67] which was endorsed a century and a half later by the Synod of Clovesho (747) where it was decreed that the *cantilena romana* should be the practice of the Anglo-Saxon church.[68] It was this tradition that Boniface took with him from England to Germany and eventually he powerfully supported the efforts of Pepin to restore regular liturgical practice in his dominions. It was at the same time that Chrodegang of Metz, a relative of Pepin's, after a visit to Rome, brought into existence his 'canons' who lived in community and undertook the celebration of the divine office but who unlike monks engaged in certain diocesan work. Thus the way was paved for the far-reaching liturgical reform of Charlemagne.

The reform initiated by Pepin, Boniface and Chrodegang shows that the history of the divine office is very much a history of its celebration. For want of the necessary books a solitary priest could not recite the office and both in the eighth century and again in the eleventh communities of priests were formed to maintain a regular life of which the celebration of the divine office was an essential part.

Before Pepin and Boniface began their reform there was a lack of liturgical books of any kind. The slow decline of the Merovingian kingdom had left Gaul in disarray and invasions from the East and the West had destroyed monasteries and churches and all that they contained. The *scriptoria* too where the books could be copied had suffered with the rest so that there was no centre left to provide texts of the Bible and the liturgical books. Such as remained were corrupt. This was one factor that prompted recourse to Rome for liturgical books. Another was the continuing prestige of Rome and the close relations that Boniface maintained with it. It was these factors that led to the extinction of the Old Gallican rite and the gradual introduction of the Roman liturgy.

The reform of Pepin seems to have been only partially successful and it needed the vision and energy of a Charlemagne to bring about a lasting change. He had created a vast empire which stretched from Italy to central Germany and although it was only loosely held together, he thought of it as a unity. Furthermore, he came gradually to think of himself as the successor of the ancient Roman emperors and the equal of the emperor who reigned in Constantinople. He was determined to produce liturgical uniformity in his dominions and he too saw Rome as the only possible source of that uniformity. He sent to Rome for a further supply of liturgical books which when they arrived included the famous Gregorian Sacramentary (the *Hadrianum*), and set up a *scriptorium* where authentic copies could be made of biblical and liturgical texts. In all this work the English monk Alcuin played a leading part.

But that was not enough for Charlemagne. He was a ruler and what he wanted must be achieved. For more than twenty years by legislation and by pressure on bishops and synods he sought to impose liturgical uniformity. As early as 789 he was insisting that all candidates for the ministry should study the Roman chant for both the Mass and the office and later, in 805, he explicitly included a knowledge of the Roman *Ordo*, that is the Roman manner of celebrating the liturgy.[69] The Roman books were adapted, copied and distributed and there must have been an immense improvement in the celebration of the liturgy. But dictation from a monarch is one thing, practice another and we know that there was resistance in certain places like the ancient liturgical centres of Milan and Lyons. What the ordinary clergy of the time made of it all is another matter and the fact that the legislation had to be repeated for years shows that the reform made headway slowly and with difficulty.

What then was this office that Charlemagne sought to impose? Although everything is not certain it can with some probability be reconstructed from the writings of Amalarius of Metz (died c. 850) who was familiar with both the Roman and the Gallican traditions.[70]

Sunday vigils retained the Roman pattern of eighteen psalms and twelve lessons, daily vigils consisted of twelve psalms and three lessons. The hour was preceded by the versicle and response and the *Venite*. To Lauds had been added a short reading and a collect now replaced the Lord's prayer. Prime had been imported from the monastic office and its *preces* had become extensive: the *Kyries*, the Lord's prayer, the creed, the *Miserere* (psalm 50) and a fixed collect. Vespers remained the same with the addition of *preces*, and Compline consisted of four psalms without antiphon but with a versicle and the *Nunc dimittis*. Clearly the Benedictine office had been exerting its influence. The daily *cursus* of hours was now complete, the monastic hours of Prime and Compline forming part of it. There was also some use of antiphons but as yet, it would seem, no hymns. Rome would not adopt these until the twelfth century. But it was also a clerical office for the distinction between the cathedral office and the monastic is no longer apparent. Its importance is that basically it was this office that became the office of the Roman rite until the reform of 1912.

The Organisation of the Liturgical Books

How far the Carolingian reform was successful is something on which we can only speculate. As far as the office was concerned, it has been reckoned that a small library of not less than ten books was necessary for the celebration of the office. Among them were the Bible, the homiliary, the book of 'sermons', the collectar, the antiphoner, the *ordo* and of course the psalter. If then the office was to become a regular practice of the clergy some organisation and simplification of the liturgical books was necessary. This, that might seem to be but a material factor, is important for it eventually affected the shape of the office.

The Bible and the psalter are the two fundamental books of the office and these had to be adapted for liturgical use. At first the reading of the bible at vigils was continuous with the exception of the greater feasts when 'proper' passages were read. But it was necessary to indicate the length of the readings and this was first done by the marking of the Bibles in such a way that the reader would know when to begin and end. St Benedict is the first witness to this procedure and it is interesting to learn that one of the first extant Bibles to be so marked is the famous *Codex Amiatinus* which was written in Northumbria about 700.[71] The next stage was (probably) the formation of *capitularia*, giving the beginnings and endings of the passages to be read. The third stage was of course the composition of lectionaries containing the passages to be read day by day and on the great feasts.[72]

Although monks and clerics were expected to know the psalter by heart, the office demanded a different arrangement of it from that of the Bible. So came into being the *psalterium liturgicum*. Another factor making its existence necessary was the addition of antiphons. Although at first these were grouped together in one place and not attached to individual psalms, it would obviously be convenient to do so.

As we have seen above,[73] in the time of Caesarius of Arles, there was a sermon at morning prayer and the notion that commentaries on the scriptures 'by well-known and orthodox Catholic writers' should be read at vigils was established by the sixth century.[74] Books of homilies from the Fathers thus became necessary and there were several collections current in the early Middle Ages. On saints' feasts it was customary to read the 'passion' or the 'legend'[75] of the martyr or saint being commemorated. For this yet another book was necessary.

The first book however that can be said to represent a convenient arrangement of certain texts was the book of collects or collectary. The origins of this kind of book can indeed be seen in the collects of the Gelasian and Gregorian Sacramentaries where they are gathered together obviously for the convenience of the user.[76] But the first examples of the book properly so called appeared in the eighth and ninth centuries. What are described as complete collectaries are two well-known English books, the Leofric Collectar, which goes back to an earlier, ninth century, exemplar, and the collectary of St Wulfstan of Worcester.[77] The latter was a good deal more than a collectary; it contains whole offices as well as the psalter, litanies and a hymnary though the collection of collects is considerable. There are collects for daily use, collects for morning and evening prayer, prayers for the little hours and *preces*. It looks like the combination of the celebrant's book with sundry private prayers. The collectary was in fact the book of the celebrant whose function it was to conclude each office with a collect. Their very number and variety made a book necessary.

All told this organisation of the books did not go very far and for a more convenient celebration of the office a further stage of development was necessary.

The Formation of the Breviary

Although there was a growing tendency to insist on the private recitation of an hour by an individual monk or cleric who for some reason had to be absent from choir, the office continued to be regarded as the celebration of a community. But if the office was to be recited conveniently, especially for small communities, some further simplification was necessary. Not only had the books to be gathered into some convenient format but a guide through the complexities of the office was also necessary. These two factors led to the formation of the 'breviary'. Until recently it was thought that the breviary was an abbreviation of the old choir office reduced to the compass of one or two handy volumes for a clergy that was becoming more mobile. Such a view is no longer tenable. First, by far the greater number of early 'breviaries' are monastic and were in fact choir books, regularly noted for singing. Secondly, they were books of from two to three hundred folios which could hardly be said to be portable.[78]

The impetus for the formation of 'breviaries' came from changed circumstances in the life of the church. After the decadence of the tenth century and with the coming of the Gregorian reform in the eleventh, there appeared smaller communities of clerics, later known as canons regular, who sought by the common life to improve the status of the clergy. If large monasteries with their precentors and other officers could find their way through the office, this was a task that was beyond the smaller community. They needed a guide which would enable them to assemble the necessary texts for different feasts and seasons and also to provide a clear 'order of service'. As we have seen above, the collectary contained certain texts for the celebrant and others that it is not easy to account for: e.g. whole offices that seem to have been models to indicate the succession of texts for other occasions. This was the book to which was eventually attached what was called an *ordo* 'indicating for each day and each liturgical hour the texts that were to be sung with their *incipits*'. It first appears in a number of *monastic* manuscripts which shows that even the monasteries needed help in this matter and the title of the document is significant *'Breviarium sive ordo* officiorum per totam anni decursionem' ('A short conspectus or order for the offices of the whole year'). This, says Salmon, is no doubt the origin of the word 'breviary' that eventually came to be used for the book containing the whole office.[79] It is to be noted that only the beginnings (*incipits*) of the texts to be used were given. For the formation of the breviary all that was necessary was to insert the full texts.

This procedure however had its disadvantages. There were the three lectionaries: the scriptural, the patristic and the hagiographical. A considerable quantity of material in themselves and the individual lessons were far longer than those of the breviaries that came into use in the thirteenth and subsequent centuries. It was here that abbreviation had to take place, to the great detriment of the office. Throughout the centuries the lectionaries have remained its weakest element. Likewise, in the older choir office there was a great variety of antiphons provided for optional use and a similar variety of collects to be used for different hours. The breviary eventually brought about the elimination of great numbers of them. It was in this way that the need for convenience brought about a change in the content of the office.

Towards Uniformity

The formation of the breviary was a gradual process and as yet there was nothing like uniformity. Religious families all had their own traditions and the great liturgical centres retained theirs. Apart from the monasteries —and they had different cutoms—no one thought that the same office should be used by everyone everywhere. Even in Rome there was a degree of liturgical pluralism. There was the office of St Peter's which retained the old Roman psalter, and there was the office of the Lateran which almost certainly did not differ greatly but which had a certain prestige as the office of the pope's residence. In the eleventh century with the reform and centralisation of church administration a third centre emerged. This was the *capella papalis* where the pope with his chaplains celebrated the office on all days when the former was not celebrating the liturgy in one of the stational churches. In the eleventh century the office of the papal chapel was the old Roman office [80] but as the chaplains became curial officials they will have had less and less time (and perhaps inclination) to celebrate the office with song and ceremony. There was a subtle change of emphasis. Although the papal chapel was very splendid, known as the *Sancta sanctorum* on account of the many relics collected there, the celebration of the office became quasi-private. The public office went on in the church of the Lateran while the 'papal' office was recited with reduced solemnity in the papal chapel. The final stage came when the office of the *capella papalis* superseded that of the Lateran Basilica. What the differences were at this time it is a little difficult to discern. It seems to have been austere and

Roman. Three-lesson-feasts were excluded in Lent and there was a sparing use of antiphons. Hymns were adopted in Rome only in the twelfth century. We may suppose too that responsories were reduced in number as these required a considerable degree of musical skill which the papal chaplains could not be expected to have.

With the coming of Innocent III (died 1216), who was himself interested in the liturgy, a further stage in the formation of the breviary was reached. First the *capella papalis* came to be known as *curia romana* and finally as *ecclesia romana* with the result that anything emanating from the papal chapel/curia came to be known as 'Roman' *tout court*. This is in fact why thirteenth century breviary was known as the office of the *ecclesia romana*.

But what was this office of the papal chapel that became the basis of the thirteenth century office that was propagated throughout Europe by the Franciscans? It has been described as an office which is 'the result of a mixture of Roman, Germano-Gallican and monastic customs' but it was substantially the old Roman monastic office. There is the same distribution of the psalter over the week, there were antiphons and responsories and a modest collection of hymns. The lessons were much longer than those of the thirteenth century book and the place given to the reading of scripture was generous: e.g. the whole of the Letter to the Romans was read in one week, the first after Christmas, its traditional place. The patristic lectionary was richer than that found in the earlier Roman office. The *Kyries* and the Lord's prayer were included in Lauds and Vespers though the concluding prayer had to be the collect of the day.[81]

The breviary known as the 'office of the *curia*' was the result of a codification that took place in the pontificate of Innocent III. For the convenience of the curial chaplains all the elements of the office, of which the *Ordo* of Innocent III seems to have been the nucleus, were gathered together though it is not clear whether the result was one book or two.[82] It was this office that in a complicated process became that of the Franciscans and which they propagated throughout Europe.[83] It was however not left untouched. It was adapted to the needs and new spirituality of the thirteenth century. To produce a book that could be said to be portable, abbreviation became necessary. The scriptural and patristic lectionaries were shortened. The importance of the Sunday liturgy was forgotten and offices of new feasts, which were shorter than the Sunday office, often superseded it. In fact, there was a steady invasion by saints' feasts of the Proper of Time and when they occurred on ferial days, they eliminated the obligation to say the supplementary offices.[84] This process would continue through the centuries, right up to the time of the reform of the rubrics in 1960. The office became the curious combination of obligation and devotional exercise. If you were not devout, you said it out of a sense of obligation; if you were, you 'enjoyed' the new offices that were so much more appealing than the old and austere texts of the classical liturgy.

The contents of the book, which hardly varied for the next seven centuries, are familiar to those who used the Roman Breviary until the appearance of the *Liturgy of the Hours* in 1971. The scattered elements that had existed in various books, the calendar, the psalter (with the canticles), the Proper of Time, with all the texts belonging to it, the sanctoral, both 'proper' and 'common', and the supplementary offices of the Blessed Virgin Mary and of the Dead, all were now combined in one book. Unlike the Pius V Breviary the rubrics came in the last place. The structure of the old Roman office did indeed remain but it was obscured by a profusion of new offices and overlaid in practice by the celebration of feasts that too often replaced the ancient offices of the Proper of Time.[85] Increasingly it was regarded as the personal obligation of the cleric and the celebration in common of the office tended to take second place to private recitation. In England, it is true, there was a certain insistence on the public recitation of the office at least on Sundays. Numerous episcopal visitations of the last part of the Middle Ages reveal that 'Mattins, Mass and Evensong' were regarded as a primary obligation of the parish priest and many were the parishioners who complained at one time or another that the clergy did not do their duty in this respect.

Nor did this 'new' office escape criticism. Salimbene of Parma, a Franciscan, complained of the length of Prime and found the eighteen psalms of Mattins too long 'especially in the summer when the fleas annoy you, the nights are short and the heat intense'.[86] On the other hand, Ralph of Tongres, a conservative and a secular priest, objected to the shortening of the office for which he blamed the papal court. For him it was a new-fangled affair, no more acceptable because it was being 'imposed' by the Franciscans.[87]

Salimbene's complaint about Prime was justified. The *officium capituli*, a purely monastic element used in monasteries as the occasion for the allocation of the day's work, had by now become part of the hour for all the clergy. The long Athanasian Creed had to be said on most of the Sundays of the year and *preces* had become a lengthy and miscellaneous collection of psalm-verses and petitions of one kind or another. It could take longer than Lauds. But there were other grounds for complaint. The calendar and its rules were imperfect, feasts acquired 'octaves' to give them greater 'solemnity', and that meant at times the commemoration of a feast for eight days. Local calendars of saints grew all the time, their offices frequently replacing that of the feria or even that of the Sunday. Non-organic elements like the gradual psalms which in Cluniac houses had been said before vigils since the tenth century as well as the penitential psalms (6, 31, 37, 50, 101, 142) on certain days, had come to be regarded as integral parts of the daily quota of prayer for the secular clergy too. Nor was that all. The supplementary offices of the Blessed Virgin Mary and of the Dead had to be recited *in addition* to the office of the day on certain days of the week.[88]

When we remember that this whole mass of verbiage had to be written by hand, that the calligraphy of the Middle Ages became less and less legible in the fourteenth and fifteenth centuries, when we recall that often only references were given to the texts to be used and the texts themselves were full of the conventional abbreviations, it is no wonder that clerics felt that the office was rather a burden than a prayer. Cranmer's was not a lone voice when he said in the preface to the Book of Common Prayer that often 'there was more business to find out what should be read, than to read it when found out'. With the coming of the Renaissance the Latinity of the breviary came under fire and the unhistorical absurdities of the 'legends' were the subject of criticism not only in the sixteenth century but in all the centuries that followed until the present day. As late as the *First* Vatican Council the lessons of the office came in for angry criticism.[89]

Not only was the Roman office in a state of confusion, there was a multiplicity of 'uses' or rites which may not have differed very greatly from one another but sufficiently to make any talk of uniformity a dream. There were in England the 'uses' of Sarum, Hereford, York and others. Everywhere there were the offices of the great religious families, the Benedictines, the Carthusians, the Dominicans and the rest and the great liturgical centres like Milan had their own offices. But a new, material, factor came into play, the invention of printing. This not only made possible an infinitely better presentation of the texts of the office but it also made possible that uniformity which was to be the mark of post-Tridentine liturgy.[90] Given the criticism of the office that was widespread at the time and the ability to produce books quickly, a reform of the office in the sixteenth century was inevitable.

Attempts at Reform—The Quiñones Breviary

We can ignore the futile attempts of some Roman humanists to 'classicise' the hymns of the breviary and their efforts to get rid as far as possible of the Christian Latin of the liturgical books. *'Salvator'* was not good enough for the Saviour; he had to be *'Servator'*.[91] The book that caught the attention of men at the time was the Breviary of Quiñones, a Franciscan and a cardinal. If his book represents a quite radical reform it is not without importance to know that it was commissioned by one pope, Clement VII, and authorised for use by another, Paul III.

Where Quiñones's breviary marked a radical change with the past was that it was intended for private recitation by the individual cleric and the fact that it was taken up by so many for so long—over thirty years—shows how weak the understanding of the prayer of the church had become. Because it was intended for private use, all the choral elements such as antiphons and responsories were suppressed.[92] The psalter was to be recited in a week but without regard for the appropriateness of certain psalms to particular hours. Each office consisted of three psalms, no more, no less. For the night office to these he added three readings, one from the Old

Testament, one from the New and a patristic or hagiographical one. A good deal of the Old Testament was read during the year and the whole of the New though his allocation of the books of the Bible to different seasons was largely traditional: thus Isaiah and the other prophets were read in Advent. The night office and Lauds were combined, as had indeed been permissible since the thirteenth century. Hymns were retained (a choral element surely!) though they were placed at the beginning of every hour. The calendar of saints was much reduced and their feasts were not allowed to break the rigid system of the psalter. The supplementary offices of the Blessed Virgin and the Dead were suppressed. Substantially Quiñones had reduced the office to the recitation of the psalter and the reading of holy scripture.[93]

The two charges that can be brought against the Quiñones's Breviary are that it was too austere and too rigid in its arrangements of the material. The possibility of different understandings of the psalms which made them adaptable for use on the greater feasts was denied by the rule that the psalter must be used every week exactly as Quiñones had arranged it. The 'colour' thus given to different feasts, seasons and hours was eliminated. The elimination of almost all the choral elements made of it a book of private prayer. The suppression of these elements gave scandal in certain quarters and although the book had a remarkable success and was even used for choral recitation, the reform that followed the Council of Trent was in conscious reaction to it. On the appearance of the Pius V breviary its use was forbidden and it looked as if this attempt at reform had proved abortive. Jungmann's article on the subject is entitled 'Why was Cardinal Quiñones reformed Breviary a failure?'. Perhaps it was not such a failure as he thought. It had an immediate though modest influence on the formation of the Book of Common Prayer[94] and a more far-reaching influence on *The Liturgy of the Hours*.

The Reformed Breviary of Pius V

The Fathers of the Council of Trent demanded a reform of the liturgical books, including the breviary but they were aware that a council cannot carry out so complicated a matter as liturgical reform must be. It was remitted to the pope. We know little enough about the commissions set up by Pius IV and Pius V[95] and all we can do is to judge their intentions on the results of their work. It is best described as a restoration. The office they produced was the old Roman office shorn of some, not all, of the medieval accretions. The night office, now officially called *matutinum*,[96] for Sundays still had eighteen psalms and twelve lessons and the daily (ferial) office twelve psalms and three lessons. Hymns, antiphons and responsories were of course retained. Sunday Lauds consisted of eight psalms, including the Old Testament canticle, or six if you count psalms 148–150 as one (they were in fact recited straight through). Vespers remained the same with five psalms. The lectionaries remained those of the later Middle Ages and the hagiographical readings went largely un-corrected.[97] The long and shapeless *preces* were retained for Lauds, Vespers and Prime and there were shorter sets for all the other hours. As before in the Roman tradition, Compline had four psalms. The supplementary offices were swept away and replaced by one or two 'suffrages' (i.e. commemoration of all the saints and in Eastertide of the cross), as in fact in the Quiñones Breviary. On the credit side was the drastic reduction of the sanctoral for it was evidently the intention of the revisers that the ferial office with its weekly course of psalmody should in fact be used.

All this was held in an apparently unbreakable system of rubrics which seemed to make variation impossible. In fact this system soon proved to be so imperfect that by the seventeenth century the situation was much as it was in the fifteenth. Saints' feasts could quite legitimately replace the ferial office and often enough the Sunday office, and since these offices were a good deal shorter, there was every temptation to have resort to this device. In addition, what Pius V had taken away, his successors spent several centuries putting back so that the calendar by the end of the nineteenth century was largely filled up for the whole year. The Sundays after Pentecost often disappeared altogether and even Lent was not sacrosanct. Here a series of 'votive' offices (e.g. that commemorating the 'Holy Winding Sheet') could supersede the liturgy of the day.

The office the revisers produced was not without its nobility. It had something of the Roman sobriety, it retained ancient texts like responsories which date from the seventh to the ninth centuries, one of the most creative periods of the Roman liturgy, and of course it was essentially a *choral* office. This kept before the mind of its users the fact that when they recited it they were engaged in the prayer of the church. When we recall what happened in the next three centuries, with its subjective devotions and sentimental pieties which all too frequently were allowed to overlay or even obliterate the liturgy of the church, we can be grateful that the revisers did what they did. Unhappily, their office proved to be pastorally impossible. If it had been intended for clerics or religious living in community, there was something to be said for it though eighteen psalms in one office is more than most can stand if we are thinking of the office in terms of *prayer*. The whole quantity was all-but crushing and when one remembers that the rubrics of the old Roman missal strongly urged that every priest should have said Mattins, Lauds *and* Prime *before* saying Mass, they were manifestly asking for something that could not be prayer even if it was physically possible to 'get through' the appalling amount of verbiage. In the centuries succeeding the Council of Trent when among other things the pastoral clergy, including the missionaries, were busier than ever before, the office came to be regarded more and more as simply a burden. The devout did their best to say it, others freely resorted to the use of the offices of saints' feasts and some got dispensations. For few was it a creative element in the spiritual life. A summary judgement on the work of the revisers must be, I think, that they 'did not take sufficient account of pastoral needs and human possibilities'.[98]

From Pius V to Pius X

In view of this situation it is not surprising that in subsequent centuries efforts at further revision were made. There was the revision of the hymns made at the behest of the Barbarini pope, Urban VIII, who himself had a weakness for writing hymns in classical metres. The rough rythms and unclassical language of the medieval hymns, some of them great poetry like the *Vexilla Regis*, offended his sensibilities and so he ordered four Jesuits to put them into a classical straight-jacket. Incongruous as some of the results were, the church was at any rate saved from the irreverent stupidities of the humanists of Leo X's time who would have had us pray to the Holy Trinity as *Triforme numen Olympi* or address the Mother of God as *Nympha candidissima*.[99]

The most notable attempt at reform was initiated by Benedict XIV (died 1758) but it came to nothing. There were the successive and varied reforms of the Neo-Gallicans of the seventeenth and eighteenth centuries which, however irregular from Rome's point of view, anticipated a number of changes that can be paralleled only in the *Liturgy of the Hours* of 1971.

The only revision of any importance in this period is that of Pius X. He (or his advisers) decided to take the old festal pattern of the Roman office for Mattins: that is, nine psalms, nine lessons (three from scripture, three patristic and the last three called 'the homily' on the gospel of the day, also from the Fathers and other ecclesiastical writers). Ferial Mattins had nine psalms and three lessons (all from scripture except in Lent). Lauds was reduced to five psalms, including the Old Testament canticle. The ancient custom of always reciting psalms 148–150 at this hour was changed. They were replaced with a single *Laudate* psalm. Vespers remained the same and the Compline psalms were reduced to three. The whole of the psalter was considerably altered in its arrangement though the psalms that were traditional for certain hours remained in place. The intention was that the whole of the psalter should normally be used in the week. This was effected by an improvement in the rubrics. Here the greatest gain was that, with rare exceptions, the Sunday office could always be said. In fact the pope brought about a reform of the whole temporal cycle. But, alas, much of his work was negated by his successors who increased the number of feasts and even imposed some of them for use on Sundays: e.g. the Feast of Christ the King. The rank of the 'octaves' of other feasts was raised so that at times the priest was condemned to saying the same texts (with a few variations) for a whole week. This in turn led to an accumulation of 'commemorations' so that at times, e.g. towards the end of June in certain years, there might be three or four of them. Even for the offices of modern saints (and there were many of them between 1925 and 1950) the 'legends' continued to be written in the old style and were often at once long and singularly uninformative. These matters and a number of others, like the length of Prime on ferial days, became increasingly the targets for criticism. Likewise, the language of the office, Latin, came to be regarded by a great number of the clergy as a barrier to prayer. Some of these criticisms were met by the decree on 'The Simplification of the Rubrics' of 1955 and further relief was afforded by the Code of Rubrics of 1960. But the whole system was manifestly breaking down and a radical reform had become necessary. This was decreed by the Second Vatican Council.

NOTES

1. If the composition of Acts is about the year 80 A.D. and if it is not granted that this prayer of this passage is 'primitive', though its very Jewishness would seem to show that it is, it is clear that a use of psalms for Christian prayer was *already* in existence when Luke wrote.

2. Cf Mark 14:26 for the psalms and for intercessions cf I Tim, 2:1, 2.

3. See J. Jeremias in *The Eucharistic Words of Jesus* (London, Eng. trans. 1966), pp. 118–122. The writer in JBC *in loc.*, rejects Jeremias's interpretation and sees the passage as no more than a general picture of the primitive community. Presumably he feels unable to pronounce on the meaning of 'the prayers' and elsewhere shows a regrettable indifference to the prayer-practices of the early church.

4. See Alexander Schmemann *Introduction to Liturgical Theology* (Faith Press, London/The American Orthodox Press, Portland, Maine, 1966), p. 43. On the next page he lists the scholars who hold this view: Oesterley, Jeremias, Dix, Gavin, Baumstark and Dugmore, though it must be remarked that as far as the prayer of the church is concerned there are considerable differences between them.

5. See Geoffrey Cuming 'La base néo-testamentaire de la prière commune' in *LMD*, 116 (1973), p. 28. Further on (p. 38) he gives another scheme which he has derived from the Pauline writings: greeting, thanksgiving, bible reading(s), instruction and exhortation, psalms (ancient and modern), doxology, kiss of peace and dismissal.

6. Canon G. Cuming in *art. cit.*, p. 26, seeks to support his view that the decalogue formed part of the early services on the basis of the 'oath' not to commit various sins. But *sacramento* is more likely to refer to baptism when, as we know later, the candidates did undertake to avoid sin and lead the Christian life. The service may have included baptism as it did in the time of Justin the Martyr forty years or less later.

7. In the following paragraph I am largely dependent on J. Jeremias, *The Prayers of Jesus* (London, 1967) and especially on his chapter 'Daily Prayer in the Primitive Church', pp. 66ff.

8. There is indeed a strong element of petition in the Blessings from 4 onwards, evidently the official 'asking-prayers' of Judaism. Cf. C. W. Dugmore, *The Influence of the Synagogue upon the Divine Office*, (2nd ed. Faith Press, 1964) pp. 115–124.

9. See L. Bouyer *Eucharistie* (Desclée, Tournai, Belgium, 1966), pp. 63–4 and A. Baumstark, *Comparative Liturgy*, Eng. trans. and ed. F. L. Cross (Mowbray, 1958), p. 38. Bouyer points out that the Hallel psalms 113–118 (Hebrew numbering) were used after the evening meal and that here 'we have the origins of Christian "Vespers".' This is more doubtful and does not take

account of the fact that it was the 110–113 group of psalms that from the sixth century at least formed the nucleus of (Sunday) Vespers. Also, in the East the evening office seems to have been built up round psalm 140. See A. Baumstark, *op. cit.* p. 112.

10. See*The Prayers of Jesus*, p. 79; but see also *The Eucharistic Words of Jesus*, p. 118 where the word is translated rather differently as meaning 'to attend worship regularly'.

11. *The Prayers of Jesus*, p. 81.

12. *Didache*, 4. Maxwell Staniforth translates 'to your prayers'. Neither the pronoun nor the plural is justified (See *Early Christian Writings*, Penguin Books, 1968, p. 229). J. B. Lightfoot (*The Apostolic Fathers*, ed. minor, 1893, p. 231) has of course quite correctly 'to prayer'.

13. In the same passage however there is an injunction to 'frequent the saints daily' (*ibid*, p. 229).

14. Dial. c. 86. Cf J. A. Jungmann *Christliches Beten in Wandel und Bestand* (München, 1969), p. 12.

15. Cf F. L. Cross *The Early Christian Fathers*, (London, 1960), pp. 23–4; and A. Hamman, *La Prière II* (Desclée, 1963), pp. 66–73.

16. Cf P. Salmon, *L'Eglise en prière*, p. 794.

17. Cf Jungmann, op. cit., p. 12. He refers to *Stromata*, vii, 49. Cf also Hamman, *La Prière*, II, p. 291.

18. For the text see *Protrepticos* IX, 84, cited by Hamman, *La Prière*, II, p. 285.

19. *Protrept.* IX, 84 in Hamman, *op. cit.,* p. 285.

20. Cf J. A. Jungmann, *The Place of Christ in Liturgical Prayer* (Geoffrey Chapman, 1965), p. 181, n. 3, who records a fragmentary text in an Oxyrhyncus papyrus which is 'allied' to the *Phōs hilaron*.

21. Hamman, *op. cit.,* p. 290 and Jungmann *Christliches Gebet*, referring to *Stromata*, VII, 40.

22. Hamman, *op. cit.,* p. 290.

23. See *De Oratione*, 25, ed. and trans. Ernest Evans (S.P.C.K. 1953), pp. 34–5. Mr Evans translates 'statutory prayers' which seems to say too much.

24. *Ad Uxorem*, II, 4.

25. *Ed. cit.*, pp. 37–41.

26. *La Tradition Apostolique*, ed. B. Botte (LQF, Münster, 1963), section 25 (for the *agape*) and section 41 for the hours. Eng. trans and ed. by Gregory Dix (S.P.C.K. 1937), XXVI, 18 and XXXV, XXXVI.

27. *Ap. Trad.* Botte, 41, p. 89; Dix, xxxv, p. 61. If the Greek was 'en ekklesia' it could mean 'in [the] assembly,' as Botte translates it though *a place* is obviously meant.

28. Whether there was a daily service for the people is not certain. Hippolytus urges deacons and presbyters to gather *daily* with their bishop when they are to teach and pray though who is to teach whom is not clear.

29. Botte 25, p. 65; Dix xxv, p. 50.

30. It is noteworthy that in 41 when Hippolytus speaks of morning prayer at home, he expects his readers to have a Bible or perhaps parts of a Bible. Perhaps this is all part of his perfectionism. How many in the back streets of Rome would have had a biblical text and if they had, would have had time to read it first thing in the morning?

31. See Balthasar Fischer '*La prière ecclésiale et familiale dans le Christianisme ancien*' in *LMD*, 116 (1973), p. 43 who describes Hippolytus's interpretation as 'a commemoration of the paschal mystery' and refers to an article by J. H. Walker in *Studia Patristica*, V (Berlin, 1962), pp. 206–212 for the observation about Mark.

32. For reasons that are obscure the language is tortuous, but the meaning is clear.

33. Cf Mk. 13:33; Lk. 21:36; I Thess. 5:17, etc.
34. Hippolytus has another notion: the whole of nature, the stars, the trees, the waters and even the angelic hosts stop their activity at midnight to pay homage to God. Christians should do likewise. He calls this a tradition though whence it comes it is difficult to say but it seems to be related in spirit to the long passage (29) that comes at the end of Tertullian's treatise on prayer.
35. *The Early Liturgy* (Notre Dame Press, U.S.A., 1959) p. 100.
36. Even Augustine was surprised to find Ambrose reading silently when he called on him. Cf F. Homes Dudden, *The Life and Times of St Ambrose* (Oxford, 1935), vol. i., p. 112.
37. As Pierre Salmon contends in several places in his treatment of the subject in *EP*.
38. *De Oratione*, xxx, 5 and cf *Origen on Prayer*, ed. and trans. by Eric George Jay (London, 1954), p. 213.
39. *Op. cit.* xxxiii, 1; E. G. Jay, p. 216–7.
40. Jungmann has pointed out that he was writing to Ambrosius, a recent convert from Gnosticism, which rejected the Old Testament Jahweh and put Christ in his place. See *Christliches Beten*. . . . pp. 18–19 and his *The Place of Christ in Liturgical Prayer*, pp. 158–9. Hymns and (private) prayers were addressed to Christ.
41. For Cassian see *La Prière des Heures*, ed. Mgr Cassien and Bernard Botte (Paris, 1963), pp. 117 ff; for the *Regula Magistri* see M. D. Knowles, '*The Regula Magistri* and the *Rule* of St Benedict' in *Great Historical Enterprises* (London, Edinburgh, etc., 1963), pp. 135 ff.
42. Dom J. Froger's view that Cassian's *novella solemnitas* was Lauds has not generally been followed. For a sufficient refutation see J. M. Hanssens, *Nature et genèse de l'office des matines* (Rome, 1952).
43. See Salmon *EP*, pp. 804–810 and B. Luykx *LMD*, 51 (1957) pp. 55–81.
44. *Ep.* 207, PG, 32, c. 764.
45. A. Baumstark holds that this is the first attestation of Ps. 50 for morning prayer. *Comparative Liturgy.* (London, 1958) p. 40, n. 1.
46. See John Wilkinson, *Egeria's Travels* (London, 1971), p. 236; for the offices, pp. 123 ff.
47. For the *Orthros* see *Apostolic Constitutions* (ed. F. X. Funk) I, vii, 47, as also for the hymn *Te decet*; for psalm 140 I, viii, 35. The compiler, usually regarded as a Syrian, also witnesses to the long dismissal at morning and evening prayer. For the *Phōs hilaron* see Basil, *De Spiritu Sancto*, xxix, 73. For Psalm 62, see *Ap. Const.* I, ii, 59.
48. See *Egeria's Travels*, trans. J. Wilkinson, (London, 1971), p. 125.
49. See B. Fischer in *LMD*, 116 (1973), pp. 42–51 and especially the thesis of R. Zerfass, *Die Schriftlesung im Kathedraloffizium Jerusalem* (LFQ, Münster, 1968). See also the reservations of the editors on the subject in the same number of *LMD*, pp. 12–3.
50. Confessions, Lib. V, ix, 17; PL 32, c. 714 and *Enarr. in psalm 66, 3* as given in Jungmann, *Pastoral Liturgy*, pp. 151–2.
51. For a convenient summary with references see F. Homes Dudden, *St Ambrose*, Vol. II, pp. 442–446.
52. *Exposit. in ps. 118*, 18, 32. Cf Homes Dudden, *op. cit.* p. 443.
53. Cf *De Virginibus*, iii, 18. Homes Dudden (p. 444) refers to Jerome: Ep. 107, 9: '*accensa lucernula reddere sacrificium vespertinum*'.
54. *Ep.* 20, 11, 13; Pl 16, c. 1039.
55. *Ep.* cvii, *Ad Laetam* (Loeb Classics, London, New York, 1933, p. 359).
56. See A. E. Burn, *Niceta of Remesiana. His Life and Works* (Cambridge, 1905). A critical edition, full of information.

57. See J. A. Jungmann, *Pastoral Liturgy* (Eng. trans. London, 1962), p. 131 and cf pp. 122–157.

58. See Jungmann, *op. cit.* pp. 147, 152, 153. Little is known of the office of the non-basilican churches, i.e. the presbyteral churches. We are safe in assuming that it consisted of morning and evening prayer for the clergy of Rome resisted attempts in the sixth century to make them attend vigils. No doubt the people attended morning or evening prayer in the presbyteral churches. Cf. P. Salmon *LMD*, 27 (1951), p. 118.

59. See G. Dix *The Shape of the Liturgy* (London, 1945), pp. 319 ff. For the modern scholars see J. A. Jungmann, *op. cit.*; Pierre Salmon 'Aux origines du bréviaire romain', *LMD*, 27 (1951), pp. 114–136 and *L'Office divin* (Paris, 1959); B. Luykz 'L'influence des moines sur l'office paroissial', *LMD*, 51 (1957), pp. 31–51, an article of crucial importance though the author tends to press the evidence too far and the word '*paroissial*' is anachronistic.

60. Salmon, *EP*, p. 818.

61. See P. Salmon, *EP*, pp. 819–820; C. Callewaert, *De Breviarii Romani Liturgia* (Bruges, 1939), pp. 51–63.

62. Cf Salmon, *EP*, pp. 819–820; C. Callewaert, *op. cit.* pp. 52–55; M. Righetti, *Storia Liturgica* (2nd ed. 1955), pp. 492, 499–502, 504–5.

63. Does this derive from the Jerusalem custom of singing a gospel *de resurrectione* on Sunday mornings?

64. See *The Rule of St Benedict*, ed. and trans. J. McCann, (London, 1972) chapter 13, p. 57.

65. Cf S. Bäumer–R. Biron, *Histoire du Bréviare* (Paris, 1905), t.I, p. 248.

66. See L. Bréhier and R. Aigrain, *Grégoire le Grand, les états barbares et la conquête arabe* (*Hist. de l'église*, Fliche et Martin, t.5, Paris, 1947), pp. 506–520.

67. If there is some doubt whether he brought the Gregorian Sacramentary with him (which may not have been compiled by this time), in the next century St Benet Biscop brought back quantities of Roman books and what is more important secured the services of John, the Chief Precentor of St Peter's, a basilican church. Whether the office was 'pure' Benedictine is, I imagine, impossible to establish. See H. Ashworth 'Did St Augustine bring the "Gregorianum" to England, *Ephemerides Liturgicae*,' 72, 1958, and other papers by the same author.

68. From the text of the decree it is clear that the whole of the liturgy was meant by *cantilena romana* and indeed if you used the Roman chant you had to use the books in which it was found.

69. Cf MGH *Scriptores*, vol. I, pp. 106, 131, as given in *DACL*, s.v. 'Charlemagne', c. 722.

70. Cf *Opera liturgica omnia*, ed. I. M. Hanssens, Rome, 1948, II, 403–465; III pp. 13–17 as given in Salmon *ODMA*, pp. 33 ff. His reservations should be noted.

71. At least it is marked for the Lamentations of Jeremiah used from an early time for vigils of the last three days of Holy Week.

72. Cf Salmon *ODMA*, pp. 26–7. The last are Gallican books. Salmon however thinks that Roman ones existed also though, as he remarks, Rome was more interested in the *order* in which the books were read.

73. p 40.

74. *Rule of St Benedict*, chapter 9.

75. From *legenda* 'something to be read'.

76. Gelasian: nos. v, lxi, lxxxi; Lib. II lxxxiii, lxxxv (ed. Mohlberg); Gregarion: nos. 202, 204 (ed. Lietzmann).

77. *The Leofric Collectar*, ed. E. S. Dewick and W. H. Frere, HBS, 45 and *The*

Portiforium of St Wulstan, HBS, 56. And see M. D. Knowles, *The Monastic Order in England* (Cambridge, 1950), p. 553 n. 5. Cf also Dame Laurentia McLachan JTS, XXX, (January 1929), pp. 174-7: '*St Wulstan's Prayer Book*'.

78. See S. J. P. van Dijk and J. Hazeldene Walker, *The Origins of the Modern Roman Liturgy* (London, 1960) pp. 32-34; P. Salmon, *ODMA*, p. 68.
79. See *ODMA*, pp. 53-60.
80. Cf M. Andrieu, *Les Ordines Romani du Haut Moyen Age* (Louvain, 1931), I, p. 519n. 1.
81. See *ODMA*, p. 151; pp. 152-170. This office can be reconstructed from an early Franciscan breviary belonging to the cathedral church of Assisi. For it and the development of the Franciscan breviary see Van Dijk-Walker, *Origins*, part III.
82. See Salmon, *ODMA*, p. 154.
83. See Salmon, *ODMA*, pp. 152-157 and Van Dijk-Walker, *Origins*, Part III.
84. For these see below, p. 50.
85. See Salmon, *EP*, pp. 839-841.
86. See Van Dijk-Walker, *Origins*, p. 1.
87. *Op. cit.* p. 3.
88. All these texts remained in breviaries until recently. They were offered for 'optional' use!
89. Cuthbert Butler, *The Vatican Council 1869-1870* (2nd ed. London, 1962), pp. 196-7. It is interesting to learn that an English bishop, Clifford of Clifton, urged that the psalter should in fact be recited in the week.
90. The same was true of the Church of England. The Book of Common Prayer could be imposed quickly because it could be printed. Even local printers had the facility to do so, like Oswen of Worcester who had the Prayer Book very quickly in circulation. See S. Morison, *English Prayer Books* (3rd ed. 1949), p. 61.
91. One has noticed this ridiculous use in even some recent Roman documents.
92. Some were put back in the second edition.
93. For a description of the Quiñones Breviary, see J. A. Jungmann, *Pastoral Liturgy*, pp. 200-214.
94. C. J. Cuming, *A History of the Anglican Liturgy* (1969), pp. 52, 69, 72-3.
95. For what is known see T. Klauser, *A Short History of the Western Liturgy* (Eng. trans. O.U.P., 1969), pp. 124-129.
96. The adjective has apparently become a noun; see the first rubric in the psalter: '*Ante Matutinum ...*'
97. A little later Baronius was allowed to make a few timid corrections but substantially lessons remained the same until their suppression in the reform of 1971. They were a scandal to the critical and edifying to the pious.
98. See the present writer's 'An Historical Sketch of the Roman Liturgy' in *True Worship* (ed. L. Sheppard, 1963), p. 76.
99. See S. Bäumer-R. Biron, *Histoire du Bréviare*, II, pp. 117-123; P. Salmon, *EP*, pp. 849-850.

ADDITIONAL NOTE TO CHAPTER III

Although as we have seen the New Testament seems to witness to the use of psalms in Christian worship, the matter is not as clear as one had supposed. Professor Fischer, writing in 1951 (*LMD*, no. 27, p. 88, footnotes 5, 6, 7), sums up scholarly opinion as it was at that time:

1. The theory that the apostolic church took over the psalter *en bloc* from the synagogue is no longer tenable.

2. Up to about the year 200 the hymns sung in the liturgy were composed by Christians (the *psalmi idiotici*, i.e. private compositions e.g. the *Phōs hilaron*).

3. The psalms were used as lessons and read.

We can readily admit that the early church did not take over the whole psalter *en bloc* for *prayer*, though they took it over with the rest of the Old Testament as 'holy scripture'. It must be a long time since anyone contended that the primitive church *sang* the whole of the psalter. It assumes an order of prayer which, as we have seen, did not exist.

Nor is there any difficulty in admitting the existence and use of 'hymns' in the second or even the first century. Clement himself is witness to their use. But both he and Tertullian (*Apol.* 39, 18, as given in *art. cit.* p. 89, n. 11) were hardly innovators and they witness to the use of psalms as prayer and, in the case of Tertullian, as sung prayer. Hippolytus too, an arch-conservative, witnesses, as we have seen, to the same use of psalms. It seems likely then that psalms were used in this way as early as the second half of the second century.

The chief text that Fischer alleges to show that the psalms were used as readings, a text that he calls 'le témoignage très probant', is the *Didascalia* V, 19, 1 in the edition of F. X. Funk pp. 288 ff (the actual phrase is on p. 291). Here we read '*legentes* Prophetas et Evangelium et *Psalmos*'. That looks 'probant' indeed. But it is a Latin translation of the Greek as it is to be found in the *Apostolic Constitutions*. Unhappily, the original Greek no longer exists and that in the A.C. is unreliable. Dom Hugh Connolly (*Didascalia Apostolorum*, Oxford, 1929, p.v) says that the 'compiler . . . dealt so freely with his source, making perpetual additions, omissions and alterations, that we can seldom feel sure that he has left a sentence exactly as he found it'. In his own translation (p. 189), which is from the fourth century Syriac (which Connolly holds is accurate), the phrase reads, 'You shall come together and watch and keep vigil (it was the Easter Vigil) all night with prayers and intercessions, and with the *reading* of the Prophets, and with the Gospel and with Psalms'. Obviously this does not say the same as the Latin–Greek versions of Funk. It does not say 'with the *reading* of psalms'. You can read it this way: 'You shall . . . keep vigil with prayers . . . and with the Gospel and with psalms', which is not at all the same thing. Perhaps some Syriac expert will have another look at the matter (though Dom Hugh Connolly was an extremely exact scholar) but as things stand the text cannot be regarded as 'probant'.

Supporting evidence, Professor Fischer alleges, is to be found in the *Peregrinatio Aetheriae* (37, 6, ed. Pétré p. 236), of the late fourth century, in which we find that on Good Friday psalms (*de passione*) were *read*. But this evidence is rather late and we know from the same source that psalms were also sung. Reading evidently did not necessarily exclude singing. The article of J. A. Jungmann (*Zeitschrift für Kath. Theol*, 72 (1950), pp. 223–226), to which he refers, adds no new evidence.

What perhaps can be deduced from all this is that we should not be surprised at Clement's mention of hymns and that he, with Tertullian and Hippolytus, does indeed, as Fischer holds, mark a turning point. The hymns had become 'radicalement compromises par les abus gnostiques' and they fell into disuse, under official church pressure.

Finally, there is the firm opinion of modern scholars (Baumstark, Bouyer, etc.) that psalms 148–150 were a contribution of the synagogue and have formed part of morning prayer from a very early date.

CHAPTER FOUR

'The Liturgy of the Hours'

In the light of the foregoing we can now consider the revised office and see where it is traditional and where it has innovated. But first we may ask why it is called 'The Liturgy of the Hours'?[1] First, it is pretty clear that the revisers had no desire to perpetuate the use of the word 'breviary' with all its misleading and unhappy associations. Perhaps too they thought that, although the whole of the liturgy in the Middle Ages was called *divinum officium*, 'divine office' was too legalistic a term. *Officia* for Cicero, as for St Ambrose after him, meant 'duties' and the office is much more than that. The revisers make clear first, that the divine office is above all prayer and is the means by which the church may fulfil the gospel injunction to 'pray always'; and secondly, that it is a prayer that is intended to consecrate the hours and the work of the day: 'Compared with other liturgical actions, the particular characteristic which ancient tradition has attached to the liturgy of the hours is that it should consecrate the course of day and night' (GI 10). This is clear from what has been said in a previous chapter and the revisers in their commentary on Lauds and Vespers repeat that the office is a celebration of the mystery of Christ in his passion, death and resurrection (GI 38, 39) and declare that the office engages the priestly intercession of Christ: 'This voice is not only that of the church, it is also Christ's. It is in the name of Christ that she prays, that is, "through Jesus Christ our Lord", and so the church continues to offer that prayer and entreaty which Christ offered during his life and which therefore has a unique effectiveness' (GI 17). What the Introduction wishes to stress is that the office is not just a pious filling up of time or even a means of personal edification. It is a celebration of the paschal mystery and we may draw the conclusion that the relationship between the eucharist and the office is a real and not simply a mental one. The office is the means by which throughout the day Christians may appropriate to themselves, through a prayer that engages the intercession of Christ, the redeeming power and love that are made available in the daily celebration of the eucharist.[2] As the Introduction has suggested, this gives to the prayer of the divine office a unique effectiveness and psychologically should give its users a great confidence.

It is however in its commentary on Lauds and Vespers that the Introduction gives the traditional teaching that the office is the celebration of the paschal mystery. Lauds 'recalls the resurrection of the Lord Jesus, the true light, enlightening every man (John 1 : 9)' and the Introduction quotes the words of St Cyprian: 'We should pray in the morning to celebrate the resurrection of the Lord ....'[3] Vespers, 'the evening sacrifice', continue the thanksgiving of the Mass and 'through the prayer (which) we offer like incense in the sight of the Lord', we recall the sacrifice 'which was given in the evening by our Lord and Saviour when he instituted the most holy mysteries of the church with his apostles' (GI 38). These are the considerations that in the beginning led to the choice of the psalms for these hours, psalms which though now distributed over a longer period are still used at these times. But perhaps the paschal character of Vespers is seen most clearly in the Sunday office which runs from Saturday evening to Sunday evening, thus keeping the ancient Jewish pattern, transposed by one day. Here the canticle from Philippians 2, the 'resurrection' psalms of Lauds (92, 117, etc.) and the psalms of Vespers (109, the great priestly psalm, and the Hallel psalms that follow), all emphasise that the church is praying through Christ who by his passion, death and resurrection brought salvation to the world.[4] This office of the Christian Sunday (for evidently Saturday is regarded as part of it) makes explicit what was contained in the old office but it does so in no uncertain manner. It must be said to be one of the most successful parts of the new office.

The Introduction also wishes to emphasise that if the office is the prayer of Christ in his church, it is also and must be prayer on the part of those who use it. This indeed is the condition of its being spiritually profitable. The office is not and never was the recitation of a certain quota of holy words. But the Introduction goes on to point out that it is a particular kind of prayer and this is an aspect of it that is often overlooked: 'The sanctification of man and the worship of God is achieved in the Liturgy of the Hours by the setting up of a *dialogue* between God and man, so that "God speaks to his people . . . and the people reply to God by song and by prayer".'[5] Worship, and particularly prayer, is a two-way traffic and the approach of God to us is far more important than our approach to him, an approach that is indeed impossible without the divine initiative. Yet our movement towards God is the very condition of our being able to take into ourselves the divine word. In practice, a realisation of this truth transforms the celebration of the office and the recommendations for times of silence throughout the new liturgy point in this direction.[6] We need to *listen*. Even the psalms convey a message for all that they are prayers addressed to God, and for that message to be heard and for the prayer to come from the heart we need calm and quiet. In the tradition that Cassian records, every psalm ended with a silence and a deep prostration. Likewise we know from experience that a silence after readings whether at the eucharist or the office allows us to assimilate the word we have listened to. In the intercessions of Lauds and Vespers silent prayer is allowed for after the official petitions of the day. It is in this general atmosphere of recollection and silence that we may expect to hear the voice of God—or to put it in another way, we may expect to receive insights for our life and situation.

The Structure of the Office

When we come to consider the structure of the office as a whole we find a surprising mixture of the old and the new. There is the insistence on the pivotal importance of Lauds and Vespers, which takes us back to the old pre-monastic 'cathedral' office. Then, none of the hours has more than three psalms (including the canticles) and the Office of Readings, replacing the former (and misnamed) 'mattins', is exactly the pattern of the Quiñones breviary with its three psalms and three readings and never any more. If Quiñones is aware of these sublunary matters he must be smiling wryly. Lauds and Vespers have become identical in structure, a process that was started by Pius X. Thirdly, as in the Quiñones book, hymns are placed at the beginning of every hour, including Compline. The sanctoral, already reduced by the Calendar of 1969, again brings the new office into line with that of Quiñones, though the rigidity of his system is avoided. All these changes represent innovations that cannot be traced back further than the sixteenth century. This is not to say, however, that they are either good or bad. Traditional elements are represented by the retention of antiphons and responsories, hymns at every hour (a non-Roman tradition) and the addition of the Lord's prayer at Lauds and Vespers is the restoration of a very ancient custom that was never wanting in the ancient office. The recitation of the psalter (except for three psalms and parts of others) 'in course' and the continuous course of scriptural and patristic readings show that this office is basically monastic, i.e. of the old Roman basilican style. The daily course of prayer, that is the number of hours to be said, represents a compromise between the monastic and the cathedral traditions. The Office of Readings evidently derives from the old monastic vigils and is presumably intended for the clergy and those religious congregations who undertake the celebration of the divine office, but are without an office of their own. On the other hand, Prime, a monastic office, has understandably been suppressed and Compline, also a monastic office, has, with some reason, been retained. Of the day hours, Terce, Sext and None, only one need be said (at the appropriate time) and thus one element of a form of prayer that was institutionalised by the monasteries though, as we have seen, goes far beyond them in time, is partially kept.

Although this office is a mixture of the old and the new, it has a character of its own. No previous office has been quite like it. As to length, it could be said to be adapted to the needs of the pastoral clergy for, at a guess, the whole of it could be recited in something less than half an hour— if anyone was so stupid as to want to do so. Whether it is adapted to the needs of the laity is another matter. One cannot but notice the multiplicity of elements of very different literary forms that are to be found in the office: antiphons in great numbers, responsories, versicles and responses, hymns as well as of course the whole of the psalter, and the three lectionaries. All this is rather a lot to take in. True, all these elements can be found in the tradition and if any apologia for the revisers is needed it is to be found in their terms of reference. The Constitution on the Liturgy (89, 90) decreed that the office should be 'revised' and not created anew. As usual, the revisers have been faithful to their commission though this should not prevent a commentator from viewing their work objectively or from making criticisms of it if they seem called for. It is now more than ten years since the Constitution on the Liturgy was promulgated and the situation of the church in general and of the clergy in particular is very different from what it was then and it would be surprising if in that period, which has been one of the most turbulent for the church in modern times, we had learnt nothing new.

Since the pattern of the office will be well known by now, there is no need to give descriptions of each of the hours. It will be more profitable to consider the rationale of the hours along the lines of the Introduction (41–80).

The Psalter

Although more will have to be said about the psalms later on, since they are so important an element of the office it is necessary to say a little about their arrangements here. The distribution of the psalter over four weeks undoubtedly makes the office more manageable as prayer for it is all but impossible to recite many psalms on end. It is difficult to keep one's attention and their literary genres are so various that one cannot respond to them individually as presumably one should. This re-arrangement, which has lightened the burden of the office, also meets the desires of the pastoral clergy who found the long series of psalms in 'mattins' difficult to handle. Moreover any over-rigid pattern has been avoided. The psalms for the Office of Readings are 'in course' over the four weeks but those for Lauds and Vespers have been chosen as more appropriate to the meaning of those hours. Certain psalms have also been reserved for Compline. The danger of monotony is largely avoided though the regular occurrence of certain psalms is not always helpful. Thus when in psalm 36 the psalmist is wrestling with the problem of evil within the terms of Old Testament revelation and comes to no very satisfactory conclusion, one does not approach it with any enthusiasm every second week. The sentiment that the wicked 'wither like grass and fade like the green of the fields' hardly seems a Christian one. Their disappearance from the face of the earth does not solve anything and as Christians we are required to convert them or to try to do so. But this is all part of a bigger problem to which we shall return.

From a practical point of view, three psalms for every hour and never any more is probably right and if you distribute the psalter over the month, you are going to run short, even with the addition of canticles. But as far as the Office of Readings is concerned this pattern sometimes gives the impression of straight-jacketing. This is particularly so in the office of the last three days of Holy Week. The 'mattins' and Lauds of these days consisted of some of the richest texts and chants of the whole year and the pattern of the former was the old 'festal' office of the Roman church. These texts, and with them their chants, have almost wholly disappeared and the lack is not made good by the 'vigils' that are suggested for these days. These vigil offices are supplementary to the Office of Readings and here if anywhere the old pattern with its texts could have been retained for the convenience of those who are in a position to use them.[7] Another oddity of this three-psalm arrangement for every hour is that sometimes the office said during the day is almost as long as Lauds or Vespers.

As for the allocation of psalms, on the assumption that you wish to use the whole psalter,[8] it must be said to be reasonably satisfactory. The traditional morning and evening psalms all find their place in Lauds and Vespers and evidently some thought has been given to the allocation of the psalms for the day hours. Psalm 118 [9] has been distributed over a number of days so that it is not necessary to recite a great deal of it on a single occasion. But two of the greatest psalms 21 and 44 (though the latter does occur in the Office of Readings) are allocated to a day hour on a Friday and Saturday respectively. They merit the best recollection one can bring to them and they would be better coming either in the Office of Reading or even in Vespers. But this may be a subjective judgement.

In the liturgical use of the psalms the Christian or fulfilled sense of holy scripture is of crucial importance and from the beginning the psalms have been used as Christian prayers.[10] But as anyone knows who used the old office it was, apart from certain great psalms like 21 or 109, impossible to carry round in your head the messianic sense or the Christian interpretation of a hundred and fifty psalms. To facilitate understanding of the psalter the revisers have done two things. They have indicated the original subject of the psalm, e.g. for psalm 103 'Praise of the God of merciful love' (which seems obvious enough in that case) and, secondly, they have added what centuries ago were called 'tituli' [11] which were a device to enable worshippers to pray 'in Christ'. Some of these are from the New Testament and some from the Fathers or early Christian writers. The former are nearly always well chosen, some of the latter say little enough. However, they are worth attending to and almost certainly in the mind of the revisers they help towards a prayerful use of the psalms. They provide a moment of recollection before reciting the psalm.[12] To sum up, if the revisers have kept the monastic pattern of psalmody, they have done what they can to secure that the psalms will be prayed rather than merely recited.

Antiphons

There is yet a third element of the psalmody that requires consideration. Every psalm throughout the psalter has its antiphon which is to be said before it but need not be repeated after it. The church of the East and the West has since the fourth century felt the need to 'personalise' the psalms so as to adapt them to different seasons, feasts and occasions. Antiphons have been used in various ways and the history of their use is not yet fully elucidated[13] though the short antiphons coming before and after the psalms derive from the Roman tradition.[14] The longer ones that still occur in Lauds and Vespers at the *Benedictus* and *Magnificat* are of Gallican and Spanish provenance, some few of them are from the Greek. For the great seasons and feasts the antiphon gives both a Christian sense to the psalm and reflects the chief significance of the celebration. In this they perform a valuable function.[15] Others, for the ferial office, usually underline a particular thought of the psalm and may have a purpose though their constant recurrence enfeebles their effect. Now that we have a title giving the subject of the psalm and another indicating its Christian sense, it is less easy to justify this considerable multiplication of texts. However, they may be used very freely. Most ambitiously they may be repeated after the strophes of a psalm and throughout its singing. For this musical settings of some complexity are needed. On the other hand, it does not appear that the whole assembly must sing or recite them. They could be sung or read by a cantor with a short pause for reflection before going on with the psalm and, as we have observed, it is not necessary to sing/recite them after the psalm. It is to be regretted however that the device has been pressed into service so relentlessly. For the daily offices where the subject of the psalms soon becomes known, they seem to be hardly necessary. In practice, their inclusion gives the office a greater appearance of complexity and makes the book bigger than it need be.

The Canticles

A feature of the new office is the great number of canticles, forty-four if the index is correct, provided for both Lauds and Vespers. For the former they are from the Old Testament and for the latter from the New. As we have seen in a previous chapter, Old Testament canticles, notably the *Benedicite*, were used in the morning office from at least the fourth century. The use of them was extended, by St Benedict especially, and they are not to be regarded as merely supplementary to the course of psalms. They have always been regarded as poems of spiritual value and like the psalms have been interpreted in a Christian sense. A good example is the Canticle of Jeremiah (31:10–14) whose meaning is indicated by the two titles: 'The joy of a liberated people'; 'Jesus had to die to reunite the children of God who had been scattered' (John 11:51–2). From the New Testament (an innovation) seven canticles have been chosen, with two extra ones, I Peter 2:21–24 for Sundays in Lent and I Timothy 3:16 for Epiphany (a happy touch this) and the Transfiguration. For Saturdays Philippians 2:6–11 is selected and it is wholly suitable for the office.[16] For *every* Sunday Revelation 19:1, 2, 5–7, is a bit high-pitched and over-decorated with numerous *Alleluias*. *Ephesians* 1 : 3–10, set for Mondays, is over-used (with a feast of Our Lady it can appear twice in a week) and again the translation needs looking at.

The Lectionaries

Of the Office of Reading the lectionaries are clearly important constituents and they must be considered at greater length further on. Here we consider them as elements of this office and take in with them the short readings of the other hours.

The reading of the scriptures 'in course' has always presented problems. To repeat a truism, the Bible is a large and very miscellaneous collection of books and at some point the decision has to be made whether you are going to include the whole of it or only part. If the latter, which parts? And then we are in danger of subjective judgements. One thing seems clear: the revisers have decided that some parts are not suitable for use in the office—which is essentially prayer—and these have been omitted. We are spared genealogical lists and catalogues of objects that run remorselessly through, for instance, the book of Exodus. Judges has been ruthlessly pruned though one wonders whether even what is left is appropriate for the office. Its barbarity strikes hard. But if you use a Bible for your scripture readings, you discover some rather odd things. The book of Ben Sirach for example is not read at all in full. Extracts from it take us over two weeks and the reason for the selections made are sometimes far to seek. That apart, there is a case here for 'extracting', for there is something relentless about the continual moralisings (of various quality) that run through fifty-one chapters. In some cases, the readings resemble a mosaic of texts from one or even two chapters. It is an odd procedure and one does not know whether it is done on critical principles or simply to make the reading more comprehensible. Perhaps the custom of reading the Bible continuously is no longer regarded as important as it once was but there are those who like to use it in that way and it is the only way you can come really to know the Bible.

However, the matter of this lectionary is a very complex one. As we see from the Introduction (146), the original intention was to provide a two-year cycle but this had to be abandoned on account of the extra bulk this would give to the book when it came to be printed.[17] The result, we are told, is that 'we have more Old Testament and less New Testament reading than originally planned'.[18] What exactly has happened to the Old Testament lectionary is difficult to discover. A prolonged examination of the texts in all three volumes would be necessary to discern the principle of selection. As it is, we have fairly evidently a truncated lectionary. Then, the two-year lectionary for week-days in the missal had to be taken into account and here the revisers have been successful in preventing overlapping. Altogether, the problem of the biblical lectionary cannot be said to have been solved and the root cause of the failure must be said to be the practical impossibility of printing anything like an adequate lectionary in an office book even if it is three volumes. And it may be asked, why try to? Every church presumably has a Bible and all that was needed was references to the appropriate passages. For clerics who have to move about a good deal, there are handy pocket-editions of the whole Bible which are easily portable.

In spite of these imperfections, the lectionary is a great improvement on the old one where the readings were sometimes reduced to mere snippets. Each reading in the new book makes sense and the length is about right. The New Testament lectionary proves in use to be very satisfactory. The divisions of the text conform for the most part to the modern critical editions which however have not been followed slavishly.[19]

Of the short readings the Introduction (45) says that they are to be regarded as true proclamations of God's word and are intended to focus attention on short sayings whose significance might be missed in the continuous reading of the Bible. This they do. Those chosen for Vespers, always from the New Testament, are sometimes quite substantial and almost always apt. For Sundays, Fridays and the greater seasons of the year, the character of these times has dictated the choice (GI 156-8).

For the second reading from the Fathers and other ecclesiastical writers the revisers have drawn on a very wide variety of sources from the East and the West (the proportion of Greek writers is particularly notable), from ancient and more modern writers, though apart from the present pope (homily for Feast of Holy Family), no living writer has been included.[20] Some may regret this and there may well be a case for the inclusion of contemporary writers. They can often 'speak to our condition' as a writer of the fourth century does not. There were no doubt good reasons for the decision though one cannot but regret the exclusion of so famous and spiritually profitable writer as Newman.[21]

One at least of the reasons why the revisers have drawn largely on the Fathers is that they wish the patristic reading to be, as far as possible, a commentary on the scripture reading. This is apparent both for the greater feasts and seasons and also for certain weeks during the year. But with the baggage of modern critical scholarship that one carries in one's mind, these commentaries are not always as acceptable as one would like them to be. There seems indeed to be an opportunity here for a new kind of spiritual writer, namely one who is completely competent in modern scriptural exegesis and who yet can draw out the meaning of the passages in question for the spiritual life.[22]

One of the most criticised parts of the former breviary was the 'legends' of the lives of saints that appeared in the second nocturn. They were not only inaccurate but sometimes sheer fabrications like the one about St Cecily of whom next to nothing is known. Again, the legends were written in a conventional literary form. Certain virtues were made pegs on which to hang a meagre amount of information about the saints' lives. Requests for their revision have been heard throughout the centuries and now the revisers have solved the problem by cutting the Gordian knot. A brief biographical note, duly reserved where facts are meagre, precedes the lesson which is either an extract from the saint's writings (if any) or an account of his life by a contemporary or near contemporary, or finally an appropriate passage from a contemporary writer. The results nearly always make acceptable reading. The *fervorino* of St Methodius of Sicily ('With full awareness this virgin empurpled her lips and cheeks and tongue by dabbing them with the light and colour of the blood of the true heavenly Lamb . . .') stands out as an unwelcome exception.

Responsories

As is now well known, the readings are followed by responsories which were one of the richest but, musically speaking, the most difficult texts of the old office. The principle underlying their use is admirable: we listen to God's word and then we ruminate on it and pray about it. The best responsories of the old system did precisely that. The chant dwelt on key phrases from the readings and turned them this way and that. But when the office is recited, they say little enough. As we know, in private recitation they may be omitted and other texts with similar content may replace them.

Hymns

When we come to consider the pattern of the individual offices we are immediately confronted with the question of the place of the hymn. From the time of St Benedict the hymns of Lauds, Vespers and Compline were placed within the body of the office. In the new office they come at the beginning of every hour. The reasons for this, according to the Introduction, are that the hymn sums up 'the particular characteristic of each hour or feast' and helps to 'draw the people into the celebration' (GI 42, 173). That is, the hymn is a popular element and it may be agreed that it is so when an office is celebrated with a community. The opening versicle and response is hardly sufficient to engage the people's attention. On the other hand, the revisers might have gone one step further and put the hymn *before* the versicle and response so that it could be sung in procession. However, there is a case for keeping the hymn where it was, at least in Lauds and Vespers. There at best it served as a meditative commentary on the short reading that preceded it and came as an interlude after the long stretch of psalmody. This function is now performed by the short responsory which in the form given has its difficulties. How is it to be set to singable music? However, it may be replaced by another hymn or verse(s) of one, so the principle is saved.

The collection of Latin hymns is extensive and drawn from many sources not hitherto used in the Roman breviary. All the great hymns of the past appear but there is much undistinguished stuff among them. All are in their pre-classical, pre-seventeenth century form and while this is satisfactory when they are sung to their proper chants, too frequently their rhythm is uneven. However, other collections of national hymns may be used (GI 178) and the editors of the English book have not hesitated to do so.

The Patterns of the Hours

Public prayer, as we have indicated above, must have a certain definable pattern if it is to be an adequate vehicle of worship for a community. It will be useful then to examine some of the individual offices. Lauds and Vespers have the same pattern and may be taken together. It is to be supposed that the revisers thought that three psalms for these offices would be sufficient and psychologically manageable though once the decision had been made to distribute the psalter over four weeks, some reduction was inevitable. The text that follows, the short reading, is of a quite different literary genre and if read slowly and followed by silence, it introduces a meditative element into the office and in this the new office marks a decisive change from the old tradition when an hour was 'gone through' without pause and sometimes almost breathlessly. The responsory prolongs the prayer. Perhaps the full value of this part of the pattern will be seen when there is a longer reading, followed by a homily which will be aimed at leading the community to prayer.[23]

Lauds and Vespers rise to a natural climax with the singing of the evangelical canticles and here, especially on the greater feasts, the antiphons that go with them and that are often of great antiquity and beauty, perform their function very well, though it must be said that in translation they sometimes appear rather pedestrian. Often they sum up the whole meaning of a feast, as for instance the antiphon to the *Benedictus* on the feast of Epiphany.[24]

In public recitation the singing of these canticles may be marked by some ceremonial and the censing of the altar at the *Magnificat* is obviously appropriate.

Up to this moment the movement of the prayer has been Godward even if in the course of it the community have recalled God's saving deeds, that is, his love towards us. But now the prayer moves in the direction of the community, of mankind who needs God's help. Hence the intercessions, the Lord's prayer and the collect. The intercessions have obviously been thought out with great care and in the course of the year they suggest petitions for almost every conceivable human need. They indeed represent a petitionary element in the office which was long desired and which was astonishingly absent from the old office.[25] If the form seems over elaborate, first (and usually) the statement of a need, then a petition and finally a response, they may in fact be used very flexibly. The response may be omitted and from time to time it will be better to do so as it is not always on all fours with the petition following the statement. Finally, time is allowed for private prayer after the official petitions and this should be used. It would also seem indicated that pauses should be made between the petitions. In this framework the Lord's prayer appears as the summing up of the whole hour and its restoration to these offices, after a long absence, can only be greeted with gratification. The collect particularises the prayer of the feast or the hour and the addition (i.e. restoration) of so many collects to the individual hours is also something to be welcomed.

There is no significant change in the hour(s) to be said during the day. The number of texts, notably the short readings, has been increased and the selection of psalms, which of course is dictated by the re-arrangement of the psalter, is somewhat different though many that were in the Pius X breviary for these hours will be found here also.[26] Compline however has suffered a considerable change and is the chief victim of an unimaginative systematisation of the liturgy which had been prevalent since the post-Tridentine reform. If you make a change in one part of the liturgy, you must make the same change everywhere else. If you think it 'a good idea' to put the hymn first in other offices, it must be put first in that of Compline. Compline has always had a special character, quiet, contemplative, summing up the day and looking on to the sleep of the night. The old office suggested this by its very pattern: a reading (even if formalised in the Roman office), from which naturally proceeded an examination of conscience, a general confession and absolution. The psalms moved forward quietly and the hymn continued in the same mood. The little chapter (which could with advantage have been varied) and the responsory turned one's thought to the coming night and the *Nunc dimittis* followed by the collect with the anthem of the Blessed Virgin Mary brought the hour to a fitting close. The place of the hymn in the new office wrecks the pattern. The examination of conscience (or in public recitation[27] the penitential act) has no obvious connection with the hymn that immediately follows it. Since the beginning of the hour has been changed and the 'blessing' (for the reader) suppressed, it was thought necessary to salvage the sentence asking for 'a quiet night and a perfect end' and this appears at the end of the office. Altogether an untidy affair. It will be said that the new Compline has the same effect. Perhaps it has, but not without jolts and bumps.

Like every liturgy the new office will reveal its virtues and defects through use over a considerable space of time. Experience may well show that if it is to become the prayer of the *people* a good deal of simplification will be necessary. This is particularly true of seasons like Lent and Advent where the pattern adopted by the revisers makes the arrangement of the book a complicated matter. The editors of the English edition have done their best to produce a reasonable arrangement but it can still be puzzling. One reason for this would seem to be the policy of the revisers in providing a very considerable number of proper texts for these seasons and the division of the seasons into two parts: the first four weeks of Lent and the special days of Advent from 17 to 24 December. The former is the more troublesome and some re-thinking of this period would seem to be necessary. Much could be done for both seasons by reducing the variety of antiphons and responsories. On the other hand, there is the fact that the office may be used with great flexibility and in the course of time there will no doubt be those who will be able to find solutions to the problems presented by the existing complexity. Already there are some who see the new office as a basis on which to build a prayer of the church for the people.[28] There is however another feature of the new office that deserves great attention. It is simply that it allows for and indeed encourages a calm, recollected manner of celebration. The titles of the psalms demand at least a moment of reflection, silences may be kept after the readings and there would seem to be no reason why similar silences should not be made at the end of the psalms before the *Gloria Patri*, especially when as in psalm 21 its content is rich. Likewise full opportunity should be taken to provide moments of silence in the course of the intercessions and if these are said kneeling (as I think they should be) the possibility of recollected prayer is real. This is one of the ways in which the unfortunate gap between private prayer, 'meditation' or whatever it has been called, can be closed. In the past it was not always realised that you cannot pray out of a vacuum. You need something to pray about and the office with its psalms, readings and intercessions provide jumping off points for personal prayer. Perhaps too it has not been sufficiently realised that the prayer of petition is essentially an approach to God, a recognition of his power and love and when that approach is made in humility of heart, the one praying is open to the movement and inspiration of the Holy Spirit. In more recent years when there has been more than a tendency to set charismatic prayer against liturgical prayer, it is important to realise that with the silences of the divine office there is a place in it for charismatic prayer. It would be a pity if the charismatic movement became associated with certain phenomena whether they be the speaking with tongues or healing. If it is anything at all, it is a movement that wishes to give free play to the movement of the Spirit in the human heart and this may be, and probably usually is, totally imperceptible to the senses or the outside world. A waiting on the Spirit within the context of liturgical prayer will strengthen both the charismatic element in the life of the church and the prayer that is called and is the prayer of the church.

NOTES

1. The official Latin edition has two titles: *Divinum Officium* (*ex sacrosancto concilio* . . .), at the top of the page and in the middle *Liturgia Horarum, iuxta Ritum Romanum*. But *Liturgia Horarum* appears on the spine and it is clear from the Introduction that the revisers intend it to be called by that name. The English translators opted for *The Divine Office* and have put 'The Liturgy of the Hours etc.' as a sub-title (See *The Divine Office*, Collins, Dwyer and Talbot, Vol. I, 1974, the edition used here). The reason was that 'Liturgy of the Hours' sounds odd in English and is over-technical. On the other hand 'The Divine Office' has long been used in English-speaking countries.

2. Even if a Christian is unable to be present at the eucharist every day, it is being celebrated continually.

3. GI 38 and Cyprian *De Orat. Dom.*, 35.

4. Of Terce, Sext and None the Introduction simply says that they commemorate the events of our Lord's passion and the first preaching of the gospel (75).

5. GI 14 and cf CL 33.

6. See GI 201–3.

7. I have noted only one of the famous responsories of *'Tenebrae'* and there are two meagre extracts from the Lamentations of Jeremiah which have been sung on these days for about fifteen hundred years. Nor should it be said that these texts, because they can only be sung in Latin if you are to retain the chants, are 'no good to the people'. They are so moving that anyone with a bi-lingual text (if he needs one) can profit from them. It may be that there are few churches able to sing them. But if they are abolished, there will be none.

8. Short of three, 57, 82, 108, the 'cursing' psalms which have been omitted 'because of certain psychological difficulties' (GI 131 – which must be regarded as a deliberate understatement) and verses from a number of others.

9. Which it is so difficult to *like*.

10. Cf for example Acts 4:23–31; and also Ephes. 5:19; Col. 3:16.

11. Not the 'titles' found in the Hebrew psalter. See P. Salmon, *Les 'tituli psalmorum' des manuscrits latins*, Paris, 1958.

12. A fourth volume of the office is expected which it is said will contain psalter-collects. See chapter IV.

13. See P. Salmon, *EP*, pp. 822–3 and J. Gelineau, *Voices and Instruments in Christian Worship* (Eng. trans. C. Howell, Collegeville, Minn, USA, 1964) pp. 107–8.

14. See P. Salmon, *EP*, p. 823.

15. For the *seasons* however the system does not always work. Thus for I Vespers of I Advent the antiphon 'Behold the Lord will come and all his holy ones with him . . .' is in no way related to the psalm (141) which is about deep suffering and affliction. Likewise, 'Rejoice and be glad, new Zion . . .' attached to a section of psalm 118 is totally out of key with it. Examples could be multiplied.

16. The translation is not always happy: 'Jesus did not count equality with God a thing to be *grasped*.' 'Grasped at' would be more correct but that was evidently too much for the RSV translators though the phrase would seem to mean 'cling to' – so J.B.

17. For details see Dom Placid Muray 'In season and out of season' in *The Furrow* (February, 1975), pp. 100–1.

18. *ibid.*

19. These editions do in fact differ from one another but the revisers do not seem to have followed the Vulgate.

20. In the draft lectionary there was one extract from Thomas Merton, but recently dead, and one (in French!) from Newman, both *ad libitum*.

21. Because he is not canonised?

22. A beginning was made by German scholars some years ago and some of their commentaries have been made available in English. Cf for example *Das Evangelium nach Matthäus* by W. Trilling in the series *Geistliche Schriftlesung* (Patmos Verlag, 1962); English translation *Gospel according to Matthew*, 2 vols (Burns and Oates, 1969). The series has been continued by Sheed and Ward.

23. GI 46 suggests that this reading may be taken either from the Office of Readings or from the Mass (and indeed from other places). But what happens when the priest-celebrant has to use these texts before or after the office? What, I

think, was needed was a supplementary lectionary, no more than references to the Bible, to be used for these longer readings.

24. A good deal could be said about the revised liturgy of the Epiphany which has heavily emphasised the western aspect of it as a feast of mission. In the eastern church, from which it came, the emphasis is on the marriage between Christ and his church. In the revised office this antiphon is distinctly isolated. The emphasis could be corrected by the substitution of Isaiah 62 : 1–5 (a bridal text) for Isaiah 52 : 7–10 (a missionary text).

25. With the exception of certain parts of the *preces* and these were stereotyped to an intolerable degree.

26. Proper antiphons for these hours seem to be an unnecessary luxury.

27. Is not public recitation of Compline something of an anomaly? For St Benedict it seems to have been a domestic act: it was said wherever the brethren were gathered for the reading of Cassian's Conferences or the Lives of the Fathers (*Rule*, c. 42).

28. The French for instance who have not (yet) committed themselves to producing a large and expensve office book. Père Roguet records that in Notre Dame, Paris, large congregations gather on Sundays for Lauds (!) and Vespers according to the new office. But he does not describe exactly what is done (see his essay, p. 78, n. 1 in *The Liturgy of the Hours*, translated by Peter Coughlan and Peter Purdue, Chapman, 1971).

CHAPTER FIVE

The Prayer of the Psalms

It is clear that in the new office the psalter has a dominant place. It is the spine of every hour. In addition to canticles from the Old and New Testaments, we are required to say eleven psalms or parts of psalms a day which means seventy-seven during the week and, as we know, the whole psalter (short of three which have been omitted) during the month. If this is a notable alleviation of the burden of reciting one hundred and fifty during a week, it still amounts to a good deal and unless we have an adequate understanding of them, it is not going to be easy to use them as prayer.

It would seem that there are many modern Christians who have difficulties in this matter, difficulties that have come from various quarters. Several generations of scholarship have revealed the psalms in all the starkness of their primitive meaning. Even the not very profound knowledge of the psalms that an average theological student acquires in the course of his studies is sufficient to show that the psalms are *Hebrew* poems, the expression of culture to which he does not belong. The God of the psalms is so often the God of battles who is fighting for a small and insignificant tribe. Up to a point we can rationalise this and then we are brought up sharp with an utterance that strikes one as barbarous: 'O give thanks to the Lord for he is good, for his great love has no end . . . The first-born of the Egyptians he smote, *for* this great love is without end . . . he flung Pharaoh and his force in the sea, *for* his great love is without end . . .' (ps. 135). A strange way of showing love, and all we can think of is the poor babies of the Egyptians and hope that the accounts of their death are no more true than the events of the Aeneid. Then in the psalms we find God manipulating nature for his own purposes; storm and flood, the crashing of trees, smoking mountains and earthquakes are all caused by God to put fear into errant Israelites or their unspeakably wicked enemies. For the psalmist sometimes sees God as his ally, set against the people of Canaan or the invading hordes from the North: 'We have heard with our own ears . . . of the things you did long ago . . . To plant them you uprooted the nations: to let them spread you laid peoples low . . .' (ps. 43) and we are reminded unhelpfully of the carnage of the Book of Joshuah. The same psalm goes on relentlessly: 'Yet now you have rejected us, disgraced us . . . though we had not forgotten you . . .' Here the note of *self*-righteousness that we hear from time to time in the psalms appears. A little too frequently the psalmist affirms that he—or the people—have done all that was required of them, and yet and yet . . . This seems to be in direct contradiction to the gospel saying: 'We have done all that we should and (yet) we are profitless servants' (Luke 17: 10). It would not be difficult to prolong the list which would perhaps look like an indictment.

Underlying these objections there is a deeper problem. As soon as you begin talking of prayer, you raise questions about God. On the one hand, our notion or image of God conditions our prayer and on the other our prayer will say much about how we regard God. The psalms can often voice the deepest and most anguished emotions known to man (psalms 21 and 68) but God dominates the scene and there is apparently little reference to 'neighbour'. To put the matter in another way, the psalms emphasise the transcendence of God giving the impression that he is all and man is nothing. It is the problem of transcendence and immanence that runs throughout religious history. Today many seem to have lost the sense of God's transcendence. God has been declared dead some time ago and by that is meant (at worst) that God is no more than part of the human process. At best, it means that modern Christians are more keenly aware of God in others, their fellow human beings, than in the traditional out-going of man to God in worship, praise and adoration. The resolution of the tension and the solution of the problem are to be found in the incarnation where God, the Lord of all things, becomes Immanuel, the God who is with us. It is perhaps for this reason that as soon as the church began using the psalms for prayer (and before that, for *kerygma* and teaching), by what seems a kind of instinct it christianised them. Of this we say something below but first we must attempt some answers to the other points.

It may be conceded that when we are confronted with the psalms and are constrained to use them we have to make a transference from one culture to another.[1] But it may be remarked that if we are to use any part of the Old Testament profitably and for that matter much of the New, we have to make this transference. Moreover, it needs to be said that the modern understanding of the psalms, the possibility of putting at least some of them in their *Sitz-im-Leben*, helps us to use them. If there are psalms, and there seem to be many of them, that are to be dated to the time of the exile, and if we remember something of the circumstances that accompanied it, if indeed we project back into that far-off age something of the experience of the millions who have suffered exile in our own times, we can appreciate the anguished accents of the psalmist who becomes the voice of his whole community. In turn, such psalms can become *our* voice, our prayer for those same people. Spatial and temporal parochialism which restricts our horizon to our own affairs is not only not true to the New Testament but it is not true to the deepest insights of the Old. It may indeed often be difficult to discern whether and if the psalmist is expressing simply his own experiences or those of the community. Yet even in psalms so deeply personal as 21 and 68 there is a sense that the sufferer is the representative of the people and that he is suffering in them and they in him. This in fact reminds us of a dimension of the psalms that at times seems to have been overlooked. Nineteenth century exegetes, who were usually brought up on a very individualistic kind of Christianity, did not, it would seem, always realise that they were dealing with the prayer book of a community. Whatever may have been the origins of certain personal psalms—and it is a perfectly proper exercise to try and discover those origins—by the time they were incorporated into the psalter they had become the expression and prayer of the people.[2] One reason why the psalter could become the prayer of the church was because it was first the prayer of the old Israel of God.

A more difficult problem is that of the relationship of God to the world and to historical events. As the merest tyro in exegesis knows the Old Testament by-passes secondary causes. If anything happens, it is God who does it. Where natural phenomena are concerned perhaps the difficulty is not so great. In the Old Testament God was involved in the human process which was not simply something that went on without him. If God was too close to natural and historical events in the Old Testament, nowadays he is thought of even by Christians as being absent from the course of history. The difficulty of course is that in the Old Testament view, God seems to be responsible for *evil* and this the Christian cannot accept. The only solution to the problem would seem to be that we must realise we are reading about God through the mentalities of successive generations of people of the Old Testament. We need to remember that when the prophets said 'Thus says the Lord' they had not a hot line to God, that the sometimes blood-curdling utterances that are part of that word are the expression of the human speaker or writer and that he is saying as best he can what the message entrusted to him is. Thus when the writer of psalm 135 seems to be exulting in the death of innocent Egyptian babes we need to remember that he was calling on an ancient and primitive tradition that is recorded in the Book of Exodus. His emphasis is not on the destruction of infants but on the power of God who brought the people of Israel out of the slavery of Egypt. It is in *this* that his love is revealed.

Perhaps in any case the Old Testament writers were not so naïve as we imagine. They could see the obverse and the reverse of the same event. *What* caused the death of the Egyptian children I think we must say we do not know. All the 'plagues' are put in a conventional framework and some are no more than the natural phenomena of Egyptian climatic conditions. The deaths happened and they were the other side of the epic story which tells of the deliverance of the people whom God loved. The same could be said of the destruction of the Egyptian army. We have to make the same considerations in our own day. Were the issues about the Second World War so clear cut in 1939? There were many who thought they were not. They were aware that even if the war was necessary it would cause a loss of life and a destruction of industry and property that would be incalculable and in the event they were right. But the western nations thought they must resist a tyranny that would have brought to an end a whole way of life which, if far from perfect, guaranteed certain fundamental human liberties. This end was achieved. This was the positive good but the evil remained and is not yet effaced.

Then there is the question of God as the 'God of battles' or even of the God of vengeance, the tribal God of this little Iron Age people who are slowly and painfully emerging into something that can be called civilisation. It may seem a poor consolation to be told that the God of the Old Testament is infinitely superior to the gods of contemporary religions but it does put us on to the track of a better understanding. In the Old Testament we have a progessive revelation of God, his image is being gradually purified and in the deepest understanding of the Old Testament writers he is not a tribal God. And so many of the psalms proclaim he is Lord of heaven and earth, the whole of creation is his and the destiny of the whole human race is in his hand. His 'jealousy' (and there is not a great deal about this in the psalter) is not an unworthy human emotion of which any decent monarch would be ashamed. It is the expression of the great love he bears to the people he has chosen. Nor are they chosen simply for their own sake. As so many of the psalms show, as so much of the prophetic writing shows, the Israelites are at once the representatives of the human race and the means chosen by God to carry his message of salvation to the whole of mankind. As we see from psalms like 95, 97 and 102, and from Isaiah 61 and 66, to mention no other passages, the final message of the Old Testament is universalist: all shall see the salvation of God. One day the posterity of Abraham will no longer be a tiny people dwelling precariously on a strip of land constantly overrun by the heathen. They will be a great nation, a universal people who will flow into a new Temple which will no longer be the shrine of a small tribe but the house of God's people. In this perspective God is the God of the whole human race whom he loves and who is the object of their love.[3] He is the God who one day will come among them, set his tent among them and indeed be one of them. It is this broad vision we need to keep in mind as we use the psalms rather than concentrating on the apparently arbitrary behaviour of God which is no more than an imperfect expression of his transcendence.

Perhaps 'transcendence' is the root of the trouble. As everyone knows there has been a vast and as yet an unended debate about this matter. In recent decades the horizontal relationship between man and man in religion and even in worship has been emphasised at the expense of the vertical relationship with God. At its simplest, the case is stated by the modern Christian in this way: he can find God in others or in the service of others and prayer has at times and by some been pronounced a useless activity. Not all in that view is to be repudiated but if the divine transcendence is rejected whether in theory or in practice, then it is difficult to see that worship and prayer in any real sense can survive. Perhaps this trend is now reaching its close, though rather from exhaustion than from a resolution of the problem.

Yet the question of the divine transcendence remains one of crucial importance. It is impossible to accept that the God of the Bible, the God of Jews and Christians alike, should be part of the world process to be conceived as in a constant state of self-perfection. That way lies either pantheism or atheism.

The reasons why some have wished to get rid of the divine transcendence are no doubt various but one of them is probably that it has seemed to deny the validity of this world order or to undervalue its importance. It is just at this point that we can see the value of the psalmists' emphasis on the involvement of God in the natural processes and in those of human history. Nowhere is the transcendence of God thrown into such high relief and yet nowhere is the sense of God being with the world and concerned in its events so strong as in the psalms. No doubt the 'science' is primitive, no doubt philosophical analysis is totally absent, no doubt we, with our post-Copernican model of the world in our minds, need to 'translate' a good deal of what is there, but the central insight is sound. As Etienne Gilson showed long ago, it is this insight, combined with the Aristotelian philosophy, that enabled the medieval philosophers to work out their rich synthesis in which God is approached through those things that are (*ea quae sunt*), things that form an essential part of the whole reality. Aquinas does indeed in one place speak of all created beings 'emanating' from the Creator in language that seems almost Gnostic (*in exitu creaturarum a primo principio . . .*) but he also sees them returning to their Origin perfected, their potentiality realised, *more* themselves than when they began their journey.[4] Dependent on God for their origin, directed towards him as their last end, they none the less achieve 'autonomy'. They *are* and they are valuable in themselves. But because they derive their being from God, they can reflect his beauty, truth and love (of which they are expressions) and through man's contemplation of them can lead him to God. The distinction between Creator and creature is always clear but so also is their essential relatedness.

This seems a far cry from the psalter but what are the psalms saying, what is psalm 8 saying ('How great is your name, O Lord our God, through all the earth. Your majesty is praised above the heavens'), if not that? The examples could be multiplied. If modern western industrialised man cannot respond to the exultation that underlies such expressions it must be because he is spiritually impoverished. For even if you are a Christian and if in practice you *exclude* God from all that really matters, you are not going to be able to praise him, to worship him or perhaps even to believe in him in any real way. Whatever may have been the defects of the people of the Old Testament they did not do that. God was real to them, God was present.

Part of the trouble about transcendence is that people have thought it meant that God was 'far away', 'up there' or 'out there'. Transcendence does not imply spatial images and when the psalmist cried 'I lift up my eyes to the mountains from where shall come my help' it is we who would be naïve in supposing that he thought God dwelt on the mountain. Sometimes one feels that the alleged inability of some to use the psalms comes from a failure to appreciate poetry! Transcendence implies 'otherness' and the radical distinction that must be made between God and things if we are not to fall into pantheism. But it may be admitted that the tension between transcendence and immanence was never wholly resolved in the Old Testament. There was a sense of God's presence, there were intimations of the Immanuel, but there could be no resolution of the tension until God had become man. It was their understanding of this radical change that enabled the first Christians to use the psalms with confidence and without *arrière-pensée* first for teaching and then for worship. This development was no doubt assisted by the translation of Yahweh in the psalms by the word '*Kyrios*' which the New Testament applied to Christ without hesitation. This brings us to what has been called the christological interpretation of the psalms.

It has been remarked that the office (as it was) was too theocentric, its users were required to glorify God 'as if the incarnation had never happened' and even if the form of the church's prayer derives from the synagogue a Christian will want 'to make it more christological'.[5] This was true of the old office, but, as we have indicated in a former chapter, this is no longer true of the new. The criticism is however made largely with the psalms and the Old Testament readings in view and these still form the major part of the Divine Office. Of the scripture lectionary we shall say something below but something further must be said about the psalms here. How can the psalms be christianised? How can we find Christ in them? How can we become aware that we are praying with Christ, about Christ and to him? These are not new questions though the need to answer them has become more acute in recent years and there has in fact been a vast amount of writing of the subject [6] which unhappily cannot even be summarised here.

Professor Fischer is quite emphatic about what he calls the 'christologisation' of the psalms. Without it, it is impossible for the Christian to use them as prayer and he finds justification for his views in the interpretation of the psalms that is assumed in the gospels and the rest of the New Testament.[7] He sees this interpretation being formed in the early church ('the church of the martyrs') in two principal ways. First, there is the christological interpretation that moves 'from above' as when the Yahweh of the Hebrew is taken as *Kyrios*, the Lord Jesus of the New Testament. The second way is the interpretation 'from below' as when the psalm is seen as giving the words of Christ—as if the *persona* of the psalm were Christ. Or the matter can be put more simply: 'for the church of the martyrs each psalm in some fashion speaks *of* Christ or *to* Christ or finally Christ is seen speaking in it'.[8] But the voice of Christ was not separated from the voice of the church so the psalm is often seen as the voice of the church, *vox ecclesiae*, which is united with that of Christ. This aspect of the matter was summed up by St Augustine in one phrase: the psalm is the voice of the whole Christ, head and body,[9] a theme that, as we know, he pursued through his vast book, the *Enarrationes in psalmos*.[10] The whole matter is expressed in the commentary of St Augustine on psalm 85 which we have quoted in the first chapter of this book: '. . . the Saviour of the Body, (Christ) prays *for* us and *in* us and we make our prayer *to* him. He prays for us *as priest*, he prays in us *as head* and we pray to him *as our God* . . . .'

This understanding of the psalms which was markedly that of the ancient Roman liturgy,[11] of course involves a major 'translation' and perhaps not everyone will be willing to make it. It may be said however that given the right disposition of mind, continual use of the psalms brings a growing realisation that the psalms are, in the deepest sense, Christian prayer. The *practical* difficulty is to discern when a psalm speaks *to* Christ as *Kyrios*, when it speaks *of* him, when it gives voice to the sentiments of Christ or when it is the voice of the church, the body of Christ. One important clue, given by the antiphons,[12] is the use the church has made of the psalms on the great feasts of the temporal cycle. Without going into technical questions of which psalms are truly messianic, it is clear that psalms like 2 and 3 (about the resurrection), psalm 22 where the Good Shepherd theme links it immediately with John 10, psalm 21 which no Christian thinks of as anything other than the voice of Christ (cf Matthew 27:46; Mark 15:34), have a Christian sense. Nor is there any doubt about a psalm like 109 or even psalm 110 which gives the covenant theme. The list could be greatly extended but there is no space for such a list here.[13] In other words, the easiest and probably the most effective way of learning the Christian interpretation of the psalms is to observe the use the church has made of them in the office of the great seasons of the year. What would be of the greatest assistance to a Christian understanding of the psalms would be a new kind of commentary, based on modern scholarship, which would take into account the whole of the Christian tradition of interpretation. Just as the typological interpretation of the scriptures has undergone close scrutiny in recent years, so we need a similar sifting for the psalms. They would stand to lose nothing and would be made more accessible to the ordinary user.

The new office has done something to bring this Christian sense of the psalms before the user by printing the second title (which may indeed in private recitation be used as an antiphon; GI 115) before the text of the psalm. These titles are drawn often enough from the New Testament (e.g. psalm 2 'They rose up against your servant Jesus, whom you had anointed' Acts 4:27) or from the Fathers and other ecclesiastical writers. Thus the title of psalm 1 interprets the 'tree that is planted beside flowing waters' as of the cross, the source of life, a phrase that evokes John 19:34. It is attributed to a writer of the second century. The 'sun' of psalm 18A is interpreted by the 'The Rising Sun (who) has come to visit us to guide our feet in the way of peace' of Luke 1:78, 79. This too is a very ancient interpretation going back to Justin the Martyr (Apol: I, 54) and represents a very bold reference for its time to *Helios*, the Sun god.[14] In a different register, namely the *vox Christi*, we find as the title to psalm 6 'Now my spirit is troubled . . .' of John 12:27. The psalm goes on 'Lord, do not reprove me in your anger, punish me not in your rage . . . Have mercy on me Lord ... my soul is racked with pain ....' Such a title suggests the interior sentiments of Christ in his passion and the use the church makes of psalms like 21, 37, 68 and some others in the Holy Week liturgy yields the same interpretation. It is indeed one of the stranger features of the early Roman liturgy that it could accept without hesitation or apology a depth of human-ness in the suffering Christ that some even today might think excessive. This interpretation is so prevalent in the liturgy of the time that it is not too much to say that it was an authentic expression of the mind of the church. If that is so, it means that we have an insight into the interior sentiments of Christ in his passion of which the gospels say very little.

All this is helpful and in using the new office we should take due notice of these titles. It is to be regretted however that a few are not really illuminating. Thus the title of psalm 146 says no more than the text of the psalm itself: 'You, O God, we worship; you, O Lord, we adore,' and the psalm goes on: 'Praise the Lord for he is good, sing to our God for he is loving' which I imagine in the view of Professor Fischer would be regarded as a christianisation 'from above': that is, 'Lord' = *Kyrios*. In one place the title contrasts very oddly with the psalm 'To you have I lifted up my eyes . . . Like the eyes of a servant on the hand of a mistress . . .'. For this the title, taken from Matthew 20:30 (and awkwardly translated), is 'The two blind men cried out: "Lord, have pity on us, Son of David".' Yes, well, of course the general sense is clear but still the point of the gospel incident is that the men could *not* see. The titles drawn from patristic works sometimes say little enough. See for example that for psalm 60: 'The prayer of a just man who looks to the things which are eternal' (St Hilary). Or let us take psalm 98, one of the most powerful psalms of the psalter which recalls so much of the history of salvation. To this is attached a saying from St Athanasius, again rather lamely translated: 'You are higher than the Cherubim; you changed the *bad state of the earth*,[15] when you came in a nature like ours.' These lapses however are comparatively rare and a study of the titles reveals that on the whole they have been successful in pointing to the Christian sense of the psalms and, it is interesting to note, they have done this most effectively by using phrases from the New Testament. There can be no sounder basis than this and the revisers have rather cleverly by-passed the scholarly debate about which psalms are 'christological' and which are not,[16] whatever criticism may be made of

details, the restoration of the titles to the psalms has done much to christianise them in practice, i.e. for those who are going to use the new book.

However, it may be said that if all this 'theology' and the device of 'titles'
are necessary, that only goes to show that it is difficult if not impossible for
the ordinary mortal to use the psalms as prayer. To this it can be answered
that all prayer needs effort of one kind or another. Even the post-Tridentine
tradition of mental prayer with its composition of place, its two or three
'points for consideration' and its resolutions or 'spiritual nosegays', demanded a good deal of work as did and do simpler forms of prayer. Few
are they who can fall on their knees and immediately get in touch with God.
Most of us need a text either from holy scripture or some other kind of
book to provide the necessary point of departure. It does not seem a great
deal to ask that people who use the psalms should take some little trouble
over them so that they can become prayer. To this we can add that there are
a number of psalms that present no difficulty at all. For centuries Christians
have used psalm 50 to express repentance, psalm 129 to express their need
of God and redemption; and psalm 130 'O Lord, my heart is not proud . . .'
is the simplest and most moving plea for the virtue of humility which needs
no reference even to the New Testament. There are others like psalm 22
of which the several metrical versions show that it has in fact become a
Christian prayer. In the Anglican tradition, in which the psalter of the
Book of Common Prayer has played so great a part, there is similar evidence to show that certain psalms have long been regarded as Christian
prayers. Some of the greatest Anglican hymns, such as 'All people that on
earth do dwell' (ps. 99) are simply paraphrases of the psalms.

If we add psalms of this kind to the very large corpus that have received
an easily discernible Christian sense in the liturgy, we shall find that we
have covered a great deal of the psalter. There remain others that are more
difficult to use prayerfully. For instance, the series of long psalms from
104–106 and psalms 77–78 recalling the chief events of Old Testament
salvation history, which from a literary viewpoint can only be regarded as
epics and not very promising material for prayer. In the new office they
have been spread out and in any case are used only during Advent, Christmas, Lent and Eastertide. They are more suitable for *reading* than for
praying and if they were appointed for use as lessons, that would be a return
to the earliest use of the psalter.[17] There are others, such as psalm 36 and
psalm 51, dealing with the problem of evil which is 'solved' in a way
that is unacceptable to a Christian, and there are passages of other psalms,
some of which have been omitted, speaking of the destruction of the wicked
or the 'enemy', which can only be described as sub-Christian. What is to be
done about them it is difficult to say. It is hardly satisfactory, as has been
suggested, to put such passages 'into parentheses' and presumably pretend
they are not there.[18] The only solution to the problem that I can see is that
the church should recognise frankly that there are still psalms and parts of
psalms in the office that the Christian cannot use or can only use by means

of a complicated exegesis. In spite of considerable modifications in the liturgical psalter of the 1971 office, it may be that the church still sees some inherent value in reciting in principle the whole of the psalter. It would seem to be a case that is still to be proved. Part of the problem of the psalter is that there is probably still too much of it in the office, and if the quantity of psalms were reduced, not simply in a single office (that is another question), but over the given period of a month, it might very well be possible to use what is left with greater spiritual profit. If the church made this decision, it would simply be returning to the earliest tradition of the prayer of the church.

Of the arrangement of the psalter in the office we note that for Lauds and Vespers all the psalms that are traditional for those hours have been retained. The ancient group 148–150 has been further divided, a process that began with the Pius X psalter but in spite of the severe criticisms of Anton Baumstark on the matter,[19] such division is a psychological necessity. To recite these psalms every day is more than most can bear. Otherwise the office follows pretty well the course of the psalter as it is in the Bible with the necessary allocation of psalms for particular hours. Sometimes this leads to uncomfortable results. For the prayer during the day of Thursday of the third week we find juxtaposed psalm 78, a lamentation over the destruction of Jerusalem and psalm 79 which is similar in mood even if its main message is 'Come, Lord Jesus'. With the section of psalm 118 they make a rather long office. As far as length goes, the same could be said of the same office for Monday of the second week; psalm 118, 41–48, psalm 39, divided into two sections. There is a great deal to be said for the Benedictine arrangements here, namely the use throughout most of the week of the gradual psalms. They are short and experience has shown that they can be prayed again and again and always have a message to deliver.

One or two other matters in connection with the use of the psalter deserve mention. The most obvious way in which the psalms have been christianised is by the addition of the short doxology (the 'Glory be to the Father . . .') to each psalm. This addition was made apparently in the fifth century and can be regarded as a permanent element to remind worshippers that they are using the psalms as Christian prayers. Dom Vandenbroucke sees in it no more than an 'extrinsic christianisation', a term that would seem to indicate that he does not think much of it. It is true I think that it has become so much 'stuffing' and we do not seem to have missed its absence in the responsorial psalm of the Mass. It is to be regretted that the older form 'Glory be to the Father, through the Son, and in the Holy Spirit', which was still current in the time of St Basil, gave way to the present form which is a relic (so old!) of the anti-Arian campaign of the fourth century. The older form would certainly remind us that always we are praying through Christ to the Father and in the Holy Spirit.[20]

The Psalm–Collects

Another means to make the use of the psalms more prayerful was the psalm-collect which was recited after a pause for silence at the end of every psalm. There is a considerable number of these collects in existence [21] and we are told [22] that they will be included in the supplementary volume to the *Liturgy of the Hours* which at the time of writing has not been published. It must be confessed that occasionally they are disappointing because arbitrary. A phrase is snatched from the psalm and prayer is built up round it perhaps regardless of context. But generally speaking they witness to the profound Christian understanding of the psalms that was current in the fifth and subsequent centuries. A few examples will give some notion of these collects.

1. From psalm 40 ('Happy the man who considers the poor and the weak') the writer expands what is almost its last verse: 'Establish me in your sight.'
'Strengthen me in your sight, Lord, and deliver us not into the hands of his enemy for you once raised us up in Christ the Lord. Send your help to us on our bed of pain; heal our souls for we have sinned against you. Guard us, give us life and make us blessed on the earth' (p. 192).

2. On a not very promising psalm 'O God you have rejected us and broken us' (59) with its curious expression about 'casting a sandal over Idumea', we have this:
'Go forth, Lord, at the head of our armies. May we be strong in the power of the Word who, when he clothed himself in our human nature, took possession of the earth (lit. *'extendit calceamentum suum in Idumea'*). Through him help us in affliction and forgive the sins of your people' (p. 142).

3. From the great eschatological psalm, 28, where God is seen enthroned in his temple ('In his temple they all cry "Glory"') the writer has seized upon that notion:
'Strengthen your people, Lord, and make us the temple of your Holy Spirit so that with pure hearts we may prepare for you an acceptable sacrifice *(holocaustum)*' (p. 78).

4. One last sample must suffice. There is much to exploit in the Messianic psalm 109 and a Spanish writer does so. The phrase *ante luciferum genitus* has caught his attention but it is only a point of departure:
'Lord, Father almighty, from your own being as from the womb before the daystar you brought forth the Son; grant that he who with you made the light of the whole world from nothing, may enlighten us with his shining glory. May he who was born into the world from the Virgin's womb, though without leaving your side, make us sharers in his passion as he promised us to be his co-heirs in glory.' (p. 242)
A little prolix perhaps as was the Spanish habit and somewhat complicated but the prayer links the worshipper with the whole redeeming work of Christ which *began* in the incarnation.

The procedure is clear. The writers of these prayers do not summarise either the theme of the psalm or its Christian meaning. They seize upon a phrase here and there and build up their prayer on it but they bring a Christian mind to the psalms and find in them the Christian message. One is inclined to say that perhaps too often they find what they want. It would be interesting to compare at length these ancient collect-prayers with some which have been written in more recent times. Space forbids but it will be useful to give one example of a modern collect for the same psalm (109) which does in fact sum up and christianise it:

'All powerful and ever-living God,
you have enthroned your Son, Jesus, at your right hand.
He was begotten of your being before the dawn
and *was raised up from the dead by the power of the Spirit.*
You have placed his enemies as a footstool under his feet.
Spread his reign by the growth of his church
and *by the sacrifice of our eternal High Priest*
give us to drink from the torrent of his graces
and make us co-heirs of his glory for ever.' [23]

The italicised phrases indicate a thorough-going christianisation of the psalm and it is clear that the collect summarises its themes. It may seem over-elaborate and indeed over-done, but the recitation of a prayer like this at the end of a psalm makes it come alive for the Christian.

Titles, antiphons, the Christian interpretation of the psalms, the *Gloria Patri*, and the collects—all this adds up to a great deal and if these 'aids to prayer' have their place, they also show that the praying of the psalms is not an easy matter. If modern people, if the young monks and clerics of whom Dom Weakland has written, are unwilling to take this trouble, then I fear they will not be able to use the psalms as Christian prayer. Whether we like it or not, we *have* to make a transference from one culture to another but in this the psalter is not unique. The whole Bible is involved and with it the question of its *sensus plenior*, the fulfilled sense of the Old Testament, about which so much has been written in the last twenty five years.[24] Without this we are condemned to reading the Old Testament as the record of an obscure pre-Christian tribe. At that level, which is not without its importance for scholarly purposes, it can hardly become *lectio divina*.

The Canticles

Two new features of the office are the very considerable increase in the number of Old Testament Canticles and the inclusion of canticles from the New Testament that apart from the *Benedictus*, the *Magnificat* and the *Nunc Dimittis* have never appeared in it before. No doubt the allocation of the psalter to a period of four weeks had something to do with the first and a growing realisation among exegetes that there are identifiable canticles in the New Testament accounts for the second. Of these additions the General Introduction has nothing to say except to record their appearance in the office (136, 137). We are left to our own surmises.

The difficulties over the Old Testament Canticles are neither greater nor less than those that effect the use of the psalms. Titles to help in their use have been added to them as to the psalms. For the most part these canticles are well chosen and include many of the great passages from Isaiah. Daniel 3 also makes a very good prayer. I am not at all sure of the value of Isaiah 38, the canticle of Hezekiah, which was in the old breviary, in spite of the new title added to it: 'I was dead, and behold I am alive and I hold the keys of death' (Revelation 1: 17, 18). The lack of a sense of an after-life in all the Old Testament literature until the last books is disconcerting and the christianisation of a text like this is unconvincing. Hezekiah did not in fact die and what he feared was complete extinction. The long Canticle of Moses, though much abbreviated (Deuteronomy 32: 1–12), remains unappealing. The Canticle of Habakkuk (also abbreviated 3: 2–4, 13a, 16–19) in spite of its corrupt Hebrew text which provides great difficulties in translation, is a good paschal hymn (compare its use in the former Good Friday service) but it takes some understanding. The Canticle of Hannah (I Samuel 2: 1–10) makes a good prayer and an explicit reference is made to the *Magnificat* by the title. There seems to have been a re-discovery by liturgicals of Ezekiel 36: 24–28 (as well as of Jeremiah 31: 10–14) in recent years; it appears an astonishing number of times everywhere in the new liturgy. A canticle one would like to have seen excluded is Ben Sira (alias *Ecclesiasticus*) 36: 1–7, 13–16 which oddly enough appeared as an epistle in the old missal for the Propagation of the Faith:

'Save us, O God of all things,
strike all the nations with terror;
raise your hand against foreign nations (!)
that they may see the greatness of your might.
Our sufferings proved your holiness to them;
let their downfall prove your glory to us . . .'

A strange way of converting people one might think. It is plainly sub-Christian and has no place in the Christian liturgy.

The use of New Testament canticles (apart from the traditional three) is an innovation and one to be welcomed. Here we are aware that we have to do with specifically Christian prayers and from this point of view they provide no difficulty. Ephesians 1: 3–10 and Colossians 1: 12–20 are very dense texts (one reason for using them in the office) but they need help from commentaries if the full richness of their content is to be appreciated. The canticles from Revelation are somewhat fabricated, verses from different places, even different chapters, being combined. The result would seem to show that the procedure was justified. All these canticles are well allocated and of course their use is restricted to Vespers. Ephesians 1 : 3–10 however is somewhat over-used. It appears in Monday Vespers and is used for feasts of the Blessed Virgin Mary, for apostles and for other saints when their anniversaries are kept as *festa*. This means that you might have to say it on Monday and again for a feast of our Lady on Tuesday and for a *festum* of a saint on Friday—altogether too much of a good thing. The reason why it has been selected for these occasions is to be found, it would seem, in the phrases 'He chose us in him . . . that we should be holy . . . He destined us in love to be his sons through Jesus Christ . . . .' The whole text in fact underlines the total dependence of the saints on Christ.

There is another question connected with these canticles, especially some of the New Testament ones. It is the matter of translation. In the Greek Ephesians 1 : 3–10 (all one sentence) goes with a fine swing which is also palpable in the Vulgate. This is made possible largely through the use of participles both in the Greek and in the Latin. Understandably modern translations bow to the necessity of breaking up the clauses if only to make the passage intelligible. In the process they have destroyed the rhythm. In the Ephesians passage (the translation is that of RSV) we have a very inelegant repetition: 'according to his purpose which he set forth in Christ./ His purpose he set forth in Christ as a plan . . . .' A different and freer form of translation would seem to be required. These texts are now being used as *prayers*, they are not the subject of learned exegesis, and while keeping as close as possible to the original text translators should be encouraged to produce more rhythmical texts that can be both said and sung with pleasure.

Finally, a word must be said about the canticle from Revelation 19 : 1–2, 5–7). It is a splendid piece of course and one is glad to see it included in the office. It is the song of the bridal church to Christ and to his Father. But not counting those of the antiphon, it is 'decorated' with no less than sixteen Alleluias of which eight may be omitted in private recitation! I fear the revisers have over-done it. Perhaps if you sing the text in *Latin* and if you have choir/cantor and assembly this could be made effective though even then the thought of doing this every Sunday of the year (except in Lent) makes one blench. In private recitation or in recitation with a small group the continual iteration of Alleluia is bizarre. I think we should be justified in using our own discretion in the matter.[25]

NOTES

1. See Rembert G. Weakland 'L'homme d'aujourdhui et l'office devin' in *LMD* (95), 1968, pp. 66 ff, conveying the criticisms of young monks and clerics.
2. It is sometimes possible to detect the redaction processes. See, for example, the last two verses of psalm 50 which seem to be a post-exilic addition and something of a contradiction of verses 18–19.
3. Cf Deut. 6.4.

4. See G. Vann, *On Being Human* London, 1933, p. 46, n. 1. The whole passage he translates as follows: 'In the coming forth of creatures from their first principle there is a sort of circling back, inasmuch as all things return as to their end to that from which in the beginning as from a principle they sprang *(prodierunt)*': *Sentences, Dist. xiv, q.2, a.2.*
5. Rembert Weakland, *art. cit.* pp. 67–8.
6. The chief authority is Balthasar Fischer. See 'Le Christ dans les psaumes', *LMD*, 27 (1951) pp. 86–109. It is a summary of his doctoral thesis of 1946. Cf also a further study by François Vandenbroucke in *QLP*, 4 (1952), pp. 149–166, 5 (1952) pp. 201–213. One can also refer to J. Daniélou *The Bible and the Liturgy*, especially chapter 11, 'Psalm XXII' (London, 1960), and L. Bouyer, *Bible et Evangile* (Paris, 1951), chapter xii.
7. See *art. cit.* pp. 105–8.
8. *Art. cit.* p. 92.
9. *Art. cit.* p. 93: *'Psalmus vox totius Christi, capitis et corporis'.*
10. *PL*, t. 36.
11. See F. Vandenbroucke *QLP*, 5 (1952) pp. 207–211.
12. *GI* 113.
13. See Vandenbroucke *art et loc cit.* who gives long lists which however refer to the old missal and breviary.
14. The same identification is made, if I remember rightly, on an early catacomb painting.
15. Ecological problems so early?
16. I am dubious in any case about this term which seems to have been devised by Professor Fischer. 'Christology' is usually taken to mean the theology of Christ, principally in the incarnation. The alternative 'the Christian sense or interpretation of the psalms' is clumsy but, as it seems to me, more accurate.
17. See B. Fischer, *LMD, num. cit.* p. 88.
18. See B. Fischer, *loc. cit.* pp. 102–3. He records that St Thérèse of Lisieux did this with a phrase from psalm 118: Inclinavi cor meum ad justificationes tuas *proper retributionem* ('I bow my heart to your commands for reward' – the reward I shall get!). *She* said 'O Jesus mine, you know that it is not for reward that I serve you but uniquely because I love you and to save souls.'
19. *Comparative Liturgy*, (London, 1958), p. 34.
20. See F. Vandenbroucke, *art. cit.* p. 150 and n. 1 for the date of its insertion. Cf also P. Salmon, *EP*, p. 822.
21. P. Verbraken *Oraisons sur les 150 psaumes* (Paris, 1967). The author has used three collections, African, Roman and Spanish. P. Salmon, *EP*, p. 821, states that six series are known.
22. *GI* 112.
23. The *Psautier de la Bible de Jérusalem*, Paris, 1961, p. 256. The collects were written by J. Gelineau and D. Rimaud. The whole edition, which does not seem to be well known, is worth attention. It has longish 'titles', is pointed for singing (in French) and of course has the collects.
24. JBC, pp. 614–619 (R. Brown).
25. There is a similar difficulty in Eastertide. Frankly, there are too many Alleluias and it is difficult to see why they should have been added to a text like 'Into your hands I commend my spirit' of Compline. In the Latin office they often worked, though even there they sometimes split an antiphon in half. The revisers seem to have retained these Alleluias without giving much thought to the matter.

CHAPTER SIX

The Lectionaries

The existence of three lectionaries in an office raises questions and calls for a more extended comment than could be given in an earlier chapter.[1] What is the purpose of a biblical lectionary and need it be printed in the office book? Why should there be a patristic lectionary and why should there be yet another for saints' feasts? We will try to answer these questions in what follows.

As we have seen in an earlier chapter, when the cathedral office was the prayer of the church there was but one lesson in morning and evening prayer and it is improbable, to say the least, that there was a continuous course. But when stable communities were established and the night office came into existence it was obviously possible to use a fixed course of reading and this is what happened. St Benedict witnesses to the existence of such a course as also to the division of the biblical material into *lectiones*. From him too we know that there was a patristic lectionary. The third, consisting of the 'passions' of the martyrs and the 'legends' of the saints appears, it would seem, in the Gallican region in the seventh century.[2] The inclusion then of a *lectio continua* of the Bible as of the patristic and hagiographical lectionaries are another instance of monastic influence on the office.

When the lessons could be read out in choir from a single book there was no problem about their length and the community or its abbot, no doubt depending on tradition, could make the necessary selection. Difficulties begin when you try to cram a lectionary into a 'breviary'. The inevitable result is, as we know, abbreviation and the problem of the Bible lectionary has never been wholly solved. The revisers of the new office have made another attempt to do so and we shall have to examine their work in due course. But before we do so, it will, I think, be profitable to look at the purpose and pattern of the old Roman lectionaries which reveal a certain understanding of the scriptures as seen in the early tradition.

The Bible Lectionary
At least in the Roman tradition the order in which the books of the Bible were read during the year was a matter of greater concern than the details of the pericopes to be used.[3]

The course of readings to be found in *Ordo* XIV (Andrieu), which may

go back to the time of Gregory the Great, is as follows: from Quinquage-
sima Sunday (i.e. approximately fifty days before Easter) until the Saturday before Palm Sunday the Roman church read the first six books of the
Bible (Genesis to Joshuah);

in Holy Week the readings were evidently 'proper': selected extracts
from Isaiah and for the last three days the Lamentations of Jeremiah;

from Easter to Pentecost the readings were from the 'Catholic Epistles',
the Acts of the Apostles and the Apocalypse;

from then until 17 October the books of Samuel, Kings and Chronicles
were read;

then, until 1 December there were the Wisdom books, Judith, Esther,
Tobit and Maccabees;

from Advent to the Epiphany Isaiah, Jeremiah and Daniel were read;

Ezekiel, the 'minor' prophets and Job filled up the rest of the time until
13 February (presumably omitted when there was an early Easter).

One book only was omitted, Esdras, perhaps says Salmon, because of the
existing doubts about the canonicity of Third and Fourth Esdras. The
letters of St Paul were allocated either to the eucharist or to the end of
vigils or to the first three lessons but in any case the reading was not continuous.[4]

Another lectionary of the eighth century and in use in the Lateran (Ordo
XIIIA-Andrieu) slightly modifies the former and provides the basis for
the lectionary that existed in the office until the recent revision.[5] The
Pentateuch, Joshuah, Judges and perhaps Ruth were read from Septuagesima to Passion Sunday when the reading of Jeremiah began. After Easter
the readings were taken from 'the Acts of the Apostles, the seven canonical
epistles and the Apocalypse' and continued until the end of the octave of
Pentecost. From then until the first Sunday of August the books of Samuel,
Kings and Chronicles were read. To August were allocated the Wisdom
books, and to September Job, Tobit, Judith, Esther and Esdras. Maccabees I and II were read in October and in November Ezekiel, Daniel and
the minor prophets. Isaiah occupied the month of December and after
Christmas until Septuagesima the epistles of St Paul were read.

The differences between the two series are not very great and we may
assume that there were reasons for this pattern. The purpose of the Bible
lectionary was not of course the scientific study of the Bible nor yet simply
a complete knowledge of the whole text though at this time and for centuries it was regarded with great reverence. In the words of Pierre Salmon,[6]
'the aim was to teach the faithful the history of salvation, its preparation,
its types, its prophecies and its fulfilment in the life and work of Christ and
its continuation in the church'. It was no coincidence then that the readings
began at Septuagesima, then regarded as the beginning of the liturgical
year, with the book of Genesis which gives the story of creation which is to
be restored by the redeeming work of Christ. Here and in the books that
followed are all the great events that prepared for the coming of Christ, and

all the types, like Abraham, the 'redemption' from Egypt, the passage through the Red Sea and the making of the covenant in the desert, that were seen as foreshadowings of the redeeming work of Christ. The Christians of that time 'read' the events of the Old Testament in the light of the New (*novum testamentum in vetere latet; vetus testamentum in novo patet*) and accepted prophecy in all simplicity as prediction. As the monks heard the words '*Ecce virgo concipiet . . .*' read out in the flickering light of a candle they instinctively translated 'Behold the Virgin (Mary) shall conceive . . . .' We have ineluctably become more sophisticated though it is a question whether we are any nearer the truth.

To continue, the oldest part of the liturgical year, the *Pentecoste*, has a lectionary that is as old as St Augustine and perhaps older, basically the Acts of the Apostles and the Apocalypse. The reason is that, as an ancient collect for the Easter vigil (quoted in the Constitution on the Liturgy (5)) has it, from the side of Christ as he lay in the sleep of death on the cross came forth the wonderful sacrament of the church. The church in Acts is seen as carrying on the redeeming word and work of Christ and that is why it is read at this time. On the broadest view the Apocalypse is to be seen as a cosmic view of human history, under the ultimate control of God, but fraught with pain, persecution and suffering which the church must endure if she is to be faithful to the Faithful Witness and to be gathered to him as his Bride 'without spot or wrinkle'. To put the matter in another way, the Apocalypse is the history of the church as she makes her painful pilgrimage from the time of the resurrection to the consummation. The 'canonical' or 'Catholic' epistles, with their 'household codes' and strong moral emphasis, may be regarded as indicating the behaviour that is proper to members of the Risen Christ.

The readings from Samuel and Kings continue the history of salvation in which David, the type of the Messiah, plays a central role. After this the pattern becomes less clear until we come to November. The Wisdom literature, with which should be included Job, can be seen as a reflection on the great saving events (as indeed so much of it is), and as a recollection in tranquillity (in the hot summer months of southern Europe!) of the significance of those events. The readings for the rest of September are somewhat miscellaneous though Tobit, Judith and Esther can be understood as typical of the great heroes and heroines who in one way or another carried forward the purpose of God. With Maccabees in October we take up again the history of salvation. The last part of the liturgical year is concerned with the Day of the Lord and the consummation of all things in Christ. Evidently, the readings from Ezekiel, Daniel and the minor prophets are appropriate for this time. Isaiah in this scheme becomes understandably the exclusive prophet of the incarnation. It is less easy to account for the letters of St Paul after Christmas but I would hazard the guess that since in the Roman liturgy of the time, as also in the Sermons of St Leo for Christmas, the redemptive aspect of the incarnation is much emphasised,

St Paul who deals with both the incarnation and the redemption in all their depth and richness, can be seen as continuing the message of the Christmas season.

Whatever we may think of the procedure—and it is to be doubted whether it was ever formally thought out—this, as far as we can discern, was the understanding of the Bible that underlay the whole scheme. The modern and more critical assessment of the 'spiritual' or fulfilled sense of holy scripture has made us more cautious in our use of it but has not, I think, invalidated the older view. In many ways it has strengthened it.[7] With minor alterations, and unhappily drastic abbreviations, this lectionary survived the centuries and was to be found in the breviary of Pius V and indeed in the breviary that has only recently been superseded by the new office.

This pattern of the lectionary, then, indicated the main purpose of the readings. There was another which is summed up in the traditional phrase *lectio divina*. The primary intent of the readings was not to give a complete verbal knowledge of the whole Bible though this is in fact what the monks achieved. Even a superficial acquaintance with the literature that came from the monasteries reveals a quite astonishing knowledge of the Latin Bible. Its texts in all its parts became part of the mind of the monks. But this was a sort of by-product. The purpose of the readings was that the monks should be able to nourish their spiritual life on the word of the Bible. Like the devout Christian of St Augustine, they listened to God's word and ruminated on it afterwards. Formal meditation of the kind typical of the post-Tridentine church seems to have been unknown in the monastic centuries and indeed for long afterwards. The monks filled their minds with the word of holy scripture and during the night office by means of the responsories meditated on their meaning, a meditation that was continued during the day. Hence the need for silence and the continued reading of the Bible in the refectory. The fruits of this system—if such it can be called—are to be seen in what scholars have called the monastic theology that preceded scholasticism and of which there are a number of examples in the lectionary of the new office. Whether and how far the pastoral clergy, even when they had the texts, were able to profit from this kind of reading is another matter. The drastic abbreviation of the scripture lessons over the centuries certainly made them less attractive.

When we come to examine the lectionary the revisers have constructed we see that they have kept substantially the pattern of the old lectionary though with very considerable changes. Responding to the requirements of Vatican II (CL 92) that a better provision of Bible readings should be made in the revised office, an attempt has been made to include practically the whole Bible in the biennial course (short of the gospels of course which appear in the Mass lectionary). This at least was the intention of the revisers but for reasons which to the knowledge of the present writer have never been made explicit, they have in fact produced a one-year cycle which seems to be a modification of the two-year cycle. I cannot pretend that I have got the matter clear. All I can do is to summarise the Introduction 145–153 and then make some observations on the lectionary as it has already appeared.

1. For Advent we have Isaiah with the addition of the book of Ruth and certain passages from Micah. This is traditional enough though the addition of Ruth seems to be an innovation, wholly appropriate as it is in this place.

2. The period after Christmas which used to begin with Romans is now occupied with Colossians 'in which the incarnation of the Lord is considered in the context of the whole history of salvation' (148).
For the second cycle the Song of Songs, interpreted as the marriage between God and his people, is prescribed but does not (yet) appear in the office book.

3. For the period after Christmas the rest of Isaiah and Baruch (absent) are prescribed.

4. Lent (Thursday after Ash Wednesday) begins with Exodus which is read during the first three weeks; then come Leviticus and Numbers, which are followed by the Letter to the Hebrews until the end of Holy Week. What was *intended* is that Deuteronomy and Hebrews should be read in cycle I and Exodus, Leviticus and Numbers in cycle II. In the book as published Deuteronomy now comes in weeks 2 and 3 of the ordinary time of the year and so will normally precede Lent. It is noteworthy that there are no readings from the Old Testament in Holy Week. Yet the revisers intended that two of the Servant Songs, and passages from Lamentations should be read in Cycle I and extracts from Jeremiah in cycle II.

5. In Easter Week I Peter is read and thereafter the Apocalypse (weeks II to V). The three Johannine letters cover the rest of the period. (There are exceptions for Sunday II and of course for the Ascension.) Originally it was intended that I Peter, the Johannine letters and the Apocalypse should be read in cycle I and the Acts in cycle II. Since Acts is to be found substantially in the Mass-lectionary this change is not catastrophic.

6. It would be tedious to detail all the books that are read from the Monday after Trinity until Advent. Suffice it to say that the history of salvation is taken up on the Monday after Trinity with readings from I and II Samuel which are followed by those from Kings I and II. But all these readings are interspersed with readings from the Pauline epistles and indeed with extracts from the prophets. Thus while the traditional arrangement can still be discerned it is clear that here the revisers have innovated. It was intended that there should be a two-year cycle (152) when these books would have been better distributed and, I suspect, there would have been a more adequate representation of them. The epistles are read in full and almost always well divided. This cannot always be said of the Old Testament readings.

Finally, the Introduction states that 'the single year arrangement is abbreviated in such a way that every year passages are selected complementary to the two-year sequence of scripture readings at (weekday) Mass' (152). A detailed examination of this would be lengthy and cannot be done here. In any case, perhaps the details do not matter over-much. Sufficient of the traditional arrangement has been preserved to make it possible to use the lectionary as *lectio divina*. At the same time, I have found it profitable to read the lessons directly from the Bible. Then one discovers the context and the many gaps left by the lectionary can be filled in. If one uses the Jerusalem Bible with its invaluable notes, particularly necessary for the prophetic literature and the Apocalypse, the reading becomes more profitable still. It is I believe, an illusion to think that we can, like medieval or even seventeenth century Christians, read the *nudus textus* with spiritual profit. Modern Christians feel that if their *lectio* is to be really *divina*, they must come as close as possible to the original meaning of the text and then go on from there.

In the light of these last considerations and of the difficulty of including a biblical lectionary in a liturgical book, one is led to question the whole policy of providing such a lectionary. Surely the clergy can be expected to possess a Bible and to read it and nowadays vast numbers of the laity have and read a Bible if not always systematically. If the argument is that 'when you are travelling' (another instance of the *argumentum ex turismo?*) it is inconvenient to carry around a Bible with you, it would have been easy enough to include a sufficient selection of Bible readings in the volume to last two or there weeks. However it can be readily agreed that the new lectionary is infinitely superior to the old. Even as it exists it presents a very great part of the Bible and, as far as I can see, the whole of the New Testament. If the insertion of certain books or parts of books here and there is a little difficult to understand, as a whole the lectionary makes sense and is a useful instrument for the pastoral and spiritual life.

The Patristic Lectionary

The Introduction (163–165) gives three reasons for the inclusion of a patristic lectionary in the office:

1. It offers a meditation on the scripture readings.

2. It gives an authentic interpretation of the word of God.

3. The readings from this lectionary teach Christians the meaning of the feasts and seasons of the liturgical year.

About the last point there can be no doubt at all and if preacher or people are to do justice to the Mass-texts it is usually necessary to look at the patristic texts as they appear in the office. But it is a little difficult to know what weight to attach to the word 'authentic'. Most of the Fathers knew no Hebrew and the Latin Fathers from Augustine onwards knew little or no Greek. Apart from a few giants like Jerome, when he is not being Origenist, Chrysostom on St Paul, and Leo in his homilies where he remains very close to his texts, we cannot look to the Fathers for a *literal* interpretation.

Even in the new lectionary there is a certain amount of allegory like this passage of Gregory of Nyssa: 'In this creation the sun is pure life; *the stars are virtues; the air is candid behaviour*; the *sea* is *depth* and the riches of wisdom and knowledge . . . *the trees bearing fruit are the observance of the commandments*' (Monday, Week 5, Eastertide). It is elegant, as Gregory always is, it is charming and the whole passage is full of New Testament echoes but it remains allegory which we are not required to take *au pied de la lettre*. What 'authentic' evidently means is that broadly the Fathers transmit the continuing Catholic tradition and in this they are peculiarly effective, as the introduction says, in their interpretation of the greater seasons and feasts.

There are other values in the patristic lectionary. Didactically they keep before us the broad spectrum of Christian writing which we ignore to our own impoverishment. It is possible for our Catholicism to be geographically broad but chronologically shallow. And the Fathers at their best, like Augustine on St John, have a depth of penetration that takes us beyond any literalist interpretation. In this, as St Benedict saw, they assist the *lectio divina* of the scriptures. At another and less important level, they remind us of the history of the church, in the sense that in various ways they suggest the continuing life of devotion and aspiration towards God which is the real history of the church. In this context it would have been helpful to append to the names of the Fathers and other writers the date of their death. Who can lay his hand on his heart and say when Aphraates flourished?[8] Nearer home is Fulgentius of Ruspe. How many of us know that he lived in the late fifth century and is an echo, often a feeble echo, of Augustine?

We must then see the patristic lectionary principally as an aid to *lectio divina* and it is clear that especially in the 'ordinary time' of the year the patristic lesson is a commentary on the scripture reading. For the great feasts it takes up one or other aspect of the scripture reading or conveys the meaning of the feast as a whole. In this respect Leo the Great, Maximus of Turin (on the paschal mystery and its consequences), St Gregory of Nazianzen and St Augustine when he is concerned more with the feast than with the exegesis of a text, are particularly effective. St Gregory the Great too, a difficult writer to 'extract', scores a bull with his homily on the Good Shepherd (Sunday 4, Eastertide). For the Easter season the revisers apparently gave up hope of finding a suitable commentator for the Apocalypse. Possibly there is no suitable candidate. In the vast literature on the Apocalypse, which has attracted every kind of oddity in the church from the second century until now, it would seem that only Andrew of Caesarea (Greek, 5th or 6th century) or Primasius (Latin, African, 6th century) are likely to provide suitable material.[9]

The same rule has been applied to the other great seasons of the year: the writers expound the mystery or the meaning of the period. Thus in the last part of Advent we find Ambrose, Bede and Bernard commenting on the infancy gospel of Luke. Leo remains the chief commentator on Christmas and Epiphany. For Holy Week we find a variety of authors and for Good Friday Chrysostom on the blood and water that flowed from the side of Christ after the piercing of his side.[10]

During Easter week when I Peter is read, the patristic readings expound various aspects of the paschal mystery. For Monday there is Melito of Sardis (c. 190), perhaps the earliest and most interesting expositor of the paschal mystery. The readings from the last three days of the week are taken from the Mystagogical Catecheses traditionally attributed to Cyril of Jerusalem. More from the same source for this week would have been welcome especially as the piece from 'an unknown author' (sometimes thought to have been Hippolytus) of the second century does not in fact say very much.

When we leave the great seasons and feasts commentary becomes difficult. The amount of material is vast, writers from East and West, writing in Syriac, Greek and Latin, not to mention a few writing in modern languages, appear in the lectionary. In time they run from Clement of Rome to Vatican II and if the generous allocation of the sub-apostolic Fathers is much to be welcomed, the way they are broken up and used from time to time as commentary (for which they are not suitable) is not so satisfactory. Hippolytus in his scripture commentaries does not suffer extraction very well but Irenaeus, who has been very carefully selected, does. In fact he is the one early writer, much used in the lectionary, who stands out above most of the others. He has important things to say and he is allowed to say them. The translation seems to be excellent, no doubt benefitting from the *Sources Chrétiennes* edition.[11] Another notable feature of the lectionary is that the revisers have drawn generously on the Greek Fathers who were poorly represented in the old. Aphraates, Ephrem and Theodore of Mopsuestia represent the Syriac Fathers. The range of Latin writers has been considerably extended and among other things the revisers have been able to take advantage of the discoveries of scholars in, for example, the matter of the sermons of St Augustine. But what is new is that writers of the monastic centuries like Isaac of Stella, William of St Thierry, as well of course as St Bernard, have been used. St Thomas Aquinas, in all the simplicity of his homiletic or expository style, St Bonaventure, and lastly the *Imitation* of Christ, represent the later Middle Ages. There has, I think, been a subtle change. The *Imitation* and the extracts from post-Tridentine writers like St John of the Cross and St Teresa turn the reading into a *lectio spiritualis* of the more modern kind. Tastes and judgements will differ but these writers and some others do not seem to be quite in harmony with the tradition of the liturgy.

But this suggests another consideration. Good as the Fathers are, at least at their best, and helpful as the more modern spiritual writers may be judged to be, often their preoccupations are not ours. It is true that a modern note is sounded by extracts from the Council documents but the question suggests itself: have contemporary writers who share our concerns no place in the lectionary? The decision was made to exclude living or recently dead writers (e.g. Thomas Merton) and perhaps with a good deal of justice. Still, it is a pity that a writer like Newman who has been teaching the church for a hundred years and whose sermons, the Plain and Parochial, so often provide superb material for the great seasons and Sundays of the year, was not included.[12] In any case there would seem to be no reason why a community or an assembly should not read a supplementary lesson from a modern author after the one given in the office.

In so vast a collection of literature it would not be surprising if there were weaker pieces and that is in fact the case. Hippolytus to Noetus (I, p. 163) does not really say very much in the extract given. Origen on Abraham is more allegorical than typological though it is a moving piece and Hilary on the beard of Aaron is more than a little fanciful. Maximus the Confessor has this on the redeeming act of Christ: 'he offered his flesh as a bait to provoke the insatiable dragon to devour the flesh which he was greedily pursuing' which suggests the 'paying of a debt to Satan' kind of soteriology. Minor and obscure writers do not come off very well. John of Naples, whoever he was,[13] has an 'élévation' of the Bossuet kind of *Dominus illuminatio mea* and Gregory of Agrigentum starts off well with one or two down to earth observations and then goes on to the 'spiritual meaning' which is really allegorical. Zeno of Verona, who can write succinctly on the paschal mystery, is not seen at his best in taking Job as a type of Christ. Dorotheus, a Greek ascetic writer of the sixth century, is not really very satisfactory on the book of Job. Tastes and needs will differ but I do not find Isaac of Stella who provides a reading on the church as the mystical body (1, 95) or William of St Thierry or Guerric d'Igny, all monastic writers, very satisfactory. The lesson of the first is over-contrived and the other two seem to be working in a tradition that is already becoming exhausted. The oddest juxtaposition I have noted is on Deuteronomy 32, the death of Moses, on which the commentary provided is from the Constitution on the Church in the Modern World on the mystery of death. I doubt whether the *death* of Moses is the point of the story.

The translations in the Divine Office of this vast and varied collection of readings seem to be good. Those of Irenaeus, as I have said, are outstandingly good. Where I have been able to test translations of other texts I have found them accurate though at times the style is a little old-fashioned.[14] Wherever possible modern translations of good quality have been used. For the rest the translators remain anonymous. In one place the translator does not seem to be very familiar with the style of St Leo. In his well-known sermon on the Passion (8) Leo has 'ordo clarior *levitarum*, et dignitas amplior *seniorum* et sacratior est unctio *sacerdotum*'. What Leo meant was 'deacons', 'presbyters' and 'bishops' and that is how I believe the passage should be translated. Finally, examination of a number of texts shows that the English translations are sometimes better than the Latin translations in the *Liturgia Horarum* which the revisers often took simply from what was available in Migne.

Obviously much more could be said of this lectionary, both for and against it. We must see it a remarkable anthology of Christian literature which should prove to be of great value to those who use it. But again, whether or not it was wise to include it in the office book is another matter. The device of a supplementary volume would have met the case and the extracts could perhaps have been even longer.

The Hagiographical Lectionary

The principles on which this lectionary is constructed have been mentioned elsewhere [15] and there is no need to repeat them. But those same principles mean that a very wide spectrum of religious literature is to be found in this lectionary: writings of the Fathers, extracts from the writings (when they exist) of canonised saints and other passages from other writers which comment suitably on the life of the saint. The decision to use this method for the saints' feasts has relieved the office of a whole mass of fiction, much of which had become the target of clerical mockery: 'to lie like a second nocturn' was a hoary clerical joke. Even the most respectable legends, like those for the offices of St Cecily and St Clement have gone and who can regret the disappearance of the wholly fictitious lesson on St Alexius? Those on the Trinitarian saints were in the same category. If a little colour has gone from the office, let us remember that it was meretricious. The Introduction insists on 'historical truth' for the lessons of the saints and in doing so is merely repeating what has been said since the sixteenth century. Whether or not these legends had any religious value may perhaps be a matter of discussion.[16] But if there is regret that some of these texts have gone, the loss is amply compensated for by the new lessons. St Gregory Nazianzen on Basil and his friendship with him is worth more than all the second-hand disquisitions from someone who never knew him. It is obviously right that we should have Athanasius on St Antony, the desert father, and who is not moved by reading Cyprian on the martyrdom of Pope Fabian? In another genre St Ambrose on St Agnes, even if all his facts are not correct, has got the spirit of the saint admirably. The contemporary account of the Japanese martyrs, St Paul Miki and his companions, has an immediacy that no other kind of writing can give. Leaping back fourteen centuries we rejoice to read an extract from the contemporary 'passion' of St Perpetua and St Felicity. This is sufficient to show that almost all these readings are apt and can be read with profit and pleasure.

But not all saints are literary geniuses nor necessarily those who write about them. You may not feel moved by reading St Angela Merici's exhortation to her nuns and the literary style of St Brigit of Sweden may be too emotional for you but a great number of these readings occur on *optional memoriae* so one is under no obligation to read them at all. It may be a shock, but surely a salutary shock, to find St Leo with a sermon on the incarnation allocated to the *memoria* of Our Lady of Mount Carmel when we remember what was there before. A reading from the *Rule* of St Benedict is preferable to even the Dialogues with all their charmingly naivety. On the other hand one regrets the absence of St Ambrose's splendid piece of rhetoric on the martyrdom of St John Baptist. It is replaced with something much tamer. Since we must end somewhere, let us rejoice in the inclusion of Thomas More's letter to his daughter Meg for the feast of St John Fisher and St Thomas More.[17]

The biographical notes before the lesson are brief, usually succint, and help to situate the saint in the history of the church.

NOTES

1. See p. 68.
2. Salmon, *EP*, pp. 826–828. Its inclusion in the Roman office is attributed to Pope Adrian I (died 795).
3. Salmon, *EP*, p. 826. For details of the Roman lectionaries described below see his *L'Office Divin* (Paris, 1959) chapter IV.
4. Salmon, *OD*, p. 137.
5. See Salmon, *OD*, pp. 137–8.
6. *Op. cit.* p. 137.
7. Cf R. Brown, *op. cit. supra*, pp. 611–619.
8. The answer is apparently *post* 345. He was the first of the Syriac Fathers (see J. Tixeront, *Précis de Patrologie*, 1927), pp. 2854–5 and ODCC s.v., p. 68. Between 1927 and 1974 (the latest edition of ODCC) it would seem that nothing further has been learned of his date.
9. See E. B. Allo, *Saint Jean, L'Apocalypse* (Paris, 1933), pp. ccxlvi, ccxlviii.
10. Good as this is one would have preferred the great sermon of Leo (*De Pass.* 8) which gives the whole mystery of the cross. It used to appear for this day in the Dominican office and is of course to be found elsewhere (Lent 5 Tuesday).
11. *Sources chrétiennes*, nos. 34, 100, 152, 153. Irenaeus wrote in Greek but much of his work survives only in a Latin translation which is so literal that unless you are able to translate it back into Greek is often obscure. And few of us can be expected to do that.
12. There were one or two extracts – in French – in the draft lectionary. Local conferences of bishops may compile supplementary lectionaries. Cf GI 162. Such supplementary lectionaries have already appeared, notably that drawn up by the monks of Orval and the lectionary of the English Benedictines (obtainable from Stanbrook Abbey, Worcestershire). An example of an extensive anthology of mostly modern writers for the Anglican Office is C. R. Campling's *The Fourth Lesson* (London, 1973, 1974), two volumes.
13. He is unknown to ODCC.
14. I have wondered whether the translations in the *Ante- and Post-Nicene Fathers*, now over seventy years old, have been used.
15. pp. 69–70.
16. See *Notitiae*, 103, Vol. II, num. 3, 1975, pp. 83–7.
17. The former has at least one lesson elsewhere.

CHAPTER SEVEN

The Hymnary

Of all the parts of the office this is the one I find it most difficult to write about. In the *Liturgia Horarum* there is a vast collection of hymns most of which seem to come from obscure medieval sources. In the *Divine Office* there is yet another collection which coincides with the former only on the greater feasts. To do justice to all this material one would have to be both a prosodist and a seasoned literary critic. The present writer is neither but as it is admitted that hymns need not always be good poetry, perhaps he may be allowed a few observations.

The Introduction (173) states that hymns have had their place in the office from early times, that their lyrical character makes them specially suited to the praise of God and that they are a popular element in the celebration of the office. There is of course a high degree of truth in those statements on the assumption that choral celebration of the office is a regular feature of the church's life. But immediately we are brought up against two problems:

1. the nature of the hymn and
2. the quantity of hymns that even a community can be expected to sing in the course of a day.

1. Although the matter is not beyond dispute, hymns seem to demand that by their nature they should be *sung*. In private recitation, which is the lot of most of the users of the office, this is obviously impossible. Can they profitably be *said*? There are those who hold that they can but at once we are brought up against the literary quality of the hymn. Everyone knows that many well-loved hymns are of poor literary quality and if you read them or say them their poverty stands out immediately so that they become a barrier and not an aid to prayer. Everyone knows too that a good melody can redeem a poor hymn and that in the last resort is why they are popular. There does not seem to be any solution along these lines.

2. If a community, especially one that is not particularly skilled in singing, is going to celebrate the office chorally, five hymns a day in addition to the psalms and canticles like the *Benedictus* and the *Magnificat*, are going to tax their powers. If the material is not particularly distinguished they will perhaps think that the effort is not worth while.

For there is yet a third difficulty. The number of really great hymns in the western church from the time of St Ambrose until today is not very great. By great hymns one means those that express an insight into a feast or season in memorable language. These because of their depth of meaning and language can be repeated year after year though hymns like *Pange, lingua gloriosi, Vexilla regis* more easily bear repetition in Latin, no doubt because in their original language they are great verse. We are faced with the problem of the shortage of really good hymns and the conclusion that was forced on me after using the office in Latin for some time was that the collection in *Liturgia Horarum* was not a very distinguished one. The Introduction (178) states that local conferences of bishops may adapt the Latin hymns 'to the nature of their language' and introduce new ones *provided* they are suited to the spirit of the hour, the season or the feast. What the editors of the *Divine Office* have done is to draw on the abundant and varied hymnology of the English tradition which to a great extent derives from the Anglican and Free Churches. To hymns from these sources they have added others, usually the translations of Caswell, Knox and a few others. The nuns of Stanbrook Abbey have made some attractive, original contributions.

The construction of the hymnary was in itself a major undertaking. A vast corpus of material had to be examined and hymns appropriate to the hour, day, season and feast had to be selected. Since a great number of these hymns were not written with the prayer of the Divine Office in view, the difficulty of selection was all the greater. If one is not always enchanted with the results it is probably because the compilers had set themselves an impossible task. The dangers of subjective criticism are considerable in this matter and this must be kept in mind in what follows.

Let us look at the provision made for Advent. We find E. Caswell's translation of *En clara vox* though drastically shortened to three verses (a quite constant practice of the compilers). This is followed by what seems to be a translation of *Conditor alme siderum* (though we are not told it is), a quite attractive piece but again only three verses. Charles Coffin's [1] hymn 'The co-eternal Son' stands out in the translation of R. Campbell as a piece of poetry. 'O Come, O Come, Emmanuel' is given in two parts. That is all and not I think sufficient for a season of four weeks.[2] One would have thought that *Verbum supernum* merited inclusion.

The provision for Christmas is more generous. There is the attractive fifteenth century hymn/poem 'A noble flow'r of Juda', *A solis ortus cardine,* attributed to Sedulius, in the translation of R. A. Knox, and the *Corde natus ex parentis* of Prudentius, translated by J. Mason Neale. Three more are given for Christmastide and two for the time after the feast of Epiphany.

For Lent there are five hymns of which 'God of thy pity . . .' and 'Jesus, think of me', by that curious fourth century bishop, Synesius, prove to be the most enduring. Among the four given for Holy Week we find of course *Vexilla regis* and 'O sacred head . . .' in the translation of R. A. Knox which seems better than the others one comes across. Eastertide is divided into two parts and if sufficient is given for the first part, a good deal of it is rather conventional. However if a community can manage it, there is nothing to stop them *singing* (it cannot be said!) 'This joyful Eastertide'³ since it is to be found in an authorised hymn-book. For the second half there is 'Come down, O love divine' and the translation of a twelfth century text by Robert Bridges 'Love of the Father, love of the Son' which one is glad to see there.

For feasts of Our Lady there are six hymns which one rejoices to see include Knox's translation of Dante's *Vergine madre, figlia del tuo figlio* (he has undoubtedly been underestimated as a translator of verse) which gives one something to think about, and a Stanbrook hymn 'Mary, crowned with living light' which stands out for its freshness. The great Anglican hymn 'The Church's one foundation' comes appropriately for the Dedication of a church.

These are but samples, but I think some of the best of what is to be found in the appendix. Others for use during the year are given in the psalter and it is here that we run into trouble. Some few are good (e.g. 'Be thou my vision') but most of them make no particular impact and some of them are extraordinarily brief. In these hymns particularly, but also in many of the others, we are confronted with another, a literary difficulty. For the most part the diction of these hymns is antiquated and their verse-forms conventional. The religious language of the nineteenth century is no longer ours and the devotional adjectives in particular have become hopelessly deflated. Nor do we any longer take to rhyming couplets as the Augustans or even the Victorians did. All these unhappy features come together in one verse of what was once a great hymn and which can still be *sung* with pleasure: 'Come Down, O love Divine.' Its second verse runs:

'Let holy charity
mine outward vesture *be*
And lowliness become mine inner clothing.
True lowliness of *heart*,
which takes the humbler *part*
and *o'er its own shortcomings weeps with loathing*'.

There is the relentless rhyming and the sort of language (perhaps dictated by the verse form) in the last line, 'weeps' and 'loathing', which we can no longer tolerate. Yet I do not think that the remedy is to modernise the diction of such hymns, as was attempted in *The Catholic Hymnal*, by changing the 'thous' and the 'thees' with their verbal cognates to 'you' and 'yours'. They are of their epoch, heavily conditioned by the time when they were written. If Latin hymns whether sung or said in Latin are more acceptable and so repeatable it is perhaps because they have a certain timelessness, even if they were written over a period of fifteen hundred years. Perhaps modern translations of these hymns should be attempted though the thing that should be aimed at is the thought underlying the verse and not simply the words themselves. But what is needed for both the office and for the rest of our liturgy is *new* hymns, new in idiom, new in metrical forms, hymns that are newly conceived and coming from new insights in the whole Christian mystery. One of the odder features of Roman Catholic hymn-writing since Faber set his hand to the work, is that we have never produced a great hymn on the church. 'Who is she that stands triumphant' is intolerably aggressive and 'Father of our fathers' is not a hymn about the church at all. It simply reflects the sentiments of the minority of England and Ireland who were emerging from the oppression of three centuries. But, alas, no more than poems do great hymns get written to order and all we can hope for is that since we have begun to use vernacular hymns in our worship we shall also gradually learn what is required.

Perhaps the poems that are included in the appendix are foreshadowings of what might come. Both Hopkins and Eliot experimented with metre and indeed with diction and although they too are now poets of an age that is ending, their example is still important. The selection of poems, which seems to have been influenced by the one to be found in *A Christian's Prayer Book*,[4] is not without significance. They are the choice of an age that had discovered the seventeenth century 'metaphysicals' and that had taken to its heart their modern equivalents, Hopkins and Eliot. We note that John Donne, Henry Vaughan (two pieces), George Herbert and Robert Herrick (the last two are not 'metaphysicals' at all) have the lion's share of the older poets and Hopkins, Muir and Eliot of the new.

Their inclusion in a book of the Divine Office is interesting. Their very presence suggests that we should use them rather as meditations than as texts simply to be recited. Poems of some religious depth obviously lend themselves to such treatment which may well give us insights into the Christian mystery. But I fear that those who are not familiar with these poets will not find them acceptable and so will not be inclined to use them. Nor are there enough of them to take one through the great seasons of the year. But that again is to raise the question of *bulk*. It is just not possible to include everything that is desirable. And when all is said and done, need there have been a hymnary included in the book? If one is saying the office at home or in church, hymnals are (presumably) available. If one is away, should one be obliged to recite snippets of undistinguished verse?

In the future however things may be different. On the assumption that the prayer of the church will evolve and will be allowed to evolve,[5] the meditative quality of poems could be incorporated in the office as *responsories*. These are intended to 'turn the reading to prayer and contemplation' (GI 106) and such responsories, both long and shorter, are provided throughout the office. For the most part they consist of short passages of scripture which echo the previous reading. But while the lapidary style of Latin lent itself to responsories, at their best pregnant in meaning and at times of great beauty, that does not seem to be the case with responsories in English. Traditionally these texts were not necessarily passages of scripture or if they were, were handled very freely. The Byzantine liturgy has a whole corpus of texts in various forms which are really poetic compositions, some of which were taken over by the old Roman liturgy: thus the *Mirabile mysterium* of Lauds (January 1st), the famous *Crucem tuam adoramus*, still used as a responsory in the Good Friday liturgy, and most famous of all the *Adorna, thalamum tuum*, a responsory in fact which remains in the office (unhappily shortened) of the Presentation of the Lord.[6] Texts such as these sensitively handled would have an acceptable place in the office. But there is no reason why we should stop there. Modern poets will respond to English texts and if they were given encouragement, that is, to be brutally practical, some promise that their work would be used in the liturgy, they could produce responsories that would enrich our office. They could even be in hymn-form provided it was not too rigid and the versicle for repetition by the assembly could be a refrain. Such a procedure would, I believe, bring relief to an office that is often prosy and might do something to re-create the whole tradition of hymn-making and hymn-singing.[7]

NOTES

1. Of Jansenist sympathies. His dates are 1676–1749.
2. Other hymns are given in the psalter but they are not seasonal.
3. *Praise the Lord*, 2nd ed. no. 205.
4. Ed. P. Coughlan, R. C. D. Jasper, Teresa Rodriguez (1972).
5. See the interesting remarks in GI 273.
6. For a list of Greek texts taken into the Roman rite see H. W. Codrington *The Liturgy of St Peter* (LQF, Münster, 1936), p. 3. It does not appear in the rite of the procession of the day but of course may be sung (cf *alii cantus apti*).
7. There are a few non-scriptural responsories in the new office which would lend themselves to the treatment suggested above.

CHAPTER EIGHT

The Intercessions

Since the intercessory prayers that have been added to the office play so important a part in it something needs to be said about the nature of intercession as well as about the texts that have been provided.

In earlier chapters of this book (I and V) we have discussed, all too summarily perhaps, some of the problems connected with prayer. In the vast debate on this subject that has been going on for some years one notes that the prayer of intercession is the one that is most questioned. There are several problematic aspects of the matter. What are we doing, what do we think we are doing, when we pray 'for fine weather'? What did we mean when, as we used to in the Litany of Saints, we asked to be delivered from earthquakes and other natural disasters? What do we think happens when we pray for other people? The petitions for innumerable 'temporal favours' like asking for a fine day for a cricket match or for 'success in exams' did much to trivialise the whole business. Much of this seems to have gone (though one wonders whether the young pray *for* anything at all), and that is gain but the problems remain and the answers are not easy to come by.

One answer, which is also a criticism, is that instead of praying for the relief of famine, say, we should get out and do something about it. If you are suffering from toothache, you do not make a novena. You go to the dentist. If someone is in distress, you go and help him in whatever way you can. Indeed, it is said that prayer on the whole is waste of time and that we should get on with the business of living even if by that is meant *Christian* living. We find God in others, we serve Christ in our neighbour and that when all is said and done is prayer. Critics of this sort say that Christians have spent too much time praying about matters they would have been much better occupied in putting right. There is a certain truth in these charges. At one time there was a mystique of suffering among Catholics which was all-but fatalistic. Suffering was 'good' for you so you did not take the natural remedies or you hesitated to do so. In a way it was Hobson's choice in earlier centuries. You might be suffering but the doctors would make you suffer more and, as like as not, kill you. Even a king like Louis XIV suffered appalling tortures at the hands of his doctors, tortures he endured with an extraordinary stoicism. Natural disasters, which included famine, were 'acts of God', of an angry God, who sent these things to punish sinful mankind. If there had been a Copernican revolution in astronomy, it took a very long time to filter down to theology and the life of prayer. God, in a way, was all too immediate. He manipulated the universe directly and everything, both good and bad, was attributed, again directly, to him.

In other words, he was, from the viewpoint of prayer, the God-of-the-gaps. When man had come to the end of what he thought possible, he invoked God to fill in the gaps. This kind of theology has been slow to disappear though its demise could be forecast with the social encyclicals of Leo XIII [1] which showed that man was not the (intended) victim of economic forces, that he has the right to shape his own destiny and that inherent in him is the power to change the conditions of human society. But it was not until Vatican II with its Constitution on the Church in the Modern World that Catholics were given a new vision of reality. This world is not an expendable extra which we should be glad to get rid of as soon as possible. It has a validity of its own, it is part of the saving purpose of God with whom man is a collaborator, a co-worker. It is his vocation to bring this world, as far as lies within his powers, to perfection and in working for the betterment of human society, in investigating the deep secrets of nature and in using them for the good of mankind, he is working out the purpose of God. All the efforts of man are to be directed towards the good life, towards the enhancement of the dignity and freedom of his fellow-men. He has a certain autonomy and is not the cat's-paw of a manipulative God. All this at the purely socio-economic level. At its deepest the document sees a certain co-inherence of the saving work of Christ and the 'tragedy' of the world. *Jesus sera en agonie jusqu'à la fin du monde*; or if you prefer St Paul, 'the whole world is groaning until it achieves its purpose and is shot through with hope that that purpose will be achieved' (Romans 8: 19, 20). In striving and suffering for that achievement man, whether he knows it or not, is sharing in the redeeming work of Christ that lies at the heart of every human endeavour so long as it is not self-orientated, so long as it is 'for others'. The natural and the supernatural are not two self-contained departments—there is but one world and Christ is present to the whole of it. If we need to get rid of the pre-Copernican universe, we need also to get rid of the two-tier system which would have us think that the natural goes one way and the supernatural goes another, as if in the intention of God, they had different ends.

At first sight this view of things does not seem to help in the matter of prayer. It seems to eliminate the need or even the possibility of praying for a whole range of things that used to be regarded as the legitimate objects of prayer. Is there any sense at all in praying for fine weather? What do we expect God to do? What I think it has done is to kill the notion that God is a means and not an end. The response to the manipulative God seems to have been an effort on the part of man to manipulate God—which is magic. If notions like that have gone, so much the better. Again, with the sense that man is a co-worker with God who has entrusted to him the perfecting of this world, he realises more clearly that in the face of the insufficiencies and evils of this world it is his task, his vocation, to remedy them. He may very well pray for the strength to perform his task, for purity of intention that he may work for others and not for himself, but that is rather different from praying for an intervention of God into the normal course of affairs. Although not all the problems connected with the prayer of petition have been solved, it is unwise to talk about a 'crisis' in the matter. What has been happening is that Christians have been absorbing new insights on prayer which have come from a renewed reflection on God and also those that have come from the new scientific way of looking at the world. In the process we have become more *adult* in our way of looking at God.

How then are we to think of prayer and in particular, the prayer of petition? We can and must eliminate from the discussion any notion of 'moving God' or trying 'to change his mind', notions that seem unhappily to remain current. We must accept that we are confronted with a world that has its own laws which are inherent in the nature of things and it is not for us to seek to 'bend' them. At the same time we are aware that we and all creation are dependent on God which in terms of language means that we are petitioners. Perhaps the basic notion of prayer is that it is a *cry*; we express our need as the infant does for its mother's milk. But this cry is but the symbol of a desire, it is a cry for *love*, a cry for the *person* who loves.[2] Prayer is in fact the expression of an inter-personal relationship: the cry is the desire for love and the response, or the gift, is the expression of a reciprocated love. That is, in her response the mother too is asking the child, the petitioner, for something, namely that the child will accept her gift. But as long as a request, even for love, is thought of in terms of satisfaction, there will always be an ambiguity, for even a mutual desire for satisfaction has an element of selfishness in it: 'it is always possible to maintain that "The Other is only granting me this so that I may duly give him satisfaction".' The problem can only be solved by stripping the request of the desire for satisfaction of need and seeing it as 'the upsurge of pure desire which is a longing for nothing else but the pure desire of the Other, or rather identification with that very desire.'

It is obvious, that this pure and unconditioned desire or identification of wills is something that exists rarely if at all among human beings, but it is a theory that fits in extraordinarily well with the teaching of the gospel and Christian tradition. The whole of the first part of the Lord's prayer, made explicit in the Matthean version, is a petition that God's will may be done. It is an effort on the part of the one praying to identify his will with God's though he does not, or only rarely, know what that will *for* him is, much less how it will be accomplished. It is also possible to see how the petitions for more particular needs fall into place in the second half of the prayer. At an even deeper level, prayer is to be seen as the response in the Spirit to the Other whom I am addressing. Or, as L. Beirnaert puts it:

'The Other to whom my words are addressed is God himself speaking and petitioning within us with inexpressible moans and cries' (Romans 8:26, 27). This too is surely the meaning of those many statements in St John's gospel that we must pray 'in the name of Christ', utterly united with him, identifying our will with his.

This too is, I believe, the teaching of St Augustine (to which I have referred in chapter 1) that prayer is an expression of desire for God, for *all* he is and wants of us. It seems also to be the final thought of St Thomas Aquinas as expressed in the *Compendium Theologiae* (II, 2). It will be as well to give the whole passage:

> The petition we address to man has not the same grounds of necessity as the one we address to God.
> When directed to a man, the petition serves to inform him of the applicant's desire or need, then *to sway the heart* of the one solicited until it yields. For prayer addressed to God, the same does not hold true. He knows our ills and our desires. And *there is no question of modifying the divine will* by means of words so that God may grant what was previously against his will. If petitionary prayer is necessary to man, the reason is that *it exercises an influence on the one who resorts to it.* When he considers his weakness, his *heart ardently desires the goal which alone matters* to the one who prays. He thereby *renders himself capable of attaining it.*[4]

This is a noble teaching on prayer and even if it does not answer all the modern objections to prayer, it states some essential principles. No question for Aquinas of 'moving' or 'changing' the divine will, no question of swaying God's heart. Secondly, he sees prayer as affecting *man*. It may shock some to hear that *man* is the object of prayer, but it is he who has to be changed if he is to be capable of attaining the goal, namely God. Thirdly, in terms that remind one of Augustine, Aquinas sees man as desiring the goal, what Augustine called the beatitude or blessedness that is to be found in God and that is God.[5] And given St Augustine's teaching in his commentary on St John's gospel on 'praying in the name', it would not be going beyond the evidence to say that for him the desire of the petitioner involves identification of his will with God's.

There is another view of prayer which throws into relief an important aspect of it though in the end the solution it offers comes close to the one set out above.[6] Prayer is the response of faith to the message, the call, the address of God, in the last resort the response to *God*, to a Person, who has revealed himself in words, the word of holy scripture. Prayer then is an expression of faith: 'faith itself is prayer, the basic form of prayer.'[7] But since we have faith in a Person, it means rather 'I believe in you' than 'I believe in it', that is teachings or doctrine.[8] But since faith means a total commitment to the Other, prayer will be an expression of that commitment.

Prayer is also spoken of as a 'conversation' or a 'dialogue' but it is important to remember that that dialogue is *initiated* by God and that our part of
it consists of *listening*, in silence. We are not to look for 'a verifiable
answer' from God. Then out of that silence we respond to God in faith and
can only grasp the import of the message by faith. But this response can take
various forms and use a variety of expressions: 'If prayer is conceived of
as "verbal faith" whose basic form is "I believe in you", then every prayer
—regardless of the words or form it chooses—must continually repeat this
phrase in endless variations, or else it is nothing more than the "empty
phrases" of the Gentiles which Jesus criticised so sharply (Mt, 6:7 ff).'
This emphasis on faith in prayer is very valuable and does more than anything else to raise it from a sub-Christian level. In language with which we
may be more familiar, it means that all prayer, since it is a response to God
in his self-revelation, is prompted by the Holy Spirit, who alone inspires
our believing. Thus we come back to Romans 8:26, 27.

But if this view is valuable it seems to need further development. Faith
seems to be the cannibal virtue; the New Testament speaks also of hope
and love. We respond 'in faith' but we must also respond *with* hope, i.e.
trust, a particularly important matter when we are dealing with the prayer
of petition, and also *with love*, for it is only then that we begin to identify
our will with that of God. We can and do also respond with joy and praise
and thanksgiving and that is presumably what is meant by 'endless
variations'. Perhaps it would be best to say that we respond to God with all
that we have and are, giving ourselves to him who gives himself to us.

Two other matters must be briefly dealt with. If it is asked why we
need to express our faith/desire in words, the answer is that God has
approached us to reveal himself in words and that language is of the very
stuff of human nature. If faith were never expressed in words it would
become unreal. Words are not mere counters of information, they are what
are called 'performative'. They bring about effects, they modify attitudes
and to pray in faith is to increase faith and in prayers of petition to increase our concern for others.[9] Faith and the prayer that springs from it
would be less than a human activity if it were never expressed in words.
However odd, then, some of the words used in prayer and worship may
seem, they are all expressions of man who is responding to God in faith.

Then there is the question of life and prayer. If prayer normally expresses itself in words, must it always do so? It is a question that did not
escape the notice of St Augustine: since prayer is desire, the desire for
God, the Christian can and does continue to 'desire' God, to have his will
directed towards union with God, *all the time*. This, for Augustine, is what
the saying 'pray without ceasing' means. This desire for God, then, is to
be found in all that we have to do, in all our daily tasks. But since our
'desire can grow cold', we need to withdraw from our work from time to
time to renew our desire, to reflect on the life of blessedness (*vita beata*)
towards which by desire and will and work we are tending.[10] The moderns

do not seem to have gone much beyond this: 'By this (continual and in-explicit prayer) we mean that a Christian to a certain extent sees his entire work . . . as an indirect form of prayer without words . . . for . . . if a person accepts his life and work in faith, then everything he does and experiences will be pervaded by faith'.[11] Put like that the statement seems to make things too easy. We need to stand back from our work from time to time, we need to try and see it under the eye of God and, as Augustine suggests, we need to renew our desire (or faith) and this we do by prayer. Without that kind of prayer we may very well live in the illusion that our life and work are 'pervaded by faith' or, if you like permeated with love, and unless we *offer* our life and work to God—for all that the offering will be prompted by 'faith'—it is all too likely to be directed towards self or to the achievement of purely materialistic purposes.

From all this we may deduce the following:

1. Prayer is the response of faith to God who has revealed himself and since God takes the initiative and our response is prompted by the Holy Spirit, prayer by its nature exists in the order of grace. It is the expression of the inter-personal relationship between God and ourselves.

2. But the response of faith can take many forms, praise, thanksgiving but also petition where adherence to God in hope and trust is peculiarly important.

3. But if the inter-personal relationship is to be one worthy of the name it is above all a response of love through which we are able, though no doubt with great and continued effort, to identify our wills with God's.

4. In prayer, including the prayer of petition and whatever we may ask for, we are seeking God's will and not our own.

5. In praying for 'the development of the peoples', for the progress of a truly human world order, we are seeking to co-operate with God, for this world is not an historical accident but is part of the saving purpose of God. There is no question of our manipulating God for purely human ends.

6. When we pray and especially when we make petitions, our prayer has an effect on *ourselves*, disposing us to attain the goal of all things, God. It will open us out to God, no doubt enlighten our minds so that we may see something of what God intends, that is, his will. With St Augustine we may say that such prayer is necessary if our desire to identify our wills with his is to be maintained.

7. When we pray for others we are asking that they may be made more capable of seeking union with God, opening their hearts to him so that they may 'desire the goal which alone matters'. Our prayer cannot bend their wills (as some seem to think) nor is it some strange 'influence' playing upon them (as others have thought) and when 'we commit others to God' we are asking that by his grace they may open themselves to him to do his will.

Against this background we can, I think, see that there is an adequate justification for the prayer of petition. Understood in this way it is not unworthy of God, it does not turn him into a benevolent dictator and it respects, without exaggerating, his transcendence. It removes prayer from the sphere of magic and it remains profoundly Christian. Perhaps not all will be satisfied with this justification but that would not be surprising. God is a mystery, the radical mystery, we know him only 'in part', dimly as in a mirror, and prayer is a mystery for it is the expression of our relationship with God. Of its effects, if we think of those as *results*, we know nothing and that is one reason why 'prayer-in-faith' and 'prayer-as-the-response-of-faith' is so supremely important. If a St John of the Cross, who had a sense of the immediacy and presence of God that is given to few, could say that in the dark night of the soul he could only cling to God in the darkness of faith, we should not be surprised if prayer is a matter of faith for us.

By what seems to be a kind of instinct Christians have felt the need for the prayer of petition throughout the centuries. Perhaps this 'instinct' is evidence of a relationship with God that is not wholly definable. It is none the less deeply rooted in the heart of man and whatever may be the imperfections of the image of God to whom he has prayed, his prayer is witness in itself of the reality of God. But if it can be described as an instinct, it has been deepened and immeasurably enriched by the revelation of the New Testament. The importance of the prayer of petition and the commands to pray are so patent in the pages of the New Testament that there is no need even to summarise them here. A single phrase of the First Letter of St John (I John 5 : 14) expresses all that is of the essence of the prayer of petition: 'We are confident that if we ask him for anything, and *it is in accordance with his will*, he will hear us.'

There is also the unbroken witness of the church from the Letter of Clement to the Corinthians through the innumerable statements of Christian writers, early and late, to the liturgies of every kind which have always included prayers of petition. In our own time they have been restored to our liturgy, first in the Mass with the inclusion of the Prayers of the Faithful, which, *pace* those who write to the newspapers, have been very acceptable to the generality of the people, and now to the Divine Office in the form of Intercessions in morning and evening prayer. The amount of material of this kind is very great and any adequate commentary on it would run to many pages. All we can do here is to single out one or two dominant features and comment upon a certain number of details.

First, there is the matter of the term: 'Intercessions'. In the Latin they are called simply '*preces*' with the intention presumably of suggesting that they are the continuation of the curious amalgam going by that name in the old office. The editors of the English *Divine Office* felt that 'prayers' was insufficiently explicit. There are other prayers in the office, there is the 'Concluding Prayer' that comes at the end of each hour. It seemed that the '*preces*' should be distinguished from all others. Then if you look into the prayers you find that they are almost wholly prayers *for* particular purposes and people. It is true that the prayers provided for the morning office are often expressions of praise, thanksgiving and dedication. But there are others that can be rightly called intercessory. Those for the evening office are almost wholly so.

A second feature of these prayers throws light on what is meant by 'intercession'. One notes with satisfaction that again and again in the introduction to the prayers the mediatorial role of Christ is prominent. The sense indicated is that the Christian, not merely as an individual but as a member of the great community of the church, is making intercession in and through Christ for the needs of mankind. All petitions are made 'in his name' and all petitions are enfolded in the unceasing prayer of Christ who is ever-living to make intercession for us. Some of the prayers are addressed to Christ himself (and in this they are different from the Prayer of the Faithful in the Mass) but he is constantly seen in relation to his Father. In a broad and general way I would say that these prayers are in the deepest sense of the New Testament *Christian* prayers where the presence of Christ is always apparent. This, I think, is one reason why they have been so warmly welcomed by those who use them.

An inspection of whole series of these prayers reveals a third feature. Although they cover almost every conceivable human need, they ask for things that are evidently in accordance with the will of God. If we are invited to pray for the betterment of the world, we do so in terms that underline our co-operation with God. If the subject of the prayer is the feeding of the hungry we ask that *men* may do what is required of them, that is, in the language of St Thomas, that they may be made capable of attaining the goal, in this case the love of others which is an integral part of loving God. If we pray for a good harvest we are asking that men will co-operate with the forces of nature to the best of their ability. There are some direct petitions for the 'healing' of the sick but they are in a distinct minority; more often they ask for God's comfort and support of the sick. Again and again the prayers ask that God may be *with* people in this or that situation or need. Equally often the prayers turn our attention and concern to others and are constant reminders of the sense of service we should have for them. A typical example is this: 'May our lives today be filled with your compassion; give us the spirit of forgiveness and a generous heart.' In this they are doing what liturgical prayer is among other things meant to do, namely they help us to realise that we are members of the community of the church and also of the human community that surrounds it. In these intercessions we pray *for* the church but often enough they show us that we are praying *as* the church: 'In the name of the church we pray . . . Be mindful of your church; keep her free from evil and make her perfect in your love' which echoes phrases of John 17. Finally, for the list could be very long, the prayers show a realism about life and its problems and an especial concern for those engaged in heavy and perhaps unrewarding work.

If the prayers are very varied, they are also adapted to the liturgical seasons. They draw out the implications of the mystery of Christ in his incarnation, passion, death, resurrection and ascension and before Pentecost there are almost continual invocations of the Holy Spirit. This again helps us to realise that the celebration of the mystery must have consequences in our living. Here are one or two examples: 'May our lives express what we celebrate at Christmas; and may its mystery enrich your church this year'; 'By your coming you showed us the faithfulness of God; keep us faithful to the promises of our baptism'; 'King of peace, your kingdom is one of justice and peace; grant that we may seek those things that will further harmony among men.' For Holy Week: 'Christ, our Redeemer, let us share in your passion by works of penance; let us attain the glory of your resurrection'; 'Lord and master, for us you became obedient even to death; keep us faithful to God's will in the darkness of our lives.'

One for Eastertide illustrates another feature of these prayers: they are constantly echoing or quoting holy scripture and very frequently are related to the readings of the Mass or office of the day: 'Let us cast out the leaven of corruption and malice; let us celebrate Christ's passover in purity and truth.' Here is another for the week before Pentecost which recalls Romans 8: 26, 27: 'Through the Holy Spirit you have made us sons of God; at all times let us pray through the Spirit to you (Christ) and the Father.' In the 'ordinary' time of the year the prayers are perhaps more practical and down to earth: 'Lord, give us your strength in our weakness; when we meet problems give us courage to face them'; and again (from the old Prime collect), 'Direct our thoughts, our words, our actions today so that we may know and do your will.' Nor do the prayers overlook certain aspects of life which too often have not figured in Christian prayer: we are invited to pray for artists and writers and all who in any way reveal the beauty and glory of God: 'Pour out your Spirit on artists, craftsmen and musicians; may their work bring variety, joy and inspiration to our lives.' Even the town-planners are not forgotten: 'We pray for all who plan and build our cities; give them respect for every human value.'

In this vast corpus of prayers it is possible that there are some that could be criticised from one viewpoint or another and that would not be surprising. It is possible that some could have benefitted from further thought and revision: God is asked a little too often to do things directly that other prayers see as being done by his creatures. What is a matter for some criticism (though I realise what an appalling task they had) is that the translators have not always been very happy in the way they have turned phrases. For instance, in the example given above for Holy Week 'works of penance' with its unhappy overtones is not the best way of translating the simple 'per paenitentiam' of the Latin; 'by penitence' or even 'by repentance' would have been better. Penitence is both a state of mind and will and expressive of an intention to proceed to action. Another example is from Thursday Vespers (Third Week): 'Turn sinners back to you.' This is very odd English. Surely it should be 'back to *yourself*' if you are going to keep that sort of sentence. It is a reflexive verb; it is the Father who is being addressed. There are several other examples of the same kind not only here but in the ICEL translation of the missal. I have to presume that it is but another example of the decline of the English language. The Latin is *'Da peccatoribus conversionem, lapsisque virtutem; omnibus paenitentiam et salutem concede'*. Very neat! For the first phrase why not 'conversion of heart': 'To sinners grant conversion of heart.' Perhaps the whole sentence could go on like this: 'To sinners grant conversion of heart, to the fallen the power to rise from their sins (this phrase is omitted) and to us all true repentance and the salvation that comes from Christ.'

Then there is the question of certain words. In Lauds for Friday of the Third Week (of the psalter) we find: 'You sent your disciples to preach the gospel ... *Bless* those men and women ....' This word occurs quite frequently and I would contend that it is unblessedly vague, especially when in the Latin there is a good strong verb: *adiuva*. The word comes in other places where the phrase goes 'Bless our families ... Bless these and those'. What I find very extraordinary throughout these prayers is the use of the word 'brothers'. A good word of course when applied to *men* but with the exception of one or two isolated phrases (as above) women nowhere appear. 'Brethren' I suppose was regarded as archaic though it has deceived far too many people into thinking that it meant both men and women whereas of course it is merely the plural of 'brothers'. For some strange reason 'sisters' was regarded as an improper word—and yet there are thousands of religious sisters throughout the world using this office who are not allowed to pray for each other but only for their 'brothers'. Elsewhere too 'sons' (of God) could often be turned 'children' who are both male and female!

When we turn to the form of the petitions, at first sight they seem a little over-complicated: the petition, divided into two parts, the whole followed by a response. The form of course is useful for those who in an assembly have no books—they can merely repeat the response but in private recitation it seems to be overloaded. However, the way we may use the petition is very flexible: 'The priest or minister says both parts of the intention and the congregation adds the invariable response, or pauses for silence; otherwise the priest or minister says only the first part and the congregation the second part of the intention' (GI 193). In private recitation then the response may be omitted. In practice it will often be best to make a silent pause after each petition and turn it into a personal prayer. One of the things that the sometimes despised prayer of petition can do for us is 'to raise our mind and heart to God'. However, if there are responses, they ought to be appropriate to the petition that has preceded them and this is not always so. Thus the response for the Second Sunday after Christmas is 'Let your birth bring peace to men' and yet in the petitions we pray (a) for the church, (b) for the pope and bishops that they may be faithful stewards and (c) that Christ will help us in our weakness and give us a share in his kingdom, all of which does not seem to have anything to do with 'peace to men'. Another petition reveals where the source of the trouble lies: 'Jesus our Saviour, in the body you were put to death . . . grant that we may die to sin and live in the power of your resurrection. *Lord, restore your kingdom in the world.*' The response which has no evident relevance to the petition is too specific. Where the responses are short and general, like 'Lord in your mercy, hear our prayer' or simply 'Lord hear us', there is no difficulty at all.

However, it must be emphasised that the intercessions are for the most part well thought out and agreeably expressed. The criticisms made here are offered in the hope that in the event of a second edition the intercessions may be reviewed and perhaps revised. Local conferences of bishops have the faculty to approve new prayers though these must follow the rules laid down in the General Instruction (184–186)—a salutary precaution! Nor should the permission to add petitions in ordinary celebrations be over-looked (188). In this way the prayers can be adapted to local needs and conditions. It is also helpful to allow a period of silence when the prayers are finished so that individuals can make their own petitions and pray to God in their hearts.

Finally, it should be noted that the intercessions are part of a whole pattern; intercessions, the Lord's prayer and the collect. All these elements, while at one time or another and in various ways giving praise and thanksgiving to God, turn the prayer of the whole hour towards ourselves so that we may appropriate and apply to our lives the content of all that has gone before. It is a sound formula, making the new office far more personal than the old and keeping a nice balance between the upward thrust of praise of God and the needs of the human community who are approaching him for help.

A Note on Collects

The very numerous collects of the new office deserve prolonged consideration but that cannot be done here. Their very number and the great variety of their content and style prohibit any adequate treatment. All we can do is to point out that they perform their proper function admirably in summing up the whole hour either in the context of the day, feast or season or in that of a particular time, e.g. (mid-day prayer or Compline). One feature that is very welcome is that apart from the greater feasts and some parts of the greater seasons, the prayer of the Mass is used only for the Office of Readings and even there there are some variations. In the daily office Lauds and Vespers, as well as the mid-day prayer and Compline, have their own collects and we are no longer required to repeat the collect of the day again and again. This has been done very deliberately not only to relieve monotony but to make the point of a particular hour (199).

The problems of translations were as great as those for the collects of the missal and it is for the users of the office to judge their value. Very generally they seem to have been welcomed.[12]

NOTES

1. In the secular sphere Hegel and Marx seem to have been the precursors of a 'theology' of social progress which largely turned on the meaning of history – a subject that has preoccupied Christian theologians for some time.
2. See L. Beirnaert, 'Prayer and Petition for Others' in *From Cry to Word* (Lumen Vitae Press, Brussels, 1968) pp. 29 ff.
3. See L. Beirnaert, *art. cit.* pp. 30, 31, which I have been summarising.
4. As quoted in *From Cry to Word*, p. 36. Emphases mine, inserted to show the difference between human requests and prayer to God.
5. St Thomas quotes part of the Letter to Proba in II–II, 83, 6. In the previous article (55, ad 2) he speaks of prayers as a conforming of our will with God's.
6. For what follows see *The Common Catechism* (Search Press, London; Seabury Press, New York, 1975), pp. 352–361.
7. p. 357.
8. *ibid.*
9. On the subject of language, see *op. cit.* pp. 354–356.
10. PL, 33, 501.
11. *The Common Catechism*, p. 361. Note the characteristic prevalence of 'faith'. We can accept our work in love and indeed in hope too. As Augustine (*loc. cit.*) says 'In faith, hope and love we pray always by unceasing desire'.
12. Since the present writer had some hand in the translation, he feels inhibited from further comment.

CHAPTER NINE

The Celebration of the Divine Office

It is very evident that it is the desire of the church that ordinary people should take part in the prayer of the Divine Office (GI 21, 22, 23, 27), especially Lauds and Vespers (GI 40). This desire and the recommendations that flow from it are firmly based on the teaching of the Constitution on the Liturgy (42) and other conciliar documents about the nature of the church. Even the local community is a manifestation, a sacrament-sign, of the great church spread throughout the world and it is there that the praise and prayer of the Christian community should have a visible presence. Priests and other ministers, if they exist, should meet together with their people to celebrate the prayer of the church whenever it is possible. Priests and clerics living in community and religious of both sexes are urged to celebrate the office in common, especially Lauds and Vespers (26, 27). Likewise, groups of lay-people who meet together for whatever purpose should also use the office as far as that is possible, and even families are urged to make parts of the office the substance of their daily prayer (27). There can be no doubt that the church wishes all to make office their prayer as far as their circumstances allow and it is equally significant that the hours recommended are Lauds and Vespers. These, as we have seen, are the pivots of the prayer of the church, summing up in themselves the essence of that prayer.

This is the ideal set before the members of the church but the reality is likely to be very different. As everyone knows, it has become increasingly difficult to assemble people for anything but eucharistic worship and attendance at that is said to be declining.[1] What then is to be done?

Before discussing practical measures it is necessary to say that Christians and perhaps especially Catholics need to have a greater conviction about the importance of prayer. Catholics particularly have a very strong feeling for the Mass and will (still) go to considerable lengths to ensure that they get to Mass on Sunday. Their appreciation of public prayer seems to be much weaker. This is understandable. Until recently the office was officially in Latin and was regarded as the peculiar exercise of the priest and if it was possible to make something of the Mass in Latin, as millions did for many centuries, the same was not true of the office. In fact for the vast majority of Catholics the office played no part in their Christian lives for over four centuries. It will not be surprising if it takes a very long time to re-integrate it into normal Christian practice. If this is to happen the whole meaning of public prayer as the prayer of the church in which Christ is actively present will have to be brought home to them. The vast teaching of the New Testament and of the Christian writers of all ages urging the necessity of prayer and its importance for Christian living will have to be broken down for them. This will have to go a good deal beyond pulpit exhortations to pray— which have never been lacking—and will have to unfold the meaning of prayer in all its richness if people are to be drawn to it. What is perhaps of even greater practical importance is that they need to be given *examples* of praying communities, or better still, of communities at prayer.

This brings us to the practicalities of the matter. It is pretty certain that Vespers will be the hour that people will be able to attend and this is the first point on which to concentrate attention.

1. Where there is a community of priests and clerics it would seem right and proper that they should recite Vespers in church at whatever hour a number of people can attend. There has been a tendency in the past for religious communities to think of the office as *their* prayer which they may indeed have agreed they were saying *for* the people but that otherwise it was no concern of theirs. When the office was in Latin there was some excuse for thinking like that. But if the church gives a mandate to priests to say the office, it does so so that they may maintain the public prayer of the church which by definition is that of the people also (GI 28 ff). One of the great advantages of a community of priests with a pastoral charge and a public church is that they are able to maintain a presence of public prayer as a normal part of the Christian life.

2. Where there is a number of priests in a parish, the same principle holds good although the practical difficulties may be greater. Priests will have a variety of functions and it may well be difficult to assemble at any given time, but some effort could be made and if only one priest can attend there will usually be a small number of people who will celebrate the office with him. The importance of the matter is not how many people are present but that there should be a fixed hour of prayer and that the prayer should be seen to go on relentlessly, irrespective of numbers.

3. Where there is only one priest in a parish, the matter becomes more difficult. With the best will in the world he cannot always be in church at the appointed hour. There will be times when he has to be absent or when he is called away. But a celebration of the office does not require the presence of a priest (GI 27) and what we need to do is to build up prayer-groups in our parishes who will undertake to be present on stated occasions and to see that the office is recited whether the priest is there or not. However, it may be conceded that in the smaller parish even this is not possible and then something simpler has to be thought of. If evening prayer cannot be said every night of the week, it may be that Saturdays and Sundays offer an opportunity. The confessional period is still usually kept on Saturday

evenings, though less frequented than formerly, and it is possible to use the first part of this period for the recitation of the office. There may only be a few people present but the main point is that the prayer of the church is said. Similarly, on Sundays even if it is not possible to have a full-scale evening service, it is possible to recite Vespers with a few people before the evening Mass. What is important is to establish that there shall be fixed times in the course of the week when the prayer of the church will be celebrated.

These simple celebrations can be enhanced by the addition of singing, first of the hymn, which in the English edition is usually familiar, and secondly of the *Magnificat* in one or other of the psalm-settings that are current. In a parish context it is also useful to make known that the people may add petitions to the intercessions whenever the office is celebrated. But even in these simple celebrations it is important that a longer scripture reading should be used and a commentary, however brief, should be given. The General Introduction suggests the use of the passage from the Office of Readings but this is not always the most apt for a mixed congregation, especially when it is from an obscurer part of the Old Testament. It is better, and I think more profitable, to take a book from the New Testament and use it fairly freely, going through it from the beginning but dwelling on what is more suitable to the group and linking one passage to another. This will ensure that those who have had to be absent for a week will know what has gone before.

It is also possible to link the celebration of the office with certain traditional Catholic devotions. A decade or two of the rosary after Vespers is acceptable. If time allows, a simple exposition of the Blessed Sacrament concluding with the blessing adds a touch of warmth and familiarity for those who are less accustomed to the austerity of the office. In some places the office is combined with the exposition of the Blessed Sacrament for the Holy Hour devotion. Here the scripture reading(s) and the homily can add depth and richness to the hour of prayer.

There is too the possibility of the house-group envisaged by the General Introduction (27). Here the prayer can be combined with a more extended reading of scripture and the homily could be of a more conversational kind. The intercessions for their part offer the opportunity of a freer kind of prayer which need not be confined to petition. Silences too could be longer so that in one office there would be formal prayer (the psalms), reading, commentary or homily, and the less formal petitions and silences which would allow for the movement of the Spirit. No doubt these possibilities have already been realised here and there and the one benefit the office brings to prayer-groups is objectivity and a wider horizon. All small groups, including sometimes the parish, have a tendency to concentrate on their own concerns and to forget the *oikoumene*, the great church and the community of mankind.

But it must be confessed that if any of these practices are to become general a considerable change of mind on the part of both the clergy and the people is necessary. The priest, badgered by legislation and long custom, has seen the office as a duty that concerned him and no one else. Notionally he knew that it was the prayer of the community but in actuality this never or only rarely affected his action. The obstacles to the way of communal celebration seemed insurmountable. The office was long and complicated and was in Latin. The Catholic laity were for the most part unfamiliar with the psalms and were not attracted by the little they knew of them. Brought up for centuries on a subjective devotionalism, which even affected their attitude to the eucharist, they were in no position to take to the 'impersonality' of the office. This phase is now passing. The laity read the Bible far more than they used to, they are confronted with a psalm or part of a psalm every Sunday and the devotions of former times seem to have much less appeal. On the other hand, the new office is a very flexible instrument, it is more personal than the old one and there are signs that people take to it once they are given the opportunity.

But there is one great material difficulty. Even the single volume office containing everything except the Office of Readings is very bulky and correspondingly expensive. There will be few lay-people who can spare £11 odd from the family budget. It is indeed difficult to understand why a volume containing only Lauds and Vespers could not be issued. This is all that is required by the laity and it should be possible to publish such a volume at a reasonable price. It is to be hoped that this will be done without delay. Otherwise the chances of the office becoming the prayer of the people are remote.[2]

Instead however of a book of the offices of Vespers and Lauds, a liturgical psalter would go a long way to meet the needs of small communities assembled for the prayer of the church. If we look at the instructions scattered throughout the General Introduction we find that there is more than one way of celebrating the office. The antiphon which need be said only at the beginning of the psalm (123) may be recited or sung by one person, a cantor or someone appointed for the task, and the community can simply listen to it. Obviously no book is needed for the reading, which is best listened to. The responsories both short and long may be replaced by some popular chant so long as it is appropriate or by silence (49). The leader of the group can give out the response to the intercessions and will read the collect. If a hymn is sung at the beginning of the office this can be taken from any authorised source. The advantage of this system is that a psalter arranged according to the offices could be produced for a small sum and would contain what is essential for a full participation in the office.

The Introduction (122) indeed suggests other ways of reciting or singing the psalms: the verses can be alternated by different groups (choir/people) or the responsorial method may be used. This latter method has its attractions and we are already familiar with it in the Mass but unless it is sung it is somewhat dull. However, the Introduction evidently favours considerable flexibility and suggests experimentation. Perhaps as the years go by we shall learn that there are many other ways of singing psalms, ways that are within the capacity of the people.

Still other possibilities are suggested by the Introduction (93–98). Lauds or Vespers may be combined with the Mass. In this case either the intro- duction of the hour *or* the introduction of the Mass liturgy is used. The three psalms are recited, then the *Gloria* and the collect of the day. The readings (with psalm and alleluia) follow and on Sundays the Prayer of the Faithful (in the form laid down for the Mass), on week-days the interces- sions of the office may be used. The Mass continues as usual until after the communion when the canticle *(Benedictus* or *Magnificat* according to the hour) is sung. The Mass then concludes in the normal way. If the evening Mass of Saturday does duty for Sunday observance this sort of celebration has much to commend it. It brings to the Mass a new element and on festive occasions, such as Pentecost, could provide an agreeable way of celebrating the feast. It is true that the two psalms and canticle of the office with the responsorial psalm of the Mass are rather a lot for one occasion but, given a greater familiarity with the psalms and an ability to sing them, the whole service could be very attractive. The allocation of psalms is balanced by the three readings of the Mass which is a quite traditional arrangement even if the *order* in which they are used is not. There would seem to be no reason why eventually the pattern of the Easter Vigil should not be adopted.[3]

The mid-day office may also be combined with the Mass and substan- tially that means simply reciting the three psalms after communion. And all these offices may be recited *after* Mass. For Vespers this means that the short reading, the intercessions and the Lord's prayer are omitted and the psalmody and the *Magnificat* are said one after another (97). This does not seem to be a very happy arrangement and it is difficult to know who would find it a convenient one.

Private Recitation

Unfortunately private or individual recitation of the office will be the lot of most secular priests for most of the time and in most places. Accord- ing to the Introduction the clergy, bishops, priests and deacons, 'who represent the person of Christ in a special way' have a mandate to pray 'to God on behalf of all the people entrusted to them and indeed for the whole world' (28). This obligation they will substantially fulfil by reciting the whole of the office but especially Lauds and Vespers, which they will not omit 'unless for a serious reason' *(ibid.)*. The recitation of the office, then, cannot be regarded as an optional extra. Yet there are well-known dif- ficulties. Many large parishes are now understaffed and even in the smaller ones the single priest has many calls upon his time and attention. The form of the office which is obviously meant for a community he sometimes finds unacceptable because unreal. To some much of the psalter is unpromising material for prayer. Finally, the many changes the office has undergone since 1955 have been the cause of disaffection among many. Before the new office appeared it was said that considerable numbers of priests were not saying the office at all. Whether the situation has improved since must be a matter of guesswork.

There is then much leeway to make up. What is to be done? Let us put aside the practical difficulties, real or alleged, for the moment. What is required is a radical change of mind and heart. The old Latin office, much of which was incomprehensible to many priests, with the heavy legal sanctions that enforced its recitation, did a great deal of harm to the practice of the prayer of the church. It was a duty to be done, a quota to be got through, rather than a prayer that would nourish the Christian life. If a priest prayed for his people it was during Mass or before or after it that he did so. If he prayed with his people it was in the form of 'devotions' of one sort or another that meant a great deal more to him and the people than anything contained in the office. The first and most fundamental truth we need to grasp is that the office, whatever may be its imperfections, is the prayer of Christ in his church. That is, just as Christ is present (in a special way) in the eucharist, just as he is present in the proclamation of the word and in the celebration of the sacraments, so is he in the prayer of the church: 'He is present when the church prays and sings for he promised: "Where two or three are gathered together in my name, there I am in the midst of them"' (CL 7; Matthew 18: 20). Just as the rest of the liturgy engages the action of Christ, so does the prayer of the church. The priest alone in his empty church is in touch with Christ who is the same yesterday, today and for ever and who is ever-living to make intercession for us. Whether we are to think that the prayer of the church has a peculiar efficacy is not the point. That we can leave to God. What is true is that it is the one certain way in which we can pray in union with Christ.

The Introduction (28) states that the bishop and the priest are leaders of the prayer of their communities and because of their special relationship with Christ by ordination they have a special duty of praying for and with their people. As the ancient text of Hippolytus, now again used for the ordination of a bishop, makes clear, prayer for the community is a specifically priestly function: 'May he exercise his priesthood without blame, serving you (leitourgounta) day and night that ceaselessly he make you propitious' (to the people). Prayer is as much a priestly function as celebrating the sacraments or preaching the word of God. Even if it seems unsatisfactory, and indeed is, that a priest has to pray so often alone, it is none the less true that when he is engaged in the prayer of the church he is praying in Christ and with the whole church spread throughout the world. But it is also important that at least from time to time he should assemble the parish community to pray with them and to make evident his role as leader of prayer in the local church. It is here perhaps that the combination of an office, say Vespers, with an evening Mass would make the point.

The old office seemed to consist of saying a given quota of words. This notion is explicitly repudiated by the new office (279). Whatever is to be said or done 'Above all, the thing to be achieved is to instil a desire for the authentic prayer of the church and a delight in celebrating the praise of God'. And speaking of different ways of reciting the psalms, the Introduction remarks 'psalms are not used just to make up a certain quantity of prayer' (121). A reply from the Congregation for Worship heavily emphasises that in the mind of the church the office is above all *prayer* and affirms that it is not necessary to vocalise the readings, which are to be regarded as nourishment for the soul and the subject-matter of meditation. Nor, it goes on, is it even necessary to pronounce the psalms; in them we should try and catch the echoes of Christ's voice. The purpose of the reform of the office was not to shorten the time of prayer but to give time to pray better. It is not a question of turning over pages or 'getting through the breviary' (*breviarium currendo legentes*) but of personal mediation. The purpose of the office, the note continues, can often be achieved without the oral pronunciation of every word, especially in the reading of the lessons.[4] It may seem odd that the clergy should have to be reminded that the office is prayer but in the past it was often not so regarded. But if it is true that the office is essentially prayer there are certain consequences to be drawn from that truth. We can say some parts of the office more slowly, we can dwell on verses of the psalms if we are so moved, we can ponder on the readings and we need not attempt to say the responsory at all. We can make use of the various devices written into the office to help our prayer. We can use the title of the psalm instead of the antiphon if we so wish. 'For a good spiritual or pastoral reason' (252) we can even occasionally change a psalm or psalms assigned to a particular day for others corresponding to the same hour. This may very well be helpful for the mid-day hour when we can use three of the gradual psalms (which are given in a place apart in the book) instead of what is laid down for the day (e.g. Thursday, Third Week, pss. 78 and 79). Above all, time is important, not in the sense that we wish to save it but in the sense that we wish to fill it. Wherever we say the office (and given its current brevity there seems to be little excuse for saying it in public places, in aeroplanes or trains), there must be an atmosphere of prayer and experience shows that this is killed if we try and 'fit in' an office in some odd moment which *seems* free—unless of course we are one of those geniuses who can switch off from activity to contemplation at a moment's notice. It should be possible for everyone with a little good will to make the office a real prayer.

Temperaments differ of course and there will be those for whom fixed forms of prayer are difficult. They prefer to follow the movement of the spirit and are happier in intimate colloquy with God.[5] Granted that is so, it must be affirmed that everyone needs some framework of prayer or it will evaporate into ineffective thoughts and longings. Let us look once again at the structure of the office. The psalms, whatever their difficulties, keep before us the vast history of God's saving work for man and prompt us to raise our minds and hearts to him in gratitude. As almost every writer on the psalms has said, they touch almost every human chord and enable us to express a range of sentiments and needs which would probably not come within our horizon. The danger of unstructured prayer is precisely that it goes round in ever-decreasing circles. Then there are the Bible readings. Sometimes they say little enough to us but in the course of the year the greater part of the Bible is unfolded before us and gives us the opportunity to reflect on God who is revealed there and on his ways with man. Even if the longer readings are not used, there are the short ones of the hours from Lauds to Compline and these too offer opportunities for moments of reflection. The Letter of St James may not be everyone's favourite reading but he has some pungent things to say about practical Christianity. Finally, the intercessions again and again remind us that our prayer must have a practical issue and they extend our vision to the whole world and to every need of mankind. It is not often that purely private prayer has so broad a vision.

There is no doubt that the devout Christian in private prayer is praying 'in Christ' but one thing that the prayer of the office does is to enable us to keep in touch with Christ throughout the seasons of the church's year. Through the office (as well of course as in the Mass) we are able to participate in the redeeming mystery of Christ which is unfolded to us in texts of all kinds in a way that is not possible in the eucharist. The whole Christian tradition from the New Testament onwards rises up to show us in this way and that, by hymns and antiphons, by readings from the Fathers, by the Christian interpretation of the psalms, we are celebrating the mystery of Christ. The *absence* of all this spells spiritual impoverishment which it is dangerous to tolerate. In urging the extended use of the office for the laity, as well as reminding the clergy of their duty, the church certainly wishes to put an end to that state of affairs.

As far as the pastoral priest is concerned, it is difficult to imagine that he cannot say Lauds and Vespers daily. Even said fairly slowly each office takes little more than ten minutes. Presumably too he says some prayer before going to bed. There remains the hour to be said sometime during the day and the Office of Reading which may indeed be said at any time. It may well be that a priest is very busy or moving about, travelling, during the day and then it will be hardly possible to say the day hour. The Office of Reading, which usually is not very long but requires a little quiet and recollection, may be a greater difficulty. But a man has to ask himself: do I ever read the Bible in any consecutive way? If not, he is doing less than his duty. If he does, he simply has to combine that with the three psalms of the office. One advantage of the office lectionary is that it keeps us up to the mark in the reading of the Bible and I do not see that we should have to keep slavishly to the passages printed in the office book. It is better—experience shows—to take the Bible text itself and to look at the context of the extracts and if, as we have said above, we use an edition like that of the Jerusalem Bible (the full one), we shall find that its introductions and notes help us to arrive at a deeper *spiritual* understanding of the text. The Bible readings can indeed become *lectio divina* that will nourish the life of the spirit.

There is of course the moral aspect of the matter, the need of some degree of self-discipline in one's life. This is easier for some than for others, easier for the old than for the young, but everyone's life must have some order (which means discipline) or it will be simply chaotic and however busy-seeming will produce but little. It is quite possible to say Lauds first thing in the morning either before Mass if the priest has to celebrate at that time or as his first duty of the day. It is not difficult to find some period of time for prayer generally and for the office in particular in the late afternoon, before the onset of the evening's work, or before Mass if it is to be celebrated in the evening. The Office of Reading may at times pose a problem. The best time seems to be later in the evening when work is done. If it is left to the morning and has to be combined with Lauds and Mass the amount of material to read and pray about is excessive. The advantage of saying this office the night before is that sometimes the readings are related to the Mass of the next day. This is particularly true of the greater feasts and a knowledge of the office texts helps in the preaching of the homily. But if there are those who find the afternoon a possible time for prayer, the Office of Reading will provide both a framework and subject-matter of the prayer.

However, it may be admitted that the Office of Reading is the one that gives most trouble and on reviewing the whole of the office as it now is, one is inclined to say that it is still not as well adapted for the pastoral life as it might be. Both the Constitution on the Liturgy and the Introduction reiterate that morning and evening prayer are the two most important offices of the day. Great emphasis is laid on this truth and, as we have seen, this is but to recall the ancient practice of the church when these offices were the prayer of the church. For Christians of today, and given the complexities of modern life, prayer in the morning and in the evening is about as much as can be asked of them. For the priest in a busy parish it is sometimes all he can manage. In any future reform of the office it is to be hoped that these factors will be taken into account. What one hopes for is that to morning and evening prayer will be added a course of scripture reading to replace the short readings that exist already. No doubt the arrangement of such a lectionary would be a matter of some complexity but no more complex than the arrangement of the one we now have. The present office lectionary takes some account of the Mass lectionary, though imperfectly. In Easter time the Acts of the Apostles are read at Mass though with large omissions and never at the office. A re-arrangement here would not be difficult and both lectionaries would benefit. At other times of the year it would be perhaps appropriate that when the Old Testament is read at Mass it should not be read in the office and *vice-versa*. Finally, if the material of the Old Testament proved to be too much for one year, we could have a two-cycle for it as we have a two-year cycle for all scripture readings during the week at Mass. In view of the very considerable omissions from the Old Testament and the 'anthologising' methods of the compilers in some places, a two-year cycle should make possible a more coherent Old Testament lectionary.

A further refinement is perhaps more disputable. As we have seen in the first chapter of this book, the oldest pattern of Christian prayer is based on the alternation of readings and psalms: the reading provides matter for reflection and the psalm that follows the means for praying about the content of the reading. This, as we know, is the pattern of the Easter Vigil and that was a *popular* service, that is, one in which great numbers of people took part. If morning and evening prayer were extended as suggested above, it is to be hoped that experiments will be made to see if such a pattern is practically possible. It might well mean that the psalm content of these offices would have to be reduced but, as we have also observed, it is possible that there are even now too many psalms in the office. It might mean that the reading would have to be divided and this would demand great skill and discretion. It may well be that there are many who do not find this pattern at all to their liking or a necessary one for liturgical prayer. So be it, but let us not close our minds to the possibilities of such a change. If, as the church desires, at least morning and evening prayer are to become a normal part of every Christian's life, the chances are that the ancient and popular pattern will prove to be the right one. As far as the pastoral priest is concerned, an office consisting of morning and evening prayer with scripture readings and intercessions would give him all that he needs and something that he could incorporate into his daily routine without strain.

Of the new office as a whole, however, it must be said that the church has to put into our hands an instrument of *prayer* and if it is to be judged over-elaborate in some ways, its rules are sane and flexible and it can be used for the purpose for which it was devised.

NOTES

1. Here as in all the allegations about a falling church practice we need hard facts, tested figures, and they are hard to come by. What seems to be the case is that the Sunday obligation is no longer regarded as seriously as it once was. This means that on any given Sunday there may be fewer people in church than formerly but it does not mean that there are fewer who are to be described as 'practising'.
2. For an account of *Daily Prayer* see *Music and Liturgy*, Spring, 1975, Vol. I, no. 3, pp. 154–5.
3. In this country as long as the Mass of Saturday evening is not allowed to count as Sunday observance, it is improbable that we shall be able to use this form of service. There will just not be a sufficient number of people.
4. *Notitiae* 82 (April, 1973), p. 150.
5. I have even heard people say that formal vocal prayer seems to them unreal and so insincere.

Index

Adrian I, Pope, 101n
agape, Hippolytus' description of, 35
Alcuin, 45
Alleluia psalms, 34, 35
Allo, E. B., *Saint Jean, L'Apocalypse*,
101n
Amalarius of Metz, 45
Ambrose, St, 57nn, 97, 101
ritual of, 39
Andrew of Caesarea, 97
Andrieu, M., *Les Ordines Romani du
Haut Moyen Age*, 59n
Angela Merici, St., 100
antiphons, 45, 46, 48, 82
in revised office, 64, 66–7, 122
Aphraates, 97, 98
Aquinas, St Thomas, 27n, 98
on fulfilment through union with
God, 8, 15nn, 80, 110, 118n
on obligation, 15n
on petitionary prayer, 110
on transcendence, 80
Aristotle, 13
Athanasius, St, 83, 100
Augustine, St, 7, 9, 15n, 39, 43, 57n
and desire for God, 3, 10, 14n, 110,
111–12, 118n
on Holy Spirit, 25
on importance of prayer of psalms,
3, 82
mission to England, 44
and patristic lectionary, 97
on union with Christ in prayer, 22

Baronius, Caesar, 59n
Basil, St, 100
'cathedral' office, 38, 39, 57n
Bäumer, S., and R. Biron, *Histoire du
Bréviare*, 58n, 59n
Baumstark, A., 85
Comparative Liturgy, 55n, 57n, 90n
Bede, St, 97

Beirnaert, L., *From Cry to Word*, 110,
118nn
Benedict, St, 37, 46
on harmony of mind and voice, 5
and patristic lectionary, 91, 97
Rule of, 5–6, 15nn
and Divine Office, 42–4, 45, 58n;
canticles, use of, 67; public reci-
tation of Compline, 75n
Benedict XIV, Pope, 54
Benedictus, 42, 123; antiphons, 67, 71;
as song of redemption, 25
Benet Biscop, St, 58n
Bernard, St, 97, 98
'Blessings', in Jewish prayer-practices,
31, 32, 55n
Bonaventure, St, 98
Boniface, St, liturgical reform, 44
Bonsirven, J., *Épître aux Hebreux*, 23,
27nn
Botte, Dom, 56nn, 57n
Bouyer, L.
Bible et Evangile, 90n
Eucharistie, 55n
Bréhier, L., and R. Aigrain, *Grégoire le
Grand*, 58n
breviary
formation of, 47–51
reform of, 51–5
Bridges, R., 104
Brigit of Sweden, St, 100
Brown, R. – see *Jerome Biblical
Commentary*
Burn, A. E., *Niceta of Remesiana*, 57n
Butler, C., *The Vatican Council 1869–
1870*, 59n

Caesarius of Arles, 40, 46
Callewaert, C., *De Breviarii Romani
Liturgia*, 58nn
Campbell, R., 103

Campling, C. R., *The Fourth Lesson*, 101n
canons regular, 47
canticles, 40
in revised office, 67, 87–9
capitularia, 46
Cassian, John, 4, 37, 57nn
Cassien, Mgr. and B. Botte (ed.), *La Prière des Heures*, 57n
Caswell, E., 103
'cathedral' office, 37–9, 40, 42–3, 64, 91
Catholic Hymnal, 104
Charlemagne, and liturgical reform, 44, 45
Christian Prayer Book, A, 105
Chrodegang of Metz, 44
Chrysostom, St John, 96, 98
Clement of Alexandria, 27n
on early pattern of prayer, 33–4, 35, 60, 61
Clement of Rome, 33
Clovesho, Synod of (747), 44
Codex Amiatinus, 46
Codrington, H. W., *The Liturgy of St Peter*, 106n
Coffin, C., 103
collects, 45, 86–7
books of (collectars), 46–7
in revised office, 117
Columbanus, 43
Common Catechism, The, 118n
community
Lord's prayer and, 18–19
need for structured prayer, 2–3, 11–13, 16
union with Christ, 21–2, 25
Compline, 41
hymns, 70
psalmody, 43, 53, 54, 65
public recitation, 72, 75n
in revised office, 64, 65, 70, 72, 117
ritual, 45
Connolly, Dom, *Didascalia Apostolorum*, 60
Cranmer, Thomas, 51
Crichton, J. D.
Christian Celebration: The Mass, 15n
'Historical Sketch of the Roman Liturgy', 59n
Cross, F. L., *Early Christian Fathers*, 56n
Cuming, G., on early prayer-service, 55nn

Cuming, G. J., *A History of the Anglican Liturgy*, 59n
Cyprian, St, 63, 100
Cyril of Jerusalem, 98

Damascene, John, 15n
Daniélou, J., *The Bible and the Liturgy*, 90n
desert monks, 36, 37
desire for God, prayer an expression of, 3, 9, 110, 111
Dewick, E. S., and W. H. Frere
The Leofric Collectar, 58n
The Portiforium of St Wulatan, 59n
Dix, Dom G., 41, 56nn
The Shape of the Liturgy, 58n
Donne, John, 105
Dorotheus, 99
Dudden, F. Homes, *Life and Times of St Ambrose*, 57nn
Dugmore, C. W., *Influence of the Synagogue upon the Divine Office*, 55n

Easter Vigil, 40
collect for, 93
pattern of, 4, 128
Egeria, and pattern of prayer, 4, 38
Eliot, T. S., 105
Ephrem, 98
Ernst, C., *Theology of Grace*, 15nn
Eucharist
communal celebration, 26
Divine Office relation to, 25, 26, 62
early Christians and, 30, 31, 33
Evans, C., *Lumen Vitae*, 27n
Evans, E., 56n
evening prayer (*see also* Vespers), 33 *et seq.*
Basil on, 38
Clement of Alexandria on, 33–4
Hippolytus on, 34–6
Tertullian on, 34

faith, prayer as response of, 110–12
'Father', use of in Lord's prayer, 16–18
Fischer, B.
on 'christologisation' of psalms, 81, 90nn
on early prayer pattern, 56n, 57n, 59–61
Froger, Dom J., 57n
Fulgentius of Ruspe, St, 97
Funk, F. X. (ed.), *Apostolic Constitutions*, 57n, 60

Gaul, 4, 40, 41, 42, 44
Gelasian Sacramentary, 46, 58nn
Gelineau, J., 90n
   *Voices and Instruments in Christian
      Worship*, 74n
*General Instruction on the Liturgy of
   the Hours*, 14, 62–3, 68, 69, 70,
   74nn, 88, 90nn
   celebration of Divine Office, 119,
      120, 121, 123, 124–5, 127
   hymnary, 103, 105, 106n
   intercession, 116, 117
   lectionary, 95–6, 99, 100
Gibbard, Father M., *Why Pray?*, 2, 14n
Gilson, E., 80
Gregorian Sacramentary, 45, 46, 58nn
Gregory of Agrigentum, 99
Gregory the Great, 43, 44, 58n, 97
Gregory of Nazianzen, St, 97, 100
Gregory of Nyssa, St, 97
Guerric d'Igny, 99

hagiographical lectionaries, 48, 69–70,
   91, 100–101
Hamman, A., *La Prière*, 27n, 56nn
Hanssens, J. M., *Nature et genèse de
   l'office des matines*, 57n
Herbert, G., 105
Hermas, Pastor of, 33
Herrick, R., 105
Hilary, St, 83, 99
Hippolytus of Rome, 98, 99
   on early pattern of prayer, 34–6, 39,
      56nn, 57n, 60, 61
   on priestly function of prayer, 124
homilies, 46
Hopkins, G. M., 105
house-groups, 121
Howell, C. H. (trans.), *Constitution on
   the Liturgy*, 5, 15n, 19, 93
   Divine Office, 19, 21, 22, 24, 41, 65,
      124, 127
Hügel, Baron von, on 'grand
   prevenience of God', 6
hymns, 34, 39, 54, 60, 61
   in revised office, 64, 70, 72, 102–6

Ignatius of Antioch, 30
Ineson, G., *One Man's Journey*, 14n
Innocent III, Pope, and formation of
   breviary, 49
intercessions, 71, 73, 126
   Aquinas on, 110
   Augustine on, 110

justification for, 112–13
   meaning of term, 113–14
   in revised office, 107–18
Irenaeus, St, 10, 98, 99, 101n
Isaac of Stella, 98, 99

Jay, E. C. (ed and trans.), *Origen on
   Prayer*, 57nn
Jeremias, J.
   Eucharistic Words of Jesus, 30, 32,
      55n, 56n
   Prayers of Jesus, 18, 27nn, 32, 55n,
      56nn
Jerome, St, 40, 96
Jerome Biblical Commentary, 27nn,
   28n, 55n, 90n, 101n
Mackenzie, J. L., on private prayer,
   15n
John of Naples, 99
Jungmann, J. A.
   Christliches Beten, 56nn, 57n
   Early Liturgy, 36, 57n
   Pastoral Liturgy, 40, 41, 52, 57n,
      58nn, 59n
   *Place of Christ in Liturgical
      Prayer*, 27n, 56n, 57n
Justin the Martyr, 33

kerygmatic service, 39, 77
Kirk, K., *Vision of God*, 15n
Klauser, T., *A Short History of the
   Western Liturgy*, 59n
Knowles, M. D.
   The Monastic Order in England, 59n
   'The *Regula Magistri* and the *Rule*
      of St Benedict', 57n
Knox, R. A., 103, 104

latreutic service, 39
Lauds (*see also* morning prayer)
   canticles, 67, 71
   celebration of, 119, 123, 126, 127
   hymns, 70
   nucleus of, 32
   paschal character, 25, 62–3
   psalmody, 42, 43, 52, 54, 65, 66
   in revised office, 64, 65, 66, 67, 70,
      71, 117, 119, 123
   ritual reform, 45, 49, 52, 53, 54,
      64
lectionaries, 46, 52, 91–101
   hagiographical, 48, 69–70, 91,
      100–101
   as *lectio divina*, 94, 96, 67

lectionaries–*cont.*
  patristic, 48, 49, 69, 91, 96–100
  in revised office, 68–70
  scriptural, 46, 48, 49, 52, 68–9,
    91–6, 97
Leo I, St, 96, 97, 98, 99, 101
Leo XIII, Pope, on man's right to shape
  destiny, 108
Leofric Collectar, 47
Lightfoot, J. B., *Apostolic Fathers*, 56n
'lighting of the lamps', 35, 39
Little Brothers of Charles de Foucauld,
  2
liturgical books, organisation of, 46–55
  breviary: formation of, 47–51;
    reform of, 51–5
  collectar, 46–7
  psalter, 46
Liturgy of the Hours (1971), 50, 52,
  54, 73n, 75n
Lord's Prayer
  as community prayer, 18–19
  in early prayer-practice, 32, 42, 43,
    45
  and filial relationship, 16–18
  as petition, 109
  and prayer of church, 19–27
  in revised office, 64
Luykz, B., 57n, 58n

McCann, Justin (trans.), *Rule of St
  Benedict*, 15n, 58n
Mackenzie, J. L., 15n
McLachan, Dame L., 'St Wulstan's
  Prayer Book', 59n
Magnificat, 42, 71, 123
  antiphons, 67
  as song of redemption, 25
Maison Dieu, La
  on prayer: Cuming, G., 55nn;
    Fischer, B., 56n, 57n, 59–61;
    Luykz, B., 57n, 58n; Salmon, P.,
    58nn
  on psalms: Fischer, B., 90nn
Martimort, A. G. (ed.), *L'Eglise en
  Prière*, 56n, 57nn, 58nn, 59nn,
  74nn, 101n.
Maximus the Confessor, St, 99
Mediator Dei, 27nn
Melito of Sardis, 98
Mersch, E., *Théologie du Corps
  Mystique*, 27n
Merton, Thomas, 74nn, 99
Methodius of Sicily, St, 70

monastic office, 37–9, 41–2, 49
  St Benedict and, 42–4
  and revised office, 64
More, St Thomas, 101
Morison, S., *English Prayer Books*, 59n
morning prayer (*see also* Lauds), 33 *et
  seq.*
  Basil on, 38
  Clement of Alexandria on, 33–4
  Hippolytus on, 34–6
  Tertullian on, 34
Muir, E., 105

Neale, J. M., 103
Newman, J. H., 69, 74n, 99
Niceta of Remesiana, and popular vigil,
  40
None, 37, 41
  psalmody, 42
  in revised office, 64

obligation, 13–14, 49
ordo, 46, 47–8
  of Innocent III, 49
Origen, 99
  on public prayer, 36–7, 57n
Oswen of Worcester, 59n

Pachomius, St, 6, 37
papal chapel, office of, 48–50
patristic lectionaries, 48, 49, 69, 91,
  96–100
Pepin II, liturgical reform of, 44–5
Peregrinatio Aetheriae, 60
petition, prayer of – *see* intercessions
Phōs hilaron, 34, 39
Pius IV, Pope, 52
Pius V, Pope, breviary of, 52–4, 94
Pius, X, Pope, breviary revision, 54, 72
Pliny, on early services, 31
Plotinus, 11
Prayer of Christ – *see* Lord's Prayer
presbyteral churches, 58n
Prime, 37, 41
  psalmody, 43
  in revised office, 64
  ritual, 45, 50, 53
Primasius, 97
private prayer
  limitations of, 125–6
  need for, 11
  and public, convergence between,
    9–10, 73

Prudentius, 103
psalm-collects, 86–7
psalms
  alleluatic, 34, 35
  antiphons, 45, 46, 66–7, 82, 122
  canticles, 87–9
  christological interpretation, 81–4,
    85–7, 90n
  doxology, 85
  in early prayer-meetings, 30, 32 et
    seq,. 59–61
  importance of, 3–4, 7–9, 126
  Lauds, 32, 42, 43, 52, 65, 66, 85
  as prayers, 66, 76–90
  in reformed office, 52, 54, 64, 65–6,
    72, 76–90, 122, 125
  titles, 82–3
  Vespers, 35, 42, 43, 52, 54, 65, 66,
    67, 85
psalterium liturgicum, 46
Psautier de la Bible de Jerusalem, 90n
public prayer
  need for, 11–13, 16, 119–20
  pattern and development of, 3–5, 33
    et seq., 71–3
  private prayer and, convergence
    between, 9–10

Quiñones Breviary, 51–2, 64

Ralph of Tongres, 50
readings, 4, 126
  in early office, 39, 40, 41, 52
  lectionaries, 46, 68–70, 91–101
  reason for, 6, 92–4, 126–7
Regula Magistri, 37, 41, 43, 57n
response to God, central to prayer, 6–7,
  10
responsories
  meditative poems as, 105–6
  in revised office, 64, 70, 105–6, 122
Righetti, M., Storia Liturgica, 58n
Rimaud, D., 90n
Roman-basilican office, 42–6, 64
Roguet, Père, 75n
Rubrics, Code of (1960), 55

saints, calendars of, 50, 52, 53
Salimbene of Parma, 50
Salmon, P., 48, 92
  L'Eglise en Prière, 56n, 57n, 58nn,
    90nn, 101nn
  L'Office Divin, 101nn

L'Office Divin au Moyen Age, 58nn,
  59nn, 74n
Sartre, J.-P., 11
Schmemann, A., Introduction to
  Liturgical Theology, 55n
scriptural lectionaries, 46, 48, 49, 52,
  68–9, 92–6, 97
Sedulius, 103
Sext, 37, 41
  psalmody, 42
  in revised office, 64
Shema (Jewish creed), 31
'Simplification of the Rubrics' decree
  (1955), 55
Spain, 4, 40, 41, 43
Staniforth, M., 56n
structured prayer
  need for, 2–3, 11–13, 125
  pattern and development of, 3–5,
    71–3
Studia Patristica, 56n
Synesius, 103

Taena Community, 2
Tenebrae, 1, 74n
Tephilla (Jewish prayer), 31–2
Terce, 37, 41
  psalmody, 42
  in revised office, 64
Tertullian, on early pattern of prayer,
  33, 34, 35, 60, 61
Theodore of Mopsuestia, 98
Thérèse of Lisieux, St, 90n
transcendance, 77, 79–81
Trent, Council of, 52
Trilling, W., The Gospel according to
  Matthew, 74n

Urban VIII, Pope, 54

Vaison, Synod of (529), 40
Van Dijk, S. J. P., and J. H. Walker,
  The Origins of the Modern
  Roman Liturgy, 59nn
Vandenbroucke, Dom, 90nn
  on doxology, 85
Vann, G., On Being Human, 89
Vatican
  Council, First, 51
  Council, Second: glory given to God
    in life and conduct, 10; liturgy
    reform, 55, 62 et seq.
Vaughan, H., 105

Verbraken, P., *Oraisons sur les 150 psaumes*, 90n
Vespers (*see also* evening prayers)
　canticles, 67, 71
　celebration of, 119, 121, 123, 126
　hymns, 70
　paschal character, 25, 63
　psalmody, 35, 42, 43, 52, 54, 65, 66, 67
　in revised office, 64, 65, 66, 67, 70, 71, 117, 119, 121, 123
　ritual of, 40, 42, 45, 49, 52, 54, 64
vigils
　Carolingian reform, 45
　early mention of, 4, 30, 36
　Easter, 4, 40, 93, 128
　institution of, 37, 38, 41, 42

popular, 39–40, 128
in revised office, 66
Vox ecclesiae and *Vox Sponsae*, Office as, 23

Walker, J. H., 56n
Weakland, Dom, 87, 89n, 90n
William of St Thierry, 98, 99
Wilkinson, J., *Egeria's Travels*, 15n, 57nn
Wulfstan of Worcester, St, collectary of, 47

Zen Buddhism, 15n
Zeno of Verona, 99
Zerfass, R., *Die Schriftlesung im Kathedraloffizium Jerusalems*, p.57n